THE CIVIL WAR

THE THIRD YEAR

THE CIVIL WAR

THE THIRD YEAR TOLD
BY THOSE WHO LIVED IT

Brooks D. Simpson, editor

THE LIBRARY OF AMERICA

Distributed to the trade in the United States
by Penguin Group (USA) Inc.
and in Canada by Penguin Books Canada Ltd.

Library of Congress Control Number: 2012935176
ISBN 978-1-59853-197-8

———

First Printing
The Library of America—234

Manufactured in the United States of America

The Civil War:
The Third Year Told by Those Who Lived It
is published with support from

THE ANDREW W. MELLON FOUNDATION

and

THE NATIONAL ENDOWMENT
FOR THE HUMANITIES

Contents

Preface

"Has there ever been another historical crisis of the magnitude
of 1861–65 in which so many people were so articulate?"
—Edmund Wilson

THIS Library of America volume is the third in a four-volume
series bringing together memorable and significant writing by
participants in the American Civil War. Each volume in the
series covers approximately one year of the conflict, from the
election of Abraham Lincoln in November 1860 to the end of
the war in the spring of 1865, and presents a chronological
selection of documents from the broadest possible range of
authoritative sources—diaries, letters, speeches, military reports, newspaper articles, memoirs, poems, and public papers.
Drawing upon an immense and unique body of American
writing, the series offers a narrative of the war years that en-
compasses military and political events and their social and
personal reverberations. Created by persons of every class and
condition, the writing included here captures the American
nation and the American language in the crucial period of their
modern formation. Selections have been chosen for their historical significance, their literary quality, and their narrative energy, and are printed from the best available sources. The goal
has been to shape a narrative that is both broad and balanced
in scope, while at the same time doing justice to the number
and diversity of voices and perspectives preserved for us in the
writing of the era.

Introduction

O<small>N</small> January 1, 1863, President Abraham Lincoln, weary from a day of greeting well-wishers and shaking hands, slowly put pen to paper and signed the Emancipation Proclamation. His signature declared free more than three million people, but the fulfillment of the proclamation's promise was highly contingent upon the course of events. Lincoln's action might be declared unconstitutional by the Supreme Court or be revoked by his successor if the Democrats won the 1864 presidential election. Above all, the success of emancipation depended on the Union winning the war, an outcome that was far from certain as the new year began.

The previous year had shown how uncertain the course of the conflict could be. After a winter and spring marked by northern victories in Kentucky, western Tennessee, northern Arkansas, coastal North Carolina, and southern Louisiana, the Union retreat during the Seven Days' Battles outside Richmond in late June sharply curtailed northern hopes that the war might be won before the end of the year. Union expectations that support for southern independence might erode in the face of battlefield reverses or the experience of occupation proved wistful. Lincoln found his faith in southern unionism misplaced, as many tepid loyalists declined to assert themselves forcefully. In turn, Confederate hopes for decisive victory in 1862 faded after late summer counteroffensives in Kentucky and Maryland ended in retreat. Both of these abortive incursions into the border states failed to rally large numbers of supporters to the secessionist cause, and in their wake expectations diminished that the British and French governments would recognize Confederate independence or offer to mediate a settlement to the conflict.

Despite these setbacks, many Confederates began 1863 confident of continued battlefield success in the east. Robert E. Lee had proved himself to be an audacious and determined commander when he drove George B. McClellan away from Richmond and routed John Pope at Manassas. Determined to retain the strategic initiative, Lee then invaded Maryland, where he barely fended off McClellan at Antietam before escaping back across the Potomac. In December he had defeated the Army of the Potomac when its new commander, Ambrose Burnside, launched an offensive across the Rappahannock at Fredericksburg. After fighting four campaigns against numerically superior opponents and besting three Union generals, Lee believed the Army of Northern Virginia was nearly invincible. Many white southerners shared his conviction, as well as Lee's deep confidence in his three principal subordinates, Thomas J. (Stonewall) Jackson, James Longstreet, and J.E.B. Stuart. But few observers could be oblivious to the human cost of Lee's four campaigns in 1862. While the Union had lost more than 70,000 men killed, wounded, captured, or missing fighting Lee, casualties in the Army of Northern Virginia under his command totaled 48,000. This was a rate of attrition that the Confederacy, with three-tenths the white male population of the free states, could not sustain indefinitely. And despite its bloody repulse at Fredericksburg, the Army of the Potomac began the new year still encamped on the northern bank of the Rappahannock, only sixty miles from Richmond.

No Union commander in 1862 had matched Lee's success. Once hailed as the "Young Napoleon" by his supporters in the press, George B. McClellan had failed to take Richmond and was judged by Lincoln to be too lethargic in the wake of Antietam. Relieved of the command of his beloved Army of the Potomac, McClellan was awaiting "further orders" at year's end. John Pope had been sent to Minnesota to fight the Dakota after his defeat at Manassas, while the disaster at Fredericksburg appeared to confirm Ambrose Burnside's own doubts about his ability to lead an army. In the west, the nearly unknown Ulysses S. Grant had emerged to national prominence with his stunning victory at Fort Donelson in February 1862, but his subsequent narrow escape from defeat at Shiloh had drawn intense criticism. Grant spent the summer and fall defending Union gains in western Tennessee and northern Mississippi before making a failed attempt to take Vicksburg at year's end that renewed doubts about his leadership. In the upper South, Don Carlos Buell, the commander of the Army of the Ohio, had turned back the Confederate invasion of

Kentucky but was then relieved by Lincoln for failing to pursue Braxton Bragg's retreating Army of Tennessee. At the turn of the year William S. Rosecrans, Buell's replacement, won a narrow victory at Stones River that forced Bragg to fall back into southern Tennessee. While the Confederacy succeeded in 1862 in retaining control of the Mississippi between Vicksburg and Port Hudson, its commanders failed at Pea Ridge, Shiloh, Iuka, Corinth, Perryville, Prairie Grove, and Stones River to win victories that would give it the strategic initiative in the west and allow it to reclaim territory lost to the Union in the first half of the year.

Support for the conflict wavered in 1862 on both sides as its cost in blood and treasure mounted, and it became increasingly hard to recruit volunteers motivated by patriotism or the desire for adventure. In the spring the Confederate Congress passed a conscription act that provoked widespread evasion and resistance throughout the South, especially in upland regions. By midyear Union authorities were also considering introducing conscription, although for the moment federal and state officials relied upon bounties and the threat of a nine-month militia draft to encourage enlistment. In the fall, Democrats capitalized on war weariness and opposition to emancipation to win state elections in Illinois, Indiana, New Jersey, and New York, and reduce the Republican majority in the House of Representatives by thirty-four seats. Although some Democrats favored continued prosecution of the war while others advocated reunion through negotiation, the party was united in its hostility to emancipation and its willingness to ask voters why white men should die so black people could be free.

It was only after months of cautious deliberation that Lincoln decided in the summer of 1862 that the immediate emancipation of the slaves in Confederate-controlled territory was necessary to save the Union. In March he had proposed using federal funds to compensate slave-owners in states that adopted plans for gradual emancipation. Determined to prevent any "radical change of our social system," representatives from the border states refused to support this proposal. At the same time, Lincoln angered many blacks and Radical Republicans by repeatedly calling for the voluntary colonization of former slaves abroad, which he earnestly believed would protect the freed people from the racial backlash he expected to follow emancipation. While Lincoln had sought support for gradual emancipation, he also signed into law a series of antislavery measures initiated by Republicans in Congress. In the spring and summer of 1862, Congress prohibited the military from returning runaway slaves, abolished slavery in the District of Columbia and the federal territories, and passed a confiscation act that created an unwieldy legal mechanism for freeing slaves held by disloyal masters. As Congress, the President, and the cabinet debated alternative courses of action, thousands of slaves had sought freedom by fleeing into Union-held territory, while thousands more were liberated by the advance of the Union armies, eroding the foundations of the "peculiar institution" from below. By year's end the prospect of enlisting blacks in the Union forces offered the promise not only of augmenting northern military power, but also of laying the foundation for claims of citizenship on behalf of those who would now help to preserve the nation.

As 1863 opened, the course of the war was as uncertain as ever. Would Lee continue his mastery over the commanders of the Army of the Potomac, and at what human cost? Would Grant take Vicksburg? Could Bragg regain central Tennessee, or would Rosecrans seize Chattanooga and open the way for a Union invasion of Georgia? Would the Union navy continue to tighten its hold on the southern coastline, or was there some way for the Confederates to break the blockade? Was the possibility of foreign intervention indeed at an end, or could it be revived in the wake of new Confederate successes? What measures would each side have to embrace to maintain their armies, and how would they affect public support for the conflict? In particular, how would the Confederacy be able to reconcile the principle of states' rights with a central government that enforced conscription and asserted the power to impose martial law? Would slaves in Confederate-controlled areas rebel or flee en masse? Would emancipation help the Union war effort, or would it only intensify opposition among Democrats to the policies of the Lincoln administration? How would Confederates, and white Union soldiers, react to the sight of black men in blue uniforms?

By the beginning of 1863 both sides had reluctantly accepted the reality that only long and hard fighting could bring the conflict to an end, although there was still a lingering hope that one great battle, an American Austerlitz or Waterloo, might go far to achieve that result. What was even more uncertain than the war's end was what would follow. If, as Lincoln said, "broken eggs can not be mended," it seemed increasingly likely that the old union was so broken by war that whatever nation—or nations—emerged from the conflict would take on radical new forms that no one could envision.

Brooks D. Simpson

Edmund DeWitt Patterson: Journal, January 20, 1863

Following the Union defeat at Fredericksburg on December 13, 1862, the opposing armies in northern Virginia faced each other across the Rappahannock River. With the Confederate Army of Northern Virginia on the southern bank was Edmund DeWitt Patterson, a native of Lorain County, Ohio, who had moved to northern Alabama shortly before the war and enlisted in the 9th Alabama Infantry in 1861. He first saw action in the Peninsula campaign during the spring of 1862, was seriously wounded at Glendale on June 30, and rejoined his regiment in late November as a lieutenant.

January 20th 1863. I have almost given up writing in my journal for the fact that I have nothing in the world to record. There is too much sameness about this kind of soldier life. One day is the repetition of the duties of the day before, and I can always tell what (in all probability) I will be doing on the same day one month ahead. Capt. Crow is often on other duty, Cannon and Chandler on detached service, and I am generally in command of the Company. Every fifth day at three o'clock P.M. I go on picket and remain twenty four hours. We stand on our side of the river and look at the Yanks. They stand on their side and look at us. Sometimes we exchange papers, though in violation of orders, and sometimes the boys trade them tobacco for coffee. Just below the dam the water is not more than three feet deep, and the boys wade out to a little shoal of rocks in the middle of the stream and meet and take a drink together, make such trades as they wish, then each returns to his own side again. I have to visit some other post in the meantime, or make it convenient to have business in another direction, for it would not do for me to see these violations of orders. And yet I like to read a New York or Philadelphia news paper.

The principal amusement of the troops now-a-days is snow-balling. A great many of them never saw any snow, or at least not enough to cover the ground, until last winter, and many of the Florida troops have never seen any at all. Sometimes whole brigades and even divisions, with their officers in command, get into a battle with snowballs. Then the sport becomes exciting, and the balls fly so thick that the opposing forces scarcely distinguish each other. I think this imitation battle is decidedly more pleasant than the real. The health of the company and regiment is much better than it was last winter. The men have become acclimated and accustomed to exposure, and it would be almost impossible to kill one of them now, by anything except a bullet. About this time last winter, quite a number of our company was sick, several of whom died. McKelvey, Fowler, Irion, Webb, and several others. Thus far our death from disease has been more than from battle. And I believe that the same thing is true with every command in the army, at least with those from the Gulf States.

Theodore A. Dodge:
Journal, January 21–24, 1863

In November 1862 President Lincoln had chosen Major General Ambrose Burnside to replace George B. McClellan as the commander of the Army of the Potomac. Burnside's failed attack at Fredericksburg in December cost the Union more than 12,600 men killed, wounded, or missing, and caused much of the army to lose confidence in his leadership. Determined to take the offensive again, Burnside decided to cross the Rappahannock four miles upriver from Fredericksburg and outflank Robert E. Lee's defensive positions from the west. One of the regiments participating in the maneuver was the 119th New York Infantry, part of the Third Division of the Eleventh Corps. Its adjutant, Theodore A. Dodge, had been commissioned as a lieutenant in the 101st New York in 1862 and had fought in the Seven Days' Battles and the Second Bull Run campaign before being wounded at Chantilly on September 1. In November 1862 he joined the 119th New York, where he served alongside his father, Nathaniel S. Dodge, the regimental quartermaster ("Q.M.").

———————

> Camp near Berea, 4 miles N.W. of Falmouth
> January 21st 1863

At last, after our numerous scares of being under orders to march at a moment's notice, we received day before yesterday orders to move "at 7 A.M. tomorrow. Further particulars will be sent," said the order, and we accordingly went to bed at 9 P.M., ready to start at any moment to carry out the provisions of any further orders that might arrive. About an hour after I had gone to sleep, an order did arrive, giving the order of march and directing our Brigade to fall in behind the 1st Brigade, which would pass our camp about 8 A.M.

This gave us a clue as to the direction in which we were to march, viz. towards Falmouth. We thought we should go to Brooke's Station, and that the Corps would be stationed along the line of communications between Aquia Creek

Landing and Burnside's Army. We were partly right. Just as we were breakfasting at 6 ¼ o'clock A.M. yesterday (20th), Lt. Stoldt, the Acting Assistant Adjutant General of our Brigade, came over with orders not to wait for the 1st Brigade but to fall into line and march at once. So, we hurried our things together and got off at 7 o'clock.

We took the road towards Falmouth, and came over the road which Stahel's Division had taken for Aquia Creek Landing and Brooke's Station; and further we found that we were destined for Hartwood Church. This point we reached about 3 P.M. and our present position about 5. The roads were good and we had a very prosperous march. Berea is on the direct road from Warrenton to Falmouth, 4 miles from the latter and consists of a fine farm house and accompanying buildings. Near this house we met Burnside's Army passing on to Banks's Ford, 4 miles from here, where a pontoon bridge is to be thrown across and the Army to pass the river. They expected to have done this last night but the wind was so high and the rain in such torrents that it was not possible. We got a little supper and then retired for the night about 8 o'clock.

The Q. M. had brought his trains along the good road at a fast pace, getting here almost as soon as we did, so that we were able to put up two tents—one for the Colonel and Lieutenant Col., and one for the Q. M. and myself. We tried to make a fire in the tent, but the stove would not draw on account of the wind, and the smoke nearly drove us wild; so we at length gave it up as a bad job, and took refuge in our cots. Towards morning, I woke up and found the wind had loosened the pins of the tent, and that it was on the point of falling. So I determined to get up and fix it. I groped about for my specs, which having found, I was trying in the dark to distinguish between the Q. M.'s boots and mine, when a sudden gust of wind raised the unfortunate tent from over our heads, and carried it several yards to leeward of its original position, when it suddenly collapsed, leaving us at the mercy of the elements. "Quarter Master!" shouted I to the cot opposite. No answer. "Quarter Master!" "What's the matter?" said he, coolly uncovering his head which had to that moment been buried in blankets. When he saw the desolation around him and the wild waving branches of the tree above him, he was filled with astonishment. It was a mercy the tent pole did not fall upon him. We roused teamsters & servants and finally got the tent pitched again. It was now nearly 6 o'clock, so we concluded to stay up and make a fire, which we accordingly did. Now (towards noon) the wind has gradually abated and there is a chance for getting fixed.

Batteries and troops are pouring on towards the river incessantly. We have just got notice that we shall stop here some time, so before night we hope to be all right again.

January 22nd 1863

Much to our surprise & gratification, a mail came this morning bringing us three letters from you. One which had been delayed since the 6th, one of the 16th and one of the 17th inst. We did not expect a mail so soon after our arrival here, and were in high glee to find our postal communications again established. We were very sorry to hear that your chilly, damp weather and east wind was afoot again and commencing his annoying attacks on your throat. What an inveterate throttler he is to be sure! He never seizes you anywhere else, but always straight at your throat. I hope, dear Mother, that his grip may be less powerful this time than his last attack.

We seem to be here to guard the communications between Aquia Landing and Burnside's Army. Stahel's Division is posted at the former place and along the R. R. to Brooke's Station, from whence to Falmouth I believe Von Steinwehr guards the R. R.; from Falmouth to Burnside his own Division along the Warrenton Turnpike. At all events, we have the post nearest the main Army, tho' if the weather should now prove so bad as to oblige us to go into winter quarters I should much prefer Aquia Landing; for a more desolate place you never saw than the one we are now occupying, rendered doubly so by rain and wind. Troops are continually passing on to the river below, and really when I see the poor wretched fellows tramping through the ankle deep mud, and remember from many sad experiences how hard such marching is, I feel as if our position were to be envied.

You have no idea of how soon the roads turn from good to bad here in Virginia. A clayey soil is hard and the very best for marching on in favorable weather, but let it rain but an hour and troops and wagons march over the road, and the mud is worse than anyone who has not been in Virginia can conceive of. The wagon train passing down to the river got stuck last night and could not move for many hours. If Burnside gets far away from the R. R. there will be the devil to pay, for the wagon trains can scarce move over the roads. You watch a train a little while and you will see horses dropping dead from sheer exhaustion every now and then. A four-horse team cannot possibly drag more than 1,000 lbs. over these roads and scarcely that.

Trains are a very different thing to manage here from what they are in Europe, where the roads are good. A turnpike here is what would be a shocking bad country lane in England. The rain ceased about 10 this evening, but the wind has not yet entirely subsided. These N. E. storms generally last 36 hours at least.

January 23, 1863

As expected, so it has come to pass. The batteries, which moved down to Banks's Ford 3 days ago, are now moving back again. It seems that Mud is really King. He sets down his foot and says, "Ye shall not pass," and lo and behold we cannot. But Mud wields more despotic sway these last two days than ever I saw him wield before. The horses sank into mud up to their bellies, and it is said down near the river you sometimes have to put sticks under the mules' necks to prevent their being engulfed in the very slough of despond. How inspirited and confident the men feel in their leaders you can well imagine. The Genl. Commanding announces to the Army of the Potomac "that they are about to meet the enemy face to face once more," says General Order No. 7, January 20th. "Go back from where you came," says order of today.

This Corps will probably wait till the Grand Divisions of Hooker and Franklin have once more waded their weary way through the mud to their old positions near Falmouth; then we shall do the same. At all events we shall have drier roads by that time, I hope. How it happens that Burnside did not make calculations upon the possibility of its raining whilst he made his move, I cannot imagine. It would seem that plans ought not to be made which rest on the favor of the elements.

The Q. M. and I pitched a new tent yesterday, and gave the one which blew from over us on the 21st to the Commissary Sergt. Owing to a scarcity of tents, the Q. M. and I have our Departments together. It is rather crowded on account of his having one clerk and I having the Sergt. Major and another clerk in the tent most of the time, but we get along tolerably well. The weather is still very damp, and as we have no flooring to our tent, cold feet are prevalent. This is however one of the minor evils. We have got out of wood today, on account of most of the rails round the farms here have been taken to corduroy the roads, and we cut down an immense oak tree close by our tents. It was a tree several hundred years old probably, & very large. We got a corporal of Co. K, who is a woodman by trade, to cut it down, and we watched with great interest to see whether he would fell it clear of the Colonel's tent and ours, which he succeeded in doing. The old tree fell with a terrible crash and thousands of branches flew up into the air like spray from a waterfall.

The other night, when the tent blew over, it broke my camp cot, and I have to set it up every night now with the greatest care, and lie still on my back all night for fear of its giving way and my coming down on to the ground. It is one of those complicated cots that pack up very small and is exceedingly difficult to mend. We have been wishing to ride down to the river these past two days, but the mud is so deep it is much too serious an undertaking.

Berea Church, January 24th 1863

A singular circumstance occurred today. The pontoons, the horses to which had been used in bringing the artillery up from the river along these excruciating roads, were being dragged up by Regiments, about 50 to each pontoon, fire engine style. This, though hard work, rather pleases the boys, & they were cheering as they came to good bits of road and running races with each other. We sat in our tents watching them on the road, about 150 yards off, when the Lieut. Col. proposed to go nearer and see what Regiments were there. As we reached the road the Lieut. Col. spoke to a young Lieutenant, who was trudging along through the mud. He turned out to be Willie Hyslop, whose family we know so well and whom we had thus singularly met. He got leave of his Colonel to come over to our tent & stay for dinner. We found him a very intelligent fellow and had a pleasant talk with him.

We asked him what the troops in his Division thought of this move. He said they quoted the proclamation, "If the Almighty is willing," and had come to the conclusion that the Almighty was not willing; that they all thoroughly laughed at Burnside, & were of the opinion that if McClellan was known to have been reinstated, not only would such cheers go up from the Army of the Potomac as were never heard, but that they would march with such a will and confidence upon Fredericksburg, either to storm the heights or to outflank the town, as would inevitably insure success. Col. P. is an inveterate opponent of McClellan, and was pumping Hyslop for his opinion, when he got the above, which *rather* took him down.

Poor Hyslop has been in active service since June '61, and is now only Lieutenant, never having been home at all. It is curious how different the chances of promotion are in different Regiments. Here is Hyslop, for example, who has been 2 years in the service, has been in almost every battle, and has served well and faithfully, and has only risen one step in all that time. Then take George Pomeroy, who has, in much less time, risen from Lieut. to Lieut. Col., and is now paymaster in the Regular Army. Some of the very best of the old Regiments are slowest in promotions.

Henry Adams to Charles Francis Adams Jr.

Henry Adams was confidential secretary to his father, Charles Francis Adams, the American minister to Great Britain. He wrote to his brother Charles, a captain in the 1st Massachusetts Cavalry serving in northern Virginia with the Army of the Potomac.

———————

London. 23 January. 1863.

My dear Charles:

I have but a moment till it grows dark and the bag closes, but I don't think I've much to say, so it don't matter. I've had a hard day's work too, as we generally do on Fridays, and am tired. We are in the dark as to movements at home since the 8th, no steamer being yet in owing I suppose to the awful gales.

We are as usual very quiet, having been dragged the rounds of the Christmas pantomimes and bored to death with them. I wish you or John were here to be funny and amuse people; you know I never could do it, and now I grow stupider and stupider every year as my hair grows thinner. I haven't even the wit left to talk to girls. I wish I were fifty years old at once, and then I should feel at home.

The Emancipation Proclamation has done more for us here than all our former victories and all our diplomacy. It is creating an almost convulsive reaction in our favor all over this country. The London Times is furious and scolds like a drunken drab. Certain it is, however, that public opinion is very deeply stirred here and finds expression in meetings; addresses to Pres. Lincoln; deputations to us; standing committees to agitate the subject and to affect opinion; and all the other symptoms of a great popular movement peculiarly unpleasant to the upper classes here because it rests altogether on the spontaneous action of the laboring classes and has a pestilent squint at sympathy with republicanism. But the Times is on its last legs and has lost its temper. They say it always does lose its temper when it finds such a feeling too strong for it, and its next step will be to come round and try to guide it. We are much encouraged and in high spirits. If only you at home don't have disasters, we will give such a checkmate to the foreign hopes of the rebels as they never yet have had.

We are all well and happy. I am at last on the point of buying a little mare and expect to have to hand her over to Mary, as her own horse is rather too much for her. Also having had my watch, hat and purse stolen at my celebrated Turkish baths, I have succeeded in obtaining a compensation of £15.0.0. with which I propose immediately to invest in a new watch. The exchange would be an inducement to invest at home, where I do not hear that my income has materially increased in spite of the superfluity of money. The mare costs £40.0.0 and will cost me at least £5.0.0 a month in keep.

Lebe wohl. Time is up and the Chief is a cussin and swearin like anythink for my letters.

Ever Yrs.

George G. Meade to Margaret Meade

A career army officer, Major General George G. Meade had led a brigade in the Seven Days' Battles and at Second Bull Run, and a division at Antietam and Fredericksburg, before becoming commander of the Fifth Corps in late December 1862. He wrote to his wife about the "Mud March" and its consequences for the Army of the Potomac.

———————

Camp near Falmouth Va.
Jany. 23d. 1863

Dear Margaret—

I have not written to you for several days (my last being on the 18th) for the reasons that I have had no opportunity & that I was aware all letters from the camp were stopped, in Washington, so that there was no use in writing.—On the 19th in the night we received orders to move the next day. On the 20th the whole army moved from the camp to a position 4 miles up the river, where crossing places had been previously selected. Every thing went off very well up to about 8 P.M. of the 20th. The army reached its position—the pontoons, artillery & all other accessories were up in time, & we all thought the next morning the bridges would be thrown over and we should be at it. But man proposes & God disposes. About 9 P.M. a terrific storm of wind & rain set in, and continued all night. At once I saw the game was up. The next day the roads were almost impassable. The pontoons, in attempting to get them to the waters edge stuck on the bank and 100 men could not budge them. Instead of 6 bridges being thrown over by *8 A.M.*, it was found late in the day that the materials of *one* only could be got to the waters-edge. Burnside visited us, and soon saw the state of the case. Still in hopes something might happen, he directed we should remain in position. All that night 21st. & the next day 22d. it continued to rain & the roads to get in such a condition, that early yesterday the 22d. I had to turn out the *whole* of my corps 15,000 men, and go to work and bridge with logs, or corduroy as it is called nearly the whole road from our camp to the crossing place 8 miles. The men worked cheerfully at this which was accomplished by early this morning, and Burnside having recalled the army to its old camp we have been all day getting our artillery back & tomorrow the infantry will return thus consuming two days to get back what it took only a few hours to get there.

I never felt so disappointed & sorry for any one in my life as I did for Burnside. He really seems to have all the elements against him. I told him warmly when I saw him how sorry I felt, and that I had almost rather have lost a limb than that the storm should have occurred. He seemed quite philosophical. Said he could not resist the elements and perhaps it was as well, for that his movement had been most strongly opposed, & some of his Generals had told him he was leading the men to a *slaughter pen*. And I am sorry to say there were many men & among them Generals high in command who openly rejoiced at the storm & the obstacle it presented.—We were very much amused to see in the papers today flaming accounts of our crossing, of the battle & Hooker's being mortally wounded. I hope you did not attach any importance to these absurd reports—which when I saw I feared you might have been anxious. I presumed the truth had been telegraphed and that you would know the storm had frustrated our plans. The plan was based on the presumption, that we would take the enemy unawares at least so far as the place of crossing was concerned and I believe but for the storm we should have succeeded in this.—What will be done now, I can not imagine. The mud is at present several feet thick wherever any wagons pass over a road, and if the weather from this time should at all resemble that of last year, it will effectively stop all operations for two months to come.—

On my return I found your letter of the 20th and two written by Markoe. I had written to Markoe, telling him it was useless for me to write to Halleck, and that my letter nominating him, was as strong an expression of my desire to have him, as any I could make, and that any further effort, would not only be unsuccessful but might bring from H— an answer that

I should not like to receive.—I am very sorry for Markoes disappointment, and would have been very glad to have him, but the thing it seems can not be effected, and there is no use, in struggling against fixed facts, besides Markoe knows I *doubted* from the first the practicality of success, and gave him distinctly to understand, that *he* must overcome in Washington the difficulties I anticipated. I can not & will not write to Halleck, because I do not believe it would be of the slightest use & I do not choose to lay myself in the power of that gentleman when I feel so confident I should fail. You can tell this to Markoe on my part, and advise him to be resigned to what can not be helped. I did not see George during our *fiasco*, tho I was at one time bivouacked near a part of his regiment but his company was not with that part. ——

Doubleday has been assigned to the *Reserves*, which is a good thing for me, for now they will think a great deal more of me than before. ——

I am very glad to hear Mr. Meredith heard such good reports of me in Washington. I see my name has gone to the Senate, all the papers say the Senate will not repeal their limiting resolution in which case my nomination can not be confirmed. I presume however the President will reappoint me after Congress adjourns, as he has done in other cases, where the Senate have tried to hand him off. ——

It is very late & I am tired so I will bid you Good bye.

Ever yours, *Geo. G. Meade*

———

Camp near Falmouth Va
Jany. 26./63—9 P.M.

Dear Margaret—

I wrote you a long letter today little thinking while I was quietly employed writing to you what momentous events were going on immediately around me. After writing to you I went out to ride for exercise & on my return at 6 P.M., found an order awaiting me announcing Maj. Genl. Hooker is in command of the Army of the Potomac & Maj. Genl. Meade in command of the Centre Grand Division. I then learned for the first time that this news arrived this morning Burnside having brought it down from Washington last night that he Burnside & all his staff had gone off this morning, and that Genls. *Sumner* & *Franklin* had both been relieved & ordered to Washington. You can readily imagine my surprise at all this, altho some such step had been talked about for some time back.—As to my commanding a Grand Division I consider it a mere temporary arrangement, as either some one of more rank will be sent or what is more likely the Grand Division organisation broken up altogether, as it was purely an invention of Burnsides, and has not I think been considered a good one. The removal of so many officers of rank however makes it certain I shall not go lower than a corps, and that is really all I particularly care for & is as much as I want.

You will doubtless be anxious to know what I think of these changes. With all my respect & I may almost say affection for Burnside, for he has been most kind & considerate towards me—I can not shut my eyes to the fact, that he was not equal to the command of so large an army. He had some very positive qualifications such as determination & nerve, but he wanted knowledge & judgement, and was deficient in that enlarged mental capacity which is essential in a commander. Another drawback, was a very general opinion among officers & men, brought about by his own assertions, that the command was too much for him. This greatly weakened his position.

As to Hooker you know my opinion of him frequently expressed. I believe my opinion is more favorable than any other of the old regular officers, most of whom are decided in their hostility to him. I believe Hooker is a good soldier. The danger he runs, is of subjecting himself to bad influences, such as *Dan Butterfield* & *Dan Sickles* who being intellectually more clever than Hooker & leading him to believe they are very influential, will obtain an injurious ascendancy over him & insensibly affect his conduct. I may however in this be wrong—time will prove. What we are now going to do remains to be seen. I have not seen Hooker since the news came & only write to tell you what is thus far known. Ever yours

Geo. G. Meade

Camp near Falmouth Va
Jany. 28. 1863

Dear Margaret—

Last evening yours of the 24th reached me. I am sorry to hear you have been sick, and still more sorry to know it has arisen from uncertainty & agitation, which it was not in my power to prevent. In the first place after the movement was determined on, I ascertained orders had been given to stop *all letters* at Acquia Creek. 2dly even if letters had been permitted to pass, it was impossible for me with my occupation & without materials to write. Again I relied on the agents of the Press to communicate the *truth*, at least sufficient to allay any unnecessary apprehensions, and never supposed *Washington canards* would be so greedily swallowed as the truth. Next time I will try & smuggle to you definite information.

Your anxiety lest I should be placed in command of the Army causes me Dearest to smile. Still I must confess when such men as Gibbons say it is talked about, it really does look serious & alarming. Yet when I look back on the good fortune which has thus attended my career I can not believe so sudden a change for the worse, can occur as would happen if I were placed in command. I think therefore we may for the present dismiss our fears on that score.—Genl. Hooker has been two days in Washington. I am looking anxiously for his return to hear what will be the result.—Before he was placed in command he was open-mouthed and constant, in his *assertions* that he did not want to command and that he *would not* command unless he was perfectly un-trammelled and allowed in every respect to do exactly as he pleased.—Now I am quite confident no such conditions will be acceded to in Washington—hence either "Fighting Joe" will have to back down, or some one else will be sent to take the command. From my knowledge of friend Hooker, I am inclined to surmise the former will be the case.—But even supposing they give him *carte-blanche* his position is any thing but enviable. This army is in a *false position* both as regards the enemy, and the public. With respect to the enemy we can literally do nothing, and our numbers are inadequate to the accomplishment of any result even if we go to the James river. On the other hand, the wise public, are under

the delusion, that we are omnipotent, and that it is only necessary to go ahead to achieve unheard of success. Of course
under such circumstances neither Cæsar, Napoleon, or any
other mighty *genius* could fail to meet with condemnation,
never mind what he did, and Hooker I fancy will find in time,
his fate, in the fate of his predecessors—in, *undue & exaggerated praise before* he does any thing, and a total absence of
reason & intelligence in the discussion of his acts, when he
does attempt any thing and a denial of even ordinary military
qualifications unless he achieves impossibilities.—Such being
the case, he certainly is not to be envied, and we may well be
satisfied that there is no chance of my being his successor.—
I think when his head is cut off the admn. will try a General of
their own kidney, either Fremont, Hunter &c

Of course so long as Hooker is absent I continue in command of the Centre Grand Division, but I am more & more
inclined to believe that his visit to Washington will result in the
abolition of the Grand Division system altogether, and the return to corps alone. In this case I infer I am bound to have a
corps for since the departure of Sumner & Franklin there are
at present only Six (6) generals ranking me viz Hooker, Couch
Sigel Slocum Smith W. F. & Sedgewick. As Hooker is in command of all & there are *8 corps*, it will make me the 6th corps
commdr. Should Reynolds be confirmed & appointed, I suppose he will rank me which would give me the 7th corps rank.
The only danger of my being reduced lower would be the
promotion of *Stoneman* on the same date as myself (Nov. 29).

This is not likely, his name not being on the list sent in, but
he has gone to Washington to try & have it done, and he will
undoubtedly have Hooker's influence in his behalf. Per contra
there is another probability, which is that Sigel will decline
serving under Hooker particularly if the Grand Divisions are
broken up, of which he has now one. So—should he leave &
both Stoneman & Reynolds be put over me I would still have
a corps. I therefore look with confidence to my not getting
lower than this. And I hope I shall retain the 5th corps as it is
one of the best including as it does the Regulars.—Humphreys
has gone to Washn to try & be made a Maj. Genl swearing he
will resign if they do not accede to his *claim.*

I believe I wrote you, he behaved with distinguished gallantry at Fredericksburg. It appears soon after the battle Burnside told him both the President & Secy. assured him solemnly that Humphreys should be immediately promoted. He now finds a long list sent to the senate including such names as *Butterfield Sickles, Berry* & others who have really done nothing, while his name is omitted, and he can not hear that there is any record in the Dept. going to shew he has ever, even been thought of. Under these circumstances he is naturally very indignant and swears he will quit the service altogether if justice is not done him. This is all *entre-nous.* Just as I had gotten this far I heard Hooker had returned, and notwithstanding it is storming & snowing violently, I rode 3 miles to his Hd. Qtrs. to see him, and have just returned.—He seemed in excellent spirits, said they had treated him en Prince in Washn. & told him he had only to ask & he should have what he wanted. He did not tell me his plans but intimated that as soon as the weather & the roads permitted he was prepared to try something. He did tell me however, as I suspected that he had *Stonemans* name put on the list of Maj. Genls thus putting another one over my head. At the same time he said my commission ought to be antedated to South Mountain tho' he said nothing about asking this for me. Well I am satisfied to take things as they are. There seems to be no justice and I am really tired of scrambling & pushing for it.

I have received your delightful letter of the 26th describing your happy relatives in the BG. & other members of your family. Pon my word I am glad I am here altho I stand a chance of being shot, than in such a position as you describe yours. Seriously why do you pay any attention to such weaknesses. Woodruff I trust in a few days will send you a soothing check, and as soon as my Decr. acct. can be paid you will be all right. Love to all. Keep up your spirits & take care of your health. Ever yours

G. G. Meade

Abraham Lincoln to Joseph Hooker

Frustrated by insubordination among his senior generals, Burnside drafted an order on January 23 transferring William B. Franklin and William F. Smith, who sought to have McClellan restored to command of the Army of the Potomac, and cashiering Joseph Hooker, who sought to command the army himself. The next day Burnside met with Lincoln at the White House and gave the President the choice of either endorsing his order or accepting his resignation. Lincoln replaced Burnside with Hooker on January 25, and then wrote to his new commander.

Executive Mansion,
Washington, January 26, 1863.

Major General Hooker:
General.

I have placed you at the head of the Army of the Potomac. Of course I have done this upon what appear to me to be sufficient reasons. And yet I think it best for you to know that there are some things in regard to which, I am not quite satisfied with you. I believe you to be a brave and a skilful soldier, which, of course, I like. I also believe you do not mix politics with your profession, in which you are right. You have confidence in yourself, which is a valuable, if not an indispensable quality. You are ambitious, which, within reasonable bounds, does good rather than harm. But I think that during Gen. Burnside's command of the Army, you have taken counsel of your ambition, and thwarted him as much as you could, in which you did a great wrong to the country, and to a most meritorious and honorable brother officer. I have heard, in such way as to believe it, of your recently saying that both the Army and the Government needed a Dictator. Of course it was not *for* this, but in spite of it, that I have given you the command. Only those generals who gain successes, can set up dictators. What I now ask of you is military success, and I will risk the dictatorship. The government will support you to the utmost of it's ability, which is neither more nor less than it has done and will do for all commanders. I much fear that the spirit which you have aided to infuse into the Army, of criticising their Commander, and withholding confidence from him, will now turn upon you. I shall assist you as far as I can, to put it down. Neither you, nor Napoleon, if he were alive again, could get any good out of an army, while such a spirit prevails in it.

And now, beware of rashness. Beware of rashness, but with energy, and sleepless vigilance, go forward, and give us victories. Yours very truly

A. LINCOLN

John A. Andrew to Francis Shaw

From the beginning of the war Frederick Douglass and other abolitionists had advocated the raising of black troops to fight for the Union. Despite opposition from the border states and northern Democrats, Congress authorized the president in July 1862 to enroll blacks as soldiers, and by the end of the year five black regiments had been formed at the initiative of Union commanders in South Carolina, Louisiana, and Kansas. After resisting calls for enlistment of blacks, President Lincoln declared in the Emancipation Proclamation that they would be "received into the armed service of the United States to garrison forts, positions, stations, and other places." Encouraged by the proclamation, John A. Andrew, the Republican governor of Massachusetts, sought and received authorization from Secretary of War Edwin M. Stanton to recruit a black regiment from among the freemen of the northern states. Andrew solicited the assistance of Francis Shaw, an abolitionist and social reformer from a wealthy and socially prominent Massachusetts family.

———————

Commonwealth of Massachusetts.
Executive Department.
Boston, Jan. 30th 1863

Francis G. Shaw, Esq. Staten Island. N.Y.
Dear Sir:
    As you may have seen by the newspapers, I am about to raise a Colored Regiment in Massachusetts. This I cannot but regard as perhaps the most important corps to be organized during the whole war, in view of what must be the composition of our new levies; and therefore I am very anxious to organize it judiciously in order that it may be a model for all future Colored Regiments. I am desirous to have for its officers —particularly for its field officers—young men of military experience, of firm Anti Slavery principles, ambitious, superior to a vulgar contempt for color, and having faith in the capacity of

Colored men for military service. Such officers must be necessarily gentlemen of the highest tone and honor; and I shall
look for them in those circles of Educated Anti Slavery Society,
which next to the colored race itself has the greatest interest in
the success of this experiment.

Reviewing the young men of the character I have described,
now in the Massachusetts service it occurs to me to offer the
Colonelcy of such a Regiment to your son, Capt Shaw of the
2nd Mass. Infantry, and the Lt. Colonelcy to Capt. Hallowell
of the 20th Mass. Infantry, the son of Mr. Morris L. Hallowell
of Philadelphia. With my deep conviction of the importance of
this undertaking in view of the fact that it will be the first
Colored Regiment to be raised in the Free States, and that its
success or its failure will go far to elevate or to depress the estimation in which the character of the Colored Americans will
be held throughout the World, the command of such a Regiment seems to me to be a high object of ambition for any officer. How much your son may have reflected upon such a
subject I do not know, nor have I any information of his disposition for such a task except what I have derived from his general character and reputation, nor should I wish him to
undertake it unless he could enter upon it with a full sense of
its importance, with an earnest determination for its success;
and with the assent and sympathy and support of the opinion
of his immediate family. I therefore beg to enclose to you the
letter in which I make him the offer of this commission, and I
will be obliged to you, if you will forward it to him accompanying it with any expression to him of your own views, and if
you will also write to me upon the subject.

My mind is drawn towards Capt. Shaw by many considerations. I am sure that he would attract the support, sympathy
and active co-operation of many besides his immediate family
and relatives. The more ardent, faithful, true Republicans and
friends of Liberty would recognize in him, a scion of a tree
whose fruit and leaves have alike contributed to the strength
and healing of our generation. So also it is with Capt. Hallowell. His father is a quaker gentleman of Philadelphia, two
of whose sons are officers in our regiments and another is a
Merchant in Boston. Their house in Philadelphia is a hospital
almost for Mass. officers, and the family are full of good works;

Mr. H. being my constant adviser in the interest of our soldiers, when sick or in distress in that city. I need not add that young Capt. H. is a gallant and fine fellow, true as steel to the cause of Human Nature, as well as to the flag of the Country.

I wish to engage the field officers and then get their aid in selecting those of the line. I have offers from "Oliver T. Beard of Brooklyn, N.Y. late Lt. Col. 48th N. Y. V." who says he can already furnish 600 men, and from others wishing to furnish men from New York, and from Conn., but I do not wish to start the regiment under a stranger to Massachusetts. Still I have written to Col. H. E. Howe to learn about Col. Beard, since he may be useful in some contingency hereafter. If in any way, by suggestion or otherwise, you can aid the purpose which is the burden of this letter, I shall receive your cooperation with the heartiest gratitude.—

I dont want the office to go begging; & if this offer is refused I wd. prefer its being kept reasonably private. Hoping to hear from you immediately on yr receiving this note, I am, with high regard, Your obt. servant & friend,

John A. Andrew.

William Parker Cutler: Diary, February 2 and 9, 1863

Congressman Thaddeus Stevens of Pennsylvania, a leading Radical Republican, introduced a bill on January 12, 1863, authorizing the enlistment of 150,000 black soldiers. After a debate in which opponents denounced the measure as "suicidal and seditious" and designed to "exterminate and drive out the white people" of the cotton states, the bill passed and was sent to the Senate. William Parker Cutler, a Republican congressman from Ohio, witnessed the final vote in the House and later discussed the issue of black soldiers with President Lincoln. The Stevens bill was withdrawn from consideration in the Senate after Henry Wilson, the Massachusetts Republican who chaired the Committee on Military Affairs, reported on February 13 that the president already had authority to enlist blacks under the Militia Act passed in July 1862.

———————

Feb 2   After a long contest over Mr Stevens bill to raise Negro regiments—it finally passed to day 83 to 54. The Democrats seemed determined to make capital out of the idea of putting a Negro on an equality with the white man—by making him a soldier. They have made every effort to rouse up the worst prejudices of the army & the people—& seem to glory & exult in the opportunity presented to degrade & tread down *Gods image* in the person of the Negro. Surely there is no solution to terrible complications of our situation except in power & strong arm of God himself. The Democrats claim a strong reaction in their favor—& seem intent only upon increasing the universal dissatisfaction & turning it all to their own account in building up a peace party. Political demagogues rule the hour—The people are bewildered & in the fog. The true friends of the govt & of the great principles which underlie this contest are groping around without a *leader*—absolutely no one to command entire confidence—& yet progress is being made daily. This vote is a recognition of the Negros *manhood*—such as has never before been made by this nation. We say in the hour of peril—come save us. "*Our God is marching on.*"

Feb 9th   Called this morning on Pres. Lincoln to present him a petition signed by—say 30 members of Congress asking him to appoint Capt Carpenter of the famous Jessie Scouts as Col. of one of the Negro regiments—in case the bill passes the Senate. He said the great difficulty he feared was the treatment these Negroes would receive at first from the rebels in case they were captured. I remarked that it was the more important that the regiments should be of good material & well officered so as to take care of themselves in a fight. He assented quickly to this—But remarked that he was troubled to know what we should do with these people—Negroes—after peace came—I remarked that I supposed the same plantations that now required their labor would then need them just as much. He said that "Whatever you and me may think on these matters peoples opinions were every thing"—He seemed to be sticking in the bank because of the popular delusion that nothing can be done with the Negro if he is *free.* Interest will settle these questions—If land owners cant get the Negroes labor for nothing—he will pay him for it—that is all. Washburne of Ill. was in the room at the same time & read a letter from Grant at Vicksburg dated Jan 29th—in which he said the canal cut there was only 9 feet wide at the top & of course was of no account. He was trying a larger one—But thought he could take the place by getting a channel through into the Yazoo & operating from the Mississippi side. The Mississippi was then bank full. Lincoln said that Richmond papers stated that the gun boat which run the Vicksburg blockade was doing mischief below.

George Templeton Strong:
Diary, February 3–5, 1863

A successful New York lawyer, Strong served as treasurer of the U.S. Sanitary Commission, a civilian organization dedicated to caring for sick and wounded soldiers and improving conditions in army camps. In his diary he considered the prospects for the Union cause.

———————

February 3. Life and Trust Company meeting this morning. To a poor man like me the talk of these wholesale moneyers, like old Joe Kernochan and Aspinwall and others, is sublime. With what irreverent familiarity do they talk of millions! At 823 afterwards.

Murray Hoffman dined here and I went at eight to Executive Committee meeting at Dr. Bellows's, where were also Gibbs and Agnew. Among other little matters that came before us was a draft for some $1,100, the third article of the sort received from Honolulu. Agnew says he expects the next big aerolite that arrives will bring us a contribution from American citizens in the moon. The success of this Sanitary Commission has been a marvel. Our receipts in cash up to this time are nearly $700,000 at the central office alone, beside what has been received and spent by auxiliaries, and the three or four millions' worth of stores of every sort contributed at our depots. It has become a "big thing," has the Sanitary Commission, and a considerable fact in the history of this people and of this war. Our work at Washington and at Louisville, our two chief nervous centres, is on a big scale, employs some two hundred agents of every sort, and costs not much less than $40,000 a month.

National affairs seem stagnant, but I suppose we shall very soon hear news of the first importance from Vicksburg and possibly from Rosecrans. I think the national destiny will be decided in the Southwest, not in Virginia. Richmond is an *ignis fatuus*. We have mired ourselves badly in trying to reach it, twice at least, and can apply our strength more advantageously at other points. I am more and more satisfied, as I have been from the first, that our true policy is to occupy every Southern port, to open the Mississippi, to keep a couple of armies in strong and comfortable and healthy positions on the rebel frontier, and then to say to Jefferson Davis, "We are not going to advance into your jungle over your muddy roads. If you want a fight, you must come to us. If you don't want it, stay where you are and let us see which party will first be starved and wearied into submission." We do not need enterprise and dash near so much as resolution and steadiness, perseverance and pluck; the passive pluck that can suffer a little and wait quietly for the inevitable result. Therein this people seems wanting. Perhaps I do it injustice, but all the symptoms of the last four months indicate a fearful absence of vital power and constitutional stamina to resist disease and pain. The way the Dirt-Eaters and Copperheads and sympathizers and compromisers are coming out on the surface of society, like ugly petechiæ and vibices, shows that the nation is suffering from a most putrescent state of the national blood, and that we are a very typhoid community here at the North.

Thank God for the rancorous, vindictive, ferocious, hysterical utterances that reach us from the South—for the speeches and the Richmond *Enquirer* editorials declaring compromise and reconstruction impossible, that "Southrons" would not take back "Yankees" even as their slaves, that Northern Democrats who talk about restoring the Union are fools and blind. Were the South only a little less furious, savage, and spiteful, it could in three months so strengthen our "Peace Democracy" as to paralyze the nation and destroy all hope of ever restoring its territorial integrity. It is strange Jefferson Davis & Co. fail to see their best move. With a few unmeaning, insincere professions of desire for reconstruction, additional Constitutional guaranties, and so forth, they could bring us grovelling to their feet and secure an armistice most profitable to them, most dishonorable and disastrous to us.

February 5. These be dark blue days. Of course, every man's duty is to keep a stiff upper lip—*fortem in arduis rebus servare mentem*—"to talk turkey" about the moral certainty of triumph at last. I do so very valiantly. It's fearful and wonderful the way I blow and brag about our national invincibility, the extent of our conquests during the last twenty months, and our steady progress toward subjugation of the South. It is the right kind of talk for the times, and is more than half true, and has materially relieved the moral and political *adynamia* of at least one man, Bidwell, already. But (between me and my journal) things do in fact look darker and more dark every day. We are in a fearful scrape, and I see no way out of it. Recognition of the "Confederacy" is impossible. So is vigorous prosecution of the war twelve months longer. This proposition is self-evident "if this court understand herself, and she think she do." How can these two contradictions be reconciled? Rabelais furnishes a case equally difficult. Jupiter created a fox that was destined never to be caught, and afterwards, by inadvertence, a dog destined to catch all foxes, so that the Olympian Ledger of Destiny could not be made to balance. If I rightly remember my learned and pious author, Jupiter got rid of the embarrassment by turning dog and fox into two stars, or two constellations, or two stones, which was a mere evasion, and no solution of the great problem he had to deal with. We are in a similar deadlock of contradiction, I fear; North cannot be defeated and South cannot be conquered. (Of course, this is taking the worst view of the case.)

Oliver W. Norton to Edwin Norton

The bugle call "Taps" was first played in July 1862 by Oliver W. Norton, who served as brigade bugler for the tune's composer, Brigadier General Daniel Butterfield. A private in the 83rd Pennsylvania Infantry, Norton had enlisted in 1861 and seen action in the Peninsula campaign and at Second Bull Run and Fredericksburg. He wrote to his brother from an army camp near the north bank of the Rappahannock.

———————

Stoneman Station, Va.,
Friday, Feb. 6, 1863.

Dear E.:—

Wicks' golden opinions of "Little Norton" may do very well to repeat at home. Perhaps he thinks, as he has said so much for me, I should return the compliment and praise him up to the skies. I can't see the point. I don't thank anybody to say that I have done more than I agreed to do, more than a soldier's duty, and if any one says I have not done my duty, send him to me to say it. I don't know what Wicks saw me do at Malvern Hill. I didn't see him at all in the fight. I was under the impression that he was "taken with a sunstroke" just before the fight commenced. At Bull Run the boys say he did "fight like the devil."

I don't care anything about what he told you of my smoking. I could have told you that long ago if I had thought you cared anything about it. You all knew when I left home that I used tobacco some, and Mother and L. particularly urged me to quit it. I wouldn't make any promises about it and continued to smoke, but a year ago last Christmas I did quit, and then I wrote home and told all about it. Well, not the first one said so much as "I'm glad," or advised me to stick to it. I waited a month or so and heard nothing, and then I thought if that was all you cared about it, if it made no difference to any of you, it didn't to me, so I went at it again. If Wicks had told you that I chewed two pounds of plug a week and a pound of opium, drank gin and gambled, would you have believed him? Well, if it makes any difference to you I will just say for your comfort that I don't.

I am glad to hear that Wicks is looking so well. The boys who saw him in Alexandria said there was nothing left of him but his mustache. If I get down so low as that, I would not be much to load down an ambulance or a hog-car, would I?

No, siree, I wouldn't take a discharge now if I could get it. You need not trouble yourself about that. If I did want one, I fancy (pardon my vanity) I could play off on the doctors and get it, but I don't want it, and I would kick a man that would offer me one. As to being the "captain's friend" I don't see the point. I despise him too much for that. Personally I have no fault to find. He has always treated me well, perhaps favored me some, but I am not the friend of the man who always has the piles or something of the sort when a fight is coming off. At Hanover Court House he couldn't keep up, at Gaines' Mill he lay behind a tree and laughed while the men fell all round him. At Malvern he shouted retreat and ran like a greyhound, and got shot in the back with a three-cornered something. Last summer at Fredericksburg when we expected a fight he was too weak to march, and we didn't see him again till after Antietam. At this last at Fredericksburg he did go in and acted something like a man, the first and last time he has done so. When we moved last, expecting another battle, he couldn't go, he had the piles. Should I be the "captain's friend"? I don't know that he has but one in the company, and he is a sort of sucker. Mrs. A. is a woman, a true woman. I respect her very much, and so does every man in the company. Nothing but that respect for her feelings prevents the company from complaining of him and having him cashiered for cowardice.

I think some of my letters must have been lost. Did you never get the one that told of Henry's watch being lost? I felt so bad about that. I would have bought a dozen rather than lost that. I kept it till we got to Antietam, waiting for a chance to send it by express, but finally after getting Mary's permission, sent it by mail, and it was never heard from. I took all the precautions I could to make it safe, did it up in a little box like an ambrotype, but the last I heard it had not arrived, and if it had, they would have told me.

I wrote you in my last how our march terminated. Did Wicks tell you anything about camp lice? I do not know that I have ever said a word about them in all my letters, but they are so plenty here that they are the subject of half the standing jokes and *bons mots* in camp. I presume you never saw one. They are the soldier's pest. I never saw one till we got to York-town. They resemble head lice in appearance, but not in habits. They don't go near the hair, but stay in the clothes, shirt and drawers. There is no way to get rid of them, but to scald them out. They will hide in the seams and nit in every hiding place possible. Cold water won't faze them. They multiply like locusts and they will fat on "onguentum." At the time we left the Peninsula they were plenty, and until we got to Antietam, more than a month, no one had a chance to wash his clothes in hot water. I do not believe there was a man in our brigade, officer, private or nigger, but was lousy. They grow to enormous size and are the most cunning and most impudent of all things that live. During the late snow storm the boys, for want of something else to do, made sleds of their jaw bones, and slid down the bank of the railroad. The other night after supper I was sitting by the fire smoking a cigar, when I felt something twitch at my pants' leg. I looked down and there was one of the "crumbs" with a straw in his mouth, standing on his hind legs and working his claws round like a crab on a fish line. I gave a kick at him, but he dodged it and sticking up his cigar squeaked out, "Give me a light."

I woke up the other night and found a regiment of them going through the manual of arms on my back. Just as I woke the colonel gave the command "charge bayonets," and the way they let drive at my sirloin was a proof of their capacity. Any one of them can throw himself into a hollow square and bite at the four corners. I would be willing to let them have what blood and meat they wanted to eat, but the devils amuse themselves nights by biting out chunks and throwing them away. Well, this is a pretty lousy leaf, ain't it? Most likely the next one will be something different if it is not.

Joe (my housemaid) is sitting by the fire picking his teeth

with a bayonet and swearing at the beef. He says it is a pity it was killed, it was tough enough to stand many a long march yet. Well, it is tough. When Burnside got stuck in the mud, the artillery harness all broke, and the only way they could get the guns out was for the men to cut their rations of beef into strips, and make tugs out of them.

Robert E. Lee to Mary Lee

After the battle of Fredericksburg the Army of Northern Virginia held a defensive line along the south bank of the Rappahannock extending from Bank's Ford, four miles above the town, to Port Royal, eighteen miles downriver. Forced to rely on the single-track Richmond & Fredericksburg railroad for its supplies, the army suffered from a shortage of food and clothing for its soldiers and forage for its animals. "Our horses & mules suffer the most," General Robert E. Lee wrote to his daughter Agnes on February 6. "They have to bear the cold & rain, tug through the mud, & suffer all the time with hunger." Lee wrote to his wife from Fredericksburg two days later.

Camp
February 8, 1863

I have just received dear Mary your letter of the 7th. I am distressed to hear of your suffering. I fear you are very imprudent, & that unless you are careful, you will reduce yourself to confinement altogether. You ought not to go out in bad weather, or to expose yourself at any time. I beg you will be careful. I send the passport for Mrs. Murdock, &c. I presume they intend returning the way they came, by Leesburg. Inform them they cannot pass through Fredericksburg. Genl Hooker has refused to permit passage through his lines here. I see in the Washington papers orders from Genl Halleck forbidding transportation of any citizens on the steamers plying between that city & Aquia Creek. All the boats &c. are reserved for the military. There is therefore no chance for them by this route. They can take the cars to Culpeper Court House & must thence find their way to Warrenton & Leesburg by private conveyance. Their best route is by flag of truce boat from City Point to Baltimore if that is permitted. But when they get home, my advice is to stay there & to let their sons & brothers alone. The men can do very well & soldiers must learn to take care of themselves. I have done however all I can. If this passport does not answer, it is useless to apply to me for another. It will take them anywhere through my lines. I know the yankees will get out of them all they know. I hope they know nothing to injure us. Not that I believe they will intentionally say or do ought to injure us, but the yankees have a very coaxing & insidious manner, that our Southern women in their artlessness cannot resist, no matter how favourable they may be to our cause or how full of good works for our men. I have not seen any of your gloves on the men, & therefore cannot say how they answer. I should think well, if they fit, & you know all your garments are warranted to do that. I advise you however to send up all you have made at once & then stop for this winter. After about a month they will be of no use. The men cannot preserve them & will throw them away. Remember me kindly to the Caskies. I cannot get down to R now. Nor can I expect any pleasure, during this war. We are in a liquid state at present. Up to our knees in mud & what is worse on short rations for men & beasts. This keeps me miserable. I am willing to starve myself, but cannot bear my men or horses to be pinched. I fear many of the latter will die. Give my love to Agnes. I wrote to her the other day. Where is she staying? As you both seem to prefer Richmond to anywhere else, you had better take a house there. Be careful of the small pox & other diseases. Tell Miss N that I told Major Talcott, after he had seen his sweetheart, he must go up & look at her for me. So she must give him a sweet look. Present me very kindly to Mrs. Jones. I sympathize with her deeply in the death of her husband. He was always a great favorite with me. Fitzhugh is still low down the Rappahannock, I believe Charlotte is with him still. But have not heard. He is 40 miles from me.

With great affection, yours
R. E. LEE

P.S. I have George as cook now. He is quite subdued but has only been here a day. I give him & Perry each 8.20 per month. I hope they will be able to lay up something for themselves.

R. E. L.

Robert Gould Shaw to Annie Haggerty

Commissioned as a second lieutenant in the 2nd Massachusetts Infantry in 1861, Captain Robert Gould Shaw saw action at Front Royal, Cedar Mountain, and Antietam. On February 3, 1863, he was visited at his camp in northern Virginia by his father Francis, who brought with him Governor John A. Andrew's offer of the colonelcy of a Massachusetts black regiment (see pp. 20–22 in this volume). Shaw initially rejected the position, then changed his mind. He wrote to his fiancée about his decision.

———————

Stafford C. H., Va.
Feb. 8, 1863
Dear Annie,

You know by this time, perhaps, that I have changed my mind about the black regiment. After Father left, I began to think I had made a mistake in refusing Governor Andrew's offer. Mother has telegraphed to me that you would not disapprove of it, and that makes me feel much more easy about having taken it. Going for another three years is not nearly so bad a thing for a colonel as a captain; as the former can much more easily get a furlough. Then, after I have undertaken this work, I shall feel that what I have to do is to prove that a negro can be made a good soldier, and, that being established, it will not be a point of honour with me to see the war through, unless I really occupied a position of importance in the army. Hundreds of men might leave the army, you know, without injuring the service in the slightest degree.

Last night I received your letter of last Sunday, February 1st. You must be at Susie's house now,—at least I judge so from Mother's telegram. As I may not receive my order to leave here for some days, do promise to stay there until I get to New York. You do not know how I shall feel if I find you are gone.

It is needless for me to overwhelm you with a quantity of arguments in favour of the negro troops; because you are with

Mother, the warmest advocate the cause can have. I am in-clined to think that the undertaking will not meet with so much opposition as was at first supposed. All sensible men in the army, of all parties, after a little thought, say that it is the best thing that can be done; and surely those at home, who are not brave or patriotic enough to enlist, should not ridicule, or throw obstacles in the way of men who are going to fight for them. There is a great prejudice against it; but now that it has become a government matter, that will probably wear away. At any rate, I shan't be frightened out of it by its unpopularity; and I hope you won't care if it is made fun of.

Dear Annie, the first thing I thought of, in connection with it, was how you would feel, and I trust, now I have taken hold of it, I shall find you agree with me and all of our family, in thinking I was right. You know how many eminent men con-sider a negro army of the greatest importance to our country at this time. If it turns out to be so, how fully repaid the pio-neers in the movement will be, for what they may have to go through! And at any rate I feel convinced I shall never regret having taken this step, as far as I myself am concerned; for while I was undecided I felt ashamed of myself, as if I were cowardly.

Good bye, dear Annie. I hope that when I arrive at Sue's door you will not be very far off.

With a great deal of love, (more every day) your

Rob

Richard Cobden to Charles Sumner

Along with his friend and parliamentary colleague John Bright, the reformer Richard Cobden was one of the leading British supporters of the Union cause. In the fall of 1862 the Liberal government led by Lord Palmerston had considered attempting to mediate an end to the American Civil War, but had decided to wait until the military situation was clearer. Cobden wrote about the impact of the Emancipation Proclamation to his friend Charles Sumner, the Massachusetts Radical Republican who chaired the Senate Committee on Foreign Relations.

————————

ATHENÆUM CLUB
LONDON, 13 Feby., 1863

Private

My dear Sumner.

If I have not written to you before it is not because I have been indifferent to what is passing in your midst. I may say sincerely that my thoughts have run almost as much on American as English politics. But I could do you no service, and shrunk from occupying your overtaxed attention even for a moment. My object in now writing is to speak of a matter which has a practical bearing on your affairs.

You know how much alarmed I was from the first lest our government should interpose in your affairs. The disposition of our ruling class, and the necessities of our cotton trade, pointed to some act of intervention and the indifference of the great mass of our population to your struggle, the object of which they did not foresee and understand, would have made intervention easy indeed popular if you had been a weaker naval power. This state of feeling existed up to the announcement of the President's emancipation policy. From that moment our old anti-slavery feeling began to arouse itself, and it has been gathering strength ever since. The great rush of the public to all the public meetings called on the subject shows how wide and deep the sympathy for personal freedom still is in the hearts of our people. I know nothing in my political experience so striking as a display of spontaneous public action as that of the vast gathering at Exeter Hall when without one attraction in the form of a popular orator the vast building, its minor rooms and passages and the streets adjoining were crowded with an enthusiastic audience. That meeting has had a powerful effect on our newspapers and politicians. It has closed the mouths of those who have been advocating the side of the South. And I now write to assure you that any unfriendly act on the part of our government, no matter which of our aristocratic parties is in power, towards your cause is not to be apprehended. If an attempt were made by the government in any way to commit us to the South, a spirit would be instantly aroused which would drive our government from power. This I suppose will be known and felt by the Southern agents in Europe and if communicated to their government must I should think operate as a great discouragement to them. For *I know* that those agents have been incessantly urging in every quarter where they could hope to influence the French and English governments the absolute necessity of *recognition* as a means of putting an end to the war. Recognition of the South, by England, whilst it bases itself on negro slavery, is an impossibility, unless indeed after the Federal government have recognized the Confederates as a nation.

So much for the influence which your emancipation policy has had on the public opinion of England. But judging from the tone of your press in America it does not seem to have gained the support of your masses. About this however I do not feel competent to offer an opinion. Nor, to confess the truth, do I feel much satisfaction in treating of your politics at all. There appears to me great mismanagement I had almost said incapacity in the management of your affairs, and you seem to be hastening towards financial and economical evils in a manner which fills me with apprehension for the future.

When I met Frémont in Paris two years ago just as you commenced this terrible war I remarked to him that the total abolition of slavery in your northern Continent was the only issue which could justify the war to the civilized world. Every symptom seems to point to this result. But at what a price is the negro to be emancipated! I confess that if then I had been the arbiter of his fate I should have refused him freedom at the cost of so much white men's blood and women's tears. I do not however blame the North. The South fired the first shot, and on them righteously falls the malediction that "they who take the sword shall perish by the sword." And it seems unlikely that after all the much despised "nigger," and not the potentates and statesmen of Europe will be the final arbitrator in the great struggle.

Let me have a line from you when your Senatorial duties have ceased on the 4th, and afford you a little leisure.

Believe me,

Yours very truly

R. COBDEN.

Isaac Funk: Speech in the Illinois State Senate

February 14, 1863

In the fall 1862 elections the Democrats won the governorships of New Jersey and New York, legislative majorities in Illinois, Indiana, and New Jersey, and gained thirty-four seats in the House of Representatives. When the new Illinois general assembly met in Springfield on January 5, 1863, the house of representatives began adopting a series of resolutions that condemned the Emancipation Proclamation, the suspension of habeas corpus, and the administration's conduct of the war, and called for an armistice and a national convention to negotiate terms of reunion. Richard Yates, the Republican governor of Illinois, described the legislature in a letter as "a wild, rampant, revolutionary body" seeking to deprive him of executive power. President Lincoln told Senator Charles Sumner that he now feared " 'the fire in the rear'—meaning the Democracy, especially at the Northwest—more than our own military chances." The fatal illness of a Democratic member prevented the anti-administration resolutions from being adopted by the closely divided state senate before the general assembly adjourned on February 14. The text of Republican senator Isaac Funk's speech from the final day of the legislative session is taken from a New York pamphlet printing titled *Copperheads under the Heel of an Illinois Farmer.*

ON THE last day of the Illinois Legislature, in February, 1863, Mr. Funk, a Senator from McLean County, delivered a speech, which is thus described and reported by the Springfield correspondent of the Chicago *Tribune*:

A great sensation was created by a speech by Mr. Funk, one of the richest farmers in the State, a man who pays over three thousand dollars per annum taxes towards the support of the Government. The lobby and gallery were crowded with spectators. Mr. Funk rose to object to trifling resolutions, which had been introduced by the Democrats to kill time and stave off a vote upon the appropriations for the support of the State Government. He said:

Mr. Speaker, I can sit in my seat no longer and see such by-play going on. These men are trifling with the best interests of the country. They should have asses' ears to set off their heads, or they are traitors and secessionists at heart.

I say that there are traitors and secessionists at heart in this Senate. Their actions prove it. Their speeches prove it. Their gibes and laughter and cheers here nightly, when their speakers get up to denounce the war and the administration, prove it.

I can sit here no longer and not tell these traitors what I think of them. And while so telling them, I am responsible, myself, for what I say. I stand upon my own bottom. I am ready to meet any man on this floor in any manner, from a pin's point to the mouth of a cannon, upon this charge against these traitors. [Tremendous applause from the galleries.]

I am an old man of sixty-five; I came to Illinois a poor boy; I have made a little something for myself and family. I pay three thousand dollars a year in taxes. I am willing to pay six thousand, aye, twelve thousand, [great cheering, the old gentleman striking the desk with a blow that would knock down a bullock, and causing the inkstand to fly in the air,] aye, I am willing to pay my whole fortune, and then give my life, to save my country from these traitors that are seeking to destroy it. [Tremendous applause, which the Speaker could not control.]

Mr. Speaker, you must please excuse me; I could not sit longer in my seat and calmly listen to these traitors. My heart, that feels for my poor country, would not let me. My heart, that cries out for the lives of our brave volunteers in the field, that these traitors at home are destroying by thousands, would not let me. My heart, that bleeds for the widows and orphans at home, would not let me. Yes, these traitors and villains in this Senate [striking his clenched fist on the desk with a blow that made the Senate ring again] are killing my neighbors' boys now fighting in the field. I dare to say this to these traitors right here, and I am responsible for what I say to any one or all of them. [Cheers.] Let them come on now, right here. I am sixty-five years old, and I have made up my mind to risk my life right here, on this floor, for my country. [Mr. Funk's seat is near the lobby railing, and a crowd collected around him, evidently with the intention of protecting him from violence, if necessary. The last announcement was received with great cheering, and I saw many an eye flash and many a countenance grow radiant with the light of defiance.]

These men sneered at Colonel Mack a few days since.* He is a small man, but I am a large man. I am ready to meet any of them in place of Colonel Mack. I am large enough for them, and I hold myself ready for them now and at any time. [Cheers from the galleries.]

Mr. Speaker, these traitors on this floor should be provided with hempen collars. They deserve them. They deserve hanging, I say, [raising his voice, and violently striking the desk;] the country would be the better of swinging them up. I go for hanging them, and I dare to tell them so, right here to their traitorous faces. Traitors should be hung. It would be the salvation of the country to hang them. For that reason I must rejoice at it. [Tremendous cheering.]

Mr. Speaker, I beg pardon of the gentlemen in this Senate who are not traitors, but true loyal men, for what I have said. I only intend it and mean it for secessionists at heart. They are here in this Senate. I see them gibe, and smirk, and grin at the true Union men. Must I defy them? I stand here ready for them, and dare them to come on. [Great cheering.] What man, with the heart of a patriot, could stand this treason any longer? I have stood it long enough. I will stand it no more. [Cheers.] I denounce these men and their aiders and abettors as rank traitors and secessionists. Hell itself could not spew out a more traitorous crew than some of the men that disgrace this Legislature, this State, and this country. For myself, I protest against and denounce their treasonable acts. I have voted against their measures; I will do so to the end. I will denounce them as long as God gives me breath; and I am ready to meet the traitors themselves, here or any where, and fight them to the death. [Prolonged cheers and shouts.]

I said I paid three thousand dollars a year taxes. I do not say

*Hon. A. W. Mack delivered a powerful speech in the Senate of Illinois, on the thirteenth of February, in opposition to the Armistice Resolutions of the "Copperheads."

it to brag of it. It is my duty, yes, Mr. Speaker, my privilege, to do it. But some of these traitors here, who are working night and day to put their miserable little bills and claims through the Legislature, to take money out of the pockets of the people, are talking about high taxes. They are hypocrites as well as traitors. I heard some of them talking about high taxes in this way, who do not pay five dollars to the support of the Government. I denounce them as hypocrites as well as traitors. [Cheers.]

The reason they pretend to be afraid of high taxes is, that they do not want to vote money for the relief of the soldiers. They want to embarrass the Government and stop the war. They want to aid the secessionists to conquer our boys in the field. They care about high taxes! They are picayune men, any how, and pay no taxes at all, and never did, and never hope or expect to. This is an excuse of traitors. [Cheers.]

Mr. Speaker, excuse me. I feel for my country, in this her hour of danger, from the tips of my toes to the ends of my hair. That is the reason I speak as I do. I can not help it. I am bound to tell these men to their teeth what they are, and what the people, the true loyal people, think of them. [Tremendous cheering. The Speaker rapped upon his desk, apparently to stop it, but really to add to its volume, for I could see by his flushed cheek and flashing eye that his heart was with the brave and loyal old gentleman.]

Mr. Speaker, I have said my say. I am no speaker. This is the only speech I have made, and I do not know that it deserves to be called a speech. I could not sit still any longer and see these scoundrels and traitors work out their hellish schemes to destroy the Union. They have my sentiments; let them, one and all, make the most of them. I am ready to back up all I say, and I repeat it, to meet these traitors in any manner they may choose, from a pin's point to the mouth of a cannon. [Tremendous applause, during which the old gentleman sat down, after he had given the desk a parting whack, which sounded loud above the din of cheers and clapping of hands.]

I never before witnessed so much excitement in an assembly. Mr. Funk spoke with a force of natural eloquence, with a conviction and truthfulness, with a fervor and pathos which wrought up the galleries, and even members on the floor, to the highest pitch of excitement. His voice was heard in the stores that surround the square, and the people came flocking in from all quarters. In five minutes he had an audience that packed the hall to its utmost capacity. After he had concluded, the Republican members and spectators rushed up and took him by the hand to congratulate him. The Democrats said nothing, but evidently felt the castigation they were receiving most keenly, as might be seen from their blanched cheeks and restless and uneasy glances.

Taylor Peirce to Catharine Peirce

Union forces were able to prevent Missouri from seceding in 1861, but the state remained bitterly divided between unionists and secessionists and became the scene of the fiercest guerrilla conflict of the war. Although the Union victory at Pea Ridge, Arkansas, in March 1862 halted Confederate attempts to invade the state, Confederate irregulars in Missouri continued to harass Union troops with ambushes and raids. Taylor Peirce mustered into the 22nd Iowa Infantry as a sergeant in August 1862 and was soon sent to southern Missouri, where his regiment guarded railroad lines, supply depots, and wagon trains. He wrote to his wife from the Ozarks describing the summary treatment often meted out to suspected guerrillas.

————————

Eminince, Mo Feby 16 1863
Dear Catharine
I again set down to write you all again. I wrote you last week but the mails are so irregular in this region that I do not know how long it will take this to reach you but Col Stone and the Chaplain leaves this for Rolla to-morrow and I think you will get it in about 6 or 7 days. I am well and in good heart. We have been on the move for 3 weeks except 3 or 4 days that we lay at West Plains. We are now about 60 miles from Rolla and will Either go to Rolla or to Pilot Knob. One Division of the army started this morning to the Knob and we will either start for that place or Rolla to morrow. The rebles are all gone from this country except some few Gurrillas and them we gather up as we go along and shoot them. They are a set of murderers and are not fit to live to encumber society. Some of the cavalry took one yesterday morning who has shot at Gen Bentons Courier the night before not knowing that the cavalry was about. So yesterday morning they caught him in his house and took him out about a mile and shot him. When we came along he was lying by the side of the road and his wife crying over him but she was no better than he for she kept on swearing

vengence against the Federals and said she would make them kiss his blood and so we left her. It looks hard to me to see a man shot and his wife and children left alone but these men are the ones that keep up the cruelties that are continually being practiced in this part of Missouri.

We have been traveling through the Ozark mountain ever since the 1st of this month and a rough country it is. There is some pretty vallies in through them and now and then a very good settlement along some stream but the land is generally stony and poor covered with oak and yellow Pine. Some of the timber is very good and some day will be valuable. We are now on the Currant River some 25 miles from the Arkansas line and 3 miles from Eminence a town with one house and a court house and jail in it and an old mill which constitutes the whole town. I have been running a mile for two or three days grinding corn for the brigade as our rations have run short and the roads are so bad that our supplies can not reach us and we have been on ½ rations for some time. But I have enough to eat all the time and more than I need but some of the large eaters grow terribly about it. I expect that we will have short allowances until we get to the Rail Road for the trains can not reach us through this god forsaken country.

Lieutenant Murray starts home in the morning and has promised to call and see you and tell you how I get along and what I am doing. And if it is possible for you to get your pictures taken I mean Cyrus & Mary & thine and the babys I would like you to send it by him. The paymaster has come and has paid me my money and as soon as I get to the Express office I will express it home.

I would send it by Murray but the Col thinks that it will be safer to keep it until we get to the office as they might be attacked by a forrageing party and robed as they will only have a small escort with them. So I concluded to keep it with me untill we get to the Rail Road. Cap Ault and I have fell out and I do not hold any communication with him any more than just what is nessessary for me to have to do my duty. He has shown himself just as damned a dog as lives and if he was not afraid of me he would be overbearing as the devil himself but I have the upper hand and he has to keep mum. The Lt can tell you about it and so you need not fear for me but I will get along all right.

I must now close for we will have to march in the morning and of course the time is precious with me. Give my love to all. Tell the children to be good and Pap will try and get home to see them this spring. Give Cyrus my best respects and tell him he could make some money following the army and buying up the worn out horses and mules and if I get my commission to raise the negroes I will come home and put him on the track.

I remain affect your husband father and brother.

Taylor Peirce

William T. Sherman to Thomas Ewing Sr. and to John Sherman

Major General William T. Sherman became the commander of the Fifteenth Corps in Ulysses S. Grant's Army of the Tennessee in January 1863. From his camp across the Mississippi River from Vicksburg, Sherman wrote to his father-in-law, Thomas Ewing Sr., and to his brother John, a Republican senator from Ohio, about the dangers posed by the press. In December 1861 the *Cincinnati Commercial* had reported Sherman to be "insane" after he was relieved from commands in Kentucky and Missouri, and in the spring of 1862 Sherman had been infuriated by sensational newspaper stories falsely claiming that his men had been bayoneted in their tents during the initial Confederate attack at Shiloh. His antagonism toward the press reached a new level after his failed assault at Chickasaw Bayou near Vicksburg on December 29, 1862. When the *New York Herald* printed a story highly critical of his leadership in the battle, Sherman had its author, correspondent Thomas W. Knox, court-martialed on charges of giving intelligence to the enemy, being a spy, and disobedience of orders. On February 18, 1863, the court-martial convicted Knox of the third charge and ordered him to be expelled from the Army of the Tennessee's lines. When Knox sought Sherman's consent to return to the army in April, Sherman wrote that he would welcome him as a soldier, but as a reporter, "my answer is Never."

Camp before Vicksburg, Feb. 17, 1863.

Hon. Thomas Ewing
Dear Sir,

Ellen has sent me the enclosed slips from the Cincinnati Commercial. The Editor evidently seems disposed to deal fairly by me, and as I have more leisure than usual now I will illustrate by examples fresh in the memory of all, why I regard newspaper correspondents as spies, & why as a Servant of an enlightened Government I feel bound in honor and in common honesty to shape my official conduct accordingly. A spy is

47

one who furnishes an enemy with knowledge useful to him &
dangerous to us. One who bears into a Fortress or Camp a
baneful influence that encourages sedition or weakens us. He
need not be an enemy, is often a trader woman or Servant.
Such characters are by all belligerents punished Summarily &
with the extremest penalties, not because they are of themselves filled with the guilty thought & intent that makes the
Madman the Burglar the Thief the Felon in civil affairs, but
because he or she endangers the safety of an army a nation or
the cause for which it is contending. Andre carried no intelligence back to Genl. Clinton but was the mere instrument used
to corrupt the fidelity of an Officer holding an important command. Washington admitted the high & pure character of
Andre but the safety of the cause demanded his punishment. It
is hard to illustrate my point by reference to our past history,
but I wish to convey the full idea that a nation & an army must
defend its safety & existence by making acts militating against
it criminal regardless of the mere interest of the instrument.
We find a scout surveying our camp from a distance in noways
threatening us but seeking information of the location strength
& composition of our forces, we shoot him of course without
asking a question. We find a stranger in our camp seeking a
stray horse & find afterwards he has been to the enemy: we
hang him as a spy because the safety of the army & the cause it
fights is too important to be risked by any pretext or chance.
Now in these modern times a class of men has been begotten
& attend our camps & armies gathering minute information of
our strength plans & purposes & publish them so as to reach
the enemy in time to serve his purposes. Such publications do
not add a man to our strength, in no ways benefit us but are
invaluable to the enemy. You know that this class published in
advance all the plans of the Manassas movement enabled Johnston to reinforce Beauregard whereby McDowell was defeated
& the enemy gained tremendous strength & we lost in comparison. I know the enemy received from the same source
some similar notice of our intended attack on Vicksburg &
thwarted our well laid scheme. I know that Beauregard at
Corinth received from the same source full details of all troops
ascending the Tennessee & acted accordingly. I know that it
was by absolute reticence only that Halleck succeeded in strik-

ing Forts Henry & Donaldson & prevented their reinforcements in time to thwart that most brilliant movement. And it was only by the absence of newspapers that we succeeded in reaching the post of Arkansas before it could be reinforced.

I *know* that the principal northern papers reach the enemy regularly & promptly & I *know* that all the vigilance of our Army cannot prevent it & I know that by this means the enemy can defeat us to the end of time. I could instance other examples but these suffice to illustrate this branch of the subject.

Another view of the case. The Northern Press either make public opinion or reflect it. By gradual steps public opinion instead of being governed governs our country. All bow to it, & even military men who are sworn officers of the Executive Branch of the Government go behind & look to public opinion. The consequence is & has been that officers instead of keeping the Executive Branch advised of all movements events or circumstances that would enable it to act advisedly & with vigor communicate with the public direct through the Press so that the Government authorities are operated on by public opinion formed too often on false or interested information. This has weakened our Executive and has created jealousies mistrust & actual Sedition. Officers find it easier to attain rank known fame and notoriety by the cheap proces of newspapers. This cause has paralized several fine armies & by making the people at home mistrust the ability of Leaders Surgeons & Quarter Masters has even excited the fears of parents so far that many advise their sons & brothers to desert until desertion & mutiny have lost their odious character. I'll undertake to say that the army of the Potomac has not today for battle one half the men whom the U.S. pays as Soldiers & this is partially the case with the army in Tennessee & here. In all armies there must be wide differences of opinion & partial causes of disaffection—*want of pay*, bad clothing dismal camps crowded transports hospitals rudely formed & all the incidents of war. These cannot be entirely avoided & newspapers can easily change them to negligence of commanders & thereby create disaffection. I do not say that the Press intends this but they have done this and are doing it all the time now I know that I made the most minute and careful preperation for the sick & wounded on the Yazoo, plenty of ambulances & men detailed in advance *to remove* the wounded—four (4) of the largest transports prepared & set aside before a shot was fired, & that every wounded man was taken from the field dressed & carefully attended immediately & yet I know that the Press has succeeded in making the very reverse impression & that many good people think there was criminal negligence. The same naked representations were made at Shiloh & I saw hundreds of Physicians come down & when our Surgeons begged & implored their help they preferred to gather up trophies & consume the dainties provided for the wounded & go back & represent the cruelty of the Army Surgeons & boast of their own disinterested humanity. I know this & that they nearly ruined Dr. Hewit one of the hardest working Surgeons in any army. I see similar attempts less successful however against Dr. McMillan not a word of truth not even a pretence of truth but it is a popular & successful theme & they avail themselves of it. What is the consequence? All officers of industry who stand by at all times through storm & sunshine find their reputations blasted & others usually the most lazy & indolent reaping cheap glory & fame through the correspondents of the Press. I say in giving intelligence to the enemy, in sowing discord & discontent in an army these men fulfil all the conditions of spies. Shall we succumb or shall we meet & overcome the evil? I am satisfied they have cost the country hundreds of millions of dollars, & brought our country to the brink of ruin & that unless the nuisance is abated we are lost. Here we are in front of Vicksburg. The attack direct in front would in our frail transports be marked by the sinking of Steamers loaded with troops, a fearful assault against hills fortified with great care by a cunning enemy. Every commander who has looked at it says it cannot be done in front it must be turned. I tried it but newspaper correspondents had sent word in advance & ample preperations were made & reinforcements to double my number had reached Vicksburg.

McClernand was unwilling to attack in front. Grant do. Then how turn the position? We cannot ascend the Yazoo to where our men can get a footing. We cannot run our frail transports past the Vicksburg Batteries then we resolve to cut a channel into Yazoo at the old pass near Delta above & into the Tensas by way of Lake Providence. Secrecy & dispatch are

the chief elements of success. The forces here are kept to occupy the attention of the enemy two steamers are floated past
the Batteries to control the River below & men are drawn secretly from Helena & Memphis to cut the canals & levies &
remove all the inhabitants so that the enemy could not have
notice till the floods of the Missippi could finish the work of
man. But what avail? Known spies accompany each expedition
& we now read in the northern papers (the same are in Vicksburg now) that our forces here are unequal to the direct assault
but are cutting the two canals above: all our plans revealed &
thwarted, the levies are cut & our plans work to a charm but
the enemy now knows our purposes & hastens above, fells
trees into the narrow head streams, cuts the side levies dis-
perses the waters & defeats our well conceived plans. Who can
carry on war thus? It is terrible to contemplate; & I say it that
no intelligent officer in this or any American army now in the
field but would prefer to have his opponent increased twenty—
yea fifty per cent if the internal informers & spies could be excluded from our camps. I know our people are full of anxiety
to hear from our armies but every soldier can & does write
home, his family can at all times hear of his welfare & if the
people could only see as I see the baneful effects of this mischeivous practise they would cry aloud in indignant tones. We
may in self defense be compelled to take the law into our own
hands for our safety or we may bend to the storm and seek a
position where others may take the consequences of this cause.
I early foresaw this result & have borne the malignity of the
Press but a day will come & that far distant when the Press
must surrender some portion of its freedom to save the rest
else it too will perish in the general wreck. I think the *Commercial* misjudges my character somewhat. I certainly am not
proud or haughty. Every soldier of my command comes into
my presence as easy as the highest officer. Their beds & rations
are as good as mine & certainly no General officer moves
about with as little pomp as I. They see me daily nightly hourly,
along the picket line afoot alone or with a Single orderly or
officer whilst others have their mighty escorts & retinue. Indeed I am usually laughed at for my simplicity in this respect.
Abrupt I am & all military men are. The mind jumps to its
conclusions & is emphatic, & I can usually divine the motive

of the insidious cotton Speculator camp follower & hypercritical humanity seeker before he discloses his plans & designs & an officer who must attend to the thousand & one wants of thirty thousand men besides the importunities of thousands of mischeivous camp followers must need be abrupt unless the day can be made more than twenty four hours long. A citizen cannot understand that an officer who has to see to the wants and necessities of an army has no time to listen to their usual long perorations & I must confess I have little patience with this class of men. To be sure policy would dictate a different course, & I know I could easily have acheived popularity by yeilding to these outside influences but I could not do what I see other popular officers do furnish transportation at Government expense to newspaper agents & supply them with public horses Seat them at my table to hear conversations of public matter give access to official papers which I am commanded to withhold to the world till my Employer has the benefit of them. I could not do these things & feel that I was an honest man & faithful servant of the Government for my memory still runs back to the time when Peter Hagner was Auditor of the Treasury, & when an officer would not take a Government nail out of a keg on which to hang his coat or feed his horse out of the public crib without charging its cost against his pay. That time is past, but must again return before the United States can regain its lost good name among the nations of the earth.

Again the habit of indiscriminate praise & flattery has done us harm. Let a stranger read our official reports & he would blush at the praise bespattered over who Regiments Divisions and Corps for skirmishes & actions where the dead & wounded mark no Serious conflict. When I praise I mean it & when troops fall into disorder I must notice it but you may read my reports in vain for an instance where troops have kept their ranks & done even moderately well but I have encouraged them to a better future. There is an unwritten history that will come out when the real soldiers come home. At the Post of Arkansas I wanted to storm the rifle pits by a Hurrah! One of my divisions faltered and in reply to my aid "How are things with you"? "Why Damn it my men are only wasting ammunition", I cautioned him to patience. "Be kind & coax along & notify me the moment you think your men are equal to the work"—hundreds heard me & yet this same officer would indulge now in extravagant boasts. I know that in trouble in danger in emergencies the men know I have patience a keen appreciation of the truth of facts & ground equalled by few and one day they will tell the truth. Many a solitary picket has seen me creeping by night examining ground before I ordered them to cross it & yet other lazy rascals ignorant of the truth would hang behind sleep or crouch around the distant camp fire till danger was passed, & then write "how Sherman with insane rashness had pushed his brave soldiers into the jaws of death."

I have departed from my theme. My argument is that newspaper correspondents & camp followers, writing with a purpose & with no data communicate facts useful to an enemy and useless to our cause & calculated to impair the discipline of the army & that the practise must cease We cannot appeal to Patriotism because news are a saleable commodity & the more valuable as it is the more pithy & damaging to our cause I am satisfied the enemy encourages this as the cheapest & most effectual weapon of war either by direct contribution of money or by becoming large purchasers of its numbers. The law gives us the means to stop it & as an army we fail in our duty to the Government to our cause & to ourselves if we do not use them.

To shew how the Press is used I will tell of another recent instance. The Captain of the Gun Boat *New Era* behaved badly, cowardly at Arkansas Post. Admiral Porter, a gallant officer sent him to Cairo in banishment. It was necessary for him to cover up his disgrace. Getting into safety nearly up to the Ohio he pretended he saw an army of 3,000 men near Island No. 10, & he shelled them away at a cost of many thousands of dollars. He alarmed the whole country & wrote his own account but not a man here believes he saw a single Guerilla. This is true of many glorious battles in the newspapers.

Our camp is about flooded & consequent idleness must form my apology for this long letter. If you think proper I have no objection to the Editor of the Commericial seeing this but I confess myself too "haughty" to allow it or anything else of mine to be printed. Affectionately

W. T. Sherman

Camp before Vicksburg,
February 18, 1863

My Dear Brother,

I have seen your speeches on the subject of absentees, filling up the army with conscripts, and the necessity of standing by the President for the sake of unity of action. So at last I see you and the Country begin to realize what we ought to have known two years ago, that individual opinions however sincere, real & honest are too various to Secure unity of action, and at last that men must forego their individual notions and follow some one Leader, the Legitimate & Constitutional one if possible. Two years of war, costly & bloody have been endured and we have arrived by sad experience at a Result that all the world knew before. If the People of the North will not learn from the experience of the world, but must go on groping in the dark for experience to develop and demonstrate the Truth of established principles of Government, why of course there is no help for it, but as a people we must pay the price.

We have reproached the South for arbitrary conduct in coercing her People—at last we find we must imitate their example —we have denounced their tyranny in filling their armies with conscripts—and now we must follow her example—We have denounced their tyranny in suppressing freedom of speech and the press, and here too in time we must follow her Example. The longer it is deferred the worse it becomes.

Who gave notice of McDowell's movement on Manassas, & enabled Johnston so to reinforce Beauregard that our army was defeated?

The Press.

Who gave notice of the movement on Vicksburg?

The Press.

Who has prevented all secret combinations and movements against our enemy?

The Press.

Who has sown the seeds of hatred so deep, that Reason, Religion and Self interest cannot eradicate them?

The Press.

What is the real moving cause in this Rebellion? Mutual hatred & misrepresentations made by a venal Press.

In the South this powerful machine was at once scotched
and used by the Rebel Government, but at the North was allowed to go free. What are the results. After arousing the passions of the people till the two great sections hate each other
with a hate hardly parallelled in history, it now begins to Stir
up sedition at home, and even to encourage mutiny in our
armies. What has paralyzed the Army of the Potomac? Mutual
jealousies kept alive by the Press. What has enabled the enemy
to combine so as to hold Tennessee after we have twice crossed
it with victorious armies. What defeats and will continue to
defeat our best plans here and elsewhere? The Press.

I cannot pick up a paper but tells of our situation here, in
the mud, sickness, and digging a canal in which we have little
faith. But our officers attempt secretly to cut two other channels one into Yazoo by an old Pass, and one through Lake
Providence into Tensas, Black Red &c., whereby we could
turn not only Vicksburg Port Hudson, but also Grand Gulf,
Natchez, Ellis Cliff, Fort Adams and all the strategic points on
the Main River, and the busy agents of the Press follow up and
proclaim to the world the whole thing, and instead of surprising our enemy we find him felling trees & blocking passages
that would without this have been in our possession, and all
the real effects of surprise are lost. I say with the Press un-
fettered as now we are defeated to the end of time. Tis folly to
say the people must have news. Every soldier can and does
write to his family & friends & all have ample opportunities for
so doing, and this pretext forms no good reasons why agents
of the Press should reveal prematurely all our plans & designs.
We cannot prevent it. Clerks of steamboats, correspondents in
disguise or openly attend each army & detachment, and presto
appears in Memphis & St. Louis minute accounts of our plans
& designs. These reach Vicksburg by telegraph from Her-
nando & Holly Springs before we know of it.

The only two really successful military strokes out here have
succeeded because of the absence of newspapers or by throwing them off the trail—Halleck had to make a simulated attack
on Columbus to prevent the Press giving notice of his intended
move against Forts Henry & Donelson. We succeeded in

reaching the Post of Arkansas before the Correspondents could reach their Papers. Now in war it is bad enough to have a bold daring enemy in great strength to our front without having an equally dangerous & treacherous foe within. I know if the People of the United States could see & realize the Truth of this matter they would agree to wait a few days for their accustomed batch of exciting news rather than expose their sons, brothers & friends as they inevitably do to failure and death. Of course I know the President & Congress are powerless in this matter & we must go on till perpetual defeat & disaster point out one of the Chief Causes. Instead of being governed by Reason, our people prefer to grope their way through personal Experience and must pay its cost. I only await a good time to Slide out & let the experiment go on at the expense of others. I have had my share & wish no more. I still have unlimited faith in Halleck & prefer that he should command the whole army than McClellan. Still I would like to have him come West. Affectionately

Sherman

Clement L. Vallandigham: Speech in Congress

February 23, 1863

Ohio congressman Clement L. Vallandigham attended the final session of the 37th Congress as a lame duck after having been defeated for reelection in October 1862. A leader of the "Peace Democrats" who opposed emancipation and the continued prosecution of the war, Vallandigham gave a lengthy speech in the House on January 14 calling for an armistice, the withdrawal of Union troops from the seceded states, and negotiations aimed at peaceful reunion. He spoke again in February as the House debated the recently introduced conscription bill. Under its terms, male citizens (and immigrants applying for citizenship) between twenty and forty-five were subject to conscription if voluntary enlistments failed to fill the recruitment quota for their district. Men who were selected by lottery to be drafted could avoid service by hiring a substitute or by paying a $300 commutation fee. The bill passed the Senate, 35–11, and the House, 115–48, and was enacted on March 3, 1863.

Mr. VALLANDIGHAM said:

Mr. SPEAKER: I do not propose to discuss this bill at any great length in this House. I am satisfied that there is a settled purpose to enact it into a law, so far as it is possible for the action of the Senate and House and the President to make it such. I appeal, therefore, from you, from them, directly to the country; to a forum where there is no military committee, no previous question, no hour rule, and where the people themselves are the masters. I commend the spirit in which this discussion was commenced by the chairman of the Military Committee, [Mr. OLIN,] and I do it the more cheerfully because, unfortunately, he is not always in so good a temper as he was to-day: and I trust that throughout the debate, and on its close, he will exhibit that same disposition which characterized his opening remarks. Only let me caution him that he cannot dictate to the minority here what course they shall pursue. But, sir, I regret that I cannot extend the commendation to the gentleman from Pennsylvania, [Mr. CAMPBELL,] who addressed the House a little while ago. His speech was extremely offensive, and calculated to stir up a spirit of bitterness and strife, not at all consistent with that in which debates in this House should be conducted. If he or any other gentleman of the majority imagines that any one here is to be deterred by threats from the expression of his opinions, or from giving such votes as he may see fit to give, he has utterly misapprehended the temper and determination of those who sit on this side of the Chamber. His threat I hurl back with defiance into his teeth. I spurn it. I spit upon it. That is not the argument to be addressed to equals here: and I therefore most respectfully suggest that hereafter all such be dispensed with, and that we shall be spared personal denunciation and insinuations against the loyalty of men who sit with me here; men whose devotion to the Constitution and attachment to the Union of these States is as ardent and immovable as yours, and who only differ from you as to the mode of securing the great object nearest their hearts.

Mr. CAMPBELL.   The gentleman will allow me—

Mr. VALLANDIGHAM.   I yield for explanation.

Mr. CAMPBELL.   Mr. Speaker, it is a significant fact that the gentleman from Ohio has applied my remarks to himself and others on his side of the House. Why was this done? I was denouncing *traitors* here, and I will denounce them while I have a place upon this floor. It is my duty and my privilege to do so. And if the gentleman from Ohio chooses to give my remarks a personal application, he can so apply them.

Mr. VALLANDIGHAM.   That is enough.

Mr. CAMPBELL.   One moment.

Mr. VALLANDIGHAM.   Not another moment after that. I yielded the floor in the spirit of a gentleman, and not to be met in the manner of a blackguard. [Applause and hisses in the galleries.]

Mr. CAMPBELL.   The member from Ohio is a blackguard. [Renewed hisses and applause in the galleries.]

Mr. ROBINSON.   I rise to a question of order. I demand

that the galleries be cleared. We have been insulted time and again by contractors and plunderers of the Government, in these galleries, and I ask that they be now cleared.

Mr. COX.   I hope my friend from Illinois will not insist on that. Only a very small portion of those in the galleries take part in these disturbances. The fool-killer will take care of them.

The SPEAKER *pro tempore*.   The Chair will have to submit the question to the House.

Mr. COX.   I hope the demand will be withdrawn.

The SPEAKER *pro tempore*.   The Chair will state, that if disorder is repeated, whether by applause or expressions of disapprobation, he will feel called upon himself to order the galleries to be cleared, trusting that the House will sustain him in so doing.

Mr. ROBINSON.   I desire the order to be enforced now, and the galleries to be cleared, excepting the ladies' gallery.

Mr. ROSCOE CONKLING.   I was going to say that I hoped the order would not be extended to that portion of the galleries.

Mr. ROBINSON.   The galleries were cautioned this afternoon.

Mr. JOHNSON.   And it is the same men who have been making this disturbance now. I know their faces well.

Mr. VALLANDIGHAM.   I think, Mr. Speaker, that this lesson has not been lost; and that it is sufficiently impressed now upon the minds of the audience that this is a legislative, and is supposed to be a deliberative, assembly, and that no breach of decorum or order should occur among them, whatever may be the conduct of any of us on the floor. I trust, therefore, that my friends on this side will withdraw the demand for the enforcement of the rule of the House.

Mr. ROBINSON.   I withdraw the demand.

Mr. VERREE.   I raise the point of order that members here, in debating questions before the House, are not at liberty to use language that is unparliamentary, and unworthy of a member.

The SPEAKER.   That is the rule of the House.

Mr. VERREE.   I hope it will be enforced.

Mr. VALLANDIGHAM.   And I hope that it will be enforced, also, against members on the other side of the Chamber.

We have borne enough, more than enough of such language, for two years past.

The SPEAKER. The gentleman from Illinois withdraws his demand to have the galleries cleared. The Chair desires to say to gentlemen in the galleries, that this being a deliberative body, it is not becoming this House, or the character of American citizens, to disturb its deliberations by any expression of approval or disapproval.

Mr. VALLANDIGHAM. The member from Pennsylvania [Mr. CAMPBELL] alluded to-day, generally, to gentlemen on this side of the House. There was no mistaking the application. The language and gesture were both plain enough. He ventured also, approvingly, to call our attention to the opinions and course of conduct of some Democrats in the State of New York, as if we were to learn our lessons in Democracy, or in anything else, from that quarter. I do not know, certainly, to whom he alluded. Perhaps it was to a gentleman who spoke not long since in the city of New York, and advocated on that occasion, what is called in stereotype phrase "the vigorous prosecution of the war," and who, but two months previously, addressed assemblages in the same State and city, in which he proposed only to take Richmond, and then let the "wayward sisters depart in peace." Now, I know of no one on this side of the Chamber occupying such a position; and I, certainly, will not go to that quarter to learn lessons in patriotism or Democracy.

I have already said that it is not my purpose to debate the general merits of this bill at large, and for the reason that I am satisfied that argument is of no avail here. I appeal, therefore, to the people. Before them I propose to try this great question —the question of constitutional power, and of the unwise and injudicious exercise of it in this bill. We have been compelled, repeatedly, since the 4th of March, 1861, to appeal to the same tribunal. We appealed to it at the recent election. And the people did pronounce judgment upon our appeal. The member from Pennsylvania ought to have heard their sentence, and I venture to say that he did hear it, on the night of the election. In Ohio they spoke as with the voice of many waters. The very question of summary and arbitrary arrests, now sanctioned in this bill, was submitted, as a direct issue, to the people of that

State, as also of other States, and their verdict was rendered upon it. The Democratic convention of Ohio assembled on the 4th of July, in the city of Columbus, the largest and best ever held in the State, among other resolutions of the same temper and spirit, adopted this without a dissenting voice:

"And we utterly condemn and denounce the repeated and gross violation, by the Executive of the United States, of the rights thus secured by the Constitution; and we also utterly repudiate and condemn the monstrous dogma, that in time of war the Constitution is suspended, or its power in any respect enlarged beyond the letter and true meaning of that instrument.

"And we view, also, with indignation and alarm, the illegal and unconstitutional seizure and imprisonment, for alleged political offenses, of our citizens, without judicial process, in States where such process is unobstructed, but by executive order by telegraph, or otherwise, and call upon all who uphold the Union, the Constitution, and the laws, to unite with us in denouncing and repelling such flagrant violation of the State and Federal Constitutions, and tyrannical infraction of the rights and liberties of American citizens; and that the people of this State CANNOT SAFELY AND WILL NOT SUBMIT to have the freedom of speech and freedom of the press, the two great and essential bulwarks of civil liberty, put down by unwarranted and despotic exertion of power."

On that the judgment of the people was given at the October elections, and the party candidates nominated by the convention which adopted that resolution, were triumphantly elected. So, too, with the candidates of the same party in the States of Wisconsin, Illinois, Indiana, Pennsylvania, New Jersey, and New York. And, sir, that "healthy reaction," recently, of which the member from Pennsylvania [Mr. CAMPBELL] affected to boast, has escaped my keenest sense of vision. I see only that handwriting on the wall which the fingers of the people wrote against him and his party and this whole Administration, at the ballot-box, in October and November last. Talk to me, indeed, of the leniency of the Executive! too few arrests! too much forbearance by those in power! Sir, it is the people who have been too lenient. They have submitted to your oppressions and wrongs as no free people ought ever to submit. But the day of patient endurance has gone by at last. Mistake them not. They will be lenient no longer. Abide by the Constitution, stand by the laws, restore the Union if *you* can restore it—not by force; you have tried that and failed. Try some other method now—the ancient, the approved, the reasonable way—the way in which the Union was first made. Surrender it not now—not yet—never. But unity is not Union; and attempt not, at your peril—I warn you—to coerce unity by the utter destruction of the Constitution and of the rights of the States and the liberties of the people. Union is liberty and consent; unity is despotism and force. For what was the Union ordained? As a splendid edifice, to attract the gaze and admiration of the world? As a magnificent temple—a stupendous superstructure of marble and iron, like this Capitol, upon whose lofty dome the bronzed image—hollow and inanimate —of freedom is soon to stand erect in colossal mockery, while the true spirit, the living goddess of liberty, veils her eyes and turns away her face in sorrow, because, upon the altar established here, and dedicated by our fathers to her worship, you, a false and most disloyal priesthood, offer up, night and morning, the mingled sacrifices of servitude and despotism? No, sir. It was for the sake of the altar, the service, the religion, the devotees, that the temple of the Union was first erected; and when these are all gone, let the edifice itself perish. Never—never— never—will the people consent to lose their own personal and political rights and liberties, to the end that you may delude and mock them with the splendid unity of despotism.

Sir, what are the bills which have passed, or are still before the House? The bill to give the President entire control of the currency—the purse—of the country. A tax bill to clothe him with power over the whole property of the country. A bill to put all power in his hands over the personal liberties of the people. A bill to indemnify him, and all under him, for every act of oppression and outrage already consummated. A bill to enable him to suspend the writ of *habeas corpus*, in order to justify or protect him, and every minion of his, in the arrests which he or they may choose to make—arrests, too, for mere opinions' sake. Sir, some two hundred years ago, men were burned at the stake, subjected to the horrors of the Inquisition, to all the tortures that the devilish ingenuity of man could invent—for what? For opinions on questions of religion —of man's duty and relation to his God. And now, to-day, for opinions on questions political, under a free Government, in a country whose liberties were purchased by our fathers by seven years' outpouring of blood, and expenditure of treasure—we have lived to see men, the born heirs of this precious inheritance, subjected to arrest and cruel imprisonment at the caprice of a President or a Secretary or a constable. And, as if that were not enough, a bill is introduced here to-day, and pressed forward to a vote, with the right of debate, indeed—extorted from you by the minority—but without the right to amend, with no more than the mere privilege of protest—a bill which enables the President to bring under his power, as Commander-in-Chief, every man in the United States between the ages of twenty and forty-five—three millions of men. And, as if not satisfied with that, this bill provides, further, that every other citizen, man, woman, and child, under twenty years of age and over forty-five, including those that may be exempt between these ages, shall be also at the mercy—so far as his personal liberty is concerned—of some miserable "provost marshal" with the rank of a captain of cavalry, who is never to see service in the field; and every congressional district in the United States is to be governed—yes, governed—by this petty satrap —this military eunuch—this Baba—and he even may be black —who is to do the bidding of your Sultan, or his Grand Vizier. Sir, you have but one step further to go—give him the symbols of his office—the Turkish bow-string and the sack.

What is it, sir, but a bill to abrogate the Constitution, to repeal all existing laws, to destroy all rights, to strike down the judiciary, and erect upon the ruins of civil and political liberty a stupendous superstructure of despotism. And for what? To enforce law? No, sir. It is admitted now by the legislation of Congress, and by the two proclamations of the President, it is admitted by common consent, that the war is for the abolition of negro slavery, to secure freedom to the black man. You tell me, some of you, I know, that it is so prosecuted because this is the only way to restore the Union; but others openly and candidly confess that the purpose of the prosecution of the war is to abolish slavery. And thus, sir, it is that the freedom of the negro is to be purchased, under this bill, at the sacrifice of every right of the white men of the United States.

Sir, I am opposed, earnestly, inexorably opposed, to this

measure. If there were not another man in this House to vote against it, if there were none to raise his voice against it, I, at least, dare stand here alone in my place, as a Representative, undismayed, unseduced, unterrified, and heedless of the miserable cry of "disloyalty," of sympathy with the rebellion and with rebels, to denounce it as the very consummation of the conspiracy against the Constitution and the liberties of my country.

Sir, I yield to no man in devotion to the Union. I am for maintaining it upon the principles on which it was first formed; and I would have it, at every sacrifice, except of honor, which is "the life of the nation." I have stood by it in boyhood and in manhood, to this hour; and I will not now consent to yield it up; nor am I to be driven from an earnest and persistent support of the only means by which it can be restored, either by the threats of the party of the Administration here, or because of affected sneers and contemptuous refusals to listen, now, to reunion, by the party of the administration at Richmond. I never was weak enough to cower before the reign of terror inaugurated by the men in power here, nor vain enough to expect favorable responses now, or terms of settlement, from the men in power, or the presses under their control, in the South. Neither will ever compromise this great quarrel, nor agree to peace on the basis of reunion; but, I repeat it—stop fighting, and let time and natural causes operate—uncontrolled by military influences—and the ballot there, as the ballot here, will do its work. I am for the Union of these States; and but for my profound conviction that it can never be restored by force and arms; or, if so restored, could not be maintained, and would not be worth maintaining, I would have united, at first —even now would unite, cordially—in giving, as I have acquiesced, silently, in your taking, all the men and all the money you have demanded. But I did not believe, and do not now believe, that the war could end in anything but final defeat; and if it should last long enough, then in disunion; or, if successful upon the principles now proclaimed, that it must and would end in the establishment of an imperial military despotism— not only in the South—but in the North and West. And to that I never will submit. No, rather, first I am ready to yield up property, and liberty—nay, life itself.

Sir, I do not propose to discuss now the question of the constitutionality of this measure. The gentleman from Ohio who preceded me, [Mr. WHITE,] has spared me the necessity of an argument on that point. He has shown that between the Army of the United States, of which, by the Constitution, the President of the United States is the Commander-in-Chief, and the militia, belonging to the States, there is a wide and clearly marked line of distinction. The distinction is fully and strongly defined in the Constitution, and has been recognized in the entire legislation and practice of the Government from the beginning. The States have the right, and have always exercised it, of appointing the officers of their militia, and you have no power to take it away. Sir, this bill was originally introduced in the Senate as a militia bill, and as such it recognized the right of the States to appoint the officers; but finding it impossible, upon that basis, to give to the Executive of the United States the entire control of the millions thus organized into a military force, as the conspirators against State rights and popular liberty desire, the original bill was abandoned; and to-day behold here a stupendous conscription bill for a standing army of more than three million men, forced from their homes, their families, their fields, and their workshops; an army organized, officered, and commanded by the servant President, now the master dictator of the United States. And for what? Foreign war? Home defense? No; but for coercion, invasion, and the abolition of negro slavery by force. Sir, the conscription of Russia is mild and merciful and just compared with this. And yet the enforcement of that conscription has just stirred again the slumbering spirit of insurrection in Poland, though the heel of despotic power has trodden upon the necks of her people for a century.

Where, now, are your taunts and denunciations, heaped upon the confederate government for its conscription, when you, yourselves, become the humble imitators of that government, and bring in here a conscription act, more odious even than that passed by the confederate congress at Richmond? Sir, the chairman of the Military Committee rejoiced that for the last two years the Army had been filled up by voluntary enlistments. Yes, your Army has hitherto been thus filled up by the men of the North and West. One million two hundred and thirty-seven thousand men—for most of the drafted men enlisted, or procured substitutes—have voluntarily surrendered their civil rights, subjected themselves to military law, and thus passed under the command and within the control of the President of the United States. It is not for me to complain of that. It was their own act—done of their own free will and accord—unless bounties, promises, and persuasion may be regarded as coercion. The work you proposed was gigantic, and your means proportionate to it. And what has been the result? What do you propose now? What is this bill? A confession that the people are no longer ready to enlist; that they are not willing to carry on this war longer, until some effort has been made to settle this great controversy in some other way than by the sword. And yet, in addition to the one million two hundred and thirty-seven thousand men who have voluntarily enlisted, you propose now to force the entire body of the people, between the ages of twenty and forty-five, under military law, and within the control of the President as Commander-in-Chief of the Army, for three years, or during the war—which is to say "for life;" ay, sir, for life, and half your Army has already found, or will yet find, that their enlistment was for life too.

I repeat it, sir, this bill is a confession that the people of the country are against this war. It is a solemn admission upon the record in the legislation of Congress that they will not voluntarily consent to wage it any longer. And yet, ignoring every principle upon which the Government was founded, this measure is an attempt by compulsion to carry it on against the will of the people. Sir, what does all this mean? You were a majority at first; the people were almost unanimously with you, and they were generous and enthusiastic in your support. You abused your power and your trust, and you failed to do the work which you promised. You have lost the confidence, lost the hearts of the people. You are now in a minority at home. And yet, what a spectacle is exhibited here to-night! You, an accidental, temporary majority, condemned and repudiated by the people, are exhausting the few remaining hours of your political life in attempting to defeat the popular will, and to compel, by the most desperate and despotic of expedients ever resorted to, the submission of the majority of the people, at home, to the minority, their servants here. Sir, this experiment has been tried before in other ages and countries, and its issue always, among a people born free, or fit to be free, has been expulsion or death to the conspirators and tyrants.

I make no threats. They are not arguments fit to be addressed to equals in a legislative assembly; but there is truth—solemn, alarming truth—in what has been said to-day by gentlemen on this side of the Chamber. Have a care, have a care, I entreat you, that you do not press these measures too far. I shall do nothing to stir up an already excited people—not because of any fear of your contemptible petty provost marshals, but because I desire to see no violence or revolution in the North or West. But I warn you now, that whenever, against the will of the people, and to perpetuate power and office in a popular Government which they have taken from you, you undertake to enforce this bill, and, like the destroying angel in Egypt, enter every house for the first-born sons of the people—remember Poland. You cannot and will not be permitted to establish a military despotism. Be not encouraged by the submission of other nations. The people of Austria, of Russia, of Spain, of Italy have never known the independence and liberty of freemen. France, in seventy years, has witnessed seven principal revolutions—the last brought about in a single day by the arbitrary attempt of the king to suppress freedom of speech and of the press, and next the free assembling of the people; and when he would have retraced his steps and restored these liberties, a voice from the galleries—not filled with clerks and plunderers and placemen—uttered the sentiments and will of the people of France, in words now historic: "It is too late." The people of England never submitted, and would not now submit, for a moment, to the despotism which you propose to inaugurate in America. England cannot, to-day, fill up her standing armies by conscription. Even the "press gang," unknown to her laws, but for a time acquiesced in, has long since been declared illegal; and a sweeping conscription like this, now, would hurl not only the ministry from power, but the queen from her throne.

Sir, so far as this bill is a mere military measure, I might have been content to have given a silent vote against it; but there are two provisions in it hostile, both to the letter and spirit of the Constitution, and inconsistent with the avowed scope and purpose of the bill itself; and, certainly, as I read them in the light of events which have occurred in the past two years, of a character which demands that the majority of this House shall strike them out. There is nothing in the argument that we have no time to send the bill back to the Senate, lest it should be lost. The Presiding Officers of both Houses are friends of the bill, and will constitute committees of conference of men favorable to it. They will agree at once, and can at any moment, between this and the 4th of March, present their report as a question of the highest privilege; and you have a two thirds majority in both branches to adopt it.

With these provisions of the bill stricken out, leaving it simply as a military measure, to be tested by the great question of peace or war, I would be willing that the majority of the House should take the responsibility of passing it without further debate; although, even then, you would place every man in the United States, between the ages of twenty and forty-five, under military law, and within the control, everywhere, of the President, except the very few who are exempt; but you would leave the shadow, at least, of liberty to all men not between these ages, or not subject to draft under this bill, and to the women and children of the country too.

Sir, these two provisions propose to go a step further, and include every one, man, woman, and child, and to place him or her under the arbitrary power not only of the President and his Cabinet, but of some two hundred and fifty other petty officers, captains of cavalry, appointed by him. There is no distinction of sex, and none of age. These provisions, sir, are contained in the seventh and twenty-fifth sections of the bill. What are they? I comment not on the appointment of a general provost marshal of the United States, and provost marshals in every congressional district. Let that pass. But what do you propose to make the duty of each provost marshal in carrying out the draft? Among other things, that he shall "inquire into and report to the Provost Marshal General"—what? Treason? No. Felony? No. Breach of the peace, or violation of law of any kind? No; but "treasonable practices;" yes, TREASONABLE PRACTICES. What mean you by these strange, ominous words? Whence come they? Sir, they are no more new or original than any other of the cast-off rags filched by this Administration

from the lumber-house of other and more antiquated despotisms. The history of European tyranny has taught us somewhat of this doctrine of constructive treason. Treasonable
practices! Sir, the very language is borrowed from the old
proclamations of the British monarchs some hundreds of years
ago. It brings up the old, identical quarrel of the fourteenth
century. Treasonable practices? It was this that called forth that
English act of Parliament of twenty-fifth Edward III, from
which we have borrowed the noble provision against constructive treason in the Constitution of the United States. Arbitrary
arrests for no crime known, defined or limited by law, but for
pretended offenses, herded together under the general and
most comprehensive name of "treasonable practices," had
been so frequent, in the worst periods of English history that,
in the language of the act of Henry IV, "no man knew how to
behave himself or what to do or say for doubt of the pains of
treason." The statute of Edward III had cut all these fungous,
toadstool treasons up by the root; and yet, so prompt is arbitrary power to denounce all opposition to it as treasonable that,
as Lord Hale observes—

"Things were so carried by parties and factions in the succeeding
reign of Richard II, that this statute was but little observed but as
this or that party got the better. So the crime of high treason was,
in a manner, arbitrarily imposed and adjudged *to the disadvantage of
the party which was to be judged*; which, by various vicissitudes and
revolutions, mischiefed all parties first and last, and left a great un-
settledness and unquietness in the minds of the people, and was one
of the occasions of the unhappiness of the king."

And he adds that—

"It came to pass that almost every offense that was *or seemed to be*
a breach of the faith and allegiance due to the king, was, by *construction, consequence, and interpretation*, raised into the offense of high
treason."

Richard II procured an act of Parliament—even he did not
pretend to have power to do it by proclamation—declaring
that the bare purpose to depose the king and to place another
in his stead, without any overt act, was treason; and yet, as
Blackstone remarks, so little effect have over-violent laws to
prevent crime, that within two years afterwards this very prince

was both deposed and put to death. Still the struggle for arbitrary and despotic power continued; and up to the time of Charles I, at various periods, almost every conceivable offense relating to the government, and every form of opposition to the king, was declared high treason. Among these were execrations against the king; calling him opprobrious names by public writing; refusing to abjure the Pope; marrying, without license, certain of the king's near relatives; derogating from his royal style or title; impugning his supremacy; or assembling riotously to the number of twelve, and refusing to disperse on proclamation. But steadily, in better times, the people and the Parliament of England returned to the spirit and letter of the act of Edward III, passed by a Parliament which now, for five hundred years, has been known and honored as *Parliamentum benedictum*, the "blessed Parliament"—just as this Congress will be known, for ages to come, as "the accursed Congress"— and among many other acts, it was declared by a statute, in the first year of the fourth Henry's reign, that "*in no time to come* any treason be judged, otherwise than as ordained by the statute of King Edward III." And for nearly two hundred years, it has been the aim of the lawyers and judges of England to adhere to the plain letter, spirit, and intent of that act, "to be extended," in the language of Erskine in his noble defense of Hardy, "by no new or occasional constructions—to be strained by no fancied analogies—to be measured by no rules of political expediency—to be judged of by no theory—to be determined by the wisdom of no individual, however wise—but to be expounded by the simple, genuine letter of the law."

Such, sir, is the law of treason in England to-day; and so much of the just and admirable statute of Edward as is applicable to our form of government was embodied in the Constitution of the United States. The men of 1787 were well read in history and in English constitutional law. They knew that monarchs and Governments, in all ages, had struggled to extend the limits of treason, so as to include all opposition to those in power. They had learned the maxim that, miserable is the servitude where the law is either uncertain or unknown, and had studied and valued the profound declaration of Montesquieu, that, "if the crime of treason be indeterminate, that alone is sufficient to make any Government degenerate into arbitrary power." Hear Madison, in the Federalist:

"As *new-fangled and artificial treasons* have been the great engines by which violent factions, the natural offspring of free governments, have usually *wreaked their alternate malignity on each other*, the convention have, with great judgment, opposed a barrier to this peculiar danger, by inserting a constitutional definition of the crime, fixing the proof necessary for conviction of it, and restraining the Congress, even in punishing it, from extending the consequences of guilt beyond the person of its author."

And Story, not foreseeing the possibility of such a party or Administration as is now in power, declared it "*an impassable barrier*" against arbitrary constructions, either by the courts or by Congress, upon the crime of treason." "Congress;" that, sir, is the word, for he never dreamed that the President, or, still less, his clerks, the Cabinet ministers, would attempt to declare and punish treasons. And yet what have we lived to hear in America daily, not in political harangues or the press only, but in official proclamations and in bills in Congress! Yes, your high officials talk now of "treasonable practices" as glibly "as girls of thirteen do of puppy dogs." Treasonable practices! Disloyalty! Who imported these precious phrases, and gave them a legal settlement here? Your Secretary of War. He it was who by command of our most noble President authorized every marshal, every sheriff, every township constable, or city policeman, in every State in the Union, to fix, in his own imagination, what he might choose to call a treasonable or disloyal practice, and then to arrest any citizen at his discretion, without any accusing oath, and without due process or any process of law. And now, sir, all this monstrous tyranny, against the whole spirit and the very letter of the Constitution, is to be deliberately embodied in an act of Congress! Your petty provost marshals are to determine what treasonable practices are, and "inquire into," detect, spy out, eaves-drop, insnare, and then inform, report to the chief spy at Washington. These, sir, are now to be our American liberties under your Administration. There is not a crowned head in Europe who dare venture on such an experiment. How long think you this people will submit? But words, too—conversation or public speech—are to be adjudged "treasonable practices." Men, women, and children are to be haled to prison for free speech. Whoever shall denounce or oppose this Administration; whoever may affirm that war will not restore the Union, and teach men the gospel of peace, may be reported and arrested upon some old grudge, and by some ancient enemy, it may be, and imprisoned as guilty of a treasonable practice.

Sir, there can be but one treasonable practice under the Constitution in the United States. Admonished by the lessons of English history, the framers of that instrument defined what treason is. It is the only offense defined in the Constitution. We know what it is. Every man can tell whether he has committed treason. He has only to look into the Constitution, and he knows whether he has been guilty of the offense. But neither the Executive nor Congress, nor both combined, nor the courts, have a right to declare, either by pretended law or by construction, that any other offense shall be treason, except that defined and limited in this instrument. What is treason? It is the highest offense known to the law, the most execrable crime known to the human heart—the crime of *læsæ majestatis*; of the parricide who lifts his hand against the country of his birth or his adoption. "Treason against the United States," says the Constitution, "shall consist ONLY in levying war against them, or in adhering to their enemies, giving them aid and comfort." [Here a Republican member nodded several times and smiled.] Ah, sir, I understand you. But was Lord Chatham guilty of legal treason, treasonable aid and comfort, when he denounced the war against the colonies, and rejoiced that America had resisted? Was Burke, or Fox, or Barré guilty, when defending the Americans in the British Parliament, and demanding conciliation and peace? Were even the Federalists guilty of treason, as defined in the Constitution, for "giving aid and comfort" to the enemy in the war of 1812? Were the Whigs in 1846? Was the Ohio Senator liable to punishment, under the Constitution, and by law, who said, sixteen years ago, in the Senate Chamber, when we were at war in Mexico, "if I were a Mexican as I am an American, I would greet your volunteers with bloody hands, and welcome them to hospitable graves?" Was Abraham Lincoln guilty, because he denounced that same war, while a Representative on the floor of this House? Was all this "adhering to the enemy, giving him aid and comfort" within the meaning of this provision?

A MEMBER.   The Democratic papers said so.

Mr. VALLANDIGHAM.   Sir, I am speaking now as a lawyer and as a legislator to legislators and lawyers acting under oath and the other special and solemn sanctions of this Chamber, and not in the loose language of the political canvass. And I repeat, sir, that if such had been the intent of the Constitution, the whole Federal party and the whole Whig party and their representatives in this and the other Chamber might have been indicted and punished as traitors. Yet, not one of them was ever arrested. And shall they or their descendants undertake now to denounce and to punish, as guilty of treason, every man who opposes the policy of this Administration, or is against this civil war, and for peace upon honorable terms? I hope, in spite of the hundreds of your provost marshals, and all your threats, that there will be so much of opposition to the war as will compel the Administration to show a decent respect for and yield some sort of obedience to the Constitution and laws, and to the rights and liberties of the States and of the people.

But to return; the Constitution not only defines the crime of treason, but in its jealous care to guard against the abuses of tyrannic power, it expressly ascertains the character of the proof, and the number of witnesses necessary for conviction, and limits the punishment to the person of the offender; thus going beyond both the statute of Edward, and the common law. And yet every one of these provisions is ignored or violated by this bill.

"No person"—

Says the Constitution—

"shall be convicted of treason"—

As just defined—

"unless on the testimony of two witnesses."

Where and when, and by whom, sir, are the two witnesses to be examined, and under what oath? By your provost marshals, your captains of cavalry? By the jailors of your military bastiles, and inside of Forts Warren and La Fayette? Before arrest, upon arrest, while in prison, when discharged, or at any time at all? Has any witness ever been examined in any case heretofore? What means the Constitution by declaring that no person shall be *convicted* of treason "unless on the *testimony of two witnesses?*" Clearly, conviction in a judicial court, upon testimony openly given under oath, with all the sanctions and safe-guards of a judicial trial to the party accused. And if any doubt there could be upon this point, it is removed by the sixth article of the amendments.

But the Constitution proceeds:

"Unless on the testimony of two witnesses *to the same overt act.*"

But words, and still less, thoughts or opinions, sir, are not acts; and yet nearly every case of arbitrary arrest and imprisonment, in the wholly loyal States, at least, has been for words spoken or written, or for thoughts or opinions supposed to be entertained by the party arrested. And that, too, sir, is precisely what is intended by this bill.

But further:

"The testimony of two witnesses to the same overt act, *or confession in open court.*"

What court? The court of some deputy provost marshal at home, or of your Provost Marshal General or Judge Advocate General here in Washington? The court of a military bastile, whose gates are shut day and night against every officer of the law, and whose very casemates are closed to the light and air of heaven? Call you that "open court?" Not so the Constitution. It means judicial court, law court, with judge and jury and witnesses and counsel; and to speak of it as anything else is a confusion of language, and an insult to intelligence and common sense. Yet, to-night, you deliberately propose to enact the illegal and unconstitutional executive orders, or proclamations of last summer, into the semblance and form of law.

"To inquire into treasonable practices," says the bill. So, then, your provost marshals are to be deputy spies to the grand spy, holding his secret inquisitions here in Washington, upon secret reports, sent by telegraph, perhaps, or through the mails, both under the control of the Executive. What right has he to arrest and hold me without a hearing, because some deputy spy of his chooses to report me guilty of "disloyalty," or of "treasonable practices?" Is this the liberty secured by the Constitution? Sir, let me tell you that if the purpose of this bill be to crush out all opposition to the Administration and the party in power, you have no constitutional right to enact it, and not force enough to compel the people, your masters, to submit.

But the enormity of the measure does not stop here. Says the Constitution:

"Congress shall make no law abridging the freedom of speech or of the press."

And yet speech—mere words, derogatory to the President, or in opposition to his administration and his party and policy, have, over and over again, been reported by the spies and informers and shadows, or other minions, of the men in power, to be "disloyal practices," for which hundreds of free American citizens, of American, not African descent, have been arrested and imprisoned for months, without public accusation, and without trial by jury, or trial at all. Even upon pretense of guilt of that most vague and indefinite, but most comprehensive of all offenses, "discouraging enlistments," men have been seized at midnight, and dragged from their beds, their homes, and their families, to be shut up in the stone casemates of your military fortresses, as felons. And now, by this bill, you propose to declare, in the form and semblance of law, that whoever "counsels or dissuades" any one from the performance of the military duty required under this conscription, shall be summarily arrested by your provost marshals, and held without trial till the draft shall have been completed. Sir, even the "sedition law" of '98 was constitutional, merciful, and just, compared with this execrable enactment. Wisely did Hamilton ask, in the Federalist, "What signifies a declaration that the liberty of the press (or of speech) shall be inviolably preserved, when its security must altogether depend on public opinion, *and on the general spirit of the people*, and of the Government?"

But this extraordinary bill does not stop here.

"No person,"

Says the Constitution,

" *No* person shall be held to answer for a capital or otherwise infamous crime, unless on a presentment or indictment of a grand jury, except in cases arising in the land and naval force, or in the militia when in actual service in time of war or public danger; nor be deprived of life, liberty, or property, without due process of law."

Note the exception. Every man not in the military service is exempt from arrest except by due process of law; or, being arrested without it, is entitled to demand immediate inquiry and discharge, or bail; and if held, then presentment or indictment by a grand jury in a civil court, and according to the law of the land. And yet you now propose by this bill, in addition to the one million two hundred and thirty-seven thousand men who have voluntarily surrendered that great right of freemen, second only to the ballot—and, indeed, essential to it—to take it away forcibly and against their consent, from three millions more, whose only crime is that they happen to have been so born as to be now between the ages of twenty and forty-five. Do it, if you can, under the Constitution; and when you have thus forced them into the military service they will be subject to military law, and not entitled to arrest only upon due process of law, nor to indictment by a grand jury in a civil court. But you cannot, you shall not—because the Constitution forbids it—deprive the whole people, also, of the United States of these rights, "inestimable to them and formidable to tyrants only," under the "war power," or upon pretense of "military necessity," and by virtue of an act of Congress creating and defining new treasons, new offenses, not only unknown to the Constitution, but expressly excluded by it.

But again:

"In all criminal prosecutions"—

And wherever a penalty is to be imposed, imprisonment or fine inflicted, it is a criminal prosecution—

"In all criminal prosecutions"—

Says the Constitution—

"the accused shall enjoy the right to a speedy and public trial, by an impartial jury of the State and district wherein the crime shall have been committed, which district shall have been previously ascertained by law; and to be informed of the nature and cause of the accusation; to be confronted with the witnesses against him; to have compulsory process for obtaining witnesses in his favor, and to have the assistance of counsel for his defense."

Do you propose to allow any of these rights? No, sir; none —not one; but, in the twenty-fifth section, you empower these provost marshals of yours to arrest any man—men not under military law—whom he may charge, or any one else may charge before him, with "counseling or dissuading" from military service, and to hold him in confinement indefinitely, until the draft has been completed. Sir, has it been completed in Connecticut yet? Is it complete in New York? Has it been given up? If so now, nevertheless it was in process of pretended execution for months. In any event, you propose now to leave to the discretion of the Executive the time during which all persons arrested under the provisions of this bill, shall be held in confinement upon that summary and arbitrary arrest; and when he sees fit, and then only, shall the accused be delivered over to the civil authorities for trial. And is this the speedy and public trial by jury which the Constitution secures to every citizen not in the military service?

"The State and district wherein the crime"—

Yes, crime, for crime it must be, known to and defined by law, to justify the arrest—

"shall have been committed, which district shall have been previously ascertained by law."

Do you mean to obey that, and to observe State lines or district lines in arrests and imprisonments? Has it ever been done? Were not Keyes and Olds and Mahoney and Sheward, and my friend here to the left, [Mr. ALLEN, of Illinois,] and my other friend from Maryland, [Mr. MAY,] dragged from their several States and districts to New York or Massachusetts or to this city? The pirate, the murderer, the counterfeiter, the thief—you would have seized by due and sworn process of law, and tried forthwith, by jury, at home; but honorable and guiltless citizens, members of this House, your peers upon this floor, were thrust, and may again, under this bill, be thrust into distant dungeons and bastiles, upon the pretense of some crawling, verminous spy and informer that they have "dissuaded" some one from obedience to the draft, or are otherwise guilty of some "treasonable practice."

"And to be informed of the nature and cause of the accusation."

How? By presentment or indictment of a grand jury. When? "Speedily," says the Constitution. "When the draft is completed," says this bill; and the President shall determine that. But who is to limit and define "counseling or dissuading" from military service? Who shall ascertain and inform the accused of the "nature and cause" of a "treasonable practice?" Who, of all the thousand victims of arbitrary arrests, within the last twenty-two months, even to this day, has been informed of the charge against him, although long since released? Yet even a Roman pro-consul, in a conquered province, refused to send up a prisoner without signifying the crimes with which he was charged.

"To be confronted with the witnesses against him."

Witnesses, indeed! Fortunate will be the accused if there be any witnesses against him. But is your deputy provost marshal to call them? Oh, no; he is only to "inquire into, and report." Is your Provost Marshal General? What! call witnesses from the remotest parts of the Union to a secret inquisition here in Washington. Has any "prisoner of State" hitherto been confronted with witnesses at any time? Has he even been allowed to know so much as the names of his accusers? Yet Festus could boast that it was not the manner of the Romans to punish any man "before that he, which is accused, have the accusers face to face."

"To have compulsory process for obtaining witnesses in his favor."

Sir, the compulsory process will be, under this bill, as it has been from the first, to compel the absence, rather, of not only the witnesses, but the friends and nearest relatives of the accused; even the wife of his bosom and his children—the inmates of his own household. Newspapers, the Bible, letters from home, except under surveillance, a breath of air, a sight of the waves of the sea, or of the mild, blue sky, the song of birds, whatever was denied to the prisoner of Chillon, and more, too; yes, even a solitary lamp in the casemate, where a dying prisoner struggled with death, all have been refused to the American citizen accused of disloyal speech or opinions, by this most just and merciful Administration.

And, finally, says the Constitution:

"To have the assistance of counsel for his defense."

And yet your Secretary of State, the "conservative" Seward —the confederate of Weed, that treacherous, dissembling foe to constitutional liberty and the true interests of his country— forbade his prisoners to employ counsel, under penalty of prolonged imprisonment. Yes, charged with treasonable practices, yet the demand for counsel was to be dealt with as equal to treason itself. Here is an order, signed by a minion of Mr. Seward, and read to the prisoners at Fort La Fayette, on the 3d of December, 1861:

"I am instructed by the Secretary of State to inform you that the Department of State of the United States *will not recognize anyone as an attorney for political prisoners*, and will look with distrust upon all applications for release through such channels; and that such applications *will be regarded as additional reasons for declining to release the prisoners.*"

And here is another order to the same effect, dated "Department of State, Washington, November 27, 1861," signed by William H. Seward himself, and read to the prisoners at Fort Warren on the 29th of November, 1861:

"Discountenancing and repudiating all such practices"—

The disloyal practice, forsooth, of employing counsel—

"the Secretary of State desires that all the State prisoners may understand *that they are expected to revoke all such engagements now existing and avoid any hereafter*, as they can only lead to new complications and embarrassments to the cases of prisoners on whose behalf *the Government might be disposed to act with liberality.*"

Most magnanimous Secretary! Liberality toward men guilty of no crime, but who, though they had been murderers or pirates, were entitled by the plain letter of the Constitution to have "the assistance of counsel for their defense." Sir, there was but one step further possible, and that short step was taken some months later, when the prisoners of State were required to make oath, as the condition of their discharge, that they would not seek their constitutional and legal remedy in court for the wrongs and outrages inflicted upon them.

Sir, incredible as all this will seem some years hence, it has happened, all of it, and more yet untold, within the last twenty months, in the United States. Under Executive usurpation, and by virtue of presidential proclamations and cabinet orders, it has been done without law and against Constitution; and now it is proposed, I repeat, to sanction and authorize it all by an equally unconstitutional and void act of Congress. Sir, legislative tyranny is no more tolerable than Executive tyranny. It is a vain thing to seek to cloak all this under the false semblance of law. Liberty is no more guarded or secured, and arbitrary power no more hedged in and limited here than under the Executive orders of last summer. We know what has already been done, and we will submit to it no longer. Away, then, with your vain clamor about disloyalty, your miserable mockery of treasonable practices. We have read with virtuous indignation in history ages ago of an Englishman executed for treason, in saying that he would make his son heir to the crown, meaning of his own tavern-house, which bore the sign of the crown; and of that other Englishman, whose favorite buck the king had killed, and who suffered death as a traitor, for wishing, in a fit of vexation, that the buck, horns and all, were emboweled in the body of the king. But what have we not lived to see in our own time? Sir, not many months ago, this Administration in its great and tender mercy toward the six hundred and forty prisoners of State, confined for treasonable practices, at Camp Chase near the capital of Ohio, appointed a commissioner, an extra judicial functionary, unknown to the Constitution and laws, to hear and determine the cases of the several parties accused, and with power to discharge at his discretion, or to banish to Bull's Island, in Lake Erie. Among the political prisoners called before him was a lad of fifteen, a newsboy upon the Ohio river, whose only offense proved, upon inquiry, to be that he owed fifteen cents the unpaid balance of a debt due to his washer-woman—possibly a woman of color—who had him arrested by the provost marshal as guilty of "disloyal practices." And yet, for four weary months the lad had lain in that foul and most loathsome prison, under military charge, lest, peradventure, he should overturn the Government of the United States; or, at least, the administration of Abraham Lincoln!

Several MEMBERS on the Democratic side of the House. Oh no; the case cannot be possible.

Mr. VALLANDIGHAM.   It is absolutely true, and it is one only among many such cases. Why, sir, was not the hump-back carrier of the New York Daily News, a paper edited by a member of this House, arrested in Connecticut, for selling that paper, and hurried off out of the State, and imprisoned in Fort La Fayette? And yet, Senators and Representatives, catching up the brutal cry of a bloodthirsty but infatuated partisan press, exclaim "the Government has been too lenient, there ought to have been more arrests!"

Well did Hamilton remark that "arbitrary imprisonments have been in all ages the favorite and most formidable instruments of tyranny;" and, not less truly, Blackstone declares that they are "a less public, a less striking, and therefore *a more dangerous engine* of arbitrary government" than executions upon the scaffold. And yet, to-night, you seek here, under cloak of an act of Congress, to authorize these arrests and imprisonments, and thus to renew again that reign of terror which smote the hearts of the stoutest among us, last summer, as "the pestilence which walketh in darkness."

But the Constitution provides further, that

"The right of the people to be secure in their persons, houses, papers, and effects, against unreasonable searches and seizures, shall not be violated, and no warrants shall issue but upon probable cause, supported by oath or affirmation, and particularly describing the place to be searched and the persons or things to be seized."

Sir, every line, letter, and syllable of this provision has been repeatedly violated, under pretense of securing evidence of disloyal or treasonable practices; and now you propose by this bill to sanction the past violations, and authorize new and continued infractions in future. Your provost marshals, your captains of cavalry are to "inquire into treasonable practices."

How? In any way, sir, that they may see fit; and of course by search and seizure of person, house, papers, or effects; for, sworn and appointed spies and informers as they are, they will be and can be of no higher character, and no more scrupulous of law or right or decency than their predecessors of last summer, appointed under Executive proclamations of no more or less validity than this bill which you seek now to pass into a law. Sir, there is but one step further to take. Put down the peaceable assembling of the people; the right of petition for redress of grievances; the "right of the people to keep and bear arms;" and finally the right of suffrage and elections, and then these United States, this Republic of ours, will have ceased to exist. And that short step you will soon take, if the States and the people do not firmly and speedily check you in your headlong plunge into despotism. What yet remains? The Constitution declares that—

"The enumeration in the Constitution of certain rights shall not be construed to deny or disparage others retained by the people."

And again:

"The powers not delegated to the United States by the Constitution, nor prohibited by it to the States, are reserved to the States respectively or to the people."

And yet, under the monstrous doctrine that in war the Constitution is suspended, and that the President as Commander-in-Chief, not of the military forces only, but of the whole people of the United States, may, under "the war power," do whatever he shall think necessary and proper to be done, in any State or part of any State, however remote from the scene of warfare, every right of the people is violated or threatened, and every power of the States usurped. Their last bulwark, the militia, belonging solely to the States when not called as such into the actual service of the United States, you now deliberately propose, by this bill, to sweep away, and to constitute the President supreme military dictator, with a standing army of three millions and more at his command. And for what purpose are the militia to be thus taken from the power and custody of the States? Sir, the opponents of the Constitution anticipated all this, and were denounced as raving incendiaries or distempered enthusiasts.

"The Federal Government"—

Said Patrick Henry, in the Virginia Convention,

"squints towards monarchy. Your President may easily become a king. If ever he violates the laws, *will not the recollection of his crimes teach him to make one bold push for the American throne?* Will not the immense difference between being master of everything and being ignominiously tried and punished powerfully excite him to make this bold push? But, sir, where is the existing force to punish him? Can he not, at the head of his army, beat down all opposition? What, then, will become of you and your rights? Will not absolute despotism ensue?"*

And yet, for these apprehensions, Henry has been the subject of laughter and pity for seventy years. Sir, the instinctive love of liberty is wiser and more far-seeing than any philosophy.

Hear, now, Alexander Hamilton, in the Federalist. Summing up what he calls the exaggerated and improbable suggestions respecting the power of calling for the services of the militia, urged by the opponents of the Constitution, whose writings he compares to some ill-written tale, or romance full of frightful and distorted shapes, he says:

"The militia of New Hampshire, they allege, is to be marched to Georgia; of Georgia to New Hampshire; of New York to Kentucky; and of Kentucky to Lake Champlain. Nay, the debts due to the French and Dutch are to be paid in militia men, instead of Louis d'ors and ducats. At one moment, there is to be a large army to lay prostrate the liberties of the people; at another moment, the militia of Virginia are to be dragged from their homes, five or six hundred miles, to tame the republican contumacy of Massachusetts; *and that of Massachusetts is to be transported an equal distance to subdue the refractory haughtiness of the aristocratic Virginians.* Do persons who

---

*And the reporter, unable to follow the vehement orator of the Revolution, adds:

"Here, Mr. Henry strongly and pathetically expatiated on the probability of the President's enslaving America, and the horrid consequences that must result."

rave at this rate imagine that their eloquence can impose any conceits or absurdities upon the people of America for infallible truths?"

And yet, sir, just three quarters of a century later we have lived to see these ravings, conceits, and absurdities practiced, or attempted, as calmly and deliberately as though the power and the right had been expressly conferred.

And now, sir, listen to the answer of Hamilton to all this— himself the friend of a strong Government, a Senate for life, and an Executive for life, with the sole and exclusive power over the militia, to be held by the national Government; and the Executive of each State to be appointed by that Government:

"If there should be an army to be made use of as the engine of despotism, what need of the militia? If there should be no army, *whither would the militia, irritated at being required to undertake a distant and distressing expedition, for the purpose of riveting the chains of slavery upon a part of their countrymen, direct their course,* BUT TO THE SEATS OF THE TYRANTS WHO HAD MEDITATED SO FOOLISH AS WELL AS SO WICKED A PROJECT; TO CRUSH THEM IN THEIR IMAGINED INTRENCHMENTS OF POWER, AND MAKE THEM AN EXAMPLE OF THE VENGEANCE OF AN ABUSED AND INCENSED PEOPLE? Is this the way in which usurpers stride to dominion over a numerous and enlightened nation?"

Sir, Mr. Hamilton was an earnest, sincere man, and, doubtless, wrote what he believed: he was an able man also, and a philosopher; and yet how little did he foresee, that just seventy-five years later, that same Government, which he was striving to establish, would, in desperate hands, attempt to seize the whole militia of the Union, and convert them into a standing army, indefinite as to the time of its service, and for the very purpose of not only beating down State sovereignties, but of abolishing even the domestic and social institutions of the States.

Sir, if your objects are constitutional, you have power abundantly under the Constitution, without infraction or usurpation. The men who framed that instrument made it both for war and peace. Nay, more, they expressly provide for the cases of insurrection and rebellion. You have ample power to do all that of right you ought to do—all that the people, your masters, permit under their supreme will, the Constitution. Confine, then, yourselves within these limits, and the rising storm of popular discontent will be hushed.

But I return, now, again, to the arbitrary arrests sanctioned by this bill, and by that other consummation of despotism, the indemnity and suspension bill, now in the Senate. Sir, this is the very question which, as I said a little while ago, we made a chief issue before the people in the late elections. You did, then, distinctly claim—and you found an Attorney General and a few other venal or very venerable lawyers to defend the monstrous claim—that the President had the right to suspend the writ of *habeas corpus*; and that every one of these arrests was legal and justifiable. We went before the people with the Constitution and the laws in our hands, and the love of liberty in our hearts; and the verdict of the people was rendered against you. We insisted that Congress alone could suspend the writ of *habeas corpus* when, in cases of rebellion or invasion, the public safety might require it. And today, sir, that is beginning to be again the acknowledged doctrine. The Chief Justice of the Supreme Court of the United States so ruled in the Merryman case; and the supreme court of Wisconsin, I rejoice to say, has rendered a like decision; and if the question be ever brought before the Supreme Court of the United States, undoubtedly it will be so decided, finally and forever. You yourselves now admit it; and at this moment, your "indemnity bill," a measure more execrable than even this conscription, and liable to every objection which I have urged against it, undertakes to authorize the President to suspend the writ all over or in any part of the United States. Sir, I deny that you can thus delegate your right to the Executive. Even your own power is conditional. You cannot suspend the writ except where the public safety requires it, and then only in cases of rebellion or invasion. A foreign war, not brought home by invasion, to our own soil, does not authorize the suspension, in any case. And who is to judge whether and where there is rebellion or invasion, and whether and when the public safety requires that the writ be suspended? Congress alone, and they cannot substitute the judgment of the President for their own. Such, too, is the opinion of Story: "The right to judge," says he, "whether exigency has arisen, must *exclusively* belong to that body." But not so under the bill which passed this House the other day.

Nor is this all. Congress alone can suspend the writ. When and where? In cases of rebellion or invasion. Where rebellion? Where invasion? Am I to be told that because there is rebellion in South Carolina the writ of *habeas corpus* can be suspended in Pennsylvania and Massachusetts where there is none? Is that the meaning of the Constitution? No, sir; the writ can be suspended only where the rebellion or invasion exists—in States, or parts of States, alone, where the enemy, foreign or domestic, is found in arms; and moreover, the public safety can require its suspension only where there is rebellion or invasion. Outside of these conditions, Congress has no more authority to suspend the writ than the President, and, least of all, to suspend it without limitation as to time, and generally all over the Union, and in States not invaded or in rebellion. Such an act of Congress is of no more validity, and no more entitled to obedience, than an executive proclamation; and in any just and impartial court I venture to affirm that it will be so decided.

But again, sir, even though the writ be constitutionally suspended, there is no more power in the President to make arbitrary arrests than without it. The gentleman from Rhode Island [Mr. SHEFFIELD] said, very justly—and I am sorry to see him lend any support to this bill—that the suspension of the writ of *habeas corpus* does not authorize arrests except upon sworn warrant, charging some offense known to the law and dangerous to the public safety. He is right. It does not; and this was so admitted in the bill which passed the Senate in 1807. The suspension only denies release upon bail, or a discharge without trial, to parties thus arrested. It suspends no other right or privilege under the Constitution—certainly not the right to a speedy public trial by jury in a civil court. It dispenses with no "due process of law," except only that particular writ. It does not take away the claim for damages to which a party illegally arrested, or legally arrested, but without probable cause, is entitled.

And yet, everywhere, it has been assumed that a suspension of the writ of *habeas corpus* is a suspension of the entire Constitution and of all laws, so far as the personal rights of the citizen are concerned, and that, therefore, the moment it is suspended, either by the President, as heretofore asserted, or by Congress, as now about to be authorized, arbitrary arrests, without sworn warrant or other due process of law, may be made at the sole pleasure or discretion of the Executive. I tell you no; and that, although we may not be able to take the body of the party arrested from the provost marshal by writ of *habeas corpus*, every other right and privilege of the Constitution and of the common law remains intact, including the right to resist the wrong-doer or trespasser, who, without due authority, would violate your person, or enter your house, which is your castle; and, after all this, the right also to prosecute on indictment or for damages, as the nature or aggravation of the case may demand. And yet, as claimed by you of the party in power, the suspension of this writ is a total abrogation of the Constitution and of the liberties of the citizen and the rights of the States. Why, then, sir, stop with arbitrary arrests and imprisonments? Does any man believe that it will end here? Not so have I learned history. The guillotine! the guillotine! the guillotine follows next.

Sir, when one of those earliest confined in Fort La Fayette— I had it from his own lips—made complaint to the Secretary of State of the injustice of his arrest, and the severity of the treatment to which he had been subjected in the exercise of arbitrary power, no offense being alleged against him, "why," said the Secretary, with a smile of most significant complacency, "my dear sir, you ought not to complain; *we might have gone further.*" Light flashed upon the mind of the gentleman, and he replied: "Ah! that is true, sir; you had just the same right to behead as to arrest and imprison me." And shall it come to this? Then, sir, let us see who is beheaded first. It is horrible enough to be imprisoned without crime, but when it becomes a question of life or death, remember the words of the book of Job—"All that a man hath will he give for his life."

Sir, it is this which makes revolutions. A gentleman upon the other side asked this afternoon which party was to rise now in revolution. The answer of the able and gallant gentleman from Pennsylvania [Mr. BIDDLE] was pertinent and just—"No party, but an outraged people." It is not, let me tell you, the leaders of parties who begin revolutions. Never. Did any one of the

distinguished characters of the Revolution of 1776 participate
in the throwing of the tea into Boston harbor? Who was it?
Who, to-day, can name the actors in that now historic scene? It
was not Hancock, nor Samuel Adams, nor John Adams, nor
Patrick Henry, nor Washington; but men unknown to fame.
Good men agitate; obscure men begin real revolutions; great
men finally direct and control them. And if, indeed, we are
about to pass through the usual stages of revolution, it will not
be the leaders of the Democratic party—not I, not the men
with me here to-night—but some man among the people,
now unknown and unnoted, who will hurl your tea into the
harbor; and it may even be in Boston once again; for the love
of liberty, I would fain believe, lingers still under the shadow of
the monument on Bunker Hill. But, sir, we seek no revolution
—except through the ballot-box. The conflict to which we
challenge you, is not of arms but of argument. Do you believe
in the virtue and intelligence of the people? Do you admit
their capacity for self-government? Have they not intelligence
enough to understand the right, and virtue enough to pursue
it? Come then: meet us through the press, and with free
speech, and before the assemblages of the people, and we will
argue these questions, as we and our fathers have done from
the beginning of the Government—"Are we right or you right,
we wrong or you wrong?" And by the judgment of the people
we will, one and all, abide.

Sir, I have done now with my objections to this bill. I have
spoken as though the Constitution survived, and was still the
supreme law of the land. But if, indeed, there be no Constitution any longer, limiting and restraining the men in power,
then there is none binding upon the States or the people. God
forbid. We have a Constitution yet, and laws yet. To them I
appeal. Give us our rights; give us known and fixed laws; give
us the judiciary; arrest us only upon due process of law; give us
presentment or indictment by grand juries; speedy and public
trial; trial by jury, and at home; tell us the nature and cause of
the accusation; confront us with witnesses; allow us witnesses
in our behalf, and the assistance of counsel for our defense;
secure us in our persons, our houses, our papers, and our effects; leave us arms, not for resistance to law or against rightful
authority, but to defend ourselves from outrage and violence;

give us free speech and a free press; the right peaceably to assemble; and above all, free and undisturbed elections and the ballot; take our sons, take our money, our property, take all else; and we will wait a little, till at the time and in the manner appointed by Constitution and law we shall eject you from the trusts you have abused, and the seats of power you have dishonored, and other and better men shall reign in your stead.

Samuel W. Fiske to the Springfield Republican

The Democratic state convention that met in Hartford, Connecticut, on February 18, 1863, nominated Thomas H. Seymour for governor. It adopted a platform denouncing "the 'monstrous fallacy' that the Union can be restored by the armed hand" and calling for a negotiated peace. Lieutenant Samuel W. Fiske of the 14th Connecticut Infantry responded in one of his regular letters to the *Springfield* (Massachusetts) *Republican*, written under the pen name Dunn Browne. Several Connecticut regiments, including Fiske's, subsequently adopted statements opposing Seymour's candidacy and the Hartford platform. The resolutions of the 14th Connecticut, possibly drafted by Fiske, called for "the earnest, thorough and rapid prosecution of the war" and declared that the regiment's sacrifices had been made "in the cause of republican government, of democracy against aristocracy, of freedom against slavery." In the election held on April 6, Governor William A. Buckingham, the Republican incumbent running on a Union ticket, defeated Seymour with 51.6 percent of the vote.

ON THE CONNECTICUT COPPERHEADS

> Camp near Falmouth, Va.
> February 25

Oh Republican! Give me a Hartford Times or some other appropriate receptacle, for I am about to vomit. I am sick, nauseated, poisoned; have taken something that, most emphatically, doesn't agree with me; have swallowed the vile and traitorous resolutions of the recent Democratic convention at Hartford, and have read in connection some of the speeches on the same occasion, filled with ribaldry and profanity just about in keeping with the whole spirit of the meeting. And I am ashamed and confounded, disgusted and grieved, to see what proportions treason has attained even in dear old New England. I knew that such things were talked in the darker sections of our western Egypt. I wouldn't have been surprised to read of proceedings a little like those at Hartford as having taken place in some very ignorant district in southern Indiana. But in Connecticut, faugh! I can't begin to express my feelings, and yet I am obliged to confess that I am one of her citizens. If the dear old state doesn't spew out of her mouth this ill-savoring Tom Seymour Democracy at the coming April election, we of the army will march North instead of South to get at the heart of the rebellion.

Talk about demoralization of the army! Well, we have fallen pretty low. We haven't the same strain of lofty patriotism in our talk as when we first came out. We have been knocked round and starved and frozen till we have some of us forgotten the distinction between a good government and its sometimes corrupt agents, and in our personal indignation we lost sight, for the moment, of our correct principles. We have said many things that were not complimentary to our lawful civil and military leaders; yes, we have said many things that we shall be ashamed of, if we ever get home; but I do still fully believe and hope that if any man should talk such foul stuff as that of this modern Hartford convention in any of our camps, we should have principle and decency enough left to roll him in one of our Virginia gutters and drum him out of camp. Thank God we are not so demoralized yet as to suffer downright, earnest treason to be talked in our presence.

But enough of such a disgusting subject. Let us roll some more pleasantly flavored morsel under our tongue to get that taste out of our mouth. Spring is coming, our time of hope, of fresh life and vigor, our time of accustomed triumph. The winter is almost over. Let us hope that the "winter of our discontent," of our discouragement, reverses and distress, shall pass away with it, and that when the mud dries up, and the grass grows green, we may also "dry up" our murmuring, and our laurels grow green. I look for a great series of spring victories like those of last year—of grand, crushing, final victories— victories that shall shut off all question of foreign intervention, make such a performance as this Hartford convention a thing for even Connecticut Seymour Democrats to be ashamed of, and take away every shadow of hope from their fellow traitors at the South. I say I am *looking* for such victories. I shall continue to *look* for them very attentively and anxiously. Oh how happy we shall all be if we only find them. Yours, as ever,

DUNN BROWNE

February 25, 1863

Charles C. Jones Jr. to Charles C. Jones Sr. and Mary Jones

Lieutenant Colonel Charles C. Jones Jr., a Confederate artillery officer serving at Savannah, wrote to his parents about the Union bombardment of Fort McAllister, which guarded the entrance to the Ogeechee River south of the city. Contrary to Jones's expectation, the Union attack on the fort was not renewed on the following day. It had been ordered by Rear Admiral Samuel F. Du Pont, who was planning an assault on Charleston Harbor, as a test of the ability of his ironclads to damage earthwork fortifications.

———————————

Savannah, *Tuesday*, March 3rd, 1863

My very dear Father and Mother,

The abolitionists, with three ironclads, four gunboats, and several mortar boats, attacked Fort McAllister this morning. They opened fire about half-past eight, and the engagement continued without intermission until near half-past four o'clock P.M. The last dispatch, which left the fort after the firing had ceased, reports that only two of our men were wounded during the whole of this protracted bombardment, and they only slightly. The carriage of the eight-inch columbiad was disabled by a shot from the enemy. A new one has been sent out; and the gun itself, which was not injured, will be remounted during the night and be all ready for action in the morning. The injury to the parapet of the fort is slight, and will be repaired during the night. The garrison is in fine spirits, and are determined to hold the fort to the last extremity. It is truly wonderful how mercifully and abundantly the good and great God of Battles has encircled our brave men with the protection of His all-powerful arm, shielding them from harm amid dangers imminent and protracted. To Him our hearts ascend in humble, fervent gratitude for the past; from Him we earnestly implore like favor in the future. If the Lord is on our side, as we honestly trust and believe He is, we will not fear what our enemies, with all their boasted strength, can do unto us.

The enemy seems determined to reduce this fort if practicable, probably with a view to the destruction of the railroad bridge. That little fort has thus far so successfully and so bravely resisted every effort on their part for its reduction that they will doubtless use every endeavor, as a matter of pride, to compass its destruction. There is no question of the fact that it is a remarkably well-constructed earthwork—well traversed. The lessons of the past and of the present so demonstrate. It is almost a miniature edition of Vicksburg. In like manner must all our defenses be conducted.

The dispatch to which I alluded above states further that the ironclads, etc., retired, apparently with a view to obtaining an additional supply of ammunition. They dropped down the river only a little way, and a store ship soon joined them and appeared to be serving out ammunition. The attack will doubtless be renewed in the morning; in fact, while I write from my office in the barracks at this 9½ P.M., I hear guns in the direction of Genesis Point. The enemy will probably continue the bombardment at intervals during the night, with a view to wearying our men and preventing the necessary repairs to the fort; and when the morning light again cleverly dawns, the attack will be renewed with vigor. We are supplying the deficiencies in ammunition caused by the expenditures of the day. It is thought that one ironclad was seriously injured. This may be, however, only *conjecture*; we hope such is the *fact*.

The land force on our side, now in the vicinity of the fort and prepared to resist any effort of the enemy to land, consists of the 29th Georgia Regiment, the sharpshooter battalion, two companies in the fort, our light battery, and some seven or more cavalry companies. With the natural advantages of the country these men, if they do their duty, ought to accomplish a great deal.

We have been reinforced at this point by the arrival of the brave General Walker. General Clingman reached the city today with his brigade of three regiments, and General Taliaferro is expected with his brigade. General Beauregard announces himself prepared to come over at any moment that his services are needed. I trust and confidently believe that we will, with the blessing of Heaven, be able successfully to defend the city from the expected attack, and to teach the enemy a fearful lesson which will not be speedily forgotten.

I am getting my light artillery in capital condition, and hope, when the opportunity presents itself, to render efficient service.

The Doctor came in this afternoon and is staying with us. Mr. Ward also returned by the Charleston train. Many, many thanks, my very dear mother, for your kind and most acceptable remembrance of us.

I am very much pained, my dear father, to hear that you are still so weak. All I can do is to hope and pray that you may soon be better, and that it would please God in tender mercy to us all to prolong your days, so precious to us all. . . . Do, my dear parents, let me know if I can do anything for you at any time, or for my dear little daughter. I wish very much to see you all, but at present it is impossible for me to leave the post of duty, for it is emphatically the fact that we know not what an hour may bring forth. . . . With warmest love to you both, my dear father and mother, and many tender kisses for my dear little daughter, I am ever

Your affectionate son,
Charles C. Jones, Jr.

Charles C. Jones Sr. to Charles C. Jones Jr.

A retired Presbyterian minister, Jones wrote to his son from one of the three plantations his family owned in Liberty County, Georgia. After suffering for years from the "wasting palsy," Jones would die peacefully at Arcadia plantation on March 16, 1863.

———————

Arcadia, *Wednesday*, March 4th, 1863

My dear Son,

Your kind favor of last evening reached us this morning, and afforded us the very information which we were anxious to receive—circumstantial and reliable. No paper from Savannah came.

Surely we have reason to bless God and take courage and fight more manfully than ever. The bombardment of Genesis Point is one of *the events* of this most eventful war. The failure of the vaunted ironclads will have a great moral effect. The enemy will have less confidence, and we stronger assurance, of being able with properly constructed fortifications and good armament, and above all with *brave men*, to repulse them. I look upon it as a special providence—an answer to prayer. Eight hours' bombardment with three ironclads and some six or seven mortar and gunboats, and only two men slightly wounded, one gun carriage injured, and the damage to the breastworks repaired in the night! We learn that the enemy has renewed the attack this morning. May it please God to help us through to the end, that they may be finally repulsed!

The effect of this affair will be most salutary upon our troops in Savannah and Charleston. Right glad am I to learn that you are still receiving reinforcements for the defense of the city, and that an excellent spirit prevails, and that our outposts are to be defended to the last extremity and the enemy fought inch by inch. That is the plan. We heard yesterday that the enemy were to be permitted to land, and the outposts were to be given up, and our forces retired within the line of the city defenses! What an idea! What would be the consequence? A regular siege approach, an accumulation of men and matériel, and the city in all probability captured! Never retire and confine ourselves within our defenses until we are forced to do it.

Am happy to know also that you are so much better, and exerting yourself with energy and judgment and with so much success in putting your batteries in the best order for service. They will no doubt play an important part if the conflict comes, and may determine the fortunes of the day—in which event I trust, my dear son, and pray that God would shield your life and your person and enable you to discharge your duty as a Christian man and as a true soldier and patriot. General Walker is a great accession. Do you observe the *mercy* in the Genesis affair? *Not a man killed*; not one *dangerously* wounded!

The presence of your dear brother with you at this time gives great comfort to Mother and myself, and must be so to you both. The Doctor would not delay, but went down to be with you and on hand with the staff of surgeons if there should be a necessity. I looked at all his fine cases of instruments, and told him I wished they might always be kept in the same capital order, but he never be called to use them on the field of battle. His visit has greatly refreshed us.

Your dear baby is quite well all to the eruption. *She walked alone for the first time Sunday, March 1st, 1863.* Mother, Daughter, Robert, and Miss Kitty Stiles all unite in love and respects to you both. The Lord bless and keep you both!

Your ever affectionate father (with a tired hand),

C. C. Jones.

Harriet Jacobs to Lydia Maria Child

Harriet Jacobs, the author of *Incidents in the Life of a Slave Girl*, had gone to the District of Columbia in the summer of 1862 and begun relief work among the former slaves who had fled there. She wrote about conditions in northern Virginia to the abolitionist Lydia Maria Child, who had edited *Incidents*, in a letter that appeared in William Lloyd Garrison's antislavery newspaper *The Liberator* on April 10, 1863.

COLORED REFUGEES IN OUR CAMPS.

The following letter is from a very worthy, intelligent woman, who was herself a slave during twenty-five years, and who is now manifesting sympathy with her long-oppressed people by nursing them in the vicinity of our camps. To do this, she not only relinquishes good wages in a family for many years strongly attached to her, but also liberally imparts from her own earnings to the destitute around her.

L. M. CHILD.

ALEXANDRIA, March 18.

Since I last wrote to you, the condition of the poor refugees has improved. During the winter months, the small pox carried them off by hundreds; but now it has somewhat abated. At present, we have one hundred and forty patients in the hospital. The misery I have witnessed must be seen to be believed. The Quakers of Philadelphia, who sent me here, have done nobly for my people. They have indeed proved themselves a Society of Friends. Had it not been for their timely relief, many more must have died. They have sent thousands and tens of thousands of dollars to different sections of the country, wherever these poor sufferers came within our lines. But, notwithstanding all that has been done, very many have died from destitution. It is impossible to reach them all. Government has erected here barracks for the accommodations of five hundred. We have fifteen hundred on the list.

Many have found employment, and are supporting themselves and their families. It would do your heart good to talk
with some of these people. They are quick, intelligent, and full
of the spirit of freedom. Some of them say to me, "The white
men of the North have helped us thus far, and we want to help
them. We would like to fight for them, if they would only treat
us like men."

The colored people could not do enough for the first regiments that came here. They had entire faith in them as the
deliverers of their race. The sight of the U.S. uniform took all
fear out of their hearts, and inspired them with hope and confidence. Many of them freely fed the soldiers at their own tables,
and lodged them as comfortably as possible in their humble
dwellings. The change is very sad. In return for their kindness
and ever-ready service, they often receive insults, and sometimes beatings, and so they have learned to distrust those who
wear the uniform of the U.S. You know how warmly I have
sympathized with the Northern army; all the more does it
grieve me to see so many of them false to the principles of
freedom. But I am proud and happy to know that the black
man is to strike a blow for liberty. I am rejoiced that Col. Shaw
heads the Massachusetts regiment, for I know he has a noble
heart.

How pitiful it is that members of any religious sect should
come here, and return home to report their observations,
without one word of sympathy for God's suffering poor! This
is suggested to me by reading the New York *Evangelist*. These
poor refugees undoubtedly have faults, as all human beings
would have, under similar circumstances. I agree with that
noble man, Gen. Saxton, who says they appear to him to be
"extremely human." As to drunkenness, I have seen but one
case. As to stealing, I wish the writer in the New York *Evangelist* had made himself acquainted with the old slave-pen here,
now used for a prison. When I last went there, I found seventy
whites and one colored man. The marriage law has been disregarded, from old habits formed in slavery, and from want of
true friends to encourage them in the observance of it now. I
wish the writer of that article could have been where I was last
night, in our rough, little, poorly-built church.

It was densely crowded; and although some alarm was

excited by the rafters giving way overhead, quiet was soon restored, and the people were deeply attentive. Eight couples
were married on this occasion. We have a day-school of eighty
scholars, and a large number attend our evening school—
mostly adults. A large sewing-circle, composed of young and
old, meet every Saturday afternoon. Three colored men teach
a school in this city for those who can afford to pay somewhat
for instruction. They have a large number of pupils, mostly
children of colored citizens; but a few of the "little contrabands" attend their school.

We are now collecting together the orphan children, of
whom there are a great number, owing to the many deaths
that have occurred of late. In justice to the refugee women, I
am bound to testify that I have never known them, in any one
instance, refuse to shelter an orphan. In many cases, mothers
who have five or six children of their own, without enough to
feed and cover them, will readily receive these helpless little
ones into their own poor hovels.

O, when will the white man learn to know the hearts of my
abused and suffering people!

HARRIET JACOBS.

William Henry Harrison Clayton to Nide and Rachel Pugh

By 1863 disaffection with the war and resistance to conscription had become widespread in many upland areas of the Confederacy, including western Virginia, eastern Tennessee, western North Carolina, northwestern Georgia, and northern Alabama. William Henry Harrison Clayton, a company clerk in the 19th Iowa Infantry, wrote from southwestern Missouri about Arkansas Unionists.

Forsyth MO.
March 26th, 1863
  Dear Uncle & Aunt:
  I take up my pen this evening for the purpose of writing a few lines to you. I have been thinking of writing for some time past, but not having anything of importance to communicate I neglected doing so.
  You will see by the heading of my letter that we are still in the same old place, where we have been for the past two months. We have been holding the "*post*" here during the time mentioned, but once or twice have thought of "driving it in the ground" and leaving but have not done so as yet. In one of my letters home a short time ago I mentioned that our forage train was attacked by the rebels and although three times as many in number as our men, they retreated after our men gave them one volley.
  The commander at Springfield hearing that there was a force marching upon this place sent down a reinforcement of about 200 men of the 13th Kansas infantry & 4 field pieces. They remained here a few days and then returned to Springfield, forage being so scarce in this part of the world that it is impossible to keep a battery here. Things quieted down until a few days ago, when a couple of suspicious looking fellows came around examining things and were caught in trying to get through the pickets after dark. They immediately were put

under guard, and one of our *Union* butternuts with them. During the night this fellow by playing secesh got out of them, that they were *spies* and were to get $300 apiece for coming here to find out our numbers and position and report them to the rebel commander at Yellville on the morning of the 24th and then it was their intention to attack us with 5000 men and some artillery. Nearly the whole regiment was set to work erecting breastworks. A number of log houses were torn down and the logs piled up and a long line of breastworks was put up in short order. We worked at them yesterday and the day before. Today the usual quiet reigns in camp, there being only a few men at work putting on the *finishing touch.*

I apprehend no attack here at the present time anyhow for we have reinforcements within a day or two's march, and they will never attack us unless they have five or six times as many as we have.

A large number of Union refugees are here or have passed through here going north. Last Sunday 20 Union men came in. They are recruits for an Arkansas regiment being made up at Fayetteville, one of them an old man 57 years of age had been shot through the left shoulder by the bushwhackers a short time before they came away. The most of them had been lying out in mountains for a good while to escape being taken to the Confederate army. Several of them were *conscripts* and were with Hindman at Prairie Grove. Hindman's army was completely demoralized at that fight. One of these men said that all in the regiment he belongs to deserted, except 3 men. They also say that Hindman had 32 regiments in that engagement. We fought them in that long-to-be-remembered fight from 10 o'clock A.M. until 4 P.M. with only 6 regiments. Blunt then came in with 3 or 4 more regiments and we cleaned them out.

We have witnessed some painful things here. Members of families have passed through going north. They generally have cattle yoked to their old ricketty wagons, and often they are driven by women or very small boys, the father being either in some of the Missouri regiments, killed by the bushwhackers, or conscripted into the rebel army. To see women trudging along through the mud, poorly clad, and driving ox teams or as I saw in one instance when five women came from Arkansas all walking, two or three of them carrying infants in their arms and several children beside about "knee high to a duck" (they were hardly old enough to walk). Some of the women carried a few articles such as tin buckets etc. and the balance of their property was packed on an old grey horse. The "secesh" had taken everything from these women because their husbands had enlisted in the Union Arkansas regiment. Such sights make the blood boil and to make a person come to the conclusion that there is no punishment severe enough for those scoundrels who have brought about the present state of affairs by their taking up arms against the best government that this world has ever seen. There is another thing that "kinder gits" us, that is the action of a set of men in the North who are blind to their own interests and are endeavoring to *kick up a fuss* in even our own state of Iowa. Would to God that some of the leading copperheads were compelled to come down to this region and if they had to live here six months I think it would cure them and they would be content to go home and stay there and let the government take its own course in putting down the rebellion. One consolation is that they find little sympathy in the army and I assure you that some of them would be roughly used if they were where the soldiers could get hold of them.

The 19th adopted a series of resolutions a short time ago assuring the people of Iowa and all others that we give the government our undivided support. We enlisted for the purpose of aiding in putting down this infernal rebellion and we intend to do so. I have heard a number of the regiment express their views in regard to these northern *traitors* for they are nothing else and always there is ten times the hatred towards the northern traitors there is to those who are in arms against us.

We have two new recruits in our company who came from Texas. They came in and desired to enlist and were taken in our company.

Today 5 more came in and have enlisted in another company. Part of them have been in the rebel service. The rebels are conscripting in Arkansas, and numbers will doubtless be compelled to go who would rather be on our side.

We have had excellent weather for 3 weeks past. Part of the time it was nearly warm enough for summertime, the ground was dry and in good order for plowing but there is none of that kind of work going on in this vicinity. The grass is coming along nicely, and the woods are beginning to put on their coat of green.

Peach trees are out in blossom. There has been a few cold mornings lately but I think not cold enough to kill the peaches.

The past winter has been very favorable as far as cold weather is concerned, to us soldiers. I have not seen the ground froze more than 2 or 3 inches during the winter. I believe I have scribbled enough for one time and will bring my letter to a close.

Uncle Nide, I know your dislike of writing but I want you to write me a letter if it is ever so short. If Uncle Sammy Clayton is at your house tell him to write also. I send my best respects to him. Tell the folks at home that I am all right. "Nincy" and Ab. Buckles are well.

Hoping this will find you as it leaves me, in the enjoyment of good health.

I remain ever your affectionate nephew,

Wm. H. H. Clayton

P.S. I suppose that Lt. Ferguson has reached home before this time. Tell him that Lt. Sommerville has been and is yet very sick. Disease typhoid fever. He was taken to a private residence about 3 miles up the river a week or two ago. Also that our devil Bill Hartson has come to the company. All quiet on White River at the present.

Henry W. Halleck to Ulysses S. Grant

Believing that his army could neither provide for nor safely transport black refugees, Major General Ulysses S. Grant issued orders in February 1863 forbidding them from coming into the Union camps near Vicksburg. Major General Henry W. Halleck had been Grant's commanding officer in the western theater before being appointed general-in-chief of the Union army in July 1862. Halleck wrote to Grant about the government's policy regarding freed slaves in advance of the arrival in early April of Brigadier General Lorenzo Thomas, the army's adjutant general, who had been sent to recruit black soldiers in the Mississippi Valley. Grant would energetically assist Thomas in his recruiting efforts, and on April 11 ordered one of his division commanders to "encourage all negroes, particularly middle aged males to come within our lines."

HEADQUARTERS OF THE ARMY,
Washington, March 31, 1863.

Maj. Gen. U. S. GRANT,
Commanding Department of the Tennessee, near Vicksburg:

GENERAL: It is the policy of the Government to withdraw from the enemy as much productive labor as possible. So long as the rebels retain and employ their slaves in producing grains, &c., they can employ all the whites in the field. Every slave withdrawn from the enemy is equivalent to a white man put *hors de combat.*

Again, it is the policy of the Government to use the negroes of the South, as far as practicable, as a military force, for the defense of forts, depots, &c. If the experience of General Banks near New Orleans should be satisfactory, a much larger force will be organized during the coming summer; and if they can be used to hold points on the Mississippi during the sickly season, it will afford much relief to our armies. They certainly can be used with advantage as laborers, teamsters, cooks, &c., and it is the opinion of many who have examined the question without passion or prejudice, that they can also be used as a military force. It certainly is good policy to use them to the very best advantage we can. Like almost anything else, they may be made instruments of good or evil. In the hands of the enemy, they are used with much effect against us; in our hands, we must try to use them with the best possible effect against the rebels.

It has been reported to the Secretary of War that many of the officers of your command not only discourage the negroes from coming under our protection, but by ill-treatment force them to return to their masters. This is not only bad policy in itself, but is directly opposed to the policy adopted by the Government. Whatever may be the individual opinion of an officer in regard to the wisdom of measures adopted and announced by the Government, it is the duty of every one to cheerfully and honestly endeavor to carry out the measures so adopted. Their good or bad policy is a matter of opinion before they are tried; their real character can only be determined by a fair trial. When adopted by the Government, it is the duty of every officer to give them such a trial, and to do everything in his power to carry the orders of his Government into execution.

It is expected that you will use your official and personal influence to remove prejudices on this subject, and to fully and thoroughly carry out the policy now adopted and ordered by the Government. That policy is to withdraw from the use of the enemy all the slaves you can, and to employ those so withdrawn to the best possible advantage against the enemy.

The character of the war has very much changed within the last year. There is now no possible hope of reconciliation with the rebels. The Union party in the South is virtually destroyed. There can be no peace but that which is forced by the sword. We must conquer the rebels or be conquered by them. The North must conquer the slave oligarchy or become slaves themselves—the manufacturers mere "hewers of wood and drawers of water" to Southern aristocrats.

This is the phase which the rebellion has now assumed. We must take things as they are. The Government, looking at the subject in all its aspects, has adopted a policy, and we must cheerfully and faithfully carry out that policy.

I write you this unofficial letter simply as a personal friend and as a matter of friendly advice. From my position here, where I can survey the entire field, perhaps I may be better able to understand the tone of public opinion and the intentions of the Government than you can from merely consulting the officers of your own army.

Very respectfully, your obedient servant,

H. W. HALLECK.

Frederick Law Olmsted to John Olmsted

In December 1862 Grant had made his first attempt to capture Vicksburg, advancing south from Oxford, Mississippi, while Sherman led a river expedition down from Memphis to the Yazoo River north of the city. The plan failed when Confederate cavalry destroyed the Union supply depot at Holly Springs, forcing Grant to retreat, and Sherman was repulsed at Chickasaw Bayou on the Yazoo. After abandoning plans for a renewed overland offensive through northern Mississippi, Grant assumed command of the river expedition on January 30. Hoping to bypass the Confederate batteries at Vicksburg, he had his troops work on a canal across a peninsula opposite the city, and tried to open a water route through a series of Louisiana lakes, rivers, and bayous to the Mississippi below the city. Grant also made two attempts to reach the Yazoo River above Vicksburg by sending expeditions to open passages through the rivers and bayous of the Mississippi Delta. The landscape architect Frederick Law Olmsted, a founder of the U.S. Sanitary Commission who served as its general secretary, visited Grant's army in late March.

Sanitary Store Boat, "Dunleith",
on the Mississippi, above Memphis;
April 1st 1863.

Dear Father,

We are returning from a visit to the army before Vicksburg, which we reached on the 22d. General Grant's command consists of four army corps: one under Gen'l Hurlbert is in Tennessee; there being detachments at Columbus; Isd No 10; New Madrid, Jackson, Helena, and considerable bodies at Corinth and Memphis. A second corps is amphibious between Helena and New Providence, under Gen'l McPherson; a third, having been recently drowned out of camp at Young's Point, near the canal across the neck, is now at Milliken's bend, ten miles above; Sherman's corps alone remains in direct observation of Vicksburg. It is camped on a series of plantations, from one to two miles above the canal. Head quarters is on the steamboat Magnolia, which lies, nose up, on the only ground which I saw, above water, outside the levee below Milliken's bend. There were a dozen large steamboats at the same place, two being quarters of Col. Bissell's Western Engineer Regiment; two ordnance boats, (loaded with ammunition) one medical store-boat; one hospital boat, several transports and forage boats, and one immense floating ware-house containing Commissary stores; also a score or two of flatboats loaded with coal. The space of ground out of water is about 1000 feet in length. At the other end of Sherman's encampment, there are half a dozen more Commissary boats. There are near here also three or four iron-clads and rams, and in the mouth of the Yazoo, which is just opposite Hd. Q., the flag boat of Admiral Porter, half a dozen mortar boats, another iron-clad, and some more rams and a naval hospital boat. Most of the Squadron, and considerable force from each army-corps were absent on the Sunflower and Blackwater expeditions, from which they were getting back as we left; the sternwheel transports, wonderfully knocked to pieces; their smoke-stacks all down, so that the black coal-smoke was thrown directly upon the hurricane decks, which were necessarily crowded with men, who must have been nearly suffocated by it.

The day after our arrival Gen'l Grant sent an aid on board our boat to take us near to Vicksburg as it would be safe to go. It was near enough to set our watches by the town-clock and to see negroes shovelling earth upon the breast-works. Bissell was building a case-mate battery for two 30 lbr Parrotts, concealed from the enemy by the levee, at the point nearest the town; from which it was intended to open fire upon their R.R. station and Commissary storehouse, the morning after we left. The next day we went with Medical Director Hewit, to look at the camps, riding on the levee, and across one plantation on a corduroy road. The ground inside the levee even, is elsewhere impassible, the ground being all soaked, where it is not flooded, with the "seepage-water" straining through and under the levees. The camps are near the levee; the tents being furnished with bedsteads made of saplings, lifting the men a few inches off the ground; the men of one battery, having been flooded out elsewhere, had pitched their tents on terraces cut in the slope of the levee; forming a very picturesque camp; the levee is here about 14 ft. high. A part of McPherson's men whom we visited opposite Yazoo pass were camped on a strip of the forest left above water, not more than fifty feet wide; the water so nearly over it, that the swell caused by our boat rolled into one of the tents. The water had risen an inch and a half during the night, and you would say it was about the most dismal place and the most dismal prospect upon which an army could be put. So here of Sherman's corps: the ground all asoak and water backing up on them in every direction except where the levee restrained it. The levee itself was lined with graves; there being no other place where the dead could be buried, on account of the water, which at once fills every cavity. These graves, which must be seen by everyone, there being no other road to travel near the camps, have helped, I suppose, to give the impression that Grant's army was in a terribly diseased state. I suppose country people would get the impression that a fearful epidemic was prevailing if they should see the burials daily occurring in any town of 40,000 inhabitants, or if they should see all the graves made within a month placed in two lines, head to foot, as they are for this army, on the levee.

In fact the health of the army, tho' not quite as good as that of the army in general, is amazingly good. You can not conceive how well and happy the men in general looked. They are mostly now well broken in, and know how to take care of themselves. Considering that they were living athletically and robustly, with plentiful air; I don't know anything that they wanted. I have enough of the Bedouin nature in my composition to envy them. I never saw men looking healthier or happier. The food is abundant, varied and most excellent in quality. I don't believe that one in fifty ever lived as well before. They were well-clothed and well-shod. If I were young and sound, I would like nothing so well as to be one of them.

We dined at Sherman's Head Quarters, which are in a planter's house in a little grove of willow oaks and Pride of China, just greened out, but dinner was served in a tent. Here I met Captain Janney, Sherman's staff-engineer, with whom I rode a couple of hours in the afternoon and whose talk I enjoyed greatly. He has had a half artist education in Paris and was warm on parks, pictures, architects, engineers and artists.

Reminiscences of Cranch and Fontainbleau; of student-life at the Politechnique and Centrale, discussions of the decoration of the Louvre, had a peculiar zest in the midst of raw upper Louisiana plantation, where nature's usual work is but half-done; looking across the River into tree-tops hung with the weird Spanish-moss, vultures floating above; shouts and turmoil of a gang of contrabands tearing down the gin-house of the plantation—Captain Janney wants the material for bridges—the drums beating and bugles sounding for evening parade behind and the distant boom of Farragut's big guns on the Hartford, pitching shells at intervals into my quondam host's, Dick Taylor's, rebel batteries at Warrenton. Another excellent fellow here was Sherman's Medical Director, McMillan, whom I have known before; indeed have met often since the war began. He was Stoneman's Medical Director on the Peninsula. He was grossly abused by the Herald's correspondent, for "entire neglect to make any provision for the wounded" at the battle of Chickasaw bluffs, whereas his arrangements were really the most complete that have ever been formed before a battle, with perhaps a single exception, and he is one of the most humane, industrious, enlightened and efficient surgeons in the Army. It is oftener than otherwise that the really good surgeons are maligned and held up to public execration, and the surgeons who always fail in an emergency pass for the best.

McMillan & Janney rode with us to call on Gen'l Steele, living in a large room of a planter's house, which had been half finished years ago, and since inhabited in its unfinished state. There were school-classics left behind on the mantel-piece. From Gen'l Steele's we rode to Gen'l Blair's also quartered in a planter's house. (The boat shakes so, it is scarcely possible to write legibly—but a pencil can be better managed).

Janney, by the way, who has charge of the Young's Point Canal and employs several hundred contrabands, and who also employed a large number while Sherman's corps was at Memphis, speaks well of the negroes as industrious, disciplinable, grateful and docile. They have less vigor and endurance than whites, can not do as much hard work and seem generally to be of weak constitution. A remarkable proportion of them are deformed or mutilated, apparently from injuries in childhood.

Nearly all bear the marks of injuries which they are unable to explain. You know that I have contended that the negro race in slavery was constantly growing in the mass less and less qualified for self dependence; the instinct of self-preservation being more and more worked out, and the habit of letting "master take care of his nigger" bred in to the race. Janney believes that slave children while more precocious than white, suffer more from accidents than the children of the poor with us. The most valuable negroes, who are also, as a rule, the cleverest, have generally been taken away from the plantations by their owners, the least enterprising and those who would be most bewildered in trying to look out for themselves, and who are worth least for army purposes, being left as they are always told to "look after things" on the plantations. Wonderfully little it is they have to look after, however. A good many who are taken away, however, contrive to escape and return to the plantation or to their relatives and friends who follow the Union army. They often show strong attachments in this way, not to their owners but to localities and to their families. Among the company which was working under him at Memphis, Captain Janney said that there was one very active, sharp, industrious and faithful fellow, who had left a plantation about twenty miles off. Soon after his good qualities had attracted Janney's attention, his owner—a rank rebel, came as they often do, with complete assurance, to ask that he should be given up to him. Janney assured him that the country needed his services and it could not be thought of at present. Some weeks after this the same negro came one morning to Janney's tent and said: "Here's a right good fowling-piece, Captain, and I want to gib it to you."

"Where did you get it?"

"Got him ob my old massa, Sah."

"How is that? What did he give you his fowling piece for?"

"Did'n gib'm me, Sah; I took 'em."

"When?"

"Last night."

"Has your master been here again?"

"No Sah, I been down dar, to de old place, myself lass night, and I see de gun, dah, and I tort he was a rebel and he ortn't to be let hab a gun, and I ort to take 'em away, tort dat wus right, Captain, wusn't it? He ain't no business wid a gun, has he? Only to shoot our teamsters wid it."

"What sent you out there?"

"Well, I went dah, Sah, for to get my wife and chile dat was dah. I tried to get 'em nodder way but I was cheated, and I had to go myself."

"What other way did you try?"

"I'll tell ou, Sah; I want my wife and chile: dey was down dah on de ole plantation. Last Sunday when we'd got our pay, I seen a white man dat libs ober dah, and he tell me if I gib him my money he get my wife for me. I had thirty dollars Sah, and I gib it to him, but my wife did'n come. So I went myself. My wife, house servant, Sah, and I creep up to de house and look into de windah: de windah was open and I heah de ole man and de ole woman dere snorin in de corner, and I put my head in and dah I see de gun standing by de fi' place. I jumped right in and cotch up de gun, and turn roun' and hold em so. Says I, 'Master, I want my wife.' 'You can take her,' says he, and he didn say another word, nor move a bit, nor Missis eider. My wife she heerd me, and she come down wid de chile and we just walk out ob de door; but I tort, I'd take de gun. He ain't no Union man and he ortn't to hab a gun, Captain. You'll take it, Sah, won't you?"

"Yes, I'll turn it in for you."

Returning to the Magnolia, we took tea with Gen'l Grant. He told me of the return of Admiral Porter and the failure of the "Sunflower" expedition. He said there seemed to be no way open to attack Vicksburg but by direct assault in front and an attempt to take it in this way would involve a frightful loss of life. He was obviously full of grave thought and concern and I avoided keeping his attention at all. He lives in the ladies' cabin of the boat, there is a sentry, or an apology for one, at the boat's gangway, but he stops no one from going on board, and there is free range in the cabin for anyone to and beyond the table, which the General, with others, writes upon, near the stern. He is more approachable and liable to interruptions than a merchant or lawyer generally allows himself to be in his office, and in my observation, citizens who had been allowed to come to the army to remove bodies of the dead for their friends; or on other pretexts, several times came in and introduced themselves to him; one man saying, "I hain't got no business with you, General, but I just wanted to have a little talk with you because folks will ask me if I did." The General had just received a number of Vicksburg papers by a deserter, which he invited me to look over. He was reading these and writing during most of the evening, while I was conversing with the gentlemen of the staff; when I rose to go, he got up and said: "I wish you would be in as much as convenient while you stay, I am not always as much occupied, as I am tonight, and whenever you see that I am not, understand that I shall be glad to talk with you." The next night I went in and had an hour's conversation with him. He is one of the most engaging men I ever saw. Small, quiet, gentle, modest—extremely, even uncomfortably, modest—frank, confiding and of an exceedingly kind disposition. He gives you the impression of a man of strong will, however, and of capacity, underlying these feminine traits. As a general, I should think his quality was that of quick common-sense judgments, unobstructed by prejudices, and deep abiding quiet resolution. He confided to me in a comic, plaintive, half humorous, half indignant way, the annoyances, obstructions, embarrassments and hindrances to which the Governors of the various Western states constantly subjected him, and keenly reviewed their various methods. The Governors of Iowa and Wisconsin were moderate in their inflictions and seemed to have some appreciation of his situation. He must do them the credit to say that they were forbearing and thoroughly patriotic. The Governor of Illinois was an amiable and weak man. He seemed to think it his business to help any citizen of Illinois to anything he wanted. "He must be in the habit of signing papers without reading them, and the quantities of letters he writes me urging me to grant favors to people who come here with them, is appalling. Favors too, which he ought to know that I have no right to grant—no more than you would have. It's very hard on me, especially when he sends women here, to get favors for their sons. It's a pastime to face a battery compared with facing a woman begging for her son, you know. These letters from the Governor of Illinois being all open letters, are written in the most earnest tone of personal and official anxiety. "He could not be more in earnest if he were pleading for his own son. And yet there are so many of them, they can't mean anything. I've been expecting a letter from him to tell me that he did not want me to pay any attention to them. It's different with the Governor of Indiana. He is perfectly cold-hearted. He seems to think, because I have some Indiana regiments, that he has a right to demand my assistance in any way he chooses, to carry out his state political arrangments. By the way, doctor, there's a lady from _____ on the _____ which arrived this afternoon, who has a great many favors to ask. I've seen her; I can't see her again. You must answer her. It's easier for you to say no to a woman than 'tis for me. Some things she wants, can be granted; some can't; you'll see how it is, when you talk with her. But don't leave it necessary for me to see her again."

I had some suggestions to make to the General; he heard me patiently, met me quickly, almost eagerly, adopted and advanced upon my views, allowed me to prepare a draft for an order in accordance with them, which next day he adopted adding one clinching sentence, and handed over to his adjutant General, who at once gave it the form of an order, signed, copied, printed and issued it. The openness of mind, directness, simplicity and rapidity of reasoning and clearness, with consequent confidence, of conclusion, of Genl Grant is very delightful. Those about him become deeply attached to him. Towards Sherman there is more than attachment, something of veneration, universally expressed, most by those who know him most intimately, from which I suspect that he has more genius than Grant.

We spent one day chiefly among the iron-clads and gun-boats. Admiral Porter is a gentlemanly, straight forward and resolute sort of man. Breese his flag-captain a smiling, cheerful and most obliging and agreeable man. He assumes friendship from the start, but, with all this, one gets an impression of strong will & great certainty that when the time comes for boarding or cutting out, he will bear his part with the same ingenuous ease and grace. Some of the new men of the navy whom we saw did not strike us so favorably. Scurvy was threatening the squadron and we put on 200 barrels of potatoes and onions on the flag-boat.

April 3d Cairo.

We have just arrived here, all quite well.
Expect to go to St. Louis this evening.
Your affectionate Son,

Fred. Law Olmsted.

John Olmsted, Esqr
Hartford, Ct

(Please send this to Washington.)

Frederick Douglass: Why Should a Colored Man Enlist?

April 1863

Frederick Douglass joined William Wells Brown, Martin Delany, Henry Highland Garnet, and other black abolitionists in recruiting men for the 54th Massachusetts Infantry. After his sons Charles and Lewis enlisted in the regiment, Douglass canvassed western and up-state New York, then spoke at public meetings in New York City and Philadelphia. By the middle of April he had sent more than one hundred recruits to the regiment's training camp at Readville, Massachusetts. This article appeared in his newspaper, *Douglass' Monthly*.

WHY SHOULD A COLORED MAN ENLIST?

THIS QUESTION has been repeatedly put to us while raising men for the 54th Massachusetts regiment during the past five weeks, and perhaps we cannot at present do a better service to the cause of our people or to the cause of the country than by giving a few of the many reasons why a colored man should enlist.

First. You are a man, although a colored man. If you were only a horse or an ox, incapable of deciding whether the rebels are right or wrong, you would have no responsibility, and might like the horse or the ox go on eating your corn or grass, in total indifference, as to which side is victorious or vanquished in this conflict. You are however no horse, and no ox, but a man, and whatever concerns man should interest you. He who looks upon a conflict between right and wrong, and does not help the right against the wrong, despises and insults his own nature, and invites the contempt of mankind. As between the North and South, the North is clearly in the right and the South is flagrantly in the wrong. You should therefore, simply as a matter of right and wrong, give your utmost aid to the North. In presence of such a contest there is no neutrality for any man. You are either for the Government or against the Government. Manhood requires you to take sides, and you are mean or noble according to how you choose between action and inaction.—If you are sound in body and mind, there is nothing in your *color* to excuse you from enlisting in the service of the republic against its enemies. If *color* should not be a criterion of rights, neither should it be a standard of duty. The whole duty of a man, belongs alike to white and black.

"A man's a man for a' that."

Second. You are however, not only a man, but an American citizen, so declared by the highest legal adviser of the Government, and you have hitherto expressed in various ways, not only your willingness but your earnest desire to fulfil any and every obligation which the relation of citizenship imposes. Indeed, you have hitherto felt wronged and slighted, because while white men of all other nations have been freely enrolled to serve the country, you a native born citizen have been coldly denied the honor of aiding in defense of the land of your birth. The injustice thus done you is now repented of by the Government and you are welcomed to a place in the army of the nation. Should you refuse to enlist *now*, you will justify the past contempt of the Government towards you and lead it to regret having honored you with a call to take up arms in its defense. You cannot but see that here is a good reason why you should promptly enlist.

Third. A third reason why a colored man should enlist is found in the fact that every Negro-hater and slavery-lover in the land regards the arming of Negroes as a calamity and is doing his best to prevent it. Even now all the weapons of malice, in the shape of slander and ridicule, are used to defeat the filling up of the 54th Massachusetts (colored) regiment. In nine cases out of ten, you will find it safe to do just what your enemy would gladly have you leave undone. What helps you hurts him. Find out what he does not want and give him a plenty of it.

Fourth. You should enlist to learn the use of arms, to become familiar with the means of securing, protecting and defending your own liberty. A day may come when men shall

learn war no more, when justice shall be so clearly apprehended, so universally practiced, and humanity shall be so
profoundly loved and respected, that war and bloodshed shall
be confined only to beasts of prey. Manifestly however, that
time has not yet come, and while all men should labor to hasten its coming, by the cultivation of all the elements conducive
to peace, it is plain that for the present no race of men can
depend wholly upon moral means for the maintenance of their
rights. Men must either be governed by love or by fear. They
must love to do right or fear to do wrong. The only way open
to any race to make their rights respected is to learn how to
defend them. When it is seen that black men no more than
white men can be enslaved with impunity, men will be less inclined to enslave and oppress them. Enlist therefore, that you
may learn the art and assert the ability to defend yourself and
your race.

Fifth. You are a member of a long enslaved and despised
race. Men have set down your submission to Slavery and insult,
to a lack of manly courage. They point to this fact as demonstrating your fitness only to be a servile class. You should enlist
and disprove the slander, and wipe out the reproach. When
you shall be seen nobly defending the liberties of your own
country against rebels and traitors—brass itself will blush to
use such arguments imputing cowardice against you.

Sixth. Whether you are or are not, entitled to all the rights
of citizenship in this country has long been a matter of dispute
to your prejudice. By enlisting in the service of your country at
this trial hour, and upholding the National Flag, you stop the
mouths of traducers and win applause even from the iron lips
of ingratitude. Enlist and you make this your country in common with all other men born in the country or out of it.

Seventh. Enlist for your own sake. Decried and derided as
you have been and still are, you need an act of this kind by
which to recover your own self-respect. You have to some extent rated your value by the estimate of your enemies and
hence have counted yourself less than you are. You owe it to
yourself and your race to rise from your social debasement and
take your place among the soldiers of your country, a man
among men. Depend upon it, the subjective effect of this one
act of enlisting will be immense and highly beneficial. You will

stand more erect, walk more assured, feel more at ease, and be less liable to insult than you ever were before. He who fights the battles of America may claim America as his country—and have that claim respected. Thus in defending your country now against rebels and traitors you are defending your own liberty, honor, manhood and self-respect.

Eighth. You should enlist because your doing so will be one of the most certain means of preventing the country from drifting back into the whirlpool of Pro-Slavery Compromise at the end of the war, which is now our greatest danger. He who shall witness another Compromise with Slavery in this country will see the free colored man of the North more than ever a victim of the pride, lust, scorn and violence of all classes of white men. The whole North will be but another Detroit, where every white fiend may with impunity revel in unrestrained beastliness towards people of color; they may burn their houses, insult their wives and daughters, and kill indiscriminately. If you mean to live in this country now is the time for you to do your full share in making it a country where you and your children after you can live in comparative safety. Prevent a compromise with the traitors, compel them to come back to the Union whipped and humbled into obedience and all will be well. But let them come back as masters and all their hate and hellish ingenuity will be exerted to stir up the ignorant masses of the North to hate, hinder and persecute the free colored people of the North. That most inhuman of all modern enactments, with its bribed judges, and summary process, the Fugitive Slave Law, with all its infernal train of canting divines, preaching the gospel of kidnapping, as twelve years ago, will be revived against the free colored people of the North. One or two black brigades will do much to prevent all this.

Ninth. You should enlist because the war for the Union, whether men so call it or not, is a war for Emancipation. The salvation of the country, by the inexorable relation of cause and effect, can be secured only by the complete abolition of Slavery. The President has already proclaimed emancipation to the Slaves in the rebel States which is tantamount to declaring Emancipation in all the States, for Slavery must exist everywhere in the South in order to exist anywhere in the South.

Can you ask for a more inviting, ennobling and soul enlarging work, than that of making one of the glorious Band who shall carry Liberty to your enslaved people? Remember that identified with the Slave in color, you will have a power that white soldiers have not, to attract them to your lines and induce them to take up arms in a common cause. One black Brigade will, for this work, be worth more than two white ones. Enlist, therefore, enlist without delay, enlist now, and forever put an end to the human barter and butchery which have stained the whole South with the warm blood of your people, and loaded its air with their groans. Enlist, and deserve not only well of your country, and win for yourselves, a name and a place among men, but secure to yourself what is infinitely more precious, the fast dropping tears of gratitude of your kith and kin marked out for destruction, and who are but now ready to perish.

When time's ample curtain shall fall upon our national tragedy, and our hillsides and valleys shall neither redden with the blood nor whiten with the bones of kinsmen and countrymen who have fallen in the sanguinary and wicked strife; when grim visaged war has smoothed his wrinkled front and our country shall have regained its normal condition as a leader of nations in the occupation and blessings of peace—and history shall record the names of heroes and martyrs—who bravely answered the call of patriotism and Liberty—against traitors, thieves and assassins—let it not be said that in the long list of glory, composed of men of all nations—there appears the name of no colored man.

Jefferson Davis to William M. Brooks

The Confederate president wrote to William M. Brooks, an Alabama lawyer who had presided over his state's secession convention, defending his choice of John C. Pemberton to lead the army defending Vicksburg. A West Point graduate from Philadelphia married to a Virginian, Pemberton had commanded the Atlantic coast defenses of South Carolina, Georgia, and Florida before being sent to Mississippi in October 1862.

———————————

Richmond, April 2 1863

My dear Sir.

Your letter of the 20th ulto, reached me in due course; and has received careful attention. Your friendly assurance of the extent to which I am honored by the confidence and esteem of my fellow-citizens is a source of sincere gratification, the more acceptable coming from one so well qualified to judge as yourself.

I was not prepared to learn the dissatisfaction which you represent as existing in regard to the assignment of Lt. Genl. Pemberton, and I hope that the distrust in his fidelity & ability to which you allude is not as great as you have been led to believe.

I selected Genl. Pemberton for the very important command which he now holds from a conviction that he was the best qualified officer for that post then available, and have since found no reason to change the opinion I then entertained of him.

If success which is generally regarded in popular estimation as evidence of qualification be so regarded in his case, I am surprised that Genl. Pemberton's merits should still be doubted. With a force far inferior in numbers to the enemy, menaced by attack at several points widely distant from each other, with no naval force to meet the enemy's fleets on the Mississippi and its tributaries by his judicious disposition of his forces and skilful selection of the best points of defense he has repulsed the enemy at Vicksburg, Port Hudson, on the Tallahatchie and at Deer Creek, and has thus far foiled his every attempt to get possession of the Mississippi river and the vast section of country which it controls.

I think that he has also demonstrated great administrative as well as military ability. He has been enabled to subsist and clothe his army without going out of his own Dept., and though within a recent period some difficulty may have arisen in the transportation of supplies, or some scarcity may have been apprehended which circumstance is, I regret to say, not confined to his command, I think he is not the less commendable for his former success in this regard & that he is entitled to confidence in his ability to overcome the difficulty and procure the requisite provisions for his troops, if indeed such may be practicable.

I still hope that "the suspicions and distrust" which you mention do not exist to any considerable extent; but however this may be, I feel assured that they are "groundless".

With reference to the fact that General Pemberton was born at the North being alleged as a justification of distrust in his fidelity to our cause, I can imagine nothing more unjust and ungenerous.

General Pemberton resigned his commission in the U.S. army on the secession of Virginia—his adopted State.—He came at once to Richmond and was one of the first officers of the U.S. army who offered his services to Governor Letcher, by whom he was immediately appointed to a field commission. He afterwards entered the service of the Confederate States in which he has risen from step to step to his present position. In addition to the other proofs which he has afforded of his devotion to the cause of the Confederate States, I may add that by coming South he forfeited a considerable fortune.

Your suggestions as to Col. I. W. Garrett shall receive due attention. I recollect him very favorably and have no doubt that your estimate of him is just. With assurances of regard and esteem I remain very respl. & truly yours

JEFFN. DAVIS.

John B. Jones: Diary, April 2–4, 1863

Food riots broke out in the spring of 1863 in Atlanta, Georgia; Salisbury, North Carolina; Mobile, Alabama; Petersburg, Virginia; and other southern cities as groups of women, many of them soldiers' wives, invaded and looted shops they believed were charging unfair prices. The largest disturbance occurred in Richmond on April 2. John B. Jones, a clerk in the Confederate war department who witnessed the riot, had recorded in his diary three days earlier the rising cost of cornmeal and potatoes while observing that meat had almost disappeared and "none but the opulent can afford to pay $3.50 per pound for butter."

———————————

APRIL 2D.—This morning early a few hundred women and boys met as by concert in the Capitol Square, saying they were hungry, and must have food. The number continued to swell until there were more than a thousand. But few men were among them, and these were mostly foreign residents, with exemptions in their pockets. About nine A.M. the mob emerged from the western gates of the square, and proceeded down Ninth Street, passing the War Department, and crossing Main Street, increasing in magnitude at every step, but preserving silence and (so far) good order. Not knowing the meaning of such a procession, I asked a pale boy where they were going. A young woman, seemingly emaciated, but yet with a smile, answered that they were going to find something to eat. I could not, for the life of me, refrain from expressing the hope that they might be successful; and I remarked they were going in the right direction to find plenty in the hands of the extortioners. I did not follow, to see what they did; but I learned an hour after that they marched through Cary Street, and entered diverse stores of the speculators, which they proceeded to empty of their contents. They impressed all the carts and drays in the street, which were speedily laden with meal, flour, shoes, etc. I did not learn whither these were driven; but probably they were rescued from those in charge of them. Nevertheless, an immense amount of provisions, and other articles, were borne by the mob, which continued to increase in numbers. An eye-witness says he saw a boy come out of a store with a hat full of money (notes); and I learned that when the mob turned up into Main Street, when all the shops were by this time closed, they broke in the plate-glass windows, demanding silks, jewelry, etc. Here they were incited to pillage valuables, not necessary for subsistence, by the class of residents (aliens) exempted from military duty by Judge Campbell, Assistant Secretary of War, in contravention of Judge Meredith's decision. Thus the work of spoliation went on, until the military appeared upon the scene, summoned by Gov. Letcher, whose term of service is near its close. He had the Riot Act read (by the mayor), and then threatened to fire on the mob. He gave them five minutes' time to disperse in, threatening to use military force (the city battalion being present) if they did not comply with the demand. The timid women fell back, and a pause was put to the devastation, though but few believed he would venture to put his threat in execution. If he had done so, he would have been hung, no doubt.

About this time the President appeared, and ascending a dray, spoke to the people. He urged them to return to their homes, so that the bayonets there menacing them might be sent against the common enemy. He told them that such acts would bring *famine* upon them in the only form which could not be provided against, as it would deter people from bringing food to the city. He said he was willing to share his last loaf with the suffering people (his best horse had been stolen the night before), and he trusted we would all bear our privations with fortitude, and continue united against the Northern invaders, who were the authors of all our sufferings. He seemed deeply moved; and indeed it was a frightful spectacle, and perhaps an ominous one, if the government does not remove some of the quartermasters who have contributed very much to bring about the evil of scarcity. I mean those who have allowed transportation to forestallers and extortioners.

Gen. Elzey and Gen. Winder waited upon the Secretary of War in the morning, asking permission to call the troops from the camps near the city, to suppress the women and children by a summary process. But Mr. Seddon hesitated, and then declined authorizing any such absurdity. He said it was a municipal or State duty, and therefore he would not take the responsibility of interfering in the matter. Even in the moment of aspen consternation, he was still the politician.

I have not heard of any injuries sustained by the women and children. Nor have I heard how many stores the mob visited; and it must have been many.

All is quiet now (three P.M.); and I understand the government is issuing rice to the people.

APRIL 3D.—Gen. D. H. Hill writes from North Carolina that the business of conscription is miserably mismanaged in that State. The whole business, it seems, has resolved itself into a machine for making money and putting pets in office.

No account of yesterday's riot appeared in the papers to-day, for obvious reasons. The mob visited most of the shops, and the pillage was pretty extensive.

Crowds of women, Marylanders and foreigners, were standing at the street corners to-day, still demanding food; which, it is said, the government issued to them. About midday the City Battalion was marched down Main Street to disperse the crowd.

Congress has resolved to adjourn on the 20th April. The tax bill has not passed both Houses yet.

Gen. Blanchard has been relieved of his command in Louisiana. He was another general from Massachusetts.

APRIL 4TH.—It is the belief of some that the riot was a premeditated affair, stimulated from the North, and executed through the instrumentality of emissaries. Some of the women, and others, have been arrested.

We have news of the capture of another of the enemy's gunboats, in Berwick Bay, Louisiana, with five guns. It is said to have been done by *cavalry*.

A dispatch just received from Charleston states that the enemy's monitors were approaching the forts, seven in number, and that the attack was commencing. This is *joyful* news to our people, so confident are they that Gen. Beauregard will beat them.

Whitelaw Reid to the Cincinnati Gazette

Writing under the pen name "Agate," Reid was the Washington correspondent for the *Cincinnati Gazette*, a Republican newspaper aligned with the party's Radical faction. Amid reports of widespread food shortages in the South, Reid considered the prospects for an early victory over the Confederacy.

1863, April 4

Now, with opening buds and stiffening roads, we are ready again, and such another spring and summer's work will bear our banners to the Gulf.

But, like the victim of lunatic periods, we begin to return to the old delusion. In bulletins from the army headquarters, speculations of the army correspondents, reasonings of the editors, speeches of Generals, declarations at Union meetings we have the old madness revived: "The rebels are nearly exhausted. Millionaires are having dealt out to them the rations of the private soldier. Four months yet must pass before they can have a new crop—before that time they must succumb."

Let us be warned in time by the experiences of eighteen months ago. The starvation theory proved folly then; it can be no less foolish now. The rebels have improved the intervening time by developing their agricultural resources. If, taken at every disadvantage, with fields sown in cotton instead of corn, and without accumulated supplies, they were able to go through the first year, each succeeding one must grow easier and easier. It is not impossible that the lack of labor has produced some inconvenience on Southern plantations and has somewhat decreased their production. Lax discipline among the slaves, consequent on the absence of their masters in the army, has doubtless tended to the same result. But on the other hand, a much greater breadth of cereals must have been sown, and much more general attention paid to the growing of live stock.

It cannot, therefore, but be as fatal a delusion now as it was in 1861, to base hopes upon the miseries produced by the blockade instead of the bayonet; or to depend upon subduing the rebels by starving them in their homes instead of routing them on the battlefield. There can be no more dangerous symptom than the recurring expressions of belief that if we "can now only hold our own a few months longer," the rebellion must fall of its own weight. A People that has accomplished what the South has in the last two years, is not to be starved out—is not likely to succumb merely from being severely let alone—*is not to be subdued, in short, save by equal pluck and superior endurance on the battlefield.* Fighting, not starving, is to win the battle and end the war, if the victory and the end are to come at all.

Charles S. Wainwright:
Diary, April 5–12, 1863

After taking command of the Army of the Potomac on January 26, Joseph Hooker reorganized its command structure and raised its morale by improving camp conditions, providing better food, and granting furloughs. President Lincoln traveled to Virginia in early April to inspect the reinvigorated army and to discuss plans for the spring campaign with Hooker. Among the troops who passed in review was the artillery of the First Corps, commanded by Colonel Charles S. Wainwright. A former officer of the New York militia, Wainwright had served in Hooker's division in the early battles of the Peninsula campaign.

———————

CAMP THREE MILES FROM BELLE PLAINE, APRIL 5, SUNDAY. We are still undisturbed in our winter quarters and several reasons are plain for our remaining so for at least a week to come. First the weather which is very uncertain and stormy; all day yesterday and extending through last night, we had one of the most severe storms of the season, wind, rain and snow. It was much like the one we had last year during the time I was loading my batteries at Liverpool Point, except that one was longer and more severe. Then General Hooker has just commenced to review the different corps of the army, and cannot well get through under a week: while the War Department has ordered a general muster of all the troops on the 10th, for the use of the provost-marshal in making drafts to fill up the regiments, and so forth. . . .

This corps was reviewed by General Hooker on Thursday. The troops are so scattered, and the ground hereabouts so broken that we could not get the whole corps out together, so it was reviewed by divisions. The Third Division was formed about half a mile from our headquarters here. Doubleday made bad work of it, for the ground was very much cramped

even for his little command of only some 3,000 men. . . .
The next day, Friday, I went over to see the Sixth Corps reviewed. The whole of it was out together, though the ground
it formed on was very rough. It is a larger corps than ours, and
certainly made a much better appearance, but I hear that General Hunt says my batteries looked decidedly the best. There is
no doubt that the Fifth and Sixth Corps under Porter and
Franklin were much better instructed and disciplined than any
of the others. Another cause for its superiority over this corps
lies in the great proportion of Pennsylvania regiments that we
have; which as a rule are, without doubt, worse officered than
any others in this army. Major DePeyster is now on duty with
Howe's division of the Sixth Corps; and made himself very ridiculous at the review by his strutting manner, which called
attention to him, while he not only did not mount his cannoneers, but also commanded "present sabres" when he passed
in review. Every officer of my acquaintance whom I met after
the review congratulated me on my major. The Twentieth
New York met General Hooker about half a mile from the review grounds and marched up with us as a sort of escort; for
the purpose of shewing the excellence of their drill. It is said
(and I believe truly) to be the best drilled regiment in the
army; their marching, and changes from company front to the
flank, and their wheeling into line on Friday were certainly
wonderful. It is a German regiment, raised in New York City,
and commanded by Colonel Von Vegesack (I don't know how
to spell the name) an officer of standing in the Swedish service,
and a very nice fellow in every way.

I hear that the President is expected down today. In case he
comes, we may very likely have all our reviewing to go over
again on a grander scale. Hooker has considerable liking for
that sort of thing when he can make it pay; and is said to have
boasted a good deal while at Washington; declaring that he
"had the finest army on this planet" and that "he could march
it straight to New Orleans." Whether or no he will prove capable of taking it as far as Richmond remains to be seen, to say
nothing of going to New Orleans. By the bye, Farragut's success on the Mississippi does not turn out to be quite so great as
at first reported. The news looks anything but very brilliant

from both west and south. Consequently, the expected capture of Charleston, Port Hudson, and Vicksburg is again postponed; and gold is once more on the rise.

APRIL 8, WEDNESDAY.   President Lincoln came down on Saturday afternoon instead of on Sunday, and arrived at headquarters quite unexpectedly. It is said that their arrival created quite a commotion on Hooker's back stairs, hustling off some of his female acquaintances in a most undignified way. Mrs. Lincoln and one of his sons came down with the President. The object of his visit seems to be to review the army, which according to present appearances will keep him here all this week. The Cavalry Corps under General Stoneman was reviewed first, on Monday. It was probably the largest body of cavalry ever seen together on this continent, there being 11,000 out, it is said. Some of the regiments looked quite well, but many were little better than ridiculous. The country here is not calculated to make fine cavalry. Our men are far too slouchy, the "setting up" and bearing of the real soldier showing much more on horseback than on foot; and the plain, simple uniform now worn in our army prevents any attempt at style, especially on such wretched horses as we have here. The horse batteries were much more creditable, and looked really finely. They are all regular batteries, except one, and in most cases are commanded by old light artillery officers. The one volunteer battery is the Sixth New York which was with me on the Peninsula. Bramhall has resigned, and Martin is now the captain. Even in the midst of the old regular batteries they keep up their reputation, in camp as well as in the field. I have been to see them several times on my way to Army Headquarters, the shortest road leading almost through their camp, and always meet with the warmest welcome.

Today the Second, Third, Fifth, and Sixth Corps were reviewed together, and made really a splendid show. There must have been 50,000 men out; the ground was fair, and the arrangements capital. It would be hard to say which of the four corps made the best appearance: the Third has, if any, turned out in a little the best style, and Sickles deserves credit for getting so good a line formed; and for the manner in which the

whole corps saluted at one time by bugle command. I rode
around with General Hooker and the reviewing party, as did
several ladies, of whom there were a large number present. . . .

APRIL 12, SUNDAY.   The reviewing is over, the President gone
back to Washington, and all once more quietly waiting for orders to move which will probably be the next excitement. On
Thursday the whole of this corps was marched down to the
plain on which the First Division was drawn up last week, and
was there reviewed by the President. The day was fine, the
view of the Potomac beautiful, the ground most capital. Reynolds and everybody worked hard, so the troops looked and
marched well; and our efforts were repaid by the generally expressed opinion that it went off altogether better than any of
the other reviews. There was one new feature in it, at any rate.
The whole of the artillery was massed, and passed in review as
one body, so that I appeared in my proper place, as an actual
commander. It was General Reynolds's own proposition, without any request on my part; whether it arose from his really
approving the brigade organization, or was only done for
convenience and effect, I do not know. The ten batteries made
quite a display, marching battery front, and looked well, although some being six and others four-gun batteries rather
broke the column. Hunt was much pleased with it. After the
review, the President, most of the general officers present, and
their ladies had a lunch at our headquarters, which Sanderson got up, and capped the satisfaction already felt with our
review. . . .

We do not yet get any direct accounts of the attempt on
Charleston: the reports through rebel sources are that Dupont's fleet was repulsed and the monitor *Keokuk* sunk. I fear
it may be true, as Charleston is almost as precious to them as
Richmond, and every effort will be made to save it; while on
our side we have anything but a desirable commander of the
land forces in old Hunter.

Everybody is reading the first report of the Congressional
Committee on the Conduct of the War. It is quite voluminous,
and comes down to the close of last year. I am trying to get
through it, but its unfairness, partiality, and in very many cases
absolute falseness make me so nervous that I can make but

little progress. The radical party, who have complete control over the Cabinet and do pretty much what they please with our weak President, seem to be determined to stick at nothing in order to punish every official who does not go all lengths with them. A small instance of this has just come out in a War Department order dismissing a volunteer lieutenant for what they call treasonable sentiments expressed in a private letter to his uncle in China!

Francis Lieber: No Party Now, But All for Our Country

April 11, 1863

A professor of history and political science at Columbia College, Francis Lieber drafted General Orders No. 100, an influential code of the laws of war issued by the Union army on April 24, 1863. Lieber gave this address at a mass meeting held in New York City to mark the anniversary of the attack on Fort Sumter. It was circulated as a pamphlet by the Loyal Publication Society, which Lieber helped organize in February 1863. Before receiving his appointment at Columbia, Lieber had taught at South Carolina College for twenty years. His eldest son had joined the Confederate army and been mortally wounded in 1862, while his other two sons served as Union officers and would survive the war.

———————

ADDRESS
READ AT THE INAUGURAL MEETING OF THE LOYAL NATIONAL LEAGUE, BY THE REQUEST OF THE LEAGUE, IN UNION SQUARE, NEW YORK, ON THE 11TH OF APRIL, 1863.

IT is just and wise that men engaged in a great and arduous cause should profess anew, from time to time, their faith, and pledge themselves to one another, to stand by their cause to the last extremity, even at the sacrifice of all they have and all that God has given them—their wealth, their blood, and their children's blood. We solemnly pledge all this to our cause, for it is the cause of our Country and her noble history, of freedom, and justice, and truth—it is the cause of all we hold dearest on this earth: we profess and pledge this—plainly, broadly, openly in the cheering time of success, and most fervently in the day of trial and reverses.

We recollect how, two years ago, when reckless arrogance attacked Fort Sumter, the response to that boom of treason-

able cannon was read, in our city, in the flag of our country—
waving from every steeple and school-house, from City Hall
and Court House, from every shop window and market stall,
and fluttering in the hand of every child, and on the head-gear
of every horse in the busy street. Two years have passed; un-
counted sacrifices have been made—sacrifices of wealth, of
blood, and limb, and life—of friendship and brotherhood, of
endeared and hallowed pursuits and sacred ties—and still the
civil war is raging in bitterness and heart-burning—still we
make the same profession, and still we pledge ourselves firmly
to hold on to our cause, and persevere in the struggle into
which unrighteous men, bewildered by pride, and stimulated
by bitter hatred, have plunged us.

We profess ourselves to be loyal citizens of these United
States; and by loyalty we mean a candid and loving devotion to
the object to which a loyal man—a loyal husband, a loyal
friend, a loyal citizen—devotes himself. We eschew the attenu-
ated arguments derived by trifling scholars from meagre etymol-
ogy. We take the core and substance of this weighty word, and
pledge ourselves that we will loyally—not merely outwardly
and formally, according to the letter, but frankly, fervently and
according to the spirit—adhere to our country, to her institutions, to freedom, and her power, and to that great institution
called the government of our country, founded by our fathers,
and loved by their sons, and by all right-minded men who have
become citizens of this land by choice and not by birth—who
have wedded this country in the maturity of their age as verily
their own. We pledge ourselves as National men devoted to
the Nationality of this great people. No government can
wholly dispense with loyalty, except the fiercest despotism ruling by naked intimidation; but a republic stands in greater
need of it than any other government, and most of all a republic beset by open rebellion and insidious treason. Loyalty is
pre-eminently a civic virtue in a free country. It is patriotism
cast in the graceful mould of candid devotion to the harmless
government of an unshackled nation.

In pledging ourselves thus, we know of no party. Parties are
unavoidable in free countries, and may be useful if they acknowledge the country far above themselves, and remain
within the sanctity of the fundamental law which protects the

enjoyment of liberty prepared for all within its sacred domain. But Party has no meaning in far the greater number of the highest and the common relations of human life. When we are ailing, we do not take medicine by party prescription. We do not build ships by party measurement; we do not pray for our daily bread by party distinctions; we do not take our chosen ones to our bosoms by party demarcations, nor do we eat or drink, sleep or wake, as partisans. We do not enjoy the flowers of spring, nor do we harvest the grain, by party lines. We do not incur punishments for infractions of the commandments according to party creeds. We do not pursue truth, or cultivate science, by party dogmas; and we do not, we must not, love and defend our country and our liberty, dear to us as part and portion of our very selves, according to party rules. Woe to him who does. When a house is on fire, and a mother with her child cries for help at the window above, shall the firemen at the engine be allowed to trifle away the precious time in party bickerings, or is then the only word—"Water! pump away; up with the ladder!"

Let us not be like the Byzantines, those wretches who quarrelled about contemptible party refinements, theological though they were, while the truculent Mussulman was steadily drawing nearer—nay, some of whom would even go to the lord of the crescent, and with a craven heart would beg for a pittance of the spoil, so that they would be spared, and could vent their party spleen against their kin in blood, and fellows in religion.

We know of no party in our present troubles; the word is here an empty word. The only line which divides the people of the North, runs between the mass of loyal men who stand by their country, no matter to what place of political meeting they were used to resort, or with what accent they utter the language of the land, or what religion they profess, or what sentiments they may have uttered in the excitement of former discussions, on the one hand, and those on the other hand, who keep outside of that line—traitors to their country in the hour of need—or those who allow themselves to be misled by shallow names, and by reminiscences which cling around those names from by-gone days, finding no application in a time which asks for things more sterling than names, theories, or platforms.

If an alien enemy were to land his hosts on your shores, would you fly to your arms and ring the tocsin because your country is in danger, or would you meditatively look at your sword and gun, and spend your time in pondering whether the administration in power, which must and can alone direct the defence of your hearths, has a right to be styled by this or that party name, or whether it came into power with your assistance, and will appoint some of your party to posts of honor or comfortable emoluments? And will any one now lose his time and fair name as an honest and brave citizen, when no foreigner, indeed, threatens your country, at least not directly, but far more, when a reckless host of law-defying men, heaping upon you the vilest vituperation that men who do not leave behind them the ingenuity of civilization when they relapse into barbarism, can invent—when this host threatens to sunder your country and cleave your very history in twain, to deprive you of your rivers which God has given you, to extinguish your nationality, to break down your liberty and to make that land, which the Distributor of our sphere's geography has placed between the old and older world as the greatest link of that civilization which is destined to encircle the globe—to make that land the hot-bed of angry petty powers, sinking deeper and deeper as they quarrel and fight, and quarrelling and fighting more angrily as they sink deeper? It is the very thing your foreign enemies desire, and have long desired. When nullification threatened to bring about secession—and the term secession was used at that early period—foreign journals stated in distinct words that England was deeply interested in the contest; for nullification might bring on secession, and secession would cause a general disruption—an occurrence which would redound to the essential benefit of Great Britain.

But the traitors of the North, who have been so aptly called adders or copperheads—striking, as these reptiles do, more secretly and deadly even than the rattlesnake, which has some chivalry, at least in its tail—believe, or pretend to believe, that no fragmentary disruption would follow a division of our country into North and South, and advocate a compromise, by which they affect to believe that the two portions may possibly be reunited after a provisional division, as our pedlers putty a broken china cup.

As to the first, that we might pleasantly divide into two comfortable portions, we prefer being guided by the experience of all history, to following the traitors in their teachings. We will not hear of it. We live in an age when the word is Nationalization, not De-nationalization; when fair Italy has risen, like a new-born goddess, out of the foaming waves of the Mediterranean. All destruction is quick and easy; all growth and formation is slow and toilsome. Nations break up, like splendid mirrors dashed to the ground. They do not break into a number of well-shaped, neatly framed little looking-glasses. But a far more solemn truth even than this comes here into play. It is with nations as with families and with individuals. Those destined by nature to live in the bonds of friendship and mutual kindliness, become the bitterest and most irreconcilable enemies, when once fairly separated in angry enmity; in precisely the same degree in which affection and good-will were intended to subsist between them. We must have back the South, or else those who will not reunite with us must leave the country; we must have the country at any price. If, however, a plain division between the North and the South could take place, who will deny that those very traitors would instantly begin to manœuvre for a gradual annexation of the North to the South? It is known to be so. Some of them, void of all shame, have avowed it. They are ready to petition on their knees for annexation to the South, and to let the condescending grantor, "holding the while his nose," introduce slavery, that blessed "corner-stone of" the newest "civilization," into the North, which has been happily purged from this evil. Let us put the heel on this adder, and bruise all treason out of its head.

As to the compromise which they propose, we know of no compromise with crime that is not criminal itself, and senseless in addition to its being wicked. New guarantees, indeed, may be asked for at the proper time, but it is now our turn to ask for them. They will be guarantees of peace, of the undisturbed integrity of our country, of law, and liberty, and security, asked for and insisted upon by the Union men, who now pledge themselves not to listen to the words, compromise, new guarantees for the South, armistice, or convention of delegates from the South and North—as long as this war shall last, until the North is victorious, and shall have established again the national authority over the length and breadth of the country as it was; over the United States dominion as it was before the breaking out of the crime, which is now ruining our fair land—ruining it in point of wealth, but, with God's help, elevating it in character, strength, and dignity.

We believe that the question of the issue, which must attend the present contest, according to the character it has now acquired, is reduced to these simple words—Either the North conquers the South, or the South conquers the North. Make up your minds for this alternative. Either the North conquers the South and re-establishes law, freedom, and the integrity of our country, or the South conquers the North by arms, or by treason at home, and covers our portion of the country with disgrace and slavery.

Let us not shrink from facts or mince the truth, but rather plainly present to our minds the essential character of the struggle in which hundreds of thousands, that ought to be brothers, are now engaged. What has brought us to these grave straits?

Are we two different races, as the new ethnologists of the South, with profound knowledge of history and of their own skins, names, and language, proclaim? Have they produced the names which Europe mentions when American literature is spoken of? Have they produced our Crawfords? Have they advanced science? Have they the great schools of the age? Do they speak the choice idiom of the cultivated man? Have the thinkers and inventors of the age their homes in that region? Is their standard of comfort exalted above that of ours? What has this wondrous race produced? what new idea has it added to the great stock of civilization? It has produced cotton, and added the idea that slavery is divine. Does this establish a superior race?

The French, ourselves, the English, the Germans, the Italians, none of whom are destitute of national self-gratulation, have ever made a preposterous claim of constituting a different race. Even the new idea of a Latin Race—a Bonaparte anachronism—is founded upon an error less revolting to common sense and common knowledge.

There is no fact or movement of greater significance in all

history of the human race, than the settlement of this great continent by European people at a period when, in their portion of the globe, great nations had been formed, and the national polity had finally become the normal type of government; and it is a fact equally pregnant with momentous results, that the northern portion of this hemisphere came to be colonized chiefly by men who brought along with them the seeds of self-government, and a living common law, instinct with the principles of manly self-dependence and civil freedom.

The charters under which they settled, and which divided the American territory into colonies, were of little more importance than the vessels and their names in which the settlers crossed the Atlantic; nor had the origin of these charters a deep meaning, nor was their source always pure. The people in this country always felt themselves to be one people, and unitedly they proclaimed and achieved their independence. The country as a whole was called by Washington and his compeers America, for want of a more individual name. Still, there was no outward and legal bond between the colonies, except the crown of England; and when our people abjured their allegiance to that crown, each colony stood formally for itself. The Articles of Confederation were adopted, by which our forefathers attempted to establish a confederacy, uniting all that felt themselves to be of one nation, but were not one by outward legal form. It was the best united government our forefathers could think of, or of which, perhaps, the combination of circumstances admitted. Each colony came gradually to be called a State, and called itself sovereign, although none of them had ever exercised any of the highest attributes of sovereignty; nor did ever after the States do so.

Wherever political societies are leagued together, be it by the frail bonds of a pure confederacy, or by the consciousness of the people that they are intrinsically one people, and form one nation, without, however, a positive National Government, then the most powerful of these ill-united portions needs must rule and, as always more than one portion wishes to be the leader, intestine struggles ensue in all such incoherent governments. It has been so in antiquity; it has been so in the middle ages; it has been so, and is so in modern times.

Athens and Sparta, Castile and Aragon, Austria and Prussia, are always jealous companions, readily turned into bitter enemies. Those of our forefathers who later became the framers of our Constitution, saw this approaching evil, and they observed many other ills which had already overtaken the confederacy. Even Washington, the strong and tenacious patriot, nearly desponded. It was a dark period in our history; and it was then that our fathers most boldly, yet most considerately, performed the greatest act that our annals record—they engrafted a national, complete and representative government on our insufficient confederacy; a government with an exclusively National executive, in which the Senate, though still representing the States as States, became Nationalized in a great measure, and in which the House of Representatives became purely National like the Executive. Virginia, which, under the Articles of Confederation, was approaching the leadership over all (in the actual assumption of which she would have been resisted by other rapidly growing states, which would inevitably have led to her Peloponnesian war)—Virginia was now represented according to her population, like every other portion of the country; not as a unit, but by a number of representatives who were bound to vote individually, according to their consciences, as National men. The danger of internal struggle and provincial bitterness had passed, and our country now fairly entered as an equal among the leading nations in the course, where nations, like Olympic chariot-horses, draw abreast the car of civilization. We advanced rapidly; the task assigned to us by Providence was performed with a rapidity which had not been known before; for we had a National Government commensurate to our land and, it seemed, adequate to our destiny.

But while thus united and freed from provincial retardation and entanglements, a new portent appeared.

Slavery, which had been planted here in the colonial times, and which had been increased in this country, by the parent government, against the urgent protestations of the colonists, and especially of the Virginians, existed in all the colonies at the time when they declared themselves independent. It was felt by all to be an evil which must be dealt with as best it might be, and the gradual extinction of which must be wisely yet surely provided for. Even Mr. Calhoun, in his earlier days, called slavery a scaffolding erected to rear the mansion of civilization, which must be taken down when the fabric is finished.

This institution gave way gradually as civilization advanced. It has done so in all periods of history, and especially of Christian history. Slavery melts away like snow before the rays of rising civilization. The South envied the North for getting rid of slavery so easily, and often expressed her envy. But a combination of untoward circumstances led the South to change her mind. First, it was maintained that if slavery is an evil, it was their affair and no one else had a right to discuss it or to interfere with it; then it came to be maintained that it was no evil; then slavery came to be declared an important national element, which required its own distinct representation and especial protection; then it was said—we feel ashamed to mention it—that slavery is a divine institution. To use the words of the great South-Carolinian, whose death we deeply mourn—of James Louis Petigru—they placed, like the templars, Christ and Baphomet on the same altar, worshipping God and Satan simultaneously. But though slavery were divine, they choked the wells of common knowledge with sand and stones, and enacted perpetual ignorance for the slave. Then the renewal of that traffic, the records of which fills far the darkest pages of European history, and which the most strenuous and protracted efforts of civilized nations have not yet wholly succeeded in abolishing, was loudly called for; and our national laws, making that unhallowed trade piracy, were declared unconstitutional. Yet still another step was to be taken. It was proclaimed that slavery is a necessary element of a new and glorious civilization; and those who call themselves conservatives plunged recklessly into a new-fangled theory of politics and civilization.

Some thirty years ago we first heard of Southern Rights. Some twenty years since we were first made familiar with the expression, Southern Principles. Within the present lustre, Southern Civilization has been proclaimed. What else remained but to invent Southern Mathematics and to decree a Southern God? And what does *Southern* mean in this connection? *South* is a word which indicates relative position in geography. Yet, in these combinations, it refers neither to geography, nor to climate, nor to product, but singly and exclusively to Slavery. Southern Rights, Southern Principles, Southern Civilization, and Southern Honor or "Chivalry," are novel phrases, to express the new idea of principles and civilization characterized and tested by the dependence of one class of people as chattel upon another. A more appalling confusion of ideas is not recorded in the history of any tribe or nation that has made any use of the terms—Rights, Principles, or Civilization.

Thus slavery came to group the different portions of our country; outside of, and indeed in hostility to, the National Government and National Constitution. The struggle for the leadership was upon us. The South declared openly that it must rule; we, in the meantime, declaring that the Nation must rule, and if an issue is forced upon us, between the South and the North, then, indeed, the North must rule and shall rule. *This* is the war in which we are now engaged—in which, at the moment this is read to you, the precious blood of your sons, and brothers, and fathers, is flowing.

Whenever men are led, in the downward course of error and passion, ultimately to declare themselves, with immoral courage, in favor of a thing or principle which for centuries and thousands of years their own race has declared, by a united voice, an evil or a crime, the mischief does not stop with this single declaration. It naturally, and by a well-established law, unhinges the whole morality of man; it warps his intellect, and inflames his soul, with bewildering passions, with defiance to the simplest truth and plainest fact, and with vindictive hatred toward those who cannot agree with him. It is a fearful thing to become the defiant idolater of wrong. Slavery, and the consequent separation from the rest of men, begot pride in the leading men of the South—absurdly even pretending to be of a different and better race. Pride begot bitter and venomous hatred, and this bitter hatred, coupled with the love of owning men as things, begot at last a hatred of that which distinguishes the whole race to which we belong, more than aught else—the striving for and love of liberty.

There is no room, then, for pacifying arguments with such men in arms against us, against their duty, their country, their civilization. All that remains for the present is the question, Who shall be the victor?

It is for all these reasons which have been stated, that we pledge ourselves anew, in unwavering loyalty, to stand by and support the Government in all its efforts to suppress the rebellion, and to spare no endeavor to maintain, unimpaired, the national unity, both in principle and territorial boundary.

We will support the Government, and call on it with a united voice to use greater and greater energy, as the contest may seem to draw to a close; so that whatever advantages we may gain, we may pursue them with increasing efficiency, and bring every one in the military or civil service, that may be slow in the performance of his duty, to a quick and efficient account.

We approve of the Conscription Act, and will give our loyal aid in its being carried out, whenever the Government shall consider the increase of our army necessary; and we believe that the energy of the Government should be plainly shown by retaliatory measures, in checking the savage brutalities committed by the enemy against our men in arms, or against unarmed citizens, when they fall into their hands.

We declare that slavery, the poisonous root of this war, ought to be compressed within its narrowest feasible limits, with a view to its speedy extinction.

We declare that this is no question of politics, but one of patriotism; and we hold every one to be a traitor to his country, that works or speaks in favor of our criminal enemies, directly or indirectly, whether his offence be such that the law can overtake him or not.

We declare our inmost abhorrence of the secret societies which exist among us in favor of the rebellious enemy, and that we will denounce every participator in these nefarious conventicles, whenever known to us. We believe publicity the very basis of liberty.

We pledge our fullest support of the government in every measure which it shall deem fit to adopt against unfriendly and mischievous neutrality; and we call upon it, as citizens that have the right and duty to call for protection on their own government, to adopt the speediest possible measures to that important end.

We loyally support our government in its declarations and measures against all and every attempt of mediation, or armed or unarmed interference in our civil war.

We solemnly declare that we will resist every partition of any portion of our country to the last extremity, whether this partition should be brought about by rebellious or treasonable citizens of our own, or by foreign powers, in the way that Poland was torn to pieces.

We pronounce every foreign minister accredited to our government, who tampers with our enemies, and holds covert intercourse with disloyal men among us, as failing in his duty toward us and toward his own people, and we await with attention the action of our government regarding the recent and surprising breach of this duty.

And we call upon every American, be he such by birth or choice, to join the loyal movement of these National Leagues, which is naught else than to join and follow our beckoning flag, and to adopt for his device—

OUR COUNTRY!

Catharine Peirce to Taylor Peirce

While her husband Taylor served with the 22nd Iowa Infantry, Catharine Peirce managed several farm and town properties, handled the family finances, and raised three young children. After his enlistment Catharine and the children had moved in with her brother, Cyrus, and his wife, Mary, who was Taylor's sister.

———————

Des Moines April/12/63
Dear Taylor
I have not got much to communicate this morning but it is sunday and I write to let thee know how we all are. We are all well to day. Cyrus is better than he has been for some time at least better than he was this time last year and I hope he will get better as the spring advances.

Dear one I sit down to write to thee not knowing what I may find to say to thee. We get no war news at this time. I suppose that the heads of affairs are trying to keep thing quiet for the present so the rebles will not know what thair at. All I have to say about it is that I hope they will do something soon that will tell and that pritty loudly too for I think that now is the time to strike a blow that will make them squirm. From what I can hear the rebles are nearly starved out and if it is true they will have to give up before long. We heard last week that there had been a bread riot among the woman and Children in Savanna and that they were in a starveing Steate and would set fire to the city if they did not get bread. It seems to me that is a big threat for woman to make but then a woman will do and dair a great deal for her starveing children. I think a pity of the poor little children but the just must suffer with the unjust. If the parents had not been such foul traitors they might still of enjoyed peace and plenty unless they belong to the class of men that are pressed into the war against their principals which I learned there are hundreds of such among the reble forces.

I can not help but feel thankful to the giver of all good that we have pleny here at the North and a fine prospect for more. The spring is opend but not as earley or as forward as it had the apperence of two or three weeks ago. But still the framework gos on gloriously. We have had no rain for some time and it is geting pritty dry so the grass is backward this season. We have had no boats up this spring and that has made teaming a good business here and wages are good generaly. The river was full enought at one time for boats to run up but I suppose that government has them all in her services to carrie provisions for the soldiers. It must take an awfull amount to supply the army that lay around Vicksburg with enough to eat.

Thee wanted me to send thy book account on Ault and a note. The note I inclose to thee. The book account I hope thee has receved before this time as I sent it some three weeks ago and also Mary's and Franks pictures. I would get little Ellis picure if I thought I could get any thing like a good one to send to thee but the artists do not like to take the picture of a baby and it is a hard matter to get them still long enough to get any like a picture. So I will wait a while and hope that thee will get home soon to see the little thing. I think he looks very much like the old hoss himself. The other Children say they want thee to come home so that they can kiss and hugg thee. They both have to kiss thair Aunt and uncle every night before they go to bed and wish one for thee. I believe I must close now. With heart felt love I remain thine Catharine. Give my respects to all that I know that thee think are deserveing of such.

Catharine A Peirce Des Moines Iowa Polk County

James A. Connolly to Mary Dunn Connolly

Following its costly victory in the battle of Stones River, December 31, 1862–January 2, 1863, the Union Army of the Cumberland had remained at Murfreesboro, Tennessee, while the Confederate Army of Tennessee occupied Tullahoma, thirty-five miles to the south. On March 20 a Union reconnaissance force of 1,300 men repulsed 3,500 Confederates near Milton, about twelve miles northeast of Murfreesboro. Major James A. Connolly of the 123rd Illinois Infantry recounted the action.

———————

Murfreesboro, Tenn., April 20, 1863.

Dear wife:

I am alone in my tent to-night, I have a good solid floor in it, an excellent fire place in one end, graced by a pair of andirons, a cheerful fire is glowing on the hearth for though the days are warm the nights are a little cool; my good *feather bed*, with *feather* pillow is waiting for me; the excellent brass band of the 19th regulars, who are encamped near us, fills the soft night air with splendid music, and while I am content as it is yet if you were here with me I should be happy. You remember when I was at home I was almost entirely out of the notion of soldiering much longer, and I really expected that by this time I should be out of the service. But I was not well then, I was petulant, ill humored, weak from my long illness, I know I was. Military rules and orders were interfering with my freedom of action and that engendered in me a rebellious spirit toward everything military, but as time has passed and my general health improved that spirit has passed away and I begin to feel somewhat the spirit of a soldier. I am a better soldier than I was before we were married, not that I am any more rash, or want to fight any more, but somehow I enter into the spirit of things here more, my experience has given me more confidence in myself, but I am in no hurry to get into any more battles, for I think we have done our full share so far. We have been under fire 15 times, we are cut down in 8 months service from 962 men to about 460, 200 of that loss being in battle and skirmish, so that all things considered I don't care to fight any more, at least until regiments in service longer than we have tried their mettle once or twice. Still I know the fighting can't be divided out that way. Fighting goes like fortunes. Some get more than their equal share while many get less. The other day when I sent you that little money package, I wrote you a short note, the first for many days; I had been unfit to do anything for ten days but grumble, although I was compelled by circumstances to be on duty. I saw your brother Jerry the day before he left his boarding place to go to his regiment. I was quite unwell then, had just got in from a hard trip of 9 days, and intended to write you next day and send it by him, but on returning to camp found an order from Division headquarters appointing me officer in charge of the Division picket for next day; I wouldn't send up an excuse of sickness but worried it through, and when I got off that duty and my report forwarded, I went back to camp, took to bed and called for calomel and jalap as the only consolation. The order for marching which the regiment had received the day I sent you that package was countermanded but issued again last evening, and at 9 o'clock this morning our whole Division started with 6 days rations in the direction of Woodbury, east of here, from there they will probably go to McMinnville and may possibly encounter the combined force of Morgan, Wheeler, Wharton and Forrest, supposed to be about 20 regiments of cavalry and mounted infantry with 6 or 8 pieces of artillery.

Our force is not more than 9 regiments of infantry, 4 pieces of artillery and 2 regiments of cavalry, but they won't dare to fight us if they can help it by running away. Since the Milton fight our men have no more fear of Morgan and his crew than they would for that many boys with guns. It is "grape vine" that Grant's and Burnsides' armies will unite with us within the next month, and then Bragg must find new camps for we will have business at Tullahoma and Chattanooga. In your last letter you say I said something about "bullet holes". I certainly did. I wrote you a long letter describing our Milton fight and telling you how and when I got my "bullet holes", one tearing away part of my saddle holster and shattering the pommel of my saddle, the other tearing away the collar of my overcoat and knocking me down slightly, all of which caused me no pain and very little uneasiness, but many of the men and officers saw me fall and the word passed along the line: "the Major is shot", but when the fighting was over and they all saw I was unhurt we had a jolly time hand shaking for a few minutes. I knew it was a mistake all the time but they didn't. I was some distance in front of the regiment when my saddle was hit, and happened to be the only officer on horseback visible to the enemy. They were in a cedar thicket and I couldn't see them but they could see me. On looking around I saw that all the other field officers were dismounted so I got out of there in a hurry, dismounted and had my horse led back by an orderly; a few minutes later while standing behind our line of men lying down, some "Johnnie" in the cedars who was a tolerably good shot sent a bullet through my overcoat collar and down I went. I expect he thought he shot me but he was badly mistaken. I was conscious all the time, knew I had fallen, but knew I was not wounded, although I was shocked as if by a galvanic battery; in three minutes I was all right again; it seems much worse in writing than the actual experience. Oh yes my clothing in the trunk; you can send it to father's if you choose, but I want it kept for myself as I hope to wear it again some day. xxxxxxxxx

Your husband.

Ulysses S. Grant to Jesse Root Grant

At the end of March Grant abandoned his attempts to open a water route around Vicksburg and began making preparations to move his army down the west bank of the Mississippi and cross the river below the city. His plan was opposed by Sherman, who favored withdrawing to Memphis and making a renewed overland advance on Vicksburg through central Mississippi. Grant persisted, and on the night of April 16 a flotilla of Union gunboats and transports successfully ran past the Vicksburg shore batteries and headed downriver in preparation for the army's crossing. Grant wrote to his father as he prepared to move south.

———————

Millikins Bend La
April 21st 1863.

DEAR FATHER,

Your letter of the 7th of April has just this day reached me. I hasten to answer your interogitories.

When I left Memphis with my past experiance I prohibited trade below Helena. Trade to that point had previously been opened by the Treasury Department. I give no permits to buy Cotton and if I find any one engaged in the business I send them out of the Department and seize their Cotton for the Government. I have given a few families permission to leave the country and to take with them as far as Memphis their Cotton. In doing this I have been decieved by unprincipled speculators who have smuggled themselves along with the Army in spite of orders prohibiting them and have been compelled to suspend this favor to persons anxious to get out of Dixie.

I understand that Govt has adopted some plan to regulate geting the Cotton out of the country. I do not know what plan they have adopted but am satisfied that any that can be adopted, except for Government to take the Cotton themselves, and rule out speculators altogether will be a bad one. I feel all Army followers who are engaged in speculating off the misfortunes of their country, and really aiding the enemy more than they possibly could do by open treason, should be drafted at once and put in the first forlorn hope.

I move my Head Quarters to New Carthage to-morrow. This whole country is under water except strips of land behind the levees along the river and bayous and makes opperations almost impossible. I struck upon a plan which I thought would give me a foot hold on the East bank of the Miss. before the enemy could offer any great resistance. But the difficulty of the last one & a half miles next to Carthage makes it so tedious that the enemy cannot fail to discover my plans. I am doing my best and am full of hope for complete success. Time has been consumed but it was absolutely impossible to avoid it. An attack upon the rebel works at any time since I arrived here must inevitably resulted in the loss of a large portion of my Army if not in an entire defeat. There was but two points of land, Hains Bluff & Vicksburg itself, out of water any place from which troops could march. These are thoroughly fortified and it would be folly to attack them as long as there is a prospect of turning their position. I never expect to have an army under my command whipped unless it is very badly whipped and cant help it but I have no idea of being driven to do a desperate or foolish act by the howlings of the press. It is painful to me as a matter of course to see the course pursued by some of the papers. But there is no one less disturbed by them than myself. I have never saught a large command and have no ambitious ends to accomplish. Was it not for the very natural desire of proving myself equal to anything expected of me, and the evidence my removal would afford that I was not thought equal to it, I would gladly accept a less responsible position. I have no desire to be an object of envy or jealousy, nor to have this war continue. I want, and will do my part towards it, to put down the rebellion in the shortest possible time without expecting or desiring any other recognition than a quiet approval of my course. I beg that you will destroy this letter. At least do not show it.

Julia and the children are here but will go up by the first good boat. I sent for her to come down and get instructions about some business I want attended to and see no immediate prospect of being able to attend to myself.

                                                    ULYSSES

David Hunter to Jefferson Davis

Major General David Hunter, the commander of the Union-held enclaves along the South Carolina and Georgia coasts, began on his own initiative to organize a regiment of freed slaves in May 1862. At the direction of Jefferson Davis, the Confederate War Department issued orders in August 1862 outlawing Hunter and declaring that any captured Union officer involved in organizing or training slaves for military service would be held for "execution as a felon." Hunter wrote to Davis without authorization from the Lincoln administration and did not carry out any acts of retaliation before being relieved of his command (for unrelated reasons) in June 1863. His letter to the Confederate leader was printed in the northern press.

HILTON HEAD, Port Royal, S. C., April 23rd. 1863.
The United States flag must protect all its defenders, white, black or yellow. Several negroes in the employ of the Government, in the Western Department, have been cruelly murdered by your authorities, and others sold into slavery. Every outrage of this kind against the laws of war and humanity, which may take place in this Department, shall be followed by the immediate execution of the Rebel of highest rank in my possession; man for man, these executions will certainly take place, for every one murdered, or sold into a slavery worse than death. On your authorities will rest the responsibility of having inaugurated this barbarous policy, and you will be held responsible, in this world and in the world to come, for all the blood thus shed.

In the month of August last you declared all those engaged in arming the negroes to fight for their country, to be felons, and directed the immediate execution of all such, as should be captured. I have given you long enough to reflect on your folly. I now give you notice, that unless this order is immediately revoked, I will at once cause the execution of every rebel officer, and every rebel slaveholder in my possession. This sad state of things may be kindly ordered by an all wise Providence, to induce the good people of the North to act earnestly, and to realize that they are at war. Thousands of lives may thus be saved.

The poor negro is fighting for liberty in its truest sense; and Mr. Jefferson has beautifully said,—"in such a war, there is no attribute of the Almighty, which will induce him to fight on the side of the oppressor."

You say you are fighting for liberty. Yes you are fighting for liberty: liberty to keep four millions of your fellow-beings in ignorance and degradation;—liberty to separate parents and children, husband and wife, brother and sister;—liberty to steal the products of their labor, exacted with many a cruel lash and bitter tear,—liberty to seduce their wives and daughters, and to sell your own children into bondage;—liberty to kill these children with impunity, when the murder cannot be proven by one of pure white blood. This is the kind of liberty —the liberty to do wrong—which Satan, Chief of the fallen Angels, was contending for when he was cast into Hell. I have the honor to be, very respectfully, Your mo. ob. serv.

D. HUNTER,
Major Gen.
Com.

Kate Stone: *Journal, April 25, 1863*

Kate Stone lived with her family at Brokenburn, a cotton plantation in what is now Madison Parish, Louisiana, about thirty miles northwest of Vicksburg. Foraging parties from the Union army camps along the Mississippi moved through the area in early 1863, seizing food and horses and encouraging slaves to leave their plantations. On March 22 Stone recorded how "two most villainous-looking Yankees" had taken her horse at gunpoint. The following day, alarmed by reports that armed former slaves were helping Union soldiers plunder neighboring plantations, she wrote: "The sword of Damocles in a hundred forms is suspended over us, and there is no escape." A month later, Stone and her family were refugees staying near Monroe, Louisiana, eighty miles west of the Mississippi. She described the incident that caused them to flee.

———————

April 25: We see that Van Dorn has had another fight and been repulsed. We can only hope Brother Coley and Dr. Buckner are safe. We will not hear for many days. Affairs look dark for our Confederacy just now.

This country is filled with refugees. Nearly all our friends are back here or on their way to Texas, where we hope to be before long. Out here the prices asked for everything are enormous. The people of Monroe seem determined to fleece the refugees. It cost us $3,000 to get a four-horse hack to bring us from Monroe here—four miles."

Having no other way of amusing myself, I may as well write the account of our flight from home and our subsequent adventures.

On Thursday, March 26, hearing that Mr. Hardison had returned from Monroe, Sister and I walked up in the afternoon to hear what news he had brought. As we approached the house, it struck me that something was wrong. As we were going through the garden George Richards came out and told us a party of Yankees and armed Negroes had just left, carrying with them every Negro on the place, most of Mrs. Hardison's and the children's clothes, and all the provisions they could manage. They were led by Charles, Mr. Hardison's most trusted servant, and they were all vowing vengeance against Mr. Hardison. They said they would shoot him on sight for moving two of his Negroes a few days before. Mr. Hardison had fortunately seen them coming and, knowing he would be arrested or perhaps killed as a conscript officer, had escaped to the woods.

We walked in and found Mrs. Hardison and the children all much excited and very angry, with flaming cheeks and flashing eyes. The Negroes had been very impertinent. The first armed Negroes they had ever seen. Just as we were seated someone called out the Yankees were coming again. It was too late to run. All we could do was to shut ourselves up together in one room, hoping they would not come in. George Richards was on the gallery. In a minute we heard the gate open and shut, rough hoarse voices, a volley of oaths, and then a cry, "Shoot him, curse him! Shoot him! Get out of the way so I can get him." Looking out of the window, we saw three fiendish-looking, black Negroes standing around George Richards, two with their guns leveled and almost touching his breast. He was deathly pale but did not move. We thought he would be killed instantly, and I shut my eyes that I might not see it. But after a few words from George, which we could not hear, and another volley of curses, they lowered their guns and rushed into the house "to look for guns" they said, but only to rob and terrorize us. The Negroes were completely armed and there was no white man with them. We heard them ranging all through the house, cursing and laughing, and breaking things open.

Directly one came bursting into our room, a big black wretch, with the most insolent swagger, talking all the time in a most insulting manner. He went through all the drawers and wardrobe taking anything he fancied, all the time with a cocked pistol in his hand. Cursing and making the most awful threats against Mr. Hardison if they ever caught him, he lounged up to the bed where the baby was sleeping. Raising the bar, he started to take the child, saying as he waved the pistol, "I ought to kill him. He may grow up to be a jarilla. Kill him." Mrs. Hardison sprang to his side, snatched the baby up, and shrieked, "Don't kill my baby. Don't kill him." The Negro turned away with a laugh and came over where I was sitting with Little Sister crouched close to me holding my hand. He came right up to us standing on the hem of my dress while he looked me slowly over, gesticulating and snapping his pistol. He stood there about a minute, I suppose. It seemed to me an age. I felt like I would die should he touch me. I did not look up or move, and Little Sister was as still as if petrified. In an instant more he turned away with a most diabolical laugh, gathered up his plunder, and went out. I was never so frightened in my life. Mrs. Hardison said we were both as white as marble, and she was sure I would faint. What a wave of thankfulness swept over us when he went out and slammed the door. In the meanwhile, the other Negroes were rummaging the house, ransacking it from top to bottom, destroying all the provisions they could not carry away, and sprinkling a white powder into the cisterns and over everything they left. We never knew whether it was poison or not.

The Negroes called and stormed and cursed through the house, calling each other "Captain" and "Lieutenant" until it nearly froze the blood in our veins, and every minute we expected them to break into our room again. I was completely unnerved. I did not think I could feel so frightened.

Mrs. Alexander went into her room hoping to prevent their robbing her bed, when one of them pointed his pistol at her and said, "I told you once before, old woman, to keep out of here and stop your jaw." Mr. McPherson and George were all the time on the gallery with Negroes guarding them with leveled guns.

After carrying on this way about two hours they lit matches, stuck them about the hall, and then leisurely took themselves off, loaded down with booty. We rushed around, put out all the matches, gathered up the few little articles left, and started at once for home. Since the Negroes declared as they moved off that they were coming back in a little while and burn every house on the place, I took the baby and Mrs. Hardison, Mrs. Alexander, and the children with George and Mr. McPherson gathered up everything of any value left, and we hurried home, reaching there spent with excitement. Mrs. Hardison was almost crazy.

As we passed through our quarters, there were numbers of strange Negro men standing around. They had gathered from the neighboring places. They did not say anything, but they looked at us and grinned and that terrified us more and more. It held such a promise of evil. Jimmy went out at once to where Mr. Hardison was in hiding to tell him his family were with us. Jimmy just escaped being shot by Mr. Hardison, who, in the dusk, took him for a Yankee. Mr. and Mrs. Hardison and the small children went off as soon as possible, not thinking it safe to remain so near home. During the night a party came to the yard looking for them, but on the house servants' assuring them that the Hardisons were gone, they did not come to the house.

We made preparations that night to move at daybreak, but something deterred us. Mamma thought she would go out and get letters of protection but later abandoned the idea. It was then too late for us to get off, and we spent a night and day of terror. The next evening the Negroes from all the inhabited places around commenced flocking to Mr. Hardison's, and they completely sacked the place in broad daylight, passing our gate loaded down with plunder until twelve at night. That more than anything else frightened Mamma and determined her to leave, though at the sacrifice of everything we owned.

We made arrangements to get Dr. Carson's skiffs and sent Webster around collecting saddles and bridles. On account of the water we could go only on horseback to take the skiffs. With much difficulty we got everything ready for the start at midnight. Aunt Laura was the only one who did not want to go. She begged Mamma to let her and Beverly stay, saying that she would get old Mr. Valentine to stay with her, but of course Mamma could not allow that. The boys brought in everything we had buried out, except Aunt Laura's silver. That had to be left packed in a barrel and buried in the yard. The boys had done it one very dark night, when they hoped all the Negroes were in their cabins as it was raining. All the servants behaved well enough except Webster, but you could see it was only because they knew we would soon be gone. We were only on sufferance.

Two days longer and we think they would all have gone to the Yankees, most probably robbing and insulting us before they left. About eleven the boys went off with their guns to have the horses saddled and brought up. After a good deal of trouble, they came. The boys carried their guns all the time. Without them I think we would never have gotten off. Webster tried every artifice to get hold of one of them, but the boys never relaxed their watch. The night was cloudy and dark with occasional claps of thunder, but we had to go then or never. We knew the news would be carried to camp, and the Yankees had forbidden citizens to leave their places. Aunt Laura, protesting all the time she could not ride, was at last after much coaxing and fixing mounted on poor Little Jack Fisher, the family pony, old and gentle, with Annie perched behind her. I took Beverly in my lap. All the others mounted, and with the baggage cart with Uncle Bob driving and Jimmy guarding it in the extreme rear, the procession moved off.

It was too dark to see the road but Johnny led off, and each one followed the shadow in front. At first Aunt Laura was loud in exclamation and complaint, until someone suggested that she would bring the Negroes down on us. That acted as a quietus, and thereafter she groaned only in spirit. Several times as the clouds lifted and it grew something lighter, I saw her pony struggling in a mud hole and Aunt Laura reeling in the saddle, but not a scream disturbed the stillness of the night. As we opened gates and rode through place after place in perfect silence, not a light was visible anywhere. After passing Out Post, the road was so bad and it was so dark that we were forced to wait for daylight. We dismounted in the middle of the road, and to Aunt Laura's surprise and amazement Mamma lay her head down in Johnny's lap and went sound asleep. Riding in the dark made her sick, and she was worn out with excitement and loss of sleep.

As soon as it was light enough to see, the sleepers were awakened, and we mounted and went on over the very worst road it was possible for ladies to travel—just a long bog from one end to the other. The morning air was pleasantly cool, and as the red light crept up the sky we heard all kinds of wild-woods sounds—squirrels chattering in the trees, birds waking with a song, the calls of the wild ducks and turkeys, and three or four deer bounding into the woods just before us.

When we reached within a mile of our place of debarkation,

the road became impassable, and we struck off into the woods. The cart had to be left there and the baggage carried on by mules. After much trouble, getting lost and riding through water up to our saddle skirts—I actually swam a bayou with Beverly in my arms—we succeeded in getting all of our party and a little of our baggage to the landing place below Mrs. Stevens'. We sent Webster back to the cart for the baggage, and no sooner was he out of sight than he mounted a horse and set off for home. He told Charles that he knew he was not going to Bayou Macon with Miss Manda and that Charles had better come on with him. Thus by his treachery we lost almost everything we brought away with us, for when we heard it, it was already too late to send back for the things. We knew the Yankees would certainly be where we were by 8 o'clock, and it was nearly that hour. We knew that we must get off at once if at all, for when the Yankees came they would turn us back. They never allow anyone to leave if they can help it. Finish this another day.

Wilbur Fisk to The Green Mountain Freeman

Private Wilbur Fisk of the 2nd Vermont Infantry began writing letters in December 1861 to *The Green Mountain Freeman* of Montpelier under the pen name "Anti-Rebel." Fisk fought in the Seven Days' Battles before being hospitalized with chronic diarrhea in September 1862. He returned to his regiment near Fredericksburg in March 1863 and wrote to the *Freeman* as the Army of the Potomac awaited the opening of the spring campaign. At the end of April Hooker had 134,000 men under his command, while Lee defended his lines along the Rappahannock with about 60,000 men.

Camp near White Oak Church, Va.
April 26, 1863

We have not moved from our old camp yet, although we came so near it once that we considered it a foregone conclusion. Last week every possible preparation was made for such an event; the usual orders were read, some more stringent and particular than ever before. The order in regard to straggling was read by the adjutant to each company separately, besides being read, according to usual custom, on dress parade, twice. Great stress was laid upon the importance of preventing a practice so demoralizing and weakening to the army. Regimental and Company officers were to be held responsible and, besides other punishments threatened, leaves of absence and furloughs would be withheld from those regiments where straggling was permitted.

The order in regard to rations informed us that we must each of us carry eight days' rations of bread, coffee and sugar, three days' rations of meat—the remaining five days' rations of meat were to be taken along on the hoof. This was making far greater provision for ourselves than had ever before been required of us, and seemed to bode heavy, fatiguing loads for our backs, or else extreme destitution in the matter of blankets

161

and extra clothing. We were not exactly ordered, but very strongly advised, to take only our rubber blankets, and leave our woollen ones in the care of the Quartermaster. Everything else, except a change of underclothing, must be left. Once before we had been ordered to send off to Washington everything worth saving that could possibly be dispensed with in a summer campaign. We thought we had been remarkably self-sacrificing and had stinted ourselves to the lowest possible extreme, but this order pressed us down another notch. Some sent off their woollen blankets and even their dress coats,— their overcoats had been sent off before. They saved nothing but their rubber blankets and their blouse coats, or fatigue jackets. Others determined to keep their woollen blankets at all hazards, and if sorely weighed down on the march, they could throw them away. Inasmuch as we didn't move, these saw the wisdom of their decision. Those that sent off all their things consoled themselves with the philosophy that they are as well off in camp without them, as they would be on the march.

But all of our preparations were nothing, as present appearances indicate. It is quite amusing, though, to be in a camp like ours on the eve of a march, and hear the debates, suggestions, and decisions in regard to a thousand little valuables,—whether they should be left behind or carried. Things of no special merit, but which had contributed to our comfort or convenience, were heedlessly thrown aside or destroyed. Many an article that a few days before would have been gladly bought at a high price, were at once valueless and could not be given away. Often a knapsack would have to be unpacked and its contents sorted over and over again, and other articles selected out and doomed to stay behind, to the no small regret of the wistful owner. No bigger article than a can for butter, or a frying-pan, would be made the subject of earnest debate, but the question, "how can we get along without them?" was confronted by one still more inexorable, "How can we carry them?" If we only knew where we were going? but we did not know that, and it was wisdom to prepare for the worst. That night it rained like a deluge, and marching the next day was rendered impracticable. It would be the merest guesswork, to undertake to tell when we shall be called upon to get ready for marching again.

The boys were never in better spirits or in better health than now, and they were never in better condition to endure the fatigues of a march than at the present time. But very few of the men are on the sick list, and those that are are mostly recruits who are not yet fully acclimated. The boys "feel their oats," as the saying is, immensely. I have never seen the time when the boys would engage in all manner of athletic sports with such eager relish as now. There is none of that thin, gloomy, woebegone expression to be seen in the faces of the men that was visible upon almost every countenance at the end of last summer's campaign. The boys never felt more *boyish* than they do now, and they never enjoyed themselves better. We can get up a sham fight that might look a little rough to some of our milder acquaintances at home, perhaps, but it passes with us as good, earnest boy's play. Rough as the Second boys have the name of being—and rough customers we certainly are, to those who are foolish enough to proclaim themselves our adversaries—a quarrel among ourselves is an unheard of thing and "difficulties" quite unknown. Almost perfect equanimity and good feeling exist throughout the entire regiment. Our guard-house remains empty, or in fact we have no guard-house at all, the apology of a thing we once had having become totally ruined and demoralized for want of use and care. The whole institution is nearly obsolete, and putting men under arrest is well nigh played out.

The 26th New Jersey regiment belongs to this brigade—a regiment of nine months men who came out here with big bounties, and, of course, has seen more hardships, endured more privations, and suffered more generally than any of the old soldiers ever dreamed of. The boys call them "two hundred dollar men," and they take wicked delight in playing their pranks on them whenever they have a chance. Our boys have no particular grudge against the Jerseys, but their mischief loving propensities must find vent somewhere and the Jersey regiment furnishes them abundant victims. It will be a long time before the boys will allow them to forget the dog scrape we got them into when we tempted them to steal a nicely dressed dog, which was duly served up to their officers in fine style. They stole it out of pure mischief and a desire not to be outstripped in that line of business by our boys; and doubtless it tasted remarkably sweet in consequence, as stolen articles proverbially do, but the joke leaked out, and it will be a long time before they will hear the last of it. It must be very provoking to them to hear the *barking* that springs spontaneously, as it would seem, from our regiment, whenever we pass the Jerseys, but nobody can tell who does it, and the Jerseys have to "grin and bear it." Our boys love to make them visits occasionally, after roll-call at night, and, as they generally come back in high glee, with a mouthful of stories to tell, it may be safely considered that the visit was a pleasant one to at least one of the parties. In one of these nocturnal visits some of our boys, for some reason or other, probably a misunderstanding, got caught, and were put into the guard-house. But the guard-house didn't hold them long. They run the guard and outrun the guard's bullets, and, though the Jerseys did their best, they couldn't imprison them again, nor tell who they were. After that our boys generously offered to stand guard for them, but our services were declined. Some time ago some officers of the Fifth advised the Jerseys to let the Second boys alone or they would find more than they could handle, and the Jerseys are beginning to think it best to accept this advice.

The paymaster made us a visit about a fortnight ago, and this has contributed not a little to keep the boys in good spirits, for there is nothing in the world that will make the boys feel so good-natured as it will to get their pockets lined with Uncle Sam's greenbacks. We received four months' pay. It made quite a little sum for us, but it is easily spent here. Some are beginning to borrow already. While every luxury (we call them luxuries, though any one but soldiers would consider the term "necessaries" more appropriate) that we have to buy rules so high, as here in the army, money is of but little account. For instance: butter is 60 cents a pound, cheese 50 cents a pound, apples 5 cents apiece, papers tobacco at the rate of nearly $3.00 a pound, whiskey $1.00 a drink or $3.00 a bottle, and so on to the end of the chapter. For five dollars a fellow could get a pretty good dinner at the sutler's. It is unnecessary, in order to tell a big story, to quote prices in Jeff's dominions; here in the Union army we can beat the rebs all hollow even in that.

The weather to-day and yesterday, has been remarkably fine. The sun shines clear and pleasant with scarcely a cloud to intervene. A stiff northwest wind has been blowing steadily, in regular April style. In Vermont it would be considered excellent weather to make sugar, as well as to dry the land and prepare it for the plow. Here it is still quite cool, and a sunny side is preferable to a shade for comfort. With this weather Virginia mud must soon disappear. Something besides mud will have to be our excuse for remaining here much longer. There has been some curious rumors afloat to account for our not moving. In the first place Gen. Hooker had broken his leg, by being thrown from a horse, and therefore could not be with the army. Then it was said that he ordered a movement to be made, but the President countermanded the order. Upon this, it is said, Hooker resigned and Fremont was now in command. They are all about equally true, probably. But whether we move or stay, as the boys say "it is all inside of the three years."

Quite a disgraceful affair occurred the other day with the 5th regiment which perhaps I ought to mention. Five or six from Co. D, of that regiment went out to a house near the picket line, for purposes too foul to mention. The guard stationed at the house was relieved, who reported his suspicions of something wrong at the nearest picket reserve. A squad of pickets was immediately sent to arrest the guilty party. They succeeded, but were fired upon and two of their number hit. I do not know the extent of the injuries received. The affair will soon undergo an investigation, and some think the death penalty will be inflicted upon one or more of the culprits.

John Hampden Chamberlayne to Martha Burwell Chamberlayne

On April 27 Hooker began an offensive designed to drive Lee out of his entrenched positions and force him either to retreat toward Richmond or fight on open ground. While Union troops prepared to cross the Rappahannock at Fredericksburg, Hooker sent three corps on a rapid march upriver. By April 30 his flanking force had crossed the Rappahannock and Rapidan rivers and reached Chancellorsville, a crossroads clearing ten miles west of Fredericksburg in the midst of an area of scrub woods and dense undergrowth known as the Wilderness. Lieutenant John Hampden Chamberlayne was a veteran Confederate artillery officer whose battery, like many in Lee's army, had been bivouacked south of Fredericksburg so as to be nearer supplies of food and forage. By the time his unit reached the front on April 30, Union troops had crossed the river just below the city and taken up positions in front of the high ground held by the Confederates.

Camp near Fredericksbg
April 30th 1863 (within 300
yards of that of Dec 12th 1862)

My dear Mother

Yesterday we received very suddenly an order to the front, distance 25 miles; starting with all the inevitable entanglements & delays about 11½ A.M. we marched some till 3 A.M. this morning, some till long after day; my Battery, as it was in the rear of the column, came in last about sunrise; our provisions followed us into camp about 12 M. today—The march was through mud, mud, mud, & cold north east rain, no sleep, no food—You who naturally think much of my hardships should only have seen the boys of my Battery almost falling asleep as they stumbled through the dark clinging mist, yet falling in at the word into knee-deep slush & mud to play at horses and push the guns up on the fagged out brutes—Some oaths and some grumbling but at bottom a will *to do it*—These men, the privates marched the 25 miles through rain, mud, & night,

166

carrying on their backs all their worldly goods & about half the time helping the horses along—The continued embarrassment such as I mention is hardly to be avoided in bad roads filled with long drawn columns of Artillery, every pause in front makes a stop in the whole line & every carriage makes the road worse until the horses to the rear carriages become cold from stopping when warm then grow restive & uncertain & finally often "baulk" (or balk), as we say, at nothing at all.

Does this begin to explain how 100 men can be of use with 4 guns? Add that each gun is drawn by six horses, driven by three drivers postilion fashion & is followed by its caisson or carriage for ammunition with three more drivers, then there are several wagoners for the Battery, a forge driver, two or three mechanics as harness makers, smiths &c, then add for each gun a sergeant & a corporal (a bugler & a flag bearer for the battery), thrown in the chances of 10 per cent being always wounded or sick & you find that 25 to a gun does not more than furnish 10 to 13 actual cannoneers, of which class one brings ammunition from the chest to the gun, one sponges & rams, one keeps the vent or touchhole closed when sponged, one primes, one fires, one aims & all assist to run the piece back when it recoils from the place of fire &c &c.

Your welcome letter reached me yesterday just as we were moving; I wrote you a scrawled line in pencil by Harrison Col. W's servant & sent by him my trunk & key; I have with me all that it is desirable or proper to carry—Please have the things aired &c from time to time—I asked that you would send by Hn the coat &c—, if not it makes little difference Yesterday I did not starve; going by to bid the Woolfolks farewell I was I might say constrained to accept a couple of huge slices of nice bread holding between them ditto meat.

We are all in the utmost spirits & confidence of success— I do not know what to think, whether we will have a battle here or not I hope we will but I am afraid not Yesterday Rhodes' formerly D. H. Hill's Divn was skirmishing; today there has been artillery at long intervals, I do not believe we have fired at all—A. P. Hill is in 1st line of reserve supporting (I believe but am not certain) both Trimble & Early, tomorrow he may be in front, if so we will be with him—I rather believe we will move up tonight or tomorrow toward the left flank toward

Orange Co Ho—My time is short to write now as you may well believe & I find I must hurry.

I have not seen V. or Mann—Hope to do so shortly—I wrote to Sister on Sunday or Monday—Love to her & to bro— Ed— & Hart—John is well, got a letter from his Mother lately, proud of it—

Give my love to all friends, I have not time to name them

And I am & always will be

Your devoted son
J H Chamberlayne

Address (except by Hn) Care Col. Crutchfield Chief Arty Jackson's Corps Army N. Va

Sarah Morgan: Diary, April 30, 1863

Sarah Morgan had fled her home in Baton Rouge, Louisiana, in August 1862 when Confederate forces unsuccessfully attempted to retake the city. She lived for eight months with relatives at Linwood, a plantation five miles northeast of Port Hudson, while her widowed mother stayed in the nearby town of Clinton. Severe food shortages and the prospect of a Union attack on Port Hudson eventually drove Morgan, her sister Miriam, and their mother from northern Louisiana in April 1863. After fruitlessly trying to find refuge in Georgia, Alabama, and Mississippi, they reluctantly decided to move in with Morgan's half brother in Union-occupied New Orleans. In September 1862 Major General Benjamin F. Butler, the Union commander at New Orleans, had ordered that any person who failed to take the oath of allegiance be registered as "an enemy of the United States." Shortly after Morgan arrived in New Orleans, Major General Nathaniel P. Banks, Butler's successor, ordered the expulsion of all registered enemies who remained within Union lines. Morgan wrote about the order on the anniversary of the death of her brother Henry, who had been killed in a duel in New Orleans in 1861.

———————

Thursday April 30th.

Was not the recollection of this day bitter enough to me already? I did not think it could be more so. Yet behold me crying as I have not cried for many and many a day. Not for Harry; I dare not cry for him. I feel a deathlike quiet when I think of him; a fear that even a deep drawn breath would wake him in his grave. And as dearly as I love you, O Hal I dont want you in this dreary world again! Not here, O Hal! Not here! Stay where you can look down on these pitiful mortals and smile at their littleness. But I would not have you among them, Hal! Stay there, where maybe one day God will call me. I will go to you, but dont wish to be back here, Harry. Long long ago I learned to say "Thy will be done," and almost to be thankful you were in your grave. Two years ago to day Hal, you folded your hands and died so quietly and meekly. Two years of trials and hardships have been spared you. Say thank

God, Harry! O safe, safe, in the heaven above pray for us, pity us, miserable creatures that we are!

To day came to us the proclamation which should link the name of Yankee to those of the inhabitants of the lower regions. Talk of the Revocation of the Edict of Nantes! Talk of Louis XIV! Of— Pshaw! my head is in such a whirl that history gets all mixed up, and all paralels seem weak and moderate in comparison to this infamous outrage. To day, thousands of families, from the most respectable down to the least, all who have had the firmness to register themselves enemies to the United States, are ordered to leave the city before the fifteenth of May. Think of the thousands, perfectly destitute, who can hardly afford to buy their daily bread even here, sent to the Confederacy, where it is neither to be earned, nor bought, without money, friends, or a home. Hundreds have comfortable homes here, which will be confiscated to enrich those who drive them out. "It is an ill wind that blows no one good."

Such dismal faces as one meets every where! Each looks heart broken. Homeless, friendless, beggars, is written in every eye. Brother's face is too unhappy to make it pleasant to look at him. True, he is safe; but hundreds of his friends are going forth destitute, leaving happy homes behind, not knowing where the crust of bread for famishing children is to come from to-morrow. He went to Gen. Bowen and asked if it were possible that women and children were included in the order. Yes, he said; they should all go, and go in the Confederacy. They should not be allowed to go elsewhere.

Penned up like sheep to starve! That's the idea! With the addition of forty thousand mouths to feed, they think they can invoke famine to their aid, seeing that their negro brothers dont help them much in the task of subjugating us. And these are the men who cry Liberty, Equality, Fraternity! These are the men who hope to conquer us! Ever unite with them? Never, never! Defenders of Charleston, Savannah, Mobile! *These* are the foes who are striving to overcome you! Deliver your cities in their hands? Die first!

O that from the Atlantic to the Rio Grande their vile footsteps should have been allowed to press our soil! Give up to them? Rather than submit, I would that, all gathered together, we should light our own funeral pyre, and old men, brave soldiers, fair women and tender children should all perish hand in hand in the bright flames we would send up to Heaven as a memorial of our toil, sorrow, and suffering.

If I was a man! O if I was only a man! For two years that has been my only cry, and to day I fairly rave about it. Blood, fire, desolation, I feel ready to invoke all, on these Yankees. Miriam and I are both desperate. If we could only get back, even to Clinton! It seems base treason to remain apparently under the protection of this hateful flag, while all of our own creed and country are sent out to starve. We would endure any thing, if we could only get mother's consent. If she would only stay with Brother, and let us go back to Clinton! For she cannot endure the privations we would have to undergo, while we could stand anything, just to get out of sight of these Yankees again. But she wont listen to it. So we will have to remain patiently here, and consequently labor under the suspicion of belonging to a side we abhor with all our souls. George and Gibbes will be frantic about it. If we could only, only get away!

Evidently, Banks had been whipped in the Attakapas. In spite of his fanfaronade of trumpets, I believe he has been outrageously beaten (as usual) and turns round to punish women and children for his defeat. The "Union" is certainly on its last legs when its generals resort to such means as getting negroes to fight its battles seeing how white men fail, and take to running women and children out of the land. You have roused the Devil in us, Banks! We women will tear you to pieces yet!

Dont care who knows I smuggled in a dozen letters! Wish I had had more!

Samuel Pickens: Diary, May 1–3, 1863

Lee responded to Hooker's flanking maneuver by dividing his already outnumbered army. Leaving 10,000 men to defend Fredericksburg, he sent Jackson and the remainder of his troops to oppose the Union forces advancing from the west. On May 1 the two sides fought at the edge of the Wilderness three miles east of Chancellorsville. When Hooker withdrew his men to defensive positions around the Chancellorsville clearing, Lee and Jackson decided to again divide their forces and seize the initiative. While Lee kept 14,000 men to face the 70,000 Union troops at Chancellorsville, Jackson marched 33,000 troops twelve miles through the Wilderness on May 2 and struck at Hooker's exposed right flank. Private Samuel Pickens had joined the 5th Alabama Infantry in the fall of 1862 and served in Jackson's corps in the division led by Brigadier General Robert E. Rodes. After writing his diary entry for May 3, Pickens was taken prisoner in the fighting around Chancellorsville.

May 1, Friday

It was Bob Price & myself who were sent fr. our Co. as guards to brstwks last eveng. at dark. We were divid. to 3 reliefs & B & I stood 1st—fr. 8 till 11. Had fire in Ditch where a place was cut out for cannon. In eveng. Yanks. threw shell over it & 1 burst just in front of it & piece passd. very near Knowland's head & struck in bank wh. K. got & showed us. We could see our signal lights on eminences on our right & faraway to left— waving occasionally. Bob & I then spread our blankets & lay front of fire expecting to sleep 6 hrs—; but just after lying a little over 3 hrs. we were waked & all the guard orderd to join Regt. wh. we found in line of battle in edge of woods, & then ('bout 2½ or 3 A.M.) movd by left flank & marchd. up the river. Roads were very wet & slippery & bad for mchg. At Hamilton's Crossing we were detained some time by a continuous & it seemed to me then an endless line of troops passing on up river by road into wh. we were then coming. There was the densest fog this morng I ever saw. We made very slow time during the morng. on acct. of the wagons in front stopping frequently. Passed many deserted camps wh. had been occup. during Winter by parts of our army. Halted between 11 & 12 near a house intended for hospital & rested, ate something & filled Canteens. I was very much exhausted & felt sick & faint fr. mching so hard thro' hot sun. Then fell in & loaded & Regts of Brig. moved on. As Col. Sam. B. Pickens of 12 Ala. passed we shook hands—& wished each other a safe passage thro' the impending battle. We then moved on down the road & came into the plank road leading fr. Culpeper C.H.? to Frdksbg. The cannon could be heard all the time firing slowly. Today for 1st time noticed trees budding & putting out new leaves. Stopped on Plank R. & piled up knap sacks & at same time our noble old Genl Robt. E. Lee passed followed by a troop of aids & couriers. He is a well set venerable looking man with white hair & beard. He passed so rapidly that I had not a good chance to see his countenance. Whether it was that he was not generally known by the troops or our silent advance towds scene of action that caused it I dont know, but he passed in silence—no cheering. All who knew him was inspired with the utmost confidence & gazed attentively upon him. We then went on further & stopped little while [   ] right flank in line of battle thro a very thick piece woods [   ] confusion not possible to preserve any thing of a line in such a thick [   ] & soon came to another road nearby [   ] with plank—as hot as could be & nearly broken down. Went by left flank along the road, passed house where there were some of 12 Va who told us they had opened the fight on Wed. & there were some wounded men on litters in yard [   ] Were orderd back a little distance & stopped—I then turned round & went still further up road [   ] wounded & prisoners. In eveng. we made a large circuit thro' woods (Brig.) passg several lines of battle lying in woods & then stopped on brstwks at edge of woods—where we washed & lay down an hour or so & [   ] mch. refreshed. Afterwds stacked arms & went bak for knap-sax —troops & artillery passing fast—men who went bak said saw 1000 troops moving. Jackson we began to see was about makg one of his favorite flank movements. We marchd on up Plank road till betwen. 9 & 10 & halted in field & orchrd. completely

broke down. Had eaten very little but as had only a biscuit left
& no prospect of getg. more concluded to keep it for Brkfst.
Carey brot us biscuits Thurs. morng. at day light & we had a
little smoked beef wh. we had lived on 2 days.

May 2, Saturday

Put down blankets. Jack, Bill Lenier & I slept together *Sat
2nd* [   ] had on the go 18 hrs. yesterday. Allowed to sleep
later than expected after day light. went to branch & took
good wash & made feel fresh. Resumed the march passing
good many troops lying along the road. Stopped to rest a few
min. & gave Matt. Jones ½ biscuit & ate the other & scrap
meat & afterwds 2 or 3 little butter crackers—whole not more
than 1 biscuit. We heard Commiss. wagons had been orderd
up & hoped wd. overtake us but in this we were disappointed.
We heard Yanks. cheering in their formal stiff way & some
boys wished Jackson would come along that we might raise a
cheer. In a little while the word was passed up lines to give way
to left—& there came Glorious old Stonewall at a sweeping
gallop—hat in hand on his sorrel horse followed by aids &
couriers. All long line troops waved hats & cheered long &
loud. I cant describe my feelings at thus seeing him suddenly
for 1st time—but my breast swelled with emotions of pride &
gratification, & all must have felt confident of success when we
shd. meet enemy. Could only see he was a younger lookg man
than I expected to see & not so stout but apparently well
made—blk hair & beard & a little bald spot on back head that
showed plainly after passing. But saw him again when we had
passed enemy's right flank & were getting round in their
rear—he gave some directions in remark. mild & cool manner
as to where he wished our Divis. to go. His hair curls round
edges of his military cap—regular features & very good looking & pleasant countenance.

(Sat. 2nd Cont) We moved on down Plank Road towds river
I think then to the right & were in the rear of Yankees Right,
& from being on Right of our lines—below Fredbg. on Thurs.
we had moved to extreme Left-flanked Yankees & got in rear
of Right of their lines. We formd line battle in woods as front
line & lay down to rest (betwn 3 & 4 P.M.) while 2 other lines
formed in rear of us to support us. When everything was ready

about 6 P.M. wh. was so late that some began to think we might not make the attack till mornig, but we were ordered forwd & had very rough time getting thro' the thick woods. By & by we heard the sharp shooters firing & we started double quick—& most terrific volleys of musketry opened on our right & such was the excitement & the desire to be doing something too, that they commencd firing in our Co. & Regt. & as they were firing around me—altho' I could not see anything & still I thought the Yanks must be there & imagined I saw blue line on opposite hillside in pines & blazed away too. Capt. Williams immediately orderd firing to be stopped that there was nothing to shoot at, & I determd not to be guilty of such folly again & did not shoot unless I had a fair mark. We loaded & started in run yelling & soon saw the blue rascals running like turkeys & our men—shooting, cheering, & pursuing as fast as they could. When Yanks got behind hill or breastwk they would stop & shoot & minute or two—but as our men would come charging upon them they'd be off again. Saw a Y. shot down & as we approached, he jumped up & started again when he was again shot down. One fell standing by tree with but of gun up to signify he surrendered. Col. Hobson called to him to drop his gun & lie down or he'd be killed—he did so & Col. H. told him to go to rear. I soon got separated from entire Co. & looking round could not see one I knew but Col. Hob. & I kept with him—he was waving sword and gallantly leading the men on. Never saw such confusion in my life—men scattered & mixed up every way. It was a running fight & difficulty was to keep near enough to Y. to shoot them. They shot at us very little—only when they'd half a little behind breast wks. (redoubts) Our men from marching all day before & that day & having nothing to eat scarcely—were so much exhausted that great many were scattered along behind a long distance & some excited fellows were firing wildly over the heads of us who were ahead & really there seemed at times as great danger of being killed by our men as by Yks. & several times we'd stop & wait for them to get up in line with us. Some fired without takg. sight up in air & I notices ball strike grd. just in front of us. Some of our men were wounded by our own side. Grt. pity theres so much confusion & men get scattered so badly—several times men were stopped

from firing into friends & I recollect joining in & screaming to
them not to do it—several times I knockd up gun Ice of fellow
in act of doing it. 1st redoubt we advanced on the artillery
stuck out pretty well & threw grape & canister like hail—a
good many of us in edge of pine thicket lay down a minute or
2 but on went our men & a shout told Yanks. were driven on.
Parts of 3 Batteries were captured that eveng. Noticed a large
N. Foundland dog—in agonies of death with a ball hole thro'
him. Some of Y. officers on horsebk. rode along lines & tried
to rally troops but all in vain. we drove them a mile & ½ or
2—till night closed in on the scene. At one time noticed flags
of 2 Regts. close together & mass of men around & fired Ice
or 2ce into them. Passed on down slope & rose another & in
edge of pines there was a horse standing. Hobson started to
it—calling to some men to catch it for him & learned afterwds
he was shot down before getting to it—he was struck in leg
above the knee—fortun. only a flesh wound. I kept on & a
wounded Yank. beckoned & called to me—shook canteen &
offered water, wh. he drank—& askd name & Regt & said he
would be ever mindful of me or somethg of sort—he was a
Lieut, & said wanted to see a Surg. that imposs. & I passed on
keeping as near Thomson with our Colors as could. He had
become separated fr. Regt. or greater part of it. Finally fell in
with Ed. Hutchinson & afterwds with Ch. Hafner & John
Cowin & Jim Arrington. We kept together & went on till near
dark when so exhausted we sat down in pines. Pretty soon
Yanks. opened with battery & shelled woods, & threw grape
everywhere. We could not go forwd or back without greatest
risk & so lay close to ground. It was terrific cannonading—
shell burst & grape cut trees all around & above us. When it
ceased a squad of men came by with some Prisoners & we
started on back to go over field & get some rations as were
very hungry. I had one crack. that had taken fr. Yank. Havre-
sak, going on & divided it with J. Arrington. As we went on
men fr. various Regts. of diff. states were calling the name of
Regt. trying to get together. Never saw such confus. & scattering. Occas. 1 or 2 & sometimes small squad of 5th Ala. fell in
with us, & went on but did n't find any plunder or rations—the
troops behind had swept them. Saw one fellow who. had 3
watches. finally we found out where Col. O'Neal was collect-

ing the Brigade & joined them. Everyone felt so grateful at coming out safely that he would shake each acquaintance warmly by hand & express delight at seeing him come out safely. 5 of our Co. were wounded—Matt Jones, Hausman, Youngblood Sr, S. Jackson & B. Price, also Col. Hobson. Stacked arms, made fires & ate supper wh. was taken fr. Yanks. the best had some time. Crackers, ham & Coffee. Yanks had 8 da. rations with them 5 in kn.sk. & 3 in Haver sk. It seems Rodes Brig. was halted late in eveng. & tried to collect & form it, but I with others had gotten separated way to right & kept on till dark—Met. Col. Pickens of 12th safe. All the boys had trophys fr. Bat. field & well supplied with oil cloths, Blankets, canteens & havresacks &c. Gave me 2 or 3 Yank. letters. Aft. sup. movd up road & to line brst wks, near Hospital. Good deal our artil going fowd. (Cannonading in front & heavy volleys musketry bright pretty night. fightg kept up as men on guard said till 12 or 1 o'clk)

May 3, Sunday

Sprd. blankts & lay on edge entrenchmts with gun & accoutremts. ready to don at moments warng. didn't even pull off boots. Up pretty early & went to spring & washd. wh. refreshg. We were waiting for Cop. Hutchinson to come up with Provision wh. he soon did but bef. could give out enemy began to shell us pretty severely & all took to trench as it wd slacken some fellows wd go up & draw for 2 or 3 around him. Then moved front in piece pines & lay few minutes when orderd forwd.

Jedediah Hotchkiss: Journal, May 2–6, 1863

Major Jedediah Hotchkiss had served on Jackson's staff since March 1862 and become the leading mapmaker in the Army of Northern Virginia. At Jackson's direction, Hotchkiss spent April 30 making maps of the Wilderness and scouting marching routes west of Fredericksburg. The following day he rode to the battlefield near Chancellorsville and distributed his maps to the Confederate division commanders.

———————————

Saturday, May 2nd. The Generals were up at an early hour and had a consultation, in the pines on the top of the hill where the Catherine Furnace road turns from the Plank Road, sitting on Yankee Cracker boxes which the enemy had left there. I went down to Mr. Welford's, where General Stuart had his quarters, and ascertained the roads that led around to the enemy's rear and came back and reported to Generals Lee and Jackson, who consulted and examined the map and then started the Second Corps down by the furnace, Rodes' division in front, and went on to the Brock road, and then up it a piece and into a private road, and so on to the Plank Road and across both Plank Roads to the Old Turnpike and formed our line of battle at the   house and with three lines of battle fell on the enemy's rear at Talley's, at precisely 6 o'clock, and after an infantry fight on our side, of 32 minutes, the enemy using infantry and artillery, we routed them and drove them completely from the field and some three miles beyond, driving them out of two lines of entrenchments and on to some breastworks when it had become dark and by accident our men fired into each other and by that fire General Jackson was wounded, having three balls through his left arm and one through his right hand, having held up both hands to urge our men to desist. The enemy had but a moment before breaking our advance and throwing it into confusion but General J. had rallied it by telling the flying men "Jackson himself calls on you to halt." The enemy took advantage of our mistake and opened a terrific volley of musketry and artillery, sweeping the roads in which our forces had become massed by the dense growth on either side and the swampy nature of the ground. Disorder reigned supreme for a few moments, the "Great Chief" being struck down; but General A. P. Hill, who had rushed to the General's side saying, "I have been trying to make the men cease firing," himself met the advance of the yankee skirmishers then formed a line of men and repulsed them, so saving General J. from capture and he was borne off in a litter by Smith and   . One of those bearing him was struck by a shell in the furious cannonade and the General received a fall. I hastened back for an ambulance and some spirits and found Dr. McGuire and sent him forward. I rode a long ways back, but could find no spirits. Mr. Lacey had left me at Tally's, at dark, and I looked for him in vain. Late at night I found my way back to the Wilderness Tavern, where General Jackson had been taken, and where he was yet in a state of stuper from the shock he had received—, not having rallied enough to have his wounds dressed. At 12, midnight, I started for General Lee's, with young Chancellor as a guide, to inform him of the state of our affairs, making a wide detour, as the enemy had penetrated our lines. I went around and struck the Catharpen road and went on and found General Lee, at his old camp, at 4 A.M., and informed him of what had occurred. Wilbourn had preceded me an hour and informed him of the General's wounds. He was much distressed and said he would rather a thousand times it had been himself. He did not wish to converse about it. I informed him of the situation of the troops and he and Colonel Long consulted and arranged for the morrow. I lay down and slept awhile. He ordered General Stuart, who had taken Jackson's command (General A. P. Hill having been struck on the leg by a shell and disabled for the time), to move around to the right and connect with the left of Anderson who was on General Lee's right and would move to the left of McLaws who was in his front, and so make a connection behind Chancellorsville which the enemy held. I spent a part of the day at General Lee's headquarters copying map, and when the enemy advanced towards the front of General Lee and made a demonstration on the rear of General Jackson's

ordnance train and artillery, near the furnace, Mr. Lacy and
myself went down the Catharpen road and made our way by
the Brock Road to General Jackson's position in time to be
present at the fight. The enemy thought we were retreating
towards Richmond when they fell on our train. They were repulsed by some of the artillery that turned back, but they soon
came on again and were held in check by the 23rd. Georgia
and the Irish Battalion until they surrounded and captured
them after an obstinate struggle, but our train escaped. After
General Jackson was wounded General Hill restored order,
aided by the gallant efforts of Major A. S. Pendleton, and several fierce encounters took place in the night, in all of which
the enemy was repulsed. The day was quite warm and pleasant
—the night clear. The trees are becoming quite green and the
apple and pear trees are in full bloom. Hooker commanded in
person on the yankee side. The musketry was incessant from 6
to 6½ P.M. and as heavy as I ever heard. Our loss was considerable. There was a slight shower in the P.M. and a thunder storm
towards the Blue Ridge during the battle.

Sunday, May 3rd. After breakfasting with General Lee he sent
me back with a message to General Stuart to press the enemy
vigorously and make the junction of our wings. The enemy had
withdrawn from the furnace so I went that way. Our men were
capturing and bringing in the yankee pickets which had been
left out. Anderson was forming his line of battle near the furnace to make the junction of the two wings, as I passed. Gen.
Lee told me to tell General Stuart that he would soon come
there in person. I went on around and down to near Tally's,
and there rested a while, being so sleepy that I could hardly
keep my eyes open. Our forces were pressing forward and
fighting severely. After resting awhile I started on to look for
my friend Boswell, whom I had not seen or heard of since the
fight. I went to where the General was wounded and there I
found him, some 20 steps in advance, by the road-side, dead,
pierced through the heart by two balls and wounded in the
leg. I was completely overcome, although I had expected it
from the state of his mind before, expecting him to be killed in
this fight. His body had been riffled of hat, glass, pistol da-
guerreotype, & c., but his look in death was as peaceful and
pleasant as in life.—I procured an ambulance and took him to

where the General was, at Wilderness Tavern, and with many tears buried him in a grave which I had dug in the family burying ground at Elwood, the home of Major J. Horace Lacey, by the side of General Jackson's arm which had been amputated and buried there. We buried him just as the moon rose, wrapped in his martial coat, Rev. B. T. Lacy making a feeling prayer. Brown, who assisted me, the two men I had employed to dig the grave, Mr. Lacy and myself were all that were present. I wept for him as for a brother; he was kind and gentle and with as few faults as most men. Peace to his memory.

We united the two wings of our army and drove the enemy, by a vigorous and bloody onset, out of his strong works at Chancellorsville and took possession of that place, the loss being very heavy on both sides. Hooker was in the Chancellor house until it was struck by a shell, he then retired to a safer place.

Brown and I slept in the yard at Elwood, on the rich and soft green carpet of its verdant slopes and our weary horses cropped the choice grass. The sight of the dead and wounded today is horrible. Warm and pleasant. A heavy dew in the morning. The woods were on fire in many places and some of the wounded must have been burnt up. Morrison was sent for Mrs. Jackson.

Monday, May 4th. Mr. Lacy aroused me up at an early hour to guide the ambulance with General Jackson and Colonel Crutchfield to Guiney's Station. I saddled up and we soon got off, going by the Brock Road to Todd's Tavern and then to Spotsylvania C. H. and on to Guiney Station. The General stood the ride very well. We passed crowds of wounded men going the same way, all cheerful and each one wishing himself the badly wounded one instead of General Jackson.—The day was quite pleasant but we had a thunder storm late in the evening. Our forces fell on the enemy today and drove them from Marye's Hill which they had taken from us, and drove them up the River; so we now have the old town again. We found the cavalry camp at Spotsylvania C. H. and the country full of wild rumors about the Yankee cavalry raids to Richmond, cutting our communications, etc. I found that our wagons at Guiney's had been sent away to avoid capture and were back again in alarm. Found Col. French at Guiney's, he having been on the train that was captured near Ashland. He said the enemy was at Chickahominy Bridge and there was nothing to keep them from Richmond & c. That the enemy had destroyed much of the Virginia Central Railroad and that Stoneman was behaving very well. Col. F. slept with me. General Jackson stood the ride very well. I washed and cleaned up and got some sleep. General Jackson came to Guiney's by General Lee's advice.

Tuesday, May 5th. We were roused up before day by a report that the enemy was coming—, that is—his cavalry, and the wagons were hitched up to depart; so I got on my horse and went over to see the General; found him cheerful, although he had not rested much; bade him good-by. He said he hoped to be soon in the field again and sent his regards to General Lee. I went by Mr. Alsop's and breakfasted with him, then on to near Fredericksburg and across to the plank road and thence on to General Lee's headquarters near Chancellorsville. I ascertained that he wanted the roads to the United States Ford, so went back by the furnace to get them and on to Mr. Stevens', where, in the P.M., there was a heavy thunder storm. After which I went on to Mr. Bullock's, a mile beyond Wilderness Run and learned from him about the roads, & c. Some young men came after him for a guide. We went to bed for a short time.

We fought the enemy near Salem Church yesterday. It was cool in the morning; the rain made the mud very deep. We have many thousand Yankee prisoners at Guiney's.

Wednesday, May 6th. We were up at 3 A.M. and off to camp. I found Gen. Stuart near Chancellorsville, asleep, the division of Gen. Rodes about moving to the enemy's right flank to dislodge him from his strong position between Chancellorsville and United States Ford. General Stuart sent me on to General Lee and told me to tell him he was satisfied the enemy was retreating. I found General Lee at his old camp and just dressing. He did not much credit the report of the enemy's retreat, and, after a cup of coffee, sent me back to tell General Stuart to press on the movement to our left. General Lee soon came up and he and General Stuart had a consultation, with the map, about the roads I had ascertained. General A. P. Hill soon came up and joined them. It rained nearly all of last night, hard, and most of to-day. It was soon ascertained that the enemy had retreated, leaving five lines of strong entrenchments which they had just thrown up. We followed them closely but they had availed themselves of the rain and darkness to make good their escape, and the mud, and the immense advantage secured to them by the other bank for artillery, prevented our doing them much damage, though we took a good many prisoners.

We spent most of the day near Chancellorsville. Orders were given for the forces to go back to their old camps. General Lee directed me to make a map of the battlefield, then General Stuart and then General A. P. Hill to whom I had reported. Late in the evening General A. P. Hill's wagons started back towards our old quarters. I went on and waited for them, but they did not come, so I started to go to Colonel Smith's quarters, but the rain, mud and darkness made me halt in a Miss. camp, where I was kindly entertained by the Sergeant of the 12th., and got a good night's rest. It has rained heavily and is quite cold.

Taylor Peirce to Catharine Peirce

Grant crossed the Mississippi with more than 20,000 men at Bruinsburg, thirty miles southwest of Vicksburg, on April 30. The following day his advancing forces engaged 6,000 Confederates under Brigadier General John S. Bowen at Port Gibson in a battle that cost each side about 800 men killed, wounded, or missing. One of the Union soldiers who fought at Port Gibson was Taylor Peirce of the 22nd Iowa Infantry, whose regiment had been sent in March from Missouri to Louisiana to serve in the Thirteenth Corps of the Army of the Tennessee.

Head Quarters 22 Iowa Inftry
Port Gibson Mississippi May 4th 1863
    Dear Catharine & all of you,
I have set down to write to you knowing that you would hear of our battle and would be very anxious about me and as soon as I found that I could send a letter I concluded to do so. On the 29th day of April we tried the experiment of bombarding the fort at Grand Gulf with the view of landing our forces at that place but the fort was impregnable being hewn out of the rock and after six hours cannonading it was found impossible to silence their guns. So the Genl concluded to run the blockade with the Transports and as they kept along side of the Steamboats and kept up such a continual roar of cannon that they did not get to injure one of them and there was not a life lost. So we were then marched down the river on the La side three miles below where we encamped for the night. Early the next morning we were then on board. There was 3 divisions one under Genl Carr one under Genl Hovey and one under Genl Ousterhouse. The whole under Comd of Genl McClernand. The whole number of men amounted to about 20 or 25 thousand men and said to be the finest army that has ever been together. We were taken down the river on the 30th of April about 10 miles to Rodney where after feeling for the

rebles and finding none we landed and drew 3 day rations and
left about 3 oclock P.M. for this place. We marched out about 6
miles and halted and eat supper. In about an hour we started
again. Our brigade being in advance we moved along sloly
expecting every minute to hear our advance Guard fire on the
reble pickets. About one oclock at night the long expected sound
was heard. After some pretty sharp firing we were opened on
by the reble battery which they had placed to rake us as we
come up a lane but oweing to our caution and silence we had
passed our whole brigade along the lane before they were
aware of it. As soon as the battery opened on us we halted and
laid down untill Harry Griffith come up with his six pieces of
cannon. As soon as he got them fixed we were moved on the
double quick around behind it into the head of a ravine where
we all laid down and at it they went and kept it up untill near
daylight when the rebles ceased to fire and we laid and slept
on our arms untill sunrise. We were all tired and anxious when
the morning came knowing that the rebles would contest the
ground to the utmost. Our regiment was ordered to support
the battery through the night and of course we lay right
where the ball and shell flew and if a man has weak nerves
then is the time he will be likely to feel it haveing to stand inactive. And the roar of the guns and this whissing of ball and
bursting of shell is terrible but thank fortune I am not of the
weak nerved kind and did not suffer from that sickning failing
called fear and am very thankfull that I am so constituted that
I do not.

Well after about an hours suspence waiting to see where the
attack was to come from as the rebles were concealed in the
cane breaks and gullies we sent a challange to them in the shape
of a shell and imediately they opened on us in earnest the ball
for the May party was opened. Our forces was in three divisions. Our regt under Carr with 21 & 23 Iowa the 8th & 18
Indianna & 11 Wisconsin formed the right wing of the army.
Genl Hovey the centre. I do not know what troops he had.
Genl Osterhouse was on the left. I suppose our lines were 3
miles in extent and the rebles under Genl Green Stacy &
Bowen all under Genl Baldwin attacked all three of our divisions at once about 7 oclock in the morning and attempted to
surround us. The Battle became general abot 9 oclock and

continued without intermission untill about 1 pm when our division made charge and the rebles gave way and retreated across the Bayou burning the bridge. That left us at liberty to go in on the Centre which we did and after some pretty hard fighting the rebles broke and run and Osterhaus had got through with his work and by sunset the whole reble army was in full flight and our victory complete. This is said to be the most unfortunate battle of the war for them. They came down in the morning with about 13,000 fresh troops boasting that they would just capture the d—d Yankee and make slaves of them. They retreated in the evening a defeated and dispairing rabble without order leaveing about 3,500 of their men behind them. The slaughter on their side was dreadful for the number engaged although they had the advantage of knowing the ground and kept hid in the cane breaks all the time just standing far enough in to keep out of sight so that they could fire out at us. But our English rifles sent their Leaden messengers in and thinned their ranks as if the plague was amongst them. Harry Griffith with his first Iowa battery tore their ranks from end to end. He is as brave as Ney. All night long we could hear him giving his commands with a clear loud voice and urging his men to give it to them while he sat or moved round amongst the guns on his horse amid a perfect shower of grape canister and shell as though it was but a May shower of rain instead of a shower of iron and seemed as unconcious of danger as when he used to walk the streets of Des Moines. Indeed our Officers all showed a bravery that was sublime. Not one of them but seemed that on his coolness and example before the men depended the fate of the battle.

Our loss is small. Our regiment was more exposed than any other but it come of the best except the 23. Our regt lost 3 killed and 12 wounded. 2 of the wounded are mortally. The rest will all get well. The 23d met the 23d Alabama and after about an hours hard fighting put them to flight. What the loss is in the 23 Iowa I have not learned certain but not much. I suppose 30 killed & wounded will cover the loss. The 23 Alabama left 360 Dead in the field or rather in the cane breaks and I suppose a number that was not discovered. We took some thing over 500 prisoners and been gathering them up ever since. I guess we will not have far short of 7 hundred. I heard we got 12 of their guns but I do not know whether it is correct or not. I do not know what the official report is but you will see it and the comments on it before you get this. We had one man wounded and none killed. Cap Ault showed considerable courage and behaved much better than I expected he would. Our Lts are good men and true and Col Stone showed us what he was as brave as he is good by the way they talk of making him governor of Iowa. Although I do not want to lose him from our regt yet I would like to see him at the head of the affairs of the State for he would give the copperheads hell and I want you to do all you can for him to get him in there. If there is a man in the world deserving it is him. Lt Col Glasgow is another here. Although I was a quarter of a mile from him I could hear him shouting to his men and telling them to give to the damd rebles and well his men obeyed him. Genl McClernand remained on the field all the time of the battle and actually sighted some of the guns himself. Old Grant heard us fighting and come on to the field about 11 oclock and when the victory was complete you ought to have heard the shout that rung out on the evening air. It was enough to pay us for all our fatigue and dangers. I am well and stouter than I have been for years although I had gone 48 hours without sleep and had to eat my meat raw with hard crackers and water and twice a little tea and marched with 40 pounds and my gun and 80 rounds of cartrige. I was able to fight the whole day among the cane breaks and ravines with the thermomater up to 90 without anything to eat. I walked 2 miles for my supper and back again on to the battle field when we lay and you had better believe I slept sound that night. After we got a little breakfast we all started after the retreating rebles but they had burned the bridges. And so we had to stop and make a bridge across bayou peirie when Genl Quinbys brigade started after them at 3 oclock P.M. of the 2 and Osterhaus and Smiths Divisions started at one oclock in the morning.

At 7 oclock we started for Grand Gulf to take the forces there and capture the battery by land but the rebs were to smart for us for they evacuated. And so we are laying now about 2 miles west SW of Port Gibson and 6 miles from Grand Gulf awaiting orders. I understand the rebs will make a stand at willow springs 18 miles from here. But I think they have either been whipped or they have not stopped there or else we would have been ordered up to assist in the fight. If they do not make a stand there they will evacuate Vicksburgh without a fight. I have just learned that the 23d lost 7 men killed and 24 wounded. Smith is safe and all the rest that you are acquainted with. Our forces engaged was abot 7,000. The rebs about 10,000. Our whole force could not get up in time to help us. I must quit as my paper is done.

Your afft Taylor

Catherine Edmondston:
Diary, May 5–7, 9, and 11–12, 1863

On May 3 Lee's army drove Union forces from the Chancellorsville clearing after several hours of intense fighting. As Hooker withdrew to a new defensive position close to the Rappahannock, Lee learned that Union troops under Major General John Sedgwick had captured Marye's Heights at Fredericksburg and were advancing on Chancellorsville. Leaving about 20,000 men to face Hooker, Lee attacked Sedgwick on May 4 at Salem Church, four miles west of Fredericksburg. After an inconclusive battle, Sedgwick withdrew across the Rappahannock on the night of May 4–5. Hooker retreated across the river the following night, ending a campaign in which the Union lost about 17,000 men killed, wounded, or missing, and the Confederates about 13,000. Catherine Edmondston followed reports of the fighting from her plantation home in Halifax County, North Carolina.

MAY 5, 1863

News last night principally rumours. The enemy under General Stoneman have made a dash into our lines and emulous of Stuart have penetrated into the heart of Va, cutting Telegraph wires, tearing up R R tracks, but as I do not know whether the particulars are authentic I will wait until they are confirmed. Rumour has it that we fought on Sunday the 3d & repulsed the enemy at every point save one & took five thousand prisoners. Stonewall Jackson and A P Hill both wounded, the first slightly, the latter severely, but we do not know whether it be true or not; in fact we do not know that there has been a fight—not even a Telegram. Matters in the West more confused than ever. I cannot keep up with them—a skirmish here at some unpronounceable unheard of before name in which we are successful & another there at some equally unknown place from which we retire. Morgan, Van Dorn, and Forrest destroy R R Bridges & tear up tracks until one would think there were none left to be destroyed. They capture one waggon train only to make room for another, but our eyes are bent now on Fredericksburg & Gen Lee. God grant him the victory. Rachel Jones came to make us a visit last night.

MAY 6, 1863

News of a Victory at Fredericksburg! Hooker is repulsed & is in retreat. More than that we cannot tell, but that fills our hearts with grateful praise. Lee telegraphs that by "the blessing of God we have gained a great Victory"—10,000 prisoners are captured, no details of our loss in either killed or Wounded. The Cavalry expedition sent out to beat up our quarters carry dismay and surprise to an unexpectant country. They have torn up the R R track between Gordonsville & Richmond, stolen horses, & captured an old engine. Beyond that they have effected nothing, but the insult is great & a burning shame which must be wiped out in blood ere it can be atoned. One of the Col's, one Davis, boasts that he is a Virginian, is familiar with the country over which he has often fox hunted! More shame to him a traitor & a renegade! Their movements are wrapped in obscurity, & they have cut the Telegraph wires so that our intercourse with the Army is destroyed for the present. The next news we hear of them will, I hope, be that they are all in the Libby Prison, but it is the most daring thing the Yankees have as yet attempted & should put us on our guard against despising our enemy.

Where is Stuart? "One blast upon his bugle horn were worth ten thousand men." Where is he that he allows the Abolitionists thus to career through our lines & pluck his Laurels unwithered from his brow?

MAY 7, 1863

News from the Rappahanock! A victory, tho dearly bought! The Abolitionists crossed, as I before stated, about 15 miles above Fredericksburg after making a feint at that point. He strongly entrenched that wing of his army which rested upon the River, but Jackson making a rapid march got into his rear beyond Chancellorsville whilst Lee made an attack in point at that point. Thus pressed, his left Flank was doubled up upon his right which lay on the River (the Rapid Ann) which he crossed in great confusion, the slaughter being terrific. In the mean time Early who had been left in command of Fredericksburg & the intrenchments there was attacked by over whelming odds under Gen Sedgwick (I wonder if he is any kin of mine) & driven from the post, Sedgwick even gaining Marye's Hill. But let me tell the rest in Lee's own words—"At the close of the battle of Chancellorsville on Sunday the enemy was reported as advancing from Fredericksburg in our rear. General McLaws was sent back to arrest his progress & repulsed him handsomly that afternoon. Learning that this corps consisted of his corps under General Sedgwick I determined to attack it & marched back yesterday with General Anderson & uniting with McLaws & Early in the afternoon, succeeded by the blessing of Heaven in driving Gen Sedgewick over the River. We have reoccupied Fredericksburg, & no enemy remains south of the Rappahanock in its vicinity." Dated May 5th.

Hooker is on the South bank of the Rappahanock, reported as entrenching & receiving reinforcements, but he is a beaten man. His prestige is gone and to God are our praises due. "With His own right hand and His holy arm hath He gotten Himself the victory." Fill our hearts with grateful praise, and may we as a nation ascribe unto God the praise due unto His name.

Jackson's wound was in this wise. At midnight on Saturday night, his troops being drawn up in line of battle, a body of men were seen a short distance in advance of our line. It being doubtful whether they were friends or enemies, Gen Jackson & staff rode forward to reconnoitre. Whilst thus engaged, his own men being unaware of his movements, mistook himself & staff for enemies & fired a volley into them instantly killing one & severely wounding Gen Jackson & Major Crutchfield. One ball struck his left arm below the elbow & ranging upwards shattered the bone near the shoulder. Another passed through his right hand. He instantly fell to the ground. His brother in Law laid down by his side to ascertain what were his wounds. In a moment the unknown troops in front who proved to be the enemy advancing captured two of his staff who were standing over him without, however, perceiving him. A stretcher was procured & four of his men were bearing him to the rear when they were all shot down. His arm has been amputated above the elbow, and the injury to his right hand is severe, one of the bones having been shot away, but it is beleived that he will recover the use of it. He is reported as doing well & Mrs Jackson—who was in Richmond has joined him. He is a heavy loss to us & the Yankees will think their defeat cheaply purchased with his life. Of course they will say that his men did it purposely & that they were demoralized—but who will beleive them?

The Cavalry raid in the vicinity of Richmond is most annoying & insulting, but they have done but little real damage besides destroying a span of the R R Bridge over the Chickahominy & delaying our communication with Fredericksburg. The damage will soon be repaired, but the additional suffering to our wounded is a serious consideration. They captured an ambulance train, destroyed the engine & paroled the wounded. A young lady having heard of their advance informed Col Duke of Wise's Legion who was, with a small detachment of men—infantry, fortunately within reach. He placed his men on the train & reached Tunstall's at the very moment that they did. Taking them thus by surprise, he killed several & captured fifteen of the marauders. They came within two miles of Richmond, stealing Mr John Young's horse from before his door in his sight. He, poor man, offered no resistance thinking Gen Lee was beaten and that this was the advance of Hooker's army. He had no time for "an abstraction" then, fond as he used to be of them.

May 9, 1863

Gen Lee's dispatch to the President dated Chancellorsville May 7th tells us that "After driving Sedgewick across the Rappahanock on the night of the 4th I (he) returned on the 5th to Chancellorsville. The march was delayed by a storm which continued all night and the following day. In placing the troops in position on the morning of the 6th to attack Gen Hooker, it was ascertained that he had abandoned his fortified position. The line of skirmishers was pressed forward until they came in range of the enemies batteries planted on the north of the Rappahanock which from the configuration of the ground completely commanded this side. His army, there-fore, escaped with the loss of a few additional prisoners." Signed R E Lee, General. So he is gone, driven back, beaten ignominiously by a far inferior force, for we had but 80,000 (eighty thousand) men all told, whilst he has 158,000 (one hundred and fifty eight). Our loss is stated on the best author-ity now attainable at nine hundred killed & six thousand wounded many of them slightly so. We lost some prisoners, but all told killed, wounded, prisoners, and missing—eight thousand covers it. Theirs is estimated at thirty thousand. We have nine thousand prisoners! We took fifty three canon & lost five on Marye's Hill, belonging to the Washington Artillery. The no of muskets captured & picked up on the battlefield is enormous. Were Lee now to advance, a large part of Hooker's Army could not fight for want of a weapon. They are piled by the side of the R R track—a wonder to the beholder. The en-emies loss in generals is heavy, including the infamous Sickles. Six are enumerated, but they are not of consequence enough to interest me. We lose one—Gen Paxton—in command of the old Stonewall Brigade. We have lost several Colonels, but as yet the details are not published. Stoneman is reported as en-camped in heavy force near Gordonsville. Ah that we could capture him! No news of importance from the West. Van Dorn is dead, but how we hear not. Forrest, Wheeler, & Morgan continue to annoy Rosencrans & capture his marauding par-ties. In Louisianna we have had a repulse. At Grand Gulf Gen Taylor was forced to retreat, which he did fighting, after two days battle. He had 3000, the enemy 20,000 men, yet he came off in good order, bringing guns & stores. One waggon (whose mule gave out) only was captured. Our loss not heavy. All quiet before Vicksburg.

MAY 11, 1863

Went out Hascosea after dinner with Mr E on horseback. Everything is terribly backward there. The garden wants work & the flowers resent the neglect by refusing to bloom. A little girl ran out from the house of one of our neighbours & stopped us to ask for some flowers for their May party next

Friday. Promised to send them, much to her gratification. Ah! me what happiness have May Queen's conferred on me in times gone by & what a contrast to the times does a Queen of May now present.

The mail came in after tea & heavy news it brought us. A chill went through my heart as Mr Edmondston unfolded the paper & I saw that it was in mourning. I felt that Jackson was dead! & so it proved! He died of pneumonia on Sunday the 10th, eight days after the amputation of his arm, died in the fulness of his reputation, the brightness of his glory, a Christian patriot, unselfish, untiring, with no thought but for his country, no aim but for her advancement. I have no heart to write more, tho the paper is full of news. I care for nothing but him. It is as tho a Divine voice has said again "Little children keep yourselves from idols." He was the nation's idol, not a breath even from a foe has ever been breathed against his fame. His very enemies reverenced him. God has taken him from us that we may lean more upon *Him*, feel that He can raise up to Himself instruments to work His Divine Will.

MAY 12, 1863

Woke up this morning with a sense of a heavy misfortune. Asked myself what had happened & remembered that Jackson was dead! Omitted to write yesterday that my nephew Thomas Jones had brought his wife to fathers. We go up to see her this morning. I shall offer her a home until the war is ended—for she cannot return into the lines of the hated enemy & since Hill's repulse at Washington, they have grown more stringent & oppressive. The papers are full of McClellan's & Burnside testimony respecting the command & conduct of the Army of the Potomac. I take little interest in any of them, or anything they say. They only offer an additional proof, if proof were wanting, that neither Lincoln, Halleck, Stanton, McClellan, Burnside, or Hooker understand the first principles of a gentleman. Deficient alike in self respect & respect for each other, they know not what is due themselves from their subordinates, or their subordinates from their own hands. Faugh! they disgust me, a set of cold blooded quill drivers. They have neither the instincts or the impulses of gentlemen.

Charles F. Morse to His Family

Captain Charles F. Morse joined the 2nd Massachusetts Infantry in 1861 and became a close friend of Robert Gould Shaw. He fought at Front Royal, Cedar Mountain, and Antietam before being appointed provost marshal of the Twelfth Corps in February 1863. During the Chancellorsville campaign Morse served as an aide to Major General Henry W. Slocum, the commander of the Twelfth Corps.

STAFFORD C. H., May 7, 1863.

I am going to give you, without any introduction, a history of this last campaign against Richmond by the army under the great Joe Hooker. I believe I have seen it and judged it fairly.

On Monday, April 27th, our corps broke camp early in the morning and marched to Hartwood Church, ten miles; there it went into camp for the night. The Eleventh and Fifth Corps also came up there and camped in our vicinity; next morning, we all moved and camped that night near Kelly's Ford. A pontoon bridge was thrown across and the Eleventh was over before daylight Wednesday; the other corps followed rapidly and the advance began towards the Rapidan. The Eleventh and Twelfth marched on the road to Germana Ford, the Fifth on the road to Ely's Ford; all three of the corps were under command of General Slocum. I was detailed, the morning of the advance, as Aide to General Slocum, and another officer was made Acting Provost Marshal. All the companies of the Second Massachusetts were sent to the Regiment. We skirmished all the way to Germana Ford; there we met quite a determined resistance; our cavalry was drawn in and the Second Massachusetts and the Third Wisconsin sent forward to clear the way; they drove everything before them and, by their heavy fire, forced the rebels at the Ford to surrender (about one hundred officers and men). We lost in this skirmish about a dozen killed and wounded.

General Slocum now determined to cross the Rapidan,

though there was no bridge and the ford was almost impassable. He sent the First and Third Brigade, (First Division,
Twelfth Corps), through the water although it was more than
waist deep, also five batteries of artillery, which took position
on the other side of the river. A bridge was then constructed,
and before daylight Thursday morning, the remainder of the
Twelfth and Eleventh Corps were across the river. By eight
o'clock, A.M., we were moving again. The rebels kept attacking
us on our flank with cavalry and artillery, and any less bold officer than General Slocum would have halted his column and
delayed the march; but he kept along steadily, detaching a
small force at intervals to repel the enemy. I had the pleasure
of superintending, at one of these skirmishes, having in charge
the Twenty-ninth Pennsylvania Regiment; we drove the rebels
before us for nearly a mile, almost capturing their artillery, taking a large number of prisoners. At about noon, we arrived at
Chancellorsville, and found the Fifth Corps already there. We
had a small cavalry skirmish, in which Colonel McVicars was
killed with about a dozen of his men, but besides that, nothing
of importance occurred that day; the troops were formed in
line of battle, but were not attacked. Up to this time you see
everything had gone well and success seemed certain.

Towards night, General Hooker arrived with his staff, and
we heard of the crossing at the U. S. Ford of the Second, Third
and First Corps. All the headquarters were in the vicinity of
the Chancellor House, a large, fine brick mansion. General
Hooker took supper with General Slocum; he didn't seem to
be able to express his gratification at the success of General
Slocum in bringing the three corps up so rapidly. Then, in the
most extravagant, vehement terms, he went on to say how he
had got the rebels, how he was going to crush them, annihilate
them, etc.

The next morning at ten, the Fifth and Twelfth Corps advanced in order of battle on two parallel roads; we soon met
the enemy and skirmished for about two miles, when they appeared in considerable force and the battle began. We were in
a splendid position and were driving the enemy when an order
came to General Slocum to retire his command to its former
position. No one could believe that the order was genuine, but
almost immediately, another of General Hooker's staff brought

the same order again. Now, perhaps, you don't know that to
retire an army in the face of an enemy when you are engaged,
is one of the most difficult operations in war; this we had to
do. I carried the order to General Geary to retire his division
in echelon by brigades, and stayed with him till the movement
was nearly completed. It was a delicate job; each brigade would
successively bear the brunt of the enemy's attack. Before the
last brigades of the Fifth and Twelfth Corps were in position,
the enemy made a furious attack on the Chancellor House;
luckily, we had considerable artillery concentrated there and
they were driven back. The next attack was on our corps, but
the enemy were severely repulsed. This about ended the fighting on Friday; we lost, I suppose, about five hundred men.

During the night, the men were kept at work digging
trenches and throwing up breastworks of logs. Our headquarters were at Fairview, an open piece of ground rising into quite
a crest in the centre. Skirmishing began at daylight next morning and continued without much result to either side, till
afternoon, when the enemy began to move, in large force, towards our right, opposite General Howard, Eleventh Corps.
This corps was in a fine position in intrenchments, with almost
open country in front of them, the right resting on Hunting
creek. At about four P.M., the Third Corps, General Sickles,
was moved out to the right of the Twelfth and advanced towards Fredericksburgh. The order then came to General Slocum that the enemy were in full retreat, and to advance his
whole line to capture all he could of prisoners, wagons, etc.
Our right, General Williams' Division, advanced without much
trouble, driving the enemy before it, but the Second Division
had hardly got out of the trenches before it was attacked with
great determination, yet it steadily retained its position. At
about five P.M., a tremendous and unceasing musketry fire
began in the direction of the Eleventh Corps. As it was necessary to know what was going on there in order to regulate the
movements of the Twelfth Corps, General Slocum and the rest
of us rode for our lives towards this new scene of action. What
was our surprise when we found, that instead of a fight, it was
a complete Bull Run rout. Men, horses, mules, rebel prisoners,
wagons, guns, etc., etc., were coming down the road in terrible
confusion, behind them an unceasing roar of musketry. We

rode until we got into a mighty hot fire, and found that no one was attempting to make a stand, but every one running for his life. Then General Slocum dispatched me to General Hooker to explain the state of affairs, and three other staff officers to find General Williams and order him back to his trenches with all haste.

I found General Hooker sitting alone on his horse in front of the Chancellor House, and delivered my message; he merely said, "Very good, sir." I rode back and found the Eleventh Corps still surging up the road and still this terrible roar behind them. Up to this time, the rebels had received no check, but now troops began to march out on the plank road and form across it, and Captain Best, Chief of Artillery of our corps, had on his own responsibility gathered together all the batteries he could get hold of, had put them in position (forty-six guns in all) on Fairview, and had begun firing at the rate of about one hundred guns a minute, into the rebels. This, in my opinion, saved our army from destruction. After delivering my message to General Hooker, I went back and tried to find General Slocum, but it was now after eight o'clock and I was unsuccessful in my search, so I took hold and tried to rally some of the cowardly Dutchmen. With the help of one cavalry orderly, I succeeded in forming a good many of them on the left of the new line, but an unusually heavy volley coming, they broke and ran like sheep. After this little episode, I again searched after the General. Towards ten, I found the rest of the staff, and soon after, we came across the General. At about eleven, the fighting stopped, but we were all hard at work getting the men of our corps into position. You see, while our First Division was advancing, the rebels had routed the Teutons and were now occupying our trenches. The Second and Third Brigades got into their former position, but the First made out only to cut through the rebels, losing a large part of its men and taking a position considerably in the rear of its former one. General Sickles fought his way through with the exception of one division and one battery, which were left out in front of our lines that night. The artillery men were hard at work all night, throwing up traverses to protect their guns, and about two in the morning we all lay down on the ground and slept until about four, when daylight began to appear. Our right was now formed by the Third, Fifth and First Corps, about five hundred yards in the rear of our first position. The rebels began the attack, as soon as there was light enough, from the left of our First Division to about the right of the Third Corps. General Birney's Division of the Third Corps was out in front of General Williams; his men behaved badly, and after a slight resistance, fell back into our lines, losing a battery.

The rebels now charged down our First Division, but were met with such a deadly fire that they were almost annihilated. Their second line was then sent in, but met the same fate, and their third and last line advanced. Our men now had fired more than forty rounds of cartridges and were getting exhausted. General Slocum sent almost every one of his staff officers to General Hooker, stating his position and begging for support; Hooker's answer was, "I can't make men or ammunition for General Slocum." Meantime, Sickles' Corps was holding its own on the right of ours, but it was rapidly getting into the same condition as the Twelfth. The rebels were driven back every time they advanced, and we were taking large numbers of prisoners and colors. All this time while our infantry was fighting so gallantly in front, our battery of forty-six guns was firing incessantly. The rebels had used no artillery till they captured the battery from Birney, when they turned that on us, making terrible destruction in General Geary's line. General Meade, Fifth Corps, now went to Hooker and entreated that he might be allowed to throw his corps on the rebel flank, but General Hooker said, "No, he was wanted in his own position." On his own responsibility, General Meade sent out one brigade, which passed out in rear of the enemy's right, recaptured a battery, three hundred of our men who were prisoners, and four hundred of the rebels, and took them safely back to their corps.

It was now after seven o'clock. Our men had fired their sixty rounds of cartridges and were still holding their position; everything that brave men could do, these men had done, but now nothing was left but to order them to fall back and give up their position to the enemy. This was done in good order and they marched off under a heavy fire to the rear of our batteries. The rebels, seeing us retreating, rushed forward their artillery and began a fearful fire. I found I could be useful to

Captain Best, commanding our artillery, so I stayed with him. I never before saw anything so fine as the attack on that battery; the air was full of missiles, solid shot, shells, and musket balls. I saw one solid shot kill three horses and a man, another took a leg off one of the captains of the batteries. Lieutenant Crosby of the Fourth Artillery was shot through the heart with a musket ball; he was a particular friend of Bob Shaw and myself; he lived just long enough to say to Captain Best, "Tell father I die happy."

The rebels came up to the attack in solid masses and got within three hundred yards, but they were slaughtered by the hundreds by the case-shot and canister, and were given back to the woods. Still not an infantry man was sent to the support of the guns. More than half the horses were killed or wounded; one caisson had blown up, another had been knocked to pieces; in ten minutes more, the guns would have been isolated. They, too, therefore, were ordered to retire, which they did without losing a gun. You see, now, our centre was broken, everything was being retired to our second line, the rebel artillery was in position, their line of battle steadily advancing across our old ground. This fire of the batteries was concentrated on the Chancellor House, Hooker's original headquarters, and it was torn almost to pieces by solid shot and was finally set on fire by a shell.

The army was now put in position in the second line; the centre was on a rising piece of ground and protected by a battery of forty or fifty guns. The Fifth Corps was on the right and was the last to fall back out of the woods and it was closely followed by the rebel masses, but these were met by such a tremendous artillery fire that they were actually rolled back into the woods. Our corps was ordered to support first the Third, afterwards the Second and Eleventh. Towards night the enemy made another desperate assault on our centre, but they were again repulsed. Our corps was now ordered to the extreme left to form behind the Eleventh. I believe that General Slocum remonstrated with General Hooker so firmly that he finally got permission to put the Twelfth Corps on the extreme left and to have only one division of the Eleventh in the trenches on his right.

You can easily see that, if the enemy once forced our right or left, our communications would at once be cut and all possibility of retreat prevented. Late that night, we lay down close beside the Rappahannock. By three o'clock next morning, we were awakened by a heavy artillery fire and shells bursting over us. Our guns replied and kept at it for about an hour, when the enemy's batteries were silenced. We now mounted our horses and rode along the lines to look at our position; we found that it was a very strong one and capable of being made very much more so.

We found that the sharpshooters were getting altogether too attentive to our party, so we moved back to our line and had hardly turned away, when a sergeant was shot dead almost on the spot where the general had been standing. All that day, our men were hard at work throwing up breastworks, cutting abattis, etc. No attack was made on us, but throughout that day and night, we heard Sedgwick fighting in the direction of Fredericksburgh.

Tuesday morning, I knew by appearances that a retreat was to be effected, as a large part of the artillery, all the ambulances, etc., were removed across the river, although the men were kept at work making line after line of trenches and breastworks. Just before dark, the order of retreat came, the Fifth and Twelfth Corps being the last to cross. About four o'clock that afternoon it began to rain in torrents. There were originally three pontoon bridges, but before most of the crossing had been effected, the river became so swollen that one of the bridges had to be taken up to piece out the other two; this caused a great delay. At about twelve, I was sent down to the ford to examine into the condition of things; it was a terrible night, the wind blowing a gale and the rain pouring, the road for a mile full of artillery. I found, at the bridge, that not a thing was moving, and learned from General Patrick that the order for retreat had been suspended and everything was to move back to its former position. This order came, remember, when half of the artillery was on the north side of the Rappahannock, the soldiers without a ration and the supply trains ten miles the other side of the river. I ran my horse back to headquarters and made my report; the telegraph was down between U. S. Ford and Falmouth, *where General Hooker was.* General Slocum wrote a dispatch, saying, that unless the movement was continued, our army would have to be surrendered within twenty-four hours; this was sent by an orderly who was ordered to kill his horse carrying it. Then to prepare for the worst, General Slocum sent one of his aides and myself back to the Ford to get our artillery ready to move back into position, that our corps might, at least, be ready to make a desperate fight in the morning; but at about two-thirty A.M., the messenger returned from General Hooker with orders for the movement to continue.

At about five, one of our divisions began to cross. The two or three succeeding hours were the most anxious I ever passed in my life. A large part of our army was massed on the south side of the river, only two bridges for the whole of it to cross, the river full to the edge of its banks; a very little extra strain would have carried away the upper bridge, and this would have swept away the lower one and all retreat would have been cut off. The rebel artillery began to fire on our troops and bridges, but was silenced by our guns; we had sixty in position on the north side.

It soon became evident that the enemy were not in force in our vicinity, but for all that, it was one of the happiest moments of my life when I saw the last of our corps over the bridge. We all started then for Stafford C. H., where our corps was ordered to its old camp. We arrived at our old headquarters at about two P.M., and found, to our joy, that our wagons had arrived and tents were being pitched. It was not until after we were in comfortable quarters that the terrible fatigue of the last ten days began to tell on us. Since we had left Stafford, we had been without wagons or blankets, with nothing to eat except pork and hard bread, and half the time not even that, and we had averaged each day at least twelve or sixteen hours in the saddle. The moment we touched a seat, we sunk into the most profound sleep and stayed in this condition for several hours. It may seem strange to you that I speak of being happy to get back into our old quarters, but you must remember that we had been through danger and hardship for ten days and had met with constant disappointment and were now safe back again where we were going to have sleep, rest, and food.

Now, let us see what this campaign shows. It seems to me that the plan was a very good one, with the exception of separating Sedgwick with thirty thousand men from the army, and that it was carried out with great success till General Hooker arrived at Chancellorsville. The next thing shown is that the commander of our army gained his position by merely brag and blow, and that when the time came to show himself, he was found without the qualities necessary for a general. If another battle had been fought on Monday, it would have been by the combined corps commanders, and the battle would have been won.

I doubt if, ever in the history of this war, another chance will be given us to fight the enemy with such odds in our favor as we had last Sunday, and that chance has been worse than lost to us. I don't believe any men ever fought better than our Twelfth Corps, especially the First Division; for two hours, they held their ground without any support, against the repeated assaults of the enemy; they fired their sixty rounds of cartridges and held their line with empty muskets till ordered to fall back. The old Second, of course, did splendidly, and lost heavily, twenty-two killed, one hundred and four wounded, ten missing; my company had five killed and eleven wounded. Lieutenant Fitzgerald was killed, Coggswell, Grafton, Perkins, and Powers, wounded. George Thompson had a narrow escape; a grape shot tore one leg of his trousers and his coat almost off and grazed his leg. Our colors got thirty new holes in them and the staff (the third one), was smashed to pieces.*

You cannot imagine the amount of admiration I have for General Slocum, for the gallant way in which he conducted himself throughout the campaign, and his skillful management of his command; then besides all that, we have been so together, that he has seemed almost like my old friends in the regiment.

I have written in this letter a pretty full account of the operations as I have seen them, and I don't believe any one has had a better chance, for during the fighting, I was at different times at every part of our lines, and in communication with General Hooker and other generals.

Our staff casualties were as follows:—Lieutenant Tracy,

*Actual loss: 31 killed and mortally wounded, 91 wounded, 7 prisoners. Total loss, 129.

badly wounded in right arm, his horse shot in four places; one of our orderlies shot and two more horses. I feel thankful to have come out unharmed from so much danger. Tracy was carrying an order to General Williams, when he was hit; somehow, he got outside our lines and was ordered to surrender; he said he thought he wouldn't, turned his horse and ran for it, while the rebels put two volleys after him.

I telegraphed, last Monday, that I was all right; I hope you received the message.

Samuel W. Fiske to the
Springfield Republican

In the spring of 1863 Fiske was promoted to captain and assigned to
the staff of a brigade in the Second Corps. The letters he wrote about
Chancellorsville from prison in Richmond were sent to the *Springfield
Republican* after Fiske was paroled to Annapolis, Maryland. They
were published on May 30, two weeks after the newspaper had erro-
neously reported that Fiske had been killed during the fighting on
May 3 and printed an obituary.

DUNN BROWNE IN DIXIE:
HOW HE HAPPENED TO GO THERE

Libby Prison, Richmond, Va.
May 9

Dear Republican: There is nothing so likely to secure an
observer from prejudice and false views and representations of
things as to take a fair look at both sides before giving his final
opinion upon any question. Your correspondent accordingly,
having already made a survey of the great rebellion from the
northern side, has now crossed the frontier and is making observations, with his usual philosophic imperturbability, upon
the southern aspect of the secesh monster. His opportunity for
this unbiased and impartial view of things came to him in this
wise.

He was acting on the staff of a general of brigade last Sabbath morning in the thick of the battle about Chancellorsville.
Things were in a decidedly mixed condition. The splendid
semi-circular line of battle of Gen. Hooker had been broken
the night before (Saturday, May 2d) by the disgraceful failure
of the 11th and 12th army corps to maintain their entrenched
position, although attacked by a greatly inferior force of the
enemy. Our brigade, the 1st in French's division, in the early

Sabbath morning was ordered to leave its position, in rifle-pits pretty well over to the left of our line, and cross over the plank-road towards the right to recover the ground, a portion of it, lost the night before. Our boys charged in splendid style through a thicket of tangled wood for half a mile or more, driving the enemy before them like chaff, slaying many, taking some prisoners and fairly running over some and leaving them in their rear. Indeed, they charged with too much impetuosity and advanced so far that they were not properly supported on the flanks and were exposed to an enfilading fire of artillery as well as musketry. To halt our line and form it anew a little further to the rear in the woods, I was sent forward by the general, together with a fine young friend, one of his aides, both on foot, as our horses were left behind as utterly imprac-ticable in that thicket of undergrowth. We had separated, he to the right and I to the left, delivered our orders to the colonels and assisted in executing it in the midst of a fire, the most dia-bolical that my eyes have yet witnessed, from front and rear (our own artillery from behind the wood occasionally dropped a shell among us) and both flanks, from at least 64 different points of the compass, I should say, and then I hastened to retrace my steps to report progress to the general.

I was hindered some little time in picking up prisoners (whom I didn't like to leave with arms in their hands in the rear of our line). I would disarm and put them in squads of 3 or 4 in the charge of some one of our slightly wounded men, first seeing that his gun was loaded and capped, and then on again till I had picked up some 20 or more of the "butternuts." Had a couple of the fellows on my hands and none of my own men in sight and was hurrying them forward by the persuasion of a cocked revolver, expecting every moment to come upon our general, when all at once pressing through a terribly dense portion of the undergrowth, I found myself face to face, at not twelve feet distance, with at least a whole regiment of the brownest and most ill-looking vagabonds that I ever set eyes on, every one of them with a gun in his hand, who were that moment rising up from behind a long line of rifle-pits they had taken from us the night before.

Here was a fix for an amiable and well disposed correspon-dent of yours, who had traveled some and ought to have known

better, to get himself into. Here was a big mouthful to swallow
for a belligerent patriot, intent on squelching the rebellion,
who had just gotten his blood up, hadn't been fighting more
than an hour, and was bound to distinguish himself before
night. Here was a capital chance for a man, who had just gotten his hand in at the business of capturing prisoners, to put a
thousand or fifteen hundred more in his bag—if they would
only let him. The undersigned is compelled to acknowledge
that in this one instance he found the situation too much for
him. He had drawn a mighty big elephant in a lottery and
didn't know what to do with him. One of the impudent
wretches he had captured a few minutes before turned round
with a grin and says, "Cap'en, I reckon things is different from
the way they was, and you'll hev to 'low you're our prisoner
now." A very sensible remark of the young man, and timely,
though he hadn't a shirt to his back and only a part of a pair of
pantaloons. Things *was* different from the way they were, with
a vengeance. I gracefully lowered my pistol to an officer who
stepped out from the ranks and presented it to him, apologiz-
ing for so doing by the remark that, "doubtless it would be
more disagreeable to a whole regiment to surrender to one
man, than to one man to surrender to a whole regiment." The
hard-hearted fellows didn't seem to care at all for my misfortune, and only laughed when I told them my story. I was
courteously treated and sent at once to the rear, minus my
pistol and trusty sword (the loss of which I the more regretted,
as it was not the purchase of money but the gift of a friend),
and so hath ended ingloriously, for the present, my military
service.

The transition from the fierce excitement of battle to the
quiet stillness of my walk of near a mile through the woods
with my guard, was so great that I could hardly realize it. It
seemed the flitting of a vision before my mind's eye. The roar
of the cannonade and rattle of the musketry sounded far away
to me, and I was like a boy rambling with a friend in the forest
of a summer morning. Not for long though could the horrid
sights and sounds of battle be put away from one's thoughts.
We soon came upon other portions of the bloody field and had
to pick our steps among mangled corpses of friend and foe,
past men without limbs and limbs without men, now seeing a

group of surgeons and assistants operating on the wounded under a tree, and now passing a group of ambulance men carrying on a stretcher some groaning sufferer. Occasionally a wounded horse struggling in his death-agony would kick at us, and occasionally a wounded secesh would mutter a curse as he saw the "d—d Yankee" pass. And in a little time we were far in the rear, and I was turned over to the care of the provost marshal, into a crowd of 1,700 captured "Yankees" about to be marched in the broiling sun, without a mouthful to eat, save the few who had their haversacks and rations with them, to Spottsylvania Court House, about 10 miles distant. Never did that nice black horse I drew a few weeks ago from provident Uncle Sam seem a more desirable underpinning to my weary fleshly tabernacle than now that I could only remember him left in the edge of that fatal forest, with my blankets and provisions on his back.

Yours, forlornly and in bonds, but yet a "prisoner of hope,"

DUNN BROWNE

May 9, 1863

PRISON REFLECTIONS ON THE CHANCELLORSVILLE FIGHT

Libby Prison, Richmond, Va.
May 11

Dear Republican: Richmond is jubilant over the great victory that the South has gained, the tremendous thrashing the chivalry has given "the best army on the planet," though to be sure their joy is fringed with mourning to-day over the funeral ceremonies of their hero, Jackson. Doubtless a great many reasons are given for our most disgraceful and disastrous defeat. There is only one real reason, and that the simplest possible. Our army didn't fight as well as that of our enemies. We had every possible advantage. Our numbers more than doubled their's till Longstreet's reinforcements came up, which didn't then bring their forces up to 100,000 to oppose our 130,000. Indeed, it would now seem that Longstreet didn't come up at all. We had the advantage of position, and no inconsiderable amount of entrenchment. Gen. Hooker's plan was admirably arranged and excellently carried out, until the fighting took place. He exposed himself in the hottest places of danger, and set an electrifying example of heroism to the whole army. The terrible loss of life among our generals shows that on the whole they were not found wanting at their posts of duty. We had men enough, well enough equipped, and well enough posted, to have devoured the ragged, imperfectly armed and equipped host of our enemies from off the face of the earth. Their artillery horses are poor, starved frames of beasts, tied on to their carriages and caissons with odds and ends of rope and strips of rawhide. Their supply and ammunition trains look like a congregation of all the crippled California emigrant trains that ever escaped off the desert out of the clutches of the rampaging Comanche Indians. The men are ill-dressed, ill-equipped and ill-provided, a set of ragamuffins that a man is ashamed to be seen among, even when he is a prisoner and can't help it. And yet they have beaten us fairly, beaten us all to pieces, beaten us so easily that we are objects of contempt even to their commonest private soldiers, with no shirts to hang out of the holes in their pantaloons, and cartridge boxes tied round their waists with strands of ropes.

I say they beat us easily, for there hasn't been much of a fight up here on the bank of the Rappahannock after all, the newspapers to the contrary notwithstanding. There was an awful noise, for I heard it. There was a tremendous amount of powder exploded, for I saw the smoke of it ascend up to heaven. There was a vast amount of running done "faced by the rear rank," but I cannot learn that there was in any part of the field very much real fighting. I have seen men from every part of the ground fought over, men from almost every division of the army, and have inquired diligently after every vestige of conflict, and not one of them all had *seen* a great deal of spirited fighting, though a good many had *heard* a vast amount of it. The particular brigade or regiment or company of each man was captured because the enemy appeared in vast numbers on their flank or in their rear. They didn't fight much because they were so unfortunately situated or surrounded that there wasn't much use in resisting. I never heard of so much cross firing and enfilading fire, and fire in the rear, in all the history of battles with which I am acquainted. Do you point to the big lists of the killed and wounded, 15,000 or 20,000 on our side, as evidence of the desperateness of the encounter? I tell you that when men get up and run out of their rifle-pits and breastworks like a flock of sheep, instead of staying in and defending them, not only they deserve to be shot, but as an actual matter of fact they do get hit and killed about four-fold what would be hurt if they did their soldierly duty like men.

Am I saying things that oughtn't to be spoken of out of school? That had better be smoothed over and explained away? I'm not certain about that. I think people ought to understand somewhere about where the truth lies, and I do not think soldiers ought to be eulogized and told that men never fought more gallantly on the face of the earth and the victory would have been theirs if their officers hadn't mismanaged, when as a matter of fact their officers gallantly did their duty and were left to be killed or captured on the field because their men turned tail and ran away from them. Mind, I don't mean to say that this was very generally the case in the late battle. But I do mean to say that according to my best information and belief the great 11th corps of our army, attacked by an inferior force of the enemy, gave way with only a shadow of resistance and ran out of their entrenchments like a parcel of frightened deer, thus making a great gap in our grand line of battle and disconcerting all our good arrangements, and opening the way for the disasters that followed. And from all I can learn the 12th corps didn't do much better, and though a very large portion of the army did their duty very fairly, I have yet to learn of any considerable body of troops that displayed that real gallantry and determination to win which only can restore a losing battle and atone for the disgraceful flight of the cowards and panic-stricken. I know of whole regiments and brigades, long and heavy lines of battle, that gave way before lines of the enemy so thin and straggling as hardly to be considered more than skirmishers. I saw regiment after regiment and brigade after brigade of those corps I have mentioned come pouring back through our reserves till they covered acres and acres of ground, enough to have made a stand against all the rebels in Virginia, and only breaking our lines and telling such cock and bull stories of being cut to pieces in front and surrounded and attacked in the rear as carried evidence of their absurdity on the very face of them, till I could have cried for shame and grief to be obliged to acknowledge myself as belonging to the same army.

Still in spite of all I have said, it is by no means the truth that our men are a parcel of cowards and poltroons. They are as brave as the average of people—quite as brave as our enemies are. But we don't fight in such a common-sense way as they do. Shall I tell you how one of our lines of battle engages? They go in fine style, steadily, in a good line and without any flinching, halt at what is held to be a desirable point, and at the command commence firing, standing, kneeling or lying down, as may be ordered. Then, as in all their previous training they have been told to load and fire as rapidly as possible, three or four times a minute, they go into the business with all fury, every man vying with his neighbor as to the number of cartridges he can ram into his piece and spit out of it. The smoke arises in a minute or two so you can see nothing where to aim. The noise is deafening and confusing to the last degree. The impression gets around of a tremendous conflict going on. The trees in the vicinity suffer sorely and the clouds a good deal. By-and-by the guns get heated and won't go off and the cartridges begin to give out. The men have become tired with their furious exertions and the excitement and din of their own firing, and without knowing anything about the effect produced upon the enemy, very likely having scarcely had one glimpse of the enemy at all, begin to think they have fought about enough and it is nearly time to retire.

Meanwhile the enemy, lying quietly a hundred or two hundred yards in front, crouching on the ground or behind trees, answer our fire very leisurely, as they get a chance for a good aim, about one shot to our 300, hitting about as many as we do, and waiting for the wild tornado of ammunition to pass over their heads, and when our burst of fighting is pretty much over they have only commenced. They probably rise and advance upon us with one of their unearthly yells as they see our fire slacken. Our boys, finding that the enemy has survived such an avalanche of fire as we have rolled in upon him, conclude he must be invincible, and being pretty much out of ammunition, retire. Now, if I had charge of a regiment or brigade, I'd put every man in the guardhouse who could be proved to have fired more than twenty rounds in any one battle; I wouldn't let them carry more than their cartridge box full (40 rounds), and have them understand that that was meant to last them pretty much through a campaign, and in every possible way would endeavor to banish the Chinese style of fighting with a big noise and smoke, and imitate rather the backwoods style of our opponents.

Whenever we choose to defeat the armies of the rebels, we can do so, and we don't need 500,000 more men to do it with either. There are men enough in Hooker's army now to march straight through to Richmond. Too many men are only an encumbrance. There isn't the general living who has shown his ability to manage properly, certainly, more than 100,000 men. All we have to do is to make up our minds not to run before an equal number of the enemy, to keep cool and save our ammunition to shoot something besides trees with, and when the butternuts find we don't run away, they will. Meanwhile, till I am able to return and effect in our army this change in their method of fighting, I have the honor to assure you that these brown-coated fellows are not so bad as they might be, only they don't furnish us any sugar to put in our coffee, nor yet any coffee to put sugar in. Yours affably,

DUNN BROWNE

May 11, 1863

Charles B. Wilder: Testimony before the American Freedmen's Inquiry Commission

May 9, 1863

The American Freedmen's Inquiry Commission, appointed by Secretary of War Edwin M. Stanton on March 16, 1863, was charged with investigating and reporting measures that would contribute to the "protection and improvement" of the newly emancipated "so that they may defend and support themselves." Its three members, Robert Dale Owen, James McKaye, and Samuel Gridley Howe, were antislavery advocates active in various social reform movements. In May the commissioners traveled to Fort Monroe in Virginia and heard testimony from Captain Charles B. Wilder, the superintendent of contrabands at the post.

May 9, 1863.

Question　How many of the people called contrabands, have come under your observation?

Answer　Some 10,000 have come under our control, to be fed in part, and clothed in part, but I cannot speak accurately in regard to the number. This is the rendezvous. They come here from all about, from Richmond and 200 miles off in North Carolina. There was one gang that started from Richmond 23 strong and only 3 got through.

Q　In your opinion, is there any communication between the refugees and the black men still in slavery?

A　Yes Sir, we have had men here who have gone back 200 miles.

Q　In your opinion would a change in our policy which would cause them to be treated with fairness, their wages punctually paid and employment furnished them in the army, become known and would it have any effect upon others in slavery?

A   Yes—Thousands upon Thousands. I went to Suffolk a short time ago to enquire into the state of things there—for I found I could not get any foot hold to make things work there, through the Commanding General, and I went to the Provost Marshall and all hands—and the colored people actually sent a deputation to me one morning before I was up to know if we put black men in irons and sent them off to Cuba to be sold or set them at work and put balls on their legs and whipped them, just as in slavery; because that was the story up there, and they were frightened and didn't know what to do. When I got at the feelings of these people I found they were not afraid of the slaveholders. They said there was nobody on the plantations but women and they were not afraid of them. One woman came through 200 miles in Men's clothes. The most valuable information we received in regard to the Merrimack and the operations of the rebels came from the colored people and they got no credit for it. I found hundreds who had left their wives and families behind. I asked them "Why did you come away and leave them there?" and I found they had heard these stories, and wanted to come and see how it was. "I am going back again after my wife" some of them have said "When I have earned a little money" What as far as that?" "Yes" and I have had them come to me to borrow money, or to get their pay, if they had earned a months wages, and to get passes. "I am going for my family" they say. "Are you not afraid to risk it?" "No I know the Way" Colored men will help colored men and they will work along the by paths and get through. In that way I have known quite a number who have gone up from time to time in the neighborhood of Richmond and several have brought back their families; some I have never heard from. As I was saying they do not feel afraid now. The white people have nearly all gone, the blood hounds are not there now to hunt them and they are not afraid, before they were afraid to stir. There are hundreds of negroes at Williamsburgh with their families working for nothing. They would not get pay here and they had rather stay where they are. "We are not afraid of being carried back" a great many have told us and "if we are, we can get away again" Now that they are getting their eyes open they are coming in. Fifty came this morning from Yorktown who followed Stoneman's Cavalry when they returned from their raid. The officers reported to their Quartermaster that they had so many horses and fifty or sixty negroes. "What did you bring them for" "Why they followed us and we could not stop them." I asked one of the men about it and he said they would leave their work in the field as soon as they found the Soldiers were Union men and follow them sometimes without hat or coat. They would take best horse they could get and every where they rode they would take fresh horses, leave the old ones and follow on and so they came in. I have questioned a great many of them and they do not feel much afraid; and there are a great many courageous fellows who have come from long distances in rebeldom. Some men who came here from North Carolina, knew all about the Proclammation and they started on the belief in it; but they had heard these stories and they wanted to know how it was. Well, I gave them the evidence and I have no doubt their friends will hear of it. Within the last two or three months the rebel guards have been doubled on the line and the officers and privates of the 99th New York between Norfolk and Suffolk have caught hundreds of fugitives and got pay for them.

Q   Do I understand you to say that a great many who have escaped have been sent back?

A   Yes Sir, The masters will come in to Suffolk in the day time and with the help of some of the 99th carry off their fugitives and by and by smuggle them across the lines and the soldier will get his $20. or $50.

Thomas Wentworth Higginson:
Journal, May 10, 1863

A writer, minister, social reformer, and radical abolitionist who had helped finance John Brown's raid on Harpers Ferry, Thomas Wentworth Higginson joined the newly organized 51st Massachusetts Infantry as a captain in September 1862. He was preparing to leave for New Bern, North Carolina, in November when Brigadier General Rufus Saxton, the Union military governor of South Carolina, offered him the command of the 1st South Carolina Volunteers, a recently formed regiment recruited from freed slaves. Higginson accepted, and in January 1863 led the regiment on a successful expedition into southern Georgia and northern Florida during which his troops gathered supplies, liberated slaves, and skirmished with Confederate forces. During a second expedition in March the 1st South Carolina briefly occupied Jacksonville, Florida, before returning to its base at Port Royal.

MAY 10

Such fun as we have had over the newspaper accounts of us. I just told Dr Rogers it was fortunate that novels were still published, that there might be truth found somewhere, since history certainly affords none; but he says if things go on so much longer we c'ant even put faith in novels. We have just seen the scrap about our picket firing—two negroes wounded—two butternuts biting the dust—all sheer fabrication. Occasionally they fire a little, at very long range & my men fire back, & that's all about it—except Gen. Hunter's pithy endorsement on the back of Gen. Saxton's letter—"Give them as good as they send —D. Hunter, Maj. Genl. Commanding"—that was to the point.

The great drawback of these Southern col'd regt's will always be the severe burden of writing they throw on officers, both field & line. I spend hours daily, & much vitality needed for

other things, in doing writing which every Col. of a white reg't
has one or more clerks detailed to do; the same with my Quartermaster, the same with my adjutant. This is inevitable; in
addition in this particular case, the Lt. col. & the Major are not
naturally bookkeepers, any more than drillmasters (neither of
them could drill either the reg't or a company ten minutes
without some serious mistake—& if we were in battle & I were
injured, a Captain would have to take command); The Sergeant Major, the only other person I can ever call on for aid in
writing, is sick, & not efficient when well, & has his own work
beside. If col'd regt's were not easier to drill & discipline than
white ones, all their officers would die, except those who had
happily never learned to write.

I d'ont wish to be severe on my field officers—Maj Strong I
should be very sorry to lose; he has no turn for drill & his
health is delicate, but he is the soul of courage, full of enterprise & resources, always amiable always ready to work. Lt.
Col. Billings is absolutely worthless.

It is Sunday noon & a wedding party is sitting under the
trees, awaiting the Chaplain. One soldier a good looking youth
in uniform coat & festive white pants & gloves; & two young
girls, jet black, in low necked white muslin dresses, shirt
sleeves, straw colored sashes, with good figures, not too stout
which they are apt to be & of the handsome shade of black.
Many have a *grimy* black, which is repulsive looking as if it
would come off—but with many the color is a very deep wine
colour which to my eye is very handsome in its way; the skin
being smoother & finer grained than ours, (Dr Rogers observes) both in the men & the women; their arms are particularly handsome, because labor seems to develop them without
making them wiry or hairy or sunburnt. We have had many
recruits lately & Dr Rogers often calls me in to admire their
fine physique or to see the common marks of the lash.

Last Sunday there was a funeral on this plantation & during
the whole sunny day a great prayer meeting of women sat
under the great live oaks before my window & sang hymn
upon hymn—an old Deborah leading off, gesticulating and
beating time with her whole body & calling on each woman
present by name. In the afternoon old men came from the

various plantations & I let the soldiers march there, instead of to our usual meeting. The women all looked neat, with handkerchiefs round their heads.

As for the wedding, this is one of the days in the quarter when they go to be married "by de book" as they call it; often letting a mere social ceremony suffice for a time.

My poor Lieuts. O'Neil & Stockdale have fared hard. After 48 days imprisonment they were tried by court martial—convicted not of desertion but of absence without leave & set at liberty as punished enough. This Gen. S. attributes to my being too mild on them in my evidence & saying too much in their favor; but he made them resign & Gen. Hunter dismisses them from service as incompetent & worthless and they forfeit all their pay, & all this because two women, who had been soldiers wives for years, couldn't make up their minds to go to New York alone! At any rate they will not return to the reg't of which I was at one time afraid.

The rapid multiplication of colored regiments is of more *personal* importance to me than to all the rest of the nation, for it is taking a load of personal responsibility off my shoulders. There is no doubt that for many months the fate of the whole movement for colored soldiers rested on the behavior of this one regiment. A mutiny, an extensive desertion, an act of severe discipline, a Bull Run panic, a simple defeat, might have blasted the whole movement for arming the blacks—& through it the prospects of the war & of a race. Now the thing is so far advanced that Africa holds many shares in the lottery of war & should the 1st S.C.V. prove a blank, others will not. The Tribune correspondent said to me the other day, "This is the only *regiment* with which the public has become familiar; in all other cases they have known at most the Division or the Brigade. (It is amusing to see, even now, how they all call my 850 a Brigade.) I have had enough of this notoriety & am very willing to be merged in an army of such regiments!

Edward O. Guerrant: Diary, May 15, 1863

Captain Edward O. Guerrant was a native Kentuckian who served as an adjutant to Brigadier General Humphrey Marshall, the commander of Confederate forces in the mountains of southwestern Virginia and eastern Kentucky. Guerrant had just returned to southeastern Kentucky from a visit to Richmond, Virginia, when he learned of Jackson's death.

Friday 15h. May 1863.
Today returned to Col. Hawkins' camps on Rock House. Williams of the battery just returned from Abingdon—Says

> *General Jackson is Dead!*
> General Jackson is Dead!

Was a nation's woe ever condensed in so few words—or a people's calamity so far beyond language to express!? O Fate "That is the unkindest stroke of all"! All other losses we have ever sustained are light in comparison with this great calamity. So mighty a warrior,—so dauntless a spirit, so pure a patriot & so devoted a Christian!—A nations homage lay at his feet—its honors crown his brow. We have not another Jackson to die! Centuries are slow in the birth of such men. The Christian Napoleon! A greater than Alexander is dead. If a nation's prayers & tears could have availed anything at a Throne of Mercy then "Stonewall" Jackson had not died! But God called him up higher—& in the ranks of a mightier army, & almost peerless in that innumerable host—stands our great Warrior.

The fire of his genius will no longer lead his invincible legions to certain victory,—& the scream of his exultant Eagles will no more echo along the bloody banks of the Rappahannock, or by the bosom of the Potomac or in the beautiful Valley of the Shenandoah—his own sweet "Valley of Virginia". But the memory of his deeds—his immortal deeds still lives—& will live while genius has an admirer—liberty a devotee—Christ a follower—or Nobility a friend & patron. If human sacrifices could have shielded his life from death's fatal stroke—a thousand —yea ten thousand lives would have been offered up on War's bloody altar that "Stonewall" Jackson might live.

But God's Eternal & wise decree has gone forth & called from the head of his veteran warriors the great commander—& He will provide another whose arm he will strengthen to drive the invaders from our soil. In Jackson's beautiful, christian resignation let us bow to the Divine decree & say "Thy will be done". From the ashes of the immortal Jackson the Genius of Liberty will rise triumphant over death and place a nation & its Great Benefactor beyond the malice or power of enemies—on the tablet of an enduring fame.

We weep over our loss—& rejoice we had such a man to die. Jackson dead is worth 10000 Hookers living. We cannot estimate our loss—It is great beyond degree. The Richmond Enquirer says we had better lost a Corps of our Army. Northern journals pay him the highest honors—acknowledging the terror of his very name—his great genius—his invincibility— & the meekness & purity of his christian character. He is styled the Modern Bonaparte. McClellan grieved over his loss— & acknowledged him to have been our greatest Executive General. He possessed more than any of our Generals, the love & confidence of our people. They idolized "Stonewall" Jackson. God's purposes are wise to have removed him. "*He gave & hath taken away*".

While reconnoitering—with Gen. A. P. Hill & both their staffs &c. in the night of Saturday 2 May Genl. Jackson was wounded by one of his own Regiments (a N.C. Regt) on Picket—& not 50 yards from the Enemy. He received two wounds in his left arm & one in his right hand. He came near bleeding to death on the field. While being borne off by four men one of them was killed & he fell from the other's shoulders & was severely hurt. His arm was amputated—but Pneumonia setting in terminated his life at Guinnea's Station on the Rappahannock R.R. on   at 3¼ P.M.

Before his death he was cheerful—. Expressed the opinion that if he had been permitted another hour of light or life on that great battle day he would have cut off Hooker's retreat by

U.S. Ford. He died delirious—his last words referring to his army. "Tell Gen Hill", said he "to prepare his division for action, & tell Major Hawkes to send forward provisions for the men."—

His remains were brought to Richmond on   where they received every honor an admiring & sorrowful people could bestow on all that was mortal of the illustrious dead. It is estimated that at least twenty thousand people crowded the avenues of the National Capitol—where he was laid in state—to behold the pallid, serene, & thoughtful countenance of the mighty, dead chieftain. He expressed a desire to be buried at "Lexington—in the Valley of Virginia"; his place of residence.

Gen Ewell, who commanded a Division under him & lost his leg at the battle of   was Genl. Jacksons choice as his successor.

It is proposed to have a bronze statue of Jackson placed in the Capitol at Richmond—that all may see the likeness of the man whose "fame is more enduring than brass"—upon whose living form they never looked. It will be a Mecca for generations to come.

As usual after some terrible defeat Mr. Lincoln has taken to his usual resort—*more men*. This time he caps the climax by calling all the armbearing population of the North into the field to "suppress the rebellion".

A grand rise from 75,000 to 4,000,000 of men!

If Thirteen Hundred & Eighty Five Thousand armed warriors are incompetent for our subjugation—what virtue is there in numbers such as his! Xerxes stands in awe at Lincoln's Abolition host *4,000,000* He never boasted half of that.

Poor Mr. Lincoln.—When will the scales of his judicial blindness fall from his eye as he beats his *obstinate, Balaams numerical horse*, & reveal the angel warrior with his retributive sword standing to stay him!? Poor man!

George Richard Browder:
Diary, May 17–26, 1863

Union troops occupied Logan County, Kentucky, in February 1862 and held it for the remainder of the war. A Methodist preacher and slave-owning farmer, George Richard Browder lived in the southern part of the county less than ten miles from the Tennessee border. Although he sympathized with the secessionist cause and believed the war to be the result of "the mad schemes of an abolition fanaticism," Browder did not join the Confederate army. "I am positively a *peace man*," he wrote in his diary in March 1863.

————————

May 15—Papers to day report Genl Vandorn & T. J. Jackson both dead—federal loss at Fredericksburg immense—say 20,000 killed & wounded. Lo the horrors of the war still crowd upon us. There is now a military order requiring all male citizens 21 years old & upward to report at Russellville & take the oath or be arrested & sent beyond the federal lines to remain until the close of the war under penalty of being shot if they return! This is a cruel & merciless order of Brig Genl Shackleford—a Cumberland Presbyterian Bro. & may give him trouble to enforce it. Who ever takes this oath under such duress is not acting of his own free will & accord. I do not know what I shall do. I am willing to do right & submit to the lawful authorities—but military men have no just right to control peaceable citizens.

May 17—There is much excitement in the country & hundreds are flocking in to take the oath of allegiance—grumbling as they go & yet swearing that they "do it of their own free will, without any mental reservation whatever." I do not see how I can conscientiously swear that I do "of my own free will" what if left to myself I should not do—& yet I must or be banished from my home & my property confiscated. Ought a Christian man to swear against his conscience to avoid suffering any more than to obtain any desired good? Is the duress sufficient to force a man so to swear or is the injunction of scripture "submit to the powers that be" a law of conscience requiring obedience to the civil or military power right or wrong! I confess that I am in some trouble about it & do not know what to do, but suppose I must submit to what I cannot avoid considering that the action is not mine—just as if I should compel my son or servant to break the sabbath, against his will. *I* should be the sabbath breaker & not he. If I were compelled to lose my hand or my head, I should of my free will give my hand to save my head—but of my *free* will would lose neither. My Hogan neighbors, arrested some weeks ago accused of harboring guerillas have been released on oath & bond. As good a man as Thos Gilbert is put under 5000 bond —accused of disloyalty! Almeda, daughter of K. C. Mason— deceased—arrested for writing to her brother in rebel army has been detained for a week or more in Russellville & now sent on to Genl Burnside for further orders. Some are wearing ball & chain & many crowded up in Russellville courthouse— charged with aiding rebellion. Oh Russellville! Little did thy people think of such scenes when they shouted & rejoiced over the entering forces of Buckner from camps Boone & Burnett a year ago last September.

The federal loss at Fredericksburg is now estimated at 30,000 & rebel loss, papers say not less—& rebels claim 50,000 stands of arms & immense supplies, clothing &c. Jackson Miss is reported captured by feds—& other federal successes. These are times of peril & trial such as I never expected to witness. C. L. Vallandigham the great statesman and orator of Ohio is condemned to close confinement in Fort Lafayette during the war for publicly denouncing the policy of the administration & warning the people that they were in danger of a military despotism. In Ky a man was arrested—taken to Louisville & imprisoned by military for speaking disrespectfully of the President! but was released. Spies & detectives are roaming the country in disguise listening for some disloyal utterance to report —& seeking by stratagem to get men to avow Southern sympathies that they may arrest them & require oath & bond— consequently men are suspicious of their servants, neighbors, & even kindred blood if they disagree in politics. Confidence is withheld—& general mistrust prevails. The papers boast of raiders burning houses—haystacks—& carrying off booty & negroes, as if they had done virtuous acts & rebels do likewise —except burning houses & taking negroes. Swearing— drunkenness & thriftless indolence are vastly increasing in the land. Altogether the picture is a gloomy one. This summer must witness an immensity of suffering—blood & death.

May 22—Went to Keysburg—was halted by some little boys on stick horses & carrying switch sabres. They said they were Morgans cavalry & would require me to go to the school house & take the oath! Even the children are full of war manoeuvres. I had a small audience, preached on Pauls prayer— Eph 3.14–21. Felt sad about the state of the country & the oath we are bound to take.

May 24—This is the great gathering day at Pleasant Grove— where all the young folks are apt to collect & dress out. It is vulgarly called "Showday." At 4—the negroes had a fine time & I preached a short sermon—Rev 14.13.

May 25—I dined with my father & others at Uncle Dicks where Lizzie was gone when I got home. We decided to go to Russellville tomorrow to comply with "order No. 18" compelling us under penalty of banishment to go to Russellville & take the oath of Allegiance—& to aid in putting down rebellion. If there be any evil in this oath let it be upon those who impose it upon us. It is not our act when forced upon us.

May 26—Bro Alexander & I went to town and took the oath & as for me I shall give no one an opportunity to convict me of violating it. The dictates of humanity I cannot disregard. I never did & will not now encourage the rebellion but as a Christian I must be humane even if I have to feed an enemy when hungry. Most of my old friends in town seemed very glad to see me & treated me most cordially.

For several days past the papers have been rejoicing over great Federal victories & the capture of great numbers of prisoners & cannon & military stores & it is believed that Vicksburg has fallen or must fall & also the greater part of the rebel

army. If this is true, it is a severe blow to the rebellion & they
have probably lost more at Vicksburg than they gained at
Fredericksburg. I feel like withdrawing my thoughts from all
public matters & trying more to be an humble Christian & get
safely out of this wicked world.

Harper's Weekly:
The Arrest of Vallandigham

May 30, 1863

Speaking at a Democratic rally in Mount Vernon, Ohio, on May 1, former congressman Clement L. Vallandigham declared that "a wicked, cruel and unnecessary" war was being waged "for the purpose of crushing out liberty and erecting a despotism; a war for the freedom of the blacks, and the enslavement of the whites." He also denounced General Orders No. 38, issued on April 13 by Major General Ambrose Burnside, which warned that "declaring sympathies for the enemy will not be allowed" in the Department of the Ohio. Burnside had Vallandigham arrested at his home in Dayton on May 5 and tried by a military commission. Charged with violating General Orders No. 38 by publicly expressing "sympathy for those in arms against the United States, and declaring disloyal sentiments and opinions, with the object and purpose of weakening the power of the Government in its efforts to suppress an unlawful rebellion," Vallandigham was convicted on May 7 and sentenced to imprisonment for the duration of the war. His application for a writ of habeas corpus was rejected by the U.S. circuit court in Cincinnati, which declined to issue a writ for a prisoner in military custody. The controversy drew the attention of *Harper's Weekly*, an illustrated journal with a circulation of more than 100,000 copies. Its editorial went to press before it became known that President Lincoln had ordered Vallandigham expelled into Confederate-held territory.

It is known that Clement C. Vallandigham, late member of Congress from Dayton, Ohio, was lately arrested at his house by order of General Burnside, tried by court-martial, and convicted of inciting resistance to the Government in the prosecution of the war. And it is reported that he has been sentenced to imprisonment in a fortress during the war. The President enjoys the power of commuting or remitting this sentence altogether; and it is the unanimous hope of the loyal North that he will remit it.

For, whether the arrest of Vallandigham was or was not a wise step, there can be very little question but his imprisonment for months, and perhaps years, in a military fortress would make a martyr of him, and would rally to his side, for the sake of liberty and free speech, an immense number of sympathizers. It would probably make him Governor of Ohio, and would impart great strength to the rapidly-decaying Copperhead sentiment of the Northwest. Notwithstanding the new lessons taught by the war, and the new duties which it has devolved upon us, we have not yet learned to look with complacency on the methods which are familiar to Old World despotisms; and the spectacle of a man immured in a prison for opinion's or words' sake shocks our feelings and arouses our anger.

It is all very well to say, as General Burnside says in his noble and patriotic reply to the Cincinnati Court, that war involves a sacrifice of liberty, and that this man Vallandigham was a pernicious and malignant enemy of his country. This we all know, and if Vallandigham would go out of the country to the rebels or any where else, loyal people would heartily rejoice. But the question is not whether Vallandigham be a traitor, or whether war involve a suspension of individual rights; it is—shall we better ourselves and help the country by locking this man up in a fortress, instead of letting him prate his seditious trash to every one who will listen? To that question the reply must be in the negative.

The mistake which has all along been made in this war by the Government and many of its agents has been not trusting the people sufficiently. Arresting seditious talkers implies a fear that the people have not sense or strength of mind enough to resist the appeals of sedition; just as the suppression or retention for a time of intelligence of a defeat implies a doubt whether the people have courage enough to bear bad news. Let us assure Mr. Lincoln, and all in authority under him, that the people of the United States have quite courage enough to bear any amount of misfortunes, and quite sense enough to withstand any amount of seditious nonsense, be it uttered ever so glibly. The only effect thus far produced by such talkers as Vallandigham has been to kill off the Copperhead sentiment in the Northwest, to reduce Fernando Wood's party to a mere corporal's guard, and to render the names of the Copperhead leaders a by-word and a reproach among honest men. Vallandigham was fast talking himself into the deepest political grave ever dug when Burnside resurrected him.

The people can be trusted to deal with traitors without any help from Washington, and those who suffer the penalty they inflict—ignominy and disgrace—never find sympathy any where. At the meeting held in this city on 18th to protest against Vallandigham's arrest not one leading man, not a single man who commands general esteem, or who carries the least weight, ventured to be present, and the performance was, on the whole, the most wretched of all the wretched fizzles that have ever been enacted in this city in the way of political meetings. Not but that every body, including the leaders of all parties, and the editors of all leading journals, regret the arrest. But Copperheadism has become so odious, and the doom of every sympathizer with treason so obvious, that not a single man who has any future to risk will jeopard it by placing himself on the record as even indirectly sympathizing with a Copperhead. So long as the people are thus firm in their loyalty it is surely superfluous for Government to interpose for their protection against traitors.

Oliver W. Norton to Elizabeth Norton Poss

Private Norton fought at Chancellorsville with the 83rd Pennsylvania Infantry under Colonel Strong Vincent. In late May Vincent became the new brigade commander, and Norton was assigned to brigade headquarters.

---

*Headquarters, Third Brigade, First Division,
Fifth Army Corps,
Crittenden's Mill, Va., June 8, 1863.*

Dear Sister L.:—

I have no letter of yours to answer, but having nothing to do and knowing that you are always glad to hear from me, perhaps I can't do better than to spend an hour jotting down for your amusement a few incidents by the way. Life at headquarters is pleasant on one account—it gives me a better opportunity to see and talk with the people of the country than I had in the regiment.

You will see by this that we have again moved. Since the 27th ult. we have been engaged in guarding the river at different points above Fredericksburg. Crittenden's Mill is some twenty miles above town and two miles back of the river. Ellis' Ford and Kempel's Ford are near, and our brigade is ordered to guard these crossings and watch the enemy on the other side. Reports of the observations have to be sent to Division headquarters every four hours of the day and night. Headquarters are at the house of a certain widow James. She has three sons in the rebel army and is a pretty loud *secesh* herself. My bivouac is in one of the old lady's tobacco houses, and there I am writing this at present, so if it smells of tobacco don't charge it to my habits. On the road up here we stopped one night at the house of a Mr. Imbray. He was a cripple and at home, but made no secret of his being *secesh* to the backbone. "I belong to the South," said he, "and my heart is with the South. If I was with the army I should shoot at you with all the power I had, but, meeting as we do, I shall not allow any difference of opinion to influence my treatment of you." (Very considerate, wasn't he, when we had the force there to enforce respect?) But it wasn't of him I meant to speak, but of his daughters. There were two, one a lady of "uncertain age," and the other not. The "not" was about eighteen, and the bitterest, rabidest, outspokenest, cantankerous-est specimen of *secesh* femininity I've come across yet. She had no objection to talk, and she commenced at me when she saw my flag, with, "Is that a Yankee flag?" "Well, the Yankees use it," said I, "but here's the Yankee flag," and I unrolled a new silk "star spangled" and waved it over her head. "Don't you think," said I, "that that's a prettier flag than the 'stars and bars?'" "No, indeed! I can't see it, sir—no, sir—give me the Confederate flag. I don't want none o' yer gridirons about me." Finally after some bantering we dropped the subject and I induced her after a chaffer to sell me two quarts of milk for half a dollar, and she offered me half a loaf of rye bread for the same price, but I preferred hard tack. "We're no way particular about prices with you all," she said. "So I see," meekly replied I. Next morning we were going, and I was bound to have some fun first, so I opened by asking her if she didn't sometimes feel lonesome with none of the young men about. "Well, sir, not lonesome enough to care to see you Yankees about." (Repulse.) "Have you any relatives in the rebel army?" "I have two brothers and a lover in the Confederate army." (Cool—that about the lover.) "Then Yankee boys stand no chance in your good graces?" "No, sir, I hate the sight of them." (Cooler yet.) "Why, I don't think you are a secessionist." (Tactics.) "Well, I am, sir, I am true to the South." (I wish I could write their pronunciation of South; it beats all the down-east you ever heard of.) "No, you are a Yankee, at least a Yankee *secesh*." "No, indeed, sir, nary drop o' Yankee blood in my veins, I tell you, sir." "Oh, but you are, begging your pardon, and I'll prove it to you." "No, sir, you can't do that, sir; better tell that to some one else. If I had any Yankee blood in me I'd let it out. Yes, indeed, I would." "Well, you acknowledge that a Yankee thinks more of property and money than anything else, don't you?" "Yes, sir, I've heard they do, and I believe it." "Yes, well, you're a Yan-

kee then. If you were a *secesh* you would go with the South
and help them. True *secesh* women do that, but your family
have some property here and you stay to take care of it and let
the South get along the best she can. You are a genuine Yankee, say what you please. You wouldn't go and share the fortunes of your 'Sunny South,' but you must stay to keep the
Yankees from destroying the property." Oh, how she did
sputter! "To think that she should be called a Yankee!" I guess
she'll get over it.

Down on the bank of the river I went into a house and met
a young married woman with a baby in her arms. She had been
pretty once and it was not age that spoiled her beauty, but
care. "Can you sell me a pie, or something good for my dinner?" said I. "A pie! sir," said she. "Well, now, sir, if I was to tell
you that I have not tasted or seen a piece of pie for more than
a year, would you believe me?" "I certainly should if you said
so. Of course I couldn't doubt a lady's word." "Sir, 'fore God
it is the truth. I have only been married 'bout a year, and my
husband, who was an overseer, came on to this place after the
fruit was all gone, and I've had no fruit. I haven't seen a bit of
sugar, nor coffee, nor tea for nigh eight months, I reckon,"
and she went on and gave me such a story of struggles to keep
alive, to get enough to keep from starving, as made all the hard
times I have ever seen seem like a life of luxury. I did pity her.
On such as she, the poor whites of the South, the burden of
this war is heaviest. She had but little sympathy for the South
or North either. She cared but little how the war ended, so it
ended soon. Poor woman, she understood but little of the
nature of the contest. She sent a little darky girl to bring in a
pan of milk. The girl came with it balanced on her head, not
touching her hands. I remarked how strange it seemed to me
to see everybody in the south carry pails on their heads. "Why,"
said she, "how do you-all carry 'em?" "In our hands." She
laughed. "I have to tote all my water up a steep bank, and, if I
toted it in my hand, it would pull me over." She gave me some
milk, and by the time I had eaten my dinner the colonel came
back from the lines, and I mounted my horse and came back
to camp.

Strawberries are ripe and I get a few. No more news from
Fredericksburg.

Robert Gould Shaw to
Annie Haggerty Shaw

The 54th Massachusetts Infantry left its training camp at Readville on
May 28 and marched through the streets of Boston before sailing for
Beaufort, South Carolina. Its departure was cheered by thousands of
spectators, including Frederick Douglass, Harriet Jacobs, and William
Lloyd Garrison, in what Shaw described as a "perfect triumph." When
Shaw arrived in Beaufort he met Colonel James Montgomery, the
commander of the 2nd South Carolina Volunteers, a regiment of
freed slaves formed in early 1863. A friend of John Brown, Montgomery had led a free-state militia in Kansas before the war and commanded Union troops fighting guerrillas in Missouri. In a letter to his
father, Shaw wrote: "He is an Indian in his mode of warfare, and
though I am glad to see something of it, I can't say I admire it. It isn't
like a fair stand up such as our Potomac Army is accustomed to." On
June 8 the 54th Massachusetts was sent to join Montgomery's regiment on St. Simon's Island, Georgia.

––––––––––––

St. Simon's Island, Ga.
Tuesday, June 9, 1863
My Dearest Annie,
    We arrived at the southern point of this island at six this
morning. I went ashore to report to Colonel Montgomery,
and was ordered to proceed with my regiment to a place called
"Pike's Bluff," on the inner coast of the island, and encamp.
We came up here in another steamer, the "Sentinel," as the
"De Molay" is too large for the inner waters,—and took possession to-day of a plantation formerly owned by Mr. Gould.
We have a very nice camping-ground for the regiment, and I
have my quarters in "*the house*"; very pleasantly situated, and
surrounded by fine large trees. The island is beautiful, as far as
I have seen it. You would be enchanted with the scenery here;
the foliage is wonderfully thick, and the trees covered with
hanging moss, making beautiful avenues wherever there is a
road or path; it is more like the tropics than anything I have

seen. Mr. Butler King's plantation, where I first went ashore, must have been a beautiful place, and well kept. It is entirely neglected now, of course; and as the growth is very rapid, two years' neglect almost covers all traces of former care.

12th.—If I could have gone on describing to you the beauties of this region, who knows but I might have made a fine addition to the literature of our age? But since I wrote the above, I have been looking at something very different.

On Wednesday, a steamboat appeared off our wharf, and Colonel Montgomery hailed me from the deck with, "How soon can you get ready to start on an expedition?" I said, "In half an hour," and it was not long before we were on board with eight companies, leaving two for camp-guard.

We steamed down by his camp, where two other steamers with five companies from his regiment, and two sections of Rhode Island artillery, joined us. A little below there we ran aground, and had to wait until midnight for flood-tide, when we got away once more.

At 8 A.M., we were at the mouth of the Altamaha River, and immediately made for Darien. We wound in and out through the creeks, twisting and turning continually, often heading in directly the opposite direction from that which we intended to go, and often running aground, thereby losing much time. Besides our three vessels, we were followed by the gunboat "Paul Jones."

On the way up, Montgomery threw several shells among the plantation buildings, in what seemed to me a very brutal way; for he didn't know how many women and children there might be.

About noon we came in sight of Darien, a beautiful little town. Our artillery peppered it a little, as we came up, and then our three boats made fast to the wharves, and we landed the troops. The town was deserted, with the exception of two white women and two negroes.

Montgomery ordered all the furniture and movable property to be taken on board the boats. This occupied some time; and after the town was pretty thoroughly disembowelled, he said to me, "I shall burn this town." He speaks always in a very low tone, and has quite a sweet smile when addressing you. I told him, "I did not want the responsibility of it," and he was only too happy to take it all on his shoulders; so the pretty little place was burnt to the ground, and not a shed remains standing; Montgomery firing the last buildings with his own hand. One of my companies assisted in it, because he ordered them out, and I had to obey. You must bear in mind, that not a shot had been fired at us from this place, and that there were evidently very few men left in it. All the inhabitants (principally women and children) had fled on our approach, and were no doubt watching the scene from a distance. Some of our grapeshot tore the skirt of one of the women whom I saw. Montgomery told her that her house and property should be spared; but it went down with the rest.

The reasons he gave me for destroying Darien were, that the Southerners must be made to feel that this was a real war, and that they were to be swept away by the hand of God, like the Jews of old. In theory it may seem all right to some, but when it comes to being made the instrument of the Lord's vengeance, I myself don't like it. Then he says, "We are outlawed, and therefore not bound by the rules of regular warfare"; but that makes it none the less revolting to wreak our vengeance on the innocent and defenceless.

By the time we had finished this dirty piece of business, it was too dark to go far down the narrow river, where our boat sometimes touched both banks at once; so we lay at anchor until daylight, occasionally dropping a shell at a stray house. The "Paul Jones" fired a few guns as well as we.

I reached camp at about 2 P.M. to-day, after as abominable a job as I ever had a share in.

We found a mail waiting for us, and I received your dear letter, and several from Father, Mother, Effie, and some business correspondence. This is the first news we have had since our departure, and I rather regained my good spirits.

Now, dear Annie, remember not to breathe a word of what I have written about this raid, to any one out of our two families, for I have not yet made up my mind what I ought to do. Besides my own distaste for this barbarous sort of warfare, I am not sure that it will not harm very much the reputation of black troops and of those connected with them. For myself, I have gone through the war so far without dishonour, and I do not like to degenerate into a plunderer and robber,—and the same applies to every officer in my regiment. There was not a deed performed, from beginning to end, which required any pluck or courage. If we had fought for possession of the place, and it had been found necessary to hold or destroy it, or if the inhabitants had done anything which deserved such punishment, or if it were a place of refuge for the enemy, there might have been some reason for Montgomery's acting as he did; but as the case stands, I can't see any justification. If it were the order of our government to overrun the South with fire and sword, I might look at it in a different light; for then we should be carrying out what had been decided upon as a necessary policy. As the case stands, we are no better than "Semmes," who attacks and destroys defenceless vessels, and haven't even the poor excuse of gaining anything by it; for the property is of no use to us, excepting that we can now sit on chairs instead of camp-stools.

But all I complain of, is wanton destruction. After going through the hard campaigning and hard fighting in Virginia, this makes me very much ashamed of myself.

Montgomery, from what I have seen of him, is a conscientious man, and really believes what he says,—"that he is doing his duty to the best of his knowledge and ability."

. . . There are two courses only for me to pursue: to obey orders and say nothing; or to refuse to go on any more such expeditions, and be put under arrest, probably court-martialled, which is a serious thing.

June 13th.—This letter I am afraid will be behindhand, for a boat went to Hilton Head this morning from the lower end of the island, and I knew nothing about it. Colonel Montgomery has gone up himself, and will not be back until Tuesday probably.

. . . To-day I rode over to Pierce Butler's plantation. It is an immense place, and parts of it very beautiful. The house is small, and badly built, like almost all I have seen here. There are about ten of his slaves left there, all of them sixty or seventy years old. He sold three hundred slaves about three years ago.

I talked with some, whose children and grandchildren were sold then, and though they said that was a "weeping day," they maintained that "Massa Butler was a good massa," and they would give anything to see him again. When I told them I had known Miss Fanny, they looked very much pleased, and one named John wanted me to tell her I had seen him. They said all the house-servants had been taken inland by the overseer at the beginning of the war; and they asked if we couldn't get their children back to the island again. These were all born and bred on the place, and even selling away their families could not entirely efface their love for their master. Isn't it horrible to think of a man being able to treat such faithful creatures in such a manner?

The island is traversed from end to end by what they call a shell-road; which is hard and flat, excellent for driving. On each side there are either very large and overhanging trees, with thick underbrush, or open country covered with sago-palm, the sharp-pointed leaves making the country impassable. Occasionally we meet with a few fields of very poor grass; when there is no swamp, the soil is very sandy.

There are a good many of these oyster-shell roads, for in many places there are great beds of them, deposited nobody knows when, I suppose. The walls of many of the buildings are built of cement mixed with oyster-shells, which make it very durable.

I forgot to tell you that the negroes at Mr. Butler's remembered Mrs. Kemble very well, and said she was a very fine lady. They hadn't seen her since the young ladies were very small, they said. My visit there was very interesting and touching.

A deserted homestead is always a sad sight, but here in the South we must look a little deeper than the surface, and then we see that every such overgrown plantation, and empty house, is a harbinger of freedom to the slaves, and every lover of his country, even if he have no feeling for the slaves themselves, should rejoice.

Next to Mr. Butler's is the house of Mr. James E. Cooper. It must have been a lovely spot; the garden is well laid out, and the perfume of the flowers is delicious. The house is the finest on the island. The men from our gunboats have been there, and all the floors are strewed with books and magazines of every kind. There is no furniture in any of these houses.

Please send this to Father, for I want him and Mother to read it, and I don't care about writing it over.

Colonel Montgomery's original plan, on this last expedition, was to land about fifteen miles above Darien, and march down on two different roads to the town, taking all the negroes to be found, and burning every planter's house on the passage. I should have commanded our detachment, in that case. The above are the orders he gave me.

Good bye for to-day, dearest Annie.

Your loving Rob

9 P.M. June 13th . . . To-morrow is Sunday, and perhaps you will be at Staten Island; at any rate, I suppose, not at Lenox; but wherever you are, I wish I could go to church with you, and saunter about in some pretty garden afterwards.

. . . There is a beautiful little church near here, almost buried in trees and moss. I have had it put to rights (it was damaged by some sailors and soldiers), and the Chaplain of the Second South Carolina Regiment is to preach there for us to-morrow.

I shall always have a service of some kind on Sunday; and if we can't always get a chaplain, I shall have one of the officers officiate. I don't feel good enough myself to undertake to teach others, as you suggest. Perhaps I shall some time. I have read some of Robertson's sermons, and think them very beautiful.

. . . I shall never let Mr. Ritchie go, if I can prevent it. He is a perfect jewel, and has been of incalculable service to us, in managing the regimental quartermaster's department. . . .

Your loving Husband

William Winters to Harriet Winters

After his victory at Port Gibson on May 1 Grant advanced northeast toward Jackson, forty miles east of Vicksburg, while his troops supplied themselves by foraging on the countryside. His forces defeated the Confederates at Raymond, May 12, and captured Jackson, May 14, frustrating attempts by General Joseph Johnston to assemble reinforcements there. While Sherman's men destroyed factories and railroads in Jackson, Grant turned most of his army west toward Vicksburg. Union victories at Champion Hill, May 16, and Big Black River Bridge, May 17, forced the Confederates to retreat inside the Vicksburg fortifications. Grant ordered assaults on the Vicksburg defenses, May 19 and May 22, both of which failed, and then began siege operations. Sergeant William Winters had enlisted in the 67th Indiana Regiment in August 1862 and fought in the Vicksburg campaign as part of the Thirteenth Corps, commanded by Major General John A. McClernand. His regiment saw action at Port Gibson, Champion Hill, Big Black River, and the May 22 assault, and lost about forty-five men killed and wounded in these engagements.

In Camp, Seige of
Vicksburg, June 9, 1863
    Dear wife,
    We are still tunneling away at the rebel works around the city and in same position as we were when I last wrote to you, with a fair prospect of remaining so for several days to come, but we will go into the city of Vicksburgh after awhile, that is shure, for we can live outside of their works longer than they can inside of them, that is certain, for we can get everything we want, and they can get nothing atall. We hear all kinds of rumors of how they are suffering for the want of water and provisions, but we cant tell which tale is the true one, and so we lett them pass for what they will fitch.
    The only thing we have here that we can rely on for certain is the roar of cannon and the rattle of musketry, but we have been taking it perfectly cool and easely since the day of the

charge. if you where here some time you would not think that we were face to face with an enemy, the men whistling and singing, sutlers selling their wares, and everything looks as if we were in camp for a big rest instead of beseigeing a rebell city.

The worst thing here is the water does not agree with the men. A good many of them are complaining with the diareah. Jacob Shut, Emanuel Sawers, and Levi Snyder are here in our hospt. they are trying to get Shut and Sawers furloughs for twenty days, but I dont know how they will succeed, but I hope they will get them as they ought to have them.

The weather for the last three days has been most intolrably hot. It looks a litle like rain to day. I hope that it will as we need it. Tom Eaton, Charly Bannes, and the rest of the boys that we left back at the river sick have all got well and are here with the regiment. I believe that the boys are all well but the three that we have here in the Hospt.

the boys are all verey mutch put out with Captain Eaton. They say that he promised to write to the most of them but he's never wrote a word to the company attall. We all hope that he is doing well. Letters from home are a scarce thing here now. We get the news from the cincinnati, st. Louis, Memphis, and Chicago papers every few days, but this is all. We got a mail the other day that had three letters in it for the 67th Reg. And that was all. Three letters in three weeks for three hundred and fifty men is a heavey mail I think.

I am not verey well and dont expect to be untill I get away from this watter. I have written this makes seven letters since I have received one from any person, but I reckon the next mail will be full of them. I hoope that we will be in Vicksburgh before I have to write again. give my love to all. Tell them I eat as many ripe blackberreys as I wanted on day before yesterday. Write soon. From your Afect Husband

Wm. Winters

Matthew M. Miller to His Aunt

One of the first battles of the war to involve significant numbers of black troops was fought on June 7 when 1,500 Confederates attacked the Union supply depot at Milliken's Bend, Louisiana, in an attempt to disrupt the siege of Vicksburg. The position was defended by about 1,000 men from the 23rd Iowa Infantry and four recently recruited black regiments, the 1st Mississippi Infantry and the 9th, 11th, and 13th Louisiana Infantry (African Descent), that had not completed their musket training. Although the Confederates succeeded in driving the defenders back to the riverbank, they broke off their attack after several hours and retreated under fire from two Union gunboats. The Confederates lost 175 men killed or wounded, the Union forces 386. Captain Matthew M. Miller of Galena, Illinois, described the fighting in a letter that was published in the *Galena Advertiser*, reprinted in other newspapers, and included in a preliminary report issued by the American Freedmen's Inquiry Commission on June 30, 1863.

MILLIKEN'S BEND, *June 10, 1863.*

DEAR AUNT: We were attacked here on June 7, about 3 o'clock in the morning, by a brigade of Texas troops, about 2,500 in number. We had about 600 men to withstand them, 500 of them negroes. I commanded Company I, Ninth Louisiana. We went into the fight with 33 men. I had 16 killed and 11 badly wounded, 4 slightly. I was wounded slightly on the head, near the right eye, with a bayonet, and had a bayonet run through my right hand near the forefinger; that will account for this miserable style of penmanship.

Our regiment had about 300 men in the fight. We had 1 colonel wounded, 4 captains wounded, 2 first and 2 second lieutenants killed, 5 lieutenants wounded, and 3 white orderlies killed and 1 wounded in the hand and two fingers taken off. The list of killed and wounded officers comprises nearly all the officers present with the regiment, a majority of the rest being absent recruiting.

We had about 50 men killed in the regiment and 80 wounded, so you can judge of what part of the fight my company sustained. I never felt more grieved and sick at heart than when I saw how my brave soldiers had been slaughtered, one with six wounds, all the rest with two or three, none less than two wounds. Two of my colored sergeants were killed, both brave, noble men; always prompt, vigilant, and ready for the fray. I never more wish to hear the expression, "The niggers wont fight." Come with me 100 yards from where I sit and I can show you the wounds that cover the bodies of 16 as brave, loyal, and patriotic soldiers as ever drew bead on a rebel.

The enemy charged us so close that we fought with our bayonets hand to hand. I have six broken bayonets to show how bravely my men fought. The Twenty-third Iowa joined my company on the right, and I declare truthfully that they had all fled before our regiment fell back, as we were all compelled to do.

Under command of Colonel Page I led the Ninth and Eleventh Louisiana when the rifle-pits were retaken and held by our troops, our two regiments doing the work.

I narrowly escaped death once. A rebel took deliberate aim at me with both barrels of his gun, and the bullets passed so close to me that the powder that remained on them burned my cheek. Three of my men who saw him aim and fire thought that he wounded me each fire. One of them was killed by my side, and he fell on me, covering my clothes with his blood, and before the rebel could fire again I blew his brains out with my gun.

It was a horrible fight, the worst I was ever engaged in, not even excepting Shiloh. The enemy cried, "No quarters," but some of them were very glad to take it when made prisoners.

Colonel Allen, of the Seventeenth Texas, was killed in front of our regiment, and Brigadier-General Walker was wounded. We killed about 180 of the enemy. The gun-boat Choctaw did good service shelling them. I stood on the breast-works after we took them, and gave the elevations and direction for the gun-boat by pointing my sword, and they sent a shell right into their midst, which sent them in all directions. Three shells fell there, and 62 rebels lay there when the fight was over.

My wound is not serious, but troublesome. What few men I have left seem to think much of me because I stood up with them in the fight. I can say for them that I never saw a braver company of men in my life.

Not one of them offered to leave his place until ordered to fall back; in fact, very few ever did fall back. I went down to the hospital three miles to-day to see the wounded. Nine of them were there, two having died of their wounds. A boy I had cooking for me came and begged a gun when the rebels were advancing, and took his place with the company, and when we retook the breast-works I found him badly wounded with one gunshot and two bayonet wounds. A new recruit I had issued a gun to the day before the fight was found dead, with a firm grasp on his gun, the bayonet of which was broken in three pieces. So they fought and died defending the cause that we revere. They met death coolly, bravely; not rashly did they expose themselves, but all were steady and obedient to orders.

So God has spared me again through many dangers. I cannot tell how it was I escaped.

Your affectionate nephew,

M. M. MILLER.

Robert E. Lee to Jefferson Davis

Despite victories at Fredericksburg and Chancellorsville, Lee worried that these triumphs did not markedly change the strategic situation. He proposed to Jefferson Davis that the Confederacy seize the initiative in the eastern theater by invading Pennsylvania, allowing the Army of Northern Virginia to gather food and forage in enemy territory and giving Lee an opportunity to weaken northern morale by winning a third consecutive victory over the Army of the Potomac. Davis agreed, and after reorganizing his army, Lee started his troops toward the Shenandoah Valley on June 3. He wrote to Davis a week later from his temporary headquarters at Culpeper Court House, thirty miles northwest of Fredericksburg.

Headquarters, Army of Northern Virginia
June 10, 1863

Mr. President:

I beg leave to bring to your attention a subject with reference to which I have thought that the course pursued by writers and speakers among us has had a tendency to interfere with our success. I refer to the manner in which the demonstration of a desire for peace at the North has been received in our country.

I think there can be no doubt that journalists and others at the South, to whom the Northern people naturally look for a reflection of our opinions, have met these indications in such wise as to weaken the hands of the advocates of a pacific policy on the part of the Federal Government, and give much encouragement to those who urge a continuance of the war.

Recent political movements in the United States, and the comments of influential newspapers upon them, have attracted my attention particularly to this subject, which I deem not unworthy of the consideration of Your Excellency, nor inappropriate to be adverted to by me in view of its connection with the situation of military affairs.

Conceding to our enemies the superiority claimed by them in numbers, resources, and all the means and appliances for carrying on the war, we have no right to look for exemptions from the military consequences of a vigorous use of these advantages, excepting by such deliverance as the mercy of Heaven may accord to the courage of our soldiers, the justice of our cause, and the constancy and prayers of our people. While making the most we can of the means of resistance we possess, and gratefully accepting the measure of success with which God has blessed our efforts as an earnest of His approval and favor, it is nevertheless the part of wisdom to carefully measure and husband our strength, and not to expect from it more than in the ordinary course of affairs it is capable of accomplishing. We should not therefore conceal from ourselves that our resources in men are constantly diminishing, and the disproportion in this respect between us and our enemies, if they continue united in their efforts to subjugate us, is steadily augmenting. The decrease of the aggregate of this army as disclosed by the returns affords an illustration of this fact. Its effective strength varies from time to time, but the falling off in its aggregate shows that its ranks are growing weaker and that its losses are not supplied by recruits.

Under these circumstances we should neglect no honorable means of dividing and weakening our enemies that they may feel some of the difficulties experienced by ourselves. It seems to me that the most effectual mode of accomplishing this object, now within our reach, is to give all the encouragement we can, consistently with truth, to the rising peace party of the North.

Nor do I think we should in this connection make nice distinctions between those who declare for peace unconditionally and those who advocate it as a means of restoring the Union however much we may prefer the former.

We should bear in mind that the friends of peace at the North must make concessions to the earnest desire that exists in the minds of their countrymen for a restoration of the Union, and that to hold out such a result as an inducement is essential to the success of their party.

Should the belief that peace will bring back the Union become general, the war would no longer be supported, and that after all is what we are interested in bringing about. When peace is proposed to us it will be time enough to discuss its terms, and it is not the part of prudence to spurn the proposition in advance, merely because those who wish to make it believe, or affect to believe, that it will result in bringing us back to the Union. We entertain no such apprehensions, nor doubt that the desire of our people for a distinct and independent national existence will prove as steadfast under the influence of peaceful measures as it has shown itself in the midst of war.

If the views I have indicated meet the approval of Your Excellency you will best know how to give effect to them. Should you deem them inexpedient or impracticable, I think you will nevertheless agree with me that we should at least carefully abstain from measures or expressions that tend to discourage any party whose purpose is peace.

With the statement of my own opinion on the subject, the length of which you will excuse, I leave to your better judgment to determine the proper course to be pursued.

I am with great respect, your obt servt

R. E. LEE
Genl

William T. Sherman to John T. Swayne

John T. Swayne, the judge of the Memphis criminal court, wrote to Sherman to protest a recent military order expelling from the city persons who refused to swear allegiance to the United States. Sherman responded to Swayne from his headquarters near Vicksburg, enclosing a letter to Major General Stephen A. Hurlbut, the Union commander at Memphis, in which Sherman endorsed the power of the military to punish spying and sedition among an occupied population but expressed doubts about the "efficiency and policy" of exacting "a 'naked oath.'"

———————

Hd. Qrs. 15th. Army Corps.
Camp on Walnut Hills, June 11, 1863

Judge Swayne, Memphis
Dear Sir,

As you can readily understand, I have about as much local business, as should engage the attention of one man, desirous of following the great revolution, which is sweeping as with whirlwind speed to destruction or Safety, I enclose you a letter, I have hastily written to General Hurlbut, which is as Specific as I ought to write. The General is a Southerner born and educated Lawyer, as well as Politician and it looks like an absurdity in one, who professes nothing of the kind to suggest to him any course of policy founded in a state of facts, of which I must be ignorant. If God himself smote Sodom and Gomorra, for departing from the law, and setting up their blind prejudice instead, surely I could not plead forbearance on the part of the U.S. if the people of Memphis are known to be conspiring against our law and safety.

But on the other hand, if the people of Memphis are acting in good faith, I will plead for them, that they be dealt with fairly honestly and even with kindness.

I fear me, that politicians and news mongers have so stirred up the vile passions of our People, and so poisoned their minds, that a government founded on public opinion, will for years to come be too unstable to curb these passions, and restrain the excesses, to which they lead, and that the U.S. Government assume the strong and dictatorial form, which alone can protect life and property.

The value of theoretical political notions, must I fear yield to that of more substantial interest. The sooner the people of the South discover this truth, and act upon it, the more will they save from the wrack of matter, that now threatens their universal ruin.

They may display heroic courage, they may elicit the admiration of the world, by the display of military genius, but they cannot stay the hand of destruction, that is now setting adrift their Slaves, occupying with fruitless muskets their adult whites, consuming and wasting their fields and improvements, destroying their roads, bridges, and the labor and fruits of near a century of undisturbed prosperity.

Men of extreme opinion and action cannot reason together and calm this tumult. It is the task allotted to such as you, and the time will come, and that soon, that even you, if you fail to act will be swept aside, helpless as a wisp of straw in the gale of wind.

Instead of appealing to Genl. Hurlbut to assist you, to escape a dangerous remote contingency, I say: think—act. Take your part and see, that some power is raised in America, that can stay the hand of strife, and substitute the rule of justice and mercy for that of force, violence and destruction.

If such men as you sit idle now, you are barred in all future Tribunals to plead for mercy and forbearance. What is a court without Power and a Sheriff? What is a Government, without Power and an Executive? Restore to our old Government its wonted power, and soon will cease this strife, and the Rights, you once prized, but now fast sinking into insignificance amidst new issues, will return and assume their natural weight.

But prolong the strife, and you may safely burn your library and turn your thoughts to some more lucrative trade than the Law.

I believe, you will receive from me in good part thoughts so crude, and it may be unreasonable. I surely wish you well. With Respect

W. T. Sherman
Maj. Genl.

Henry C. Whelan to Mary Whelan

The largest cavalry battle of the war was fought on June 9 when 11,000 Union troops crossed the Rappahannock and attacked 10,000 Confederate cavalrymen deployed around Brandy Station, five miles northeast of Culpeper Court House. Although they were taken by surprise, the Confederates eventually drove the Union forces from the field. The Confederates lost about 500 men killed, wounded, or missing, and the Union about 900. Major Henry C. Whelan of the 6th Pennsylvania Cavalry described the battle to his sister.

Thursday Morning, June 11/63.
Old Camp under the Oaks near
Catletts Station, Va.

On Monday the 8th we marched from here at 3 P.M. and halted near the ford for the night—no fires—and all kept perfectly quiet. At 3 in the morning we were again in the saddle and our Regiment, at the head of the Regular Brigade, crossed the river, when fighting immediately began. The Rebels fell back slowly, until they gained a good position, when they made a stand. Whilst I was by the side of Haseltine, talking with him, a number of shots hissed close by us, and a minute after, Harry's magnificent horse "Medor" fell, shot through the flank. About 15 minutes later we were ordered to advance on the woods from which the enemy were annoying us with sharp shooters. We had with us then five, Captain Treichel's Company A; Company D, Lieut. White; Company F, Captain Davis; Company K, Lieut Colliday; and Company L, Captain Leiper—the other five Companies were on duty on the north side of the river and joined us later in the day. Leiper's Company advanced as skirmishers, and Major Morris led the two squadrons, he at the head of the first, I of the second. We passed through the woods, being heavily shelled on our left by the enemy's batteries. When we came through to the open, we found a whole brigade of Stuart's Cavalry drawn up to receive us. We dashed at them, squadron front with drawn sabres, and as we flew along—our men yelling like demons—grape and cannister were poured into our left flank and a storm of rifle bullets on our front. We had to leap three wide deep ditches, and many of our horses and men piled up in a writhing mass in those ditches and were ridden over. It was here that Major Morris' horse fell badly with him, and broke away from him when he got up, thus leaving him dismounted and bruised by the fall. I didn't know that Morris was not with us, and we dashed on, driving the Rebels into and through the woods, our men fighting with the sabre alone, whilst they used principally pistols. Our brave fellows cut them out of the saddle and fought like tigers, until I discovered they were on both flanks, pouring a cross fire of carbines and pistols on us, and then tried to rally my men and make them return the fire with their carbines.

I found we were rapidly getting hemmed in, so I, as rapidly as possible, gathered together the remnant of our Regiment and dashed out of the woods, only to find that hundreds of grey devils occupied both sides of the open;—and because we had not been supported, we were completely surrounded. Then came a *race for life*—I shook the reins on poor little "Lancer's" neck, and he dashed off with the speed of a deer, passed by scores of yelling demons, who devoted most of their attention and shots to me. How many were fired at once I am afraid to guess, as it would look like exaggeration. I had to dash to the right and to the left to avoid and get between them, and a dozen of them fired so close to me that I almost felt the hot breath of their pieces—one officer rode close up on my right side and levelled his pistol. I stooped under his arm on "Lancer's" neck as he fired, and gave him a hissing right cut with my sabre as I flew by—I then dropped my sabre on my wrist and drew my pistol and fired at all who came too close—I passed a dismounted Rebel officer so close that I could have cut his head off. An Irishman, of Company K, who was splendidly mounted, stuck to me like a leech, and called out from behind: "Major, there's an officer—shall I cut him down?" I saw his horse was killed and he himself stood defenceless, so I told the man to let him alone. That Irishman cried out, when I cut the rebel who fired his pistol at me: "Good for you, Major", and gave a regular Irish whoop.

Oh! What a fearful ride, full two miles of ground covered with dead and wounded men and horses, wide ditches, which my dear sorrel cleared like an antelope, and all the time pursued and fired at by those grey blood-hounds, who kept yelling for me to surrender. To get rid of some of them, I made a desperate dash at a stone wall about 5 feet high, which "Lancer" topped like a bird. After that, only four or five continued the chase, until I caught sight of some of our Cavalry and rode for them across the country, over a deep creek and two wide ditches and one more stone wall. I found they were a Company of the 2nd Regulars, Captain Rodenbaugh, of Easton. As soon as I joined them, the Rebels broke out of the woods, five times the number of Rodenbaugh's men, so he wheeled about and started his men back by fours at a gallop. I rode along with them, and going through a narrow gate their horses got jambed and piled up in a horrid kicking mass—poor "Lancer" was almost crushed—I could only see part of his head, some grey horse's legs were right over his neck, and I was crushed in so tight, with horses on both sides, that I could not move. Strange to say, after much kicking, groaning and rolling about, I managed to get "Lancer" partly free; and then he struggled out with me, considerably bruised, and his hind leg bleeding. It was only a minute perhaps, but it seemed hours of horror, to be pinioned and fettered by a writhing mass of heavy horses, and the murderous Rebels coming up to shoot or stab us in the back.

"Lancer" was no sooner free than away he sped like an arrow from the bow, and bore me back safe, though covered with dust and bruised and weary. The men I got together, who made their way back from the charge, only numbered about one small squadron. I was reinforced by Frazier's squadron, from the other side of the river, and sent to take possession of a stone wall which the Rebels were trying to get with their skirmishers.

The enemy, in about an hour, brought so strong a force against the place that they ordered me to take the balance of my Company and to garrison this wall. I had to take them over an open field, about six hundred yards, through a perfect tempest of shell, grape, canister, solid shot and rifle bullets. I took them at a full run, but before we reached the wall, poor Captain Davis was shot dead with a grape shot; two of Frazier's men, together with their horses, were literally smashed by a solid shot; a large number of men were wounded, and horses killed. Going to and down at that wall was decidedly the hottest place I was ever in. A man could not show his head or a finger without a hundred rifle shots whistling about you. We saw negroes with white teeth grinning firing at us with long rifles. I was obliged to ride three times up and down that fearful place with the air almost solid with lead.

At last, when the 5th Cavalry men, who were out of ammunition, left to return, the Rebels charged in number 3 to 1 of us; and we were forced to fall back. I had just sprung on poor "Lancer's" back when there came a rifle ball right through his flank, and the noble little fellow could move no more. He fell with and although in that hail storm of iron and lead I could have sat down and cried. I own that my eyes filled with tears as I walked slowly away. In a moment my orderly, Ward, of Company C, rode up to me, sprung to the ground, and said, "Major, take my horse—I have a carbine, and can get back safe on foot". I mounted and rode back, whilst Ward turned and shot a Rebel who was robbing "Lancer" of his saddle blanket. Lieut. Lennig was lost at that place, whether killed, wounded or taken prisoner, we don't know. How I escaped through all I can't imagine. I was only grazed on the left wrist, and didn't know it till I saw my wrist bathed in blood. The shot which killed "Lancer" passed close to my thigh through the saddle bag and piercing Bulwer's "What will he do with it", which was strapped to the saddle bag. I will send the book to you by mail. It has some of "Lancer's" blood upon it. All the rest of that day we were engaged constantly under severe fire from artillery and small arms, until we fired away all our ammunition, and about five in the afternoon the regular brigade, exhausted by 14 hours hard fighting, retired to the other side of the river.

The conduct of officers and men of the 6th Penna. Cavalry is spoken of in the highest terms by all. General Buford says the regiment has covered itself with glory, but at a fearful expense. We lost six officers and over one hundred men killed, wounded and missing, and took 347 men and 18 officers into the fight. Our loss is thus one third of the whole command engaged.

Our charge on the Rebel brigade is said by all to have been the finest feature of the fight and leaving us unsupported to cut our own way back is severely blamed on—"somebody".

I have tried to give you as faithful account as I could, but such a crowd of terrible incidents is almost impossible to describe. Charley Leiper was cut across the forehead by a sabre, but he fought like a Turk with pistol and sabre, was surrounded and disarmed, but still stuck to his horse and striking with his fists finally broke away and escaped. Haseltine was twice struck by spent balls, one hurting him quite severely. Eight of our officers had their horses shot away under them. Lennig had two horses shot, and so had White. Colliday was lost in the charge—Rudolph Ellis was shot in the leg during the afternoon. He was quite close to me—he and Leiper were sent to Washington. I recovered the body of Capt. Davis and sent it to Washington with the Chaplain there to be embalmed and sent home. He is a great loss to the Regiment and is deeply mourned.

Abraham Lincoln to Erastus Corning and Others

The arrest and trial of former congressman Clement L. Vallandigham were widely criticized by Democrats and by some Republicans. In private President Lincoln and his cabinet regretted General Burnside's actions, but, as Lincoln wrote Burnside, "being done, all were for seeing you through with it." After commuting his prison sentence to banishment, the President wrote a public letter responding to resolutions protesting Vallandigham's arrest adopted at a public meeting in Albany, New York. (The meeting was presided over by Erastus Corning, a Democratic congressman and president of the New York Central Railroad.) Lincoln's letter appeared in the press on June 15, four days after the Ohio Democratic convention nominated Vallandigham for governor.

EXECUTIVE MANSION
Washington.
June 12, 1863.

Hon. ERASTUS CORNING *and others:*

GENTLEMEN: Your letter of May 19, inclosing the resolutions of a public meeting held at Albany, N. Y., on the 16th of the same month, was received several days ago.

The resolutions, as I understand them, are resolvable into two propositions—first, the expression of a purpose to sustain the cause of the Union, to secure peace through victory, and to support the Administration in every constitutional and lawful measure to suppress the Rebellion; and secondly, a declaration of censure upon the Administration for supposed unconstitutional action, such as the making of military arrests. And, from the two propositions, a third is deduced, which is that the gentlemen composing the meeting are resolved on doing their part to maintain our common government and country, despite the folly or wickedness, as they may conceive, of any Administration. This position is eminently patriotic, and as such I thank the meeting and congratulate the nation for it. My own purpose is the same; so that the meeting and myself have a common object, and can have no difference, except in the choice of means or measures for effecting that object.

And here I ought to close this paper, and would close it, if there were no apprehension that more injurious consequences than any merely personal to myself might follow the censures systematically cast upon me for doing what, in my view of duty, I could not forbear. The resolutions promise to support me in every constitutional and lawful measure to suppress the Rebellion; and I have not knowingly employed, nor shall knowingly employ, any other. But the meeting, by their resolutions, assert and argue that certain military arrests, and proceedings following them, for which I am ultimately responsible, are unconstitutional. I think they are not. The resolutions quote from the Constitution the definition of treason, and also the limiting safeguards and guarantees therein provided for the citizen on trials for treason, and on his being held to answer for capital or otherwise infamous crimes, and, in criminal prosecutions, his right to a speedy and public trial by an impartial jury. They proceed to resolve "that these safe-guards of the rights of the citizen against the pretensions of arbitrary power were intended more *especially* for his protection in times of civil commotion." And, apparently to demonstrate the proposition, the resolutions proceed: "They were secured substantially to the English people *after* years of protracted civil war, and were adopted into our Constitution at the *close* of the Revolution." Would not the demonstration have been better if it could have been truly said that these safeguards had been adopted and applied *during* the civil wars and *during* our Revolution, instead of *after* the one and at the *close* of the other? I, too, am devotedly for them *after* civil war, and *before* civil war, and at all times, "except when, in cases of rebellion or invasion, the public safety may require" their suspension. The resolutions proceed to tell us that these safeguards "have stood the test of seventy-six years of trial, under our republican system, under circumstances which show that, while they constitute the foundation of all free government, they are the elements of the enduring stability of the Republic." No one denies that they have so stood the test up to the beginning of the present Rebellion, if we except a certain occurrence at New-Orleans; nor does any one question that they will stand the same test much longer after the Rebellion closes. But these provisions of the Constitution have no application to the case we have in hand, because the arrests complained of were not made for treason—that is, not for *the* treason defined in the Constitution, and upon conviction of which the punishment is death—nor yet were they made to hold persons to answer for any capital or otherwise infamous crimes; nor were the proceedings following, in any constitutional or legal sense, "criminal prosecutions." The arrests were made on totally different grounds, and the proceedings following accorded with the grounds of the arrests. Let us consider the real case with which we are dealing, and apply to it the parts of the Constitution plainly made for such cases.

Prior to my installation here, it had been inculcated that any State had a lawful right to secede from the national Union, and that it would be expedient to exercise the right whenever the devotees of the doctrine should fail to elect a President to their own liking. I was elected contrary to their liking; and, accordingly, so far as it was legally possible, they had taken seven States out of the Union, had seized many of the United States forts, and had fired upon the United States flag, all before I was inaugurated, and, of course, before I had done any official act whatever. The Rebellion thus began soon ran into the present Civil War; and, in certain respects, it began on very unequal terms between the parties. The insurgents had been preparing for it more than thirty years, while the Government had taken no steps to resist them. The former had carefully considered all the means which could be turned to their account. It undoubtedly was a well-pondered reliance with them that, in their own unrestricted efforts to destroy Union, Constitution, and law, all together, the Government would, in great degree, be restrained by the same Constitution and law from arresting their progress. Their sympathizers pervaded all departments of the Government and nearly all communities of the people. From this material, under cover of "liberty of speech," "liberty of the press," and "habeas corpus," they hoped to keep on foot among us a most efficient corps of spies, informers, suppliers, and aiders and abettors of their cause in a thousand ways. They knew that in times such as they were in-augurating, by the Constitution itself, the "habeas corpus" might be suspended; but they also knew they had friends who would make a question as to *who* was to suspend it; meanwhile, their spies and others might remain at large to help on their cause. Or, if, as has happened, the Executive should suspend the writ, without ruinous waste of time, instances of arresting innocent persons might occur, as are always likely to occur in such cases; and then a clamor could be raised in regard to this, which might be, at least, of some service to the insurgent cause. It needed no very keen perception to discover this part of the enemy's programme, so soon as, by open hostilities, their machinery was fairly put in motion. Yet, thoroughly im-bued with a reverence for the guaranteed rights of individuals, I was slow to adopt the strong measures which by degrees I have been forced to regard as being within the exceptions of the Constitution, and as indispensable to the public safety. Nothing is better known to history than that courts of justice are utterly incompetent to such cases. Civil courts are orga-nized chiefly for trials of individuals, or, at most, a few indi-viduals acting in concert; and this in quiet times, and on charges of crimes well defined in the law. Even in times of peace, bands of horse-thieves and robbers frequently grow too numerous and powerful for the ordinary courts of justice. But what comparison, in numbers have such bands ever borne to the insurgent sympathizers, even in many of the loyal States? Again: a jury too frequently has at least one member more ready to hang the panel than to hang the traitor. And yet, again, he who dissuades one man from volunteering, or in-duces one soldier to desert, weakens the Union cause as much as he who kills a Union soldier in battle. Yet this dissuasion or inducement may be so conducted as to be no defined crime of which any civil court would take cognizance.

Ours is a case of rebellion—so called by the resolutions be-fore me—in fact, a clear, flagrant, and gigantic case of rebel-lion; and the provision of the Constitution that "the privilege of the writ of habeas corpus shall not be suspended, unless when, in cases of rebellion or invasion, the public safety may require it," is *the* provision which specially applies to our pres-ent case. This provision plainly attests the understanding of those who made the Constitution, that ordinary courts of justice are inadequate to "cases of rebellion"—attests their purpose that, in such cases, men may be held in custody whom the courts, acting on ordinary rules, would discharge. Habeas corpus does not discharge men who are proved to be guilty of defined crime; and its suspension is allowed by the Constitution on purpose that men may be arrested and held who cannot be proved to be guilty of defined crime, "when, in cases of rebellion or invasion, the public safety may require it." This is precisely our present case—a case of rebellion, wherein the public safety *does* require the suspension. Indeed, arrests by process of courts, and arrests in cases of rebellion, do not proceed altogether upon the same basis. The former is directed at the small per centage of ordinary and continuous perpetration of crime; while the latter is directed at sudden and extensive uprisings against the Government, which at most, will succeed or fail in no great length of time. In the latter case, arrests are made, not so much for what has been done, as for what probably would be done. The latter is more for the preventive and less for the vindictive than the former. In such cases, the purposes of men are much more easily understood than in cases of ordinary crime. The man who stands by and says nothing when the peril of his Government is discussed, cannot be misunderstood. If not hindered, he is sure to help the enemy; much more, if he talks ambiguously—talks for his country with "buts" and "ifs" and "ands." Of how little value the constitutional provisions I have quoted will be rendered, if arrests shall never be made until defined crimes shall have been committed, may be illustrated by a few notable examples. Gen. John C. Breckinridge, Gen. Robert E. Lee, Gen. Joseph E. Johnston, Gen. John B. Magruder, Gen. William B. Preston, Gen. Simon B. Buckner, and Commodore Franklin Buchanan, now occupying the very highest places in the Rebel war service, were all within the power of the Government since the Rebellion began, and were nearly as well known to be traitors then as now. Unquestionably if we had seized and held them, the insurgent cause would be much weaker. But no one of them had then committed any crime defined in the law. Every one of them, if arrested, would have been discharged on *habeas corpus* were the writ allowed to operate. In view of these and similar cases, I think the time not unlikely to come when I shall be blamed for having made too few arrests rather than too many.

By the third resolution, the meeting indicate their opinion that military arrests may be constitutional in localities where rebellion actually exists, but that such arrests are unconstitutional in localities where rebellion or insurrection does *not* actually exist. They insist that such arrests shall not be made "outside of the lines of necessary military occupation, and the scenes of insurrection." Inasmuch, however, as the Constitution itself makes no such distinction, I am unable to believe that there *is* any such constitutional distinction. I concede that the class of arrests complained of can be constitutional only when, in cases of rebellion or invasion, the public safety may require them; and I insist that in such cases they are constitutional *wherever* the public safety does require them; as well in places to which they may prevent the Rebellion extending as in those where it may be already prevailing; as well where they may restrain mischievous interference with the raising and supplying of armies to suppress the Rebellion, as where the Rebellion may actually be; as well where they may restrain the enticing men out of the army, as where they would prevent mutiny in the army; equally constitutional at all places where they will conduce to the public safety, as against the dangers of rebellion or invasion. Take the particular case mentioned by the meeting. It is asserted, in substance, that Mr. Vallandigham was, by a military commander, seized and tried "for no other reason than words addressed to a public meeting, in criticism of the course of the Administration, and in condemnation of the Military orders of the General." Now, if there be no mistake about this; if this assertion is the truth and the whole truth; if there was no other reason for the arrest, then I concede that the arrest was wrong. But the arrest, as I understand, was made for a very different reason. Mr. Vallandigham avows his hostility to the War on the part of the Union; and his arrest was made because he was laboring, with some effect, to prevent the raising of troops; to encourage desertions from the army; and to leave the Rebellion without an adequate military force to suppress it. He was not arrested because he was damaging the political prospects of the Administration, or the personal interests of the Commanding General, but because he was damaging the Army, upon the existence and vigor of which the life of the Nation depends. He was warring upon the Military, and this gave the Military constitutional jurisdiction to lay hands upon him. If Mr. Vallandigham was not damaging the military power of the country, then his arrest was made on mistake of fact, which I would be glad to correct on reasonably satisfactory evidence.

I understand the meeting, whose resolutions I am considering, to be in favor of suppressing the Rebellion by military force—by armies. Long experience has shown that armies cannot be maintained unless desertions shall be punished by the severe penalty of death. The case requires, and the law and the Constitution sanction, this punishment. Must I shoot a simple-minded soldier boy who deserts, while I must not touch a hair of a wily agitator who induces him to desert? This is none the less injurious when effected by getting a father, or brother, or friend, into a public meeting, and there working upon his feelings till he is persuaded to write the soldier boy that he is fighting in a bad cause, for a wicked Administration of a contemptible Government, too weak to arrest and punish him if he shall desert. I think that in such a case to silence the agitator, and save the boy is not only constitutional, but withal a great mercy.

If I be wrong on this question of constitutional power, my error lies in believing that certain proceedings are constitutional when, in cases of rebellion or invasion, the public safety requires them, which would not be constitutional when, in the absence of rebellion or invasion, the public safety does *not* require them: in other words, that the Constitution is not, in its application, in all respects the same, in cases of rebellion or invasion involving the public safety, as it is in time of profound peace and public security. The Constitution itself makes the distinction; and I can no more be persuaded that the Government can constitutionally take no strong measures in time of rebellion, because it can be shown that the same could not be lawfully taken in time of peace, than I can be persuaded that a particular drug is not good medicine for a sick man, because it can be shown not to be good food for a well one. Nor am I able to appreciate the danger apprehended by the meeting that the American people will, by means of military arrests during the Rebellion, lose the right of Public Discussion, the Liberty of Speech and the Press, the Law of Evidence, Trial by Jury, and Habeas Corpus, throughout the indefinite peaceful future, which I trust lies before them, any more than I am able to believe that a man could contract so strong an appetite for emetics during temporary illness as to persist in feeding upon them during the remainder of his healthful life.

In giving the resolutions that earnest consideration which you request of me, I cannot overlook the fact that the meeting speak as "Democrats." Nor can I, with full respect for their known intelligence, and the fairly presumed deliberation with which they prepared their resolutions, be permitted to suppose that this occurred by accident, or in any way other than that they preferred to designate themselves "Democrats" rather than "American citizens." In this time of national peril, I would have preferred to meet you upon a level one step higher than any party platform; because I am sure that, from such more elevated position, we could do better battle for the country we all love than we possibly can from those lower ones where, from the force of habit, the prejudices of the past, and selfish hopes of the future, we are sure to expend much of our ingenuity and strength in finding fault with, and aiming blows at each other. But, since you have denied me this, I will yet be thankful, for the country's sake, that not all Democrats have done so. He on whose discretionary judgment Mr. Vallandigham was arrested and tried is a Democrat, having no old party affinity with me; and the judge who rejected the constitutional view expressed in these resolutions, by refusing to discharge Mr. Vallandigham on habeas corpus, is a Democrat of better days than these, having received his judicial mantle at the hands of President Jackson. And still more, of all those Democrats who are nobly exposing their lives and shedding their blood on the battle-field, I have learned that many approve the course taken with Mr. Vallandigham, while I have not heard of a single one condemning it. I cannot assert that there are none such. And the name of President Jackson recalls an instance of pertinent history: After the battle of New-Orleans, and while the fact that the treaty of peace had been concluded was well known in the city, but before official knowledge of it had arrived, Gen. Jackson still maintained martial or military law.

Now, that it could be said the war was over, the clamor against martial law, which had existed from the first, grew more furious. Among other things, a Mr. Louiallier published a denunciatory newspaper article. Gen. Jackson arrested him. A lawyer by the name of Morel procured the United States Judge Hall to issue a writ of habeas corpus to release Mr. Louiallier. Gen. Jackson arrested both the lawyer and the judge. A Mr. Hollander ventured to say of some part of the matter that "it was a dirty trick." Gen. Jackson arrested him. When the officer undertook to serve the writ of habeas corpus, Gen. Jackson took it from him, and sent him away with a copy. Holding the judge in custody a few days, the General sent him beyond the limits of his encampment, and set him at liberty, with an order to remain till the ratification of peace should be regularly announced, or until the British should have left the Southern coast. A day or two more elapsed, the ratification of a treaty of peace was regularly announced, and the judge and others were fully liberated. A few days more, and the judge called Gen. Jackson into court and fined him $1,000 for having arrested him and the others named. The General paid the fine, and there the matter rested for nearly thirty years, when Congress refunded principal and interest. The late Senator Douglas, then in the House of Representatives, took a leading part in the debates, in which the constitutional question was much discussed. I am not prepared to say whom the journals would show to have voted for the measure.

It may be remarked: First, that we had the same Constitution then as now; secondly, that we then had a case of invasion, and now we have a case of rebellion; and, thirdly, that the permanent right of the People to Public Discussion, the Liberty of Speech and the Press, the Trial by Jury, the Law of Evidence, and the Habeas Corpus, suffered no detriment whatever by that conduct of Gen. Jackson, or its subsequent approval by the American Congress.

And yet, let me say that, in my own discretion, I do not know whether I would have ordered the arrest of Mr. Vallandigham. While I cannot shift the responsibility from myself, I hold that, as a general rule, the commander in the field is the better judge of the necessity in any particular case. Of course, I must practice a general directory and revisory power in the matter.

One of the resolutions expresses the opinion of the meeting that arbitrary arrests will have the effect to divide and distract those who should be united in suppressing the Rebellion, and I am specifically called on to discharge Mr. Vallandigham. I regard this as, at least, a fair appeal to me on the expediency of exercising a Constitutional power which I think exists. In response to such appeal, I have to say, it gave me pain when I learned that Mr. Vallandigham had been arrested—that is, I was pained that there should have seemed to be a necessity for arresting him—and that it will afford me great pleasure to discharge him so soon as I can, by any means, believe the public safety will not suffer by it. I further say that, as the war progresses, it appears to me, opinion, and action, which were in great confusion at first, take shape, and fall into more regular channels, so that the necessity for strong dealing with them gradually decreases. I have every reason to desire that it should cease altogether, and far from the least is my regard for the opinions and wishes of those who, like the meeting at Albany, declare their purpose to sustain the Government in every constitutional and lawful measure to suppress the Rebellion. Still, I must continue to do so much as may seem to be required by the public safety.

A. LINCOLN

William Henry Harrison Clayton to Amos and Grace Clayton and to George Washington Clayton and John Quincy Adams Clayton

The 19th Iowa Infantry was sent downriver from Missouri in June 1863 to join the Union forces investing Vicksburg and assigned to the Seventeenth Corps, commanded by Major General James B. McPherson. William Henry Harrison Clayton, the clerk of Company H, described the siege to his parents and to his younger brothers.

––––––––––––––––––

Camp of 19th Iowa Infantry
In the rear of Vicksburg
June 18th, 1863

Dear Father & Mother:

Having a few spare moments, I thought that I would improve them by writing and give you an account of our movements since leaving Young's Point, LA. at which point I last wrote.

We left there on the 12th, marching across the bend, and reached the river 3 or 4 miles below Vicksburg and in full view of the town.

We have 5 or 6 steamboats below Vicksburg that are used for carrying troops, supplies, etc. across to Warrenton. Some of these run the blockade and are pretty well used up. The *Forest Queen* is a nice sidewheel boat, the others are stern-wheelers. The ram *Switzerland* was there and is as good as ever. When running the blockade a ball passed into one of her boilers and let the steam out in a hurry but did no other damage. Several gunboats are stationed there to watch the river. The *Tuscumbia* is a large boat and looks like a large turtle with its back out of water.

We crossed to Warrenton 6 or 8 miles below Vicksburg, on

the *Silver Wave*. Her guards had been nearly all torn off some how and was a hard looking boat.

At Warrenton we remained over night. Here I saw 3 large guns that were captured by our forces at Grand Gulf. They are having them brought up and will soon have them planted opposite some of the Rebel forts here. The Rebels had a pretty strong earthwork at Warrenton & places fixed with railroad iron and logs to protect the men. All is destroyed now.

We first used our shelter tents at Warrenton. They do well enough to keep off the sun but will not turn much rain. Each tent is composed of two pieces about 3 yards square and is for two men each of whom carries his piece and one pole each about 4 ft. long, when the two pieces composing it are put together. When we pitch tents we button the two pieces together, fix the "sticks" in the center and stake down two ends. The sides are open and permit the air to circulate freely!

On the 13th we marched 3 or 4 miles towards our lines and camped that night. On the 14th we took our present position, to the left of the center. We are camped *under* a hill side, to shelter us from the Rebel shells which come over occasionally. It is not a mile straight across to the Rebel line. We, that is Co. "H" and 5 other companies of the 19th were on picket yesterday & last night.

We acted more as skirmishers than anything else. We were strung along behind logs and stumps and kept popping away whenever we would see a shadow of a Rebel, our guns with the sights raised to 300 yards would strike their outer works every time, some of their pickets were not more than 150 yards from us, but they had holes in the ground so that we would not see them and could only tell where they were by the smoke when they discharged their guns. The discharge of small arms is almost constant along the line, but they don't do much damage on either side. A fellow has to keep his head pretty low though, for some ball would whistle by, very close. Occasionally the heavy artillery takes a turn and makes things "git."

I and one of our boys yesterday, saw 5 or 6 "Rebs" on their works some distance off, and thought that we would see how close we could shoot to them. We raised the gun sights to 800 yards. He shot and we could notice that one got out of that place in a hurry. I then shot at them standing all together in an embrasure of a fort, the dust flew up close by them. It was not more than 2 minutes before *boom* went a gun and a shell came crashing over us. They fired three times but hit no one.

Our forces along this part of the line have advanced several hundred yards, and will be apt to go farther, not however without digging in on the right and center. Our boys are close under their guns, so close that they cannot fire them. Some of the 15th Iowa boys have been down to see their friends. They said that they had worked in the trenches not more than 20 yds. from their forts.

I expect the people of the North are getting impatient because Grant does not take Vicksburg, but if they were here for themselves they would not wonder at the delay. It is certainly the roughest country I ever seen. The hills are not so very high, but the whole country is nothing but a succession of hills and hollows about like some places on the Buckles farm.

The Rebels have forts thrown up about 200 or 300 yds. apart all along their line, with heavy guns mounted and forts in the rear of these, making the place almost impregnable. I do not believe that another place in the country could be found that is so naturally fortified. They had forts outside of our present lines that they evacuated, that would have been hard to take. The hills in places rise abruptly, and look almost as though they had been drawn up purposefully for a fort. The boys who have been here since the siege began appear to be in good spirits. They say that it will be almost impossible for Johnston to get in with reinforcements. The timber has been cut down for miles and we have a large force on Big Black watching him. I don't see what Pemberton is holding out so long for. It looks almost impossible for reinforcements to reach him. I suppose he will hold out until his provisions give out, and that may be sometime longer. Deserters say that they are living on quarter rations. The weather here is right warm. The magnolia trees are in full bloom. There is lots of them in the woods. I saw some green figs a day or two ago. Peaches are nearly full size. The blackberries are ripe in this part of the world. Corn is out in tassel in places. I have not seen much around here but I suppose there is plenty of it growing further back.

I was a good deal surprised to see the cane here grow where

it does. I always thought that grew in swamps or in the low grounds, but here it grows on the hills. Where we are camped it is thick, some of it 25 or 30 feet long.

The boys are all well at present. I had an idea that the change would make us sick, but it has not made much of a difference in the sick list yet. John Stone is one of our company cooks. The cooks do nothing but get our "grub" ready for eating, have no other duty to perform. Mooney is cooking for the col. and captain. He is a very good hand at the business. There is a little insect that bothers us a great deal. They are called "jiggers," "chickers," or something like it. They are little red things not bigger than a pin point. They stick like a tick and raise little places like muskuits bites. As I expected the furlough business has *played out*, I suppose no more will be granted until after Vicksburg is taken.

Give my respects to all friends.

I remain your affectionate son,

W. H. H. Clayton

Camp of the 19th Iowa
In the rear of Vicksburg
June 28, 1863

Dear Brothers:

I received John's letter of the 7th a few days ago and was glad to hear from you again.

I have nothing of interest to write, but thought that I would send a few lines to let you know that I am well and getting along finely.

We have been here two weeks. Nothing of especial importance has transpired along our part of the line.

We have mounted several siege guns since we came here. They fire on the Rebels occasionally and make them hunt their holes. The Rebels fired at us considerably for a few days after our arrival here but since then have not fired much, only when our guns opened upon them, and for some days past they fired none at all.

Yesterday however they opened on our battery from a mortar that they had planted under a hill so that our guns could not reach them. Our camp is in range of their shells and some that came over the battery made us lay "kinder" close. The pieces flew around considerably but luckily no one was hurt.

There has been no firing on either side today. It is said that our gun boats got range of the mortar that disturbed us and silenced it. I hope it is so for it is not pleasant to hear shells buzzing around. The blamed things are apt to burst and the pieces go every direction. We have been on picket 4 times since we came here. The last two times we were up or awake all night. One night it rained the whole night slowly. I tell you, I would not have taken a good deal for my gum blanket that night. We laid within a few hundred yards of a brigade of Rebels, so we have learned since from prisoners. There was nearly two companies of us, we were there to prevent a movement on our guns. The 94th Ill. and 20th Wis. have taken 20 or 30 prisoners since we came here by charging upon their (the Rebels) rifle pits. But such work don't pay. The last *sortie* of this kind was by a company of the 94th. They took 8 men, and had one mortally wounded, he died an hour or two later, and another wounded so that it will render him unfit for service. The Rebels could have the rifle-pit defended by eight more men, right away, for it was not held by our men. Thus by the operation we lost two men and the Rebels got rid of feeding 8. I think the more men we can keep in there, the sooner will it surrender. There is no telling anything about how long it will hold out. Some prisoners & deserters say that they have not got much provision and others that they have enough to last 2 or 3 months. There has been no mail received here for several days. It is reported in camp that letters from here do not go further than Memphis. I think if such was the case we would not be allowed to send them from camp. I would like very much to hear how the Rebel raid into Pennsylvania terminated. We have no news later than June 17th. It takes a letter at least 10 days to come from Iowa here. We are in as bad a position to get news as we were when at Forsyth away down in Missouri. It is 10 or 12 miles around our line and we know no more what is going on at the other end of the line than you do. Sometimes it is reported that they have had a big fight on the right or in the center, and they have heard that we have had a battle here when there was nothing of the kind. We would like to get the St. Louis daily papers so that we could get news from Vicksburg!

The weather is very warm especially so in the sun. We lay around in the shade the most of the time when not on duty. The boys stand the change much better than I expected, but of course the sick list is larger than it was at Salem. Co. "H" has 47 men for duty, and 7 or 8 sick. The water here is not very good. We get it by digging 10 ft. It goes rather hard after being used to good spring water. The Chequest boys stand it "Bully" all being able for their rations.

There has been an oven erected here, and all our flour is baked and issued in loaves by the quartermaster. I like it much better than the biscuits our cooks make. I never did like hot or warm bread, but have had to get used to it, and sometimes glad to get anything in the bread line. We get half our bread rations in hard crackers.

Col. Kent was honored today by a visit from Mrs. Wittemeyer, U.S. Sanitary Commission agent, from Iowa. I suppose she is on a tour of inspection. Gen. Herron was also here today.

Well I must quit writing for the present. I want you to write whenever you can.

I remain your affectionate brother,

W. H. H. Clayton

Charles B. Haydon: Journal, June 20, 1863

A veteran of the Peninsula campaign, Second Bull Run, and Fredericksburg, Captain Charles B. Haydon was a company commander in
the 2nd Michigan Infantry. In March 1863 his regiment was transferred from Virginia to Kentucky, and in mid-June it was sent up the
Yazoo River fifteen miles from Vicksburg to help guard against a
possible Confederate attempt to relieve the city. Haydon recorded his
impressions the day after his arrival at his new post.

JUNE 20, 1863   We are really down South—Latitude 32° 20′,
a degree south of Charleston, on a line with the great desert of
Africa. Everything looks new and at this point not very pleas-
ing. The hills are not high but the ground is in all conceivable
shapes & so full of ravines as to be almost impassable. The
water is brackish & bad, very bad. The woods are oak, bass-
wood, sycamore, cottonwood, magnolia, palmetto &c. They
are so full of underbrush, briars, nettles, poisonous weeds and
such like that it is very unpleasant & difficult to get through
them. The trees are loaded with the long grey Southern moss
which hangs from the limbs in clusters & sheets from 2 to 10
feet in length (perpendicular) and swings loose in the wind.
This gives to everything a sort of dull sombre appearance. It
looks old, very old, as though everything was on the decline.

Canebrakes such as we buy at home for fish poles are very
abundant & are used by the men for almost everything. There
are some *alligators*, a good many snakes, lizards everywhere,
plenty of mosquitoes, flies, bugs, tarantulas, horned frogs &
other infernal machines too numerous to mention. I have not
been far into the woods. I went up to the edge once to day &
very cautiously looked in a little way then walked off. I am not
much afraid of snakes but I do not wish to provoke any unnecessary collision. They say that in the woods snakes & lizards
tumble down on your head every few steps but could not

swear to that. There are blackberries & wild plums in abundance, ripe & inviting.

There was terrific firing at Vicksburgh this m'g commencing before daylight. How I wish we could go down to the front where there is something doing. I saw Lt. Col. May and several other acquaintances from Michigan.

Our Regt. got very drunk on the way here. Moore and Montague had their hands full with Co. E. I have had experience enough in loading drunken soldiers onto boats & cars. They act like devils. If they should act so when sober it would not take long to adjust matters but in this case you have to tolerate some things which you would not at any other time. The men know perfectly well that as a rule the officers want to get drunk as bad as they do & that if it were not for the responsibility & their presence they would.

Still I do not believe that many of them would drink much after they had been out of the army a few days. A soldier never knows one day where he may be the next & his hold on the future being so uncertain he crowds the present to the utmost. "Eat drink & be merry for to morrow you die." I know by experience how powerfully those words appeal to the desires & if I do not indulge in wine as others do I presume it is only because other things please me more.

After some months of hard fare you arrive in a city. There is no one there who knows you except comrades who never tell tales. You have money & opportunity. Everything within you says there is no law or restraint here. Do as you please. "Let joy be unconfined." It may be your last chance. Everyone seems to think you are doing exactly right & to be anxious to help you in all your undertakings. Be careful & you will meet your Chaplain or hear his voice in the next room. But enough of this. Those who have tried it know all about it & those who have not can never learn from mere description.

There must be an increase of sickness if we remain here long. I am not much afraid of disease but can see the possibility of hard times ahead. The darkies are jubilant. "God bless Massa Lincum" say they all. They do nothing now but gather blackberries & plums to sell together with their master's property to soldiers. I saw a planter try to stop one who threw down his hoe & was walking off. He called out to him "where are you going?" "Oh I'se gwine to 'list—yah, yah, yah" was the reply & off he went & three others after him.

Their employment as soldiers is looked upon here with much more favor than in the Army of the Potomac. They are pretty well posted & are nearly all anxious to fight. It is thought here that they will make good soldiers. I find that my late journey amounts to about 2000 miles & that of the Regt. to about 1200 miles. There is no further need of troops in this vicinity.

William T. Sherman to
Ellen Ewing Sherman

Sherman wrote to his wife several days after Grant assigned him command of the forces guarding against a possible Confederate attempt to relieve Vicksburg.

———————

Camp on Bear Creek,
20 miles N.W. of Vicksburg.
June 27, 1863.

Dearest Ellen,

I am out here studying a most complicated Geography and preparing for Joe Johnston if he comes to the relief of Vicksburg. As usual I have to leave my old companions & troops in the trenches of Vicksburg, and deal with strange men, but I find all willing & enthusiastic. Although the weather is intensely hot, I have ridden a great deal, and think I know pretty well the weak and strong points of this extended Line of Circumvallation, and if Johnston comes I think he will have a pretty hard task to reach Vicksburg, although from the broken nature of the country he may feign at many points and attack but on one. Black River the real Line is now so low it can be forded at almost any point and I prefer to fight him at the Ridges along which all the Roads lead. Of these there are several some of which I have blocked with fallen trees and others left open for our own purposes, and which will be open to him if he crosses over—Our accounts of his strength & purposes are [   ] as the [   ] of fact of deserters & spies [   ] are. I [   ] to be governed by what I suppose he will do, under the pressure of opinion that must be brought to bear on him to relieve a brave & beleaguered Garrison. I suppose he made large calculations on obstructing the River at some point above us, and it seems the Boats coming down & going up receive shots at various points along the River, but thus far reinforcements and supplies have reached us without serious check. My Line extends from the Railroad Bridge on Black River, around to Haines Bluff, both of which are entrenched. I have some works at intermediate points, but if Johnston crosses the fight will be mostly by detachments along the narrow Ridges with which the country abounds, and along which alone Roads can be made.

The siege of Vicksburg progresses. From my camp I hear the booming of cannon, telling of continued battering. My trenches had connected with the main ditch before I left, and had I remained I think by this time we should have made a push for the Bastion in my front. I hear every day, that things remain status quo. I left Charley at Head Qrs. to continue his inspections and Hugh in command of his Brigade which is on the main approach. He say he writes often to his wife and to you all. [   ] I have [   ]—He is very stubborn & opinionated, but has his Brigade in good order, which is the only test to which I refer in official & military matters. I must not favor him or Charley unfairly, as it would do them no good & me much harm. You will feel sure that each has as much of my thoughts and affections as can be spared for the thousands subject to my orders & care. My military family numbers by the tens of thousands and all must know that they enjoy a part of my thoughts and attention. With officers & soldiers I know how to deal but am willing to admit ignorance as to the People who make opinion according to their contracted Knowledge & biassed prejudices, but I know the time is coming when the opinion of men "not in arms at the countrys crisis, when her calamities call for every man capable of bearing arms" will be light as to that of men who first, last & all the time were in the war. I enclose a slip which came to me by accident, describing our Leaders here. Were I to erase the names you would not recognize one, although the narrative meant to be fair & impartial.

I meet daily incidents which would interest you but these you will have to draw out on cross examination when we meet —I find here a Mrs. Klein only child of Mrs. Day of New Orleans & niece of Tom Bartley [   ] and will continue to befriend them. They have a son in the Confederate Army now in Vicksburg, a lad some 18 years of age. The day I approached Vicksburg, my advance Guard caught a Confederate soldier

and a negro, servant to George Klein, carrying a letter to the
father at his Country refuge near here. Of course the negro
was sent north and the letter read. It contained much useful
information, and among other things he described the loss of
the Battery of Guns at Champion Hill in which he used the
Expression, "We lost our Guns, but they will do the Yankees
no good, for we broke up the carriages and hid the Guns in a
Ravine" so this boy of Ohio birth is not very loyal, though he
was with John Sherman during his Electioneering Canvas
which resulted in Lincolns Election. Mr. Klein father continually exclaims, "they cant hold out much longer—their provisions must be out &c." but the enemy in Vicksburg in my
judgment shows no abatement of vigorous resistance or short
food—with every house in sight of our lines marked with the
Hospital Flag—Orange Yellow. We cant show a hand or cap
above our rifle pits without attracting a volley. But of course
there must be an end to all things & I think if Johnston do not
make a mighty effort to relieve Vicksburg in a week they will
cave in.

I would at this moment be in the saddle, but have sent a
Brigade down to Black River to examine a certain Ford where
one of our Pickets was fired on last night by Cavalry. I rather
think two of our patrols came together & mistook. Nobody
was hurt but I must watch closely, as I know Joe Johnston will
give me little time to combine after he moves. He may approach from the North North East or East, all of which routes
I am watching closely, but it will be necessary to draw from
two quarters to reinforce one, and it will be exceedingly difficult to judge from signs the Real point from the Feints. Their
cavalry is so much better than ours, that in all quick movements they have a decided advantage.

As I am now on my second sheet, and as I am listening for
signs of action at a Ford in the bottom 3 miles off, I might as
well go on and punish you with a surfeit after the manner of
your affectionate son & uncle, and bosom friend, Lt. Col.
Charley Ewing. My Head Qrs. here are in a tent by the Road
side, where one forks down to Bear Creek & the other goes
along down to Black River direct. I have with me the invariable Hill who still puts me on a damned allowance of segars &
whiskey & insists on blacking my boots & brushing my clothes

in & out of season. Boyer my orderly is also here, with my
horses Dolly, Abner, Sam and a new one recently presented me
by General Steele called Duke. Dolly carries me when I explore
—Sam & Duke when I expect to be shot at. Yesterday morning with Dolly, Boyer, McCoy & Hill aids and a small escort I
started on a circuit visiting outposts & pickets—At a Mrs.
Fox's I found as is the case of all farms here a bevy of women
waiting patiently the fate of husbands & sons penned up in
Vicksburg—one of them a Mrs. Eggleston, whose pretty children I noticed asked me if I were the Genl. Sherman of New
Orleans—of course not—She asked because a Mrs. Wilkinson
was a great friend of his—What Mrs. Wilkinson? a Mrs. Wilkinson of New Orleans. Where was she? spending the day at another Mrs. Fox, Parson Fox about a mile further on—As my
route lay that way I rode up the yard of Parson Fox. A company
of Iowa men lay in the shade on picket, and about a dozen
ladies sat on the broad balcony. I rode up close saluted the ladies & inquired for Mrs. Wilkinson a small old lady answered—
I asked if she were of Plaquemine Parish—Yes—Where was her
husband the General? Killed on the Plains of Manassas, fighting for his Country," with a paroxism of tears at tearing open
the old wound, and all the women looking at me as though I
had slain him with my own hand—I knew him well, he was a
direct descendant of the General Wilkinson of the old wars,
and was once a client of your father, I think in the famous
Land case of Penrose St. Louis. He had a son at Alexandria
about whom we corresponded a good deal. When I left Louisiana I regarded him as an Union man and had forgotten that
he was killed at Manassas at the first Battle—After the old lady
had cooled down a little I inquired for the Son. He is in Vicksburg, and the mother has got this near to watch his fate. Do,
oh do General Sherman spare my son, in one breath and in
another, that Lincoln was a tyrant and we only Murderers,
Robbers, plunderers and defilers of the houses and altars of an
innocent & outraged People. She and all the women were real
secesh, bitter as gall & yet Oh do General Sherman protect my
son. The scene set all the women crying, and Dolly & I concluded to go into the more genial atmosphere out in the Fields
& Woods. I doubt if History affords a parallel of the deep &
bitter enmity of the women of the South. No one who sees

them & hears them but must feel the intensity of their hate. Not a man is seen—nothing but women, with houses plundered, fields open to the cattle & horses, pickets lounging on every porch, and desolation sown broadcast—Servants all gone and women & children bred in luxury, beautiful & accomplished begging with one breath for the soldiers Ration and in another praying that the Almighty or Joe Johnston will come & kill us, the despoilers of their houses and all that is sacred—Why cannot they look back to the day & the hour when I a stranger in Louisiana begged & implored them to pause in their course, that secession was death, was everything fatal, and that their seizure of the public arsenals was an insult that the most abject nation must resent or pass down to future ages an object of pity & scorn. Vicksburg contains many of my old pupils & friends. Should it fall into our hands I will treat them with kindness, but they have sowed the wind & must reap the whirlwind. Until they lay down their arms, and submit to the rightful authority of their Government, they must not appeal to me for mercy or favors—The weather is very hot, though the nights are cool—wild plums abounded, have ripened and are gone. Blackberries are now as abundant as ever an army could ask, and are most excellent—Apples & peaches & figs are ripening, and of all these there will be an abundance even for our host. Corn too is in silk & tassel and soon Roasting ears will give our soldiers an additional tendency to sickness —advice, orders & remonstrance are all idle. Soldiers are like children, and eat, eat all the time. Water is very poor & scarce on the hills but is found in moving brooks down in the chasms and hollows of Clear & Bear Creeks near which all my Camps are—I have written Minnie & Willy & sent the latter some fishing poles from the "Battle Field"—Tell Tom & Lizzy they must write me also. Tell them all that actually I have hardly time to write to you and I get tired of writing more than I used to—Love to all yrs. ever

Sherman

INVADING THE NORTH:
MARYLAND AND PENNSYLVANIA, JUNE 1863

Edmund DeWitt Patterson: Journal, June 24–30, 1863

Lieutenant Edmund DeWitt Patterson of the 9th Alabama Infantry had fought at Marye's Heights and Salem Church during the Chancellorsville campaign. He marched north in June as part of the Third Corps of the Army of Northern Virginia, commanded by Lieutenant General A. P. Hill. The advance forces of Lee's army defeated the Union garrison at Winchester in the Shenandoah Valley on June 15 and crossed into Pennsylvania on June 22.

———————

Near Boonesboro, Md. Wednesday the 24th.   This morning bright and early we crossed the Potomac at Mill Ford one mile below Shepherdtown. The water from three to four feet deep. It was a little cool but we were all in such fine spirits that we didn't mind it. We came up on the hill near Sharpesburg and halted for an hour or two; while there General Wright and staff rode into town and all came near being captured. All escaped but the General's son, who could not ride fast on account of the loss of a leg which he parted with at Manassas. The squad who made the charge escaped before our infantry could reach them. Passed through Sharpesburg which is a hard looking dilapidated old town, and which still shows the marks of the battle fought there. The battle of Sharpsburg, or Antietam as the Yankees have it, will long be remembered. We have had an easy march today, and are now camping in a pretty meadow, in a valley three miles from Boonesboro.

Hagerstown, Md. Thurs. 25th.   Passed through Boonesboro this morning just as the sun was rising bright and glorious over the South Mountain. Everything on the road looks strange to us coming as we do from the desolate fields of Virginia. Here we see houses, barns filled with grain, fine stock etc. Today we met a fine large drove of beef cattle going to the rear. Some of the boys who have fully realized the effects of the war at their own houses are fairly itching to retaliate, but Gen'l. Lee's order issued the morning we crossed into Md. is too strict. The majority of the people seem to be "loyal" tho we find quite a number who are with us heart and soul, though not bodily. Fungston seems to contain quite a number of families who are Southern sympathizers. We reached this place at one o'clock this evening, and quite a number of the boys have been in the city. I preferred to remain in camp.

Two miles from Green Castle, Penn. Friday the 26th of June. This morning Capt. Harry Lee, Jim Crow and I left camps about daylight and came into the city of Hagerstown. Had an old fashioned time. Patronized the barber shop, hotel, and saloon, and as it bade fair to rain all day we laid in a supply of the "needful." About 8 o'clock our command passed through Middlebury. Crossed the Pennsylvania and Maryland line at 11 o'clock precisely. Jim Crow, Van Whitehead and I persuaded an old gentleman to show us exactly where the line ran and then standing with one foot in Maryland and the other in Pennsylvania, we finished the contents of a canteen, drinking some pretty heavy toasts. Green Castle seems to be a pretty little town but intensely "loyal." It would probably be more so, if it had passed through what many of the towns in the South have, tried with fire. Gen'l. A. P. Hill passed us on the march looking ready for a fight.

Saturday the 27th. On the march again. Passed through Marion and Chambersburg. While passing through the latter place Gen'l. Lee rode up the column speaking kindly to acquaintances and passed on. The boys never cheer him, but pull off their hats and worship. The females of Chambersburg seem to be very spiteful, make faces, sing "Rally round the flag," wave their little banners etc. I think if they had a hole burned out in their town about the size and extent of that which the Yankees burned in Florence or Athens, Alabama, these patriotic females would not be quite so saucy. A widow in the place discovered the knapsack of her deceased husband in the command, she wished it and the soldier gave it to her. He had picked it up on the battlefield of "Gaine's Mills," where we fought the "squirrel tail rifles." I suppose that her husband has gone to that home from whence etc., such is war. We reached this place, Fayetteville, a little before sun down, and Jim and I went out and took supper with a good old Pennsylvania farmer; plenty of everything, especially apple butter, the first I have tasted since I left Ohio.

Fayetteville, Sunday Evening, 28th.   I have been down town nearly all day sauntering about up and down the streets. No preaching either in camps or in town. Some of the boys have been "capturing" chickens. It is against positive orders, but I would not punish one of them, for as Joe McMurray says, it's not half as bad as they did, to his mother and sisters in Alabama, for they not only took such things, but took the rings from his sisters' fingers, and earrings from their ears, besides cursing and abusing them. It is well that Joe isn't General in Chief for he would try what virtue there is in fire, as well as the sword.

Tues. 30th.   Still at Fayetteville, but there is something on the tapis, for yesterday Heath's and Pender's divisions left, and have gone in the direction of Gettysburg. I took dinner yesterday at the hotel, and at night Jim Crow, Dick Hobbs and I went out about two miles into the country to get supper, and had a most magnificent time. The young lady was Union but called herself a "copperhead." I would not mind being bitten by her a few times. On our way back as we were coming through the town we serenaded the citizens with "The Bonnie Blue Flag," "The Sunny South Forever," etc. Don't think it was appreciated though. Hood's and McLaws' divisions passed through town late this evening. Met several of my old friends in the 4th Alabama. Also saw Cousin Frank. Had but little time to talk to him. Was on brigade guard today, and kept things *straight* around the hotel, took dinner there, and so won the heart of the old landlord that he filled my canteen with cherry brandy. I pronounce him a "gentleman and scholar and a judge of the article."

Lafayette McLaws to Emily McLaws

A West Point graduate who joined the Confederate army in 1861 and fought in the Seven Days' Battles, Antietam, Fredericksburg, and Chancellorsville, Major General Lafayette McLaws commanded one of the three divisions in the First Corps of the Army of Northern Virginia, led by Lieutenant General James Longstreet. When McLaws wrote to his wife on June 28, Longstreet's and A. P. Hill's corps were camped around Chambersburg, while the Second Corps, commanded by Lieutenant General Richard Ewell, was divided between Carlisle and York. After learning on the night of June 28 that the Army of the Potomac had left northern Virginia and reached Frederick, Maryland, Lee issued orders for his army to reunite at either Cashtown, seventeen miles east of Chambersburg, or at Gettysburg, another eight miles farther to the east.

Head Quarters Division
June 28'/63
Camp near Chambersburg, Pa

My Dear Emily

My command arrived at this place, this morning at 10 oclock, and joined the rest of the Corps camped near this place.

We left Martinsburg in Virginia on the 26th at five oclock in the morning, and fording the river, camped three Brigades near Wmsport and one brigade with my artillery near Hagerstown. I camped in an open lot in the town. The ford at Wmsport is a very good one the men crossing without difficulty. The Chesapeake and Ohio Canal which runs along the river bank on the north side, was dry, the aquaduct having been blown up. The track of the Baltimore and Ohio Canal running along the canal was also destroyed—from Martinsburg to the river, eleven miles, the houses were all closed, the curtains drawn and the people either absent or invisible—showing an evident dislike to our cause. It was remarked as we went into Martinsburg that the magnificent farm of the Honl. Charles J

Faulkner who was the Adjutant General of General Jackson was in a beautiful state of cultivation, not a stone of his fences injured and the laborers at work with their teams, collecting the clover which has been cut and cured. While on the other side of the road, the fences were down, the crops destroyed, the grounds trampled and everything wearing the appearance of places which had long ago been deserted and devastated. The secret was out, when we visited the town and was told that Mrs Faulkner had not long since returned from Washington, and on the evening our troops first entered the town she had issued tickets for a large party to be given to the Yankee officers. Her daughters were also constantly visiting the Yankee families and were being visited by them and the Yankee officers generally, and that the greatest cordiality existed between them.

The farms we saw lying in waste were those of southern families who were not so devoted to Yankeedom. There was no welcome given us in Martinsburg, except by a very few and those of the ladies who exhibited any cordiality I noticed were clothed in silks, and de lames & muslins, and all the finery of a thriving Yankee town. Many women & children made faces at us as we marched along, and although we could not hear them, we could see their mouths moving, and from their expressions knew they were giving us their maledictions. As we crossed into Williamsport, the people were more friendly but yet all the shops were closed and the houses generally deserted or exhibiting no signs of being inhabited. One lady said she was delighted to see us. Shook hands very cordially. Said she expected to be sent over the river if the enemy should ever return but did not care. Shortly after I went to the window to get some water and seeing a boy of nine or ten in the room with the blue blouse of a Yankee. I Said "You are a Yankee Sir"; the boy said nothing but held down his head. The young lady before mentioned said to him "Speak up buddy and tell him you are no Yankee." "Yes but I am one" asserted the boy. And I remarked "Children take their opinions from their older sisters and brothers & they always tell the truth" and rode away. The family within looking as if they had been caught in a falsehood.

I camped three Brigades near Wmsport and one near Hagerstown with four batteries and camped in the town myself

(Hagerstown) where a good many persons called to see me
and I was invited to supper and breakfast. I went to supper and
had nothing better than I usually have at home; in camp, did
not mention the breakfast. Was introduced to Mr Roman formerly Member of Congress from Maryland, and went to his
house for a few minutes. Found him a very polished gentleman, and his wife and niece good specimens of southern ladies.
I was very glad to meet them as I thus had in my mind to
contrast between the southern gentleman and ladies and the
very different species I soon encountered. As I crossed the line
into Pennsylvania. At Green Castle on the road to Chambersburg. Several young ladies were assembled engaged in scoffing
at our men as they passed, but they were treated with contempt
or derision. I heard of nothing witty said by any of them. It
was made evident however that they were not ladies in the
southern acceptations of the word. The men I spoke to acknowledged that the brutalities practiced by their troops, upon
the southern people, fully justified our retaliating and were
surprised at our moderation—the poorer classes told me that
our troops behaved better to them than their own did. Arrived
at & marched through Chambersburg on 28th, a town of five
thousand inhabitants perhaps more. And camped two miles
east of it on the Harrisburg Road. Then arrived in camp on the
29th & destroyed about four miles of the rail road leading
then to Harrisburg. The people of Chambersburg are decidedly. The men dare not show it but by their looks, the women
tried to be sarcastic on various occasions but succeeded in
being vulgar only. They are a very different race from the
southern. There is a coarseness in their manners and looks and
a twang in their voices—which grates harshly on the senses of
our men; the distinction of class, the poor & sick is very
marked. Every one speaks for peace at any price, and since war
has been brought to their own homes, they look desponding
to the last degree, and begin to believe that they have been
vastly deceived by engaging in it— I have found no one to
speak of Lincoln as a man of either capacity or patriotism,
every one even the women think he is under abolition influence entirely, and they assert boldly that freedom should not
be the lot of the negro. To day I moved camp seven miles on
the Gettysburg Road, to Greenwood a small village, sending

one brigade two miles on to Caledonia, where Thadeus Stevens, the abolition Member of Congress from Penna who introduced the bill for the employment of negro troops, had large iron works. They were burned by our troops however, and are now in ashes & total ruin—

My division mail rider was caught by the enemy, in Hagerstown on his way here with letters.

When you write, therefore you must be cautious and particular. This may be captured also & I am particularly cautious as you may observe.

You may send this letter to WmR to be returned to you.

Give much love to the children, and ask them to write me, also to sister Laura & Bet. —Good night and much love from your devoted husband L.

Alpheus S. Williams to Irene and Mary Williams

When Lee began to move his army away from Fredericksburg, Hooker proposed crossing the Rappahannock and advancing on Richmond, but Lincoln directed him to instead make Lee's army his objective. Hooker started moving his army north on June 13 along a route that kept it between Lee's forces and Washington and began crossing the Potomac on June 25. By then, the President had become frustrated by Hooker's requests for reinforcements and his inability to work with General-in-Chief Henry W. Halleck. When a dispute with Halleck led Hooker to submit his resignation, Lincoln accepted it and named Major General George G. Meade to replace him. Brigadier General Alpheus S. Williams, a former officer in the Michigan militia who commanded a division in the Twelfth Corps, wrote to his daughters about the change in command.

––––––––––––––

Frederick, Md., June 29, 1863.

My Dear Daughters:

I have a moment in the office of Dr. Steiner of the Sanitary Commission to tell you where I am. We left Leesburg on Friday last, the 26th inst., and marched across the river at Edwards Ferry on pontoons and encamped that night at the mouth of the Monocacy. The next day we marched to within a mile of Knoxville, which Rene will remember is within two miles of the Longbridges on the Baltimore & Ohio Railroad, where we generally took the railroad for Baltimore. The Saturday's march was too tedious and fatiguing for me to go to the Longbridges. Besides, I did not get my brigades in camp until after dark. The whole line of march was crowded by baggage wagons and trains. I expected to march through Sandy Hook towards Williamsport but during the night was ordered to march my division towards Frederick. I reached this place yesterday afternoon, when a change of commanders was announced, Meade superceding Hooker.

It was intimated that we should remain at this place a day or so, but at 2.30 this morning I was awakened by a messenger ordering my division to march towards Taneytown at 5 A.M. I was camped in a fine grove and had a great desire for sleep after three days' fatiguing marches, but there is no help under orders. Besides, we are filled with an idea that the Rebels are getting into Pennsylvania, and of course we are bound to go on, cost what of human flesh it may. For myself, I am rejoiced at the change of commanders. I have said very little in my letters, but enough for you to guess that I had no confidence in Hooker after Chancellorsville. I can say now, that if we had had a commander of even ordinary merit at that place the army of Jackson would have been annihilated. I cannot conceive of greater imbecility and weakness than characterized that campaign from the moment Hooker reached Chancellorsville and took command.

I am not much of a military genius, but if I could have commanded the Army of the Potomac at Chancellorsville I would have wagered my life on being in Richmond in ten days! All we are suffering now in shame and mortification and in the great risk of losing the whole fortunes of the war is the legitimate result of the weakness which characterized that campaign. Since then, and as the results of that campaign, our army has been reduced over 50,000 men, two-thirds by expiration of term of service of three-months' and two-years' troops, and yet not one soldier has been added to our forces. All winter, by the natural disintegration of armies, we have been running down at the rate of 20 per cent per annum; add to this 35 to 40,000 men discharged by expiration of service and 25,000 killed and wounded in battle and you have at least 85,000 men in this army less now than last December, and this, too, at the season when active field duties commence. I have in my division less than half the men I had in January last, when I reached Stafford Court House. I think my division is a fair sample of the Army of the Potomac.

You see we have a great task before us to preserve the Republic. It is reported that the Rebels are 110,000 strong in infantry, with 20,000 cavalry. I think the report is greatly exaggerated, but they have been all winter recruiting by conscription, while we have been all winter running down. Still, I don't despair. On the contrary, now with a gentleman and a soldier in command I have renewed confidence that we shall at least do enough to preserve our honor and the safety of the Republic. But we run a fearful risk, because upon this small army everything depends. If we are badly defeated the Capital is gone and all our principal cities and our national honor. That this dilemma could have been suffered by men deputed to care for the safety of the Republic is indeed disheartening. That our northern people could sit down in search of the almighty dollar, when their all is depending upon this conflict, is indeed passing strange. If we fail in this war, be assured there is an end of northern prosperity. The Rebels in Baltimore and Washington will dictate terms and these terms will humiliate and destroy us. I would I had an archangel's voice to appeal to the patriotism (if there be any left) in the North!

I sent you a sort of journal of a few days we were in Leesburg, excepting two or three of the last. Those were devoted to putting the forts in good condition for the Rebels and making several miles of rifle pits and breast works.

Love to all; my column has passed and I must follow. This is a hasty scrawl, but I know with you better than none. Keep writing me. I am full of faith and yet fearfully anxious. There must be a decisive battle, I think, soon, but you will hear of it before this reaches you, probably. Possibly the enemy may withdraw, and I am not without hope that we may strike them on a weak flank exposure.

Whatever may happen, be contented and resigned, and believe it is all for the best. In nations, as in individuals, we must believe there is a "Divinity which shapes our ends, rough hew them as we will."

Your Affectionate Father,
A.S.W.

Samuel W. Fiske to the Springfield Republican

Following his parole to Annapolis, Fiske was exchanged, allowing him to return to duty as a brigade staff officer in the Second Corps. He wrote his dispatch as the Army of the Potomac continued to march northward.

TOWARD GETTYSBURG

Uniontown, Md.
June 30

Dear Republican: There is a deal of romance about this business of war. We lay us down at night under heaven's glorious canopy, not knowing if at any moment the call to arms may not disturb our slumbers. We wake at reveille, cook and eat our scanty breakfast, thankful if we have any to dispose of in that way. At the bugle-call we strike tents, put on our harness and packs, and start off, not knowing our direction, the object of our march, or its extent; taking everything on trust, and enjoying as much as possible the varied experience of each passing hour; and ready for a picnic or a fray, a bivouac, a skirmish, a picket, a reconnaissance, or a movement in retreat. There is no life in which there is more room for the exercise of faith than in this same soldierly life of ours—faith in our own good right arms, and in the joint strength and confidence of military discipline; faith in the experience and watchfulness of our tried commanders (happy if they be not tried and found wanting); faith in the ultimate success of our country's good and holy cause; faith in the overruling care and protection of Almighty Jehovah, who holdeth the movements of armies and nations, as also the smallest concerns of private individuals, in His hand.

Our marches for the last few days have been through the

most lovely country, across the state of Maryland to the east of Frederick City. There is not a finer cultivated scenery in the whole world, it seems to me; and it was almost like going to Paradise from—another place; the getting-out of abominable, barren, ravaged Old Virginia into fertile, smiling Maryland. It is a cruel thing to roll the terrible wave of war over such a scene of peace, plenty, and fruitfulness; but it may be that here on our own soil, and in these last sacrifices and efforts, the great struggle for the salvation of our country and our Union may successfully terminate. Poor Old Virginia is so bare and desolate as to be only fit for a battle-ground; but it seems that we must take our turn too, in the Northern states, of invasion, and learn something of the practical meaning of war in our own peaceful communities. I sincerely hope that the scare up in Pennsylvania isn't going to drive all the people's wits away, and prevent them from making a brave defense of homes, altars, and hearths. When I read in a paper to-day of the "chief burgess" of York pushing out eight or ten miles into the country to find somebody to surrender the city to, I own to have entertained some doubts as to the worthiness and valor of that representative of the dignity of the city. It would be well for the citizens of Pennsylvania to remember that Lee's soldiers are only men, after all, and that their number is not absolutely limitless, and that they have not really the power of being in a great many places at the same time.

Also, that, if they wish to enable the proper military authorities to defend them understandingly, it will be just as well to see to the accuracy of the information they carry, and not magnify a half-dozen cavalrymen into a huge invading army. It is the very best time in the world now for everybody to keep cool, and use a little common sense. When there isn't any danger near, it doesn't matter much about that. The simple truth is, that the enemy cannot by any possibility, leaving many of his men behind to keep his long line of communications open, carry into Pennsylvania anything like the number of forces we can bring to meet him; and it is only the circumstance of our being frightened to death at the audacity of his movement that can save him from repenting most ruefully the audacity of his crossing the Potomac northward. We of the unfortunate "grand army," to be sure, haven't much reason to make large promises; but we are going to put ourselves again in the way of the butternuts, and have great hopes of retrieving, on our own ground, our ill fortune in the last two engagements, and, by another and still more successful Antietam conflict, deserve well of our country.

Our troops are making tremendous marches some of these days just past; and, if the enemy is anywhere, we shall be likely to find him and feel of him pretty soon. For sixteen days we have been on the move, and endure the fatigues of the march well. There is much less straggling, and much less pillaging, than in any march of the troops that I have yet accompanied. Our men are now veterans, and acquainted with the ways and resources of campaigning. There are very few sick among us. The efficient strength, in proportion to our numbers, is vastly greater than when we were green volunteers. So the Potomac Army, reduced greatly in numbers as it has been by the expiration of the term of service of so many regiments, is still a very numerous and formidable army. An innocent "Dunker" (if you know that religious denomination), at whose house we staid last night, thought that he had seen pretty much all the people of the world when a corps or two of our forces had passed his house.

We passed, in our march up the Potomac, the field of the two Bull Run battles; and I was much shocked to find such great numbers of the bodies of Union soldiers lying still unburied. Their skeletons, with the tattered and decaying uniforms still hanging upon them, lie in many parts of last year's battle field, in long ranks, just as they fell; and in one place, under a tree, was a whole circle of the remains of wounded soldiers, who had been evidently left to die under the shade of which they had crawled, some of them with bandages round their skeleton limbs, one with a battered canteen clasped in his skeleton hand, and some with evidence, as our boys fancied, of having starved to death. On one old broken cart lies what is left of eight Union soldiers, left to decay as they were laid to be borne off the field, and the vehicle struck, probably, by a cannon ball. In many instances the bodies which were partially or hastily buried are now much uncovered; and a grinning skull meets our gaze as you pass, or a fleshless arm stretches out its ghastly welcome.

Still it is wonderful to notice how quickly and how kindly Nature covers up the traces of murderous conflict on her face. The scars are mostly healed, verdure reigns, and beauty smiles over the bloody field; and save in a lonely chimney here and there, and the ghastly sights I have above referred to, which result from human neglect and barbarity, and are not to be charged at all to Nature, you would not suspect your feet were pressing the sod that one year and two years ago was reddened in human gore.

Enough of moralizing for the present, and "a little more sleep and a little more slumber" for the heavy eyelids of one who was in the saddle fifteen hours out of the last twenty-four, and expects to be as many more in the next twenty-four. No news except that which can be gathered from the date of this epistle. Yours truly,

DUNN BROWNE

June 30, 1863

Arthur James Lyon Fremantle: Diary, July 1–4, 1863

Fighting broke out northwest of Gettysburg on the morning of July 1 when a Confederate infantry division advancing from Cashtown encountered two dismounted Union cavalry brigades defending the town. Both sides brought up reinforcements, and by the end of the day Lee and Meade had committed their armies to a battle that would eventually involve 83,000 Union and 75,000 Confederate troops. Arthur James Lyon Fremantle was a lieutenant colonel in the British army who took six months leave in early 1863 in order to visit the Confederacy. Fremantle entered Texas from Mexico on April 2, and met with Joseph E. Johnston in Mississippi, Braxton Bragg in Tennessee, and Jefferson Davis in Richmond before joining the Army of Northern Virginia in the Shenandoah Valley on June 22. Shortly after the battle of Gettysburg Fremantle crossed the lines in western Maryland and traveled to New York City, where he witnessed the draft riots before sailing for England on July 15. His diary was published in London shortly before Christmas as *Three Months in the Southern States: April–June 1863*, and was reprinted in both New York and Mobile in 1864.

———————

1st *July* (Wednesday).—We did not leave our camp till noon, as nearly all General Hill's corps had to pass our quarters on its march towards Gettysburg. One division of Ewell's also had to join in a little beyond Greenwood, and Longstreet's corps had to bring up the rear. During the morning I made the acquaintance of Colonel Walton, who used to command the well-known Washington Artillery, but he is now chief of artillery to Longstreet's *corps d'armée*. He is a big man, *ci-devant* auctioneer in New Orleans, and I understand he pines to return to his hammer.

Soon after starting we got into a pass in the South Mountain, a continuation, I believe, of the Blue Ridge range, which is broken by the Potomac at Harper's Ferry. The scenery through the pass is very fine. The first troops, alongside of whom we rode, belonged to Johnson's division of Ewell's corps. Among them I saw, for the first time, the celebrated "Stonewall" Brigade, formerly commanded by Jackson. In appearance the men differ little from other Confederate soldiers, except, perhaps, that the brigade contains more elderly men and fewer boys. All (except, I think, one regiment) are Virginians. As they have nearly always been on detached duty, few of them knew General Longstreet, except by reputation. Numbers of them asked me whether the General in front was Longstreet; and when I answered in the affirmative, many would run on a hundred yards in order to take a good look at him. This I take to be an immense compliment from any soldier on a long march.

At 2 P.M. firing became distinctly audible in our front, but although it increased as we progressed, it did not seem to be very heavy.

A spy who was with us insisted upon there being "a pretty tidy bunch of *blue-bellies* in or near Gettysburg," and he declared that he was in their society three days ago.

After passing Johnson's division, we came up to a Florida brigade, which is now in Hill's corps; but as it had formerly served under Longstreet, the men knew him well. Some of them (after the General had passed) called out to their comrades, "Look out for work now, boys, for here's the old bulldog again."

At 3 P.M. we began to meet wounded men coming to the rear, and the number of these soon increased most rapidly, some hobbling alone, others on stretchers carried by the ambulance corps, and others in the ambulance wagons. Many of the latter were stripped nearly naked, and displayed very bad wounds. This spectacle, so revolting to a person unaccustomed to such sights, produced no impression whatever upon the advancing troops, who certainly go under fire with the most perfect nonchalance. They show no enthusiasm or excitement, but the most complete indifference. This is the effect of two years' almost uninterrupted fighting.

We now began to meet Yankee prisoners coming to the rear in considerable numbers. Many of them were wounded, but they seemed already to be on excellent terms with their captors, with whom they had commenced swapping canteens, tobacco, &c. Among them was a Pennsylvanian colonel, a miserable object from a wound in his face. In answer to a question, I heard one of them remark, with a laugh, "We're pretty nigh whipped already." We next came to a Confederate soldier carrying a Yankee color, belonging, I think, to a Pennsylvania regiment, which he told us he had just captured.

At 4.30 P.M. we came in sight of Gettysburg, and joined General Lee and General Hill, who were on the top of one of the ridges which form the peculiar feature of the country round Gettysburg. We could see the enemy retreating up one of the opposite ridges, pursued by the Confederates with loud yells. The position into which the enemy had been driven was evidently a strong one. His right appeared to rest on a cemetery, on the top of a high ridge to the right of Gettysburg, as we looked at it.

General Hill now came up and told me he had been very unwell all day, and in fact he looks very delicate. He said he had had two of his divisions engaged, and had driven the enemy four miles into his present position, capturing a great many prisoners, some cannon, and some colors. He said, however, that the Yankees had fought with a determination unusual to them. He pointed out a railway cutting, in which they had made a good stand; also, a field in the centre of which he had seen a man plant the regimental color, round which the regiment had fought for some time with much obstinacy, and when at last it was obliged to retreat, the color-bearer retired last of all, turning round every now and then to shake his fist at the advancing rebels. General Hill said he felt quite sorry when he saw this gallant Yankee meet his doom.

General Ewell had come up at 3.30, on the enemy's right (with part of his corps), and completed his discomfiture. General Reynolds, one of the best Yankee generals, was reported killed. Whilst we were talking, a message arrived from General Ewell, requesting Hill to press the enemy in the front, whilst he performed the same operation on his right. The pressure was accordingly applied in a mild degree, but the enemy were too strongly posted, and it was too late in the evening for a regular attack. The town of Gettysburg was now occupied by Ewell, and was full of Yankee dead and wounded. I climbed up a tree in the most commanding place I could find, and could form a pretty good general idea of the enemy's position, although the tops of the ridges being covered with pine-woods, it was very difficult to see anything of the troops concealed in them. The firing ceased about dark, at which time I rode back with General Longstreet and his Staff to his headquarters at Cashtown, a little village eight miles from Gettysburg. At that time troops were pouring along the road, and were being marched towards the position they are to occupy to-morrow.

In the fight to-day nearly 6,000 prisoners had been taken, and 10 guns. About 20,000 men must have been on the field on the Confederate side. The enemy had two *corps d'armée* engaged. All the prisoners belong, I think, to the 1st and 11th corps. This day's work is called a "brisk little scurry," and all anticipate a "big battle" to-morrow.

I observed that the artillerymen in charge of the horses dig themselves little holes like graves, throwing up the earth at the upper end. They ensconce themselves in these holes when under fire.

At supper this evening, General Longstreet spoke of the enemy's position as being "very formidable." He also said that they would doubtless intrench themselves strongly during the night.* The Staff officers spoke of the battle as a certainty, and the universal feeling in the army was one of profound contempt for an enemy whom they have beaten so constantly, and under so many disadvantages.

2d July (Thursday).—We all got up at 3.30 A.M., and breakfasted a little before daylight. Lawley insisted on riding, notwithstanding his illness. Captain —— and I were in a dilemma for horses; but I was accommodated by Major Clark (of this Staff), whilst the stout Austrian was mounted by Major Walton. The Austrian, in spite of the early hour, had shaved his cheeks and *ciréd* his mustaches as beautifully as if he was on parade at Vienna.

Colonel Sorrell, the Austrian, and I arrived at 5 A.M. at the

---

*I have the best reason for supposing that the fight came off prematurely, and that neither Lee nor Longstreet intended that it should have begun that day. I also think that their plans were deranged by the events of the first.

same commanding position we were on yesterday, and I climbed up a tree in company with Captain Schreibert of the Prussian army. Just below us were seated Generals Lee, Hill, Longstreet, and Hood, in consultation—the two latter assisting their deliberations by the truly American custom of *whittling* sticks. General Heth was also present; he was wounded in the head yesterday, and although not allowed to command his brigade, he insists upon coming to the field.

At 7 A.M. I rode over part of the ground with General Longstreet, and saw him disposing of M'Laws's division for to-day's fight. The enemy occupied a series of high ridges, the tops of which were covered with trees, but the intervening valleys between their ridges and ours were mostly open, and partly under cultivation. The cemetery was on their right, and their left appeared to rest upon a high rocky hill. The enemy's forces, which were now supposed to comprise nearly the whole Potomac army, were concentrated into a space apparently not more than a couple of miles in length. The Confederates inclosed them in a sort of semicircle, and the extreme extent of our position must have been from five to six miles at least. Ewell was on our left; his headquarters in a church (with a high cupola) at Gettysburg; Hill in the centre; and Longstreet on the right. Our ridges were also covered with pine-woods at the tops, and generally on the rear slopes. The artillery of both sides confronted each other at the edges of these belts of trees, the troops being completely hidden. The enemy was evidently intrenched, but the Southerners had not broken ground at all. A dead silence reigned till 4.45 P.M., and no one would have imagined that such masses of men and such a powerful artillery were about to commence the work of destruction at that hour.

Only two divisions of Longstreet were present to-day—viz., M'Laws's and Hood's—Pickett being still in the rear. As the whole morning was evidently to be occupied in disposing the troops for the attack, I rode to the extreme right with Colonel Manning and Major Walton, where we ate quantities of cherries, and got a feed of corn for our horses. We also bathed in a small stream, but not without some trepidation on my part, for we were almost beyond the lines, and were exposed to the enemy's cavalry.

At I P.M. I met a quantity of Yankee prisoners who had been

picked up straggling. They told me they belonged to Sickles's corps (3d, I think), and had arrived from Emmetsburg during the night. About this time skirmishing began along part of the line, but not heavily.

At 2 P.M. General Longstreet advised me, if I wished to have a good view of the battle, to return to my tree of yesterday. I did so, and remained there with Lawley and Captain Schreibert during the rest of the afternoon. But until 4.45 P.M. all was profoundly still, and we began to doubt whether a fight was coming off to-day at all. At that time, however, Longstreet suddenly commenced a heavy cannonade on the right. Ewell immediately took it up on the left. The enemy replied with at least equal fury, and in a few moments the firing along the whole line was as heavy as it is possible to conceive. A dense smoke arose for six miles; there was little wind to drive it away, and the air seemed full of shells—each of which appeared to have a different style of going, and to make a different noise from the others. The ordnance on both sides is of a very varied description. Every now and then a caisson would blow up—if a Federal one, a Confederate yell would immediately follow. The Southern troops, when charging, or to express their delight, always yell in a manner peculiar to themselves. The Yankee cheer is much more like ours; but the Confederate officers declare that the rebel yell has a particular merit, and always produces a salutary and useful effect upon their adversaries. A corps is sometimes spoken of as a "good yelling regiment."

So soon as the firing began, General Lee joined Hill just below our tree, and he remained there nearly all the time, looking through his field-glass—sometimes talking to Hill and sometimes to Colonel Long of his Staff. But generally he sat quite alone on the stump of a tree. What I remarked especially was, that during the whole time the firing continued, he only sent one message, and only received one report. It is evidently his system to arrange the plan thoroughly with the three corps commanders, and then leave to them the duty of modifying and carrying it out to the best of their abilities.

When the cannonade was at its height, a Confederate band of music, between the cemetery and ourselves, began to play polkas and waltzes, which sounded very curious, accompanied by the hissing and bursting of the shells.

At 5.45 all became comparatively quiet on our left and in the cemetery; but volleys of musketry on the right told us that Longstreet's infantry were advancing, and the onward progress of the smoke showed that he was progressing favorably; but about 6.30 there seemed to be a check, and even a slight retrograde movement. Soon after 7, General Lee got a report by signal from Longstreet to say *"we are doing well."* A little before dark the firing dropped off in every direction, and soon ceased altogether. We then received intelligence that Longstreet had carried every thing before him for some time, capturing several batteries, and driving the enemy from his positions; but when Hill's Florida brigade and some other troops gave way, he was forced to abandon a small portion of the ground he had won, together with all the captured guns, except three. His troops, however, bivouacked during the night on ground occupied by the enemy this morning.

Every one deplores that Longstreet *will* expose himself in such a reckless manner. To-day he led a Georgian regiment in a charge against a battery, hat in hand, and in front of everybody. General Barksdale was killed and Semmes mortally wounded; but the most serious loss was that of General Hood, who was badly wounded in the arm early in the day. I heard that his Texans are in despair. Lawley and I rode back to the General's camp, which had been moved to within a mile of the scene of action. Longstreet, however, with most of his Staff, bivouacked on the field.

Major Fairfax arrived at about 10 P.M. in a very bad humor. He had under his charge about 1,000 to 1,500 Yankee prisoners who had been taken to-day; among them a general, whom I heard one of his men accusing of having been "so G—d d—d drunk that he had turned his guns upon his own men." But, on the other hand, the accuser was such a thundering blackguard, and proposed taking such a variety of oaths in order to escape from the U.S. army, that he is not worthy of much credit. A large train of horses and mules, &c., arrived to-day, sent in by General Stuart, and captured, it is understood, by his cavalry, which had penetrated to within 6 miles of Washington.

3d July (Friday).—At 6 A.M. I rode to the field with Colonel Manning, and went over that portion of the ground which, after a fierce contest, had been won from the enemy yesterday evening. The dead were being buried, but great numbers were still lying about; also many mortally wounded, for whom nothing could be done. Amongst the latter were a number of Yankees dressed in bad imitations of the Zouave costume. They opened their glazed eyes as I rode past in a painfully imploring manner.

We joined Generals Lee and Longstreet's Staff: they were reconnoitring and making preparations for renewing the attack. As we formed a pretty large party, we often drew upon ourselves the attention of the hostile sharpshooters, and were two or three times favored with a shell. One of these shells set a brick building on fire which was situated between the lines. This building was filled with wounded, principally Yankees, who, I am afraid, must have perished miserably in the flames. Colonel Sorrell had been slightly wounded yesterday, but still did duty. Major Walton's horse was killed, but there were no other casualties amongst my particular friends.

The plan of yesterday's attack seems to have been very simple —first a heavy cannonade all along the line, followed by an advance of Longstreet's two divisions and part of Hill's corps. In consequence of the enemy's having been driven back some distance, Longstreet's corps (part of it) was in a much more forward situation than yesterday. But the range of heights to be gained was still most formidable, and evidently strongly intrenched.

The distance between the Confederate guns and the Yankee position—*i. e.*, between the woods crowning the opposite ridges —was at least a mile—quite open, gently undulating, and exposed to artillery the whole distance. This was the ground which had to be crossed in to-day's attack. Pickett's division, which had just come up, was to bear the brunt in Longstreet's attack, together with Heth and Pettigrew in Hill's corps. Pickett's division was a weak one (under 5,000), owing to the absence of two brigades.

At noon all Longstreet's dispositions were made; his troops for attack were deployed into line, and lying down in the woods; his batteries were ready to open. The general then dismounted and went to sleep for a short time. The Austrian officer and I now rode off to get, if possible, into some commanding position from whence we could see the whole thing without being exposed to the tremendous fire which was about to commence. After riding about for half an hour without being able to discover so desirable a situation, we determined to make for the cupola, near Gettysburg, Ewell's headquarters. Just before we reached the entrance to the town, the cannonade opened with a fury which surpassed even that of yesterday.

Soon after passing through the toll-gate at the entrance of Gettysburg, we found that we had got into a heavy cross-fire; shells both Federal and Confederate passing over our heads with great frequency. At length two shrapnel shells burst quite close to us, and a ball from one of them hit the officer who was conducting us. We then turned round and changed our views with regard to the cupola—the fire of one side being bad enough, but preferable to that of both sides. A small boy of twelve years was riding with us at the time: this urchin took a diabolical interest in the bursting of the shells, and screamed with delight when he saw them take effect. I never saw this boy again, or found out who he was.

The road at Gettysburg was lined with Yankee dead, and as they had been killed on the 1st, the poor fellows had already begun to be very offensive. We then returned to the hill I was on yesterday. But finding that, to see the actual fighting, it was absolutely necessary to go into the thick of the thing, I determined to make my way to General Longstreet. It was then about 2.30. After passing General Lee and his Staff, I rode on through the woods in the direction in which I had left Longstreet. I soon began to meet many wounded men returning from the front; many of them asked in piteous tones the way to a doctor or an ambulance. The further I got, the greater became the number of the wounded. At last I came to a perfect stream of them flocking through the woods in numbers as great as the crowd in Oxford-street in the middle of the day. Some were walking alone on crutches composed of two rifles, others were supported by men less badly wounded than themselves, and others were carried on stretchers by the ambulance corps; but in no case did I see a sound man helping the wounded to the rear, unless he carried the red badge of the ambulance corps. They were still under a heavy fire; the shells were continually bringing down great limbs of trees, and carrying further destruction amongst this melancholy procession. I saw all this in much less time than it takes to write it, and although astonished to meet such vast numbers of wounded, I had not seen *enough* to give me any idea of the real extent of the mischief.

When I got close up to General Longstreet, I saw one of his regiments advancing through the woods in good order; so, thinking I was just in time to see the attack, I remarked to the General that "*I wouldn't have missed this for any thing.*" Longstreet was seated at the top of a snake fence at the edge of the wood, and looking perfectly calm and imperturbed. He replied, laughing, "*The devil you wouldn't! I would like to have missed it very much; we've attacked and been repulsed: look there!*"

For the first time I then had a view of the open space between the two positions, and saw it covered with Confederates slowly and sulkily returning towards us in small broken parties, under a heavy fire of artillery. But the fire where we were was not so bad as further to the rear; for although the air seemed alive with shell, yet the greater number burst behind us.

The General told me that Pickett's division had succeeded in carrying the enemy's position and capturing his guns, but after remaining there twenty minutes, it had been forced to retire, on the retreat of Heth and Pettigrew on its left. No person could have been more calm or self-possessed than General Longstreet under these trying circumstances, aggravated as they now were by the movements of the enemy, who began to show a strong disposition to advance. I could now thoroughly appreciate the term bulldog, which I had heard applied to him by the soldiers. Difficulties seem to make no other impression upon him than to make him a little more savage.

Major Walton was the only officer with him when I came up—all the rest had been put into the charge. In a few minutes Major Latrobe arrived on foot, carrying his saddle, having just had his horse killed. Colonel Sorrell was also in the same predicament, and Captain Goree's horse was wounded in the mouth.

The General was making the best arrangements in his power

to resist the threatened advance, by advancing some artillery, rallying the stragglers, &c. I remember seeing a General (Pettigrew, I think it was)* come up to him, and report that "he was unable to bring his men up again." Longstreet turned upon him and replied with some sarcasm: "*Very well; never mind, then, General; just let them remain where they are: the enemy's going to advance, and will spare you the trouble.*"

He asked for something to drink: I gave him some rum out of my silver flask, which I begged he would keep in remembrance of the occasion; he smiled, and, to my great satisfaction, accepted the memorial. He then went off to give some orders to M'Laws's division. Soon afterwards I joined General Lee, who had in the mean while come to that part of the field on becoming aware of the disaster. If Longstreet's conduct was admirable, that of General Lee was perfectly sublime. He was engaged in rallying and in encouraging the broken troops, and was riding about a little in front of the wood, quite alone—the whole of his Staff being engaged in a similar manner further to the rear. His face, which is always placid and cheerful, did not show signs of the slightest disappointment, care, or annoyance; and he was addressing to every soldier he met a few words of encouragement, such as, "All this will come right in the end: we'll talk it over afterwards; but, in the mean time, all good men must rally. We want all good and true men just now," &c. He spoke to all the wounded men that passed him, and the slightly wounded he exhorted "to bind up their hurts and take up a musket" in this emergency. Very few failed to answer his appeal, and I saw many badly wounded men take off their hats and cheer him. He said to me, "This has been a sad day for us, Colonel—a sad day; but we can't expect always to gain victories." He was also kind enough to advise me to get into some more sheltered position, as the shells were bursting round us with considerable frequency.

Notwithstanding the misfortune which had so suddenly befallen him, General Lee seemed to observe every thing, however trivial. When a mounted officer began licking his horse for shying at the bursting of a shell, he called out, "Don't whip

*This officer was afterwards killed at the passage of the Potomac.

him, Captain; don't whip him. I've got just such another foolish horse myself, and whipping does no good."

I happened to see a man lying flat on his face in a small ditch, and I remarked that I didn't think he seemed dead; this drew General Lee's attention to the man, who commenced groaning dismally. Finding appeals to his patriotism of no avail, General Lee had him ignominiously set on his legs by some neighboring gunners.

I saw General Willcox (an officer who wears a short round jacket and a battered straw hat) come up to him, and explain, almost crying, the state of his brigade. General Lee immediately shook hands with him and said cheerfully, "Never mind, General, *all this has been* MY *fault*—it is *I* that have lost this fight, and you must help me out of it in the best way you can." In this manner I saw General Lee encourage and reanimate his somewhat dispirited troops, and magnanimously take upon his own shoulders the whole weight of the repulse. It was impossible to look at him or to listen to him without feeling the strongest admiration, and I never saw any man fail him except the man in the ditch.

It is difficult to exaggerate the critical state of affairs as they appeared about this time. If the enemy or their general had shown any enterprise, there is no saying what might have happened. General Lee and his officers were evidently fully impressed with a sense of the situation; yet there was much less noise, fuss, or confusion of orders than at an ordinary field-day; the men, as they were rallied in the wood, were brought up in detachments, and lay down quietly and coolly in the positions assigned to them.

We heard that Generals Garnett and Armistead were killed, and General Kemper mortally wounded; also, that Pickett's division had only one field-officer unhurt. Nearly all this slaughter took place in an open space about one mile square, and within one hour.

At 6 P.M. we heard a long and continuous Yankee cheer, which we at first imagined was an indication of an advance; but it turned out to be their reception of a general officer, whom we saw riding down the line, followed by about thirty horsemen. Soon afterwards I rode to the extreme front, where there were four pieces of rifled cannon almost without any infantry support. To the non-withdrawal of these guns is to be attributed the otherwise surprising inactivity of the enemy. I was immediately surrounded by a sergeant and about half-a-dozen gunners, who seemed in excellent spirits and full of confidence, in spite of their exposed situation. The sergeant expressed his ardent hope that the Yankees might have spirit enough to advance and receive the dose he had in readiness for them. They spoke in admiration of the advance of Pickett's division, and of the manner in which Pickett himself had led it. When they observed General Lee they said, "We've not lost confidence in the old man: this day's work won't do him no harm. 'Uncle Robert' will get us into Washington yet; you bet he will!" &c. Whilst we were talking, the enemy's skirmishers began to advance slowly, and several ominous sounds in quick succession told us that we were attracting their attention, and that it was necessary to break up the conclave. I therefore turned round and took leave of these cheery and plucky gunners.

At 7 P.M., General Lee received a report that Johnson's division of Ewell's corps had been successful on the left, and had gained important advantages there. Firing entirely ceased in our front about this time; but we now heard some brisk musketry on our right, which I afterwards learned proceeded from Hood's Texans, who had managed to surround some enterprising Yankee cavalry, and were slaughtering them with great satisfaction. Only eighteen out of four hundred are said to have escaped.

At 7.30, all idea of a Yankee attack being over, I rode back to Moses's tent, and found that worthy commissary in very low spirits, all sorts of exaggerated rumors having reached him. On my way I met a great many wounded men, most anxious to inquire after Longstreet, who was reported killed; when I assured them he was quite well, they seemed to forget their own pain in the evident pleasure they felt in the safety of their chief. No words that I can use will adequately express the extraordinary patience and fortitude with which the wounded Confederates bore their sufferings.

I got something to eat with the doctors at 10 P.M., the first for fifteen hours.

I gave up my horse to-day to his owner, as from death and exhaustion the Staff are almost without horses.

4th July (Saturday).—I was awoke at daylight by Moses complaining that his valuable trunk, containing much public money, had been stolen from our tent whilst we slept. After a search it was found in a wood hard by, broken open and minus the money. Dr. Barksdale had been robbed in the same manner exactly. This is evidently the work of those rascally stragglers, who shirk going under fire, plunder the natives, and will hereafter swagger as the heroes of Gettysburg.

Lawley, the Austrian, and I, walked up to the front about eight o'clock, and on our way we met General Longstreet, who was in a high state of amusement and good humor. A flag of truce had just come over from the enemy, and its bearer announced among other things that "General Longstreet was wounded, and a prisoner, but would be taken care of." General Longstreet sent back word that he was extremely grateful, but that, being neither wounded nor a prisoner, he was quite able to take care of himself. The iron endurance of General Longstreet is most extraordinary: he seems to require neither food nor sleep. Most of his Staff now fall fast asleep directly they get off their horses, they are so exhausted from the last three days' work.

Whilst Lawley went to headquarters on business, I sat down and had a long talk with General Pendleton (the parson), chief of artillery. He told me the exact number of guns in action yesterday. He said that the universal opinion is in favor of the 12-pounder Napoleon guns as the best and simplest sort of ordnance for field purposes.* Nearly all the artillery with this army has either been captured from the enemy or cast from old 6-pounders taken at the early part of the war.

At 10 A.M. Lawley returned from headquarters, bringing the news that the army is to commence moving in the direction of Virginia this evening. This step is imperative from want

---

*The Napoleon 12-pounders are smooth-bore brass guns, with chambers, very light, and with long range. They were invented or recommended by Louis Napoleon years ago. A large number are being cast at Augusta and elsewhere.

of ammunition. But it was hoped that the enemy might attack during the day, especially as this is the 4th of July, and it was calculated that there was still ammunition for one day's fighting. The ordnance train had already commenced moving back towards Cashtown, and Ewell's immense train of plunder had been proceeding towards Hagerstown by the Fairfield road ever since an early hour this morning.

Johnson's division had evacuated during the night the position it had gained yesterday. It appears that for a time it was actually in possession of the cemetery, but had been forced to retire from thence from want of support by Pender's division, which had been retarded by that officer's wound. The whole of our left was therefore thrown back considerably.

At 1 P.M. the rain began to descend in torrents, and we took refuge in the hovel of an ignorant Pennsylvanian boor. The cottage was full of soldiers, none of whom had the slightest idea of the contemplated retreat, and all were talking of Washington and Baltimore with the greatest confidence.

At 2 P.M. we walked to General Longstreet's camp, which had been removed to a place three miles distant, on the Fairfield road. General Longstreet talked to me for a long time about the battle. He said the mistake they had made was in not concentrating the army more, and making the attack yesterday with 30,000 men instead of 15,000. The advance had been in three lines, and the troops of Hill's corps who gave way were young soldiers, who had never been under fire before. He thought the enemy would have attacked had the guns been withdrawn. Had they done so at that particular moment immediately after the repulse, it would have been awkward; but in that case he had given orders for the advance of Hood's division and M'Laws's on the right. I think, after all, that General Meade was right not to advance—his men would never have stood the tremendous fire of artillery they would have been exposed to.

Rather over 7,000 Yankees were captured during the three days; 3,500 took the parole; the remainder were now being marched to Richmond, escorted by the remains of Pickett's division. It is impossible to avoid seeing that the cause of this check to the Confederates lies in the utter contempt felt for the enemy by all ranks.

Wagons, horses, mules, and cattle captured in Pennsylvania, the solid advantages of this campaign, have been passing slowly along this road (Fairfield) all day: those taken by Ewell are particularly admired. So interminable was this train that it soon became evident that we should not be able to start till late at night. As soon as it became dark we all lay round a big fire, and I heard reports coming in from the different generals that the enemy was *retiring*, and had been doing so all day long. M'Laws reported nothing in his front but cavalry videttes. But this, of course, could make no difference to General Lee's plans: ammunition he must have—he had failed to capture it from the enemy (according to precedent); and as his communications with Virginia were intercepted, he was compelled to fall back towards Winchester, and draw his supplies from thence. General Milroy had kindly left an ample stock at that town when he made his precipitate exit some weeks ago. The army was also incumbered with an enormous wagon-train, the spoils of Pennsylvania, which it is highly desirable to get safely over the Potomac.

Shortly after 9 P.M. the rain began to descend in torrents. Lawley and I luckily got into the doctors' covered buggy, and began to get slowly under way a little after midnight.

Samuel Pickens: Diary, July 1–3, 1863

On the morning of July 1 two divisions of the Army of Northern Virginia's Second Corps began marching from Heidlersburg to Cashtown, but then changed direction after Lieutenant General Richard Ewell, the corps commander, learned of the Confederate advance on Gettysburg. Serving with the 5th Alabama Infantry, one of the regiments in the division commanded by Robert E. Rodes, was Private Samuel Pickens, who had been quickly exchanged after his capture at Chancellorsville. Pickens recorded his regiment's part in the fighting on July 1 and in the subsequent Confederate attempts to capture Cemetery Hill, which, along with the adjoining Culp's Hill, anchored the northern end of the Union defensive line.

July 1, Wednesday

Left camp this morning at 6:30 A.M. & marched 7 miles on the Chambersburg road to Middletown, where we turned to the left on the Gettysburg road. As we approached the town we heard the cannonading & formed a line of battle about 2 miles off & advanced upon the Yankees. Our Regt. was on the left of the Brigade & as it moved forward it made a partial right wheel & thus kept us at a double quick march all the time; & as it was an excessively hot day & we were going through wheat fields & ploughed ground & over fences, it almost killed us. I was perfectly exhausted & never suffered so from heat & fatigue in my life. A good many fell out of ranks being completely broken down & some fainted. We halted & lay down for some time at a fence & witnessed an artillery duel between one of our batteries stationed about 150 yds. in front of us & a Yankee battery away to our left. 5 or 6 dead horses & 1 or 2 broken caissons or gun carriages were left by our battery when it moved off. Our Regt. then went forward, for the rest of the Brigade had gone on while we had been left to guard the space between our Brigade & Doles' which was on our left & prevent either from being flanked. We came up with the

Brig., however, at a fence where it had halted and there our
Company was sent forward to a barn to act as sharp-shooters.
There were some N.C. sharp-shooters there who had shot
away all their cartridge. Wm. Stokes was wounded before getting to the barn, & Joe Brown while in it. We kept up pretty
brisk firing at the Yankees, but it seemed as if we could do very
little execution as they were so far off & behind a fence in the
woods, though they made the bullets whistle over us. After the
Brig. passed on we ran out of the barn & through an open
field where the bullets were flying thick & went down on the
left to a lane where the Regt. was. I never saw troops so scattered & in such confusion. We were under a heavy fire from
the front & a cross fire from the left & pretty soon had to fall
back to a fence where the Brig. was rallied by Col. O'Neal &
Genl Rodes. Paul Lavender was coming off wounded & asked
Lt. Jones (in commd. of Co.) to let me help him. I got three
of the ambulance corps of the 26th Regt. & a litter & had to
carry Paul about a mile to get to a Surgeon. Mr. Mushat extracted the ball & after waiting in vain all the evening for an
ambulance to take the wounded to the Hospital, I set out to
find the H. & get ambulances, which I succeeded in doing
after a long walk & a deal of difficulty. The scenes about the
Hospital were the most horrible I ever beheld. There were the
poor wounded men lying all over the yard, moaning & groaning, while in the barn the terrible work of amputating limbs
was going on, and the pallid limbs lying around presented a
most disagreeable sight. As soon as I could get 2 ambulances
we set out & had to go a very roundabout way, so by time we
got to the wounded it was some time after night & they had
been put in a house & were so comfortable they did not want
to be moved, so the ambulances were dismissed to return in
the morning. In the mean time our troops had driven the
Yankees and were in possession of the town of Gettysburg.
When our Brig. was reformed it moved up & took position
along the Rail-road to the right of town. Oh! what terrible
work has been done to-day. The loss in our Brig. was very
heavy—particularly in our Regt. I was much affected on learning that my warm friend & mess-mate Tean Nutting had been
mortally wounded & died in a short time on the field. He was
at his post with the colors. A nobler, more generous or braver

boy never lived. He was a great favorite & will be much missed. Marched 14 ms. before getting in fight.

July 2, Thursday

The ambulances came this morning and conveyed the wounded to the Hospitals, & I, with Cruse Coleman returned to the Regiment. The town is full of the enemy's wounded & every large building has been made a hospital. David Barnum brought from town a havresack of candy, plenty of lemons & other nice things which were a great treat. It was pretty quiet during the morning while we were placing our artillery in position. Gilliam J. told us that 80 pieces were being massed on a hill to our right. After a while they opened all around & the cannonading was terrific: almost as rapid as musketry. Late in the evening our Divis. was moved forward in line of battle & as we advanced upon the hill where the Yankees had all their artillery & troops massed we expected to have to charge it, but it was then after dark & we lay a while in a wheat field & then went back in town. The loss in our Regt. in killed, wounded & missing is 226. The no. that left camp was 380; but a great many fell out of ranks, & Col. Hall thinks that not many over 300 went into the fight—so our loss was very heavy, & nearly all killed or wounded, for there are only————missing. In our Co. ("D") the loss is:—

Killed   —   George Nutting
Wounded —   P. H. Lavender—thigh.
                    J. L. Wright—shoulder.
                    J. M. Brown—foot.
                    Wm Stokes—leg—& Prisoner.
                    Wm A. Lenier—hand—& Prisoner.
Prisoners —   Jas. Burton.
                    J. T. Knowlan.
                    J. C. Ray

July 3, Friday

We lay in line along one of the streets last night & this morning our Brigade with the exception of our Regt. was sent down on the left with Johnson's Divis. & participated in the fight. Our Regt. was attached to Doles' Brig. & stayed in town during the morning—while our Co. was sent to the edge of town as sharp-shooters. We built breast works and remained there till evening. An occasional minnie ball whizzed over us & a shell passed through a stable or crib beside us & exploded immediately after. The Regt. then moved up with Doles' Brig. & lay in line of battle in a lane. There was no shade, & the heat of the sun was almost insupportable. A heavy cannonading was kept up—a great many shells passing over us—and some from our own batteries exploded over our line & killed men in Doles', Ramseur's &, I think, Iversons Brigades. It was either very inferior ammunition or great carelessness on the part of the gunners. Saw Tom Biscoe in town to-day. His looks shewed plainly that he had seen hard service. His Brigade (Hays') made a desperate charge upon *the Hill* last night & took a battery, but were not supported & had to fall back. Tom is now in command of the 5th La. Regt.

Francis Adams Donaldson: Narrative of Gettysburg, July 2–3, 1863

A company commander in the 118th Pennsylvania Infantry, Captain Francis Adams Donaldson had fought at Ball's Bluff, Fair Oaks, Shepherdstown, Fredericksburg, and Chancellorsville. His regiment was assigned to the Fifth Corps, which advanced from Union Mills, Maryland, to Hanover, Pennsylvania, on July 1, then turned west and marched until 3:30 A.M. on July 2, when it halted four miles east of Gettysburg. On the afternoon of July 2 Meade learned that Major General Daniel E. Sickles, the commander of the Union Third Corps, had moved his men forward from the low-lying southern part of Cemetery Ridge toward slightly higher ground along the Emmitsburg Road, forming a salient with its apex at a peach orchard and opening a large gap in the Union lines. As Longstreet's corps began its attack on the exposed Third Corps, Donaldson's brigade was sent to help defend a stony hill south of the peach orchard against an assault by Lafayette McLaw's division. (The hill adjoined farmer John Rose's wheat field, which would become the scene of some of the day's fiercest fighting.) The next day Donaldson was posted on the northeast slope of Big Round Top, at the southern end of the Union defensive line. He recorded his experiences on July 2–3 as part of a long letter to his aunt, Eliza Ann Nice, written on July 21.

July 2nd. I slept about an hour then arose, brushed the dew from my hair and looked around me. The woods were a scene of busy stir, here and there the blue smoke was curling up in playful wreaths from our bivouac fires, while the men were cooking coffee or otherwise preparing to take the road again. About 5 A.M. our division moved out into the open ground beyond the woods and commenced to deploy for action, the regiments being formed at deploying distance in close column. It was a beautiful sight to see, as far as the eye could reach, regiment after regiment in mass, with colors unfurled, upon a line as straight as a die, while the death like silence pervading all made the senses keen to note every trifling incident.

It took some time to satisfactorily arrange us, but finally the order came to move forward, and with a firm tread and muskets at the right shoulder, the movement commenced. Over fields and fences went the silent moving mass, while nothing was heard save an occasional caution from our Colonel as to the guide, and the singular noise made by the tramping of so many thousands of feet thro' the crushing leaves and grass, while the atmosphere was heavy with the pennyroyal smell so peculiar to all battlefields. As we gradually approached the rising ground in front, from beyond which musketry firing could be distinctly heard, a change of direction to the right was made, which after continuing for some time was changed again to the front.

We halted in a piece of woods to the front of which our army was then engaged, and from the length of time we remained here, I presume were upon the reserve. After listening for a long time to the intermittent firing, the battle suddenly became very animated, the deafening and unceasing roar of artillery making the earth fairly quake. By its long continuance and regularity, all felt that if not pushing the enemy they were certainly not getting the advantage of our people, and as we had received no orders to load, our help was evidently not needed. Drawing this inference I determined to avail myself of an opportunity to indulge in a bath, a pond of inviting water being but a short distance to the rear of our regiment. I stripped myself, rushed eagerly into the water and was soon splashing and dashing about like a dolphin, when noticing some very curious weeds sticking to my person, I hastened out to rid myself of them, when to my astonishment I found them to be leeches. I postponed further bathing. After this little episode nothing was to be done but to sit down and listen to the firing, which was now becoming terrible, the shells whistling above us and plunging away beyond our ammunition trains which were directly to the rear of us.

My feelings at this time can be readily described, as but one thought was paramount, a hope that the troops in front would be able to thrash the confederates without our aid, for with rest comes a dislike for bloody encounters. With this thought uppermost and while considering our probable chances for continuing this *soft* thing, even then, amid the thunder of the artillery bursting upon my ear, the missiles flying and the sound of musketry piercing the air, I, before I was aware of it, grew drowsy, my eyelids grew heavy and shut, thus closing out the warlike scene, and I was asleep. I know not how long I had been sleeping when suddenly I was awakened by the cry of "fall in," which was quickly responded to by all. As the men took their places in line, still laughing and jesting among themselves, the order to load was given, which at once put a stop to all trifling, and by its peculiar significance made the blood leap suddenly in the veins, and the choking sensation to rise in the throat, as each realized that we were about to take an active part in the battle going on in front. The enemy were shelling our lines furiously which seemed to indicate a general assault.

At 3:30 P.M. we moved by the left flank, and our regiment, being on the left of the brigade, of course now became the advance. Already the battle was raging fearfully ahead, and strings of ambulances with the wounded and mangled fellows were passing to the rear. As nearer and nearer we approached the field, shells could be seen bursting in vast quantities, while ammunition wagons and limber boxes were being hurried forward, and the usual confusion, noise and bustle of the rear of an immense army during a battle met our eye, and, I may add, left an unpleasant feeling upon us.

We now entered the woods which appeared to crown an eminence whose sides, full of rocks and boulders, sloped away towards the enemy, and were at once amid the dreadful bursting shells, which, however, flew past us and did no harm. At this point I saw an orderly leading a splendid black horse which was limping along on three legs, the other having been shot off at the hoof. Inquiring to whom it belonged, I learned that Capt. John Fassitte of General Birney's staff, its owner, fearing harm would come to this fine animal, had mounted another and sent it to the rear for safety, but just as our column was reached, a shell had struck the poor beast and he would now have to be killed. At this moment Captain Crocker came to me and asked my opinion of the present movement. I replied that judging from the heavy musketry fire going on to the front, I had no doubt our movement was intended to support a threatened point, or to retrieve a disaster which had already happened; certainly the peculiar rebel cheer now heard above every other sound would indicate that they had been success-ful somewhere.

A few minutes after, we formed in line immediately to the rear of a very thin line of battle that looked to me like a skir-mish line, which retired as soon as we were posted. Our bri-gade was now rapidly drawn up in the following order: 118th P.V. on the right, 22nd Massachusetts on the left, 1st Michigan in rear of the 22nd Mass., and the 18th Mass. in rear of the right of the 1st Michigan and left of our regiment. We had in our brigade all told but 425 men, the balance, having straggled during the night before, had been collected, formed into a stragglers brigade, and taken into a different part of the field. The reason the 1st Mich., and 18th Mass. were not in line was because the 2nd brigade crowded us to such an extent there was no room for them, and they therefore acted as supports. . . . Our position was in all respects a good one. We were on the edge of a heavy growth of timber, with rocks and huge boul-ders scattered about forming ample protection, and just be-yond, the hill fell off to quite a slope, up which the enemy would have to reach us. Upon our immediate right a battery of brass guns was posted which was, even now, being served with wonderful rapidity. Shortly before the engagement com-menced on our part we were moved slightly to the rear, which allowed the 1st Mich. to get into line. . . . Nearly one half of our regiment was refused on the right in order to prevent flanking. The skirmishers were but a short distance to the front, and I greatly feared many of them would be unable to get back, owing to the extreme eagerness of the men to open fire, and I particularly cautioned my company to be extremely careful and allow our people to get in before firing.

At this moment Private Jas. Godfrey, the man I had forced into the company the day before, came to me with his watch and pocket book, also a letter to his wife saying, "Here, Cap-tain, take these things and if I get killed send them to my wife, I am going to show the boys how to fight today, I have been called coward long enough." I could not help smiling at what this action implied, altho' of course not so intended, as I was as likely to be killed as he, but taking him by the hand and giving it a good honest squeeze and a terrible shake, I said, "Well done Godfrey, I knew you were sound at heart and I will write to your wife of your conduct this day, here, take a pull at this," and stepping behind a tree I let him have my canteen. Well, I really thought the poor fellow would certainly choke in his eagerness to get the rum down him. When I thought he had enough I sent him back to the company, and shortly after saw him standing, in advance of all with sleeves rolled up, musket aport, and foot firmly planted awaiting the development of events. I now felt very badly for the skirmishers as I was sure Godfrey was certainly one of them.

During all this time the enemy were making their charge, and from the rapid firing of the battery on our right, I judged, were drawing closer and closer to our line, altho' as yet unseen by us. The roar of the artillery was deafening, and from the excited manner of the gunners all efforts had evidently failed to check the onset. The voice of the officer commanding the guns could be heard loudly calling for "canister," while the surrounding objects were becoming less and less distinct from the sulphurous smoke occasioned by such rapid firing. Soon was heard a startling volley of musketry towards the left of our brigade, another and another followed in a wild and continuous rattle as the enemy's column came within range. The scene now beggars description. The deafening shouts of the combatants, the crash of artillery, the trembling ground beneath us, the silent and stricken countenances of the men, the curtain of smoke over all and its peculiar smell, made up a picture never to be forgotten by any who witnessed it.

As the enemy's columns came nearer, the artillery was served with shell with short fuse, which burst at once upon leaving the gun, scattering destruction broadcast. Our skirmishers now came running rapidly towards us, and a moment after, the enemy's column was seen moving at a quick pace obliquely along our front, very many of them in their shirt sleeves, and all appearing to be loading and firing as they came steadily up the hillside in the face of the battery, which seemed to be their objective point. Our regiment now opened and in a few minutes were at it pell mell loading and firing as rapidly as possible.

So eager were the men to fight that I did not notice one of
them taking advantage of the trees and rocks, but all standing
bravely up to the work and doing good execution.

As I passed up and down in rear of the company speaking to
the men and directing their firing, I noticed one of them like a
blazing Vesuvius, standing a yard to two in front of all, be-
grimed with powder, hatless and shouting as he fired his piece,
"Give them hell boys," and by his extraordinary behavior making himself the most conspicuous object in our whole line. It
was Godfrey, who by his determined bravery had actually assumed a leadership among his hitherto jeering comrades, and
now had several of them loading his and their own muskets
for him to discharge. Passing thro' the line I took my place beside him to observe more closely the movements of the enemy,
who were now so near that the countenances of many of them
were quite distinct. I noticed one man in particular on the
right of a division, as it seemed to me, with big broad brimmed
hat on the back of his head, large black whiskers and eyes directed towards our regiment, as in evident fear of danger from
that quarter, he looked the personification of physical daring
as he rammed a cartridge into the musket he held at a trail.
Altho' I know he was the object of several shots specially directed at him, yet I saw him gradually move away apparently
unhurt, and finally with his comrades disappear altogether in
the dense smoke of the guns.

Our line now became somewhat broken and open as the
men, after firing, would step back to load, but this is generally
the case in all stationary lines of battle. A cheer now broke
forth, the smoke was rent, and the rebels dashed in upon the
battery with a savage yell. The artillery men retreated somewhat to the rear dragging their guns with them by ropes,
which in anticipation of a catastrophe had been fastened to
them.

Running to the rear of my company to prevent any movement looking towards a retreat, for all saw that our position
was now untenable as the cannon were virtually in the hands
of the enemy, I was met by Capt. Richd. W. Davids, who was
slowly walking towards me. Upon stopping to see what was
wanted, he said, "Capt., I am hit." "Where?," said I. "Thro'
the stomach and bowels," said he, at the same time placing his

hand upon his waist belt. "You had better go to the rear," cried I, and he started to do so, but had not gone more than twenty steps before he fell, and I knew that death had come upon him. I was the last person he ever spoke to upon this earth, and mine the ears to hear the last utterance of as brave and noble a gentleman as ever trod God's green footstool.

Nothing could now stop the rebel onset, and the shouts of rage and defiance rose up amid the roar of musketry as they swarmed upon the cannon. In a moment our guns were lost and the enemy in fierce numbers were crowding upon our right and rear. Our line wavered, trembled and commenced to give ground, when Maj. Herring, in a clear and distinct voice heard by the whole command above the din and roar of battle, cried, "Change front to rear on 10th company," and as upon parade the men performed the movement of swinging round to right angles with the line previously held, thus compelling the enemy to continue on a longer circle in order to outflank and get to our rear. This, however, they continued to do, and at last we were compelled reluctantly to fall back. Our retreat was as follows—1st Mich. and 118th P.V. immediately to the rear, the 18th and 22d Mass. by the left flank to the 3rd brigade. Our regiment was pushed back directly among the ammunition trains, but the men still kept up a straggling fire as they retreated.

Soon after we commenced to give way Maj. Biddle, of Genl. Meade's staff, and I am not sure but the general himself, appeared and entreated, prayed and called upon the men for God sake to halt, not to give way, that this was the only portion of the line broken, to think of the safety of the ammunition train, that the whole army would have to retreat—but to no purpose, for with dogged silence the men retired slowly and without apparent panic or hurry, for they were perfectly well satisfied of the impossibility of longer holding their ground.

While this was happening, observing Capt. Crocker lingering behind, I allowed the men to pass me and went back to see what could possibly detain him amid such extreme danger. With a manner perfectly cool and collected he said it was too bad our boys had not stood their ground longer, and that he wanted to see how many the enemy numbered and what they would do next. It was a strange sight to look upon. The rebels were crowding up in great numbers but appeared unable to realize the extent of their success, and were standing cheering and yelling without attempting to pursue or even to fire upon our retreating line. Turning to me Crocker seized the pistol I held in my hand and discharged the two remaining barrels at the mass in front of us, then suddenly taking to his heels beat a rapid retreat quickly followed by me.

Our regiment continued to fall slowly back for a few minutes longer, when all at once it was brought to a stand still by a yell so fierce and terrible that the very blood seemed to curdle in our veins, while a sound as of a hurricane was swept towards us. It was the crushing of leaves and twigs made by the Pennsylvania Reserves coming up in mass, at the double quick, arms at the right shoulder, bayonets fixed and with Genl. Crawford on horseback at their head, hat in hand, waving it excitedly as he led the most terrific charge I ever witnessed. With diabolical screeches and shouts they pressed forward, struck the bewildered enemy and by very force of the onset sweeping every living thing before them, retaking the cannon, crushing under foot and bayonetting all who for a moment attempted a resistance and finally pushing back the whole rebel line up over and beyond a hill of considerable height upon our left which had evidently been occupied by them. In the meantime the 2nd and 3rd brigade had been performing a movement rarely occuring in battle, resisting a bayonet charge; and it was give and take with them, no quarter being shown on either side. The 16th Mich. of the 2nd brigade was nearly annihilated, their colonel being bayonetted several times thro' the stomach and bowels as he sat on horseback, and died at his post, not having yielded an inch of ground. This bloody work could not last long and the 2nd brigade gave ground slowly, and was about to retire altogether when a cheer arose, and a line of glistening steel was seen approaching. It was the 20th Maine, 83rd and 10th Penna. of the 3rd brigade, together with the Penna. Reserves, who, having just cleared our front, now did the same for the hard pressed 2nd. I have been told that the 16th Mich. bayonetted every living rebel, wounded or unhurt, that fell into their hands, in retaliation for the loss of their Colonel. Such was the ending of this conflict from out of which our command so narrowly escaped annihilation or capture. We remained at the spot where we had halted and adjusted our line, while the 6th Corps, just arrived, formed line to our rear, and Penna. Reserves continuing to the front. After these dispositions we prepared for the night.

I must mention more prisoners had been taken than we had men in the brigade, these unfortunates being caught between us and the charging Reserves. I went among them eagerly questioning right and left for news of the 22nd Virginia Regt., and from what I could learn, that regiment is with Bradley Johnson and was not engaged today. The prisoners, one and all, seemed rejoiced to have passed safely thro' such a "blazing Hell" as they termed the fire we poured upon them. They say we have no idea of the tremendous slaughter made among their people and are unable to explain how it was they escaped unhurt. One man told me they thought it was militia they were to encounter and rather took comfort from being beaten by old soldiers. About 8 o'clock P.M. the ammunition wagons unloaded at our regiment enough cartridges to have supplied a whole division. Surely this seemed to me a most uncalled for waste, as we really did not need more than an additional thirty rounds per man, and these boxes would therefore be abandoned when most probably some other portion of the field would need them.

At last the battle was hushed and all was still, night veiled the earth. Its gloomy shades were thickened by a sulphurous cloud that like a pall hung sadly over the field. The woods and fields were strewn with the wounded and dying, and with the ghastly forms of the dead. It is indeed remarkable that men can lie down and sleep so tranquilly when they know the danger that awaits them on the morrow, when they hear the cries of the already mangled, when they know that the dead lie strewn around and that with the early dawn of the coming day, the work of death will be resumed as all felt it would surely be, now that the whole army was up and the enemy had been repulsed.

July 3rd. At day break we were moved to the left and took position on the summit of quite a high hill from which the Reserves had driven the enemy last evening, and we had now a commanding view of the whole field. The ground in front was heavily wooded and the enemy occupied the base of the hill, while our skirmishers were unable to push forward but a short distance from the line . . . and vast numbers of dead and wounded encumbered the ground, and to make the sight more horrifying, wild hogs were seen feeding on some of the badly torn bodies. The troops who had occupied this place last night had erected a substantial stone breastwork from the loose boulders and broken fragments that covered the mountains.

Just after we had been established in our new position a rebel officer was seen leisurely walking towards our line, with his hands in pockets, segar in mouth and without sword or weapon of any kind, while his jacket was thrown open in careless abandon. The skirmishers allowed him to walk into their line, and he was greatly astonished and mortified to learn he was a prisoner. He said he was Genl. Heth's Adjutant General, had left his command but a few minutes before and strolled along not supposing for a moment the "Yanks" were so near. He betrayed considerable feeling as he was led to the rear by two privates who were instructed to deliver him to Genl. Meade.

During the morning nothing of moment was done on either side and with the exception of a cannon shot now and then, everything remained perfectly quiet. Availing myself of the presence of the chaplain, who had come up in order to talk seriously to the men and distribute tracts among them, I wrote home that I had thus far escaped unhurt, the chaplain promising to forward any letters given him. Our men, wherever they could, gathered up the wounded enemy and carried them to the rear. I talked to one poor fellow who was shot thru' the breast, the lungs most probably, and who had been placed upon a stretcher and left to await the return of the ambulance men. He was suffering great anguish from thirst and was scarcely able to articulate his gratitude for the kindness shown by those from whom he had expected other treatment. The poor fellow was not as sanguine as he would liked to have been as to the final result of the battle, as our men looked to him so healthy, well fed and clothed, and yet capable of making a stout fight behind such splendid breastworks. He was an intelligent attractive man of about 45 years, and was exceedingly gentlemanly in his speech, always thanking us for any attention. I gave him some water and whiskey which appeared to help him considerably, and was sorry when compelled to leave him so helpless and alone.

About 1 o'clock, there suddenly burst forth the deafening crash of what appeared to me to be the whole of the enemy's artillery. I went to my post to see what was the occasion of this sudden concentration of the enemy fire that was making the ground rock as in the throes of an earthquake. The air was soon filled with a hissing, bursting torrent, while the men crouched low along the line. Standing on a rock I could see the smoke rising up along the whole of the enemy's position, and supposed they were about to try and beat us out by the weight of their artillery. The sun shone gloriously, making objects quite distinct in the distance, and I could see puffs of smoke from our own guns which were now replying. Retiring to the rear of our line, I sought shelter from the screaming and exploding shells, but could find none, so was compelled, along with many others, to sit still and endure this trial of the nerves for at least two hours. There was scarcely a second that we were free from shot or shell, and I never remembered to have seen so many solid shot thrown before. The missiles were sent one after the other so rapidly that a constant, prolonged and connected whizzing was maintained. Shells were exploded in front, now in the rear of us and frequently over our heads, solid shot came rushing madly, crashing and tearing among the trees, while the air was filled with fragments and the suspense was horrible to endure. During this time Capt. O'Neill and myself were sitting together on a piece of shelter tent which protected us from the damp ground. We had very little to say to one another and were very close together for protection, as it were. A shell bursting rather nearer than usual over our heads caused us to huddle still closer, while our very hearts ceased to beat as we listened to the singing of a fragment that seemed to be coming rapidly towards us. With one look we read in each others faces the alarm both felt, and saw the impossibility of avoiding the terrible death dealing missile. As we sat motionless—breathless,—it dashed furiously between my knees, and with a thud and splash of dirt, buried itself deep into the ground. I dug up the ragged piece of metal, felt its sharp edges, and put it into my haversack as a memento of the narrow escape I had made.

After enduring the fire of the rebels for at least two hours there was again a lull in the storm of battle, the artillery gradually slackened and finally ceased altogether. We could observe the field to be free from troops, the rebel infantry being within the woods. I now ran back to see after the poor wounded reb we had left on the stretcher, and found him torn to atoms and the stretcher to shreds. Poor fellow, he had been killed by his own friends, how terrible that must be, and what agony it must have been to him to have lain there fearful, not of his enemies, but lest he should be killed by his own people. Well, he was mortally wounded in the first place, and is now better off.

For a time everything continued to remain perfectly calm and quiet. Such quiet is always ominous; it betokens preparation for something of vital importance. Our own men we could not see owing to the woods, but the line could be easily traced as it stretched away to the right in the shape of an exceedingly shallow semicircle. We could clearly observe the movements of the enemy should they make any, and, I can add, all eyes were eagerly rivetted on their line to see what they would do next. About 4 P.M. they began to show themselves at the edge of the woods and to manifest signs of an intended attack. Our batteries again opened, but the rebs appeared firm and proceeded in two lines to advance in splendid order. There seemed to be a heavy body upon their rear and flank, apparently as supports, all forming a mass, I should say, of at least eight or ten thousand men, who were being pushed forward in the face of our whole army upon some point considerably to the right of our position. There was nothing to hinder anyone in our whole line from witnessing their advance, and the eagerness with which each man gazed upon this magnificent spectacle was evidence that all felt a terrible crisis was approaching. On every side could be heard men questioning the capability of our line resisting so tremendous an onset. After proceeding some distance to the front, the enemy appeared to move obliquely to the left, owing, no doubt, to the severe fire from the batteries near us. They again changed to the front, however, after proceeding a short distance, and came up in the face of all our artillery. They continued to move on unflinchingly, and it was a grand sight to see them, their splendid behavior calling forth bursts of admiration from us all. A piece of woods considerably to our right and beyond which the enemy's column soon passed shut out from our sight the finale of this desperate charge, but our ears were soon greeted by the tremendous roar of musketry, whilst a curtain of smoke ascended to the tops of the trees and remained there to tell us that a desperate fight was in progress. This state of things continued for some time and we were uncertain as to the result, when presently a few men were seen running from beyond the woods, followed by others, and at last whole clusters of the enemy were seen scampering to the rear as fast as possible, but it was also noticed that not one third of those who, but a few moments before had gone forward so bravely, returned; they had all been killed or wounded and the charge was unsuccessful. This latter fact we knew, as the enemy soon opened again their artillery fire to cover the retreat of their men, and we accepted the sign by giving a fearful shout for the victory gained.

Elizabeth Blair Lee to Samuel Phillips Lee

Elizabeth Blair Lee wrote to her husband, a Union naval officer commanding the squadron blockading the North Carolina coast, from the Maryland estate of her politically prominent family. Her father, Francis Preston Blair, was an adviser to Andrew Jackson who now counseled President Lincoln; her brother Montgomery was postmaster general; and her brother Frank was a former Republican congressman from Missouri who now commanded a division at Vicksburg.

———————

Silver Spring

My Dear Phil   We are here still on tiptoe with all eyes turned towards the north West where I have felt all day that a mortal combat was going on for our Country's life & I think our troops are more alive to the exigencies of the country ever before— besides Meade has just done what the Rebels did two years ago— ordered the instant death of the recreant— if this had been done by Grant we would have had Vicksburg. & saved many brave men by punishing the Cowards & preventing their Contagion from spreading— & that is one reason why the Rebels fight well Our political Generals are afraid to deal with our Army according to Military discipline— I have great hopes of Mead   the whole family are people of talent & energy & as he was born in Spain he can never be President— thus will not be warred upon by Politicians or get a tete monte himself

Letters today from Frank who writes confidently They know that Bragg's army are coming on them. but says they have now means to cope with them— but Grant hopes to be in Vicksburg before they turn to fight Joe Johnston— Frank encloses a letter to him from Sherman giving the history of Genl McClellands dismissal by Grant

A letter today from Meade to the P says yesterday at 3 olk— he had all his Army concentrated but 2 corps were so prostrated for an immense march that he would not attack until today— Our Army lay in full view of the enemy I think Lee will retreat if it is possible— Our two corps 1st & 11th got the best of the fight with Longstreet & Hill until they were reinforced by Ewell— when it became a drawn battle— Mead says they got our field of battle & the wounded which gives them therin the Victory in all else the battle was a drawn one— I send you a poster which is cast on every wall in New York— Your devoted Lizzie No news from Silver Spring today— Father rides to the Fort in a few minutes— Mother is very content here—

July 3, 1863

Washington   July 4, 1863
Dear Phil   Mother Blair & I have just returned from the Country where we went after a 7 olk breakfast— We found everything in good order & as quietly beautiful as ever— birds were joyous & dogs gave Blair a riotous welcome and I think all three of us were heartily sorry to come back to the City— altho entirely comfortable here

The news from the Armies is favorable but scarcely decisive enough for my appetite but I confess to some relief about things for our Army was *not* concentrated as rapidly as the enemy & I feared bad results from the fatigue & *scramble* with which it was collected— but Meade has only had it in hand 6 days— & in that time has fought three of them— he is in good position & on the defensive to get his men rested & in hand for an assault— Betty says there was an artillery train by this door today which took three quarters of an hour to pass— I have just asked Brother for the news & he says nothing especial—

Blair is firing of his small artillery in the alley under the window where he first realized that his Country had a birthday— & this one will long be remembered by the Nation & Lee's retreat will sanctify it anew in the feelings of the people— He commenced his Retreat at 3 olk this morning— Now I hope Meade will show his energy of which none of his family I've known lack— that is *the* trait of the race— especially in a quarrel or fight— but George & Robt— who was my friend always kept themselves out of the family feuds—

I recieved a letter from Apo inviting me most cordially to come stay with her says it will be a comfort to her as well as of service to Blair & me— the journey is too long to go alone besides I am loth to leave my mother who said to me I cannot last long under such trials— & yet a little while after she was amused by Blair   I feel I am a comfort to her & it is a great one to your own affecate Lizzie

Sunday July 5/63 I was too late getting in town to have this mailed yesterday, I went next door with it & there met your Secy with a dispatch in his hand— he said it was a matter of business— Dalhgren son a Capt. intercepted a letter of Jeff Davis' to Robt. Lee which developes their plan of this perilous campaign out of which he is trying now to extricate himself— the plan was for Lee to lead off Hooker just as he has done— take Harrisburg & then strike for Phila & Baltimore & Cut off all our Railroad resources— when Beauregard was to strike in at the rear of Washington led by Stuart— but when Cooper came to ordering off Beauregard— Jeff objected it seems that he had not been taken in confidence by Cooper & Lee— & his intercepted letter shows this fact— & he explains how impossible it is to part with Beauregard— that the Yankees are at the White House & threatening Charleston from which place he has had to reinforce Johnston & through the mercy of God we are saved by Jeff fears— for if Beauregard had accompanied Stuart last Saturday this day a week ago— Washington would now have been in the hands of the Rebels— that you & I know—

Meade would pursue Lee instantly but has to stop to get food for his men!! this I heard the President say when we met him at the White House door— where we took Blair to see the fireworks in which he was disappointed— And he also said that Meade said he was not yet certain whether Lee was beating a retreat— or in search of a good stronghold— at which to have another fight— You see the details of the battles so I need not dwell upon them I shall return home tomorrow— but Nothing is sure in this world. Your own   Lizzie

Joshua Lawrence Chamberlain to George B. Herendeen

On the afternoon of July 2 Brigadier General Gouverneur K. Warren, the chief engineer of the Army of the Potomac, discovered that, aside from a detachment of signalmen, there were no Union troops on Little Round Top, a hill at the southern end of the battlefield that dominated the Union defensive positions along Cemetery Ridge. Warren's urgent request for troops reached Colonel Strong Vincent, a brigade commander in the Fifth Corps, who hurried his men onto the hill as it came under Confederate assault. A professor of rhetoric and modern languages at Bowdoin College, Joshua Lawrence Chamberlain joined the 20th Maine Infantry in August 1862 and saw action at Shepherdstown and Fredericksburg before becoming the regiment's commander in late May 1863. He described his part in the battle for Little Round Top in a report sent to a brigade staff officer. Eventually regiments from two Union brigades secured the position, although both brigade commanders—Vincent and Brigadier General Stephen H. Weed—as well as artillery battery commander First Lieutenant Charles Hazlett were killed. (A longer version of Chamberlain's report to Lieutenant Herendeen was published in 1889 in *The War of the Rebellion: a Compilation of the Official Records of the Union and Confederate Armies.* Although it was dated July 6, 1863, it was actually written by Chamberlain in 1884 after the War Department told him that his original report had been lost.)

Head Quarters 20th Maine Vols.
Field near Gettysburg, Pa.
July 6th 1863

Lieut,

In compliance with orders from Brigade Hd. Qrs. I have the honor to submit the following Report of the part taken by the 20th Regt. Maine Vols, in the action of July 2d and 3d near Gettysburg, Pa.

On reaching the field at about 4 P.M. July 2d, Col. Vincent

commanding the Brigade, placing me on the left of the Brigade and consequently on the extreme left of our entire line of battle, instructed me that the enemy were expected shortly to make a desperate attempt to turn our left flank, and that the position assigned to me must be held at every hazard.

I established my line on the crest of a small spur of a rocky and wooded hill, and sent out at once a company of skirmishers on my left to guard against surprise on that unprotected flank.

These dispositions were scarcely made when the attack commenced, and the right of the Regt. found itself at once hotly engaged. Almost at the same moment, from a high rock which gave me a full view of the enemy, I perceived a heavy force in rear of their principal line, moving rapidly but stealthily toward our left, with the intention, as I judged, of gaining our rear unperceived. Without betraying our peril to any but one or two officers, I had the right wing move by the left flank, taking intervals of a pace or two, according to the shelter afforded by rocks or trees, extending so as to cover the whole front then engaged; and at the same time moved the left wing to the left and rear, making a large angle at the color, which was now brought to the point where our left had first rested.

This hazardous maneuvre was so admirably executed by my men that our fire was not materially slackened in front, and the enemy gained no advantage there, while the left wing in the mean time had formed a solid and steady line in a direction to meet the expected assault. We were not a moment too soon; for the enemy having gained their desired point of attack came to a front, and rushed forward with an impetuosity which showed their sanguine expectations. Their astonishment however was evident, when emerging from their cover, they met instead of an unsuspecting flank, a firm and ready front. A strong fire opened at once from both sides, and with great effect—the enemy still advancing until they came within *ten paces* of our line, where our steady and telling volleys brought them to a stand. From that moment began a struggle fierce and bloody beyond any that I have witnessed, and which lasted in all its fury, a full hour. The two lines met, and broke and mingled in the shock. At times I saw around me more of the enemy than of my own men. The edge of conflict swayed to and fro—now one and now the other party holding the contested ground. Three times our line was forced back, but only to rally and repulse the enemy. As often as the enemy's line was broken and routed, a new line was unmasked, which advanced with fresh vigor. Our "sixty rounds" were rapidly reduced: I sent several messengers to the rear for ammunition, and also for reinforcements. In the mean time we seized the opportunity of a momentary lull, to gather ammunition and more serviceable arms, from the dead and dying on the field. With these we met the enemy's last and fiercest assault. Their own rifles and their own bullets were turned against them. In the midst of this struggle, our ammunition *utterly failed.* The enemy were close upon us with a fresh line, pouring on us a terrible fire. Half the left wing already lay on the field. Although I had brought two companies from the right to its support, it was now scarcely more than a skirmish line. The heroic energy of my officers could avail no more. Our gallant line writhed & shrunk before the fire it could not repel. It was too evident that we could maintain the *defensive* no longer. As a last, desperate resort, I ordered a *charge.* The word "fix bayonets" flew from man to man. The click of the steel seemed to give new zeal to all. The men dashed forward with a shout. The two wings came into one line again, and extending to the left, and at the same time wheeling to the right, the whole Regiment described nearly a half circle, the left passing over the space of half a mile, while the right kept within the support of the 83d Penna. thus leaving no chance of escape to the enemy except to climb the steep side of the mountain or to pass by the whole front of the 83d Penna. The enemy's first line scarcely tried to run—they stood amazed, threw down their loaded arms and surrendered in whole companies. Those in their rear had more time and gave us more trouble. My skirmishing company threw itself upon the enemy's flank behind a stone wall, and their effective fire added to the enemy's confusion. In this charge we captured three hundred & sixty eight prisoners, many of them officers, and took three hundred stand of arms. The prisoners were from four different regiments, and admitted that they had attacked with a Brigade.

At this time Col. Rice commanding the Brigade (Col. Vincent having been mortally wounded) brought up a strong support from Genl. Crawford's command, and 3000 rounds of ammunition. The wounded and the prisoners were now sent to the rear, and our dead gathered and laid side by side.

Shortly after Col. Rice desired me to advance and take the high steep hill, called "Wolf Hill" or "Round Top" half a mile or more to our left and front, where the enemy had assembled on their repulse—a position which commanded ours in case the assault should be renewed.

It was then dusk. The men were worn out, and heated and thirsty almost beyond endurance. Many had sunk down and fallen asleep the instant the halt was ordered. But at the command they cheerfully formed their line once more, and the little handful of men went up the hill, scarcely expecting ever to return. In order not to disclose our numbers—as I had now but two hundred guns—and to avoid bringing on an engagement in which I was sure to be overpowered, I forbid my men to fire, and trusted to the bayonet alone. Throwing out two small detachments on each flank, we pushed straight up the hill. The darkness favored us, concealing our force and preventing the enemy from getting range so that their volleys went over our heads, while they deemed it prudent to retire before us. Just at the crest we found more serious difficulty and were obliged to fall back for a short time. We advanced again with new energy, which the knowledge of our isolated and perilous position rendered perhaps desperate, and carried the desired point. We took twenty five prisoners in this movement, among them some of the staff of Genl. Laws. From these officers I learned that Hoods whole Division was massed but a short distance in front, that he had just prepared to advance and take possession of the heights, and was only waiting to ascertain the number and position of our force. I posted my command among the rocks along the crest in line of battle, and sent two companies in charge of judicious officers to reconnoitre the ground in front. They reported a large body of the enemy in a ravine not more than two or three hundred yards distant. I therefore kept these two companies out, with orders to watch the enemy, while our main line, kept on the alert by occasional volleys from below, held its position among the rocks throughout the night. In the meantime the 83d

Penna. and the 5th & 12th Penna Reserves came up and formed as a support. The next day at noon we were relieved by the 1st Brigade.

We were engaged with Laws' Brigade, Hood's Div. The prisoners represented themselves as from the 15th and 47th Alabama and the 4th and 5th Texas Regts. The whole number of prisoners taken by us is three hundred & ninety three—of arms captured three hundred stand. At least one hundred and fifty of the enemy's killed and wounded were found in front of our first line of battle.

We went into the fight with three hundred & fifty eight guns. Every pioneer and musician who could carry a musket was armed and engaged. Our loss is one hundred & thirty six —thirty killed, one hundred & five wounded—many mortally —and one taken prisoner in the night advance. Often as our line was broken and pierced by the enemy, there is not a man to be reported "missing."

I have to regret the loss of a most gallant young officer, Lt. W. L. Kendall, who fell in the charge also Capt. C. W. Billings mortally wounded early in the action, and Lieut. A. N. Linscott mortally wounded on the crest of "Wolf Hill." Our advantage was dearly bought with the loss of such admirable officers as these.

As for the conduct of my officers and men, I will let the result speak for them. If I were to mention any, I might do injustice by omitting some equally deserving. Our roll of Honor is the three hundred & eighty officers and men who *fought at Gettysburg.*

My thanks are due the 83d Penna, Capt Woodward comdg. for their steady and gallant support, and I would particularly acknowledge the services of Adjt. Gifford of that Regt. who exposed himself to the severest fire to render me aid.

> Very respectfully
> Your obdt. servt.
> J. L. Chamberlain
> Col. 20th Maine Vols.

Lt. Geo. B. Herendeen,
Act. Asst. Adjt. Genl.
3d Brigade 1st Div. 5th Corps.

Henry Livermore Abbott to Josiah Gardner Abbott

A veteran of Ball's Bluff, Fair Oaks, the Seven Days, Fredericksburg, and Chancellorsville, Captain Henry Livermore Abbott commanded a company in the 20th Massachusetts Infantry. His regiment reached the Gettysburg battlefield early on July 2 and was posted along with the rest of the Second Corps at the center of the Union line on Cemetery Ridge. On the afternoon of July 3, as Lee sent about 13,000 men against the Union center, the section of Cemetery Ridge defended by the 20th Massachusetts came under attack by two brigades from the division commanded by Major General George E. Pickett.

July 6 / 1863
Near Gettysburg Pa

My dear Papa,

When our great victory was just over, the exultation of victory was so great that one didn't think of our fearful losses, but now I cant help feeling a great weight at my heart. Poor Henry Ropes was one of the dearest friends I ever had or expect to have. He was one of the purest-minded, noblest, most generous men I ever knew. His loss is terrible. His men actually wept when they showed me his body, even under the tremendous cannonade, a time when most soldiers see their comrades dying around them with indifference. Col. Hall, I believe, means to mention him in his report. He says that of every body in the army, Henry was the only one he knew that was fighting simply from patriotism, & that he would himself almost have given his life to have had Ropes lived to see the splendid victory he always so earnestly hoped for. I cant cease to think of him, whenever I am alone, which is pretty frequent now that we have only 3 left. All our pique against Revere too had long ceased, since we saw him on the march struggling so nobly with his physical weakness, & he is regretted as such a man should be. Then there is poor Macy with a hand gone. Herbert Mason hit too, with Ropes my most intimate friend here, two of the finest & bravest officers that ever fought in this war. Just as he was going off from the hospital, with a consideration that wounded men going home very rarely feel for those left, he send me his brandy, tobacco, &c a perfect God-Send at the time. Patten too, who is going to be mentioned by Col. Hall for the gallantry, with which he held his outpost, when the skirmishers on both flanks had run, & our whole fire in the direst confusion had gone over him. In deed with only two officers besides myself remaining, I cant help feeling a little spooney when I am thinking, & you know I am not at all a lachrymose individual in general. However I think we can run the machine. Our losses are—of 13 officers, 3 killed, 7 wounded. Of 231 enlisted men, 30 killed, 84 wounded, 3 missing, total 117, with officers, aggregate 127. I haven't time to give you an account as I have to write to Mr. Ropes, & John Revere, also to Paines father. (Paine was one of the finest officers I have ever seen though only 17 years of age). The enemy, after a morning of quiet on our part of the line, (a little to the right of the left center) began the most terrific cannonade with a converging fire of 150 pieces that I ever heard in my life & kept it up for 2 hours, almost entirely disabling our batteries, killing & wounding over half the officers & men & silencing most of the guns. The thin line of our division against which it was directed was very well sheilded by a little rut they lay in & in front of our brigade by a little pit, just one foot deep & one foot high, thrown up hastily by one shovel, but principally by the fact that it is very difficult to hit a single line of troops, so that the enemy chiefly threw over us with the intention of disabling the batteries & the reserves which they supposed to be massed in rear of the batteries in the depression of the hill. In the former object they were successful, in the latter they were better than successful. The one brigade brought up in support had to be retired 2 miles, & no other reserves could be brought up, for any massing of troops would under that fire would have proved their own destruction, without their being of any service to us. No infantry in the world could have been massed under that fire for half an hour. The rebels thus left us entirely unsupported & advanced with perfect confidence, after ceas-

ing their artillery, our artillery being so well knocked up that
only one or two shots were fired into them which however
were very well aimed & we could see tumble over squads in
the rebel lines. Had our batteries been intact, the rebels would
never have got up to our musketry, for they were obliged to
come out of the woods & advance from a half to 3/4 of a mile
over an open field & in plain sight. A magnificent sight it was
too. Two brigades in two lines, their skirmishers driving in
ours. The moment I saw them, I knew we should give them
Fredericksburg. So did every body. We let the regiment in
front of us get within 100 feet of us, & then bowled them over
like nine pins, picking out the colors first. In two minutes there
were only groups of two or three men running round wildly,
like chickens with their heads off. We were cheering like mad,
when Macy directed my attention to a spot 3 or 4 rods on our
right where there were no pits, only, a rail fence. Baxter's
Pennsylvania men had most disgracefully broken, & the rebels
were within our line. The order was immediately given to fall
back far enough to form another line & prevent us being
flanked. Without however waiting for that, the danger was so
imminent that I had rushed my company immediately up to
the gap, & the regiment & the rest of the brigade, being there
some before & the rest as quick as they could. The rail fence
checked the main advance of the enemy & they stood, both
sides, pegging away into each other. The rows of dead after the
battle, I found to be within 15 and 20 feet apart, as near hand
to hand fighting as I ever care to see. The rebels behaved with
as much pluck as any men in the world could, they stood there
against the fence, until they were nearly all shot down. The
rebels batteries, seeing how the thing was going, pitched shell
into us, all the time, with great disregard of their own friends
who were so disagreeably near us. Gen Webb who commands
the Philadelphia brigade in his official report has given Hall's
brigade the credit of saving the day, after his own men had run
away. A miserable rowdy named Hays comdg. the 3rd div. of
our corps, who was not engaged at all in the musketry fire,
claims I believe all the credit of the thing. So look out for false
stories in papers. Dont confound this fellow with Hays comdg
the corps, who is said to be a good officer, & who got up just
after the fight, Hancock commanding the corps & Gibbon

comdg the div, a splendid officer, being both wounded. Our lines were something of this form.

The field was mostly open where we all were with scarcely a perceptible rise, comanded by the rebel side, on the centre a little wooded still better commanded by the rebel side, on the right, I am told, wooded & rocky, both parties contending for the slopes towards us. The mountains facing our left were out of cannon range. On the right they were not, but I am told, of such a nature that the rebels could have only got so little artillery into position, that our superior number of batteries would soon have knocked them into pie, notwithstanding their commanding hight, which accounts for what at first was very strange to me, why the rebs didn't shell us out, since the hights near the right center commanded the entire field around the centre, where it is very narrow. Moreover our line of retreat was so narrow that it was easy, if our left was turned to cut us off from it. Had the rebels driven in our left (they twice tried it & I have told you how near they came to it,) it would have been all up with us. The advantages of our position were that the comdg. general could over look almost the whole line, a rare thing in this country, & that moving on the chord of the circle while the enemy moved on the arc, we could reinforce any part of the line from any other part much quicker than they could, an advantage which Meade availed himself of admirably in the first day's rebel attack, but which their shell fire prevented him from doing in the second day's. In person, Meade is a tall, thin lantern-jawed respectable covey, wearing spectacles, looking a good sort of a family doctor. Uncle John Sedgewick, as have most other of our good officers, long ago told us that McClellan was the first choice, Franklin the 2nd,

& Meade the 3rd. An extremely good officer you see, with no vanity or nonsense of any kind, knowing just exactly what he could do & what he couldn't. Our troops were so elated by the removal of Hooker, both Generals, line officers & men, & by the feeling that they were on their own soil, that perhaps they deserve fully as much credit as the generalship of Meade. I dont know however. I am afraid Meade would hardly have conducted an invasion into Va. as well.

I find I am getting a good deal longer than I meant to be, so I will conclude with asking you to thank mama for the things she sent. Wm Kelly was delighted & the tobacco for me came just when I was starting on the march without any. You can imagine what a godsend it was.

I suppose you have all been suffering a great deal of anxiety, but how thankful you must be now that certainty doesn't bring you the same grief that the Ropes family have. God grant we may have no bad news from Fletcher. My love of course to all the family including George & Mary Welch. Tell them to be sure & write how John is. We miss him terribly.

Your aff. son,
H. L. Abbott

I have had no mail since leaving Falmouth.

Lafayette McLaws to Emily McLaws

As the Army of Northern Virginia retreated through Maryland, Major General Lafayette McLaws wrote about his division's actions at Gettysburg. The unexpected resistance his troops encountered around the peach orchard was caused by the advance of the Union Third Corps toward the Emmitsburg road in the early afternoon of July 2.

Headquarters Division
July 7th/63

My Dear Wife

Since I wrote you last we have had a series of terrible engagements out of which God has permitted me to come unscathed again. On the 1st of July we left Chambersburg and went across the mountains by Fayetteville and Greenwood to Cashtown and camped within five miles of Gettysburg. Where we heard that there had been a considerable battle fought between the forces of the enemy and the Corps of Genls Ewell and Hill, resulting in the route of the enemy with a loss of several thousand prisoners. The next morning we moved around Gettysburg towards the Emmitsburg road, to arrive at the *Peach orchard*, a small settlement with a very large Peach Orchard attached. The intention was to get in rear of the enemy who were supposed to be stationed principally in rear of Gettysburg or near it. The report being that the enemy had but two regiments of infantry and one battery at the Peach orchard. On arriving at the vicinity of the Orchard, the enemy were discovered in greater force than was supposed, and two of my Brigades were deployed to face the enemy, and the other two in the rear as reserve; ten or twelve pieces were put in position, and fire opened— General Longstreet sent word that he was satisfied there was but a small force of the enemy in front and that I must proceed at once to the assault. On examination it was discovered that the enemy were in much greater force than was expected, and the assualt was delayed, but again delayed and finally I was directed not to assault until General Hood was in position. Gen H had gone around above me to the right, and found that the enemy were very strongly posted on two rocky hills, with artillery and infantry and before he could aid me it was necessary to carry one of the hills—the one nearest to him—which was done by his troops after a desperate encounter, and my division was then ordered in readiness, and as Genl Hoods success became apparent, the Brigades of Kershaw and Semmes were ordered to advance and then those of Barksdale and Wofford, gallantly our men swept the enemy before them, away from the Peach orchard and on to the woods and hills beyond with great slaughter. The enemy in crowds running to our lines. The right Brigades attempted to storm the second hill which was very steep and rocky and bare of trees towards the top, their efforts were however vain and we were obliged to desist. We however occupied the woods beneath the hills, and remained during the night. Genl Barksdale, commanding the Mississippi Brigade was killed, Genl Semmes badly wounded. Colonel Carter of the 13th Miss killed, Colonel Griffin of the 18th Miss & Col Holder 17th Miss. badly wounded, Col de Saussure 15th S.C. killed, Lt. Col. Fiser 17th Miss. Wounded, &c &c. —The loss in my Division was near twenty four hundred, the heaviest of the war, and many of the most valuable officers in the whole service have been killed. Thus ended the battle of the Peach orchard. In place of there being but two regiments of infantry and one battery, the enemy were in very great force, very strongly posted and aided by very numerous arty. I think the attack was unnecessary and the whole plan of battle a very bad one. Genl Longstreet is to blame for not reconnoitering the ground and for persisting in ordering the assault when his errors were discovered. During the engagement he was very excited, giving contrary orders to every one, and was exceedingly overbearing. I consider him a humbug—a man of small capacity, very obstinate, not at all chivalrous, exceedingly conceited, and totally selfish. If I can it is my intention to get away from his command. We want Beauregard very much indeed, his presence is imperatively called for. On the 3d inst, all our available arty was put in position along our lines, and commenced the most tremendous artillery fire I expect ever heard on our continent. We had several hundred cannon and the enemy as many more; finally our troops assaulted the centre, and gained the enemies batteries but were compelled to relinquish our hold and retire to our lines of the day previous to the assualt—where we remained until the next day, when were retired at dark without molestation and reached this place 2 miles from Hagerstown last night about ten oclock. Our men very much fatigued and foot sore, but not disheartened.

The retirement was necessary because it became important to re-establish our communications with the government.

Give a thousand kisses to my dear children, and my dear wife a thousand kisses to you also, and much love indeed. The mail is waiting & I write in a hurry.

Your devoted husband
LM

Be careful in writing as the last mails were captured by the enemy and were of course read by all, & may be published.

Cornelia Hancock to Her Cousin
and to Ellen Hancock Child

The battle of Gettysburg cost the Confederates about 28,000 men killed, wounded, or missing, while Union losses totaled about 23,000. Cornelia Hancock, a young Quaker woman from New Jersey, went to Gettysburg with her brother-in-law, Dr. Henry T. Child, to help care for the wounded. (She was not related to Major General Winfield Scott Hancock, the commander of the Union Second Corps.) Hancock arrived at Gettysburg on the evening of July 6 and began working in an army field hospital the next day.

––––––––––––––

Gettysburg, Pa. July 7th, 1863.

My dear cousin

I AM very tired tonight; have been on the field all day—went to the 3rd Division 2nd Army Corps. I suppose there are about five hundred wounded belonging to it. They have one patch of woods devoted to each army corps for a hospital. I being interested in the 2nd, because Will had been in it, got into one of its ambulances, and went out at eight this morning and came back at six this evening. There are no words in the English language to express the sufferings I witnessed today. The men lie on the ground; their clothes have been cut off them to dress their wounds; they are half naked, have nothing but hard-tack to eat only as Sanitary Commissions, Christian Associations, and so forth give them. I was the first woman who reached the 2nd Corps after the three days fight at Gettysburg. I was in that Corps all day, not another woman within a half mile. Mrs. Harris was in first division of 2nd Corps. I was introduced to the surgeon of the post, went anywhere through the Corps, and received nothing but the greatest politeness from even the lowest private. You can tell Aunt that there is every opportunity for "secesh" sympathizers to do a good work among the butternuts; we have lots of them here suffering fearfully. To give you some idea of the extent and numbers of the wounds, four surgeons, none of whom were idle fifteen minutes at a time, were busy all day amputating legs and arms. I gave to every man that had a leg or arm off a gill of wine, to every wounded in Third Division, one glass of lemonade, some bread and preserves and tobacco—as much as I am opposed to the latter, for they need it very much, they are so exhausted.

I feel very thankful that this was a successful battle; the spirit of the men is so high that many of the poor fellows said today, "What is an arm or leg to whipping Lee out of Penn." I would get on first rate if they would not ask me to write to their wives; *that* I cannot do without crying, which is not pleasant to either party. I do not mind the sight of blood, have seen limbs taken off and was not sick at all.

It is a very beautiful, rolling country here; under favorable circumstances I should think healthy, but now for five miles around, there is an awful smell of putrefaction. Women are needed here very badly, anyone who is willing to go to field hospitals, but nothing short of an order from Secretary Stanton or General Halleck will let you through the lines. Major General Schenk's order for us was not regarded as anything; if we had not met Miss Dix at Baltimore Depot, we should not have gotten through. It seems a strange taste but I am glad we did. We stay at Doctor Horner's house at night—direct letters care of Dr. Horner, Gettysburg, Pa. If you could mail me a newspaper, it would be a great satisfaction, as we do not get the news here and the soldiers are so anxious to hear; things will be different here in a short time.

CORNELIA

Gettysburg—July 8th, 1863.

My dear sister

We have been two days on the field; go out about eight and come in about six—go in ambulances or army buggies. The surgeons of the Second Corps had one put at our disposal. I feel assured I shall never feel horrified at anything that may happen to me hereafter. There is a great want of surgeons here; there are hundreds of brave fellows, who have not had their wounds dressed since the battle. Brave is not the word; more, more Christian fortitude never was witnessed than they exhibit, always say—"Help my neighbor first he is worse." The Second Corps did the heaviest fighting, and, of course, all who were badly wounded, were in the thickest of the fight, and, therefore, we deal with the very best class of the men—that is the bravest. My name is particularly grateful to them because it is Hancock. General Hancock is very popular with his men. The reason why they suffer more in this battle is because our army is victorious and marching *on* after Lee, leaving the wounded for citizens and a very few surgeons. The citizens are stripped of everything they have, so you must see the exhausting state of affairs. The Second Army Corps alone had two thousand men wounded, this I had from the Surgeon's head quarters. I cannot write more. There is no mail that comes in, we send letters out: I believe the Government has possession of the road. I hope you will write. It would be very pleasant to have letters to read in the evening, for I am so tired I cannot write them. Get the Penn Relief to send clothing here; there are many men without anything but a shirt lying in poor shelter tents, calling on God to take them from this world of suffering; in fact the air is rent with petitions to deliver them from their sufferings.

C. HANCOCK

Direct boxes—E. W. Farnham, care of Dr. Horner, Gettysburg, Penna. for Second Corps Hospital. Do not neglect this; clothing is shockingly needed. We fare pretty well for delicacies sent up by men from Baltimore.

If you direct your letters Miss Hancock, Second Corps, Third Division Hospital, do not scruple to put the Miss to it, and leave out Cornelia, as I am known only by that cognomen. I do not know when I shall go home—it will be according to how long this hospital stays here and whether another battle comes soon. I can go right in an ambulance without being any expense to myself. The Christian Committee support us and when they get tired the Sanitary is on hand. Uncle Sam is very rich, but very slow, and if it was not for the Sanitary, much suffering would ensue. We give the men toast and eggs for breakfast, beef tea at ten o'clock, ham and bread for dinner, and jelly and bread for supper. Dried rusk would be nice if they were only here. Old sheets we would give much for. Bandages are plenty but sheets very scarce. We have plenty of woolen blankets now, in fact the hospital is well supplied, but for about five days after the battle, the men had no blankets nor scarce any shelter.

It took nearly five days for some three hundred surgeons to perform the amputations that occurred here, during which time the rebels lay in a dying condition without their wounds being dressed or scarcely any food. If the rebels did not get severely punished for this battle, then I am no judge. We have but one rebel in our camp now; he says he never fired his gun if he could help it, and, therefore, we treat him first rate. One man died this morning. I fixed him up as nicely as the place will allow; he will be buried this afternoon. We are becoming somewhat civilized here now and the men are cared for well.

On reading the news of the copperhead performance, in a tent where eight men lay with nothing but stumps (they call a leg cut off above the knee a "stump") they said if they held on a little longer they would form a stump brigade and go and fight them. We have some plucky boys in the hospital, but they suffer awfully. One had his leg cut off yesterday, and some of the ladies, newcomers, were up to see him. I told them if they had seen as many as I had they would not go far to see the sight again. I could stand by and see a man's head taken off I believe—you get so used to it here. I should be perfectly contented if I could receive my letters. I have the cooking all on my mind pretty much. I have torn almost all my clothes off of me, and Uncle Sam has given me a new suit. William says I am very popular here as I am such a contrast to some of the office-seeking women who swarm around hospitals. I am black as an Indian and dirty as a pig and as well as I ever was in my life—have a nice bunk and tent about twelve feet square. I have a bed that is made of four crotch sticks and some sticks laid across and pine boughs laid on that with blankets on top. It is equal to any mattress ever made. The tent is open at night and sometimes I have laid in the damp all night long, and got up all right in the morning.

The suffering we get used to and the nurses and doctors, stewards, etc., are very jolly and sometimes we have a good

time. It is very pleasant weather now. There is all in getting to
do what you *want* to do and I am doing that.

The First Minnesota Regiment bears the first honors here for
loss in the late battle. The Colonel was wounded—Lieutenant
Colonel, Major, and Adjutant. They had four captains killed
outright and when they came out of battle, the command devolved on the First Lieutenant. Three hundred and eighty-four
men went into battle, one hundred and eighty were wounded
and fifty-four killed. The Colonel I know well; he is a very fine
man. He has three bullets in him; has had two taken out by
Dr. Child, the other he got in at Antietam and it is there yet. I
do hope he will recover. Most of the men are from New York
here now; they are very intelligent and talk good politics.
McClellan is their man mostly. Meade they think sympathizes
with McClellan and therefore they like him. Hooker is at a very
low ebb except as they think he fed them well—a circumstance
that soldiers make great account of. Such feeders you never
saw.

Pads are terribly needed here. Bandages and lint are plenty.
I would like to see seven barrels of dried rusk here. I do not
know the day of the week or anything else. Business is slacken-
ing a little though—order is beginning to reign in the hospital
and soon things will be right. One poor fellow is hollowing
fearfully now while his wounds are being dressed.

There is no more impropriety in a *young* person being here
provided they are sensible than a sexagenarian. Most polite
and obliging are all the soldiers to me.

It is a very good place to meet celebrities; they come here
from all parts of the United States to see their wounded. Senator Wilson, Mr. Washburn, and one of the Minnesota Senators
have been here. I get beef tenderloin for dinner.—Ladies who
work are favored but the dress-up palaverers are passed by on
the other side. I tell you I have lost my memory almost entirely, but it is gradually returning. Dr. Child has done very
good service here. All is well with me; we do not know much
war news, but I know I am doing all I can, so I do not concern
further. Kill the copperheads. Write everything, however trifling, it is all interest here.

From thy affectionate
C. HANCOCK

Catharine Peirce to Taylor Peirce

Catharine Peirce wrote with news of home to her husband, a soldier with the 22nd Iowa Infantry at Vicksburg. She would later receive a letter Taylor had written to her on July 4 announcing that the "Gibralter of America has fallen."

———————————

Des Moines City July 5th 1863

I sit down to write feeling a little bad again not having had a letter for two weeks but I will try and be patient hopeing thee is well and that I will get one in a few days more. We are all well to day. Cyrus seems to be in a better condition this two weeks than he has been for a long time. I do not know whather it is Ayers medicine that is helping him or not. We have had a very pleasant summer so far with the exception of a few very warm days but our fourth was not near so hot as it was last year I do not think. We had a very nice celebration on the fair ground and a real good addres by a Mr Palmer in favour of the war the Union and the Soldeirs and death to all Copperheads and rebel sympathisers. It was a good thing and just suited my stile. The speaker went on to say that Goverment must be sustained and the soldiers cared for at all hazards but Dear me I can not write half of the good that was spoken in behalf of our Country and our Countrys cause. Mary received a letter from Rachel day before yesterday. R writes they are all well but Aunt Hannah she is no better and there appears very little prospect of her ever being any better. Rachel writes very gloomily of the times. The Rebels have got up into Penn and are doing a great amount of damage. But if thee has a chance to see the Union papers thee will know more about what they are doing than I can write, but it seem as our army in the east has not or can not attane much some how or other. What is the reason I am shour I can not tell. It seemed to me if they let the rebles overrun them there that there is very little hope

346

for our beloved Country. But I still hope and trust there is still a just God in heaven that will set the Nation right one of these days, wheather we live to see it or not Dear Taylor. I can not write to do any good or that will be interesting to thee for the simple reason that I do not know of any thing of interest to write of.

I have not had any news from Jasper Co for a week or more. Mr Vowel and his wife was up here about two weeks ago and gave me the full news. There is nothing of importance except deaths. Preston Caloson was killed at the Battle of Black river Bridge and Willis Greens son also but I expect thee has seen the account of the killed before this time. Vowel says that there is no thing doing in Newton this summer to a mount to any thing. He thinks if the railroad should mis it a few miles that it will die a naturel death and that right soon they have got the cars runing to Grenell now and are working on this side. They say thair are going to grade Skunk bottom this fall but it may not be done if the Draft gos on. The baby is siting on the floor by side me and is beginig to fuss and I will have to close.

With love I remain thy wife Catharine

William Henry Harrison Clayton to Amos and Grace Clayton

With no hope of relief or resupply, Lieutenant General John C. Pemberton opened surrender negotiations at Vicksburg on July 3. Grant initially demanded an unconditional surrender, but then agreed to parole the garrison in order to avoid having to transport 30,000 prisoners to Illinois; he also hoped that many of the paroled Confederates would return home and spread disaffection with the war. Pemberton's army capitulated on July 4, ending a nine-week campaign that had cost the Union about 9,000 men killed, wounded, or missing. William Henry Harrison Clayton of the 19th Iowa Infantry witnessed the surrender.

———————

Vicksburg, Miss.
July 5th, 1863
    Dear Father & Mother:
    It is with great pleasure that I pen the following lines. Yesterday, the "*glorious* Fourth of July" was made doubly so, by the *surrender*, and *occupation* of this, the strongest rebel position in their Confederacy.
    It was an event that we, and I suppose the whole Northern people, have been patiently waiting for, for months past, and what is better than all it fell without the necessity of storming the works and thus losing numbers of valuable lives.
    We have *starved* them out, they held out until they could do so no longer, and they were compelled to come to terms.
    I saw from the Keosauqua papers that there was to be celebrations on the Fourth at a number of places in the county, one being at Lebanon. I would have given anything almost if I could by some means, have been conveyed from here, there and given the joyful news. What a celebration there would have been had you only known the situation here. I imagine that copperheads would have looked down their noses and wish

themselves hid from the gaze of exultant loyal people. My sincere wish now is, that Lee and his army may get the *devil* from Hooker or someone else. I think that the Rebs would be about *played out*.

Hostilities ceased here on the 3rd before noon, they had hoisted a flag of truce. Negotiations were pending until the morning of the Fourth, when they surrendered.

I have not yet learned the terms. The prisoners are still in places they occupied yesterday morning. On the 3rd when firing ceased, our boys laid down their guns and went over to their rifle pits and forts and had quite a chat with them. It looked singular to see men, who but a few minutes previously were shooting at each other, mingle together and shake hands, and be as friendly, apparently, as brothers, but such is among the incidents of war.

Our batteries had been well supplied with ammunition and it was the intention to celebrate the Fourth on a *grand* scale, by shelling the town's 7 fortifications, but owing to the surrender only the National salute was fired, with blank cartridges.

We received orders, and at 9½ o'clock Ormes' brigade started for the inside of the fortifications. It was very hot and dusty and the march was very fatiguing. It is but a short distance from here to our old camp, but by the wagon road it is 2 or 3 miles. We are a mile or two from the town but as we are inside the works, considered that we are in Vicksburg, and began my letter accordingly. We received orders before we started in to *not cheer* or make any demonstration upon coming in. The Rebs were surprised at our conduct, and were as friendly as could be expected under the circumstances. Some of them are fine looking fellows, and some are very reasonable and admit that they are defending a bad cause. I have talked with a number that say they will fight no more if they can possibly help it. I was talking to one awhile ago close by an earthwork where our regimental flag was waving to the breeze. He said it looked better to him yet, than any other flag. I have looked in vain for the Rebel flag (the stars & bars) but have not seen it *yet*. I have seen their battery flags flying at the different forts. That of Georgia is a red flag with two black stripes diagonally across it, another flag was white with a large spot in the center. I asked a fellow this morning what kind of flag they had, but he could not tell me, he said they had several kinds but could describe none.

If we had charged these works there would have been great loss of life, for they have an abundance of ammunition and the works command each other so that if one should be taken there is two or three others ready to open upon it. They say that we never could have taken the place if they had plenty of provision, but I think it would have been taken anyhow.

They acknowledge that we did as much work in a nights time building forts and digging rifle-pits as they could do in a week. They say that we are western troops or the place never would have been taken. They seem to think that eastern troops do not possess the valor of western troops. After we entered the works the gunboats above steamed down and each fired the National salute as she rounded to. A number of boats came down during the day, screaming and blowing around as though glad to once more pass the spot so long barricaded.

Numbers of the prisoners say that they have had but one biscuit a day, and a piece of meat about the size of a persons finger, twice a day for two weeks past. The meat gave out toward the last, and I have it from a number of them that they actually eat mule-meat. They say that if the place had not been surrendered when it was they would not have stood it much longer, but laid down their arms and refused to fight longer. We have made a *big* haul, from 20 to 30,000 prisoners, the same number stands of arms and *lots* of field artillery & heavy guns, and any quantity of ammunition for them. It has been the most glorious event of the war. I would not have missed being here for a good deal. Herron's command occupies the right of their defenses or the left of our army, being below town. I received a letter from Lizzie Cooper yesterday. All were well excepting Aunt Agness who was no better. She said that there was considerable excitement there in regard to the Rebel invasion, but that preparations were being made to give them a warm reception if they should make their appearance there. The boys are all well and are pleased to be present at the fall of Vicksburg.

Give my respects to all my friends.

Your affectionate son,

W. H. H. Clayton

P.S. As I write the poor devils are running around trading tobacco for bread or anything to eat. There is so many that it takes a long time to issue provisions to them. Our boys have given them all that we could spare. They have drawn tobacco since they came here & have plenty.

The 19th had but one man wounded during our three weeks stay here. We have been lucky, were as much exposed as the other regiments that had some killed and wounded but we passed through without loss.

William T. Sherman to
Ellen Ewing Sherman

Sherman wrote to his wife on July 5, four days before the Confederate garrison at Port Hudson, Louisiana, surrendered to Major General Nathaniel P. Banks. The fall of Port Hudson, which had been under siege since May 22, would give the Union control of the entire length of the Mississippi River.

Camp near Black River,
20 miles east of Vicksburg,
July 5, 63

Dearest Ellen,

You will have heard all about the capitulation of Vicksburg on the 4th of July, and I Suppose duly appreciate it. It is the event of the war thus far. Davis placed it in the scale of Richmond, and pledged his honor that it should be held even if he had to abandon Tennessee. But it was of no use, and we are now in full possession. I am out and have not gone in to See, as even before its surrender Grant was disposing to send me forth to meet Johnston who is and has been since June 15 collecting a force about Jackson to raise the siege. I will have Ords corps, the 13th (McClernands) Shermans 15th and Parkes 9th. All were to have been out last night but Vicksburg & the 4th of July were too much for one day and they are not yet come. I expect them hourly. I am busy making 3 bridges to cross Black River and Shall converge on Bolton and Clinton and if not held back by Johnston shall enter Jackson, and then finish what was so well begun last month and break up all the Railroads & bridges in the Interior so that it will be impossible for armies to assemble again to threaten the River.

The capture of Vicksburg is to me the first gleam of daylight in this war—It was strong by nature, and had been strengthened by immense labor & stores—Grant telegraphs me 27,000 prisoners, 128 Field Guns and 100 siege pieces—add to these, 13 Guns, & 5000 Prisoners at Arkansas Post, 18 Guns & 250 prisoners at Jackson, 5 Guns & 2000 prisoners at Port Gibson —10 heavy Guns at Grand Gulf, 60 field Guns & 3500 prisoners at Champion Hill, and 14 heavy Guns at Haines Bluff, beside the immense amounts of ammunition, shot shells, horses, wagons &c. make the most extraordinary fruits of our six months campaign. Here is Glory enough for all the Heros of the West, but I content myself with Knowing & feeling that our enemy is weakened so much, and more yet by failing to hold a point deemed by them as essential to their empire in the South West. We have ravaged the Land, and have sent away half a million of negros so that this country is paralyzed and cannot recover its lost strength in twenty years.

Had the Eastern armies done half as much war would be substantially entered upon. But I read of Washington, Baltimore & Philadelphia being threatened & Rosecrans sitting idly by, writing for personal favor in the newspapers, and our Government at Washington chiefly engaged in pulling down its leaders. Hooker now consigned to retirement. Well I thank God, we are far from Washington and that we have in Grant not a Great man or a hero—but a good, plain sensible kindhearted fellow. Here are Grant, & Sherman & McPherson, three sons of Ohio, have achieved more actual success than all else combined and I have yet to see the first kindly notice of us in the State, but on the contrary a system of abuse designed & calculated to destroy us with the People & the Army: but the army of the Tennessee, those who follow their colors & do not skulk behind in the North, at the Hospitals & depots far to the Rear, Know who think & act, and if Life is spared us our Countrymen will realize the Truth. I shall go on through heat & dust till the Mississipi is clear, till the large armies of the enemy in this quarter seek a more secure base, and then I will renew my hopes of getting a quiet hour when we can grow up among our children & prepare them for the dangers which may environ their later life. I did hope Grant would have given me Vicksburg and let some one else follow up the enemy inland, but I never suggest anything to myself personal, and only what I deem necessary to fulfil the purposes of war. I know that the capture of Vicksburg will make an impression the world over, and expect loud acclamations in the North West, but I heed more its effects on Louisiana & Arkansas. If Banks succeed as he now must at Port Hudson, and the army in Missouri push to Little Rock, the Region west of the Mississipi will cease to be the Theater of war save to the Bands of Robbers created by war who now prefer to live by pillage than honest labor. Rosecrans army & this could also, acting in concert, drive all opposing masses into the recesses of Georgia & Alabama, leaving the Atlantic slopes the great Theater of War.

I wish Halleck would put a Guard on the White House to keep out the Committees of preachers Grannies & Dutchmen that absorb Lincolns time & thoughts, fill up our thinned Ranks with conscripts, and then handle these vast armies with the Single thought of success regardless of who shall get the personal credit and Glory.

I am pleased to hear from you that occasionally you receive Kindness from men out of regard to me. I know full well there must be a large class of honest people north who are sick of the wrangling of officers for power and notoriety and are sick of the silly flattery piled by interested parties on their favorites. McClernand the only sample of that List with us played himself out, and there is not an officer or soldier here but rejoices he is gone away. With an intense selfishness and lust of notoriety he could not let his mind get beyond the limits of his vision and therefore all was brilliant about him and dark & suspicious beyond. My style is the reverse. I am somewhat blind to what occurs near me, but have a clear perception of things & events remote. Grant possesses the happy medium and it is for this reason I admire him. I have a much quicker perception of things than he, but he balances the present & remote so evenly that results follow in natural course. I would not have risked the passing the Batteries at Vicksburg & trusting to the long route by Grand Gulf & Jackson to reach what we both knew were the key points to Vicksburg, but I would have aimed to reach the same points by Grenada—But both arrived at the same points and though both of us Knew little of the actual ground, it is wonderful how well they have realized our military calculations.

As we sat in Oxford last November we saw in the future what we now realize and like the architect who sees developed the beautiful vision of his Brain, we feel an intense satisfaction at the realization of our military plans. Thank God no president was near to thwart our plans, and that the short sighted Public could not drive us from our object till the plan was fully realized.

Well the campaign of Vicksburg is ended, and I am either to begin anew or simply make complete the natural sequences of a finished Job. I regard my movement as the latter, though you and others may be distressed at the guesses of our newspaper correspondent on the Spot (Cairo) and made to believe I am marching on Mobile, or Chattanooga or Atlanta. The weather is intensely hot, and dust terrible I may have to march far & long, but unless Johnston fight at Clinton or Jackson I will not expect more than affairs of Cavalry till my return.

Dayton brought me the clothes, but the truth is I never undress now except semioccasionally to put on clean under clothes. For near two months I have slept in my clothes ready to jump to the saddle, for I have been close upon an enemy since we crossed the Mississipi near two months ago. I have just written to Brooks Bros. New York to send me two Coats & two pants—Sweat & dust have made my clothes shabby, and the bushes have made me ragged below the Knee. Hill takes admirable care of things and I can always get clean drawers, socks & shirts by asking for them. Indeed I distress him sometimes by wearing shirts & socks too long. Still we manage to get along most admirably. He is the most faithful fellow I ever saw—and my nigger Carter keeps my horses seat fat. So I am well off—Hammond is with me as cranky as ever, but as long as he can find buttermilk he lives. He has found some secesh relations and at this moment has gone to Bovina to See a cousin, a handsome widow? whose husband is in Vicksburg. Oh the wail of these secesh Girls when Vicksburg surrendered. They cried and tore their hair, but I told them they had better not—they would survive the humiliating thought and eat whatever bread with as much relish as they ever did the corn dodgers of Aunt Dinah—now Gone to the Land of Linkum. It is hard to see as I do here an old preacher Mr. Fox, 40 years resident on this spot, with 17 children born to him lawfully & 11 still alive—carrying wood and milking cows. Two months ago he had a dozen house servants & 40 field hands, but now all gone, fences open & corn eaten up—garden pillaged by soldiers, house gutted of all furniture &c., indeed desolation, and he & his family compelled to appeal to us for the Soldier's Ration. This you will say is the judgment of God, but stiff necked he dont see it.

Yesterday I expected to cross Black River today but the troops have not come out from the siege, but I hope to cross Black tomorrow and see who are behind the saucy pickets that sit their horses so jauntily in the Cornfield beyond.

Charley has written you, we are all well—Love to all the folks. Yrs. Ever

W. T. Sherman

William Winters to Harriet Winters

Sergeant William Winters of the 67th Indiana Infantry had described the ongoing bombardment of Vicksburg to his wife on June 21: "For six hours our artilery opened on the rebel works at six oclock and poured it into them untill thenn, and such a roar of canon as was never heard in this neck of the woods before." After the surrender Winters surveyed the result of weeks of shelling.

_____

Division Hospital, rear of Vicksburgh, July 6th, 1863

Dear Wife,

Vicksburgh is ours!

Pemberton surrendered on the 4th, and such a day was never known in this country, I know, for we had got tired of laying here in these hollows and pounding without doing verey mutch aparent good, but the rebs had to come to it at last, but they held out as long as they had any thing to eat and actuly eat mule beef before they surendered.

I was down to the city on yesterday afternoon and took a stroll through the town looking at the work of destruction which is visable on every hand. The effects of our mortor shell is frightfull to look at, for where ever they struck they lef a frightful mark. I saw houses that shells from our mortor had struck and went straight down through from the roof to the cellar and the hole was large enough to drop a bushell basket through and some would take out nearly one whole side [   ]. When they struck the ground before bursting, they left a queer looking hole. Some of them left a place resembling a potatoe hill where the potatoes had cracked the hill all open, only in size they looked as if a cow was buried on the top of the ground. Others again would throw the dirt about and leave a hole that would hid a hogshead, and the efect of the shot and shell in some places is terible to look at. I saw one house that had 27 round shot holes in it and I dont know how many from musket balls and fragments of shell, but it was an awfull sight.

And then the greatest curiosity was the caves in the hill side that the citisens have dug to protect themselves from the deadly misels that our guns were constatly hurling into their midst. They cut them with the roof arched and the side of them trimmed down very smooth, and there was this rush carpet laid down to walk upon and nicly tacked around over the walls and ceiling so as to keep their clothes clean; and from the looks, every family in the city must of had one or more as the hills are perfectly full of them. I counted 20 in one roe in one place and sixteen in another, and I had not time to take particular notice. I only saw those that I walked pased.

This city looks dirty and disgraceful, a great many of the residents having left for safer quarters some 2 months ago, and the dust is so deep and dry that it has setled all over everything and gives the place a forlorn and forsaken apearance. And then to see those poor sick rebels lying about dirty and raged! Everything around them looks filthy and greasey and the atmosphere is full of a nasty, sickening, humid smell ariseing from the decaying animal matter and ofals of one kind and another that is laying around in every direction. The quarters where their men stay are perfectly filthy, and their hospitals are but verey litle better. those in the field are no better. I should like to have you see the diferenace between where I have my men quartered at and one of those rebel hospitals, as they choose to call them. I have my men all upon cots and with bed sacks filled with cotton, a clean white sheet spread over that, and then I made them all put on clen white shirts and red flanel drawers, and they look realey comfortable. And then I keep the tents and quarters swept up clean, and I think if some of those rebel surgeons would come out and look at our division Hospital they would think that our sanitary societies at home were doeing a noble work and they would go back and make their men keep themselves more clean and tidy. We have not nearly the amount of sickness that they have, notwithstanding they are in their own climate and we are not. I saw a great maney that were nearly eat up with the scurvey, something we have not been troubled with as yet, having had only a few cases and those were not bad.

I took a strole down along the levey, and it was perfectly crowded with rebs looking at our gun boats and steam boats.

The wharf was crowded for a mile with boats, something that plenty of the rebels had never saw, having lived away back in the interior. And it was amusing to hear the remarks that some of them would make as the sailors from the gun boats would come off from their boats to see what damage their firing had done to the rebel town and fortifacations. Whenever the rebels would see a black sailor with his white pants and blue shirt they would swear at an awful rate.

But the most of them dont want to be paroled at all. They say they want to go north untill this war is over as they are tired of it, or if they cant do that they want to take the oath of alegiance and then go north untill the war is over, as they are satisfied of how the thing is going. Some of them, however, swear that they will fight us as long as they live or have a foot of ground to fight upon, but they are only the fewest [   ].

We are going to send Joe gambold up the river to Memphis or some other place, as there is no chance for him to get well down here.

the Regiment left yesterday in morning for to try old Joe Johnson a fight if he will stop for them to do it. we heard to day noon that they had him surounded some where between here and Jackson, but I dont know how true it is.

Well, I guess I have written enough for this time. this is rebel paper that come from Vicksburgh. Give my love to all and write oftener. I haven't received but one letter in three weeks, and there was from wes the [   ].

Wm. Winter

tell the folks that I am well.

P.S. I wish you had some peaches like I paid a dime for a half a dozen of yesterday—if I had only had some cream.

Bill

Joe gamboled leaves for the river this afternoon.

Bill

What do you think of rebel letter paper? And then what is the matter with Mat Beavers? Is she mareed yet to Jotham Sleare?

Benjamin B. French: Journal, July 8, 1863

A longtime Washington resident and former clerk of the House of Representatives, Benjamin B. French was appointed commissioner of public buildings for the capital in September 1861.

———————

Wednesday, July 8. "*Vicksburg has fallen!*" Since 2 o'clock yesterday I suppose I have heard that said a thousand times. "It is a glorious victory," and I trust we shall soon have more of the same sort. Rumor already has it that Port Hudson is captured, and I believe if our army does all its duty Lee's army will scarcely ever see old Virginia soil again *as an army*. It is already awfully used up and is fast being pushed to annihilation. Richmond must soon go, and then poor Jeff will be driven to his wits end. My guess is that the Rebs. will soon find themselves a set of poor, miserable wretches, and they will cry to come back into our glorious Union! I see National glory in the future such as the past has never seen. Slavery forever abolished! The South populated and thriving under Free labor & Free rule! No more Cotton lords, but plenty of Cotton Commons, and all the land pouring out its productions & becoming immensely rich! Industry, Wealth, Happiness, Virtue, all marching hand in hand, and millions of voices raising their thanks to God for His goodness in doing good to all. Oh how manifest it is to my mind that *He* is now working out the future goodness and greatness of this, his chosen people, by the sore affliction and sacrifice of War! My Faith in the glorious result has not wavered a single instant since the Rebel cannon opened on Fort Sumter, and I think now I have a perfectly realizing sense of what our future is to be; and to the goodness and honesty of Abraham Lincoln, who has acted, in my beliefs, as the servant of the Most High God in all that he has done, do we owe all that we are to be.

The weather was very dry nearly all June. The Potomac was very low and easily fordable. Lee's army crossed as easily as the Israelites crossed the Red Sea, but no sooner were they well away from its Northern bank than the rain began to fall, and it has been raining almost continually till the river has risen so much as not to be fordable at any point, & Lee & his whole army are caught, & must be captured! Is not the finger of Providence as clear in this as it was to the Israelites of old when they escaped so miraculously from Pharaoh & his Hosts? I think it is. Then—

> Sound the loud timbrel o'er Egypt's dark sea,
> JEHOVAH hath triumphed! *His* people are FREE!

Catherine Edmondston: Diary, July 8–11, 1863

On her North Carolina plantation Catherine Edmondston struggled to make sense of conflicting reports regarding events in Pennsylvania and Mississippi.

———————

JULY 8, 1863

News! News! News!—so much of it that I do not know how to begin to tell it! There has been a battle, a terrible battle at Gettysburg in Penn. We get Yankee accounts alone of it, but from their gasconade, bluster, & boasting, we pick the grain of wheat & are sure that the modest telegram which announces to us that Meade is falling back to Baltimore & Lee pursuing him is true. We lose three Brigadier's, Garnett, Barksdale, & Kemper killed—Pender & Scales wounded. I know none of the Col's so do not enumerate them. On their side the loss is heavier, including Reynolds, said to be the best General they have. He commanded the 3d army corps. Sickles, the infamous, loses his leg, so he will assassinate no more men because the world had discovered what he had long known & winked at. They have taken 2,000 (two thousand), we twelve thousand prisoners! The slaughter terrific both sides admit. The bridge over the Susquehanna at Wrightsville has been destroyed, whether by us or them I cannot understand. Gen Lee has issued orders for the government of his army in the enemy's country so widely different from those that emanate from the pens of their Generals that I preserve it for contrast. Read it & then turn to Pope's and Steinwehr's! A no 20.

These twelve thousand prisoners of ours refuse their parole, in order I suppose to embarras us & weaken Lee by the guard which they will force him to send with them. They deserve to be shot but we are, fortunately for them, too much under the law of Knightly honour & chivalry to give them their deserts.

The Yankee papers report that Johnson has cut Grant to peices & that Vicksburg is releived, but it does not elate us in the least, for we do not beleive it. The accounts from Louisiana are very fine but too good & a little contradictory. Brashear city has been taken by Gen. Dick Taylor. Magruder threatens New Orleans. Banks has fallen back from Port Hudson with only five thousand men & more to the same effect. It does not affect us much. We know not how much to beleive & Gettysburg eclipses all else. The news from Tennessee & Bragg is bad, *very* bad. He has fallen back from Tallahoma & virtually abandoned Tenn and part of North Ala, but we must not yet blame him. He may have been weakened by reinforcing Johnson in order to rescue Vicksburg. Let us wait before we condemn him. The damage done to the R R at Magnolia is slight, but a handful of miscreants have scoured the country burning & destroying everything before them, under Gen Martins very nose too! Murad the Unlucky I call him.

Went with Father and Mama to call on Mrs Clark & Miss Hines. Mrs James Smith poor thing did not make her appearance, being too much distressed about her brother, Col Evans, of whose fate they are yet in ignorance. How I pity those poor people who have friends at Gettysburg! What agony they must endure. From Mr Smith we learned that the enemy under the German Gen Weitzel had advanced to Williamston which they occupied & burned a few more houses. Col Martin holds Rainbow Banks where he is strongly entrenched. Brisk firing has been heard there today. The Yankees may intend only a diversion or they may be coming up to destroy the Gunboat now building. A few hours will determine. Gettysburg, however, absorbs every thought, so that we almost forget our own fate in that of our Army.

JULY 9, 1863

Glorious news, too good to be true! We hear unofficially that the fight was renewed on Sunday. Gen Hill made a feint of falling back. Meade pressed on when the two wings commanded by Ewell & Longstreet swept round & enclosed the entire Yankee Army; 40,000 men laid down their arms. Now this cannot be true. So large a number of men would not surrender in an open plain & in their own country. The Telegraph has played pranks with its message. I will not transcribe the flying rumours, the reports brought by "reliable gentlemen" & "wounded officers." There has been a fight & victory seems to incline to our side. We *hope* but we dare not beleive as yet.

Came brother yesterday afternoon, like "Widrington" in "*doleful dumps*," beleives a wild rumour gotten up I fancy by speculation to the effect that Vicksburg has capitulated. We laugh at it in spite of what we hear Com Barron says about its want of provisions & Johnston's weakness. Mr E & himself armed themselves & went down to the store with the intention if need was of keeping on & volunteering under Col Martin at Rainbow but met the good news on the road that we had ambushed the enemy at Gardner's bridge & that they had retired leaving ten of their number dead on the field, for which God be praised! Ah! for news from Penn! God keep Gen Lee. Give him wisdom & to his men endurance, obedience, & moderation.

JULY 10, 1863

Grant me patience with the news! I know not what to beleive! I hate to fill my Journal with rumours & yet it will be no truthful expositor of our lives if I fail to relate the state into which these uncertain Telegrams have brought us. One tells us that the fight was not renewed on Sunday, consequently the 40,000 men whom it reported as refusing parole were *not* captured & Lee is not pressing Meade who is not falling back to Baltimore, but per contra *Lee* it is who is falling back to Hagerstown. Now which is true? But our perplexities do not end here. A Dispatch which freezes the marrow in our bones, signed, too, Joseph E Johnston, tells Mr Seddon that Vicksburg has capitulated, that the garrison march out with the honours of war, officers wearing their side arms. This no one seems to beleive tho it is countersigned by one of Johnson's staff. The impression is that the wires have been tampered with by sugar speculators.

The news from the North Via Fortress Monroe inform us that Grant is retiring, that Vicksburg is releived, that Banks has been driven from Port Hudson, cries aloud for succour for N O & says Louisiana is slipping from the grasp. Then, too, another telegram from Loring dated Jackson tells us of his successes on the 'Big Black,' news of Dick Taylor's & Magruder's victories, one at Port Hudson the other in the Teche, whilst another has it that they have joined forces. I take refuge in utter unbeleif. I wish I could convince myself that the war is a myth, a hideous dream, but alaas! it presses too heavily to be thrown off like an incubus. There is but one comfort left—that our *Government* unlike the Yankee despotism does not lie. Its official Dispatches are all true, for they come from Gentlemen & through Gentlemen's hands do they pass until they reach us. So when we see 'R E Lee' signed to a dispatch we can rely on it, as there is no Telegraph to be tampered with by unprincipled speculators, as we hope and beleive is the case with Johnston's reported Dispatch. Vicksburg cannot have fallen! Not ten days ago they drove 300 mules out of the city. Surely, Yankee tho he is, Pemberton is not a traitor! He must have been able to inform Johnston of his situation. I cannot beleive it. As for the news from Penn, I never expected so much as they gave us, so am not depressed when they take the surplusage away. Give me the bare fact of a *Victory* & I am content without a "*rout*." I have been so occupied with public that I have omitted all mention of private matters.

Last week we had a freshet in the River, a heavy one which drowned a large portion of our corn. We hoped, however, to save much of it, as the water remained up but a short time. These hopes, however, are all crushed, for a second rise higher & slower than the first is now in progress. The crop is all re-submerged & much that escaped last week is destroyed this. It is a heavy blow. The loss to Father and Mr Edmondston is heavy, heavier to Father than to Patrick, for the Low grounds proper at Looking Glass are not in cultivation this year. But God has sent it. We must not repine.

I have been very unwell for some days & the suspense about public matters, the wearing anxiety about Vicksburg, & the uneasiness about the river do not help to make me better. Hannah More's ill "*bile*"—oppresses me. I leave our killed & wounded until they are authenticated. I hope they are exagerated. Petigru again wounded!

JULY 11, 1863

I have no heart to write. Vicksburg has fallen! It is all true. No lying speculator has imposed upon us. Pemberton has surrendered! As yet it is all dark. We are told that they were reduced to the verge of starvation & yet 200 mounted men of the garrison have been paroled & have reached Jackson, the officers allowed to march out with their side arms, retain their *horses* & private property. Now who ever heard of a beleagured city starving with horses & mules in it? Pemberton drove 500 mules out of his lines not ten days since & now lo, he is starving. The garrison surrendered on the 4th of July. I would have waited until the 5th & not have sullied our national anniversary with such an act. My doubts of Pemberton return. He is a Pennsylvanian & his heart cannot be in the cause as ours is. Can he be a traitor? I am not willing to trust him. I could have born the disaster better had it come to us through a Southern hand.

Ah! Mr Davis, Mr Davis, have we not suffered enough from Northern Generals. Remember Lovel & New Orleans & now comes Pemberton & Vicksburg to crown that first disaster! Just at the moment of triumph too. Banks driven from Port Hudson and Johnston nearly ready to fall on Grant. We remember Pemberton's blunders before he was shut up in Vicksburg, blunders which his defence of it had almost made us forget, & then his bluster about holding out whilst there was a "pound of Mule's flesh" left. Think of Londonderry, think of Antwerp, & then think of marching out with 200 mounted men besides officers, horses & citizen's "stock," which now they are "in haste to remove." We remember all this I say, & thoughts too bitter for words rise in our hearts against *this Northerner, this Pemberton*! The truth will never be known, smothered in a court of Inquiry, as was Lovels conduct at New Orleans. Grant me patience O Lord! grant me patience. Let me see Thy hand in it & make me cease to repine at the instruments Thou hast chosen to chastise us with!

From Lee's army we get only Northern accounts through lying newspapers in Yankee pay & tho they are depressing enough, we do not credit them. They have it that Lee is beaten & in full retreat, demoralized & scattered & that Meade's victorious army presses on him whilst French & Milroy's late command & a host of other generals in Buckram bar his retreat across the Potomac. They will "fight him eight hours" by "Shrewsbury clock" no doubt. We know from our operator at Martinsburg that he is at Hagerstown, a retreat certainly but rendered necessary on account of his wounded & thirteen Thousand prisoners with whom he is encumbered. The Yankees say he left his wounded on the field, not one word of which we beleive. In the face of their victory Keyes & his marauders are ordered immediately to Washington. Eastern Va is deserted by them & if Lee had been beaten surely they are not such fools as not to reinforce him & send him before he recover from the shock in a triumphant "On to Richmond" march. I have not said so much of Keyes as I ought perhaps. Latterly, he has long since ceased to give us uneasiness & has merely been ravaging the country, burning & destroying with the usual Yankee wickedness, barbarity, and wantonness.

D H Hill has been more than a match for him & he is now gone back to his master Lincoln. I do not tell all the Yankees say of our pretended defeat. I shall have the truth soon from our own side. We are sad enough today without their lies to madden us in addition. What with the loss of Vicksburg & our crop, well may we say—"The King does not dine today." At present prices we lose $30,000 worth of corn by this rise (Father, brother, & Patrick I mean), a heavy blow, but we are in God's hands. We see Him in it & do not murmur, but when a human instrument like Pemberton peirces us, we feel it deeply & keenly, tho' it is God still who allows it. We should remember that.

Suffolk has been evacuated, not a Yankee left in it after thirteen months occupation. An order was issued to burn it, but before it could be carried into execution Lee was over the border & fearing retaliation, Dix countermanded his barbarous edict. So, we go. Grant's army is marching on Jackson, "burning every dwelling that they come to on their route," women & helpless children turned without food or shelter into the woods & fields. How long O Lord? how long?

George Hamilton Perkins to Susan G. Perkins

Confederate forces attacked Donaldsonville, Louisiana, on June 28 as part of an offensive designed to relieve Port Hudson by disrupting Union river traffic along the Mississippi and threatening to recapture New Orleans. After the Union garrison repelled the assault, the Confederates set up artillery batteries along the levee about ten miles below the town. Lieutenant Commander George Hamilton Perkins, a Union naval officer, commanded the *New London*, a wooden screw steamer armed with five guns. When Port Hudson fell on July 9, the *New London* was sent downriver carrying dispatches reporting the surrender. Perkins described his encounter with the shore batteries to his sister. The capture of Port Hudson caused the Confederates to withdraw from the river bank, and on July 16 an unescorted cargo ship from St. Louis safely arrived in New Orleans.

JULY 29, 1863.

Since I wrote you last I have been through more excitement, and it seems to me as if I had been in more danger, than ever before in my life; and I am going to try and describe to you my last trip in the New London.

I had passed the Whitehall Point batteries in her successfully five times, but on the sixth trip, when the New London was returning to New Orleans, just as she was passing those batteries, at about quarter past one, on the morning of the 10th of July, the enemy discovered her, and opened with artillery and sharpshooters. One shot struck the New London's boiler, which exploded, severely scalding six men, and another shot penetrated the steam drum. This disabled the vessel, and I ordered her to be run towards the eastern bank, but the escaping steam made it impossible for the helmsman to remain at the wheel, and the ship grounded within range of the battery. The gunboat Winona, which had been ordered to escort the New

London, past Whitehall Point, ran away, at the first shot, and was out of sight by this time. I fired rockets to inform her of my danger and to summon her to my assistance, but received no response.

We were at the mercy of the sharpshooters, and every shot dealt death and destruction. My first lieutenant was shot through the head, and the men now became so terrified that they began to leap overboard. I then ordered a boat to be manned and kedged off the ship astern, till she drifted down stream out of the way of the upper battery. But the most powerful fortification of the battery was still below us; so I towed the ship to the eastern bank and made her fast; but danger pursued me here, and it was soon plain that I had only gained a respite from the murderous fire, for I could see the enemy cutting embrasures to move their guns down for a better range, and I knew that daylight would seal the fate of my ship and crew.

I determined to save them if I could. I sent the ship's company ashore under the protection of the levee, where they could use their muskets to repel an attack, and stationed pickets along the road. I then despatched messengers by land to Donaldsonville, where General Weitzel was, for assistance, and sent a boat by the river to the Monongahela and Essex with the same request. These two ships were stationed some miles below on the river to protect an encampment of our troops on the eastern bank.

The messengers returned from Donaldsonville saying no assistance could be rendered; while, with regard to the success of those I sent by the river, I felt very doubtful, so much was the passage of the Whitehall Point batteries dreaded. Just at this time information was brought me that a force of rebel cavalry—five hundred strong—was only a few miles in the interior. I felt desperate, for I realized the whole peril of the situation, and I was determined that my ship and crew should not fall into the hands of the enemy. I resolved to follow the dictates of my own judgment. I knew that upon a personal application Weitzel would at once grant me anything I wanted. I went ashore and, capturing a horse that was tied to a fence, I rode back to Donaldsonville. Arrived opposite I signaled to the Princess Royal to send a boat for me, and, to save time, I first demanded assistance from her senior officer; this he thought fit to refuse.

The Princess Royal was one of our gunboats stationed at Donaldsonville to protect and help Weitzel. I immediately hastened to him, and without delay he started a body of troops down the river for my assistance. But when I returned to the spot where I had left the New London, I found her gone, and I concluded—rightly, as it afterwards proved—that the boat I had sent early in the morning had succeeded in reaching our ships, and that they had come up and taken her off. I found afterwards that it was the ironclad Essex, and it towed her directly to New Orleans.

This was a great relief to me, for now the lives of my men were safe, and the ship was still under its own flag; but I began to realize that my own position was now one of considerable danger. I fastened the horse I had so unceremoniously borrowed, to the spot I first found him, and then hired a negro to drive me, in any sort of vehicle he could get, down the levee road to our lines. This proved to be a carry-all harnessed to a mule; but it was the best he could do. I took the back seat and laid my loaded pistols by my side close under my hand. At the negro's earnest entreaty, I put on my uniform coat wrong-side out, that it might not attract attention, and so I started—a Union officer, miles from our troops—on my passage through the enemy's country, along a road where rebel troops, bands of guerillas, and sharpshooters were usually in constant movement. Yet by some rare fortune it happened, just at this time, that my chief danger—except the overhanging peril of the whole situation—was not incurred until I approached our lines, except that around a grocery shop, which I passed, there were lounging a group of armed rebels. My driver was terribly frightened at this, and kept saying, "Set back, massa, for God's sake, set back! Mebbe dey won't see you!" And then whipped up his mule till we were safe beyond their reach.

But I had been seen and suspected by the rebel troops on the other side of the river, and they had sent a boat and some soldiers across to capture me. They reached the bank on my side, landed, and came up the road to intercept me, just as I was nearing our lines. Fortunately all this was perceived by our troops, and a body of cavalry was sent out, which captured the rebels, and conducted me in safety to the camp by one and the same proceeding. Here I found one of our ships—the Monongahela—and I went on board of her in a perfectly exhausted condition. Flinging myself in a bunk I slept soundly for hours, undisturbed by the fact that a short time before, while lying in that very same place, the Captain of the Monongahela —Abner Read—had been killed by a rebel shot which penetrated the ship's side and struck him, and that his dead body was then on board, being conveyed to New Orleans.

I roused myself very early next morning in order to continue my journey to New Orleans in a commissary wagon, but when daylight dawned, I saw a gunboat coming down the river in command of my friend Captain Cooke, and I went on board of her, and made the rest of my trip by water.

Charles B. Haydon: Journal, July 11, 1863

On July 4 Grant ordered Sherman to move east and drive Joseph E.
Johnston's forces away from Jackson. Captain Charles B. Haydon of
the 2nd Michigan Infantry described a skirmish fought on July 11, five
days before the Confederates evacuated the city.

———————

JULY 11   We were up at 3 A.M. I had very little supper & no
breakfast. Our clothes are constantly wet with sweat & having
no water to wash we are suffering terribly from sores, erup-
tions & a breaking out of the skin which makes one almost raw
& feels as though he were in the fire.

A little before sunrise the 2d was deployed as skirmishers
covering the front of our brigade and connecting with others
on the right & we all slowly advanced. The skirmishers had
orders to advance till they drew the fire of the rebel batteries if
possible. We had gone but a little way when some Regts. to the
right of us which seemed to be resting carelessly received a
brisk fire which appeared to be pretty effective. They moved to
the rear in very quick time, sent out skirmishers & advanced
again. A few shots fell near but no one was struck. We moved
forward across a very difficult ravine & gained good cover
under a fence with an open field beyond.

Here we encountered a moderate but well directed fire from
skirmishers at long range. The whistling of the balls animated
the men greatly. Chas. Smith of my Co. recd a severe shot in
the leg & some others of the Regt. were struck. We lay here abt
an hour when an order came to advance at double quick. We
had before us abt 100 rods of open field, then a narrow steep
ravine through which runs a brook, then a hill, thick bushes,
further on a corn field fence with rifle pits at a short distance.
Between us & the fence there were as we have since learned
three Regts. of Infantry.

We crossed the open at a run & without much loss, the men

full of fire, yelling like devils, Kearney's name being uppermost in their cry. I never felt more eager. Their skirmishers flew before us. We sprang down into the ravine & up the other bank. I tumbled back once & did not get up as quick as most of the others. When I did I found a narrow terrace & another steep bank. The Co. had all halted at the bank & seemed waiting to see who should go up first. I swore a most substantial oath (being indignant at them for stopping) & then we all made a dash at the hill.

It was so steep that only three or four got up at first. The Rebs were about three rods off. I made abt half the distance to them when I was whirled around & laid on my back suddenly, very suddenly & in a manner which left no doubt in my mind that I was hit. All who came up with me shared the same fate.

When I first became conscious, which was very soon, I lay on my back wondering what was to come next. I tried to get up but could not stir so much as a finger, nor could I speak although I could see & hear all that was doing, the trees above & the bullets around. Our men had halted at the brink of the hill so that I lay between the fires. I tried two or three times to rise but finding I could not move I began to reflect on other matters. I now observed that my hands were laid across my breast & in fact that my whole position was that of the greater part of those killed in battle. I then began to question myself as to whether I were not really dead.

I soon discarded this idea but still felt certain that I must die very soon. My whole feeling became one of wonder & curiosity as to the change which I believed I was about to experience. I was in no pain bodily & no mental anxiety. After abt 2 minutes I heard Sergt. Keyser of my Co. cry out to the men "G-d d--n your souls are you going to leave the Capt. lying there?" A second after he with eminent danger to himself sprang forward & caught me by the arm. The instant he touched me I sprang to my feet. Just then the Regt. went past on a charge driving the enemy before them. I tried to give my Co. a word of encouragement but my throat was so full of blood that I strangled when I attempted to speak.

With the aid of the Sergt. I walked back to the brook & lay down partly in it. He gave me water to drink & poured it over me in large quantities. I soon got up again & with his aid walked back 50 to 60 rods & lay down again. I could speak pretty well now but still threw up large quantities of blood from the lungs. I was soon able to walk again & started but met some men with a stretcher who carried me to the field hospital. But for the aid of the Sergt. I should have fallen into the hands of the enemy as the Regt. being wholly unsupported was very soon compelled to fall back.

My Co. numbered for the fight 18 men & 2 officers. One man was killed & four wounded. Both officers were wounded, Lt. Montague receiving a severe flesh wound below the knee. The Regt. lost 58 killed & wounded. I never saw better fighting done but the want of support rendered it of little avail beyond the mere number of the enemy killed which was however very considerable.

On arriving at the Hospt. my wound was dressed, my chances of recovery discussed, some encouragement was given by the Surgeons & I resolved to get well. I was laid on a blanket under a tree & soon after ate a good dinner to make up for the want of breakfast. No very severe pain to day. The ball struck me in the right shoulder abt an inch below the collar bone & passed out just at the lower edge of the shoulder blade.

John Hay: Diary, July 11–15, 1863

Lee began his retreat from Gettysburg on July 4, the same day a Union cavalry raid destroyed the Confederate pontoon bridge at Falling Waters, West Virginia. Meade started his pursuit the next day. The movements of both armies were slowed by heavy rain that made the Potomac unfordable. By July 12 Meade's army reached the defensive lines Lee established to protect the crossing at Williamsport, Maryland, six miles upriver from Falling Waters. John Hay had lived in the White House since 1861 while serving as one of Lincoln's principal secretaries. He recorded the President's response to subsequent events.

----

11 JULY 1863, SATURDAY

The President seemed in a specially good humor today, as he had pretty good evidence that the enemy were still on the North side of the Potomac and Meade had announced his intention of attacking them in the morning. The Prest. seemed very happy in the prospect of a brilliant success. He had been rather impatient with Gen Meade's slow movements since Gettysburg, but concluded today that Meade would yet show sufficient activity to inflict the Coup de grace upon the flying rebels.

12 JULY 1863, SUNDAY

Rained all the afternoon, have not yet heard of Meade's expected attack.

13 JULY 1863, MONDAY

The President begins to grow anxious and impatient about Meade's silence. I thought and told him there was nothing to prevent the enemy from getting away by the Falling Waters, if they were not vigorously attacked. Eckert says Kelly is up on their rear. Nothing can save them, if Meade does his duty. I doubt him. He is an engineer.

14 JULY 1863, TUESDAY

This morning the Prest. seemed depressed by Meade's despatches of last night. They were so cautiously & almost timidly worded—talking about reconnoitering to find the enemy's weak place and other such. He said he feared he would do nothing.

About noon came the despatch stating that our worst fears were true. The enemy had gotten away unhurt. The Prest was deeply grieved. We had them within our grasp" he said. "We had only to stretch forth our hands & they were ours. And nothing I could say or do could make the Army move."

Several days ago he sent a despatch to Meade which must have cut like a scourge but Meade returned so reasonable and earnest a reply that the Prest concluded he knew best what he was doing & was reconciled to the apparent inaction which he hoped was merely apparent.

Every day he has watched the progress of the Army with agonizing impatience, hopes struggling with fear. He has never been easy in his own mind about Gen Meade since Meades General Order in which he called on his troops to drive the invader from our soil. The Prest. says "This is a dreadful reminiscence of McClellan. The same spirit that moved McC. to claim a great victory because Pa & Md were safe. The hearts of 10 million people sank within them when McClellan raised that shout last fall. Will our Generals never get that idea out of their heads? The whole country is *our* soil."

15 JULY 1863, WEDNESDAY

Went with R.T.L. around town to concert saloons. Saw some very queer dancing and singing at one place and some very tolerable singing at a great hall where mann sauft and trinkt and raucht.

R. T. L. says the Tycoon is grieved silently but deeply about the escape of Lee. He said "If I had gone up there I could have whipped them myself." I know he had that idea.

Abraham Lincoln to Ulysses S. Grant

Although Lincoln praised Grant's Vicksburg campaign as "one of the most brilliant in the world" in a letter to a congressman on May 26, the President had had doubts about his leadership. Concerned by allegations that Grant was incompetent, opposed to emancipation, and frequently drunk, Lincoln and Secretary of War Stanton had sent Charles A. Dana as a special emissary to Grant's headquarters in the spring of 1863. Aware of the nature of Dana's mission, Grant took him into his confidence, and Dana's favorable reports helped reassure the President. Lincoln received definitive news of the surrender of Vicksburg on July 7 and wrote his first personal note to Grant six days later.

———————————

Executive Mansion,
Washington, July 13, 1863.

Major General Grant
My dear General
I do not remember that you and I ever met personally. I write this now as a grateful acknowledgment for the almost inestimable service you have done the country. I wish to say a word further. When you first reached the vicinity of Vicksburg, I thought you should do, what you finally did—march the troops across the neck, run the batteries with the transports, and thus go below; and I never had any faith, except a general hope that you knew better than I, that the Yazoo Pass expedition, and the like, could succeed. When you got below, and took Port-Gibson, Grand Gulf, and vicinity, I thought you should go down the river and join Gen. Banks; and when you turned Northward East of the Big Black, I feared it was a mistake. I now wish to make the personal acknowledgment that you were right, and I was wrong.

Yours very truly
A. LINCOLN

Abraham Lincoln to George G. Meade

On the afternoon of July 14 Halleck telegraphed Meade that "the escape of Lee's army without another battle has created great dissatisfaction in the mind of the President." Meade replied within ninety minutes, describing Lincoln's "censure" as "undeserved" and asking to be relieved of his command. The President wrote this letter in response, but never signed or sent it, and Meade remained the commander of the Army of the Potomac.

————————————

Executive Mansion,
Washington, July 14, 1863.

Major General Meade

I have just seen your despatch to Gen. Halleck, asking to be relieved of your command, because of a supposed censure of mine. I am very—*very*—grateful to you for the magnificient success you gave the cause of the country at Gettysburg; and I am sorry now to be the author of the slightest pain to you. But I was in such deep distress myself that I could not restrain some expression of it. I had been oppressed nearly ever since the battles at Gettysburg, by what appeared to be evidences that yourself, and Gen. Couch, and Gen. Smith, were not seeking a collision with the enemy, but were trying to get him across the river without another battle. What these evidences were, if you please, I hope to tell you at some time, when we shall both feel better. The case, summarily stated is this. You fought and beat the enemy at Gettysburg; and, of course, to say the least, his loss was as great as yours. He retreated; and you did not, as it seemed to me, pressingly pursue him; but a flood in the river detained him, till, by slow degrees, you were again upon him. You had at least twenty thousand veteran troops directly with you, and as many more raw ones within supporting distance, all in addition to those who fought with you at Gettysburg; while it was not possible that he had received a single recruit; and yet you stood and let the flood run

down, bridges be built, and the enemy move away at his leisure, without attacking him. And Couch and Smith! The latter
left Carlisle in time, upon all ordinary calculation, to have
aided you in the last battle at Gettysburg; but he did not arrive. At the end of more than ten days, I believe twelve, under
constant urging, he reached Hagerstown from Carlisle, which
is not an inch over fiftyfive miles, if so much. And Couch's
movement was very little different.

Again, my dear general, I do not believe you appreciate the
magnitude of the misfortune involved in Lee's escape. He was
within your easy grasp, and to have closed upon him would, in
connection with our other late successes, have ended the war.
As it is, the war will be prolonged indefinitely. If you could not
safely attack Lee last monday, how can you possibly do so
South of the river, when you can take with you very few more
than two thirds of the force you then had in hand? It would be
unreasonable to expect, and I do not expect you can now effect much. Your golden opportunity is gone, and I am distressed immeasureably because of it.

I beg you will not consider this a prossecution, or persecu-
tion of yourself. As you had learned that I was dissatisfied, I
have thought it best to kindly tell you why.

Samuel Pickens: Diary, July 14, 1863

Samuel Pickens of the 5th Alabama Infantry described his crossing of the Potomac at Williamsport. The pontoon bridge at Falling Waters used by Longstreet's and A. P. Hill's corps had been rebuilt by Confederate engineers after the July 4 cavalry raid that destroyed its predecessor.

———————————

July 14, Tuesday
    Late yesterday evening the troops left the breastworks quietly & commenced falling back, leaving one Regt. from each Brig. to fill the space occupied by the Brig. Our Regt. was one of the no. that remained. The Yankees soon found that most of our troops were gone & commenced a brisk skirmishing & on the left charged with a double line of skirmishers, & a line-of-battle; but Ramseur's sharpshooters fought splendidly & 3 or 4 pieces of artillery at the breastworks where we were, opened on them & they charged back again. About 8 or 9 O'clock the remaining Regts. fell back, while only our sharpshooters and a few Cavalry were left along the lines. We marched about two miles along behind the ridge on which are our fortifications, & where fires were left burning. What a splendid position we occupied! I think if the Yankees had attacked Genl Lee he would have whipped them badly. We had very rough, muddy, & bad marching before reaching the pike, which was itself perfectly sloppy; & to make it still more disagreeable there was a light rain falling for a while. The road was so blocked up with troops that we did not get on very fast, & when we got to Williamsport we found it crowded with soldiers. Here we had to *stand* & wait an hour or more, for there was no place to sit down as the streets were ankle deep with mud & water. Finally we moved on down towards the River, but every few yards the column would halt—so that we were just creeping along at a most fatiguing pace. We went to a ford several hundred yards

higher up the river than where we crossed before—going up the aqueduct through water that smelt very offensively. As soon as we got near the river we knew the men were wading, by the yelling & hallooing that we heard. The Potomac being swollen, was very wide & was over waist deep. The water felt cool when we first entered it, but afterwards very pleasant. We waded two & two side by side, holding on to each other in order to resist the current better & be more steady. There were orders for the men to hang their cartridge-boxes around their necks, but a great many failed to do it & there was a considerable amount of ammunition damaged & destroyed by getting wet. Our clothes, blankets (partly) & havresacks all got wet, which increased our load & made it very disagreeable marching after crossing. The banks were muddy & on this side so steep & slippery that it was difficult to scuffle up it. We were very tired & confidently expected to stop directly after getting over the river, but on we went without stopping. Although the distance from Hagerstown was only about six miles, & we were on our feet from 8 or nine O'clock last night, it was day-break when we got across the Potomac. We passed by "Falling Water" where our Pontoon bridge spanned the river, on which Longstreet's & A. P. Hill's Corps were crossing & also the artillery & wagon trains. At 6 or 7 O'clock this morning we came to a halt. After being on our feet the whole night—marching on a sloppy pike, & stopped to rest only once (5 or 10 mins.) during the whole trip. Oh! it was a killing march. It beggars description. We waded into a little pond where we stopped and washed the mud off our pants, socks and shoes, then made fires and dried our clothes—after which we lay down and slept. At 11½ A.M., though we were called up & marched on 3 or 4 miles & camped in a nice piece of woods. As we had gotten our rations wet—what little we had—David Barnum & several others went out & killed two hogs. We broiled the meat at the fire & ate one for supper. I had the pleasure of hearing from home to-day by a letter from Jamie. Happy to hear Mama has, at last gotten rid of the Standenmeyers—having dismissed them. Our Mess was up till 10 or 11 O'clock P.M. cooking. Marched 8 or 9 miles from Williamsport.

George Templeton Strong: Diary, July 13–17, 1863

The first draft lottery conducted in New York City under the 1863 conscription act was held on July 11. Two days later a mob attacked the draft office at Third Avenue and 46th Street, beginning five days of violence in which at least 105 people were killed. The riots were eventually suppressed by several regiments of Union troops, some of which had fought at Gettysburg. Strong recorded his attempts to persuade the authorities to take early and decisive action against the rioters.

———————————

July 13, MONDAY.   A notable day. Stopped at the Sanitary Commission office on my way downtown to endorse a lot of checks that had accumulated during my absence, and heard there of rioting in the upper part of the city. As Charley is at Newport and Bidwell in Berkshire County, I went to Wall Street nevertheless; but the rumors grew more and more unpleasant, so I left it at once and took a Third Avenue car for uptown. At the Park were groups and small crowds in more or less excitement (which found relief afterwards, I hear, in hunting down and maltreating sundry unoffending niggers), but there was nothing to indicate serious trouble. The crowded car went slowly on its way, with its perspiring passengers, for the weather was still of this deadly muggy sort with a muddy sky and lifeless air. At Thirteenth Street the track was blocked by a long line of stationary cars that stretched indefinitely up the Avenue, and I took to the sidewalk. Above Twentieth Street all shops were closed, and many people standing and staring or strolling uptown, not riotously disposed but eager and curious. Here and there a rough could be heard damning the draft. No policemen to be seen anywhere. Reached the seat of war at last, Forty-sixth Street and Third Avenue. Three houses on the Avenue and two or three on the street were burned down: engines playing on the ruins—more energetically, I'm told, than they did when their efforts would have been useful.

The crowd seemed just what one commonly sees at any fire, but its nucleus of riot was concealed by an outside layer of ordinary peaceable lookers-on. Was told they had beat off a squad of police and another of "regulars" (probably the Twelfth Militia). At last, it opened and out streamed a posse of perhaps five hundred, certainly less than one thousand, of the lowest Irish day laborers. The rabble was perfectly homogeneous. Every brute in the drove was pure Celtic—hod-carrier or loafer. They were unarmed. A few carried pieces of fence-paling and the like. They turned off west into Forty-fifth Street and gradually collected in front of two three-story dwelling houses on Lexington Avenue, just below that street, that stand alone together on a nearly vacant block. Nobody could tell why these houses were singled out. Some said a drafting officer lived in one of them, others that a damaged policeman had taken refuge there. The mob was in no hurry; they had no need to be; there was no one to molest them or make them afraid. The beastly ruffians were masters of the situation and of the city. After a while sporadic paving-stones began to fly at the windows, ladies and children emerged from the rear and had a rather hard scramble over a high board fence, and then scudded off across the open, Heaven knows whither. Then men and small boys appeared at rear windows and began smashing the sashes and the blinds and shied out light articles, such as books and crockery, and dropped chairs and mirrors into the back yard; the rear fence was demolished and loafers were seen marching off with portable articles of furniture. And at last a light smoke began to float out of the windows and I came away. I could endure the disgraceful, sickening sight no longer, and what could I *do?*

The fury of the low Irish women in that region was note-worthy. Stalwart young vixens and withered old hags were swarming everywhere, all cursing the "bloody draft" and egging on their men to mischief.

Omnibussed down to No. 823, where is news that the Colored Half Orphan Asylum on Fifth Avenue, just above the reservoir, is burned. "*Tribune* office to be burned tonight."

Railroad rails torn up, telegraph wires cut, and so on. If a quarter one hears be true, this is an organized insurrection in the interest of the rebellion and Jefferson Davis rules New York today.

Attended to business. Then with Wolcott Gibbs to dinner at Maison Dorée. During our symposium, there was an alarm of a coming mob, and we went to the window to see. The "mob" was moving down Fourteenth Street and consisted of just thirty-four lousy, blackguardly Irishmen with a tail of small boys. Whither they went, I cannot say, nor can I guess what mischief the handful of *canaille* chose to do. A dozen police-men would have been more than a match for the whole crew, but there were no policemen in sight.

Walked uptown with Wolcott Gibbs. Large fire on Broadway and Twenty-eighth Street. Signs of another to the east, said to be on Second Avenue. Stopped awhile at Gibbs's in Twenty-ninth Street, where was madame, frightened nearly to death, and then to St. Nicholas Hotel to see the mayor and General Wool. We found a lot of people with them. There were John Jay and George W. Blunt and Colonel Howe and John Austin Stevens, Jr., all urging strong measures. But the substantial and weighty and influential men were not represented; out of town, I suppose. Their absence emboldened Gibbs and myself to make pressure for instant action, but it was vain. We begged that martial law might be declared. Opdyke said that was Wool's business, and Wool said it was Opdyke's, and neither would act. "Then, Mr. Mayor, issue a proclamation calling on all loyal and law-abiding citizens to enroll themselves as a vol-unteer force for defense of life and property." "Why," quoth Opdyke, "that is *civil war* at once." Long talk with Colonel Cram, Wool's chief of staff, who professes to believe that ev-erything is as it should be and sufficient force on the ground to prevent further mischief. Don't believe it. Neither Opdyke nor General Wool is nearly equal to this crisis. Came off disgusted. Went to Union League Club awhile. No comfort there. Much talk, but no one ready to do anything whatever, not even to telegraph to Washington.

We telegraphed, two or three of us, from General Wool's rooms, to the President, begging that troops be sent on and stringent measures taken. The great misfortune is that nearly all our militia regiments have been despatched to Pennsylvania. All the military force I have seen or heard of today were in Fifth Avenue at about seven P.M. There were two or three feeble companies of infantry, a couple of howitzers, and a squadron or two of unhappy-looking "dragoons."

These wretched rioters have been plundering freely, I hear. Their outbreak will either destroy the city or damage the Copperhead cause fatally. Could we but catch the scoundrels who have stirred them up, what a blessing it would be! God knows what tonight or tomorrow may bring forth. We may be thankful that it is now (quarter past twelve) raining briskly. Mobs have no taste for the effusion of cold water. I'm thankful, moreover, that Ellie and the children are out of town. I sent Johnny off to Cornwall this afternoon in charge of John the waiter.

July 14. Eleven P.M. Fire bells clanking, as they have clanked at intervals through the evening. Plenty of rumors throughout the day and evening, but nothing very precise or authentic. There have been sundry collisions between the rabble and the authorities, civil and military. Mob fired upon. It generally runs, but on one occasion appears to have rallied, charged the police and militia, and forced them back in disorder. The people are waking up, and by tomorrow there will be adequate organization to protect property and life. Many details come in of yesterday's brutal, cowardly ruffianism and plunder. Shops were cleaned out and a black man hanged in Carmine Street, for no offence but that of Nigritude. Opdyke's house again attacked this morning by a roaming handful of Irish blackguards. Two or three gentlemen who chanced to be passing saved it from sack by a vigorous charge and dispersed the popular uprising (as the *Herald*, *World*, and *News* call it), with their walking sticks and their fists.

Walked uptown perforce, for no cars and few omnibi were running. They are suppressed by threats of burning railroad and omnibus stables, the drivers being wanted to reinforce the mob. Tiffany's shop, Ball & Black's, and a few other Broadway establishments are closed. (Here I am interrupted by report of a fire near at hand, and a great glare on the houses across the Park. Sally forth, and find the Eighteenth Ward station house, Twenty-second Street, near First Avenue, in full blaze. A splendid blaze it made, but I did not venture below Second Avenue, finding myself in a crowd of Celtic spectators disgorged by the circumjacent tenement houses. They were exulting over the damage to "them bloody police," and so on. I thought discretion the better part of curiosity. Distance lent enchantment to that view.)

At 823 with Bellows four to six; then home. At eight to Union League Club. Rumor it's to be attacked tonight. Some say there is to be great mischief tonight and that the rabble is getting the upper hand. Home at ten and sent for by Dudley Field, Jr., to confer about an expected attack on his house and his father's, which adjoin each other in this street just below Lexington Avenue. He has a party there with muskets and talks of fearful trouble before morning, but he is always a blower and a very poor devil. Fire bells again at twelve-fifteen. No light of conflagration is visible.

Bellows's report from Gettysburg and from Meade's headquarters very interesting. Thinks highly of Meade. Thinks the battle around Williamsport will be tolerably evenly matched, Lee having been decidedly beaten a week ago, but not at all demoralized. But there's a despatch at the Union League Club tonight that Lee has moved his whole army safely across, except his rear guard, which we captured.

A good deal of yelling to the eastward just now. The Fields and their near neighbour, Colonel Frank Howe, are as likely to be attacked by this traitor-guided mob as any people I know. If they *are*, we shall see trouble in this quarter, and Gramercy Park will acquire historical associations. O, how tired I am! But I feel reluctant to go to bed. I believe I dozed off a minute or two. There came something like two reports of artillery, perhaps only falling walls. There go two jolly Celts along the street, singing a genuine Celtic howl, something about "Tim O'Laggerty," with a refrain of pure Erse. Long live the sovereigns of New York, Brian Boroo *redivivus* and multiplied. Paddy has left his Egypt—Connaught—and reigns in this promised land of milk and honey and perfect freedom. Hurrah, there goes a strong squad of police marching eastward down this street, followed by a company of infantry with gleaming bayonets. One A.M. Fire bells again, southeastward,

"Swinging slow with sullen roar." Now they are silent, and I shall go to bed, at least for a season.

July 15. Wednesday begins with heavy showers, and now (ten A.M.) cloudy, hot, and steaming. Morning papers report nothing specially grave as occurring since midnight. But there will be much trouble today. Rabbledom is not yet dethroned any more than its ally and instigator, Rebeldom.

News from the South is consolatory. Port Hudson surrendered. Sherman said to have beaten Joseph Johnston somewhere near Vicksburg. Operations commencing against Charleston. Bragg seems to be abandoning Chattanooga and retiring on Atlanta. *Per contra*, Lee has got safely off. I thought he would. . . . Lots of talk and rumors about attacks on the New York Custom-house (*ci-devant* Merchants' Exchange) and the Treasury (late Custom-house). Went to see Cisco and found his establishment in military occupation—sentinels pacing, windows barricaded, and so on. He was as serene and bland as the loveliest May morning ("so cool, so calm, so bright") and showed me the live shell ready to throw out of the window and the "battery" to project Assay Office oil-of-vitriol and the like. He's all right. Then called on Collector Barney and had another long talk with him. Find him well prepared with shells, grenades, muskets, and men, but a little timid and anxious, "wanting counsel," doubtful about his right to fire on the mob, and generally flaccid and tremulous—poor devil!

Walked uptown with Charley Strong and Hoppin, and after my cup of coffee, went to Union League Club. A delegation returned from police headquarters, having vainly asked for a squad of men to garrison the clubhouse. *None can be spared.* What is worse, we were badly repulsed in an attack on the mob in First Avenue, near Nineteenth Street, at about six P.M. Fired upon from houses, and had to leave sixteen wounded men and a Lieutenant Colonel Jardine in the hands of these brutes and devils. This is very bad indeed. But tonight is quieter than the last, though there seems to be a large fire downtown, and we hear occasional gun-shots.

At the club was George Biggs, full of the loudest and most emphatic jawing. "General Frémont's house and Craven's to be attacked tonight, Croton mains to be cut, and gas works destroyed," and so on. By way of precaution, I had had the bathtubs filled, and also all the pots, kettles, and pails in the house. . . . Twelve-thirty: Light as of a large fire to the south.

July 16. Rather quiet downtown. No trustworthy accounts of riot on any large scale during the day. General talk downtown is that the trouble is over. We shall see. It will be as it pleases the scoundrels who are privily engineering the outbreak —agents of Jefferson Davis, permitted to work here in New York.

Omnibusses and railroad cars in full career again. Coming uptown tonight I find Gramercy Park in military occupation. Strong parties drawn up across Twentieth Street and Twenty-first Streets at the east end of the Square, by the G House, each with a flanking squad, forming an L. Occasional shots fired at them from the region of Second or First Avenue, which were replied to by volleys that seem to have done little execution. An unlucky cart-horse was knocked over, I hear. This force was relieved at seven by a company of regulars and a party of the Seventh with a couple of howitzers, and there has been but a stray shot or two since dark. The regulars do not look like steady men. I have just gone over to the hotel with John Robertson and ordered a pail of strong coffee to put a little life into them.

Never knew exasperation so intense, unqualified, and general as that which prevails against these rioters and the politic knaves who are supposed to have set them going, Governor Seymour not excepted. Men who voted for him mention the fact with contrition and self-abasement, and the Democratic Party is at a discount with all the people I meet. (Apropos of discount, gold fell to one hundred and twenty-six today, with the city in insurrection, a gunboat at the foot of Wall Street, the Custom-house and Treasury full of soldiers and live shells, and two howitzers in position to rake Nassau Street from Wall to Fulton!!!!)

Every impression that's made on our people passes away so soon, almost as if stamped on the sand of the sea-beach. Were our moods a little less fleeting, I should have great hope of permanent good from the general wrath these outrages have provoked, and should put some faith in people's prophesyings that Fernando Wood and McCunn, and the New York *Herald*, and the Brookses and others, are doomed henceforth to obscurity and contempt. But we shall forget all about it before next November. Perhaps the lesson of the last four days is to be taught us still more emphatically, and we have got to be worse before we are better. It is not clear that the resources of the conspiracy are yet exhausted. The rioters of yesterday were better armed and organized than those of Monday, and their inaction today may possibly be meant to throw us off our guard, or their time may be employed perfecting plans for a campaign of plundering and brutality in yet greater force. They are in full possession of the western and the eastern sides of the city, from Tenth Street upward, and of a good many districts beside. I could not walk four blocks eastward from this house this minute without peril. The outbreak is spreading by concerted action in many quarters. Albany, Troy, Yonkers, Hartford, Boston, and other cities have each their Irish anti-conscription Nigger-murdering mob, of the same type with ours. It is a grave business, a *jacquerie* that must be put down by heroic doses of lead and steel.

Dr. Peters and Charley Strong called at eleven P.M. They have been exploring and report things quiet except on First Avenue from Nineteenth to Thirtieth Street, where there is said to be trouble. A detachment of the Seventh Regiment, five hundred or six hundred strong, marched to that quarter from their armory an hour ago.

July 17.   The Army of Gramercy Park has advanced its headquarters to Third Avenue, leaving only a picket guard in sight. Rain will keep the rabble quiet tonight. We are said to have fifteen thousand men under arms, and I incline to hope that this movement in aid of the rebellion is played out.

Emma Holmes: Diary, July 16–19, 1863

Nine Union ironclads attempted to enter Charleston Harbor on April 7, 1863, but were repulsed by artillery fire from Fort Sumter and several shore batteries. Following the failure of the naval expedition, Brigadier General Quincy A. Gillmore made plans to capture Morris Island at the southern entrance to the harbor and use it to bombard Fort Sumter. Union troops landed on the southern end of Morris Island on July 10 and made an unsuccessful assault the following day on Battery Wagner (also known as Fort Wagner) on the northern end. Emma Holmes, the daughter of a plantation owner, followed the battle for the harbor from the city of Charleston.

Thursday 16 Our troops on James I. made a reconnaissance & found negro troops to oppose them—scarcely a white officer among them—at the first discharge they fled, pursued by our men, who mowed them down, & would have cut them to pieces, but one of our officers, put a stop to it, saying he wished some captured to be hung as an example & 16 were taken— most of the gentlemen think it decidedly a wrong step, as many nice questions will now be involved—if we hang them, will not the Yankees retaliate upon our men—they are fiendish enough to delight in the idea—yet it is revolting to our feelings to have them treated as prisoners of war as well as injurious in its effects upon our negroes—however they were brought to the city, barefoot, hatless & coatless & tied in a gang, like common runaways—

Friday morning I was much surprised to receive a message from Carrie saying Mary Jane & Hattie & herself had "run the blockade" but expected to leave next day for Summerville & begging me to go to see her—just as I was starting determined to make a great effort to walk so far, "our good Dr." came in to visit his patients, & said he would drive me up—he is almost the only person who fully understands & appreciates my weakness & debility—the girls arrived soon after I did, & most happy were we to meet once more—Dr. White & Sims also came in at different times, so I had quite a pleasant day seeing old friends—Isaac driving me down after tea—by the bye, he has sold his pet horse Prince, a beautiful animal, $2000 having been offered him for it & he now drives a remarkably fine large pair of mules, for which he has already been offered $1600—

Lee has recrossed the Potomac, in admirable order, and the army in splendid trim and spirits, without loss, though continual skirmishing took place, in which the gallant Gen. J. J. Pettigrew was mortally wounded & has since died—this time his death is certain, as Henry Young, his aid, telegraphed the fact—Lee's move has surprised one half the community, & pleased the other—the latter thinking he had gone too far from his base of supplies and communication, particularly as the still frequent heavy rains, which by the bye are now ruining the fine crops everywhere made the Potomac almost impassable —It is said, that the President ordered the recrossing of the river, much to Lee's anger & mortification & that he said if it were not for his country he would resign—His retreat from Gettysburg was strategic, to draw Meade's army from the high hills behind which they took refuge—President Davis has called out all *male residents* of the Confederacy, capable of bearing arms, between 18 & 45. The New York Herald of the 14th gives an account of a tremendous riot which took place there in the attempt to enforce the Conscription Act—it is headed—"The Draft. Tremendous Excitement in the City. Popular Opposition to enforcement of the Conscription— Enrolling Offices in Eight Districts Demolished. Two whole blocks of houses in Third Avenue, near Broadway burned. Military ordered out. Several Citizens & Soldiers killed, Arrival of the Police; and their attack, on the Crowd, Police Dispersed, some killed, others badly beaten—Superintendent Kennedy severely wounded. An Armory destroyed, Raid on negroes, Colored Orphan Asylum laid in ashes Hotels burnt, two mansions sacked, Tribune office attacked, as negro hanged— etc—etc—Everybody and every thing was in a state of excitement, cannon planted in the streets & troops guarding the Post office, & Newspaper offices & hotels—every negro seen by the mob was either murdered or cruelly beaten, and altogether a most demoniac scene—I am glad the Yankees are suffering a touch, even though such a faint one, of the horrors they have committed or tried to incite in our midst—

They have just made another raid on Pon Pon carrying off hundreds of negroes & burning & destroying the most elegant residences & barns etc. of Messrs. Heyward Manigault, Edward Barnwell & Col. Morris, Mrs. Hayne & others—

Saturday 18th. From daylight this morning the enemy was bombarding Battery Wagner furiously; they have over 70 guns concentrated from their various batteries & Monitors, & they fired at the rate of 20 shots a minute—it was intended to demoralize our troops, preparatory to the assault which commenced at dark—I spent a good part of the day with an excellent spy glass watching the Ironsides and four Monitors; I could see almost every discharge, & when the Yankee shells struck the earth, sending up a tall column of sand; I did not feel at all alarmed or excited; I had become so accustomed to the cannonading—but watched everything with intense interest. The Ironsides lay like a huge leviathan, long, low & black, discharging broadsides, while at her side, but nearer to Morris Island, lying between herself & land was a Monitor, whose peculiar black turrets were instantly recognizable, so distinctly defined against the sky are their huge black forms—Our batteries on Morris I. & Sumter slowly replied, but with excellent effect; during the morning the Yankee columns were formed for an attack, but our grape & canister drove them back with considerable loss. I could with a glass, see not only the signalling from our various forts and batteries, but from the Yankee observatory on Folly Island, which is high above the trees I was wishing so much I could read their dispatches & found later that Mr. Westervelt had done so, & intercepted Gilmore's orders for a general attack on our batteries Saturday night, so our men were ready for them—

Just as we were going to dinner cousin John's Baltimorean friend from the Marion Artillery, Mr. Jenkins (who had like himself, come to the city sick, & gone to the Roper Hospital, where he had received great attention from various ladies including cousin Beck & aunt Amelia) came to get a view of the bombardment; he is a delicate looking, very gentlemanly young man, who quite interested us—cousin Christopher & others came later, for the same purpose, and the Battery was thronged with spectators; during the afternoon I received a note from Carrie, saying the Summerville plan had been necessarily given up, as Mr. Hughes might be ordered off with the Bank to Columbia at any time, so Carrie intended remaining here till obliged to leave, then go to Camden, & wished me to come and stay with her—At such a time when everything of interest was concentrated on the Battery, & I am not able to walk down there, it really is a sacrifice to friendship to come up into the interior of the town; however, I determined to enjoy a last walk on the Battery & with Miss Ellen, promenaded till dark, watching the beautiful effect of the broad flashes of light at every discharge, which illuminated the sky; on our return found Gen. Gonzales, who had been on the housetop for a long time, in cousin Beck's piazza, & I could not help being amused to think how war had leveled ceremony all were obliged to pass through her chamber, where she was busily writing by a bright gas light the room was of course neatly arranged, but the pavilion down, etc. & as he was halfway through, some question was asked, and a long & interesting conversation ensued, which decidedly cheered all parties—He said the reason those lower batteries on Morris I. had not been completed was, that instead of sending their negroes, the planters preferred paying the fines, consequently instead of the three or four thousand laborers needed, there were only twenty odd at one time, & we did not even have troops enough to build them, for we had sent 10,000 men to Miss—& had only about three regiments here & if the Yankees had dared, they could have taken the city before, but now there was no cause for apprehension, at present, at least, & he had written for his wife, (he married Miss Elliott of Savannah) to come to the city if she wished & he promised to tell cousin B. when he thought it time for her to leave—Men were not what we wanted on Morris I. we had plenty now, but heavier guns, which were being rapidly supplied there, & on Sullivan's I. If Battery Wagner were taken, the Yankees' troubles would only commence, he said, for it would be a work of time to erect batteries to reduce Sumter & every day was gain to us. he had recommended Beauregard to strengthen the officer's quarter's there, the weakest side, by taking away the floors & making a wall of compressed cotton on a flooring of wet sand & Battery

Bee, on Sullivan's I. is as strong as Sumter & heavier guns are being put on Moultrie, so even if Sumter were taken, the city was not necessarily lost. I was really glad I had seen him, & was very much pleased with him—Just after Isaac called for me, & everything seemed so quiet up in Beaufain St. that we all slept as quietly as possible, little dreaming of what a sanguinary engagement was going on almost at our doors—

Sunday morning we learned what a tremendous assault had been made & how gloriously repulsed—about eight Saturday evening the Yankees advanced in six columns, as Willie Ramsey has since described to me, in perfect line of battle—our men waited till within 800 yards, then opened on them with grape & canister, which mowed huge gaps in their ranks; they would waver for a moment, then close up and move steadily on, again to be cut down—again and again were assaults made, & in the darkness & melie two or three hundred gained a position on the magazine, where they planted their flag & held it for more than an hour, it being some little time before they were discovered—a call for volunteers to dislodge them was made & numbers instantly stood forth—and in doing so, we lost the majority of our killed & wounded, among them Capt. Ryan of the Irish Volunteers, a very brave man killed & Maj. David Ramsey severely wounded—After having made other desperate assaults, they were finally driven off—They had expected our men to be completely demoralized by the incessant cannonading, & William White who was down there with Ramsey, assisting in erecting a mortar battery, says nothing can be more demoralizing, for the men to be cooped up all day in the close bomb proofs, with this awful never-ending roaring & whistling —the nerves kept in such a state of intense excitement—Our loss is about 24 killed & 70 wounded—sad to say, Lieut. Col. Simpkins, commanding the fort, a most gallant & excellent officer was killed, & Capt. William S. Stone dangerously wounded by our own men. Clingman's North Carolinians having fired into them by mistake, & Yankee prisoners say their troops did the same—it is fearful to think of such a battle in the darkness, with the roar of artillery mingled with the rattle of musketry. Capt. Warren Adams & William Sinkler wounded slightly, also Lieut. Wm. Clarkson, & William Macbeth very badly in the leg Willie Ramsey says may lose both it & his life—my old acquaintance Lieut. James Powe, whose gallantry is highly spoken, is also wounded—

William W. & William R. have both given us accounts of the fight & say they had heard of "piles of dead Yankees" & "bodies three deep" but never saw it till now, when they actually would be four deep, one on the other, as they fell forward, in every conceivable attitude—it was an awful sight in the ditch below the parapet—The Yankees sent a flag of truce, seeking the body of Col. Putnam, acting Brigadier a splendid looking man, grandson of Gen. Israel Putnam, & requesting to bury their dead—the first request was granted, the latter refused, as it was thought they only wanted an opportunity of close inspection, & the answer was we would bury their dead & take care of their wounded, many of whom however must have been carried off—we buried 600 among them numerous field officers, as well as captains & lieutenants, & beyond our lines the enemy buried over 200; among them about 150 negroes, and a good many of them were among the 230 wounded brought to the city, many so severely they will certainly die— and a negro has been put alternately with a Yankee in the hospital, much to their disgust, but our surgeons told them as they had put them on an equality they must abide the consequences —Their loss in killed, wounded & prisoners must 1500—Col. Shaw of Massachusetts was buried with eleven negroes over him—among the wounded prisoners is a remarkable intelligent negro from Bermuda, educated in the military school there— having no employment at home & needing support for his mother, he went to New York & Boston to seek it, & found large bounties being offered to volunteers, & as he had nothing else to provide his mother with, he joined the army & was made a sergeant—he says, when the column to assault was formed, the general rode up to the negro regiment commanded by Shaw, & told them to charge bravely, remembering if they faltered, 10,000 bayonets were behind them, & he says they marched with the bayonets almost in their backs. He curses the Yankees fearfully, for a set of vile cowards & wretches—

Sunday morning Carrie & I went to Grace Church & heard Rev. Mr. Seabrook; Sims & the girls & Edward dined with us, & in the evening Hanna & Mr. H. came down, having heard a report of W. Ramsey's death & feeling anxious about their brother—they said they heard a telegram had just been received from Louis Stark, saying Tom Ferguson was better—constant heavy skirmishing has been taking place between Grant's & Johnson's army, in which we repulsed them handsomely two or three times, but we finally evacuated Jackson again, Bragg seems to be quiet again, while Morgan is "*raiding*" in Indiana & scaring Hoosierdom out of its senses—

Walter H. Taylor to Richard Taylor

A member of Robert E. Lee's personal staff since 1861, Major Walter H. Taylor served as his adjutant during the Gettysburg campaign. He wrote to his brother from the Shenandoah Valley about the recent battle in Pennsylvania and its consequences. (Walter H. Taylor was not related to the Confederate general Richard Taylor.)

Camp near Winchester
17 July 1863

Presuming that Mary Lou may have left Richmond before this I will address myself to you and get you to forward this letter after reading it to our people wherever they may be.

I have written twice and telegraphed once since the late battle in Pennsyla giving assurance of the safety of Rob and myself and, as far as I know, of all our immediate friends. I hope these advices have been received & that all anxiety on our account has been allayed.

I was rejoiced to hear that John was unhurt up to the 24th of last month and trust that ere this you have received later tidings from him and that he is well. But for the loss of prisoners & the morale effect I would not much regret the fall of Vicksburg. Our people make a sad mistake when they attempt to hold such isolated points & attach so much importance to their being held successfully. After the enemy had obtained possession of the reach between Vicksburg & Pt. Hudson and held the same with their gunboats, I regarded the two points as of no more importance than any other two points on the Miss river. We could have prevented the free navigation of the stream by means of light and moveable batteries, and by concentrating our forces been enabled perhaps to have successfully resisted Grant's advance into the interior. Even now it seems to me affairs are terribly deranged out west. If Genl Johnston feels too weak to attack Grant, or rather felt too weak to attempt to relieve Pemberton, why so weaken Bragg to such an extent to make him powerless to resist Rosecrans? Division and not concentration seems to be the order of the day out there. But it is not proper to criticise yet, nor do I blame anyone particularly; only it looks to me as if there was some lack of judgment or some mismanagement.

As regards our own affairs, I wish I could write you an account in full of all that has transpired since we left the Rappahannock but I cannot now do this. Indeed you are already aware of all that happened up to our arrival at Gettysburg and engagements at that place. On the first day we were eminently successful. We fought two corps of their army with two divisions & a fraction of ours and drove them handsomely, capturing a number of prisoners & reducing the two corps to less than half their strength. The Northern papers admit a loss in one corps of 66 per cent.

On the second day we were also successful & drove them from a very strong position, capturing some cannons & many prisoners. But now we came to a position that was a sort of Gibraltar. Their two flanks were protected by two insurmountable, impracticable rocky mountains. It was out of the question to turn them. We reached the very base of the stronghold only to find almost perpendicular walls of rock. Besides the natural advantages of the place the enemy had strengthened themselves very much by artificial works. There was no opportunity whatever for a successful flank movement and on the third day two divisions assaulted a position a little to the left of their centre. Pickett's division of Virginians here immortalized itself. Its charge was the handsomest of the war as far as my experience goes and though it carried the works and captured a number of guns, it was not well supported by the division on its left, which failed to carry the works in its front & retired without any sufficient cause, thereby exposing Pickett's flank. The enemy then moved on Pickett's left & forced him to retire. The loss I suppose in killed, wounded & missing was about half of his command, which however was very small, consisting of only 3 reduced brigades.

Tho not much affected by this repulse, it was deemed inexpedient to make any more attempts to carry this place by assault. It was beyond our strength, simply this. If we had have had say 10,000 more men, we would have forced them back. As it was they did not resist Pickett but fled before him & had the supporting or second division performed its part as well, the result would have been different. On the next day we waited patiently for the enemy to attack us. This they did not do nor have they at any time since either attacked or manifested any desire to attack us. They retired from Gettysburg before we did and only claimed a victory after they had discovered our departure.

They only followed us with a little cavalry & horse artillery & their attempts to annoy our rear were ridiculous and insignificant. We took our time to Hagerstown, though to tell the truth we could not have moved rapidly had we desired it, for it rained in torrents incessantly, as indeed it did the whole month we were north of the Potomac. We arrived at Hagerstown & did not even hear of the enemy in our vicinity. Why he did not attempt to intercept us must appear remarkable to those who believe his lies about his *grand victory*. After four or five days he made his appearance. This time we had selected the ground and were most anxious for an attack. Our ordnance wagons had been replenished, we had enough to eat & the high waters of the Potomac gave no concern, if the enemy would only attack us.

We could not wait there for weeks & do nothing, nor could we afford to attack him in position, but if he would attack us, we would rejoice exceedingly. This the rascals dared not do, and their army, as they say, anxious to meet us again & flushed (as they say) with victory, did meet us & what next? They went to work fortifying as hard as they could and as I have discovered from their papers since, anticipated an attack from us. As they manifested no intention of fighting us, it was necessary or at least proper for us to leave our position and go where we could subsist. We threw a bridge over the Potomac & in face of this tremendous Yankee army flushed with victory (?) came into Virginia without the slightest annoyance from the enemy, but the elements were certainly against us. I never saw it rain so hard and our poor fellows had a hard time of it, I can tell you. The Yankees must organize a new army before they can again enjoy an "On to Richmond." We crippled them severely & they cannot now make any formidable aggressive movement.

We are again restive & ready for work. I will not hide one truth—that our men are better satisfied on this side of the Potomac. They are not accustomed to operating in a country where the people are inimical to them & certainly every one of them is today worth twice as much as he was three days ago. I am persuaded that we cannot without heavy acquisitions to our strength invade successfully for any length of time. Indeed had we been eminently successful at Gettysburg, in all probability we would have been obliged to make the same movements we have. Posterity will be astonished when the *facts* of this war are made known to see against what *odds* this little army contended. Even you would be surprised if I were to give you the figures of the Yankee army and our own.

I have just received Sister's letter of the 13th and am grieved to see that she has not received my letter. I wrote immediately after the fight & hoped she certainly would have rec'd it as soon as the Dept did the Genl's dispatches, which it accompanied. I did not know before that Mother had returned to Norfolk, tho I had received a letter stating she was detained in Annapolis. I try to be resigned & imagine that tho it now seems hard to us, some good will result from their cruel treatment of our household. God ordains all things well & I am assured we have only to wait patiently to see the good in this instance. We must get her some money if possible, or else she must borrow from the banks on some of her stocks or her real estate. I will send a draft to you by first safe opportunity for her half year's interest on her Virginia stock.

I expect Mrs Parks will write to Norfolk & advise of the safety of all of us.

Unlike most people I think Peace is near at hand & more probable now than when we entered Pennsylvania, that is, provided Genls Grant & Rosecrans are not allowed to overrun the whole west & do as they please. If they are confined to the fall of Vicksburg & that of Pt Hudson all will be well, but if allowed to go where & when they please without any genuine show of resistance, why then we can't say what the result will be. What the North is to be taught in order to secure peace is that a few military successes do not at all affect the ultimate result. Let them know that a success here and one there only prolongs the war without rendering our conquest by any

means probable & they will not be able to resist the propositions of the Peace party in the North. Europe too may now
think that we are weak in the knees & about to collapse and as
sure as they do for fear of a reunion they will certainly recognize the independence of the South. The last thing they desire
is to see us restored to the Union & if they see any apparent
probability of it, they will move Heaven & Earth to prevent it.

Give my love to all at home when you write to Sally or
Marcia and to all in Richmond. Aff yr bro

Walter

James Henry Gooding to the
New Bedford Mercury

The 54th Massachusetts Infantry returned to Hilton Head, South Carolina, from coastal Georgia in late June and was assigned to the force attacking Charleston. On July 11 the regiment landed on James Island, located between Morris Island and the mainland. (The low-lying, marshy islands south of the harbor were separated from each other by a series of tidal creeks and inlets.) After skirmishing with Confederate troops on James Island, the 54th Massachusetts was sent to Morris Island on July 18 to take part in a second attack on Fort Wagner. When his brigade commander offered Colonel Shaw the honor of having his regiment lead the assault, Shaw accepted. That evening the 54th Massachusetts led 5,000 men in an advance that at one point had to move forward along a strip of sand less than one hundred feet wide. Private James Henry Gooding was a sailor from New Bedford who enlisted in the 54th Massachusetts in February 1863. The following month he began writing regular letters to the *New Bedford Mercury*, where his account of the battle of Fort Wagner appeared on August 1.

Morris Island, July 20, 1863

Messrs. Editors:—At last we have something stirring to record. The 54th, the past week, has proved itself twice in battle. The first was on James Island on the morning of the 16th. There were four companies of the 54th on picket duty at the time; our picket lines extending to the right of the rebel battery, which commands the approach to Charleston through the Edisto river. About 3 o'clock in the morning, the rebels began harassing our pickets on the right, intending, no doubt, to drive them in, so that by daylight the coast would be clear to rush their main force down on us, and take us by surprise. They did not suppose we had any considerable force to the rear of our pickets on the right, as Gen. Stevenson's brigade was plain in sight on the left; and their plan, I suppose, was to

rush down and cut Gen. Stevenson off. They made a mistake—
instead of returning fire, the officer in charge of the pickets
directed the men to lie down under cover of a hedge, rightly
expecting the rebels to advance by degrees toward our lines.
As he expected, at daylight they were within 600 yards of the
picket line, when our men rose and poured a volley into them.
That was something the rebels didn't expect—their line of
skirmishers was completely broken; our men then began to fall
back gradually on our line of battle, as the rebels were advancing their main force on to them. On they came, with six pieces
of artillery and four thousand infantry, leaving a heavy force to
drive Gen. Stevenson on the left. As their force advanced on
our right, the boys held them in check like veterans; but of
course they were falling back all the time, and fighting too.
After the officers saw there was no chance for their men, they
ordered them to move on to a creek under cover of the gunboats. When the rebels got within 900 yards of our line of
battle, the right wing of Gen. Terry's brigade gave them three
volleys, which checked their advance. They then made a stand
with their artillery and began shelling us, but it had no effect
on our forces, as the rebels fired too high. The 6th Connecticut battery then opened fire on them from the right, the John
Adams and May Flower from the creek between James and
Cole Islands, and the Pawnee and a mortar schooner from the
Edisto, when the rebels began a hasty retreat. It was a warmer
reception than they had expected. Our loss in the skirmishing
before the battle, so far as we can ascertain, was nine killed, 13
wounded, and 17 missing, either killed or taken prisoners; but
more probably they were driven into the creek and drowned.
Sergeant Wilson, of Co. H, was called upon to surrender, but
would not; he shot four men before he was taken. After he was
taken they ordered him to give up his pistol which he refused
to do, when he was shot through the head.

The men of the 54th behaved gallantly on the occasion—so
the Generals say. It is not for us to blow our horn; but when a
regiment of white men gave us three cheers as we were passing
them, it shows that we did our duty as men should.

I shall pass over the incidents of that day, as regards individuals, to speak of a greater and more terrible ordeal the 54th
regiment has passed through. I shall say nothing now of how

we came from James to Morris Island; suffice it to say, on Saturday afternoon we were marched up past our batteries, amid
the cheers of the officers and soldiers. We wondered what they
were all cheering for, but we soon found out. Gen. Strong
rode up, and we halted. Well, you had better believe there was
some guessing what we were to do. Gen. Strong asked us if we
would follow him into Fort Wagner. Every man said, yes—we
were ready to follow wherever we were led. You may all know
Fort Wagner is the Sebastopol of the rebels; but we went at it,
over the ditch and on to the parapet through a deadly fire; but
we could not get into the fort. We met the foe on the parapet
of Wagner with the bayonet—we were exposed to a murderous fire from the batteries of the fort, from our Monitors and
our land batteries, as they did not cease firing soon enough.
Mortal men could not stand such a fire, and the assault on
Wagner was a failure. The 9th Me., 10th Conn., 63d Ohio,
48th and 100th N.Y. were to support us in the assault; but
after we made the first charge, everything was in such confusion that we could hardly tell where the reserve was. At the
first charge the 54th rushed to within twenty yards of the
ditches, and, as might be expected of raw recruits, wavered—
but at the second advance they gained the parapet. The color
bearer of the State colors was killed on the parapet. Col. Shaw
seized the staff when the standard bearer fell, and in less than a
minute after, the Colonel fell himself. When the men saw their
gallant leader fall, they made a desperate effort to get him out,
but they were either shot down, or reeled in the ditch below.
One man succeeded in getting hold of the State color staff, but
the color was completely torn to pieces.

I have no more paper here at present, as all our baggage is at
St. Helena yet; so I cannot further particularize in this letter.
Lieut. Grace was knocked down by a piece of shell, but he is
not injured. He showed himself a great deal braver and cooler
than any line officer.

J. H. G.

Our correspondent gives a list of killed, wounded and missing. It is the same that we have already published.

Lewis Douglass to Amelia Loguen

The July 18 assault on Fort Wagner cost the Union 1,515 men killed, wounded, or captured, while the 1,800 Confederate defenders lost 222 men. Casualties in the 54th Massachusetts were 272 men killed, wounded, or captured, more than two-fifths of the regiment. Among the survivors was Sergeant Major Lewis Douglass, Frederick Douglass's eldest son, who wrote about the battle to Amelia Loguen, his future wife.

———————

MORRIS ISLAND. S. C. July 20

MY DEAR AMELIA: I have been in two fights, and am unhurt. I am about to go in another I believe to-night. Our men fought well on both occasions. The last was desperate we charged that terrible battery on Morris Island known as Fort Wagoner, and were repulsed with a loss of 300 killed and wounded. I escaped unhurt from amidst that perfect hail of shot and shell. It was terrible. I need not particularize the papers will give a better than I have time to give. My thoughts are with you often, you are as dear as ever, be good enough to remember it as I no doubt you will. As I said before we are on the eve of another fight and I am very busy and have just snatched a moment to write you. I must necessarily be brief. Should I fall in the next fight killed or wounded I hope to fall with my face to the foe.

If I survive I shall write you a long letter. DeForrest of your city is wounded George Washington is missing, Jacob Carter is missing, Chas Reason wounded Chas Whiting, Chas Creamer all wounded. The above are in hospital.

This regiment has established its reputation as a fighting regiment not a man flinched, though it was a trying time. Men fell all around me. A shell would explode and clear a space of twenty feet, our men would close up again, but it was no use we had to retreat, which was a very hazardous undertaking. How I got out of that fight alive I cannot tell, but I am here.

My Dear girl I hope again to see you. I must bid you farewell
should I be killed. Remember if I die I die in a good cause. I
wish we had a hundred thousand colored troops we would put
an end to this war. Good Bye to all Your own loving

Write soon
LEWIS

Charlotte Forten: Journal, July 20–24, 1863

The daughter of a prominent Philadelphia black family and an active abolitionist, Charlotte Forten became one of the first black school-teachers in the Sea Islands when she arrived on St. Helena Island, South Carolina, in October 1862. Forten met Robert Gould Shaw in early July when the 54th Massachusetts was posted to St. Helena, and wrote in her journal: "What purity what nobleness of soul, what exquisite gentleness in that beautiful face!"

Monday, July 20. For nearly two weeks we have waited, oh how anxiously for news of our regt. which went, we know, to Morris Is. to take part in the attack on Charleston. To-night comes news oh, so sad, so heart sickening. It is too terrible, too terrible to write. We can only hope it may not all be true. That our noble, beautiful young Colonel is killed, and the regt. cut to pieces! I cannot, cannot believe it. And yet I know it may be so. But oh, I am stunned, sick at heart. I can scarcely write. There was an attack on Fort Wagner. The 54th put in advance; fought bravely, desperately, but was finally overpowered and driven back after getting into the Fort. Thank Heaven! they fought bravely! And oh, I still must hope that our colonel, *ours* especially he seems to me, is not killed. But I can write no more to-night.

Beaufort, July 21. Came to town to-day hearing that nurses were sadly needed. Went to Mrs. L.'s. Found Col. H. and Dr. R. there. Mrs. L. was sure I sh'ld not be able to endure the fatigues of hospital life even for a few days, but I thought differently, and the Col. and Dr. were both on my side. So at last Mrs. L. consented and made arrangements for my entering one of the hospitals to-morrow.

It is sad to see the Col. at all feeble. He is usually so very strong and vigorous. He is going North next week. The Dr. is looking very ill. He is quite exhausted. I shall not feel at peace until he is safe in his northern home. The attachment between these two is beautiful, both are so thoroughly good and noble. And both have the rarest charm of manner.

Wednesday, July 22. My hospital life began to-day. Went early this morning with Mrs. L. and Mrs. G., the surgeon's wife, saw that the Dr. had not finished dressing the wounds, and while I waited below Mrs. S. gave me some sewing to do —mending the pantaloons and jackets of the poor fellows. (They are all of the 54th.) It was with a full heart that I sewed up bullet holes and bayonet cuts. Sometimes I found a jacket that told a sad tale—so torn to pieces that it was far past mending. After awhile I went through the wards. As I passed along I thought "Many and low are the pallets, but each is the face of a friend." And I was surprised to see such cheerful faces looking up from the beds. Talked a little with some of the patients and assisted Mrs. G. in distributing medicines. Mrs. L. kindly sent her carriage for me and I returned home, weary, but far more pleasantly impressed than I had thought possible, with hospital life.

Thursday, July 23. Said farewell to Col. H. who goes North in the "Arago" today. Am very sorry that Dr. R. c'ld not go with him, not having been able to get his papers. He is looking so ill. It makes me very anxious. He goes to Seaside for a few days. I hope the change, and Mrs. H.'s kind care will do him good. Took a more thorough survey of the hospital to-day. It is a large new brick building—quite close to the water,— two-storied, many windowed, and very airy—in every way well adapted for a hospital. Yesterday I was employed part of the time in writing letters for the men. It was pleasant to see the brave, cheerful, uncomplaining spirit which they all breathed. Some of the poor fellows had come from the far west—even so far as Michigan. Talked with them much to-day. Told them that we had heard that their noble Colonel was not dead, but had been taken prisoner by the rebels. How joyfully their wan faces lighted up! They almost started from their couches as the hope entered their souls. Their attachment to their gallant young colonel is beautiful to see. How warmly, how enthusiastically they speak of him. "He was one of the best little men in the world," they said. "No one c'ld be kinder to a set of men than he was to us." Brave grateful hearts! I hope they will ever prove worthy of such a leader. And God grant that he may indeed be living. But I fear, I greatly fear it may be but a false report. One poor fellow here interests me greatly. He is very young, only nineteen, comes from Michigan. He is very badly wounded—in both legs, and there is a ball—in the stomach—it is thought that cannot be extracted. This poor fellow suffers terribly. His groans are pitiful to hear. But he utters no complaint, and it is touching to see his gratitude for the least kindness that one does him. Mrs. G. asked him if he w'ld like her to write to his home. But he said no. He was an only son, and had come away against his mother's will. He w'ld not have her written to until he was better. Poor fellow! that will never be in this world.*

Another, a Sergeant, suffers great pain, being badly wounded in the leg. But he too lies perfectly patient and uncomplaining. He has such a good, honest face. It is pleasant to look at it—although it is black. He is said to be one of the best and bravest men in the regiment.

When I went in this morning and found my patients so cheerful some of them even quite merry, I tho't it c'ld not be possible that they were badly wounded. Many, indeed have only flesh wounds. But there are others—and they among the most uncomplaining—who are severely wounded;—some dangerously so. Brave fellows! I feel it a happiness, an honor, to do the slightest service for them. True they were unsuccessful in the attack of Fort Wagner. But that was no fault of theirs. It is the testimony of all that they fought bravely as men can fight, and that it was only when completely overwhelmed by superior numbers that they were driven back.

Friday, July 24. To-day the news of Col. Shaw's death is confirmed. There can no longer be any doubt. It makes me sad, sad at heart. They say he sprang from the parapet of the fort and cried "Onward, my brave boys, onward"; then fell, pierced with wounds. I know it was a glorious death. But oh, it is hard, very hard for the young wife, so late a bride, for the invalid mother, whose only and most dearly loved son he was, —that heroic mother who rejoiced in the position which he occupied as colonel of a colored regiment. My heart bleeds for her. His death is a very sad loss to us. I recall him as a much

*He has since recovered. I am surprised to hear.

loved friend. Yet I saw him but a few times. Oh what must it be to the wife and the mother. Oh it is terrible. It seems very, very hard that the best and the noblest must be the earliest called away. Especially has it been so throughout this dreadful war.

Mr. P. who has been unremitting in his attention to the wounded—called at our building to-day, and took me to the Officers Hospital, which is but a very short distance from here. It is in one of the finest residences in Beaufort, and is surrounded by beautiful grounds. Saw Major Hallowell, who, though badly wounded—in three places—is hoped to be slowly improving. A little more than a week ago I parted with him, after an exciting horseback ride, how strong, how well, how vigorous he was then! And now thoroughly prostrated! But he with all the other officers of the 54th, like the privates, are brave, patient—cheerful. With deep sadness he spoke of Col. Shaw and then told me something that greatly surprised me;—that the Col. before that fatal attack had told him that in case he fell he wished me to have one of his horses—He had three very fine spirited ones that he had brought from the North. (I afterward found this to be a mistake. He only wished me to take charge of the horses until they c'ld be sent North to his wife.—) How very, very kind it was! And to me, almost a perfect stranger. I shall treasure this gift most sacredly, all my life long.

Maria Lydig Daly: Diary, July 23, 1863

The daughter of a wealthy New York family of Dutch-German ancestry, Maria Lydig Daly supported the war effort through contributions
to the Women's Central Association for Relief and other charitable
activities. Her husband, Charles P. Daly, was an Irish-American
Catholic active in Democratic politics who served as chief judge of
the New York City Court of Common Pleas (the highest court in the
city). She wrote about the draft riots shortly after their suppression.
In early August Horatio Seymour, the Democratic governor of New
York, would ask that the draft be suspended in his state. Lincoln refused, and on August 19 conscription resumed in New York City
under a heavy military guard.

───────────────

July 23, 1863

At last the riot is quelled, but we had four days of great
anxiety. Fighting went on constantly in the streets between the
military and police and the mob, which was partially armed.
The greatest atrocities have been perpetrated. Colonel O'Brian
was murdered by the mob in such a brutal manner that nothing in the French Revolution exceeded it. Three or four Negroes were hung and burned; the women assisted and acted
like furies by stimulating the men to greater ferocity. Father
came into the city on Friday, being warned about his house,
and found fifteen Negroes secreted in it by Rachel. They came
from York Street, which the mob had attacked, with all their
goods and chattels. Father had to order them out. We feared
for our own block on account of the Negro tenements below
MacDougal Street, where the Negroes were on the roof, singing psalms and having firearms.

One night, seeing a fire before the house, I thought the
time had come, but it proved to be only a bonfire. The Judge
sallied out with his pistol, telling me that if he were not at
home in five minutes to call up the servants. This mob seems
to have a curious sense of justice. They attacked and destroyed

many disreputable houses and did not always spare secessionists. On Saturday (the fifth day) we went up to see Judge Hilton, who thought me very courageous, but I felt sorry for
Mrs. Hilton upon hearing that she had been so terribly frightened. She gave me such details that I came home too nervous
to sleep. In Lexington Avenue, houses were destroyed. One
lady before whose house the mob paused with the intention of
sacking it, saved her house by raising her window, smiling, and
waving her handkerchief. Mr. Bosie's brother was seized by a
rioter who asked him if he had $300.

"No," said he.

"Then come along with us," said the rioter, and they kept
him two hours. Mrs. Hilton said she never saw such creatures,
such gaunt-looking savage men and women and even little
children armed with brickbats, stones, pokers, shovels and
tongs, coal-scuttles, and even tin pans and bits of iron. They
passed her house about four o'clock on Monday morning and
continued on in a constant stream until nine o'clock. They
looked to her, she said, like Germans, and her first thought was
that it was some German festival. Whilst we sat there, we heard
occasional pistol shots, and I was very glad that I had ordered
a carriage to take us home. The carriage, it seems, was very
unwillingly sent since the livery-stable keeper was so much
afraid.

Every evening the Judge *would* go out near eleven o'clock,
to my great distress. But he threatened to send me into the
country if I objected (which I dreaded still more), so I kept
quiet. Leonard, the Superintendent of Police in our neighborhood, said the draft could not be enforced; the firemen are
against it, as well as all the working classes.

Among those killed or wounded have been found men with
delicate hands and feet, and under their outward laborers'
clothes were fine cambric shirts and costly underclothing. A
dressmaker says she saw from her window a gentleman whom
she knows and has seen with young ladies, but whose name
she could not remember, disguised in this way in the mob on
Sixth Avenue.

On Sunday we went to see Mrs. Jarvis and Mr. James T. Brady,
who had just arrived from Washington. I saw Susanna Brady,
who talked in the most violent manner against the Irish and in

favor of the blacks. I feel quite differently, although very sorry and much outraged at the cruelties inflicted. I hope it will give the Negroes a lesson, for since the war commenced, they have been so insolent as to be unbearable. I cannot endure free blacks. They are immoral, with all their piety.

The principal actors in this mob were boys, and I think they were Americans. Catherine, my seamstress, tells me that the plundering was done by the people in the neighborhood who were looking on and who, as the mob broke the houses open, went in to steal. The police this morning found beds, bedding, and furniture in the house of a Scotch Presbyterian who was well off and owned two cows and two horses. The Catholic priests have done their duty as Christians ministers in denouncing these riotous proceedings. One of them remonstrated with a woman in the crowd who wanted to cut off the ears of a Negro who was hung. The priest told her that Negroes had souls. "Sure, your reverence," said she, "I thought they only had gizzards."

On Sunday evening, Mr. Dykes came in. He had seen Judge Pierrepont, who had gone to Washington with others to see what can be done. Mr. Dykes thinks that New York, being a Democratic city, may expect little indulgence from the Administration. The Judge went up to see General Dix, now in command here, who says that the government is determined to carry the draft measure through at all costs. Yesterday we went to the wedding of Lydia Watson in Westchester County. Mr. Adie told the Judge that there was a secessionist plot to burn all the houses in the neighborhood on Thursday night, that he had heard that his had been exempted by vote, and that the principal instigator and mover in it was one of the richest and most influential men in the neighborhood. The purpose of the plot was to intimidate the government and prevent conscription. Mrs. Harry Morris, who I hear has been very violent in her invectives against the North, wished to know if the soldiers could be relied upon. I told her entirely so, that they declared they would rather fight these traitors at home who made this fire in their rear whilst they were risking their life to preserve order and the laws than the rebels. For her comfort, I told her that the mob had destroyed the houses of secessionists. I frightened her, I think, not a little.

Herman Melville: The House-top

Although Herman Melville was living in Pittsfield, Massachusetts, during the draft riots, some of his family and friends experienced the violence firsthand, among them his cousin Henry Gansevoort, a Union cavalry officer who helped restore order in the city. "The House-top" first appeared in *Battle-Pieces and Aspects of the War*, published in August 1866. (The footnote to the poem in this volume originally appeared as an endnote in *Battle-Pieces*.)

The House-top.
A Night Piece.
(JULY, 1863.)

No sleep. The sultriness pervades the air
And binds the brain—a dense oppression, such
As tawny tigers feel in matted shades,
Vexing their blood and making apt for ravage.
Beneath the stars the roofy desert spreads
Vacant as Libya. All is hushed near by.
Yet fitfully from far breaks a mixed surf
Of muffled sound, the Atheist roar of riot.
Yonder, where parching Sirius set in drought,
Balefully glares red Arson—there—and there.
The Town is taken by its rats—ship-rats
And rats of the wharves. All civil charms
And priestly spells which late held hearts in awe—
Fear-bound, subjected to a better sway
Than sway of self; these like a dream dissolve,
And man rebounds whole æons back in nature.[i]

NOTE[i]
"I dare not write the horrible and inconceivable atrocities committed," says Froissart, in alluding to the remarkable sedition in France during his time. The like may be hinted of some proceedings of the draft-rioters.

Hail to the low dull rumble, dull and dead,
And ponderous drag that shakes the wall.
Wise Draco comes, deep in the midnight roll
Of black artillery; he comes, though late;
In code corroborating Calvin's creed
And cynic tyrannies of honest kings;
He comes, nor parlies; and the Town, redeemed,
Gives thanks devout; nor, being thankful, heeds
The grimy slur on the Republic's faith implied,
Which holds that Man is naturally good,
And—more—is Nature's Roman, never to be scourged.

Henry Adams to
Charles Francis Adams Jr.

News of Lee's defeat and the surrender of Vicksburg reached London on July 19. Henry Adams shared his reaction with his brother, who had fought with the 1st Massachusetts Cavalry in the Gettysburg campaign.

———————————

23 July. 1863.

I positively tremble to think of receiving any more news from America since the batch that we received last Sunday. Why can't we sink the steamers till some more good news comes? It is like an easterly storm after a glorious June day, this returning to the gloomy chronicle of varying successes and disasters, after exulting in the grand excitement of such triumphs as you sent us on the 4th. For once, there was *no* drawback, unless I except anxiety about you. I wanted to hug the army of the Potomac. I wanted to get the whole of the army of Vicksburg drunk at my own expense. I wanted to fight some small man and lick him. Had I had a single friend in London capable of rising to the dignity of the occasion, I don't know what mightn't have happened. But mediocrity prevailed and I passed the day in base repose.

It was on Sunday morning as I came down to breakfast that I saw a telegram from the Department announcing the fall of Vicksburg. Now, to appreciate the value of this, you must know that the one thing upon which the London press and the English people have been so positive as not to tolerate contradiction, was the impossibility of capturing Vicksburg. Nothing could induce them to believe that Grant's army was not in extreme danger of having itself to capitulate. The Times of Saturday, down to the last moment, declared that the siege of Vicksburg grew more and more hopeless every day. Even now, it refuses, after receiving all the details, to admit the fact, and only says that Northern advices report it, but it is not yet

confirmed. Nothing could exceed the energy with which everybody in England has reprobated the wicked waste of life
that must be caused by the siege of this place during the sickly
season, and ridiculed the idea of its capture. And now, the announcement was just as though a bucket of iced-water were
thrown into their faces. They couldn't and wouldn't believe it.
All their settled opinions were overthrown, and they were left
dangling in the air. You never heard such a cackling as was kept
up here on Sunday and Monday, and you can't imagine how
spiteful and vicious they all were. Sunday evening I was asked
round to Monckton Milnes's to meet a few people. Milnes
himself is one of the warmest Americans in the world, and received me with a hug before the astonished company, crowing
like a fighting cock. But the rest of the company were very
cold. W. H. Russell was there, and I had a good deal of talk
with him. He at least did not attempt to disguise the gravity of
the occasion, nor to turn Lee's defeat into a victory. I went
with Mr Milnes to the Cosmopolitan Club afterwards, where
the people all looked at me as though I were objectionable. Of
course I avoided the subject in conversation, but I saw very
clearly how unpleasant the news was which I brought. So it has
been everywhere. This is a sort of thing that can be neither
denied, palliated, nor evaded; the disasters of the rebels are
unredeemed by even any hope of success. Accordingly the
emergency has produced here a mere access of spite; preparatory (if we suffer no reverse) to a revolution in tone.

It is now conceded at once that all idea of intervention is at
an end. The war is to continue indefinitely, so far as Europe is
concerned, and the only remaining chance of collision is in the
case of the iron-clads. We are looking after them with considerable energy, and I think we shall settle them.

It is utterly impossible to describe to you the delight that we
all felt here and that has not diminished even now. I can imagine the temporary insanity that must have prevailed over the
North on the night of the 7th. Here our demonstrations were
quiet, but ye Gods! how we felt! Whether to laugh or to cry,
one hardly knew. Some men preferred the one, some the other.
The Chief was the picture of placid delight. As for me, as my
effort has always been here to suppress all expression of feeling, I preserved sobriety in public, but for four days I've been

internally singing Hosannahs and running riot in exultation.
The future being doubtful, we are all the more determined to
drink this one cup of success out. Our friends at home, Dana,
John, and so on, are always so devilish afraid that we may see
things in too rosy colors. They think it necessary to be corre-
spondingly sombre in their advices. This time, luckily, we had
no one to be so cruel as to knock us down from behind, when
we were having all we could do to fight our English upas influences in front. We sat on the top of the ladder and didn't care
a copper who passed underneath. Your old friend Judge Goodrich was here on Monday, and you never saw a man in such a
state. Even for him it was wonderful. He lunched with us and
kept us in a perfect riot all the time, telling stories without
limit and laughing till he almost screamed.

I am sorry to say however that all this is not likely to make
our position here any pleasanter socially. All our experience has
shown that as our success was great, so rose equally the spirit
of hatred on this side. Never before since the Trent affair has it
shown itself so universal and spiteful as now. I am myself more
surprised at it than I have any right to be, and philosopher
though I aspire to be, I do feel strongly impressed with a desire
to see the time come when our success will compel silence and
our prosperity will complete the revolution. As for war, it
would be folly in us to go to war with this country. We have
the means of destroying her without hurting ourselves.

In other respects the week has been a very quiet one. The
season is over. The streets are full of Pickford's vans carting
furniture from the houses, and Belgravia and May Fair are the
scene of dirt and littered straw, as you know them from the
accounts of Pendennis. One night we went to the opera, but
otherwise we have enjoyed peace, and I have been engaged in
looking up routes and sights in the guide book of Scotland.
Thither, if nothing prevents and no bad news or rebel's plot
interferes, we shall wend our way on the first of August. The
rest of the family will probably make a visit or two, and I propose to make use of the opportunity to go on with Brooks and
visit the Isle of Skye and the Hebrides, if we can. This is in
imitation of Dr Johnson, and I've no doubt, if we had good
weather, it would be very jolly. But as for visiting people, the
truth is I feel such a dislike for the whole nation, and so keen a

sensitiveness to the least suspicion of being thought to pay court to any of them, and so abject a dread of ever giving anyone the chance to put a slight upon me, that I avoid them and neither wish them to be my friends nor wish to be theirs. I haven't the strength of character to retain resentments long, and some day in America I may astonish myself by defending these people for whom I entertain at present only a profound and lively contempt. But at present I am glad that my acquaintances are so few and I do not intend to increase the number.

You will no doubt be curious to know, if, as I say, I have no acquaintances, how the devil I pass my time. Certainly I do pass it, however, and never have an unoccupied moment. My candles are seldom out before two o'clock in the morning, and my table is piled with half-read books and unfinished writing. For weeks together I only leave the house to mount my horse and after my ride, come back as I went. If it were not for your position and my own uneasy conscience, I should be as happy as a Virginia oyster, and as it is, I believe I never was so well off physically, morally and intellectually as this last year.

I send you another shirt, and a copy of the Index, the southern organ, which I thought you would find more interesting this week than any other newspaper I can send. It seems to me to look to a cessation of *organised* armed resistance and an ultimate resort to the Polish fashion. I think we shall not stand much in their way there, if they like to live in a den of thieves.

Ever

George G. Meade to Henry W. Halleck

Meade remained sensitive to criticism of his pursuit of Lee's army after Gettysburg. On July 28 Halleck wrote to Meade, praising him for handling his troops during the battle "as well, if not better, than any general has handled his army during the war," and expressing continued confidence in his leadership. Halleck also told Meade that he "should not have been surprised or vexed at the President's disappointment at the escape of Lee's army," adding that Lincoln "felt no little impatience" at Lee's "unexpected escape." Meade replied from his headquarters at Warrenton in northern Virginia.

———————

UNOFFICIAL.]

HEADQUARTERS ARMY OF THE POTOMAC,
July 31, 1863.

Major-General HALLECK,
General-in-Chief:

MY DEAR GENERAL: I thank you most sincerely and heartily for your kind and generous letter of the 28th instant, received last evening. It would be wrong in me to deny that I feared there existed in the minds of both the President and yourself an idea that I had failed to do what another would and could have done in the withdrawal of Lee's army. The expression you have been pleased to use in your letter, to wit, "a feeling of disappointment," is one that I cheerfully accept and readily admit was as keenly felt by myself as any one. But permit me, dear general, to call your attention to the distinction between disappointment and dissatisfaction. The one was a natural feeling, in view of the momentous consequences that would have resulted from a successful attack, but does not necessarily convey with it any censure. I could not view the use of the latter expression in any other light than as intending to convey an expression of opinion on the part of the President that I had failed to do what I might and should have done. Now, let me say, in the frankness which characterizes your letter, that perhaps the President was right; if such was the case, it was my duty to give him an opportunity to replace me by one better fitted for the command of the army. It was, I assure you, with such feelings that I applied to be relieved. It was not from any personal considerations, for I have tried in this whole war to forget all personal considerations, and have always maintained they should not for an instant influence any one's actions.

Of course you will understand that I do not agree that the President was right, and I feel sure when the true state of the case comes to be known, that however natural and great may be the feeling of disappointment, no blame will be attached to any one.

Had I attacked Lee the day I proposed to do so, and in the ignorance that then existed of his position, I have every reason to believe the attack would have been unsuccessful, and would have resulted disastrously. This opinion is founded on the judgment of numerous distinguished officers, after inspecting Lee's vacated works and position. Among these officers I could name Generals Sedgwick, Wright, Slocum, Hays, Sykes, and others.

The idea that Lee had abandoned his lines early in the day that he withdrew, I have positive intelligence is not correct, and that not a man was withdrawn till after dark. I mention these facts to remove the impression, which newspaper correspondents have given the public, that it was only necessary to advance to secure an easy victory. I had great responsibility thrown on me. On one side were the known and important fruits of victory, and, on the other, the equally important and terrible consequences of a defeat. I considered my position at Williamsport very different from that at Gettysburg. When I left Frederick, it was with the firm determination to attack and fight Lee, without regard to time or place, as soon as I could come in contact with him; but after defeating him, and requiring him to abandon his schemes of invasion, I did not think myself justified in making a blind attack simply to prevent his escape, and running all the risks attending such a venture. Now, as I said before, in this, perhaps, I erred in judgment, for I take this occasion to say to you, and through you to the President, that I have no pretensions to any superior capacity for the post he has assigned me to; that all I can do is to exert my utmost efforts and do the best I can; but that the moment those who have a right to judge my actions think, or feel satisfied, either that I am wanting or that another would do better, that moment I earnestly desire to be relieved, not on my own account, but on account of the country and the cause.

You must excuse so much egotism, but your kind letter in a measure renders it necessary. I feel, general, very proud of your good opinion, and assure you I shall endeavor in the future to continue to merit it.

Reciprocating the kind feeling you have expressed, I remain, general, most truly and respectfully, yours,

GEO. G. MEADE,
Major-General.

Robert E. Lee to Jefferson Davis

Lee wrote to Davis in response to a July 27 note from the Confederate president that has not been found. It enclosed a clipping from the
Charleston Mercury, possibly a dispatch from Richmond on July 18
that referred to "the ill-timed Northern campaign, which cost us
Vicksburg, with the States of Mississippi and Tennessee, and endan-
gered Charleston." The *Mercury* was owned by Robert Barnwell Rhett
and edited by his son, Robert Barnwell Rhett Jr., both bitter political
opponents of the Davis administration.

————————

Camp, Culpeper
July 31, 1863

Mr. President:

Your note of the 27 enclosing a slip from the *Charleston
Mercury* relative to the battle of Gettysburg is received. I much
regret its general censure upon the operations of the army, as it
is calculated to do us no good either at home or abroad. But I
am prepared for similar criticism & as far as I am concerned
the remarks fall harmless. I am particularly sorry however that
from partial information & mere assumption of facts that injustice should be done any officer, & that occasion should be
taken to asperse your conduct, who of all others are most free
of blame. I do not fear that your position in the confidence of
the people, can be injured by such attacks, & I hope the official
reports will protect the reputation of every officer. These cannot be made at once, & in the meantime as you state much
falsehood may be promulgated. But truth is mighty & will
eventually prevail. As regards the article in question I think it
contains its own contradiction. Although charging Heth with
the failure of the battle, it expressly states he was absent
wounded. The object of the writer & publisher is evidently to
cast discredit upon the operations of the Government & those
connected with it & thus gratify feelings more to be pitied
than envied. To take notice of such attacks would I think do

423

more harm than good, & would be just what is desired. The delay that will necessarily occur in receiving official reports has induced me to make for the information of the Department a brief outline of operations of the army, in which however I have been unable to state the conduct of troops or officers. It is sufficient to show what was done & what was not done. No blame can be attached to the army for its failure to accomplish what was projected by me, nor should it be censured for the unreasonable expectations of the public. I am alone to blame, in perhaps expecting too much of its prowess & valour. It however in my opinion achieved under the guidance of the Most High a general success, though it did not win a victory. I thought at the time that the latter was practicable. I still think if all things could have worked together it would have been accomplished. But with the knowledge I then had, & in the circumstances I was then placed, I do not know what better course I could have pursued. With my present knowledge, & could I have foreseen that the attack on the last day would have failed to drive the enemy from his position, I should certainly have tried some other course. What the ultimate result would have been is not so clear to me. Our loss has been very heavy, that of the enemy's is proportionally so. His crippled condition enabled us to retire from the country comparatively unmolested. The unexpected state of the Potomac was our only embarrassment. I will not trespass upon Your Excellency's time more. With prayers for your health & happiness, & the recognition by your grateful country of your great services

I remain truly & sincerely yours

R. E. LEE

Hannah Johnson to Abraham Lincoln

It is not known if President Lincoln ever saw this letter, which is preserved in the National Archives in the records of the adjutant general's office.

—————————

Buffalo July 31 1863

Excellent Sir   My good friend says I must write to you and she will send it   My son went in the 54th regiment. I am a colored woman and my son was strong and able as any to fight for his country and the colored people have as much to fight for as any. My father was a Slave and escaped from Louisiana before I was born morn forty years agone   I have but poor edication but I never went to schol, but I know just as well as any what is right between man and man. Now I know it is right that a colored man should go and fight for his country, and so ought to a white man. I know that a colored man ought to run no greater risques than a white, his pay is no greater his obligation to fight is the same. So why should not our enemies be compelled to treat him the same, Made to do it.

My son fought at Fort Wagoner but thank God he was not taken prisoner, as many were   I thought of this thing before I let my boy go but then they said Mr. Lincoln will never let them sell our colored soldiers for slaves, if they do he will get them back quck he will rettallyate and stop it. Now Mr Lincoln dont you think you oght to stop this thing and make them do the same by the colored men   they have lived in idleness all their lives on stolen labor and made savages of the colored people, but they now are so furious because they are proving themselves to be men, such as have come away and got some edication. It must not be so. You must put the rebels to work in State prisons to making shoes and things, if they sell our colored soldiers, till they let them all go. And give their wounded the same treatment. it would seem cruel, but their no other way, and a just man must do hard things sometimes, that shew him to be a great man. They tell me some do you will take back the Proclamation, don't do it. When you are dead and in Heaven, in a thousand years that action of yours will make the Angels sing your praises I know it. Ought one man to own another, law for or not, who made the law, surely the poor slave did not. so it is wicked, and a horrible Outrage, there is no sense in it, because a man has lived by robbing all his life and his father before him, should he complain because the stolen things found on him are taken. Robbing the colored people of their labor is but a small part of the robbery   their souls are almost taken, they are made bruits of often. You know all about this

Will you see that the colored men fighting now, are fairly treated. You ought to do this, and do it at once, Not let the thing run along   meet it quickly and manfully, and stop this, mean cowardly cruelty. We poor oppressed ones, appeal to you, and ask fair play. Yours for Christs sake

Hannah Johnson.

Hon. Mr. Lincoln   The above speaks for itself   Carrie Coburn

Frederick Douglass to George L. Stearns

In a proclamation issued on December 23, 1862, Jefferson Davis ordered that former slaves captured while fighting for the Union be
turned over to state authorities to be tried for the capital offense of
insurrection. His policy was extended by a joint resolution of the Confederate Congress, adopted on May 1, 1863, to apply to free blacks
from the North. In practice, captured black soldiers were either summarily executed, returned or sold into slavery, or used for forced labor
by the Confederate army. Angered by the Lincoln administration's
apparent unwillingness to retaliate, Douglass announced his refusal to
continue recruiting black soldiers in a public letter to George L.
Stearns that appeared in *Douglass' Monthly*. (A wealthy Boston abolitionist who had financially supported John Brown, Stearns had been
commissioned by Governor Andrew to recruit for the 54th Massachusetts and in turn had enlisted Douglass and other black abolitionists in the effort.) In fact, Lincoln had issued an order on July 30
declaring that to "sell or enslave any captured person, on account of
his color, and for no offence against the laws of war, is a relapse into
barbarism and a crime against the civilization of the age." The order
specified that "for every soldier of the United States killed in violation
of the laws of war, a rebel soldier shall be executed," and that for
every one enslaved, "a rebel soldier shall be placed at hard labor on
the public works."

Rochester, August 1st, 1863

My Dear Sir:

Having declined to attend the meeting to promote enlistments, appointed for me at Pittsburgh, in present circumstances, I owe you a word of explanation. I have hitherto
deemed it a duty, as it certainly has been a pleasure, to cooperate with you in the work of raising colored troops in the free
states, to fight the battles of the Republic against the slaveholding rebels and traitors. Upon the first call you gave me to
this work, I responded with alacrity. I saw, or thought I saw a
ray of light, brightening the future of my whole race as well as

that of our war troubled country, in arousing colored men to
fight for the nation's life, I continue to believe in the black
man's arm, and still have some hope in the integrity of our
rulers. Nevertheless, I must for the present leave to others the
work of persuading colored men to join the Union Army. I
owe it to my long abused people, and especially of them already in the army, to expose their wrongs and plead their
cause. I cannot do that in connection with recruiting. When I
plead for recruits I want to do it with all my heart, without
qualification. I cannot do that now. The impression settles
upon me that colored men have much overrated the enlight-
enment, justice and generosity of our rulers at Washington. In
my humble way I have contributed somewhat to that false estimate. You know, that when the idea of raising colored troops
was first suggested, the special duty to be assigned them, was
the garrisoning of forts and arsenals in certain warm, unhealthy
and miasmatic localities in the South. They were thought to be
better adapted to that service than white troops. White troops,
trained to war, brave and daring, were to take fortifications,
and the blacks were to hold them and keep them from falling
again into the hands of the rebels.—Three advantages were to
arise out of this wise division of labor. 1st. The spirit and pride
of white troops was not to waste itself in dull and monotonous
inactivity in fort-life. Their arms were to be kept bright by
constant use. 2dly. The health of the white troops was to be
preserved. 3dly. Black troops were to have the advantage of
sound military training, and be otherwise useful at the same
time that they should be tolerably secure from capture by the
rebels, who early avowed their determination to enslave and
slaughter them in defiance of the laws of war. Two out of the
three advantages, were to accrue to the white troops. Thus far
however, I believe that no such duty as holding fortifications
has been committed to colored troops. They have done far
other and more important work than holding fortifications. I
have no special complaint to make at this point, and I simply
mention it to strengthen the statement that from the beginning of this business it was the confident belief among both
the colored and white friends of colored enlistments that
President Lincoln as Commander-in-Chief of the army and
navy would certainly see to it, that his colored troops should

be so handled and disposed of as to be but little exposed to capture by the rebels, and that—if so exposed—as they have repeatedly been from the first, the President possessed both the disposition and the means for compelling the rebels to respect the rights of such as might fall in their hands. The piratical proclamation of President Davis announcing Slavery and assassination to colored prisoners was before the country and the world. But men had faith in Mr. Lincoln and his advisers. He was silent, to be sure, but charity suggested that being a man of action rather than words, he only waited for a case in which he should be required to act. This faith in the man enabled us to speak with warmth and effect in urging enlistments among colored men. That faith, my dear Sir, is now nearly gone. Various occasions have arisen during the last six months for the exercise of his power in behalf of the colored men in his service. But no word comes from Mr. Lincoln or from the War Department, sternly assuring the Rebel Chief that inquisitions shall yet be made for innocent blood. No word of retaliation when a black man is slain by a rebel in cold blood. No word was said when free men from Massachusetts were caught and sold into slavery in Texas. No word is said when brave black men who according to the testimony of both friend and foe, fought like heroes to plant the star spangled banner on the blazing parapets of Fort Wagner, and in doing so were captured, some mutilated and killed, and others sold into slavery. The same crushing silence reigns over this scandalous outrage as over that of the slaughtered teamsters at Murfreesboro.— The same as over that at Millikens Bend and Vicksburg. I am free to say, my dear sir, that the case looks as if the confiding colored soldiers had been betrayed into bloody hands by the very Government in whose defense they were heroically fighting. I know what you will say to this; you will say; "wait a little longer, and after all, the best way to have justice done to your people is to get them into the army as fast as possible." You may be right in this; my argument has been the same, but have we not already waited, and have we not already shown the highest qualities of soldiers and on this account deserve the protection of the Government for which we are fighting? Can any case stronger than that before Charleston ever arise? If the President is ever to demand justice and humanity for black soldiers, is not this the time for him to do it? How many 54ths must be cut to pieces, its mutilated prisoners killed and its living sold into Slavery, to be tortured to death by inches before Mr. Lincoln shall say: "Hold, enough!"

You know the 54th. To you, more than any one man belongs the credit of raising that Regiment. Think of its noble and brave officers literally hacked to pieces while many of its rank and file have been sold into a slavery worse than death, and pardon me if I hesitate about assisting in raising a fourth Regiment until the President shall give the same protection to them as to white soldiers. With warm and sincere regards,

Frederick Douglass

Since writing the foregoing letter, which we have now put upon record, we have received assurance from Major Stearns, that the Government of the United States is already taking measures which will secure for the captured colored soldiers, at Charleston and elsewhere, the same protection against slavery and cruelty, extended to white soldiers. What ought to have been done at the beginning, comes late, but it comes. The poor colored soldiers have purchased this interference dearly. It really seems that nothing of justice, liberty, or humanity can come to us except through tears and blood.

Frederick Douglass:
The Commander-in-Chief and His Black Soldiers

August 1863

This article appeared in *Douglass' Monthly* along with the letter to Stearns.

———————————

Whatever else may be said of President Lincoln, the most malignant Copperhead in the country cannot reproach him with any undue solicitude for the lives and liberties of the brave black men, who are now giving their arms and hearts to the support of his Government. When a boy, on a slave plantation the saying was common: "Half a cent to kill a Negro and half a cent to bury him."—The luxury of killing and burying could be enjoyed by the poorest members of Southern society, and no strong temptation was required to induce white men thus to kill and bury the black victims of their lust and cruelty. —With a Bible and pulpit affirming that the Negro is accursed of God, it is not strange that men should curse him, and that all over the South there should be manifested for the life and liberty of this description of man, the utterest indifference and contempt. Unhappily the same indifference and contempt for the lives of colored men is found wherever slavery has an advocate or treason an apologist. In the late terrible mobs in New York and elsewhere, the grim features of this malice towards colored men was everywhere present. Beat, shoot, hang, stab, kill, burn and destroy the Negro, was the cry of the crowd. Religion has cursed him and the law has enslaved him, and why may not the mob kill him?—Such has been our national education on this subject, and that it still has power over Mr. Lincoln seems evident from the fact, that no measures have been openly taken by him to cause the laws of civilized warfare to be observed towards his colored soldiers. The slaughter of blacks taken as captives, seems to affect him as little as the slaughter of beeves for the use of his army. More than six months ago Mr. Jefferson Davis told Mr. Lincoln and the world that he meant to treat blacks not as soldiers but as felons. The threat was openly made, and has been faithfully executed by the rebel chief. At Murfreesboro twenty colored teamsters in the Federal service, were taken by the rebels, and though not soldiers, and only servants, they were in cold blood—every man of them—shot down. At Milliken's Bend, the same black flag with its death's head and cross-bones was raised. When Banks entered Port Hudson he found white federal prisoners, but no black ones. Those of the latter taken, were no doubt, in cold blood put to the sword. Today, news from Charleston tells us that Negro soldiers taken as prisoners will not be exchanged, but sold into slavery—that some twenty of such prisoners are now in their hands. Thousands of Negroes are now being enrolled in the service of the Federal Government. The Government calls them, and they come. They freely and joyously rally around the flag of the Union, and take all the risks, ordinary and extraordinary, involved in this war. They do it not for office, for thus far, they get none; they do it not for money, for thus far, their pay is less than that of white men. They go into this war to affirm their manhood, to strike for liberty and country.—If any class of men in this war can claim the honor of fighting for principle, and not from passion, for ideas, not from brutal malice, the colored soldier can make that claim preeminently. He strikes for manhood and freedom, under the forms of law and the usages of civilized warfare. He does not go forth as a savage with tomahawk and scalping knife, but in strict accordance with the rules of honorable warfare. Yet he is now openly threatened with slavery and assassination by the rebel Government—and the threat has been savagely executed.

What has Mr. Lincoln to say about this slavery and murder? What has he said?—Not one word. In the hearing of the nation he is as silent as an oyster on the whole subject. If two white men are threatened with assassination, the Richmond Rebels are promptly informed that the Federal Government will retaliate sternly and severely. But when colored soldiers are so threatened, no word comes from the Capitol. What does this silence mean? Is there any explanation short of base and scandalous contempt for the just rights of colored soldiers?

For a time we tried to think that there might be solid reasons of state against answering the threats of Jefferson Davis—but the Government has knocked this favorable judgment from under us, by its prompt threat of retaliation in the case of the two white officers at Richmond who are under sentence of death. Men will ask, the world will ask, why interference should be made for those young white officers thus selected for murder, and not for the brave black soldiers who may be flung by the fortunes of war into the hands of the rebels? Is the right to "life, liberty and the pursuit of happiness" less sacred in the case of the one than the other?

It may be said that the black soldiers have enlisted with the threat of Jefferson Davis before them, and they have assumed their position intelligently, with a full knowledge of the consequences incurred. If they have, they have by that act shown themselves all the more worthy of protection. It is noble in the Negro to brave unusual danger for the life of the Republic, but it is mean and base in the Republic if it rewards such generous and unselfish devotion by assassination, when a word would suffice to make the laws of war respected, and to prevent the crime. Shocking enough are the ordinary horrors of war, but the war of the rebels toward the colored men is marked by deeds which well might "shame extremest hell." And until Mr. Lincoln shall interpose his power to prevent these atrocious assassinations of Negro soldiers, the civilized world will hold him equally with Jefferson Davis responsible for them. The question is already being asked: Why is it that colored soldiers which were first enlisted with a view to "garrison forts and arsenals, on the Southern coast"—where white men suffer from climate, should never be heard of in any such forts and arsenals? Was that a trick? Why is it that they who were enlisted to fight the fevers of the South, while white soldiers fight the rebels are now only heard of in "forlorn hopes," in desperate charges always in the van, as at Port Hudson, Milliken's Bend, James Island and Fort Wagner? Green colored recruits are called upon to assume the position of veterans. They have performed their part gallantly and gloriously, but by all the proofs they have given of their patriotism and bravery we protest against the meanness, ingratitude and cruelty of the Government, in whose behalf they fight, if that Government remains longer a silent witness of their enslavement and assassination. Having had patience and forbearance with the silence of Mr. Lincoln a few months ago, we could at least imagine some excuses for his silence as to the fate of colored troops falling by the fortunes of war into the hands of the rebels, but the time for this is past. It is now for every man who has any sense of right and decency, to say nothing of gratitude, to speak out trumpet-tongued in the ears of Mr. Lincoln and his Government and demand from him a declaration of purpose, to hold the rebels to a strict account for every black federal soldier taken as a prisoner. For every black prisoner slain in cold blood, Mr. Jefferson Davis should be made to understand that one rebel officer shall suffer death, and for every colored soldier sold into slavery, a rebel shall be held as a hostage. For our Government to do less than this, is to deserve the indignation and the execration of mankind.

Walt Whitman to Lewis Kirk Brown

Walt Whitman was living in Brooklyn and working as a freelance journalist when he learned in December 1862 that his brother George had been wounded at Fredericksburg. Whitman traveled to northern Virginia, where he learned that his brother's wound was slight. After visiting army hospitals and camps around Falmouth, he accompanied a group of wounded soldiers to Washington. Whitman would remain in the capital until June 1864, visiting military hospitals while working part-time as a government clerk. One of the soldiers he befriended in the Armory Square Hospital was Lewis Kirk Brown of Elkton, Maryland. Wounded in the leg by a shell at Rappahannock Station, Virginia, on August 19, 1862, Brown lay in the open for four days before being brought to Washington. His wound did not heal, and in January 1864 his left leg would be amputated below the knee. The operation was successful, and Brown lived until 1926.

———————

Washington, August 1, 1863.
Both your letters have been received Lewy—the second one came this morning, & was welcome, as any thing from you will always be, & the sight of your face welcomer than all, my darling—I see you write in good spirits, & appear to have first rate times—Lew you must not go around too much, nor eat & drink too promiscuous, but be careful & moderate, & not let the kindness of friends carry you away, lest you break down again, dear son—I was at the hospital yesterday four or five hours, was in Ward K—Taber has been down sick, so he had to lay abed, but he is better now, & goes around as usual—Curly is the same as usual—most of the others are the same—there have been quite a good many deaths—the young man who lay in bed 2 with a very bad leg is dead—I saw Johnny Mahay in ward E,—poor fellow, he is very poorly, he is very thin, & his face is like wax—Lew I must tell you what a curious thing happened in the Chaplain's house night before last—there has been a man in Ward I, named Lane, with two fingers amputated,

very bad with gangrene, so they removed him to a tent by
himself—last Thursday his wife came to see him. She seemed a
nice woman but very poor. She stopt at the Chaplain's—about
3 o'clock in the morning she got up & went to the sink, &
there she gave birth to a child, which fell down the sink into
the sewer runs beneath, fortunately the water was not turned
on—the Chaplain got up, carried Mrs. Lane out, & then
roused up a lot of men from the hospital, with spades &c. dug
a trench outside, & got into the sink, & took out the poor little
child, it lay there on its back, in about two inches of water—
well, strange as it may seem, the child was alive, (it fell about
five feet through the sink)—& is now living & likely to live, is
quite bright, has a head of thick black hair—the Chaplain took
me in yesterday, showed me the child, & Mrs. Jackson, his
wife, told me the whole story, with a good deal I haven't told
you—& then she treated me to a good plate of ice cream—so
I staid there nearly an hour & had quite a pleasant visit. Mrs.
Lane lay in an adjoining room. Lew, as to me & my affairs
there is nothing very new or important—I have not succeeded
in getting any employment here yet, except that I write a little,
(newspaper correspondence &c) barely enough to pay my
expenses—but it is my fault, for I have not tried hard enough
for anything—the last three weeks I have not felt very well—
for two or three days I was down sick, for the first time in my
life, (as I have never before been sick)—I feel pretty fair to-day
—I go round most every day, the same as usual—I have some
idea of giving myself a furlough of three or four weeks, &
going home to Brooklyn, N Y but I should return again to
Washington, probably. Lew, it is pretty hot weather here, & the
sun affects me—(I had a sort of sun stroke about five years
ago.)—You speak of being here in Washington again about the
last of August—O Lewy how glad I should be to see you, to
have you with me—I have thought if it could be so that you &
one other person & myself could be where we could work &
live together, & have each other's society, we three, I should like
it so much—but it is probably a dream—Well, Lew they had
the great battle of Gettysburgh, but it does not seem to have
settled anything, except to have killed & wounded a great
many thousand men—It seems as though the two armies were

falling back again to near their old positions on the Rappahannock—it is hard to tell what will be the next move—Yet Lewy
I think we shall conquer yet—I don't believe it is destined that
this glorious Union is to be broken up by all the Sesech South,
or Copheads north either—Well my darling I have scribbled
you off something to show you where I am & that I have rec'd
your welcome letters—but my letter is not of much interest,
for I don't feel very bright to-day—Dear son you must write
me whenever you can—take opportunity—when you have
nothing to do, & write me a good long letter—Your letters &
your love for me are very precious to me, for I appreciate it all
Lew, & give you the like in return. It is now about 3 o'clock &
I will go out & mail this letter, & then go & get my dinner—
So good bye Lewy—good bye my dear son & comrade & I
hope it will prove God's will that you get well & sound yet, &
have many good years yet—.

WALT

Address my letters care Major Hapgood paymaster U S A at
cor. 15th & F st Washington D C

———————

Washington
August 11 1863

Dear Lewy,

I thought I would write you a few lines to day—I suppose
you rec'd a letter from me eight or nine days ago—I hope this
will find you in good health & spirits—I wrote to you not to
go about too much, & eat & drink too freely, & I must repeat
the caution—a fellow can keep himself in good condition by a
little care & prudence—

Well Lewy the presentation to Dr. Bliss came off last Saturday evening—it was in Ward F—the beds were all cleared out,
the sick put in other wards—the room cleaned, hung with greens
&c. looked very nice—the instruments were there on exhibition the afternoon. I took a view of them, they were in four
cases, & looked very fine—in the evening they were presented
—speeches were made by one & another—there was a band of
music &c—I stopt about 20 minutes, but got tired, and went

off among the boys that were confined to their beds—the room was crowded, and everything passed off right I heard—

Lewy, we had the hottest weather here I ever experienced—it has been now about ten days, & no let up yet—Yesterday & last night was the hottest, no rain for sometime & the air prickly & burning—Still I am enjoying very good health, thank God,—better this last week than I have had for two or three months—I have some thought of going on to New York for a short time, as I have not been home now in eight months, but if I do, I shall pretty surely return here before long—Lewy the draft has been put through here in Washington the past week—they drafted lots of Secessionists & quite a good many darks—(I wonder if it wouldn't be a good plan to draft all of both them kinds)—I don't hear any particular war news,—the Army of the Potomac is down around Warrenton—there are conscripts arriving there to fill up the regts. more or less every day—it will be a great & sudden change of life to many, especially such weather as this.—I believe I told you in my last letter about the strange way the baby was born in the Chaplain's —Well the baby is alive and growing like a pig, & the father Mr. Lane is getting well, Mrs. Lane ditto—Dr. Bliss is just going off on a furlough—the Chaplain & wife have left on a furlough—Taber & the rest in Ward K are all right—there have been quite a good many deaths in hospital the past week or so, the heat is bad for the poor wounded men—Well Lewy I must now wind up—I send you my love my darling son & comrade, & request you to write me soon as convenient, how you are getting along & all about things—I will write again before very long, till then good bye & God bless you dear son.

WALT WHITMAN

Address care Major Hapgood paymaster U S A cor 15th St & F st Washington D C

———————

Washington
August 15 1863

Lewy, your letter of August 10 came safe, & was glad to hear all about you, & the way you are spending the time—Lew you must be having first rate times out there,—Well you need something to make up what you have suffered—You speak of being used well out there—Lewy I feel as if I could love any one that uses you well, & does you a kindness—but what kind of heart must that man have that would treat otherwise, or say anything insulting to a crippled young soldier, hurt in fighting for this union & flag? (well—I should say damned little man or heart in the business)—Should you meet any such you must not mind them, dear comrade, & not allow your feelings to be hurt by such loafers—(I agree with you that a rebel in the Southern army is much more respectable than a Northern Copperhead.) Dear son, when I read about your agreeable visit of a week, & how much you enjoyed yourself, I felt as much gratified as though I had enjoyed it myself—& I was truly thankful to hear that your leg is still doing well, & on the gain—you must not mind its being slowly, dear son, if it only goes forward instead of backward, & you must try to be very careful of your eating and drinking &c. not indulge in any excesses & not eat too much flummery, but generally plain food, for that is always best, & it helps along so much.—Lewy I believe I wrote you an acc't of the presentation to Dr. Bliss—he is now off North for three weeks—Dr. Butler, (ward D) is in charge—some of the doctors & wardmasters have been drafted —poor Johnny Mahay is not in very good spirits—he was to have an operation performed before Bliss went, but he went off and did not do it—Johnny is pretty low some days—Things in Ward K are pretty much the same—they had some improvements in the Hospital, new sinks, much better, & the grounds in front & between the wards nicely laid out in flowers & grass plots &c.—but Lew it has been awful hot in the wards the past two weeks, the roofs burnt like fire—There is no particular war news,—they are having batches of conscripts now every day in the Army—Meade is down on the Upper Rappahannock & fords & around Warrenton—Lee stretches down toward Gordonsville, they say his headquarters is there—folks are all looking toward Charleston,—if we could only succeed there, I don't know what Secesh would do—the ground seems to be slipping more & more from under their feet—Lew, the *Union* & the *American Flag* must conquer, it is destiny—it may be long, or it may be short, but that will be the result—but O what precious lives have been lost by tens of thousands in the struggle already—Lew you speak in your letter how you would like to see me—well my darling I wonder if there is not somebody who would be gratified to see you, & always will be wherever he is—Dear comrade, I was highly pleased at your telling me in your letter about your folks' place, the house & land & all the items—you say I must excuse you for writing so much foolishness,—nothing of the kind—my darling boy when you write to me, you must write without ceremony. I like to hear every little thing about yourself & your affairs,—you need never care how you write to me Lewy, if you will only—I never think about literary perfection in letters either, it is the *man* & the *feeling*—Lew, I am feeling pretty well but the sun affects me a little, aching & fulness on the head—a good many have been sun-struck here the last two weeks—I keep shady through the middle of the day lately—Well my dear boy I have scribbled away any thing for I wanted to write you to-day & now I must switch off—good by my darling comrade, for the present, & I pray God to bless you now & always. Write when you feel like it, Lewy. Don't hurry.

WALT.

Address still care Major Hapgood, paymaster U S A at cor 15th & F st Washington D C

George E. Stephens to the Weekly Anglo-African

Although enlistees in the 54th Massachusetts had been promised equal pay with white soldiers, in June 1863 the War Department decided otherwise. It ruled that black soldiers would receive the pay authorized by the Militia Act of July 17, 1862, which had envisioned that blacks would serve mainly as military laborers. Privates and non-commissioned officers would both be paid $10 a month minus a $3 clothing allowance, at a time when white privates received $13 a month plus $3.50 for clothing. Among the soldiers who protested against this discrimination was Sergeant George E. Stephens, a Philadelphia native who had fought at Fort Wagner. Stephens wrote about the 54th Massachusetts in one of his regular letters to the *Weekly Anglo-African*, an influential black newspaper in New York. The regiment would remain on Morris Island until January 1864, when it was sent to Florida.

In Camp,
Morris Island, S.C.,
Aug. 7, 1863.
Mr. Editor: Since I wrote my last letter the startling news of the mobs, riots, incendiarism, pillage and slaughter, recently so rife in the North, particularly in New York City, has reached here. You may judge what our thoughts and feelings were as we read bulletin after bulletin depicting to the life the scenes of violence and bloodshed which rivaled and even surpassed in their horrors, those which were perpetrated in Paris, during the bloody French Revolution, for we are yet to find an instance there where the orphan was ruthlessly assailed, or women and children murdered and maltreated without cause or provocation, simply for belonging to another race or class of people.

What cause or provocation have the New York rabble for disloyalty to their country, and for their bloody, atrocious assaults on my countrymen? Are we their enemies? Have we tyrannized over them? Have we maltreated them? Have we robbed them? Are we alien enemies? And are we traitors? Has not the unrequited labor of nearly four million of our brethren added to the country's wealth? Have we not been loyal to the country, in season and out of season, through good report and evil? And even while your mob-fiends upheld the assassin knife, and brandished the incendiary torch over the heads of our wives and children and to burn their homes, we were doing our utmost to sustain the honor of our country's flag, to perpetuate, if possible, those civil, social, and political liberties, they, who so malignantly hate us, have so fully enjoyed. Oh! how causeless, senseless, outrageous, brutal, and violative of every sentiment of manhood, courage and humanity these attacks on our defenseless brethren have been!

Fearful as these mobs have been, I trust they may prove to be lessons, though fearful ones, to guide the popular and loyal masses in the country, in all times of national emergency and peril, for when the services of every citizen or denizen of the country are imperatively required to defend it against powerful and determined foes, either foreign or domestic, and there can be found a strong minority ready and willing to subvert the government by popular violence and tumult or a base submission unworthy the meanest varlet of some monarchy; much less the boasted citizens of this great and magnificent country, it will bring still more forcibly to their minds the truism that "eternal vigilance is the price of liberty."

These mobs are the stepping-stones upon which base traitors and demagogues hope to mount into arbitrary power, and to overawe and subvert liberty and law. They seek anarchy; and despotism, they think, must succeed. First anarchy, then despotism. They make the negro the catspaw or victim; but the loyalist and the friend of law and order cannot fail to see that every blow directed against the negro is directed against them. Our relation to the government is and has been that of unflinching, unswerving loyalty. Even when the government, by its every precept and practice, conserved the interests of slavery, and slaves were hunted down by United States soldiers and surrendered to traitorous slave-masters, the conduct of the negro was marked with distinguished loyalty. The instances

are too numerous to cite of their braving the most fearful
dangers to convey valuable information to the Union armies,
and for this, the half yet untold, such has been our reward.
Does not Milliken's Bend and Port Hudson furnish a chapter
of valor and faithful loyalty? Is there no justice in America—or
are we doomed to general massacre, as Mr. Blair said we would
be, in the event of the issue of the President's Emancipation
proclamation? If this be our doom let us prepare for the worst.

The siege of Charleston has not yet commenced. The preparations of Gen. Gillmore are very ample. There is no doubt
that this citadel of treason will fall. Every one is impatient at
the delay; but the siege of a stronghold upon which all of the
engineering skill of the rebel Confederacy has been lavished,
cannot be planned and matured in a day. They harass our fatigue
parties considerably with their shells, but they only succeed in
killing and wounding one or two men a day. These shells are
very disagreeable at first, but after one is under them a while
he can learn to become accustomed to them. The men sing,
dance, and play cards and sleep as carelessly within range of
them as if they were no more harmful than so many soap
bubbles.

This Morris Island is the most desolate heap of sand-hills I
ever saw. It is so barren that you cannot find so much as a
gypsum weed growing. Our situation is almost unbearable.
During the day the sun is intensely hot, and this makes the
sand hot; so we are sandwiched between the hot sun and the
hot sand. Happily, the evenings are cool and bracing—so
much so, that woolen blankets are not uncomfortable. The
bathing is most delightful. I think Morris Island beach the
most magnificent on the whole Atlantic coast. Had we in
the North such a bathing shore, it would soon eclipse Newport, Atlantic City or Long Branch, and the other bathing re-
sorts. The beach at some points is at least one-third of a mile in
width, descending at an almost imperceptible angle into the
more refreshing breakers.

There is quite a stir in the camp of the 54th just at this moment, created by an attempt on the part of the Paymaster and
Col. Littlefield of the 4th Connecticut volunteers (who has
been temporarily assigned to the command of our regiment
since the death of Col. Shaw, our lamented commander) to

pay us off with the paltry sum of $10 per month, the amount paid to contrabands. Col. Littlefield had the men drawn up in their company streets, and addressed them in a style something like this: "Gentlemen, I know that you are in want of money. Many of you have families who are dependent on you for support. The Paymaster refuses to pay any of the colored troops more than $10 per month. I have no doubt that Congress, when it meets next December, will pay you the balance of your pay. The government, in paying you this sum, only advances you this amount—it is not considered paying you off." Only one company consented to take this sum. The rest of the regiment are highly incensed at the idea that after they have been enlisted as Massachusetts soldiers, and been put into the active service of the United States government, they should be paid off as the drafted ex-slaves are. The non-commissioned officers are to be paid the same as the privates.

There is to be, according to the Colonel's and Paymaster's arrangement, no distinction. Our First Sergeants, Sergeant-Major, and other Sergeants are to be paid only $10 per month. Now, if this $10 per month is advanced by the Paymaster, and he is so confident or certain that the next Congress will vote us the pay that regularly enlisted soldiers, like the 54th, generally receive, why does he not advance the privates and non-commissioned officers their full pay? Or does he not fear that the next Congress may refuse to have anything to do with it, and conclude that if we could receive $10 and make out until then, we could make out with that amount to the end of our term? To offer our non-commissioned officers the same pay and reducing them to the level of privates, is, to say the least, insulting and degrading to them.

Then, again, if we are not placed on the same footing with other Massachusetts soldiers, we have been enlisted under false pretenses. Our enlistment itself is fraudulent. When Gov. Andrew addressed us at Readville on the presentation of our colors, he claimed us as Massachusetts soldiers. Frederick Douglass, in his address to the colored people to recruit the 54th, and who penned it by the authority of Gov. Andrew, declares that we form part of the quota of troops furnished by the State of Massachusetts. If this be the case, why make this invidious distinction? We perform the same duties of other

Massachusetts troops, and even now we have to perform fatigue duty night and day, and stand in line of battle from 3 to 5 A.M. with white soldiers, and for all this, not to say anything of the many perils we necessarily encounter, we are offered $10 per month or nothing until next December or January! Why, in the name of William H. Seward, are we treated thus? Does the refusal to pay us our due pander to the pro-slavery Cerberus? Negroes in the navy receive the same pay that the Irish, English, German, Spanish or Yankee race do, and take it as a matter of course. Why, sir, the State of Massachusetts has been rebuked and insulted through her colored soldiers, and she should protect us, as Gov. Andrew has pledged his word she would. Since our regiment has been in this department, an attempt has been made to substitute the dark for the light-blue pantaloons of the U. S. army. This was at St. Helena. Col. Shaw rejected them, and we continue to wear the uniform of the U.S. Infantry corps.

The ever-memorable anniversary of British West India Emancipation was observed by the non-commissioned officers of the 54th, by calling, on the 1st instant, a meeting, and passing a series of resolutions. This meeting was organized by the appointment of Sergeant-Major Douglass, Chairman, and Sergt. Fletcher, Co. A, Secretary. A long list of Vice-Presidents were appointed, representing nearly every State. Commissary-Sergeant Lee represented South Carolina; Sergt. Grey, Massachusetts; Sergt. Swails, Pennsylvania. A Committee, consisting of Sergts. Francis, Stephens, Barquet, Johnson and Gambier, presented the following resolutions, which were passed:

1. Resolved, That we look with joy upon the example set by Great Britain twenty-nine years ago in liberating the slaves in her West India Islands, thereby making a long stride in the pathway of civilization, and eliciting the gratitude of enthralled millions everywhere—contributing largely to influence the people of this country to seek the overthrow of that system which has brought the nation to the verge of dissolution. We hail with more than gratification the determination of our government to follow her great and good example as evinced by that glorious instrument of January 1st, 1863, proclaiming freedom to slaves of rebels in Southern States—the desire to purchase those in loyal States—the decision of Attorney-General Bates, and the

calling to its aid the strong arms and loyal hearts of its black citizens.

2. Resolved, That we have another day added to our small family of holidays; we hail the 1st of January as twin-sister to the 1st of August; and as we have met together within six miles of the birthplace of secession to commemorate this day, we trust that on the 1st day of January next, by the blessing of God on our arms, the city of Charleston will ring with the voices of free men, women and children shouting, "Truly, the day of Jubilee has come."

3. Resolved, That while we look forward with sanguine hope for that day, and have the arms in our hands to help bring it about, we will use them, and put forth all our energies, and never cease until our ears shall hear the jubilant bell that rings the knell of slavery.

4. Resolved, That in our humble opinion the force of circumstances has compelled the loyal portion of this nation to acknowledge that man is physically the same, differing only in the circumstances under which he lives, and that action—true, manly action, only—is necessary to secure to us a full recognition of our rights as men by the controlling masses of this nation; and we see in the army, fighting for liberty and Union, the proper field for colored men, where they may win by their valor the esteem of all loyal men and women—believing that "Who would be free, themselves must strike the blow."

5. Resolved, That we recognize in the brilliant successes of the Union armies the proofs that Providence is on our side; that His attributes cannot take sides with the oppressor.
Private John Peer, Co. B, died at 6 o'clock P.M. this instant.

G. E. S.

Robert E. Lee to Jefferson Davis

As the controversy over the Pennsylvania campaign continued in the southern press, several Richmond newspapers defended Lee, while the *Charleston Mercury* declared that it "is impossible for an invasion to have been more foolish and disastrous." A widely reprinted dispatch by Peter W. Alexander, a war correspondent for the *Savannah Republican*, questioned Lee's decision to continue attacking at Gettysburg after the first day of the battle. Lee wrote to the Confederate president from his headquarters near Orange Court House, about thirty miles west of Fredericksburg.

———————————

Camp Orange
8 Aug 1863

Mr President

Your letters of 28 July & 2 Aug have been recd., & I have waited for a leisure hour to reply, but I fear that will never come. I am extremely obliged to you for the attention given to the wants of this Army & the efforts made to supply them. Our absentees are returning, & I hope the earnest & beautiful appeal made to the country in your proclamation, may stir up the virtue of the whole people & that they may see their duty & perform it. Nothing is wanted but that their fortitude should equal their bravery to ensure the success of our cause. We must expect reverses, even defeats. They are sent to teach us wisdom & prudence, to call forth greater energies & to prevent our falling into greater disasters. Our people have only to be true & united, to bear manfully the misfortunes incident to war & all will come right in the end. I know how prone we are to censure, & how ready to blame others for the nonfulfilment of our expectations. This is unbecoming in a generous people & I grieve to see its expression. The general remedy for the want of success in a military commander is his removal. This is natural & in many instances proper. For no matter what may be the ability of the officer if he loses the confidence of his troops, disaster must sooner or later ensue. I have been prompted by these reflections more than once since my return from Penna. to propose to your Excy the propriety of selecting another commander for this army. I have seen & heard of expression of discontent in the public journals at the result of the expedition. I do not know how far this feeling extends in the army. My brother officers have been too kind to report it, & so far the troops have been too generous to exhibit it. It is fair however to suppose that it does exist, & success is so necessary to us that nothing should be risked to secure it. I therefore in all sincerity request your Excy to take measures to supply my place. I do this with the more earnestness because no one is more aware than myself of my inability for the duties of my position. I cannot even accomplish what I myself desire. How can I fulfil the expectations of others? In addition, I sensibly feel the growing failure of my bodily strength. I have not yet recovered from the attack I experienced the past spring. I am becoming more & more incapable of exertion, & am thus prevented from making the personal examinations & giving the personal supervision to the operations in the field which I feel to be necessary. I am so dull that in making use of the eyes of others I am frequently misled. Every thing therefore points to the advantages to be derived from a new commander, & I the more anxiously urge the matter upon your Excy from my belief that a younger & abler man than myself can readily be attained. I know that he will have as gallant & brave an army as ever existed to second his efforts, & it would be the happiest day of my life to see at its head a worthy leader; one that would accomplish more than I could perform & all that I have wished. I hope your Excy will attribute my request to the true reason. The desire to serve my country & to do all in my power to ensure the success of her righteous cause. I have no complaints to make of any one but myself. I have recd. nothing but kindness from those above me & the most considerate attention from my comrades & companions in arms. To your Excy I am specially indebted for uniform kindness & consideration. You have done every thing in your power to aid me in the work committed to my charge, without omitting anything to promote the general welfare. I pray that your efforts may at length be crowned with success & that you may long live to enjoy the thanks of a grateful people— With sentiments of great esteem I am very respectfully & truly yours

R E LEE
Genl

Jefferson Davis to Robert E. Lee

Lee would reply to this letter on August 22 by asking Davis to accept his resignation "whenever in your opinion the public service will be advanced" by a change in command. In conclusion, he wrote: "Beyond such assistance as I can give to an invalid wife and three houseless daughters I have no object in life but to devote myself to the defense of our violated country's rights."

Richmond, Va., Augt. 11, 1863.

Yours of the 8th. inst. has been received. I am glad to find that you concur so entirely with me as to the want of our country in this trying hour, and am happy to add that after the first depression consequent upon our disasters in the West, indications have appeared that our people will exhibit that fortitude which we agree in believing is alone needful to secure ultimate success.

It well became Sydney Johnston when overwhelmed by a senseless clamor to admit the rule that success is the test of merit, and yet there has been nothing which I have found to require a greater effort of patience than to bear the criticisms of the ignorant, who pronounce everything a failure which does not equal their expectations or desires, and can see no good result which is not in the line of their own imaginings. I admit the propriety of your conclusions, that an officer who loses the confidence of his troops should have his position changed, whatever may be his ability; but when I read the sentence, I was not at all prepared for the application you were about to make. Expressions of discontent in the public journals furnish but little evidence of the sentiment of an army. I wish it were otherwise even tho' all the abuse of myself should be accepted as the results of honest observation. I say, I wish I could feel that the public journals were not generally partisan nor venal.

Were you capable of stooping to it, you could easily sur-round yourself with those who would fill the press with your laudations, and seek to exalt you for what you had not done rather than detract from the achievements which will make you and your army the subject of history and object of the worlds admiration for generations to come.

I am truly sorry to know that you still feel the effects of the illness you suffered last Spring, and can readily understand, the embarrassments you experience in using the eyes of others, having been so much accustomed to make your own recon-naissances. Practice will however do much to relieve that embarrassment, and the minute knowledge of the country which you have acquired will render you less dependent for topographical information.

But suppose, my dear friend, that I were to admit, with all their implications, the points which you present, where am I to find that new commander who is to possess the greater ability which you believe to be required. I do not doubt the readiness with which you would give way to one who could accomplish all that you have wished, and you will do me the justice to be-lieve that if Providence would kindly offer such a person for our use, I would not hesitate to avail of his services.

My sight is not sufficiently penetrating to discover such hid-den merit if it exists, and I have but used to you the language of sober earnestness, when I have impressed upon you the propriety of avoiding all unnecessary exposure to danger be-cause I felt our country could not bear to lose you. To ask me to substitute you by some one in my judgment more fit to command, or who would possess more of the confidence of the army, or of the reflecting men in the country is to demand an impossibility.

It only remains for me to hope that you will take all possible care of yourself, that your health and strength may be entirely restored, and that the Lord will preserve you for the important duties devolved upon you in the struggle of our suffering country, for the independence which we have engaged in war to maintain. As ever very respectfully & truly yrs.

JEFFN. DAVIS

Wilbur Fisk to
The Green Mountain Freeman

Private Fisk of the 2nd Vermont Infantry had fought with the Sixth Corps at Marye's Heights and Salem Church during the Chancellorsville campaign and been posted to a reserve position at Gettysburg. He wrote from northern Virginia about the routines of camp life and their impact on the civilians living nearby.

————————————

Camp near Warrenton, Va.
Aug. 10, 1863

This camp is, I believe, without an official name at present. We are within about five miles of Warrenton, and about two from what was once the village of Waterloo. Warrenton is on your left, and Waterloo on your right as we face the enemy. You will perceive since writing my last we have moved our camp once more. This remarkable event occurred last Wednesday. I cannot say whether it was a military necessity, or a military convenience, or some other motive that prompted the change, but so far as my humble opinion can judge, I think the move a wise and judicious one. We went almost directly back to where we were encamped at first, only swinging in a half a mile or so nearer the Rappahannock. This may not be quite so good a camping place as that, but it is better than the last one, and makes a very acceptable compromise between the two. So, having become somewhat domesticated in our new position, I see no better way of employing one of the fairest mornings here that Virginia ever saw than by writing a line or so to my always welcome visitor, the *Freeman*. To be sure, nothing has transpired worth noticing, and there is nothing to write about; but incessant talkers and scribblers can generally manage to make themselves sufficiently troublesome without the aid of these superfluous auxiliaries.

Living in camp is a peculiar kind of life, but like every other situation one may become so accustomed to it that the evil and the good bear a relation to each other very nearly approaching to what may be found in almost any other pursuit. It may often seem dull and irksome, imposing burdensome restraints and duties not at all agreeable, but only the croaker will say the days are all dark and cheerless. We certainly have had hardships and privations to endure, and sometimes pretty severe ones, too; but we have also, now and then, a time for sport, joyous, health-inspiring, and full of fun. We have our games of chess, backgammon, draughts, cards, and others, to make merry many a dull, listless hour. We get occasionally a book to read, sometimes a paper, or what is often better than either, a letter from home. These last are the chinks that fill up many a useless, if not burdensome, hour, presenting to the soldier's mind something tangible that his thoughts will love to dwell upon. Many hours are pleasantly spent in answering these letters, many in visiting our friends in other portions of the camp, many more in fishing and foraging; and thus the day often closes before we are aware or wish to have it.

Since we formed our new camp we have been employed principally in making our tents comfortable and convenient. I would like to introduce the reader in to our camp this morning that he might see what pleasant houses we can improvise at short notice and very little expense. If you can imagine a pole or rail, whichever happens to be the handiest, elevated a little higher than one's head and held horizontally by two crotches, or by being strapped to two other rails that are perpendicular, which are inserted in the ground, one at each end, you have an idea of the first starting point in putting up a tent. The principal difficulty in all this is to get an ax or hatchet to cut a pole or sharpen the stake that is to be driven into the ground; but sometimes a big jack-knife will answer the purpose. The next thing is to throw our tent, which is nothing more nor less than two pieces of cotton or linen cloth, about five feet square buttoned together, over this ridge-pole and fasten the lower edge, or eaves, to small stakes as near the ground as we have calculated to have the tent come. The boys generally prefer from two to three feet. Here then is a tent for two men. Others can join on to the ends indefinitely, thus making a continual line of tents and have it all one. Along the centre of this we can build our bunks, running lengthwise, if we have tents sufficient, at a convenient height from the ground, making us a good seat or lounge in the day-time, and a bed for the night, or we can build them crosswise, if we prefer, and thus economize the room. Being open all around, the tent has the freest circulation of air, and we escape the unhealthy damp of living on the ground. Some of the boys fix themselves up stands for writing-desks, and cupboards for their cups, plates, and fragments of rations. Many other conveniences are constructed as necessity demands, or ingenuity invents. Generally we provide ourselves with all the proudest aristocrat needs to ask for, while the whole establishment would be costly at five dollars.

But in order to tell the whole story, which seeing I have begun I might as well continue, it will be necessary to speak of the manner in which the boys often procure the boards to build and ornament their singular habitations. The rapid disappearance however of barns and sometimes houses in the vicinity of where a new camp is being formed disclosed the secret. In our last camp the boys had begun to render their location quite pleasant and tasteful, supposing that the promise to stay there was made in good faith, and were quite loth to leave in consequence. Boards were plenty there as the Village had been vacated but not entirely destroyed. Every building there, of whatever description that was not occupied was speedily sacrificed to the boys' greediness for comfortable tents. They had been polluted with the heresy of secession, and the boys could not be made to feel any compunction for their downfall. As soon as a building was struck it was doomed. The first blow became a signal for a general attack, and soon all that was left would be a few scattering timbers and fragments of boards, while the road to camp would be lined with soldiers sweating under their loads of plunder.

There was one old miller left in the village of Waterloo, and I believe he is the last of his race in that spot. The village was burnt last summer or destroyed when we came, except one negro shanty. It used to contain two stores, a woollen factory besides the grist mill and blacksmith shop. Waterloo is on the Hedgeman river or Rappahannock proper, which stream is the southern boundary of Fauquier County of which Warrenton is the capitol. It is about sixty miles from Washington in a direction a little south of west. It is represented as having been a very thrifty place but like many of her sister towns it has become totally crushed out by this desolating war.

The camp of the 2nd regiment since moving from Waterloo, is on a small ridge crowned with a grove of bushes which unfortunately was not so extensive but that both ends of the regiment extended out into open sunlight. The 3rd, 4th and 6th are camped near by; the 5th are guarding Thompson's Ford. We have found lumber much more difficult to obtain here than at Waterloo. "But where there is a will there is a way" and where there is plenty of boards only two miles distant, who would be willing to lie in the dirt and go without them? Certainly not Vermonters, if we may judge from the throng that has been continually streaming back to that place over the hills and brooks and coming again with a load such as no lazy man would ever put on his shoulders. The officers had teams to bring their boards, but the men being more independent brought theirs on their backs. By dint of much perseverance and industry we have again established ourselves in camp pretty much to our satisfaction. Next week I may be able to chronicle another move.

Perhaps some one will question the constitutionality of our confiscating secesh boards and buildings in the manner I have described. I can only say it is a way we have of managing affairs here, and our officers had much rather help than hinder us. This morbid tenderness towards secesh property has been stifled by the rebels themselves, in their uncivilized conduct toward Union people when the power has been with them. Still I must confess it looks a little barbarous to go into a man's door yard, almost, as we did the miller's at Waterloo and tear down his barn and shed under his very eyes. This "erring brother" could only look demurely on and witness the progress of the destruction; he was powerless to prevent it. But they not only tore down his buildings they carried away his garden fence and ransacked and spoiled his garden. Excuse me reader, but I too went into that garden to help harvest the immature crop, and should have carried out my intentions, perhaps, but when I saw the woman and one of her children looking in sorrowful submission from the window at the wasteful destruction going on in their own garden—and it was a pretty one—my courage failed me, and I withdrew without taking so much as a pod of peas or a handful of potatoes. I never was caught stealing sheep or any thing of that sort, but I fancied I then had a very realizing sense of such a culprit's self-importance. It is impossible I suppose in war time but that such offences will come, and doubtless, in most cases they are well enough deserved, but when they are to happen to women and children that appear innocent in this case, I thought it would be as safe for me in the end to shirk the responsibility, and let them come through some one else; and certainly it was as consistent with my inclination on this particular occasion. Generally I am not behind when secession sinners are being punished after this fashion.

Frederick Douglass to George L. Stearns

On August 10 Douglass visited the capital, where, with the help of Senator Samuel C. Pomeroy, a Radical Republican from Kansas, he was able to meet with Secretary Stanton and President Lincoln. In his conversation with Stanton, Douglass agreed to help recruit black troops in Mississippi with the understanding that he would be commissioned as an officer. When the War Department failed to send the commission, Douglass would refuse to go south as a civilian.

Head Quars 1210 Chestnut St
Phila Aug 12th 1863

Maj Geo. L Stearns.
A.A.G. USV &c
    Dear Sir.

    According to your request I paid a flying visit to Washington. I spent the entire day (Monday) in calling upon the Heads of Depts there and other influential persons. I had the good fortune, early in the morning after reaching there, of meeting with Senator Pomeroy who at once offered to accompany me and facilitate my mission. First I called on Secty Stanton at the War Department who kindly granted me an interview of about thirty minutes which must be considered a special privilege in view of the many pressing demands upon his time and attention. His manner was cold and business like throughout but earnest.

    I at once gave him in brief my theory of the elements of negro character which should be had in view in all measures for raising colored troops. I told him that the negro was the victim of two extreme opinions. One claimed for him too much and the other too little. That it was a mistake to regard him either as an angel or a demon. He is simply a man and should be dealt with purely as such. That a certain percentage of negroes were brave and others cowardly. That a part were ambitious and aspiring and another part quite otherwise and that the theory in practice of the Government in raising colored troops should conform to these essential facts. The Secty instantly inquired in what respect the present conditions of colored enlistments conflicted with the views I had expressed. I answered "In the unequal pay accorded to colored soldiers and in the fact that no incentive was given to the ambition of colored soldiers and that the regulations confined them to the dead level of privates or non-commissioned officers." In answer the Secty went into an interesting history of the whole subject of the employment of Colored Troops briefly mentioning some of the difficulties and prejudices to be surmounted. Gave a history of the bill drawn up by himself, giving equal pay, the same rations, the same uniforms, and equipments, to colored troops as to White, and spoke with much apparent regret that his bill, though passed in the House was defeated in the Senate on what he considered quite an insufficient reason alleging that the President already possessed necessary powers to employ colored troops.

I told Mr Stanton that I held it to be the duty of Colored men to fight for the Government even though they should be offered but subsistance and arms considering that we had a cause quite independent of pay or place. But he quickly responded, "That he was in favor of giving the same pay to black as to white soldiers and also of making merit the criterion of promotion further stating his readiness to grant commissions to any reported to him by their superior officers for their capacity or bravery." The conclusion of our conversation was, that Gen Thomas was now vigorously engaged in organizing colored troops on the Mississippi and that he (the Secty) wished me to report to Gen Thomas and cooperate with him in raising said troops. I told the Secty that I was already at work under the direction of Major Stearns and that I thought that he would still need my services. But the Secty thought I had better report as aforesaid, adding that he would send me sufficient papers immediately. Thus you see, My dear Sir, that you have sent me to Washington to some purpose. Mr Stanton was very imperative in his manner, and I did not know but that you had suggested this prompt employment of me, from the fact that you inquired as to my willingness to go South in this work. My interview with Mr Stanton was free from compliments of every kind. There was nothing from him to me, nor from me to him, but I felt myself stopped in regard to your own efficient services not so much from his manner as from what I knew to be your own wishes.

From the War Office I went directly to the White House. Saw for the first time the President of the United States. Was received cordially and saw at a glance the justice of the popular estimate of his qualities expressed in the prefix "*Honest*" to the name of Abraham Lincoln. I have never seen a more transparent countenance. There was not the slightest shadow of embarrassment after the first moment. The drift of my communication to the President, except that I thanked him for extending equal protection to Colored Prisoners of War, was much the same as that to the Secty of War. I desired only to say so much as to furnish a text for a discourse from Mr Lincoln himself. In this I was quite successful for the President instantly upon my ceasing to speak proceeded with an earnestness and fluency of which I had not suspected him, to vindicate his policy respecting the whole slavery question and especially that in reference to employing colored troops. I need not here repeat his views. One remark, however, of his was of much significance. He said he had frequently been charged with tardiness, hesitation and the like, especially in regard to issuing his retaliatory proclamation. But had he sooner issued that proclamation such was the state of public popular prejudice that an outcry would have been raised against the measure. It would be said "Ah! We thought it would come to this. White men were to be killed for negroes. His general view was that the battles in which negroes had distinguished themselves for bravery and general good conduct was the necessary preparation of the public mind for his proclamation. But the best thing said by the President was "I have been charged with vacillation even by so good a man as Jno. Sherman of Ohio, but" said he "I think the charge cannot be sustained. No man can say that having once taken the position I have contradicted it or retreated from it." This remark of the President I took as our assurance that whoever else might abandon his anti slavery policy President Lincoln would stand firm to his. My whole interview with the President was gratifying and did much to assure me that slavery would not survive the War and that the

Country would survive both Slavery and the War. I am very sorry my Dear Sir, not to see you before leaving. I should be glad to have a line from you if convenient before I leave Rochester.

With Great Respect and Regard

Your Obt Servant
(Signed) Fredk Douglass

William H. Neblett to
Elizabeth Scott Neblett

Galveston, Texas, had been captured by a Union expeditionary force on October 4, 1862, then retaken by the Confederates on New Year's Day in 1863. Among the soldiers posted there was William H. Neblett, a lawyer and farmer from Grimes County who had enlisted in March 1863 as a private in the 20th Texas Infantry. Neblett wrote from Harrisburg (now part of Houston) to his wife, Elizabeth, who was managing their farm while raising five children. The mutiny he described among some of the troops of the Galveston garrison ended when their commanders promised to improve their food and grant limited furloughs.

———————

Harrisburg Texas
Aug 18th/63
Dear Lizzie

Yours of the 11th inst was recd a few days since. It is really astonishing how much pleasure it gives me to receive a letter from home and although there is no news related still the fact that all are well is sufficient to make the heart thrill with joy. There is a member of Capt. Dickie's Co here who says he left Orange yesterday week. He says John Scott was well & the Co well pleased with their situation. Two letters came to John after he left both of which I forwarded to him at Orange. We arrived here on the 16th and will remain here until 1st of Sept unless some unexpected order moves us. There has been considerable insubordination among the troops in Galveston lately. Col Lucketts Reg recently from the Rio Grande were furnished it seems with corn meal with worms in it. They refused to drill unless flour was furnished. Debray ordered all the troops on the Island including Lucketts out to the parade ground. All supposed it was for General Inspection but when the troops arrived Lucketts men still not suspecting anything were ordered to stack their arms, which they did. Their guns were taken away and the parade dismissed to their respective quarters. Since then Cooks Reg have demanded furlough and are in a state of insubordination have or did in one instance turn the guns of one of the Forts on the city declaring that they would fire on the town and troops if any attempt was made to disarm them. Yesterday Lucketts Reg was sent from the Island and are near here now and Browns Battallion sent down. This Co received orders also to go back to Galveston yesterday but the Bayou City being out of order the order was countermanded. I fear there will be some trouble if not blood-shed before the matter is settled. Gen Magruder passed here on the way to Galveston yesterday.

There is a great deal of demoralization in the Regiments here. From what I can hear such is not the case with the troops East of the Mississippi or those who have been in active service from Texas. I notice that you are quite despondend in your last letter and am sorry to see it. For my own part I have never lost hope even for a moment and moreover I do not think it prob-able that Texas will be invaded within the next six months by any force formidable enough to make head against the forces in Texas and moreover I think that within the next six months France will recognize our Independence & be followed soon by England & other powers. You ask what are you to do in case the yankees get to Grimes. This is like providing for a re-mote contingency but still one in the limits of possibility. In such a case all the advise I can give is to harness up your horses and have the wagon & oxen to help haul what provisions &c with all the wagons. The direction you go will have to be de-termined by the direction the yanks come from. I do not think an attempt will be made to subjugate Texas until East of the Mis is subjugated & at least until our great armies are whiped & dispersed. I do not anticipate any such direful result as this, and although the fall of Vicksburg was a sad reverse of fortune & the capture of Morgan one of less magnitude still I do not think such things should alarm the country into inaction or submission. You ask me what should be done on the farm. I cannot well answer the question. I want the hogs taken care of, and the pork hogs kept growing so that when the mast falls they will grow fast and fatter. I also wish that piece of new ground cleared up this month if possible. I suppose you have heard something of the bagging rope twine & salt which I was to get from Houston. I want the cotton hauled to the Gin & as soon as Ginned sent to [   ] of Houston who pay the Rail Road freight on the cotton while I am to pay the freight on the Bagging Rope Twine and salt. I also wish the cotton weighed and the weights kept so that I may know how much there is. As soon as the cotton is sold buy what you wish of flour and any other things. Calico is $4.00 per yard but it is best to buy & if I am where I can get it I will buy you some. Confederate money is going down fast & I believe as soon as the war ends it will be perfectly worthless and it may be so before then. Bonds may be worth something but there will be an effort made after the war to repudiate them unless they are in the hands of foreigners and the fear of a war prevents repudiating of such as are held by them. For this reason the money you get for the cotton had best be spent in paying debts contracted since the war and for such things as you wish. Have the seed saved from the cotton sent to McCune I shall want at least half of it for planting next year. The balance can be used for feeding the oxen this Winter & next Spring. I agreed to let McCune have a few bushels to plant (say 4 or 5 bus).

I am glad to hear that Bettie is getting well of her cholic. I hear that there is prevailing east of Lake Creek putrid soar throat or Diptheria and has been quite fatal. I feel uneasy sometimes about our children on that account. Tell Mary to write me another letter when you write again. I expect you had better try and get old Keifer to come and curry your leather about the first of Sept. You can get him to do so I expect for $10. or 12.00. Get him also to blacken the calf and coon skins. I expect you had better look out for some person to make your shoes and Marys & Walters. If you could get McDonald's negro to do so at $2 or 3.00 per day it will be about as cheap as you may expect, & you may have to pay $4 or 5.00 to get shoes for yourself made fit to wear. Perhaps you had better write to Mrs Mc Donald on the subject. I am in good health.

yours affectionately
Wm H Neblett

P.S. The following is used by the soldiers here for flux very sucessfully. Tea spoon full of salt and Table spoon full of vinegar with a little water to be repeated after every operation.

Richard Cordley:
Narrative of the Lawrence Massacre

Born in Ohio in 1837, William C. Quantrill taught school in Illinois and worked a farm in eastern Kansas before turning to rustling and slave-catching shortly before the war. In 1862 he became the leader of a guerrilla band based in Jackson County, Missouri. Commissioned by the Confederacy as a captain of partisan rangers, Quantrill engaged in an increasingly bitter conflict with the Union army and "Jayhawker" raiders from Kansas. On August 21, 1863, he led more than 400 men (among them the future bank robbers Cole Younger and Frank James) across the border in an attack on Lawrence. After killing more than 180 men and teenage boys, the raiders eluded pursuing Union cavalry and escaped into the wooded hills of western Missouri. Richard Cordley was the minister of the Plymouth Congregational Church in Lawrence and editor of *The Congregational Record*. Despite the destruction of his office during the raid, Cordley was able to write a narrative of the massacre for the September–October 1863 number of his church publication.

THE LAWRENCE MASSACRE.

The destruction of Lawrence had no doubt been long contemplated by the rebels of the border. Ever since the war commenced, rumors have been constantly reaching us of the maturing of such a purpose. Each rumor called forth efforts for defense. The people had become so accustomed to alarms as to be almost unaffected by them. At several times the prospect had been absolutely threatening. This was especially the case after the battle of Springfield, and again after the capture of Lexington by the rebels. The people had never felt more secure than for a few months preceding the raid of last August. The power of the rebellion was broken in Missouri, and the Federal force on the Border, while it could not prevent depredations by small gangs, seemed to be sufficiently vigilant to prevent the gathering of any large force. No rumors of danger had been received for several months.

Still many of the citizens did not feel that the place was entirely safe. Mayor Collamore, early in the summer, prevailed upon the military authorities to station a squad of soldiers in Lawrence. These soldiers were under command of Lieut. Hadley, a very efficient officer. Lieut. Hadley had a brother on Gen. Ewing's staff. About the first of August this brother wrote him that his spies had been in Quantrell's camp—had mingled freely with his men—and had learned from Quantrell's clerk, that they purposed to make a raid on Lawrence about the full of the moon, which would be three weeks before the actual raid. He told his brother to do all he could for the defense of the town, to fight them to the last, and never be taken prisoner, for Quantrell killed all his prisoners. Lieut. Hadley showed this letter to Mayor Collamore, who at once set about the work of putting the town in a state of defense. The militia was called out, pickets detailed, the cannon got in readiness, and the country warned. Had Quantrell's gang come according to promise, they would have been "welcomed with bloody hands to hospitable graves." Some one asked Quantrell, when in Lawrence, why he did not come before when he said he would. He replied, "You were expecting me then—but I have caught you napping, now."

It may be asked, why the people of Lawrence relaxed their vigilance so soon after receiving such authentic evidence of Quantrell's intentions? The city and military authorities made the fatal mistake of keeping the *grounds of their apprehensions a profound secret*. Nobody knew the reason of the preparation. Rumors were afloat, but they could not be traced to any reliable source. Companies came in from the country, but could not ascertain why they were sent for, and went home to be laughed at by their neighbors. Unable to find any reliable ground of alarm, people soon began to think that the rumors were like the other false alarms by which they had been periodically disturbed for the last two years. The course of the military authorities tended to strengthen this view.

Mayor Collamore sent to Fort Leavenworth for cannon and troops. They were at once sent over, but were met at Lawrence by a dispatch from Headquarters at Kansas City, ordering them back. A few days after, the squad of soldiers under Lieut. Hadley were ordered away. It was evident, therefore, that the military authorities at Kansas City, who ought to know, did not consider the place in danger. The usual sense of security soon returned. Citizens were assured that Quantrell could not penetrate the military line on the border without detection. They felt sure, too, that he could not travel fifty miles through a loyal country without their being informed of the approach of danger. The people never felt more secure, and never were less prepared, than the night before the raid.

REBEL SPIES.

There is no doubt Quantrell had spies in Lawrence for weeks before the raid, who kept him constantly informed of the condition of things. The sense of security felt by the people was so great, that everybody was permitted to go and come as he pleased. The familiarity of the rebels with the place and the people, abundantly proved this. Several of them, in all probability, came up the night before. One, asking where Jim. Lane was, was told that he was out of town. "No, he is not," replied the rebel, "did n't I see him at the railroad meeting last night?" Some ladies and gentlemen returning late the night before, saw horsemen stationed at the outskirts of the town. Supposing them to be citizen pickets they took no notice of the fact. So the town was guarded that night by rebel pickets. The design was doubtless to notice if any messenger came in to warn of danger, and to be sure that no alarm was given. They showed that they were familiar with the common expressions of the town. As they were riding round and doing their work of death, one cries to another—"Quantrell is coming!" "No he 'aint," says another, "he can't get here!"

THE APPROACH.

Quantrell assembled his gang about noon on the day before the raid, and started towards Kansas about two o'clock. They crossed the border between five and six o'clock, and struck directly across the prairie toward Lawrence. He passed through Gardner, on the Santa Fe road, about eleven o'clock at night.

Here they burned a few houses and killed one or two citizens. They passed through Hesper, ten miles southeast of Lawrence, between two and three o'clock. The moon was now down and the night was very dark and the road doubtful. They took a little boy from a house on Captain's Creek near by, and compelled him to guide them into Lawrence. They kept the boy during their work in Lawrence, and then Quantrell dressed him in a new suit of clothes, gave him a horse and sent him home. They entered Franklin about the first glimmer of day. They passed quietly through, lying upon their horses, so as to attract as little attention as possible. The command, however, was distinctly heard—"Rush on, boys, it will be daylight before we are there. We ought to have been there an hour ago." From here it began to grow light, and they traveled faster. When they first came in sight of the town they stopped. Many were inclined to waver. They said "they would be cut to pieces and it was madness to go on." Quantrell finally declared that *he* was going in, and they might follow who would. Two horsemen were sent in ahead to see that all was quiet in town. Those horsemen rode through the town and back without attracting attention. They were seen going through the Main street, but their appearance there at that hour was nothing unusual. At the house of Rev. S. S. Snyder a gang turned aside from the main body, entered his yard and shot him. Mr. Snyder was a prominent minister among the United Brethren. He held a commission as lieutenant in the Second Colored Regiment, which probably accounts for their malignity.

Their progress from here was quite rapid, but cautious. Every now and then they checked up their horses as if fearful to proceed. They were seen approaching by several persons in the outskirts of town, but in the dimness of the morning and the distance, they were supposed to be Union troops. As they passed the house of Mr. Joseph Savage, half a mile from town, one of them entered the yard and called at the door. Mr. Savage was just up and was washing himself. Having weak eyes, he was longer washing them, and was delayed thereby in going to the door. When he opened the door the rebel was just going out of the gate. His weak eyes doubtless saved his life, as he did not suspect the character of his visitor. They passed on in a body till they come to the high ground facing the Main street, when the command was given—"Rush on to the town!" Instantly they rushed forward with the yells of demons. The attack was perfectly planned. Every man knew his place. Detachments scattered to every section of the town, and it was done with such promptness and speed that before people could gather the meaning of their first yell, every part of the town was full of them. They flowed into every street and lane like water dashed upon a rock. Eleven rushed up to Mount Oread, from which all the roads leading into the town could be seen for several miles out. These were to keep watch of the country round about, lest the people should gather and come in upon them unawares. Another and larger squad, struck for the west part of the town, while the main body, by two or three converging streets, made for the hotel. The first came upon a camp of recruits for the Kansas Fourteenth. On these they fired as they passed, killing seventeen out of twenty two. This attack did not in the least check the speed of the general-advance. A few turned aside to run down and shoot fugitive soldiers, but the company rushed on at the command—"To the hotel!" which could be heard all over the town. In all the bloody scenes which followed, nothing equalled, in wildness and terror, that which now presented itself. The horsemanship of the guerrillas was perfect. They rode with that ease and abandon which are acquired only by a life spent in the saddle amid desperate scenes. Their horses scarcely seemed to touch the ground, and the riders sat with bodies and arms perfectly free, with revolvers on full cock, shooting at every house and man they passed, and yelling like demons at every bound. On each side of this stream of fire, as it poured in towards the street, were men falling dead and wounded, and women and children half dressed, running and screaming—some trying to escape from danger and some rushing to the side of their murdered friends.

THE CAPTURE OF THE HOTEL.

They dashed along the main street, shooting at every straggler on the sidewalk, and into almost every window. They halted in front of the Eldridge House. The firing had ceased and all was silence for a few minutes. They evidently expected resistance here, and sat gazing at the rows of windows above them, apparently in fearful suspense. In a few moments, Captain Banks, Provost Marshal of the State, opened a window and displayed a white flag, and called for Quantrell. Quantrell rode forward, and Banks, as Provost Marshal, surrendered the house, stipulating for the safety of the inmates. At this moment the big gong of the hotel began to sound through the halls to arouse the sleepers. At this the whole column fell back, evidently thinking this the signal for an attack from the hotel. In a few moments, meeting with no resistance, they pressed forward again, and commenced the work of plunder and destruction. They ransacked the hotel, robbing the rooms and their inmates. These inmates they gathered together at the head of the stairs, and when the plundering was done, marched them across the street on to Winthrop street under a guard. When they had proceeded a little distance, a ruffian rode up, and ordered a young man out the ranks, and fired two shots at him, but with no effect. One of the guard at once interposed, and threatened to kill the ruffian if one of the prisoners was molested. Quantrell now rode up and told them the City Hotel, on the river bank, would be protected, because he had boarded there some years ago and was well treated. He ordered the prisoners to go in there, and *stay in*, and they would be safe. The prisoners were as obedient to orders as any of Quantrell's own men, and lost no time in gaining the house of refuge. This treatment of the prisoners of the Eldridge House shows that they expected resistance from that point, and were relieved by the offer of surrender. They not only promised protection, but were as good as their word. Other hotels received no such favors, and had no such experience of rebel honor.

At the Johnson House they shot at all that showed themselves, and the prisoners that were finally taken and marched off, were shot a few rods from the house, some of them among the fires of the burning buildings. Such was the common fate of those who surrendered themselves as prisoners. Mr. R. C. Dix was one of these. His house was next door to the Johnson House, and being fired at in his own house, he escaped to the Johnson House. All the men were ordered to surrender. "All we want," said a rebel, "is for the men to give themselves up,

and we will spare them and burn the house." Mr. Dix and
others gave themselves up. They marched them towards town,
and when they had gone about two hundred feet, the guard
shot them all, one after another. Mr. Hampson, one of the
number, fell wounded, and lay as if dead till he could escape
unseen. A brother of Mr. Dix remained in the shop, and was
shot four times through the window, and fell almost helpless.
The building was burning over his head, and he was compelled
to drag himself out into the next building, which fortunately
was not burned. The air was so still that one building did not
catch fire from another.

After the Eldridge House surrendered, and all fears of resistance were removed, the ruffians scattered in small gangs to all
parts of the town in search of plunder and blood. The order
was "to burn every house and kill every man." Almost every
house was visited and robbed, and the men found in them
killed or left, according to the character or whim of the captors. Some of these seemed completely brutalized, while others
showed some signs of remaining humanity. One lady said that
as gang after gang came to her house, she always met them
herself, and tried to get them to talking. If she only got them
to talking, she could get at what little humanity was left in
them. Those ladies who faced them boldly, fared the best.

SCENE IN TOWN.

It is doubtful whether the world has ever witnessed such a
scene of horror—certainly not outside the annals of savage
warfare. History gives no parallel, where an equal number of
such desperate men, so heavily armed, were let perfectly loose
in an unsuspecting community. The carnage was much worse
from the fact that the citizens could not believe that men could
be such fiends. No one expected an indiscriminate slaughter.
When it was known that the town was in their possession, everybody expected they would rob and burn the town, kill all
military men they could find, and a few marked characters. But
few expected a wholesale murder. Many who could have escaped, therefore, remained and were slain. For this reason the
colored people fared better than the whites. They knew the
men which slavery had made, and they ran to the brush at

the first alarm. A gentleman who was concealed where he could see the whole, said the scene presented was the most perfect realization of the slang phrase, "Hell let loose," that ever could be imagined. Most of the men had the look of wild beasts; they were dressed roughly and swore terribly. They were mostly armed with a carbine and with from two to six revolvers strapped around them. It is doubtful whether three hundred such men were ever let perfectly loose before.

INSTANCES OF RESISTANCE.

The surprise was so complete that no organized resistance was possible. Before people could fully comprehend the real state of the case, every part of the town was full of rebels, and there was no possibility of rallying. Even the recruits in camp were so taken by surprise that they were not in their places. The attack could scarcely have been made at a worse hour. The soldiers had just taken in their camp guard, and people were just waking from sleep. By some fatal mistake, the authorities had kept the arms of the city in the public armory, instead of in each man's house. There could be no general resistance therefore from the houses. When the rebels gained possession of the main street, the armory was inaccessible to the citizens, and the judicious disposition of squads of rebels in other parts of the town, prevented even a partial rally at any point. There was no time nor opportunity for consultation or concert of action, and every man had to do the best he could for himself. A large number, however, did actually start with what arms they had towards the street. Most saw at once that the street could not be reached, and turned back. Some went forward and perished. Mr. Levi Gates lived about a mile in the country, in the opposite direction from that by which the rebels entered. As soon as he heard the firing in town, he started with his rifle, supposing that a stand would be made by the citizens. When he got to town he saw at once that the rebels had possession. He was an excellent marksman and could not leave without trying his rifle. The first shot made the rebel jump in his saddle, but did not kill him. He loaded again and fired one more shot, when the rebels came on him and killed him; and after he was dead, brutally beat his head in pieces.

Mr. G. W. Bell, County Clerk, lived on the side hill over-looking the town. He saw the rebels before they made their charge. He seized his musket and cartridge box with the hope of reaching the main street before them. His family endeavored to dissuade him, telling him he would certainly be killed. "They may kill *me*, but they cannot kill the principles I fight for. If they take Lawrence they must do it over my dead body." With a prayer for courage and help he started. But he was too late. The street was occupied before he could reach it. He endeavored then to get round by a back way, and come to the ravine west of the street. Here he met other citizens. He asked, "Where shall we meet?" They assured him it was too late to meet anywhere, and urged him to save himself. He turned back, apparently intending to get home again. The rebels were now scattered in all directions, and he was in the midst of them. A friend urged him to throw his musket away, which he did. Finding escape impossible, he went into an unfinished brick house, and got up on the joists above, together with another man. A rebel came in and began shooting at them. He interceded for his friend, and soon found that the rebel was an old acquaintance who had often eaten at his table. He appealed to him in such a way that he promised to save both their lives for old acquaintance sake, if they would come down. They came down, and the rebel took him out to about twenty of his companions outside. "Shoot him! Shoot him!" was the cry at once. He asked for a moment to pray, which they granted, and then shot him with four balls. His companion was wounded and lay for dead, but afterwards recovered. The treacherous rebel who deceived and murdered him, afterwards went to his house, and said to his wife, who was ignorant of her husband's fate: "We have killed your husband and we have come to burn his house." They fired it, but the family saved it. Mr. Bell was a man of excellent character, and leaves a wife and six children to miss and mourn him.

REBELS COWARDLY AS WELL AS BRUTAL.

What little resistance was offered to the rebels, developed their cowardice as much as the general license given them developed their brutality. On the opposite bank of the river twelve soldiers were stationed. When the rebels first came into town, they filled Massachusetts street clear to the river bank, firing into every house, and robbing every stable. They even attempted to cut the rope of the ferry. But these brave boys on the opposite side made free use of their rifles, firing at every butternut that came in sight. Their minnie balls went screaming up the street, and it was not many minutes before that section of the town was pretty much deserted; and if one of the ruffians by chance passed along that way, he was very careful not to expose himself to the bullets from across the river. The result was, all that section of the town which stretched along the river bank was saved. In this section stood Gov. Robinson's house, which was the first inquired for. Here was the armory, which they took possession of early, but left it with the most of its guns unharmed.

Another evidence of their cowardice was shown in the fact, that very few stone houses were molested. They shunned almost all houses which were closed tightly, so that they could not see in, when the inmates did not show themselves. There is a deep ravine, wooded but narrow, which runs almost through the centre of the town. Into this many citizens escaped. They often chased men into this ravine, shooting at them all the way. But *they never followed one into the ravine itself,* and seldom followed up to the brink. Whenever they came near to it, they would shy off as if expecting a stray shot. The cornfield west of the town was full of refugees. The rebels rode up to the edge often, as if longing to go in and butcher those who had escaped them, but a wholesome fear that it might be a double game, restrained them. A Mrs. Hindman lives on the edge of this cornfield. They came repeatedly to her house for water. The gang insisted on knowing what "was in that cornfield?" She, brave woman, replied, "Go in and see. You will find it the hottest place you have been in to-day." Having been in to carry drink to the refugees, she could testify to the heat. The rebels took her word and left. So every little ravine and thicket round the outskirts of the town were shunned as if a viper had been in it. Thus scores of lives were saved that would otherwise have been destroyed.

In almost every case where a determined resistance was offered, the rebels withdrew. Mr. A. K. Allen lives in a large brick house. A gang came to his door and ordered him out. "No!" replied the old gentleman, "if you want anything of me, come where I am—I am good for five of you." They took his word for it, and he and his house were thenceforth unmolested. The two Messrs. Rankin were out in the street trying to gain a certain house, when they were overtaken by six of the ruffians. They at once turned and faced their foes, drew their revolvers, and began to fire, when the whole six broke and fled. The cowards evidently did not come to fight, but to murder and steal.

INCIDENTS.

We can only give a few of the incidents of the massacre as specimens of the whole. The scenes of horror we describe must be multiplied till the amount reaches one hundred and eighty, the number of killed and wounded.

Gen. Collamore, Mayor of the city, was awakened by their shouts around his house. His house was evidently well known, and they struck for it first to prevent his taking measures for defense. When he looked out, the house was surrounded. Escape was impossible. There was but one hiding place—the well. He at once went into the well. The enemy entered the house and searched for the owner, swearing and threatening all the while. Failing to find him, they fired the house and waited round to see it burn. Mrs. Collamore went out and spoke to her husband while the fire was burning. But the house was so near the well that when the flames burst out they shot over the well, and the fire fell in. When the flame subsided, so that the well could be approached, nothing could be seen of Mr. Collamore or the man who descended into the well with him. After the rebels had gone, Mr. Lowe, an intimate friend of Gen. Collamore, went at once down the well to seek for him. The rope supporting him broke, and he also died in the well, and three bodies were drawn from its cold waters.

At Dr. Griswold's there were four families. The doctor and his lady had just returned the evening before from a visit east. Hon. S. M. Thorp, State Senator, Mr. J. C. Trask, Editor of the State Journal, Mr. G. W. Baker, Grocer, with their ladies, were boarding in Dr. Griswold's family. The house was attacked about the same time as Gen. Collamore's. They called for the men to come out. When they did not obey very readily, they assured them "they should not be harmed—if the citizens quietly surrendered, it might save the town." This idea brought them out at once. Mr. Trask said, "If it will help save the town, let us go." They went down stairs and out of doors. The ruffians ordered them to get into line, and to march before them towards town. They had scarcely gone twenty feet from the yard before the whole four were shot down. Dr. Griswold and Mr. Trask were killed at once. Mr. Thorp and Mr. Baker wounded, but apparently dead. The ladies attempted to come to their husbands from the house, but were driven back. A guard was stationed just below, and every time any of the ladies attempted to go from the house to their dying friends, this guard would dash up at full speed, and with oaths and threats drive them back. After the bodies had lain about half an hour, a gang rode up, rolled them over and shot them again. Mr. Baker received his only dangerous wound at this shot. After shooting the men, the ruffians went in and robbed the house. They demanded even the personal jewelry of the ladies. Mrs. Trask begged for the privilege of retaining her wedding ring. "You have killed my husband, let me keep his ring." "No matter," replied the heartless fiend, and snatched the relic from her hand. Dr. Griswold was one of the principal druggists of the place; Mr. Thorp was State Senator; Mr. Trask, Editor of the State Journal, and Mr. Baker one of the leading grocers of the place. Mr. Thorp lingered in great pain till the next day, when he died. Mr. Baker, after long suspense, recovered. He was shot through the neck, through the arm, and through the lungs.

The most brutal murder was that of Judge Carpenter. Several gangs called at his house and robbed him of all he had—but his genial manner was too much for them, and they all left him alive and his house standing. Toward the last, another gang came more brutal than the rest. They asked him where he was from. He replied, "New York." "It is you New York fellows that are doing the mischief in Missouri," one replied, and drew his revolver to shoot him. Mr. Carpenter ran into the house, up stairs, then down again, the ruffian after him and firing at him at every turn. He finally eluded them and slipped into the cellar. He was already badly wounded, so that the blood lay in pools in the cellar where he stood for a few minutes. His hiding place was soon discovered, and he was driven out of the cellar into the yard and shot again. He fell mortally wounded. His wife threw herself on to him and covered him with her person to shield him from further violence. The ruffian deliberately walked round her to find a place to shoot under her, and finally raised her arm and put his revolver under it, and fired so that she could see the ball enter his head. They then fired the house, but through the energy of the wife's sister, the fire was extinguished. This sister is the wife of Rev. G. C. Morse, of Emporia, who was making her first visit to her sister's house. The Judge had been married less than a year. He was a young man, but had already won considerable distinction in his profession. He had held the office of Probate Judge for Douglas county, and a year ago was candidate for Attorney General of the State.

Mr. Fitch was called down stairs and instantly shot. Although the second ball was probably fatal, they continued to fire until they lodged six or eight balls in his lifeless body. They then began to fire the house. Mrs. Fitch endeavored to drag the remains of her husband from the house, but was forbidden. She then endeavored to save his miniature, but was forbidden to do this. Stupified by the scene, and the brutality exhibited towards her, she stood there gazing at the strange work going on around her, utterly unconscious of her position or her danger. Finally one of the ruffians compelled her to leave the house, or she would probably have been consumed with the rest. Driven out, she went and sat down with her three little ones in front, and watched the house consumed over the remains of her husband. Mr. Fitch was a young man of excellent character and spirit. He was one of the "first settlers" of Lawrence, and taught the first school in the place. He was a member of the Congregational Church, and very active in both Church and Sabbath School. He was the man always to stand in the "gap." If there was anything which others had left undone, he was the man to see it and do it. If a subscription for library, papers or any other object in Church or Sabbath School, fell short of the needed amount, he always made up the deficiency. All these things were done so quietly, that few ever knew of them. He was a firm but quiet man, taking little part in public affairs, and it seems strange that the rebels should have exhibited towards him such malignity. The only explanation is, that they were enraged by the Union flag which the children had set up on the wood pile.

Mr. Sargent, another member of the same Church, and a most excellent Christian man, was shot with his wife clinging to him. The revolver was placed so near as to burn his wife's neck. He lingered some ten days and then died.

James Perine and James Eldridge were clerks in the "Country Store." They were sleeping in the store when the attack was made and could not escape. The rebels came into the store and ordered them to open the safe, promising to spare their lives. The moment the safe door flew open, they shot both of them dead and left them on the floor. They were both very promising young men, about seventeen years of age.

Mr. Burt was standing by a fence, when one of the rebels rode up to him and demanded his money. He handed up his pocket-book, and as the rebel took the pocket-book with one hand, he shot Mr. Burt with the other. Mr. Murphy, a short distance up the same street, was asked for a drink of water. He brought out the water, and as the fiend took the cup with his left hand he shot his benefactor with his right hand. Mr. Murphy was over sixty years of age. Mr. Ellis, a German blacksmith, ran into the corn in the Park, taking his little child with him. For some time he remained concealed, but the child growing weary began to cry. The rebels outside, hearing the cries, ran in and killed the father, leaving the child in its dead father's arms. Mr. Allbranch, a German, was sick in bed. They ordered the house cleared that they might burn it. The family carried out the sick man on the mattrass, and laid him in the yard, when the rebels came out and killed him on his bed, unable to rise. These are a species of cruelty to which savages have never yet attained.

But even the fiendishness of these deeds was surpassed. Mr. D. W. Palmer, formerly of Andover, Mass., but one of the early settlers of Kansas, kept a gun shop just south of the business part of the town, on the main street. His position prevented escape, but he and his shop were spared till near the last. As a large gang of drunken rebels were going out, they came upon his shop. Mr. Palmer and another man were standing by the door. They fired upon them, wounding both, and then set fire to the shop. The shop being old and all of wood, without plastering, burned rapidly. While it was burning, the rebels took up the wounded men, bound their hands together and threw them into the burning shop. A woman who was standing on the opposite sidewalk, says she saw the poor men get up among the flames and endeavor to come out, but were pushed back by the guns of the torturers. The fire having consumed the bandages from their hands, she saw Mr. Palmer throw up his hands, and cry, "O God, save us!" and then fall lifeless among the embers. The fiends all this time stood around the building shouting and cheering, and when the poor men fell dead, they gave one shout of triumph and passed on. We have been slow to believe this terrible story; but two reliable persons, in full sight, witnessed the scene, and a score of circumstances corroborate it. It comes the nearest to the old description of the fiends around the pit of anything we have ever heard.

The most severely wounded man was Mr. Thornton. After being awakened by the firing in the street and around him, he remained up stairs till the house was burning. He then came down and ran. The rebels fired at him, inflicting three wounds in his hip. As he was attempting to get over some bars into a yard, another shot struck him back of the shoulder and passed down through the whole length of the back and out at the hip. His wife followed him and clung to him to shield him from further violence. The rebel sat on his horse over them, and finally got his pistol between the two and fired again, the ball going through his hat, grazing his eye and passing through his cheek. The fellow then cried out—"I can kill you," and began beating him over the head with the butt of his revolver, till the poor man fell senseless from exhaustion. The brute, not yet satisfied, leveled his revolver to shoot him again, but the wife flew at him, exclaiming, "You are not going to shoot him again," and pushed the revolver aside. The fellow soon left, supposing his victim dead. Mr. Thornton still lives, but both his legs are helpless. He will probably be a cripple for life.

Age was no protection. Many of the oldest people in town were the most brutally murdered. It was said Quantrell ordered his men to burn no churches and kill no ministers. Still they burned the Colored Church in Lawrence, and the Congregational Church of Wakarusa. They did not set fire to the Colored Church, but they set fire to a little wood shanty right under its walls, and must have designed to burn the Church, as they must have known the Church would catch from the shanty, and there could be little object in burning the one except for the sake of burning the other. The Church at Wakarusa was just finished. It was five miles from Lawrence (south), and they took it on their way out. While it was burning, the whole band gathered around, cheering and yelling, as if they were doing some specially congenial work. The first and the last man killed were preachers—Rev. Mr. Snyder was the first, and Mr. Rothrock—a Dunkard preacher—the last. Mr. Rothrock was an old man of very excellent character. He lived ten miles south of the town, and on their way out several rebels stopped at his house and ordered breakfast. His wife cooked them a good breakfast which they ate with good relish. After rising, they inquired about the old gentleman, and some one told them "he was a preacher." "We intend to kill all the d—d preachers," and at once shot him and left him for dead. He lived, however, and may recover. Rev. H. D. Fisher, they hunted like a wild beast, and it was almost a miracle that he was not burned in his house. Rev. Mr. Paddock they inquired for repeatedly, shot into his house and shot at him. Rev. R. Cordley they asked for in a number of places, as "that negro preacher," "negro harborer," and as "that abolition preacher who had been preaching at Kansas City." A lady, hoping to save his house, told one of them to whom it belonged, supposing they would spare a minister's house. He immediately whirled his horse round and rode up to the house and set it on fire. However others might have fared, there can be no doubt but these three would have been killed if they had been found.

As we said before, age was no protection. Mr. Longley lived about a mile from town. He was about sixty years of age. He was a very quiet, peaceable man, taking no part in public affairs, any further than to perform the duties of a private citizen and a Christian. He and his wife were living quietly on their farm. Two of the pickets stationed outside the town, while their bloody work was being done in town, come to his house.

His wife begged them to be merciful. "They were old people and could not live long at best." They heeded none of her entreaties, but shot the old gentleman in his yard. The first shot not doing its work, they shot again and again, and then proceeded to burn the house. Through the energy of the old lady, the fire was put out and the house saved.

THE COLORED PEOPLE.

The colored people were pursued with special malignity, but they knew the character of their old masters so well that they all ran who could, at the first alarm. Few, comparatively, were killed, therefore. Most of the killed were the old and decrepid, who could not run. Old Uncle Frank, as he was called, was about ninety years old. He was born in "Old Virginia." He said when he first came to Lawrence, "When I was a slave I pray de Lord to let me go some whar so as I could tend meetins all I wanted to. And now de Lord has answered my prayer." He was a short, heavy set man, lame with "rheumatiz," and compelled to hobble round on his cane. Still he would work, getting a job of chopping at one place and a job of hoeing at another. In this way, he earned what little his simple habits required. He always worked faithfully and did his work well, though slow. When the rebels came he was unable to escape. He was seen and shot. He fell and was left for dead. After a while, when he thought himself unobserved, he got up and endeavored to escape. Some of the rebels seeing him, dashed upon him and killed him.

"Uncle Henry" was another decrepid old negro. He hid in a barn, and was killed, and burned up in the building. Old man Stonestreet was a Baptist preacher among the colored people. He was about sixty. He also was killed, as was Mr. Ellis, another old man of about sixty. Anthony Oldham was another preacher and a man of fine character and of great influence. He was shot in his own door in the presence of his daughter.

ESCAPES.

There were many hair-breadth escapes. Many escaped to the cornfields near to town; others escaped to the "friendly brush" by the river bank. The ravine which runs almost through the centre of the town, proved a safe refuge to scores. The cornfield west of town and the woods east, were all alive with refugees. Many hid in the "Park" which was planted with corn. Many others, who could get no further, hid among the weeds and plants in their gardens. Mr. Strode, colored blacksmith, had a little patch of tomatoes, not more than ten feet square. He took his money and buried himself among the vines. The rebels came up and burned his shop, not more than ten feet off, but did not discover him.

Mr. Hampson, of whom we spoke before, lay wounded close by a burning building. It would be certain death to show signs of life. His wife, therefore, who stood by him, asked one of the rebels to help her carry her husband's body away from the flames. He took hold of Hampson and carried him out of reach of the fire without discovering that he was alive. As soon as she could, his wife helped him on to a hand-cart, and covered him up with rags, and then drew the whole away out of danger. The rebels she passed thought her crazy for "drawing off that load of old rags."

One of the most wonderful escapes was that of Rev. H. D. Fisher. We give an account of it in his own words, in a letter to a friend in Pittsburg:

"When Quantrell and his gang came into our town, almost all were yet in their beds. My wife and second boy were up, and I in bed, because I had been sick of quinsy. The enemy yelled and fired a signal. I sprang out, and my other children, and we clothed ourselves as quick as it was possible.

I took the two oldest boys and started to run for the hill, as we were completely defenceless and unguarded. I ran a short distance, and felt I would be killed. I returned to my house, where I had left my wife with Joel, seven years old, and Frank, six months old, and thought to hide in our cellar. I told Willie, twelve years old, and Eddie, ten years old, to run for life, and I would hide. I had scarcely found a spot in which to secrete myself, when four murderers entered my house and demanded of my wife, with horrid oaths, where that husband of hers was, who was hid in the cellar. She replied, "The cellar is open; you can go and see for yourselves. My husband started over the hill with the children." They demanded a light to search. My wife gave them a lighted lamp, and they came, light and revolvers in hand, swearing to kill me at first sight. They came within eight feet of where I lay, but my wife's self-possession in giving the light had disconcerted them, and they left without seeing me. They fired our house in four places; but my wife by almost superhuman efforts, and with baby in arms, extinguished the fire. Soon after, three others came and asked for me. But she said, 'Do you think he is such a fool as to stay here? They have already hunted for him, but, thank God! they did not find him.' They then completed their work of pillage and robbery, and fired the house in five places, threatening to kill her if she attempted to extinguish it again. One stood, revolver in hand, to execute the threat if it was attempted. The fire burned furiously. The roof fell in, then the upper story, and then the lower floor; but a space about six by twelve feet was by great effort kept perfectly deluged with water by my wife to save me from burning alive. I remained thus concealed as long as I could live in such peril. At length, and while the murderers were still at my front door and all around my lot, watching for their prey, my wife succeeded, thank God, in covering me with an old dress and a piece of carpet, and thus getting me out into the garden and to the refuge of a little weeping willow covered with 'morning-glory' vines, where I was secured from their fiendish gaze and saved from their hellish thirst for my blood. I still expected to be discovered and shot dead. But a neighbor woman who had come to our help, aided my wife in throwing a few things saved from the fire over and around the little tree where I lay, so as to cover me more securely."

Mr. Riggs, District Attorney, was set upon by the vilest ruffian in the lot. His wife rushed to his side at once. After a short parley the man drew his revolver and took aim. Mr. Riggs pushed the revolver aside and ran. The man started after him, but Mrs. Riggs seized hold of the bridle rein and clung to it till she was dragged round a house, over a wood pile, and through the yard back on to the street again. Mr. Riggs was still in sight, and the man was taking aim at him again, when Mrs. Riggs seized the other rein and timed his horse round, and Mr. Riggs was beyond reach. All this time the man was swearing and striking at her with his revolver, and threatening to shoot her.

Old Mr. Miner hid among the corn in the Park. Hearing the racket around Mr. Fisher's house near by, he ventured to the edge of the corn to gratify his curiosity. He was seen and immediately shot at. He ran back into the corn, but had not proceeded far before he heard them breaking down the fence. The corn was evidently to be searched. He ran, therefore, *through* the corn, and lay down among the weeds beyond. The weeds only partially covered him, but it was the best he could do. He had scarcely lain down, when the rebels came dashing through the corn, and stationing a picket at each corner of the field to prevent escape, they searched the field through but found no one. They did not happen to look among the grass almost at their very feet.

Near the centre of the town was a sort of out-door cellar with a very obscure entrance. A woman, whose name we have been unable to obtain, but who ought to be put on record as one of the heroines of that day, took her station at a convenient distance from this cellar. Every poor fugitive that came into that region, she directed into this hidden cellar. Thus eight or ten escaped from the murderers. Finally, the rebels noticing that their victims always disappeared when they came into this locality, suspected this woman of aiding in their escape. They demanded of her that she should show their hiding place. She refused. One of them drew his revolver, and pointing it at her, said, "Tell us or I will shoot you." "You may shoot me," answered the brave woman, "but you will not find the men." Finding they could not intimidate her, they left.

Mr. Bergen was wounded and then taken off with six or eight other prisoners. After taking them a short distance, their captors shot all of them dead but Mr. Bergen. He was lying down exhausted from loss of blood, and for some reason they passed him by. There he lay among the dead, feigning death. After lying a short time, a rebel rode up, and discovering he was not dead, took aim at his head and fired. He felt the ball pass and instinctively dropped his head, and the rebel supposing he had completed his work, rode off. His head was now brought under the body of a young man who had been killed with the rest. There he lay, the living under the dead, till the rebels left town. At one time, the young man's mother came to wash the blood from the face of her murdered son. Mr. Bergen begged her not to move her son's body, as his only hope of life was in lying still with his head under the lifeless corpse.

Several saved themselves by their ready wit. An officer in the camp of recruits, when the attack was made, ran away at full speed. He was followed by several horsemen, who were firing at him continually. Finding escape impossible, he dashed into the house of a colored family, and in the twinkling of an eye, slipped on a dress and a shaker bonnet, passed out of the back door and walked deliberately away. The rebels surrounded the house, and then some of them entered and searched, but found no prey.

A son of John Speer hid for some time under the side-walk. The fire soon drove him into the street, which was full of rebels. He went boldly up to them and offered his services in holding horses. They asked his name, and thinking that the name Speer would be his death warrant, he answered "John Smith," and he remained among them unharmed to the last.

One man was shot as he was running away, and fell into a gutter. His wife, thinking him killed, began to wring her hands and scream. The rebel thinking from this her husband was dead, left. As soon as he was gone, the man said, "Don't take on so, wife, I don't know as I am hit at all." And so it proved.

Mr. Winchell, being hard pressed, ran into Mr. Reynolds' house (Episcopal Minister's). Mrs. Reynolds at once arrayed him in female attire, and shaved off his whiskers with a pen knife, and set him in a rocking chair with a baby in his arms, and christened him "Aunt Betsie." The rebels searched the house, but did not disturb "Aunt Betsie."

THE SCENE AFTER THE MASSACRE.

As the scene at their entrance was one of the wildest, the scene after their departure was one of the saddest that ever met mortal gaze. Massachusetts street was one bed of embers. On this one street, seventy-five buildings, containing at least twice that number of places of business and offices, were destroyed. The dead lay all along the side-walk, many of them so burned that they could not be recognized, and could scarcely be taken up. Here and there among the embers, could be seen the bones of those who had perished in the buildings and been consumed. On two sides of another block, lay seventeen bodies. Almost the first sight that met our gaze, was a father, almost frantic, looking for the remains of his son among the embers of his office. The work of gathering and burying the dead soon began. From every quarter they were being brought in, until the floor of the Methodist Church, which was taken as a sort of hospital, was covered with dead and wounded. In almost every house could be heard the wail of the widow and orphan. The work of burial was sad and wearying. Coffins could not be procured. Many carpenters were killed and most of the living had lost their tools. But they rallied nobly and worked night and day, making pine and walnut boxes, fastening them together with the burnt nails gathered from the ruins of the stores. It sounded rather harsh to the ear of the mourner, to have the lid *nailed* over the bodies of their loved ones; but it was the best that could be done. Thus the work went on for three days, till one hundred and twenty-two were deposited in the Cemetery, and many others in their own yards. Fifty-three were buried in one long grave. Early on the morning after the massacre, our attention was attracted by loud wailings. We went in the direction of the sound, and among the ashes of a large building, sat a woman, holding in her hands the blackened skull of her husband, who was shot and burned in that place. Her cries could be heard over the whole desolated town, and added much to the feeling of sadness and horror which filled every heart.

THE RESULT.

The whole number of persons known to be killed, or who died from wounds, was one hundred and forty-three. It is probable some others were killed and burned and never found. There were about twenty-five wounded, most of them severely. Only two of the wounded have since died—the rest are recovering. Several men are now walking our streets who had balls through their heads or lungs.

The loss of property has been variously estimated; some putting it as low as $750,000, and others as high as $2,500,000. We think it cannot fall below $1,500,000.

The business of the place was mainly on Massachusetts

street, between Winthrop and Warren—a space of about 1,800 feet. This was one continued line of stores on both sides. In this space about seventy-five buildings were destroyed. Only one block, containing two stores, remained, and those two stores were robbed. On the lower end of the street there also remain two or three small buildings and one grocery store. In other parts of the town there were about seventy-five dwelling houses burned. As many more were fired, but saved by the women. The loss in buildings and goods could be very nearly estimated. But these by no means constitute the whole. All the rooms over the stores were occupied as offices or by families. The loss in the Eldridge House alone was beyond all the estimates yet made. The original cost of the house is said to have been $70,000. In the lower story were five stores and a law office. In these stores were doubtless $60,000 in goods. There were sixty inmates in the hotel, with their personal baggage. Many of these were families boarding permanently, with all their personal and household goods there. Estimating the building at its original cost, the loss in that house would not fall much short of $150,000. Then almost every house in town was robbed, and every man, woman and child that could be found.

On their way out of town, also, the rebels burned a large share of the farm houses along their route for about ten miles, when they were overtaken by citizens in pursuit.

In this narrative we have not pretended to give all the details, but only a part of those that have come to our knowledge in the regular performance of duty. Every house has a story almost as thrilling as any to which we have referred.

Lawrence has been stunned by the blow, but not killed. We feel confident she will rise from her ashes stronger than ever.

Ulysses S. Grant to Abraham Lincoln

After the fall of Vicksburg Grant wrote to Halleck and proposed mounting a campaign against Mobile, Alabama. On August 9 President Lincoln wrote to Grant that while an expedition against Mobile was "tempting," the ongoing French intervention in Mexico made him "greatly impressed with the importance of re-establishing the national authority in Western Texas as soon as possible." Lincoln added that Brigadier General Lorenzo Thomas was returning to the Mississippi Valley to raise more black troops, and observed that recruiting blacks "works doubly, weakening the enemy and strengthening us." In closing, the President asked if Grant had received his letter of July 13 (p. 377 in this volume). Grant replied from Cairo, Illinois, where he had been visiting with his family.

———————————

Cairo Illinois
August 23d 1863,

HIS EXCELLENCY A. LINCOLN
PRESIDENT OF THE UNITED STATES,
SIR:

Your letter of the 9th inst. reached me at Vicksburg just as I was about starting for this place. Your letter of the 13th of July was also duly received.

After the fall of Vicksburg I did incline very much to an immediate move on Mobile. I believed then the place could be taken with but little effort, and with the rivers debouching there, in our possession, we would have such a base to opperate from on the very center of the Confederacy as would make them abandon entirely the states bound West by the Miss. I see however the importance of a movement into Texas just at this time.

I have reinforced Gen. Banks with the 13th Army Corps comprising ten Brigades of Infantry with a full proportion of Artillery.

I have given the subject of arming the negro my hearty sup-

488

port. This, with the emancipation of the negro, is the heavyest blow yet given the Confederacy. The South rave a greatdeel about it and profess to be very angry. But they were united in their action before and with the negro under subjection could spare their entire white population for the field. Now they complain that nothing can be got out of their negroes.

There has been great difficulty in getting able bodied negroes to fill up the colored regiments in consequence of the rebel cavalry runing off all that class to Georgia and Texas. This is especially the case for a distance of fifteen or twenty miles on each side of the river. I am now however sending two expeditions into Louisiana, one from Natchez to Harrisonburg and one from Goodriche's Landing to Monroe, that I expect will bring back a large number. I have ordered recruiting officers to accompany these expeditions. I am also moving a Brigade of Cavalry from Tennessee to Vicksburg which will enable me to move troops to a greater distance into the interior and will facilitate materially the *recruiting service.*

Gen. Thomas is now with me and you may rely on it I will give him all the aid in my power. I would do this whether the arming the negro seemed to me a wise policy or not, because it is an order that I am bound to obey and do not feel that in my position I have a right to question any policy of the Government. In this particular instance there is no objection however to my expressing an honest conviction. That is, by arming the negro we have added a powerful ally. They will make good soldiers and taking them from the enemy weaken him in the same proportion they strengthen us. I am therefore most decidedly in favor of pushing this policy to the enlistment of a force sufficient to hold all the South falling into our hands and to aid in capturing more.

Thanking you very kindly for the great favors you have ever shown me I remain, very truly and respectfully

your obt. svt.
U. S. GRANT
Maj. Gn.

Jonathan Worth to Jesse G. Henshaw

Between July and September 1863 about one hundred "peace meet-ings" were held in North Carolina, most of them in the central Pied-mont region of the state. Some of the speakers at the rallies called for negotiations with the North resulting in Confederate independence, while others advocated reunion on terms that would preserve slavery. William H. Holden, the editor of the Raleigh *North Carolina Stan-dard* and an opponent of secession in 1861, became the leader of the "Peace Party." His support for an "honorable peace" caused a breach with his political ally, Governor Zebulon B. Vance, a critic of the Davis administration who supported continued prosecution of the war. A successful lawyer from the Piedmont region who had opposed se-cession, Jonathan Worth was elected state treasurer in 1862. He wrote about the peace movement to Jesse G. Henshaw, a farmer and mill owner in Randolph County. The peace meetings ended in early Sep-tember after Confederate soldiers ransacked Holden's newspaper of-fices and Governor Vance issued a proclamation denouncing the movement. Nevertheless, candidates who advocated seeking an "honorable peace" would win six out of ten seats when the state voted in the fall for representatives to the Second Confederate Con-gress.

RALEIGH *Aug. 24, 1863.*

*   *   *   *   *   *   *

I hardly know whether I am in favor of the peace meetings or not. On the one hand, it is very certain that the President and his advisers will not make peace, if not forced into it by the masses and the privates in the army. Their cry echoed by al-most every press is: "Independence, or the last man and the last dollar." The North will not make peace on the basis of Independence. The real question which nobody—not even Holden—will squarely present is, shall we fight on with certain desolation and impoverishment and probable ultimate defeat; or make peace on the basis of reconstruction? Nearly every public man—every journal, political and religious, and every politician, in the fervor of their patriotism, has vociferously declared in favor of "the last man and the last dollar" cry. These classes cannot be consistent unless they still cry war. Many believe the masses in their saner hours, never approved the war and would rather compromise on the basis of the Constitution of the U. S. with such additional securities against any future rupture as could be agreed on. If there be any sense in peace meetings they mean reconstruction. They may rather do mischief if they are not so imposing as to force the administration to reconstruction. They will be impotent and mischievous if the *army* is still for war to the last man and the last dollar. I do not know the sentiments of the rank and file of the army.

I am for peace on *almost any terms* and fear we shall never have it until the Yankees dictate it. Upon the whole I would not go into a peace meeting now or advise others to go into one, particularly in Randolph—but I have no repugnance to them in other places and see no other chance to get to an early end of this wicked war, but by the action of the masses who have the fighting to do. If an open rupture occur between Gov. V. and Mr. Holden, it will be ruinous to us. There ought to be none and I trust there will be none. There is no difference between them that justifies a breach. The Governor concedes the right of the people to hold meetings and express their wishes, but he deems such meetings inexpedient and tending to dissatisfaction and disorganization in the army and that no honorable peace can be made, after we cease to present a strong military front. The Gov. acts consistently and in the eminent difficult position he occupied, I doubt whether any pilot could manage the crippled ship in such a storm with more skill. Repress all expressions of dissatisfaction against him. He values the extravagant eulogiums of the fire-eaters at their worth. They are playing an adroit game. They would get up dissention between the Gov. and Holden and then break up the Conservative party and seize the helm of Government.

NEW SALEM.

John M. Schofield to Thomas Ewing Jr.

Four days after the Lawrence massacre Major General John M. Schofield, the Union commander in Missouri, proposed draconian measures against the border counties that sheltered Quantrill. By the time he received Schofield's letter, Brigadier General Thomas Ewing Jr., the commander of the Missouri border district (and William T. Sherman's brother-in-law), had already taken action. On August 25 Ewing ordered the expulsion within fifteen days of the entire population of Jackson, Cass, Bates, and northern Vernon counties, except for the residents of five garrisoned towns. Ewing's General Orders No. 11 would be enforced mainly by Union troops from Kansas, who expelled between 10,000 and 20,000 persons from the border district and burned most of its houses, barns, and crops. Quantrill's men would remain in western Missouri until early October, when they killed more than eighty Union soldiers at Baxter Springs in southeastern Kansas before escaping to Texas.

HEADQUARTERS DEPARTMENT OF THE MISSOURI,
Saint Louis, August 25, 1863.

Brigadier-General EWING,
Commanding District of the Border, Kansas City, Mo.:

GENERAL: I inclose a draught of an order which I propose to issue in due time. I send it to you in order that you may make the necessary preparations for it. Such a measure will, of course, produce retaliation upon such loyal people as may be exposed to it, and they should, as far as possible, be removed to places of safety before the execution of the order is commenced or the purpose to execute it is made public. Also, it is necessary to be quite certain that you have the power to put down the rebel bands and prevent retaliation like that recently inflicted upon Lawrence, if, indeed, that can be regarded or was intended as an act of retaliation. My information relative to that distressing affair is too imperfect to enable me to judge accurately on this point. But it occurs to me as at least probable that the massacre and burning at Lawrence was the immediate consequence of the inauguration of the policy of removing from the border counties the slaves of rebels and the families of bushwhackers. If this is true, it would seem a strong argument against the wisdom of such policy. You are in position to judge of all this better than I can. At all events, I am pretty much convinced that the mode of carrying on the war on the border during the past two years has produced such a state of feeling that nothing short of total devastation of the districts which are made the haunts of guerrillas will be sufficient to put a stop to the evil. Please consider the matter fully and carefully, and give me your views in regard to the necessity for the application of such severe remedy, and of the wisdom of the method proposed. I will be guided mainly by your judgment in regard to it. If you desire the order to be issued as I have written it, or with any modifications which you may suggest, please inform me when you are ready for it.

Very respectfully, your obedient servant,

J. M. SCHOFIELD,
Major-General.

A band of robbers and murderers, under the notorious Quantrill, has been for a long time harbored and fed by the disloyal people of Jackson, Cass, and Bates Counties, Missouri, and have driven out or murdered nearly all the loyal people of those counties; and, finally, on the —— of the present month these brigands, issuing suddenly from their hiding-places, made a descent upon the town of Lawrence, in Kansas, and in the most inhuman manner sacked and burned the town, and murdered in cold blood a large number of loyal and unoffending citizens. It is manifest that all ordinary means have failed to subdue the rebellious spirit of the people of the counties named, and that they are determined to harbor and encourage a band of scoundrels whose every object is plunder and murder. This state of things cannot be permitted longer to exist, and nothing less than the most radical remedy will be sufficient to remove the evil. It is therefore ordered that the disloyal people of Jackson, Cass, and Bates Counties will be given until the —— day of ——— to remove from those counties, with such of their personal property as they may choose to carry away. At the end of the time named all houses, barns, provisions, and other property belonging to such disloyal persons, and which can be used to shelter, protect, or support the bands of robbers and murderers which infest those counties, will be destroyed or seized and appropriated to the use of the Government. Property situated at or near military posts, and in or near towns which can be protected by troops so as not to be used by the bands of robbers will not be destroyed, but will be appropriated to the use of such loyal or innocent persons as may be made homeless by the acts of guerrillas or by the execution of this order. The commanding general is aware that some innocent persons must suffer from these extreme measures, but such suffering is unavoidable, and will be made as light as possible. A district of country inhabited almost solely by rebels cannot be permitted to be made a hiding-place for robbers and murderers, from which to sally forth on their errands of rapine and death. It is sincerely hoped that it will not be necessary to apply this remedy to any other portion of Missouri. But if the people of disloyal districts wish to avoid it, they must unite to prevent its necessity, which is clearly in their power to do.

This order will be executed by Brigadier-General Ewing, commanding District of the Border, and such officers as he may specially detail for the purpose.

Abraham Lincoln to James C. Conkling

Lincoln was invited by his old friend James C. Conkling to address a mass meeting in Springfield, Illinois, on September 3. Unable to attend, he sent Conkling a public letter accompanied by a personal note: "I can not leave here now. Herewith is a letter instead. You are one of the best public readers. I have but one suggestion. Read it very slowly." On August 31 Lincoln would send a telegram adding a passage ("I know as fully . . . good faith," pp. 497.29–498.3 in this volume) that alluded to a letter he had recently received from Ulysses S. Grant (pp. 488–489 in this volume). The Conkling letter was widely printed in the northern press.

Executive Mansion,
Washington, August 26, 1863.

Hon. James C. Conkling
My Dear Sir.

Your letter inviting me to attend a mass-meeting of unconditional Union-men, to be held at the Capital of Illinois, on the 3d day of September, has been received.

It would be very agreeable to me, to thus meet my old friends, at my own home; but I can not, just now, be absent from here, so long as a visit there, would require.

The meeting is to be of all those who maintain unconditional devotion to the Union; and I am sure my old political friends will thank me for tendering, as I do, the nation's gratitude to those other noble men, whom no partizan malice, or partizan hope, can make false to the nation's life.

There are those who are dissatisfied with me. To such I would say: You desire peace; and you blame me that we do not have it. But how can we attain it? There are but three conceivable ways. First, to suppress the rebellion by force of arms. This, I am trying to do. Are you for it? If you are, so far we are agreed. If you are not for it, a second way is, to give up the Union. I am against this. Are you for it? If you are, you should say so plainly. If you are not for *force*, nor yet for *dissolution*, there only remains some imaginable *compromise*. I do not believe any compromise, embracing the maintenance of the Union, is now possible. All I learn, leads to a directly opposite belief. The strength of the rebellion, is its military—its army. That army dominates all the country, and all the people, within its range. Any offer of terms made by any man or men within that range, in opposition to that army, is simply nothing for the present; because such man or men, have no power whatever to enforce their side of a compromise, if one were made with them. To illustrate—Suppose refugees from the South, and peace men of the North, get together in convention, and frame and proclaim a compromise embracing a restoration of the Union; in what way can that compromise be used to keep Lee's army out of Pennsylvania? Meade's army can keep Lee's army out of Pennsylvania; and, I think, can ultimately drive it out of existence. But no paper compromise, to which the controllers of Lee's army are not agreed, can, at all, affect that army. In an effort at such compromise we should waste time, which the enemy would improve to our disadvantage; and that would be all. A compromise, to be effective, must be made either with those who control the rebel army, or with the people first liberated from the domination of that army, by the success of our own army. Now allow me to assure you, that no word or intimation, from that rebel army, or from any of the men controlling it, in relation to any peace compromise, has ever come to my knowledge or belief. All charges and insinuations to the contrary, are deceptive and groundless. And I promise you, that if any such proposition shall hereafter come, it shall not be rejected, and kept a secret from you. I freely acknowledge myself the servant of the people, according to the bond of service—the United States constitution; and that, as such, I am responsible to them.

But, to be plain, you are dissatisfied with me about the negro. Quite likely there is a difference of opinion between you and myself upon that subject. I certainly wish that all men could be free, while I suppose you do not. Yet I have neither adopted, nor proposed any measure, which is not consistent with even your view, provided you are for the Union. I suggested compensated emancipation; to which you replied you wished not to be taxed to buy negroes. But I had not asked you to be taxed to buy negroes, except in such way, as to save you from greater taxation to save the Union exclusively by other means.

You dislike the emancipation proclamation; and, perhaps, would have it retracted. You say it is unconstitutional—I think differently. I think the constitution invests its commander-in-chief, with the law of war, in time of war. The most that can be said, if so much, is, that slaves are property. Is there—has there ever been—any question that by the law of war, property, both of enemies and friends, may be taken when needed? And is it not needed whenever taking it, helps us, or hurts the enemy? Armies, the world over, destroy enemies' property when they can not use it; and even destroy their own to keep it from the enemy. Civilized belligerents do all in their power to help themselves, or hurt the enemy, except a few things regarded as barbarous or cruel. Among the exceptions are the massacre of vanquished foes, and non-combatants, male and female.

But the proclamation, as law, either is valid, or is not valid. If it is not valid, it needs no retraction. If it is valid, it can not be retracted, any more than the dead can be brought to life. Some of you profess to think its retraction would operate favorably for the Union. Why better *after* the retraction, than *before* the issue? There was more than a year and a half of trial to suppress the rebellion before the proclamation issued, the last one hundred days of which passed under an explicit notice that it was coming, unless averted by those in revolt, returning to their allegiance. The war has certainly progressed as favorably for us, since the issue of the proclamation as before. I know as fully as one can know the opinions of others, that some of the commanders of our armies in the field who have given us our most important successes, believe the emancipation policy, and the use of colored troops, constitute the heaviest blow yet dealt to the rebellion; and that, at least one of those important successes, could not have been achieved when it was, but for the aid of black soldiers. Among the commanders holding these views are some who have never had any affinity with what is called abolitionism, or with republican party politics; but who hold them purely as military opinions. I submit these opinions as being entitled to some weight against the objections, often urged, that emancipation, and arming the blacks, are unwise as military measures, and were not adopted, as such, in good faith.

You say you will not fight to free negroes. Some of them seem willing to fight for you; but, no matter. Fight you, then, exclusively to save the Union. I issued the proclamation on purpose to aid you in saving the Union. Whenever you shall have conquered all resistance to the Union, if I shall urge you to continue fighting, it will be an apt time, then, for you to declare you will not fight to free negroes.

I thought that in your struggle for the Union, to whatever extent the negroes should cease helping the enemy, to that extent it weakened the enemy in his resistance to you. Do you think differently? I thought that whatever negroes can be got to do as soldiers, leaves just so much less for white soldiers to do, in saving the Union. Does it appear otherwise to you? But negroes, like other people, act upon motives. Why should they do any thing for us, if we will do nothing for them? If they stake their lives for us, they must be prompted by the strongest motive—even the promise of freedom. And the promise being made, must be kept.

The signs look better. The Father of Waters again goes unvexed to the sea. Thanks to the great North-West for it. Nor yet wholly to them. Three hundred miles up, they met New-England, Empire, Key-Stone, and Jersey, hewing their way right and left. The Sunny South too, in more colors than one, also lent a hand. On the spot, their part of the history was jotted down in black and white. The job was a great national one; and let none be banned who bore an honorable part in it. And while those who have cleared the great river may well be proud, even that is not all. It is hard to say that anything has been more bravely, and well done, than at Antietam, Murfreesboro, Gettysburg, and on many fields of lesser note. Nor must Uncle Sam's Web-feet be forgotten. At all the watery margins they have been present. Not only on the deep sea, the broad bay, and the rapid river, but also up the narrow muddy bayou, and wherever the ground was a little damp, they have been, and made their tracks. Thanks to all. For the great republic— for the principle it lives by, and keeps alive—for man's vast future,—thanks to all.

Peace does not appear so distant as it did. I hope it will come soon, and come to stay; and so come as to be worth the keeping in all future time. It will then have been proved that, among free men, there can be no successful appeal from the ballot to the bullet; and that they who take such appeal are sure to lose their case, and pay the cost. And then, there will be some black men who can remember that, with silent tongue, and clenched teeth, and steady eye, and well-poised bayonet, they have helped mankind on to this great consummation; while, I fear, there will be some white ones, unable to forget that, with malignant heart, and deceitful speech, they have strove to hinder it.

Still let us not be over-sanguine of a speedy final triumph. Let us be quite sober. Let us diligently apply the means, never doubting that a just God, in his own good time, will give us the rightful result. Yours very truly

A. LINCOLN.

Ulysses S. Grant to Elihu B. Washburne

Henry Wilson, a Republican from Massachusetts, was the chairman of the Senate Committee on Military Affairs. On July 25 he wrote to Illinois Republican congressman Elihu B. Washburne, Grant's political patron since 1861, praising Grant for favoring the overthrow of slavery. Wilson added that he hoped Grant would remain with the Army of the Tennessee and not accept a reported offer of the command of the Army of the Potomac, where, he warned, Grant would be "ruined" by envious men "in and out of that army." Washburne sent Wilson's letter to Grant, who responded from his headquarters at Vicksburg.

———————

Vicksburg Mississippi
August 30th 1863.

Hon. E. B. Washburn,
Dear Sir;

Your letter of the 8th of August, enclosing one from Senator Wilson to you, reached here during my temporary absence to the Northern part of my command; hence my apparent delay in answering. I fully appreciate all Senator Wilson says. Had it not been for Gen. Halleck & Dana I think it altogether likely I would have been ordered to the Potomac. My going could do no possible good. They have there able officers who have been brought up with that army and to import a commander to place over them certainly could produce no good. Whilst I would not possitively disobey an order I would have objected most vehemently to taking that command, or any other except the one I have. I can do more with this army than it would be possible for me to do with any other without time to make the same acquaintance with others I have with this. I know that the soldiers of the Army of the Ten. can be relied on to the fullest extent. I believe I know the exact capacity of every General in my command to command troops, and just where to place them to get from them their best services. This is a matter of no small importance.

Your letter to Gen. Thomas has been delivered to him. I will make an effort to secure a Brigadiership for Col. Chetlain with the colored troops   Before such a position will be open however more of these troops will have to be raised. This work will progress rapidly.

The people of the North need not quarrel over the institution of Slavery. What Vice President Stevens acknowledges the corner stone of the Confederacy is already knocked out. Slavery is already dead and cannot be resurrected. It would take a standing Army to maintain slavery in the South if we were to make peace to-day guaranteeing to the South all their former constitutional privileges.

I never was an Abolitionest, not even what could be called anti slavery, but I try to judge farely & honestly and it become patent to my mind early in the rebellion that the North & South could never live at peace with each other except as one nation, and that without Slavery. As anxious as I am to see peace reestablished I would not therefore be willing to see any settlement until this question is forever settled.

Rawlins & Maltby have been appointed Brigadier Generals. These are richly deserved promotions. Rawlins especially is no ordinary man. The fact is had he started in this war in the Line instead of in the Staff there is every probability he would be to-day one of our shining lights. As it is he is better and more favorably know than probably any other officer in the Army who has filled only staff appointments. Some men, to many of them, are only made by their Staff appointments whilst others give respectability to the position. Rawlins is of the latter class.

My kind regards to the citizens of Galena.

Your sincere friend
U. S. GRANT

Charles Francis Adams to Lord Russell

Under the Foreign Enlistment Act of 1819, British subjects were forbidden to arm or equip ships to be used by foreign belligerents at war with a power friendly with Great Britain. The Confederate naval agent James D. Bulloch circumvented the law by having unarmed warships built in English shipyards and then arranging for them to be equipped with guns and ammunition outside of British territory. Despite repeated protests by Charles Francis Adams, the U.S. minister to Great Britain, the Palmerston government failed to prevent the construction and sailing of the commerce raiders *Florida*, *Alabama*, and *Georgia*. Bulloch had also contracted with the Laird shipyard in Liverpool for the building of two large ironclad rams, and then devised the stratagem of selling them to a French broker purportedly acting for the Egyptian government. On July 11, 1863, Adams sent the first of a series of letters to the British foreign secretary, Lord Russell, protesting the construction of the rams and providing evidence of their true destination. In his reply of September 1 Russell described most of the evidence as hearsay and said the government had no legal grounds to interfere. Adams responded in this letter with a warning that became famous after it was published in January 1864. In fact, Russell had given orders on September 3 for the rams to be detained in port. The British government seized the ships in October, and they were purchased by the Royal Navy in May 1864.

LEGATION OF THE UNITED STATES,
London, September 5, 1863.

MY LORD: At this moment, when one of the iron-clad vessels is on the point of departure from this kingdom, on its hostile errand against the United States, I am honored with the reply of your lordship to my notes of the 11th, 16th and 25th of July, and of the 14th of August. I trust I need not express how profound is my regret at the conclusion to which her Majesty's government have arrived. I can regard it no otherwise than as practically opening to the insurgents free liberty in this kingdom to execute a policy described in one of their late publications in the following language:

"In the present state of the harbor defences of New York, Boston, Portland, and smaller northern cities, such a vessel as the Warrior would have little difficulty in entering any of these ports and inflicting a vital blow upon the enemy. The destruction of Boston alone would be worth a hundred victories in the field. It would bring such a terror to the 'blue-noses' as to cause them to wish eagerly for peace, despite their overweening love of gain, which has been so freely administered to since the opening of this war. Vessels of the Warrior class would promptly raise the blockade of our ports, and would even, in this respect, confer advantages which would soon repay the cost of their construction."

It would be superfluous in me to point out to your lordship that this is war. No matter what may be the theory adopted of neutrality in a struggle, when this process is carried on in the manner indicated, from a territory and with the aid of the subjects of a third party, that third party to all intents and purposes ceases to be neutral. Neither is it necessary to show that any government which suffers it to be done fails in enforcing the essential conditions of international amity towards the country against whom the hostility is directed. In my belief it is impossible that any nation, retaining a proper degree of self-respect, could tamely submit to a continuance of relations so utterly deficient in reciprocity. I have no idea that Great Britain would do so for a moment.

After a careful examination of the full instructions with which I have been furnished, in preparation for such an emergency, I deem it inexpedient for me to attempt any recurrence to arguments for effective interposition in the present case. Under these circumstances, I prefer to desist from communicating to your lordship even such further portions of my existing instructions as are suited to the case, lest I should contribute to aggravate difficulties already far too serious. I therefore content myself with informing your lordship that I transmit, by the present steamer, a copy of your note for the consideration of my government, and shall await the more specific directions that will be contained in the reply.

I seize this opportunity to pray permission of your lordship to correct a clerical error inadvertently made in my note of the 3d instant, in inserting the date of two notes of mine as having received the express approbation of my government. The intention was to specify only one, that of the 11th of July. The correction is not material, excepting as it conforms more strictly to the truth.

I pray your lordship to accept the assurances of the highest consideration with which I have the honor to be, my lord, your most obedient servant,

CHARLES FRANCIS ADAMS.

Right Honorable EARL RUSSELL, *&c.*, *&c.*, *&c.*

Charles C. Jones Jr. to Mary Jones

Lieutenant Colonel Jones, a Confederate artillery officer, wrote to his mother in Georgia about the ongoing siege of Charleston. While Union artillery fire forced the evacuation of Fort Wagner on September 7 and demolished much of Fort Sumter, the siege would continue until February 1865.

———————

James Island, *Sunday*, September 6th, 1863

It is Sabbath morning, my dear mother, but it is a very difficult matter to realize the fact. All day yesterday, all last night, and all day up to this hour, Battery Wagner has been subjected to a most terrific bombardment. Over one hundred were killed and wounded within its walls yesterday. No human being could have lived for one moment upon its walls or upon its parade. Against it were hurled the combined projectiles fired from the ironsides and the various mortar and Parrott batteries of the enemy located at different points on Morris Island. As their shells in numbers would explode in the parapet and within the fort, Wagner would seem converted into a volcano. Never was any battery called upon to resist such a bombardment, and I fear that it is now held more as a matter of military pride than anything else. It is very questionable whether this should be done.

In full view of everything on yesterday afternoon, from Battery Haskell, which was firing upon the enemy, I witnessed the progress of the siege. The gunnery of the Federals was wonderful. Wagner could not answer a single shot. The enemy last night assaulted Battery Gregg, which is located on the extreme north point of Morris Island, and were repulsed. God be praised for that; for had Gregg been carried, the entire garrison at Wagner would have been captured. I would not be surprised if the enemy assaulted Wagner tonight. That portion of the parapet looking towards the south of Morris Island has been knocked very much to pieces, and the sand crumbled into the ditch. In the very nature of things it cannot be held very much longer.

As a port of commercial ingress and egress Charleston is gone; but my impression at present is that the enemy will never be able to obtain possession of the city itself. It may be destroyed in whole or in part by the shells of the enemy, but it is questionable whether they can ever hold it as a site. The inner defenses are as yet intact, and the large Blakely gun is nearly mounted. Three ironclad gunboats are in the harbor, ready to attack the enemy in the event of their endeavoring to enter with their fleet.

We know not what a day may bring forth, but I trust that we may all be enabled, by God's blessing, to do our heroic duty under any and every circumstance. This life is a terrible one, but must be endured. Do, my dear mother, kiss my precious little daughter for me. Assure all at home of my sincerest love. And believe me ever

Your affectionate son,
Charles C. Jones, Jr.

James Island, *Wednesday*, September 9th, 1863
My very dear Mother,

I write simply to assure you and my dear little daughter and all at home of my constant remembrance and truest love.

The enemy yesterday attacked, with the ironsides and four monitors, Fort Moultrie, and were repulsed after a severe and prolonged bombardment. Last night an assault was made by them in barges upon Fort Sumter. The assault was signally repelled. We captured nineteen commissioned officers, one hundred and two noncommissioned officers and privates, and six barges. It is supposed that we killed and wounded and drowned between two and three hundred of the rascals. Our ironclads performed signal service. We captured also the flag which floated from Sumter when that fort was surrendered by Anderson, and which the enemy had brought in the expectation of again planting it upon the walls of that fort.

Day before yesterday I proceeded to the Stono with three

light batteries to engage the sloop of war *Pawnee*; but she would not come within range, and after firing a few random shots retired.

Through God's great mercy I am still quite well. I think matters are assuming a rather more favorable aspect, and if the enemy will only delay a little longer any contemplated attack by the way of James Island, we will have completed a new and formidable line of defenses. The enemy will find it a very difficult matter to enter the harbor. What I most fear is the partial destruction of the city by the long-range Parrott batteries of the Federals located on Morris Island. The scoundrels are busy as bees placing them in position, and apparently are training them upon the city and our James Island batteries. Our batteries are always firing, night and day.

Do, my dear mother, kiss my precious little daughter for me. Give best love to all at home. And remember me ever as

Your affectionate son,
Charles C. Jones, Jr.

I have had no letter from home yet.

Raphael Semmes:
Journal, September 16–24, 1863

A bark-rigged sailing ship equipped with an auxiliary steam engine, the *Alabama* was built at the Laird shipyard in Liverpool. She left port on July 29, 1862, and was armed with eight guns off the Azores before being commissioned as a Confederate warship on August 24. Her captain was Raphael Semmes, who had entered the U.S. Navy in 1826 and risen to the rank of commander before resigning his commission in 1861. As captain of the Confederate raider *Sumter*, he had captured eighteen American merchant ships between July 1861 and January 1862 before seeking refuge at Gibraltar. Unable to repair his ship, Semmes went to England and was given command of the new raider. While almost all of the ship's officers were Confederates, the crew of the *Alabama* had been recruited in Liverpool and served for double their normal wages and the promise of prize money. By the time she reached Simon's Town in British South Africa, the *Alabama* had sunk a Union gunboat, captured or burned fifty-four American whalers and merchant ships, and was being pursued by the U.S.S. *Vanderbilt*. After leaving Simon's Town, the Confederacy's most destructive raider would sail through the East Indies and into the South China Sea before returning to the Indian Ocean in the new year.

Wednesday, September 16.—Weather very fine. At daylight lighted fires and at 8 A.M. went ahead under steam. Saw nothing during nearly a whole day's steaming, except a bark (neutral) toward evening. At 3 P.M. doubled the Cape of Good Hope and steamed into the anchorage at Simon's Town, where we came to at about 4:30 P.M. The *Vanderbilt* had left on Friday last and was reported to have hovered near the cape for a day or two. Greatly discouraged by the news from home— Vicksburg and Port Hudson fallen, Rosecrans's army marching southward, and Lee having recrossed the Potomac. Our poor people seem to be terribly pressed by the Northern hordes of

Goths and Vandals, but we shall fight it out to the end, and the end will be what an all-wise Providence shall decree.

Thursday, September 17.—Weather good. Called on the admiral and received a visit from the captain of the *Narcissus*, Bickford. Various misrepresentations had been made to the admiral as to my proceedings since I left, etc., by the U. S. consul, which I explained away. Spent an agreeable half hour with the admiral and his lady. There being no coal here—the *Vanderbilt* having taken it all—I made arrangements for it to be sent to me from Cape Town. Visited the Dutch transport.

Friday, September 18.—Weather pleasant. Took a long stroll up the hills, permitting the men to visit the shore on liberty, and they are behaving badly, as usual.

Saturday, September 19.—The steamer *Kadie* arrived with coals for me from Cape Town. Hauled her alongside and commenced coaling. Walked on shore and lunched with Captain Bickford. Dispatched letters for the mail steamer for England. Liberty men drunk and few returning. Dined with the admiral. A very pleasant party, composed entirely of naval officers—the captains of the ships present, the captain superintendent of the dockyard, etc. After dinner the young ladies made their appearance in the drawing-room and we had some music.

Sunday, September 20.—Weather very fine. Heeled ship over to get at the copper around the blowpipe, which was worn off. Visited the shore at half past 9, took a long walk, dropped in upon the port captain, and went to church, Father Kiernan saying mass. He is an earnest, simple-minded Irish priest, with a picturesque little church on the hillside, and a small congregation, composed chiefly of soldiers and sailors, a seaman serving mass, Captain J. H. Coxon and a couple of the lieutenants of the squadron being present. Liberty men returning in greater numbers to-day; the money is giving out and the drunk wearing off.

Monday, September 21.—Morning cloudy. At daylight hauled the steamer alongside again, and recommenced coaling. Called to see the ladies at the admiral's after the dinner, and walked through their quite extensive garden, winding up a ravine, with a rapid little stream of water passing through it. Afternoon rainy.

Tuesday, September 22.—Morning cloudy, with showers of rain; wind hauling to the S. E., and the weather clearing toward noon. Coaling. A large number of liberty men on shore yet. The Yankee consul, with usual unscrupulousness, is trying to persuade them to desert, and the drunken and faithless rascals will, many of them, no doubt, sell themselves to him. With one or two exceptions the whole crew have broken their liberty—petty officers and all. With many improvements in the character of the seaman of the present day in regard to intelligence, he is as big a drunkard and as great a villain as ever. Finished coaling this afternoon. Equinoctial weather, blustering and rainy.

Wednesday, September 23.—Refitting the fore-topmast. Some twenty men still absent. A few are picked up by the Simon's Town police for the sake of the reward; and the sailor landlords, those pests of all seaports, are coming on board and presenting bills against the drunken rascals for board, etc. Of course these claims are not listened to. It is a common contrivance with Jack and these sharks to endeavor to extort money out of their ships. The process is simple enough. The landlord gives Jack a glass or two of bad liquor, and, it may be, a meal or two, and it is agreed between them that a bill of twenty times the value received shall be acknowledged. The land shark charges in this exorbitant way for the risk he runs of not being able to get anything. Knowing the villains well, I did not permit them to impose upon me.

Thursday, September 24.—Blowing a gale from the S. E. Waiting for the chance of getting over my deserters from Cape Town. Informed by telegraph in the afternoon that it was useless to wait longer, as the police declined to act. It thus appearing that the authorities declined to enable me to recover my men, 14 in number, enough to cripple my crew, I received on board 11 vagabonds, hungry and nearly shirtless, to take passage with me out to my own dominions, the high seas; thus very nearly setting off the number I had lost. Having a high respect for her Majesty, I made no contract with these fellows in her dominions. Informed by telegrams from Cape Town that vessels had arrived reporting the *Vanderbilt* on two successive days off Cape Agulhas and Point Danger. The moon being near its full, I preferred not to have her blockade me in

Simon's Bay, as it might detain me until I should have a dark moon, and being all ready for sea, this would have been irksome, and so, the gale having lulled somewhat toward 9 P.M., I ordered steam got up, and at half past 11 we moved out from our anchors. The lull only deceived us, as we had scarcely gotten underway before the gale raged with increased violence, and we were obliged to buffet it with all the force of our four boilers. The wind blew fiercely, but still we drove her between 5 and 6 knots per hour in the very teeth of it. Nothing could exceed the peculiar, weird-like aspect of the scene, as we struggled under the full moonlight with this midnight gale. The surrounding mountains and highlands, seemingly at a great distance in the hazy atmosphere, had their tops piled with banks of fleecy clouds remaining as motionless as snow banks, which they very much resembled, the cold south wind assisting the illusion; the angry waters of the bay breaking in every direction and occasionally dashing on board of us; the perfectly clear sky, with no sign of a cloud anywhere to be seen, except those piled on the mountains already mentioned; and the bright full moon shedding her mysterious rays on all surrounding objects, illuminating, yet distancing objects; all these were things to be remembered. And last, the revolving light on the cape at regular intervals lighting up the renowned old headland. We passed the cape at about 3 A.M., and bearing away gave her the trysails reduced by their bonnets and close-reefed topsails; and I turned in to snatch a brief repose before the toils of another day should begin.

William T. Sherman to
Henry W. Halleck

In a private letter of August 29, Halleck told Sherman that the "question of reconstruction in Louisiana, Mississippi, and Arkansas will soon come up for decision of the government." Hoping that the President would "consult opinions of cool and discreet men," Halleck wished to solicit the views of generals who knew the region. Sherman replied from his headquarters on the Big Black River, where his corps had been resting during the extreme heat and drought of summer. Halleck later told him that Lincoln had read his letter carefully.

---

private and confidential

Head Qrs. 15 Army Corps.
Camp on Big Black Miss. Sept. 17. 63
Maj. Genl. Halleck, Comdr. in Chief, Washington, D.C.
Dear General,

I have received your letter of Aug. 29, and with pleasure confide to you fully my thoughts on the important matter you suggest, with absolute confidence that you will use what is valuable, and reject the useless or superfluous.

That part of the Continent of North America Known as Louisiana, Mississipi, and Arkansas is in my judgment the Key to the Whole Interior. The valley of the Mississipi is America, and although Railroads have changed the scenery of intercommunication, yet the water channels still mark the Lines of fertile land, and afford carriage to the heavy products of it. The inhabitants of the country on the Monongehela, the Illinois, the Minnesota, the Yellowstone and Osage are as directly concerned in the security of the Lower Mississipi as are those who dwell on its very banks in Louisiana, and now that the nation has recovered its possessions, this Generation of men would make a fearful mistake if we again commit its charge to a People liable to mistake their title, and assert as was recently done that because they dwelt by sufferance on the Banks of this mighty stream they had a right to control its navigation. I would deem it very unwise at this time, or for years to come, to revive the State Governments of Louisiana &c. or to institute in this Quarter any Civil Government in which the local People have much to say. They had a Government, and so mild & paternal that they gradually forgot they had any at all, save what they themselves controlled; they asserted an absolute right to seize public monies, Forts, arms, and even to Shut up the national avenues of travel & commerce. They chose War. They ignored & denied all the obligations of the Solemn Contract of Government and appealed to force.

We accepted the issue, and now they begin to realize that War is a two edged sword, and it may be that many of the Inhabitants cry for Peace. I know them well, and the very impulses of their nature, and to deal with the Inhabitants of that part of the South which borders the Great River, we must recognise the classes into which they have naturally divided themselves.

1st The Large Planters, owning Lands, slaves and all kinds of personal property. These are on the whole the ruling Class. They are educated, wealthy, and easily approached. In some districts they are bitter as gall, and have given up, slaves, plantations & all, serving in the armies of the Confederacy, whereas in others they are conservative. None dare admit a friendship to us, though they Say freely that they were opposed to disunion and war. I *know* we can manage this class, but only by *action*. Argument is exhausted, and words have not their usual meaning. Nothing but the Logic of events touches their understanding, but of late this has worked a wonderful change. If our Country were like Europe, crowded with people, I would say it would be easier to replace this population than to reconstruct it subordinate to the Policy of the Nation, but as this is not the case it is better to allow them with individual exceptions gradually to recover their plantations to hire any species of labor and adapt themselves to the new order of things. Still their friendship and assistance to reconstruct order out of the present Ruin cannot be depended on. They watch the operations of our Armies, and hope still for a Southern Confederacy that will restore to them the slaves and privileges which they feel are otherwise lost forever. In my judgment we have two more battles to win before we should even bother our minds with the idea of restoring civil order, viz. one near Meridian in November, and one near Shreveport in February and March where Red River is navigable by our Gunboats. When these are done, then & not till then will the Planters of Louisiana, Arkansas & Mississipi submit. Slavery is already gone, and to cultivate the Land, negro or other labor must be hired. This of itself is a vast revolution and time must be afforded to allow men to adjust their minds and habits to the new order of things. A civil Government of the Representative type would suit this class far less than a pure Military Rule, one readily adapting itself to actual occurrences, and able to enforce its laws & orders promptly and emphatically.

2nd. The smaller farmers, mechanics, merchants and laborers:

This class will probably number ¾ of the whole, have in fact no real interest in the establishment of a Southern Confederacy, and have been led or driven into war, on the false theory that they were to be benefitted somehow, they Knew not how. They are essentially tired of the War, & would slink back home if they could. These are the real Tiers-etat of the South and are hardly worthy a thought for they swerve to & fro according to events they do not comprehend or attempt to shape. When the time for reconstruction comes, they will want the old political system, of caucuses, Legislatures &c. something to amuse them, and make them believe they are achieving wonders, but in all things they will follow blindly the lead of the Planter. The Southern Politicians who understand this class use them as the French do their masses. Seemingly consulting their prejudices they make their orders and enforce them. We should do the same.

3rd. The Union men of the South. I must confess I have little respect for this class. They allowed a clamorous set of demagogues to muzzle & drive them as a pack of curs. Afraid of shadows, they submit tamely to squads of dragoons and permit them without a murmur to burn their cotton, take their horses, corn and everything; and when we reach them, they are full of complaints, if our men take a few fence rails for firewood, or corn to feed our horses. They give us no assistance or information, and are loudest in their complaints at the smallest excess of our Soldiers. Their sons, horses arms and everything useful are in the army against us, and they stay at home claiming all the exemptions of peaceful citizens. I account them as nothing in this Great Game.

4th. The young Bloods of the South, sons of Planters, Lawyers about Town, good billiard players & sportsmen. Men who never did work, or never will. War suits them: and the rascals are brave, fine riders, bold to rashness, and dangerous subjects in every sense. They care not a "sous" for niggers, land or anything. They hate Yankees "per se" and don't bother their brains about the Past, present or Future. As long as they have a good horse, plenty of Forage and an open Country they are happy. This is a larger class than most men suppose, and are the most dangerous set of men which this war has turned loose upon the world. They are splendid riders, shots, and utterly reckless. Stuart, John Morgan, Forrest, and Jackson are the types & leaders of this class. They must all be killed, or employed by us before we can hope for Peace. They have no property or future & therefore cannot be influenced by anything except personal considerations. I have two Brigades of these fellows to my Front, commanded by Cosby of the old army and Whitfield of Texas, Stephen D. Lee in command of the whole. I have frequent interviews with the officers, and a good understanding; and am inclined to think when the resources of their country are exhausted we must employ them. They are the best Cavalry in the world, but it will tax Mr. Chase's Genius of Finance to supply them with horses. At present horses cost them nothing for they take where they find, and dont bother their brains, who is to pay for them. Same of the corn fields which have, as they believe been cultivated by a good natured people for their special benefit. We propose to share with them the free use of these cornfields planted by willing hands that will never gather them.

Now, that I have sketched the People who inhabit the District of Country under consideration, I will proceed to discuss the Future. A Civil Government for any part of it would be simply ridiculous. The People would not regard it, and even the Military Commanders of the antagonistic party would treat it lightly. Governors would be simply petitioners for military assistance to protect supposed friendly interests, and Military

Commanders would refuse to disperse & weaken their armies for military reasons. Jealousies would arise between the two conflicting powers, and instead of contributing to the end we all have in view, would actually defer it. Therefore I contend that the interest of the United States, and of the real parties concerned, demand the continuance of the simple military Rule till long after *all* the organized armies of the South are dispersed, conquered and subjugated. All this Region is represented in the Army of Virginia, Charleston, Mobile and Chattanooga. They have sons & relations in each and naturally interested in their fate. Though we hold military possession of the Key Points of this country, still they contend & naturally that should Lee succeed in Virginia, or Bragg at Chattanooga, that a change would occur here also. We cannot for this reason attempt to reconstruct parts of the South as we conquer it, till all idea of the establishment of a Southern Confederacy is abandonned. We should avail ourselves of the lull here, to secure the Geographical points that give us advantage in future military movements, and Should treat the idea of Civil Government as one in which we as a nation have a Minor or subordinate interest. The opportunity is good to impress on the population the Truth that they are more interested in Civil Government than we are, and that to enjoy the protection of Laws, they must not be passive observers of events, but must aid and Sustain the constituted authorities in enforcing the Laws: they must not only submit themselves, but pay their taxes, and render personal services when called on.

It seems to me in contemplating the past two years history, all the people of our country north, south, east & west have been undergoing a Salutary Political Schooling, learning lessons which might have been taught by the History of other People; but we had all become so wise in our own conceit, that we would only learn by actual experience of our own.

The people even of small & unimportant localities north as well as south, had reasoned themselves into the belief that their opinions were superior to the aggregated interest of the whole nation. Half our territorial nation rebelled on a doctrine of secession that they themselves now scorn, and a real numerical majority actually believed, that a little state was endowed with such sovereignty, that it could defeat the Policy of the Great Whole. I think the present war has exploded that notion, and were this war to cease now, the experience gained though dear would be worth the expense.

Another Great & important natural Truth is still in contest and can only be solved by War. Numerical majorities by vote is our Great Arbiter. Heretofore all have submitted to it in questions left open, but numerical majorities are not necessarily physical majorities. The South though numerically inferior, contend they can whip the Northern superiority of numbers, and therefore by natural Law are not bound to submit. This issue is the only real one, and in my judgement all else should be deferred to it. War alone can decide it, and it is the only question left to us as a People.

Can we whip the South? If we can, our numerical majority has both the natural and constitutional right to govern. If we cannot whip them they contend for the natural right to Select their own Government, and they have the argument. Our Armies must prevail over theirs, our officers, marshals and courts must penetrate into the innermost recesses of their Land before we have the natural right to demand their submission. I would banish all minor questions, and assert the broad doctrine that as a nation the United States has the Right and also the Physical Power to penetrate to every part of the National domain, and that we will do it—that we will do it in our own time and in our own way, that it makes no difference whether it be in one year, or two, or ten or twenty: that we will remove & destroy every obstacle, if need be take every life, every acre of land, every particle of property, every thing that to us seems proper, that we will not cease till the end is attained, that all who do not aid are enemies, and we will not account to them for our acts. If the People of the South oppose they do so at their peril, and if they stand by mere lookers on the domestic tragedy, they have no right to immunity, protection or share in the final Result.

I even believe and contend further, that in the North every member of the Nation is bound by both natural & constitutional Law to "maintain and defend the Government against all its opposers whomsoever." If they fail to do it, they are derelict, and can be punished, or deprived of all advantage arising from the labors of those who do—If any man north or south withholds his share of taxes, or physical assistance in this crisis of our History, he could and should be deprived of all voice in the future Elections of this country and might be banished or reduced to the condition of a Denizen of the Land.

War is upon us. None can deny it. It is not the act of the Government of the United States but of a Faction. The Government was forced to accept the issue or submit to a degradation fatal & disgraceful to all the Inhabitants. In accepting war it should be pure & simple as applied to the Belligerents. I would Keep it so, till all traces of war are effaced, till those who appealed to it are sick & tired of it, and come to the emblem of our Nation and Sue for Peace. I would not coax them, or even meet them half way, but make them so sick of war that Generations would pass before they would again appeal to it.

I know what I say, when I repeat that the insurgents of the South sneer at all overtures looking to their interest. They Scorn the alliance with Copperheads: they tell me to my face that they respect Grant, McPherson and our brave associates who fight manfully & well for a principle, but despise the Copperheads & sneaks, who profess friendship for the South, and opposition to the War, as mere covers to their Knavery & poltroonery.

God knows that I deplored this fratricidal war as much as any man living, but it is upon us a physical fact; and there is only one honorable issue from it. We must fight it out, army against army, and man against man, and I know and you Know, and civilians begin to realize the fact, that reconciliation and reconstruction will be easier through and by means of strong, well equipped & organised armies than through any species of conventions that can be framed. The issues are made & all discussion is out of place and ridiculous.

The Section of 30 pounder Parrott Rifles now drilling before my tent is a more convincing argument than the largest Democratic or Union meeting the State of New York could assemble at Albany: and a simple order of the War Department to draft enough men to fill our Skeleton Regiments would be more convincing as to our national perpetuity, than an humble pardon to Jeff Davis and all his misled host.

The only Government now needed or deserved by the States

of Louisiana, Arkansas and Mississipi now exists in Grants Army. It needs simply enough privates to fill its Ranks, all else will follow in due season. This army has its well defined code of Laws and Practice, and can adapt itself to the wants and necessities of a city, the country, the Rivers, the Sea, indeed to all parts of this Land. It better subserves the interest and Policy of the General Government and the People prefer it to any weak or servile combination, that would at once from force of habit revive & perpetuate local prejudices and passions. The People of this country have forfeited all Right to a voice in the Councils of the Nation. They Know it and feel it, and in after years they will be the better citizens from the dear bought experience of the present Crisis. Let them learn now, and learn it well that good citizens must obey as well as command. Obedience to law, absolute yea even abject is the lesson that this war under Providence will teach the Free & enlightened American Citizen. As a Nation we will be the better for it.

I never have apprehended Foreign Interference in our family quarrel. Of course Governments founded on a different & it may be antagonistic principle with ours, would naturally feel a pleasure at our complications: but in the end England & France will join with us in jubilation in the triumph of a Constitutional Government over Faction: even now the English manifest this. I do not profess to understand Napoleons design in Mexico, but I do not see that his taking military possession of Mexico concerns us. We have as much territory as we want. The Mexicans have failed in self Government and it was a question to what nation she would fall a prey. That is solved, and I dont see that we are damaged. We have the finest part of the North American Continent, all we can people & take care of, and if we can suppress rebellion in our Land and compose the strife generated by it, we will have people, resources & wealth which if well combined can defy interference from any and every quarter. I therefore hope the Government of the U.S. will continue as heretofore in collecting in well organized armies the physical strength of the nation, apply it as heretofore in asserting the national authority, persevering without relaxation to the end. This whether near or far off is not for us to say, but fortunately we have no choice. We *must* succeed. No other choice is left us but degradation.

The South must be ruled or will rule. We must conquer them or ourselves be conquered. There is no middle course.

They ask and will have nothing else, and all this talk of compromise is bosh, for we know they would even now scorn and despise the offer.

I wish this war could have been deferred for twenty years, till the superabundant population of the North could flow in and replace the losses sustained by War, but this could not be, and we are forced to take things as they arise.

All therefore I can now venture to advise is the pushing the draft to its maximum, fill the present Regiments to as large a standard as possible, and push this War, "pure and simple."

Great attention should be paid to the discipline of our armies, for on them will be founded the future stability of our Government. The Cost of the War is of course to be considered, but finances will adjust themselves to the actual state of affairs, and even if we would, we could not change the cost. Indeed, the larger the cost now, the less will it be in the end, for the End must be attained somehow regardless of cost of Life and Treasure, and is merely a question of Time. Excuse so long a letter. With great respect your friend & servant

W. T. Sherman
Maj. Genl.

William W. Heartsill:
Journal, September 17–28, 1863

The opposing armies in the battle of Stones River, December 31, 1862–January 2, 1863, had each lost about one-third of their men killed, wounded, or missing. In the six months that followed, the Union Army of the Cumberland under Major General William S. Rosecrans had remained at Murfreesboro, Tennessee, while the Confederate Army of Tennessee under General Braxton Bragg occupied Tullahoma, thirty-five miles to the south. Rosecrans began advancing on June 23 and executed a series of flanking maneuvers that forced Bragg to retreat across the Tennessee River on July 6. After pausing to repair bridges and build up supplies, Rosecrans resumed his offensive on August 16. By crossing the Tennessee downriver from Chattanooga, he again outflanked Bragg and forced him to evacuate the town, a strategic railroad junction, on September 8. As Rosecrans advanced into the mountains of northwest Georgia, Bragg received reinforcements from Mississippi, eastern Tennessee, and Virginia. The two armies skirmished on September 18, then began fighting the next day in the dense woods along the western side of West Chickamauga Creek, about eight miles south of Chattanooga. William W. Heartsill had enlisted in 1861 in the W. P. Lane Rangers, a Texas cavalry company that was captured at Arkansas Post in January 1863. Exchanged in April, the men of the Lane Rangers joined an infantry brigade led by Brigadier General James Deshler. As part of the division commanded by Major General Patrick Cleburne, Deshler's Brigade fought on the Confederate right wing at Chickamauga, attacking the Union lines south of Winfrey Field at dusk on September 19 and at the southern end of Kelly Field the following morning.

Whartons Cavalry is passing down the mountain and in 15 minutes firing of small arms commences and now as the sun is rising the fire is quite lively only one shot from the Big guns up to this time. The firing with Whartons men is waxing warm. 7 oclock our Cavalry has just charged the enemy and compelled him to fall back with a loss of one killed (a Geo Captain) and 8

521

wounded. 8 oclock our Batterries are keeping up the music on the right verry lively the enemy remains quiet except his sharp shooters. ½ past 8 all is now quiet General orders No 108 from Gen Bragg announcing the check of the enemy twice in his attempt at flanking and that now this army would press forward and compell him to fight even on his own ground. Gen B. calls upon his men to stand as true as in the days of Murfreesboro Shiloh Perryville & victory will crown our arms. To the world wee can say from what wee have seen that the Army of Tennessee is enthusiastic & will come out victorious if the Enemy will give us any thing like a fair showing. Either Ewell or Longstreet is here with troops from Va. at 1 oclock Adams Brigade comes up our Brigade goes to the foot of the Pass at 3. our Batterys open again on the enemy without a reply, at 4 oclock the small arms are rattling lively again, at 5 our Brigade is thrown forward on the right and now at sunset our Company is thrown forward along the fence of a cornfield with orders to hold the Woods in our rear at all hazzards and while I am writing the enemy is not idle They are some 1½ miles in front of us & The Smokey sides of Look out mountain looms up still beyon them while clouds of smoke and dust plainly indicates that they are preparing as well as wee for the deadly work of tomorrow. If wee are not greatly mistaken this time tomorrow will see many a throbing heart cease many that will be cold and stiff in death that little think twill be him. wee know not our fate and would not if wee could but leave all to him who governs the world as well as the lives of mortal man

Sept 18 The pickets kep up a slow but continious rattle of musketry all night, but our lines was not molested. At daybreak wee were called in an now at sunup are resting at the foot of the pass. 7 oclock all the infantry is gone and our Co is ordered to bring up the rear Some Cavalry are left to guard the Gap. Wee Soon wind up the mountain and at 10 oclock wee pass within two miles of Lafayett. Two miles farther on the road and now wee can plainly hear connonnading in the direction of Lee & Gordons mills, on the road wee meet Capt Nutt from the Hospital also Lawrence & McCain They thinking it too hazardous to cross the Mississippi river come back to share our fate for Good or bad. 12 oclock wee have been ordered to our Brigade and are now resting in a meadow This is

the first fall day and by the by a fine one for fighting Fall in Fall
in comes ringing down the Brigade and of course I stop writing and fall in. one mile on the road and the cannonnading is
geting loud thick and fast and the prospects are magnificent
for us to get into a brush this evening one ock and wee are
now in line of Battle on the right of the road and in verry good
trim for a fight The evening wears away evry moment we expected to start and now at Sunset all is quiet From what I can
see wee have plenty of troops and if Rosy will give us an opportunity he will see that the ocupation of East Tennessee is
dearly bought. The clouds are flying from North to South and
as wee are all siting around our Camp fires chating over the
pending fight the first chilly winds of Autumn is blowing about
our ears. A great many of the men have not even one Blanket
and now as I am just rolling up in my old Green army coat to
roll down on a pile of leaves to think and dream of comeing
events or of loved ones at home oh how many aching hearts
would be ore our country did they but know wha a few days
will bring forth Cruel Cruel war and thrice cruel invaders that
come to drench our sunny south in blood and drag us to worse
than slavery Up southrons and strike for God and our native
land may the God of the right hover ore our Battle flag and
may our independance be dated, from the begining of this
pending contest that it is to be one of the most sanguinary and
decisive battles of the war no one doubts. Wee close for the
night while at evry camp fire nothing but the coming struggle
is discused

Sept 19 This morning is still cool but the day promises to be
verry pleasant. at 7 oclock cannonading is ringing some three
miles toward Chattanooga and now at 8 all is quiet Courrirs
are dashing to and fro all in perfect motion. our position here
is at present the reserve of the extreme left Gen Hills HcQts
are some two hundred yards down the road on the right at the
forks of the road one leading to Chattanooga the other west
toward Lookout mountain 10 oclk the roar of Battle is pealing
forth on the right. The cannonnading is terrific wee cannot
hear the small arms on account of the distance and hills on our
right 11 oclk The battle still rages we have rumors that Breck-
enridge & Longstreet have crossed the Chicamauga driving
the enemy before them The rattle of musketry is now geting

close at ½ past 11 wee are called into lines and expect to moove at any moment. ¼ to 12 wee moove to the right other troops are pooring down the valley. at 12 the fight is raging verry heavy. This fight decides whether this shall be a long or a short war our Boys are confidend. Wee march quick and double quick for 5 miles and have the pleasure of wading the chicamauga below Lee & Gordons mills. The fireing is now on our left and is quite lively wee pass 150 prisoners in one group and several smaller squads some are wounded. At 5 oclock wee are now about the center of the army the firing is verry heavy on our left for the past 4 hours The fight has raged with unceasing furry our boys at sunset have driven them some two miles. wee have just passed annother squad of prisoners. Our wounded are scatered around in large numbers at dark Deshlers Brigade is on the front and the fight is increasing on our right and continues until 8 oclock our Brigade participated on the right and Col Wilkes Regt. took 250 prisons and now at 9 oclock all is quiet we are the front line. Wee have seen 7 yankee stand of collors and some 4 or 5 hundred prisoners from the fight on our extreme left at L & Gs mills wee have no news. The 7th Texas is heare some of the Boys saw Capt Talley of Marshall who is now nobly braving dangers for his native state. Nearly all the Texans are here and will give a good account of The Lone Star State. Wee manuver all night do not get a particle of sleep wee pass over a large number of Dead Yankes

Sept 20 Annother sunday and evry prospect of a fierce conflict between mighty armies at day break wee advance in line of Battle wee are waiting paitiently for the dread conflict of to day. The woods wee are now show evidence of the fierce fight of yesterday There is an abundance of Dead Yankees scatered around. our Litter corps have carried all the enemys wounded to the rear that can be found. 7 oclock skirmishing has commenced in front. 8 oclock the artillery has just opened Cheathams men are opening the Ball fineley. Gens Brag & Hill have just passed to the front at 9 oclock Deshlers brigade is ordered forward. wee front forward about face right & left flank quick and double quick for about 3 miles and take our position in the center on a ridge amidst a perfect storm of Grape stoom solid shot and minie balls which are pooring in on us from the valley beyond. Wee lay down and thus escape destruction at 9 oclock Gen Deshler is killed by shell it is usless to pass eulogies upon Gen D. for to know him was to love him and evry man in his Brigade regrets his death. Col Wilks is wounded therefore the Command fall upon Col Mills—our Brigade holds the position althou the enemy try evry means to disloge us at 3 oclock the fight became general and until sun set never did the roar of Battle peal louder it seemed that the verry heavens and earth shook and then the triumphant shout that went up at sun set our Boys are driving them back in fact they are in full retreat our victory is completed and now at 9 oclock I am writing by a federal Camp fire wee have captured a good number of Prisoners and several Battery wee must wait for particulars. our Brigade lost about 200 killed & wounded. Our Company* two wounded and four missing none of the W P L Rs were wounded. Wee have to night passed over part of the Battle ground and find the Yanks in perfect heaps. wee have work before us for Rosey will certainly hold us a lively string for the next few days it is bed time I must sleep for our work is fairly begun

Sept 21 This is a lovely morning and a perfect calm succeeds yesterdays Battle, wee can get no particulars of yesterdays work but it is satisfactory all our missing are in except Alvin Anderson but think he is not hurt. Deshlers Brigade held a position that two other brigades failed in. The Enemy has splendid brest works in our front & on the right Their works were made of large logs notched and fited close. They were stongly fortified but our Boys were too determined for them Clebourns Division suffered severly expecially Woods Brigade 8 oclock Anderson comes in all right. The loss of our Brigade is heavier than wee at first thought it will run up to near 400 killed and wounded. Sunset and wee are still at our last nights camp and from what wee can learn, Meinhier Rosecrance is in full retreat to chattanooga wee can form nothing like an acurate list of killed wounded & prisoners Wee have orders to be ready to march at a moments notice. our army is in motion Northward and day light may see us several miles from this camp. a stroll over part of the Battle field this evening was any thing els but

*Benge slightly wounded

pleasant wee can but forgive an Enemy even as savage a foe as the Federal Soldiers is when wee see him stiff in death or suffering from wounds. The sight was truly hart rending The enemys dead greatly outnumber ours The woods caught fire last night and a number of the dead are badly burned but it was unavoidable at dark wee fall in and march toward Chattanooga for two miles then take a right hand road Company C & Nutts Co were flankers on the left and a sweet time wee had through corn fields meadows over hills & hollows across ravines and up cliffs & Bluffs & at 2 oclock wee camp but dont ask us where at for wee do not know but think wee are in the neighbourhood of Graysville or Chicamauga Depot

Sept 22 This morning wee are awakened by the welcome words come and draw your rations which command is obeyed verry punctually by evry man. Upon looking around wee are camped on the south bank of the Chicamauga and about 3 miles from the Depo. as to what is up by this moovment none of us have the least idea but I guess Rosy will find that Corpl Bragg is wide awake. Wee marched two miles and camp once more in old Tennessee. Maj Van Zandt of the 7th Tex came over to see us this evening from him wee learn that Lieutenant L R Bayless of our Co died at Pine Bluff Ark some months ago also that several others of the Company are dead but he had forgoten their names. This camp is about 5 miles East of Chattanooga.

Sept 23 At 7 oclock wee march and 3 miles wee reach the top of Missionary Ridge here The view of Lookout Valley is verry fine while the fortifications and suburbs of Chattanooga is to our right along the river in front of us looms up Lookout mountain. at the fork of the Ridge wee file to the left and cross our line of Battle and from along the ridge near two miles from the foot of Lookout mountain The enemy is verry active and it is believed he is evacuating the place as Smoke is bursting forth from different parts of the Town and clouds of dust indicate such a moovment. at 2 oclock wee march in colum and in 1 mile of Town are again thrown into line our Brigade is on the right of Gen Breckenridges Division. The Enemy have evry few minutes made known his presents by shelling us from the fortifications—at sunset orders from Gen Bragg announcing a complete victory and rout of the enemy on the field of

Chicamauga and that too over superior numbers He however reminds us that while wee drop a tear to our brave comrades who fell by our sides on the hard fought Battle of the 18th 19 & 20 of Sept wee must now press forward to new victorys and drive the invaders from our land So Gen Bragg has named the Battle field and the thrilling victory of Chicamauga will send a throb of joy and thanksgiving throughout our land. Wee hardly think the enemy will give us battle on this side of the river but to morrow will tell what his intentions are

Sept 24 At day break this morning the Feds commenced shelling our lines and kepp it up quite brisk for an hour and now at 8 oclock skirmishing is going on to our left & near the foot of the mountain Longstreet is on the left at 8 oclock all is quiet. At 9 wee fall back and form a line along the foot of the ridge our artillery is in position 50 yards in front. here wee remain until Sunset The enemy keeping up a continuous but slow cannonading all day. our artillery has advanced some 200 yards There is a little sharp shooting going on and from the direction of the cannonading on the right & left our forces must bee surrounding the Enemy. It is now growing dark the valley is full of smoke & dust which prooves activity of troops below. To morrow old Lookout mountain will I think shake to its foundation with the roar of Battle. Wee dread the nights as they are so verry cool and the days are verry warm. The common expression of the Boys is freeze in the night & thaw in the day. While I am writeing Longstreets artillery is thundering away to the left near Lookout and in fact it seems to be even beyon the mountain. Lawrence & McCain have gone to the rear verry sick Leaving of the Rangers present Lt. Smith Sergt Heartsill & Elgin—Privates A H M Vanderson—Bence Beard & Watson. Hamlett is at his post as the Boys call him 3rd doctor In our line of Artillery in front of us is 36 pieces, forty yards apart making 678 artillery horses in one line look out Rosey or somebody will get hurt.

Sept 25 Wee rested finely until midnight when the rapid fire of musketry in front of us soon aroused us and by the time wee were in line cannon was belching forth and at the dead calm hour of midnight the moon shining lovely a sharp little battle is rageing in Lookout Valley. wee are thrown forth in front of our artillery and in an hour all is quiet Can you guess what

commenced the fight to night twas this the Federal pickets had
their super brought out to them and was just gathering around
to eat when our boys who are allways wide a wake made a dash
upon them and after a slight resistance they took to their heels
and left their super to the Rebs Two Boxes passed by us while
in line containing Bread &cc so much for bringing Eatiables in
sight of starving Rebles after all was quiet wee are ordered
back to our old position and pass the remainder of the night
without molestation—and at day light this morning wee are
thrown forward again and are some ¼ mile in front of our line
of artillery nothing but an occasional shot from the pickets to
remind us that Roseys men are near us and to keep a sharp
look-out. 8 oclock The yanks are busy building brest works
while their Bands keep up one continuous strain of music. At
11 oclock wee back again to the ridge and at 12 wee forward
and take a position 600 yards from the foot of the ridge and
by sunset wee have first rate brest works made of rails Rocks
and Logs. Slow cannonadeing is going on to our left, wee are
verry well fixed for minie balls and grape but wont do for 12
pounders wee will do the best wee can four of the Co return
from the Hospital in the number is Snediker and wee are glad
to see him improving so finely. Wee are verry much in hopes
wee may get to rest to night but it is doubtful. and now for a
snack and then down in the dirt for a nights rest behind brest
works

Sept 26. This morning at daybreak our Pickets advance and
drove the enemy to his intrenchments now at 8 oclock all is
quiet except our Boys strengthing their works. It is reported
that only about 5000 Federals are now in Chattanooga. Longstreet has possesion of the Rail Road below town thereby
forcing the enemy to evacuate the place by crossing the
mountina oposite. It is also reported that Forrest has captured
a large number of wagons loaded with commissary stores verry
good if true Some wounded men by this mornings skirmish
have just passed. They say they killed several yankees Wee spent
the remainder of the day without molestation and now preparing for another nights rest behind our works

Sept 27. All is quiet even the Pickets appear to have reaver-
ance for the sabath for scarcly a shot has been fired to this time
9 oclock. Wee receiv orders to strengthen our works as our

artilleryists will give us a bit of fun on to morrow. Wee all work
finely in fact I blistered my hands I hardly think twould have
been the case at any other work. But men will work at brest
works when they will work at nothing els. Capt Nutt called at
Gen Braggs HcQts and is satisfied that wee will get to cross
the river after this campaign is over. Weaver returned & ready
for the fun

Sept 28 The morning wears away and wee learn that the
order to open fire this morning was countermanded at any rate
there has been no firing up to this time 12 oclock. at 10 oclock
wee witnessed the shooting of a deserter he left his command
at Tullahoma July 1st and was caught after the fight on the
Chickamaga having joined the Federals he had on the Federal
Uniform After prayer by an aged minister the guilty man
kneeling the command was given Aim Fire and Henry Roberts
of Co K 26th Tenn paid the penalty of his crime Wee have had
the pleasure of seeing a large *number of Harrison County
Boys sience the late Battle in the Number Lieutenants Allen
Woodson & Lipscombe also Charley & Jno Bedell Jno Smith
Dan Dapplemyer Jno Weebb Jim Bradfield Ringold Hynson.
Wee are sorry to learn that several were wounded in the number is Felix Johnson Henry Mills Lee Sanders & Joe Alford &
Howell Lewis. but hope to meet all the Boys one more in
Marshall when the trials and privations of camp life is over and
the war at an end then wee can talk over our strugle for independance and laugh at our hairbreadth escapes long marches
through mud dust Rain hail storm winter & Summer In after
days wee will think of the Rapidan Raphanoc Patomac Chica-
homini Big Black Peal Tennessee Yazzoo Chicamauga and
other waters by whose sides our camp fires have glittered and
when the Battles of Raymond Jackson Fort Doneldson Ark
Post Richmond Gettysburg 2nd Manasses Shepherdstown
Chickamauga and scores of other are mentioned wee will remember that Texans bled upon that day and sealed our caus
with patriots Blood Those are days to come the present wee
are now enjoying in Brest works ½ mile in front of the enemy
works. our rations are brought to us evry day cooked and they
are of verry short allowance in fact rather too much so I am

*H Rains Engine Mundon Curry Atkins Lee Ward Blalack Lieut Perry.

sure wee could eat as much more. Wee must not however complain as it is some distance to our nearest Depot station and then wee have the consolation of knowing if Rosey get any thing to eat he must haul it over cumberlane mountains as our forces have possession of the Railroads above and below the Town This condition of affairs will certainly force a fight or retreat from the enemy in a few days. If a fight is the result I think wee are fully prepared

John S. Jackman:
Diary, September 18–21, 1863

John S. Jackman had enlisted in 1861 in the Confederate 5th Kentucky Infantry (later redesignated the 9th Kentucky) and saw action at Shiloh and Stones River. His regiment formed part of the 1st Kentucky Brigade, commanded at Chickamauga by Brigadier General Ben Hardin Helm, the husband of Mary Todd Lincoln's half-sister Emilie. On the morning of September 20 the brigade was posted to the Confederate right flank where, as part of the division commanded by Major General John C. Breckinridge, it repeatedly assaulted Union troops fighting from behind log breastworks at the northern end of Kelly Field. At midday James Longstreet (who was on detachment with two divisions from Lee's army) launched an attack that discovered a quarter-mile gap in the Union center and split Rosecrans's army in two. While Rosecrans and the Union right wing fled toward Chattanooga, Major General George H. Thomas withdrew his troops on the left onto a ridge and held the position for several hours before withdrawing at nightfall. Dismayed by his heavy losses in men and artillery horses, Bragg did not occupy the heights overlooking Chattanooga until September 23 and chose to besiege the town rather than assault it.

Sept. 18th.—About noon came to the road leading off to where the wagon train is encamped, we left the wagon, and started for the regiment. Part of the time our road led over steep hills, and had a very tiresome walk. In the evening, a party of us left the main road to make a "near cut." There were 4 of us—Capt. N., 1st Seg't, J. F. of his company, Dr. S., our Ass't Surg., and myself. We could hear the cannon booming occasionally. At night we stopped at a cabin on the roadside, and got a good supper. Then adjourned to a neighboring pine-thicket, where we passed the night, nearly freezing, as blankets were scarce.

Sept. 19th.—On the road early. Stopped at a well to wash and breakfast. A lady seeing us, sent out some butter and milk. Five miles brought us to the regiment near Glass' Mills. The brigade had just crossed Chicamauga River at Glass' Ford to support Cobbs' and Slocums' batteries, & the wickedest artillery duel ensued, I ever saw. Slocum and Cobb had to "limber to the rear" and move their batteries back across the river. There were several of our regiment wounded—three afterward, died of their wounds. About the middle of the afternoon moved a mile or two further to the right and halted in line of battle sending out skirmish line. While here we could hear the battle raging further to the right. But before sundown, our division again commenced moving to the right. At sundown, and a little after dark, the musketry rattled incessantly. I don't believe I ever heard heavier volleys of small arms. The word came back that Cleburn was driving the enemy on the right. Having to move 5 or 6 miles, we continued our march until sometime after dark and the night being black, we had a deal of trouble. We at last crossed the Chicamauga at Alexander's Bridge, and not far from the bridge we stopped in an old field for the night. We built a large fire, yet not having any blankets with me, I did not sleep any. The night was very cold and my large overcoat came in good place.

Sept. 20th.—Before daylight, the division moved to take position in line of battle. After we had stopped for the night, the field band had been sent to the rear with the horses of the field and staff, and were not back in time; so the Col., etc., had to "foot it." The Col. left me at the fire to tell the musicians where to bring the horses. Daylight came and a heavy frost was on the ground. I waited until long after sunup, yet the drummers did not come; so I shouldered a long bundle of blankets intended to be put on the horses, and started for the regiment. I had to pass over the ground where Cleburn had fought the evening before. The dead of both sides were lying thick over the ground. I saw where six Federal soldiers had been killed from behind one small tree, and where eight horses were lying dead, harnessed to a Napoleon gun. Men and horses were lying so thick over the field, one could hardly walk for them. I even saw a large black dog lying mangled by a grape. In the rear of the brigade, I found our ambulance, and put the blankets in it, then went on to the regiment. The boys were lying in line of battle, and cracking jokes as usual. Many of them I noticed to be in the finest spirits were in a few minutes afterwards numbered with the slain. All the time the skirmishers about two hundred yards on advance, were very noisy. About 10 o'clock A.M. Maj. Wilson rode up to Gen'l Helm, who was sitting against a tree in "rear" of our regiment, talking to Col. C., and gave him the verbal order from Breckinridge to advance in fifteen minutes, and adjust his movements to the brigade on the right. The General got up and mounted his horse, laughing and talking as though he was going on parade. I had intended to go along with the infirmary corps, but as the drummers had not come up with the horses, Col. C., ordered me to go back and see if I could find them. I had not gone far, before I came to several of our boys that had been wounded on the skirmish line and as the shells were tearing up the ground about them, which makes a helpless man feel very uncomfortable, I helped put them in an ambulance and sent them to a hospital. I went a little farther, in hopes of finding the drummers, but they were nowhere to be found. I then started back for the regiment. The rattle of musketry was kept up pretty lively. As I passed along over the field, could see all the little gullies were packed full of straggling soldiers, (but I saw none of our Brigade among them) avoiding the shells. When I got to the regiment it was just falling back under a heavy fire, having charged three times unsuccessfully. The regiment was greatly reduced—by half at least—Col. C. had been wounded. Out of our company, my old friend J. H. had fallen with others and many had been wounded. Gen'l Helm had received a mortal wound and had to be borne to the hospital on a litter. Lt. Col. W., in command of the regiment, had me to ride the general's horse back to the hospital. Our brigade hospital was more than a mile from the field, across the Chicamauga. The wounded, I found, scattered over a half acre of ground—all out of our brigade too. Here I found one of the refugee drummers on Col. H's horse, which I immediately rode to the regiment, piloting Maj. Hope and others to the brigade. The sun was then getting low and Col. W. immediately despatched me on his horse to the wagon train, or cook wagons, to hurry up the rations, the boys, not having had much to eat for two or three days. I had not been long gone, when our troops advanced again on the extreme right, and this time our brigade went over the enemy's works. The loss though, was nothing, compared to that of the morning fighting. When I got to the cook train, our wagon had gone to the regiment with rations, which I had accidentally passed in the darkness. I then rode back to the hospital, and stayed until morning.

Sept. 21st.—As soon as it was light enough to see how to ride, I started for the regiment. I found them lying around loose, in line of battle, waiting orders. A skirmish line was soon after sent forward to find the enemy, but he had withdrawn during the night. The Army of Tennessee, *for once* had beaten the enemy in an open field fight. Gen'l Bragg rode along the lines, and everywhere was loudly cheered. We tried to get tools to bury our boys, but could not. Late in the evening, was sent with orders to the hospital, and remained there all night. After I had left, the brigade started towards Chattanooga. A detail was left to bury the dead.

Kate Cumming:
Journal, September 28–October 1, 1863

Kate Cumming had begun her nursing service with the Confederate army in April 1862 when she volunteered after the battle of Shiloh. After spending two months caring for sick and wounded soldiers at Corinth and Okolona in northern Mississippi, she returned home to Mobile, Alabama. She then began serving as a hospital matron in Chattanooga in September 1862, the same month the Confederate Congress authorized paid positions for women in the army medical department. Evacuated from Chattanooga in July 1863, Cumming was working at a hospital in Newnan, Georgia, when she learned of the fighting at Chickamauga. On September 26 she recorded news of the death of several Confederate officers and wrote: "Alas! what scenes of horror does not even the word victory bring up before us!" Out of an army of about 65,000, the Confederates lost more than 18,000 men killed, wounded, or missing in the battle, while Union losses totaled more than 16,000 men out of about 60,000.

September 28.—Last evening, Rev. Dr. Husten made a speech at the depot, calling on the people to send up provisions and nurses to Chickamauga, for the purpose of feeding and nursing the wounded, as General Bragg has gone with his whole army to take Chattanooga, and requires the services of every man who is able to travel, and there are not enough left to take care of the sufferers. Our cooks have been up all night long, cooking food to send up. The same has been done in all the other hospitals.

This morning Mrs. Johnston called, and I went with her to a meeting, which was held in town, about the wounded.

Dr. Heustis addressed us, and presented a picture of suffering that would have wrung the heart of the most hardened, and said he had only told us about our own men; that if they were in such distress we could guess in what state the prisoners were.

He told us the principal thing needed was something to eat, and he believed that in one place where the men were lying, that if a basket full of biscuits was put down in the midst of them, they would let out a shout of joy that would rend the air. He had worked day and night while there, dressing wounds and giving the men water to drink, and said he believed many persons could be kept busy doing nothing but the latter. He urged all the men to go that could possibly do so; said that ladies could not go yet, as there is no place for them to stay. The enemy had destroyed a portion of the railroad, and the wounded had to be taken to a place called the "Burnt Shed," some twenty miles distant from the battlefield, there to await transportation on the cars.

Colonel Colyer of Tennessee made a very stirring speech, and was ready himself to go. A collection was then taken up, and many hundreds of dollars given. Mrs. J. introduced me to Dr. Heustis. I told him I was very anxious to go; I knew I could get some place to stay, as I was well acquainted in that neighborhood; the Burnt Shed being only a short distance from Cherokee Springs. He tried to persuade me not to think of it. On my way home I met our chaplain, Mr. Green, who told me he was going, and that if I wished I could go with him, and stay with a very nice lady, a friend of his. I intend leaving this afternoon, and am busy collecting what I can to take with me. Dr. Devine has just received a box full of delicacies from Mississippi, for troops from that state. It is impossible to send any thing to the army at present. He has given me some nice wine and other things.

Some of the ladies of the place intend going up in a few days, but none are ready to go at present. Mrs. Colonel Griffin gave me a black man for a servant.

October 6.—Left here on the 28th ult., about 3 o'clock A. M. The cars were densely crowded with soldiers returning to their commands. When we arrived at the Burnt Shed, found that the rail track had been finished to Ringgold; so we passed on to that place. As I was familiar with it, I went to the nearest building, which had been the Bragg Hospital.

There was no light to be seen any place, excepting that which came from a fire outside, around which stood a crowd of shivering soldiers.

Wounded men, wrapped in their blankets, were lying on the balcony. I went into a room which was filled with others in the same state; some of whom were suffering for want of water. They all seemed perfectly resigned; the more so as we had been victorious. How they seemed to glory in it!

After finding a vacant room to put my baggage in, I went to our old friend, Mrs. Evans. She was delighted to see me, said she had often wondered what had become of Mrs. W. and myself.

She had passed through the fearful ordeal of having been under the fire of the enemy; and she was obliged to live in the woods for some days.

I remained there until after breakfast; then I went down to the main hospital, where I was introduced to the surgeon in charge, Dr. Ussery. He gave me bandages to roll; I was assisted by a young man by the name of Dearing, from Kentucky, who was disabled by being wounded in one of his arms. Mr. Green and the colored man were kept busy all day dressing wounds.

Mr. D. and myself sat on the up-stairs gallery, where we could see the wagon trains come in with their precious burdens. As many as fifty came in at one time. We rolled bandages until the afternoon, and could scarcely supply the demand. The surgeons were getting the wounded men ready to send off on the train. I was rejoiced when we were told we had rolled enough for that day. This work had been quite a trial for me, as I had been compelled to see our poor fellows brought in as they were taken from the field hospital, and I had no chance of doing any thing for them.

There had been no rain for some time, and the wagons raised the dust in clouds, and when the men were taken out of them they were almost as black as negroes.

I took the blackberry wine which Dr. D. had given me and put it in a bucket of water, which made a nice drink. With it and something to eat, Mr. D. and I went down and waited on the men; I never saw any thing relished as much as it was. When we came to Mississippians, and told them it was from Mississippi, they relished it still more. I wondered if the ladies of Mississippi who made it had the least idea by whom and where it would be used.

While in one of the rooms a gentleman came up to me and said he was rejoiced to see me, and that I was the first lady he had seen there. He told me these men were Kentuckians, and that he was leaving on the train with some wounded. He said any attention I paid to these sufferers he would take as a personal favor.

After he left I asked one of the men who he was, and was informed he was Professor Pickett, a Baptist minister, and chaplain of a Kentucky brigade, and that he was a true Christian and zealous patriot, and had done much good in the cause.

We went into the cars which were filled with the wounded. Mr. D., while waiting on the patients, ran the risk of having his arm again broken, as he had the use of but one hand.

About dark I took some cloth for bandages and went to Mrs. Evans's to remain all night. On reaching there I met a widow lady, Mrs. ——. I asked Mrs. E. what the ladies of the place were doing, as not one of them had visited the hospital that day; and I said, if they would all roll bandages, that would be all I would ask of them. Mrs. —— did not seem to like my remarks, and said the surgeons had never asked them, and that the Federals had taken all the cloth they had to make bandages with. I answered her that I supposed the surgeons thought the ladies did not need asking, and that there was plenty of cloth at the hospitals. She said she would work at them to-morrow. She then assisted me with what I had.

Colonels Walter and Hays, who were stopping at Mrs. E.'s, came in. Colonel W. said, word for word, what I had about the ladies; only added that such neglect pained him very much. To this Mrs. —— said nothing.

I think these two gentlemen were there for the purpose of seeing that the wounded were properly cared for. I believe they are on General Bragg's staff. Colonel W. was very talkative. He spoke highly of the Mobile ladies and their beauty; said it was a dangerous place for any one who was at all susceptible of the tender passion, and that, fortified as he was by age and a wife, he nearly lost his heart. Both of these men seemed high-toned gentlemen; such as most all our educated southerners are.

Next morning, the 30th, I arose early, and took a hurried

breakfast, and when leaving asked Mrs. —— if she intended coming for the bandages. She answered, with emphasis, "I never go to hospitals, but will send for them."

On reaching the hospital, to my joy and surprise, I found that Dr. Stout had arrived early in the morning, and with him a hospital corps of surgeons and nurses; among them my kind friends, Dr. Burt and Mrs. Ellis. I knew that now the wounded would be well cared for.

Dr. Stout and his corps had been at the "Burnt Shed" for some days. He told me that when he went there, he found quite a number of regimental surgeons, and, to his sorrow, nearly all were intoxicated. He had done what he could to have every thing put in as good order as the place would admit of. He also said that no words could tell the amount of good which had been done by the Georgia Relief Committees; that had it not been for them, many of our men would have died of starvation. Part of the Atlanta Committee (I think it was) was then with him. He introduced me to some of the members; among them was Neal Brown, ex-governor of Tennessee, who was a Unionist when the war broke out; but after seeing how badly the Federal government acted, joined our side.

I had made up my mind, on seeing so many there to take care of the wounded, that I would go right back to Newnan, as I had left Mrs. W. quite sick, and much work to do.

I have always had a great desire to go on a battle-field. I can not call it idle curiosity; but a wish to see and know the most of every thing, so that I might judge for myself, and know how I may be of service.

There was a Mrs. Weir, from Griffin, Georgia, who had come to nurse her son. He had lost a leg, and was at a private house near the battle-field. This lady told me she had a young friend, whose corpse she had heard was still on the battle-field unburied. She kindly asked me to go with her.

The field was some fifteen miles distant; so we had to watch our chances of getting a conveyance. There were wagons coming in all the time with the wounded, but none going back that day; so an opportunity for getting out seemed slender. Mr. Dearing was on the watch for us. A very nice-looking covered private wagon came, and after depositing its load, Mr. D. requested the owner to take us; but he stoutly refused,

saying his horses were completely worn out. Mr. D. then told
him that there was one of the ladies who had nursed at least
one thousand Confederates, and was very anxious to go out to
the field. He immediately drew up and invited us all in, Mr. D.
going with us.

We found our kind driver quite intelligent and very talkative.
He related to us many anecdotes of the late battle. His name
was Tedford. The first line of battle was formed on his farm,
but I believe was moved before there was any fighting. His
wife's pantry had suffered from our own men. She was ordered
out of the house, and took shelter in the woods. After the
battle, when the men found the house deserted, they went in
and took every thing they could get; even taking some preserves which Mrs. T. had hid away in an attic. They also took
her clothes and tore them up; the latter might have been done
for the benefit of the wounded, which Mr. T. seemed to think.
He did not grumble, for he was too happy about our having
gained the victory for that.

The battle was partly fought at Tedford's Ford, on his
brother's farm, and he said that the havoc made there was very
great.

He related an incident to us about his brother, or one of his
neighbor's sons, who had been in the service during the war.
He had been on duty at a post far south, and had been sent to
Bragg's army when it was reinforced. He was killed on or near
his father's farm.

We traveled over the roughest roads I ever was on. I thought,
if this was the road our wounded had to come, they must indeed suffer; and, sure enough, we met what seemed to me
hundreds of wagons, with their loads, going to Ringgold. We
also saw many wounded men wending their way on foot, looking wearied enough. We stopped and spoke to them; all were
cheerful.

On arriving at Mr. Strickland's house, where Mrs. Weir's son
was, Mr. T. begged me to go on to Mr. Hunt's, where part of
Hindman's Division Hospital was. He told me that there was a
nice young lady there, Miss H., who was doing a great deal for
the wounded, and he was certain she would be delighted to
have my help. The temptation was a great one. I was anxious
to see what a field hospital was like, and to know if I could be

of any service; and another thing, I had heard nothing certain regarding my brother. He was in Hindman's division; so I thought by going there I might hear from him.

On our way we met Dr. Ray, who had just heard of a brother being badly wounded, and was on his way to see him. He and the other surgeons had had a hard time since leaving us. They had wandered two days on foot in search of head-quarters, or any one who could tell them where to go. They had been all that time without food, but had come across a pig, which they had *pressed*. They had quite a number of nurses with them. I think he said they were at Claiborne's Division Hospital, and if I recollect the number rightly, he told me the first day they went there, there were no less than twelve hundred men to attend. This seems almost incredible, but we have had many more wounded than killed. He also told me that at first they had neither food to give the men or cloth to dress their wounds, and that at present rags were very scarce. I promised to send them some, and go and see them.

Mr. Hunt's house was a small cottage, surrounded by a garden. In the latter were tents, flies, and sheds, which were filled with wounded.

I went to the house with Mr. T., who introduced me to one of the surgeons. He informed me that this was Managault's Brigade Hospital, and also that Captain Chamberlain and Lieutenant Cooper of the Twenty-fourth Alabama Regiment were lying badly wounded in the house. I went in to see them; found them lying on the floor, but on mattresses. They were old friends, and glad to see me. Captain C. looked very badly, as besides his being wounded his health was delicate.

I was introduced to Miss Hunt, a very nice-looking young girl, and as I had already heard much of her kindness to the soldiers, knew she was a true southern woman.

My wounded friends informed me that Lieutenant Bond of the company of which my brother is a member had been to see them, and but one man had been killed in the company.

Captain C. introduced me to the surgeons—Drs. Cochran of the Twenty-fourth Alabama Regiment, Gibbs, and Gourie, who had charge of the hospital; the latter I had met before in Chattanooga. Dr. C. took me around to see the Mobilians—an old man by the name of Chillion, Mr. New, and Mr. Brown—neither of whom I had seen before. Mr. Chillion is a brother of Mr. C., a well-known Roman Catholic priest. He is now in his seventieth year, and has been in the service since the commencement of the war. He went through the Kentucky campaign, and every other in which the Twenty-fourth Alabama Regiment has been, and kept up as well as the youngest man. The poor old man actually cried when he found out who I was. He is a Frenchman, and I could scarcely make him understand me. He requested me to write to Mrs. Chaudron and Mrs. Perey Walker of Mobile, and let them know where he was. The men were lying on bunks made out of branches of trees.

I visited the room where Mr. Hunt and his family were. They had been driven from every corner of their house, which was filled with wounded, and had taken shelter in a small kitchen. I don't know how many there were, but this room was sleeping-room, dining-room, kitchen, and every thing else for the whole family. In it were two bedsteads, and some of the family were then lying sick. I heard no grumbling or complaint from any of them, with the exception of the old man, who sat by the fire, and it is not much to be wondered that he murmured a little.

Before the battle his farm was stocked and his barn filled with grain, and now he has nothing left but the house over his head. Winter is coming on, and with it want and starvation for him and his family; as all the neighbors for miles around had shared the same fate, he could expect no aid from them.

Before the battle the enemy had full possession of that country, and helped themselves to what they wanted. After the battle our troops took what was left, the houses being empty, as the inmates were forced to fly from the bullets. There had been fighting in Mr. H.'s yard, and many killed there.

It was in this house that Captain O'Brien had breathed his last. He lived two days after he was wounded.

When Miss H. and I retired for the night, we went up into a loft in the house, which had no flooring. We had to be careful for fear of falling through the plastering. It was filled with furniture, which had been taken out of the rooms. We had a mattress, with which we made a comfortable bed.

The next morning when Miss H. got up, as there were no windows, it was as dark as night. The ceiling was so low we could not stand upright. On coming down-stairs we found it raining in torrents, and as there were so many persons crowded together, it was any thing else but comfortable. The surgeons ate in the hall, and very kindly asked me to take breakfast with them, but I declined; I felt as if I never should eat again. The scenes with which I was surrounded had taken away all my appetite. They sent me a cup of pure coffee, which did me more good than any thing I ever took in my life. I think if Cowper had drank coffee instead of tea, he would have found it a still more cheering beverage.

I found my two friends much better than they were the evening previous. I had a small basket with me, into which I had put a few articles on leaving Ringgold, thinking I might meet some one on the road who would need them. I had no idea when leaving Ringgold of visiting any of the hospitals, as I had been told I could be of no service in them, or I should have taken plenty of every thing with me. I had a few biscuits and a box of sardines; the latter I received from the Mobile Hebrew Military Aid Society while I was in Chattanooga. I divided them around, and they seemed to be relished.

The Georgia Aid Society had as yet done nothing for this hospital. There seemed to be no food of any kind, excepting corn-bread and bacon, provided by the government; any thing else was private property. What cooking was done for the patients was done outside in the rain.

I found I could be of little service there, and became very anxious to get back to where I had left Mrs. Weir, as I knew I could very readily get a conveyance from there to Ringgold. Mr. D. tried everywhere to get some kind of a wagon, but his efforts were of no avail. He went to Mr. Tedford's to ask him for his, but our men had broken into his barn the evening before, and taken what little corn he had left to feed his mules, and he had gone in search of provender.

It rained so hard that I found it impossible to visit the patients. I was gratified to see how much solicitude the surgeons exhibited for them. They were out in the rain nearly all the morning, trying to make the patients as comfortable as possible. They said that the rain was pouring down on some of them, but it could not be avoided. They informed me that from what they had heard of many of the other brigade hospitals, the men were in a much worse plight than theirs. They blamed Dr. Foard for not attending to their wants, or appointing a deputy. They had a number of patients who were ready for transportation, but there were no wagons.

I asked what Drs. Foard and Flewellyn were doing, and said that I thought these hospitals their especial care. Was answered, "They were watching General Bragg look at the army."

There was a man there who had his arm cut off on the late battle-field, and he was not only walking about, but nursing the others, and apparently quite well.

I assisted Miss Hunt in making some arrow-root, and showed how she could prepare it without milk, as that article was scarce. Captain C. had a little wine, which made it very nice. There were no chickens or eggs to be had for miles around.

I have always found eggnog the best thing ever given to wounded men. It is not only nourishing, but a stimulant.

Miss H. is very pleasant, well educated, and intelligent. She was assiduous in her attention to the suffering.

Captain C. was expecting his wife, and Lieutenant C. his mother. I should like to have remained until these ladies came, but I could not.

Deus's Brigade Hospital I wished to visit, but the rain prevented me. I heard there were some Mobilians wounded there, among them Mr. Murray, adjutant Thirty-sixth Alabama Regiment.

As we found it impossible to get a wagon, Drs. Gourie and Gibbs kindly offered the use of their horses, which was gratefully accepted. Miss H. loaned me her saddle and skirt.

I took leave of my two Mobile friends with many regrets. I had seen numbers die from such wounds as theirs, and did not know but this might be the last time we would meet on earth.

As we rode out of the yard I tried to look neither to the right or left, for I knew there were many pairs of eyes looking sadly at us from the sheds and tents. I could do nothing for them, and when that is the case I try to steel my heart against their sorrows.

I saw men cooking out in the rain; it seemed like hard work keeping the fire up; a perfect war between the two elements; all around had a most cheerless aspect.

As we rode out the tents of the different field hospitals came in view; when we thought of the inmates and their sufferings, it only served to add to the gloom.

I looked in the direction of the battle-field, and thought of the nameless dead who were there. A nation weeps for them, and that day nature, like Rachel, was shedding tears for her children, because they were not.

I thought of the awful conflict which had so recently raged between brother and brother. "O, what a field of fratricide was there!" it makes one cry out in anguish, as did brave Faulkland of old. "Peace! peace! when will it come? Alas! who can tell?"

Jefferson Davis: Speech at Missionary Ridge

October 10, 1863

After laying siege to Chattanooga, Bragg sought to replace two of his corps commanders, Leonidas Polk and D. H. Hill (no relation to A. P. Hill), for their alleged poor performance and disobedience before and during the battle of Chickamauga. At the same time, many of Bragg's generals blamed him for having failed to pursue aggressively Rosecrans's defeated army and capture Chattanooga, and twelve of them had written to Jefferson Davis asking that Bragg be relieved. On October 9 Davis arrived at Bragg's headquarters on Missionary Ridge and tried to resolve the conflict. In a meeting with Bragg and his senior generals, four of his corps commanders—James Longstreet, Simon Bolivar Buckner, Benjamin F. Cheatham, and Hill—called for Bragg's replacement. The next day Davis addressed the army's senior officers and about one hundred soldiers from the porch of a farmhouse. His remarks were reported in the Marietta, Georgia, *Confederate* and later reprinted in other newspapers. Before leaving the Army of Tennessee on October 14, Davis would decide to retain Bragg as its commander and transfer Polk and Hill to other posts.

He began by paying a warm tribute to their gallantry, displayed on the bloody field of Chickamauga, defeating the largely superior force of the enemy, who had boasted of their ability to penetrate to the heart of Georgia, and driving them back, like sheep, into a pen, and protected by strong entrenchments, from which naught but an indisposition to sacrifice, unnecessarily, the precious lives of our brave and patriotic soldiers, prevented us from driving them. But, he said, they had given still higher evidence of courage, patriotism, and resolute determination to live freemen, or die freemen, by their patient endurance and buoyant, cheerful spirits, amid privations and suffering from half-rations, thin blankets, ragged clothes, and shoeless feet, than given by baring their breasts to the enemy.

He reminded them that obedience was the first duty of a soldier, remarking that when he was a youth a veteran officer said to him: "My son, remember that obedience is the soldier's first duty. If your commanding officer orders you to burn your neighbor's house down, and to sit on the ridge-pole till it falls in, do it." The President said, this is an exaggerated statement of the duty, but prompt, unquestioning obedience of subordinates to their superiors could not be too highly commended. If the subordinate stops to consider the propriety of an order, the delay may derange the superior's whole plan, and the opportune moment for achieving a success or averting a defeat may be irretrievably lost.

He alluded to the boast of our enemy that, on the occupation of East Tennessee, they would heavily recruit their army and subjugate us with the aid of our own people; but the boast had not been fulfilled. He said the proper course to pursue towards the misguided people of East Tennessee was, not to deride and abuse them, but to employ reason and conciliation to disabuse them of their error; that all of us had once loved and revered the old flag of the Union; that he had fought under its folds, and, for fifteen years, had striven to maintain the Constitution of our fathers in its purity, but in vain. It could not be saved from the grasping ambition for power and greed of gain of the Yankees, and he had to relinquish it. The error of the misguided among us was, that they clung longer than we to what was once a common sentiment and feeling of us all, and, he repeated, they must be reasoned with and conciliated.

In closing, he expressed his deep conviction of our eventual success under the blessing of Providence, and expected the army of Tennessee, when they should resume active operations, not to pause on the banks of the Cumberland, but to plant our banners permanently on the banks of the Ohio.— This, he believed, would be done. As the humble representative of the people he returned their grateful thanks to the army of Tennessee for what they had already accomplished, and fervently invoked the blessing of Almighty God upon all officers and men comprising it.

Oliver W. Norton to Elizabeth Norton Poss

At Gettysburg Norton's brigade had played a crucial role in holding Little Round Top for the Union at the cost of more than 120 men killed or mortally wounded, including the brigade commander, Colonel Strong Vincent. "There is no one to fill his place," wrote Norton, who had served as Vincent's brigade bugler. "Oh, how we loved him!" Norton served at brigade headquarters for another three months before seeking a new position in the army.

> *Home of the Sanitary Commission,*
> *Washington, D. C., Oct. 15, 1863.*

Dear Sister L:—.

My mind has been in such a muddle since I came to Washington that I cannot remember whether I have written to you since I came here or not. I know I have answered your last letter, but I believe I did that in camp, and though I have not heard from you since, it seems time to write again, so here it is.

First, what I am doing here. If you have not heard, you are wondering if I have at last got into a hospital. Not very, at least I am not under medical treatment.

You know that, with my restless disposition, I could not be contented as brigade bugler while there was a possibility of doing better. As long ago as last May I began to work for a commission in a colored regiment. I wrote to Galusha A. Grow for advice. (I presume you noticed the record of that in my diary and wondered what that was about.) I heard nothing from him till this fall, when I received a letter recommending me to the notice of C. W. Foster, Major and Assistant Adjutant General, Chief of Colored Bureau, and requesting that I might be examined. It was dated September 21st. I immediately made an application to Major Foster, enclosing this letter, and in due time received an order from the War Department permitting me to appear for examination before the board of which Major General Casey is president. I reported to the board on the 1st of October and was informed that I could not be examined for a week or two yet, and was sent to this place to stay in the meantime.

Second, my prospects. When I first came here I had a very poor idea of the qualifications requisite to pass a successful examination. I knew I was as well qualified as half the officers of my regiment and I hoped to get through. Now I find that none are commissioned who are not qualified to hold the same rank in the regular army, and I begin to feel very small indeed. A man is required to show, first, a thorough knowledge of Casey's Tactics (and the examination is very severe in this), then a good knowledge of geography and history, arithmetic, algebra and geometry. Then the "Army Regulations," "Articles of War," muster and pay rolls, etc., etc., in fact be fully as well posted for second lieutenant as colonel of volunteers. Since I have been here two lieutenant colonels and many line officers have been rejected as unfit for second lieutenants.

After all this comes a searching physical examination, and no matter how well a person is posted, if the surgeon does not pronounce him sound in every respect, he is rejected. Knowing all this you may believe that my hopes of success are very small indeed. However, I shall try, and if I succeed shall be very agreeably disappointed, and I shall consider it no small honor, either. I am studying all I can, but I cannot fix my mind to study as I once could. Two years and a half in the army vetoes that.

I left the army at Culpeper. To-day they are reported at Bull Run, and the air is full of rumors of another great battle on that already famous field. For the first time, if so, the "Third Brigade" has been in a fight without me. I confess to no little anxiety for the result. Our army, I know, is weakened. The Eleventh and Twelfth corps have been sent to Rosecrans, and the First, Second, Third, Fifth and Sixth comprise the whole of our army. The papers say that "Meade is only falling back to seek a field," but I don't believe it. If he had the force, the fields at Culpeper are just as good as those at Bull Run, where the rebels have the memory of two victories. However, I will not croak, but hope for the best.

From Pennsylvania and Ohio we have glorious news. Curtin is re-elected by 30,000 majority and Brough has beat

Vallandigham 100,000. That is a greater victory for Pennsylvania than the battle of Gettysburg. It is a victory for the country. Copperheads are nowhere and the elections speak in unmistakable terms the determination of the people to support the administration. It cannot but have its influence on the South and on the war.

Jefferson Davis: Speech at Wilmington

After leaving the Army of Tennessee, Davis toured through Alabama, eastern Mississippi, Georgia, and South Carolina before arriving in Wilmington on November 5. His speech, delivered from a balcony on Market Street, was reported in the *Wilmington Journal* the following day.

———————————

November 5, 1863

The President in reply returned his thanks to the people of Wilmington and to Mr. Wright as their organ, for the cordial welcome they had given him. He was proud to be welcomed by such an enthusiastic concourse of North Carolinians to the soil of the ancient and honored town of Wilmington. He hoped that Wilmington, although frequently menaced, might be forever free from the tread of an invading foe. He knew well the importance of her harbor, now the only one through which foreign trade was carried on, and he trusted that the valor of her people, assisted by the means which the government would send to her defence would be fully adequate for that purpose. He had given for the defence of Wilmington one of the best soldiers in the Confederate army—one whom he had seen tried in battle and who had risen higher and higher as dangers accumulated around him. What other means the government could command had been sent here, and in case of attack such additions would be made to the garrison in men and arms as would, he believed, enable Wilmington to repulse the foe, however he might come, by land or by sea.

The President urged upon all their duty to do a full part in the present great struggle, the issues of which were on the one hand freedom, independence, prosperity—on the other hand, subjugation, degredation and absolute ruin.—The man who could bear arms should do so. The man who could not bear arms, but had wealth, should devote it freely to the support of the soldiers and to taking care of their widows and orphans.

Those who for the necessities of civil government, or for the carrying on of industrial pursuits deemed essential to the country, were exempt from the general service, were still bound to take part in the local defence; even the old man who was unable to bear arms, must, in the course of long years have acquired an influence, which should be exerted to arouse those in his neighbourhood to fresh zeal and renewed exertions in support of the cause in which all are so deeply interested. If we were unanimous, if all did their duty manfully, bravely disinterestedly, then our subjugation would be impossible; but if, neglecting the interests of the country, and only anxious to heap up sordid gain, each man attended only to his own private interests, then would it be found that such gains were accumulated only to fall into the hands of the plundering Yankees. The soldier who had fought bravely for his country, although he could leave his children no other fortune, would leave them rich in an inheritance of honor, while the wealth gathered and heaped up in the spirit of Shylock, in the midst of a bleeding country, would go down with a branding and a curse.

Since the President had last passed through Wilmington he had travelled far and visited many portions of the country, and in some he had found ruin and devastation marking the track of the vandal foe. Blackened chimneys alone remained to mark the spot where happy homes once stood, and smouldering ashes replaced the roofs that had sheltered the widow and the orphan. Wherever the invader had passed the last spark of Union feeling had been extinguished, and the people of the districts which the Yankees had supposed subjugated were the warmest and most devoted friends of the Confederacy.

He had visited the army of the West, had gone over the bloody battle field of Chickamauga, and a survey of the ground had heightened his admiration for that valor and devotion, which, with inferior numbers, had overcome difficulties so formidable, and after two days' fighting had achieved a glorious victory, the routed foe only finding shelter under the cover of night.

He had visited Charleston, where the thunder of the enemy's guns is heard day and night hurling their fiercest fire against Sumter, and still the grand old fortress stands grim, dark and silent, bidding defiance to the utmost efforts of the foe. He had visited the other points about Charleston, and had found the spirit of the people and of the troops alike resolute and determined. The Yankees were anxious to crush what they called the nest of the rebellion. He believed that it would stand, spite of their utmost efforts for its capture. It had his best prayers for its safety. God bless the noble old city!

The President said that in North Carolina, as elsewhere, the contact of the Yankees had thoroughly extinguished every spark of Union feeling wherever they had come. The Eastern portion of the State which had suffered most from the enemy was perhaps the most loyal and devoted portion of the whole State; and North Carolina as a State had not been behind any other in the number of troops she had given to the armies of the Confederacy. In every field, from great Bethel, the first, to Chickamauga, the last, the blood of North Carolinians had been shed and their valor illustrated, and if she had fewer trumpeters than some others to sound her fame, the list of killed and wounded from every battle-field attested her devotion and bore witness to her sacrifices. North Carolina might well be proud of her soldiers in the armies of the Confederacy.

We are all engaged in the same cause. We must all make sacrifices. We must use forbearance with each other.—We are all liable to err. Your Generals may commit mistakes; your President may commit mistakes; *you* yourselves may commit mistakes. This is human and for this proper allowance must be made. We must cultivate harmony, unanimity, concert of action. We must, said the President, beware of croakers—beware of the man who would instil the poison of division and disaffection because this section or that section had not got its full share of the spoils and the plunder, the honors and the emoluments of office. Did we go into this war for offices or for plunder?—did we expect to make money by it? If so, then he and others, who, like him, had lost all—had seen the product of years swept away, had been woefully mistaken. But we had not gone into this war from any such ignoble motives, and no such narrow considerations ought to control appointments. Merit and merit alone should be the criterion. And merit *had* been found, and North Carolinians had received and now held a full proportion of the high positions in the army. He here alluded to General Bragg, a native son of North Carolina.

If, there were those who yielded to despondency, who despaired of the Republic, who were willing to submit to degradation, they were not to be found in the ranks of the army, where all was confidence and determination. Those who complained most, were those who had made the fewest sacrifices, not the soldiers who had made the most.

In the changing fortunes of war, we may for a time be driven back, but with a resolute purpose and united effort we would regain all that we had lost, and accomplish all that we had proposed. Freed from the shackles imposed upon us by our uncongenial association with a people who had proved themselves to be ten times worse than even he had supposed them to be, the Confederate States would spring forward in a career of happiness and prosperity surpassing the dreams of the most sanguine.

The President again returned thanks for his kind and enthusiastic reception, and withdrew.

Walter H. Taylor to Bettie Saunders

In the last week of September two corps from the Army of the Potomac were sent west to reinforce Rosecrans, leaving Meade with
about 75,000 men camped around Culpeper, Virginia. Although the
detachment of Longstreet and his two divisions had left him with
only 45,000 men, Lee decided to take the offensive. Starting on October 9, Lee's army marched west and then north, turning Meade's
right flank and causing him to withdraw along the Orange & Alexandria railroad to Centreville, forty miles to the north of Culpeper. On
October 14 A. P. Hill lost more than 1,300 men killed, wounded, or
captured in a battle with the Union rear guard at Bristoe Station,
ending Confederate hopes of cutting off the Union retreat. Unable to
supply his army near Centreville, Lee turned south on October 18 and
withdrew behind the Rappahannock. On November 7 a Union night
attack overran the Confederate bridgehead at Rappahannock Station,
capturing 1,600 prisoners. Lee then retreated across the Rapidan, and
by November 10 the two armies had returned to their previous positions. Major Walter H. Taylor, Lee's adjutant, wrote to his fiancée
after the campaign ended.

––––––––––

Camp near Orange CHo
15 November 1863
 For the first time I think since the commencement of the
war Sunday has come upon me unawares. I had persuaded
myself that it was to come on the 16th of the month and all day
yesterday and this morning I have imagined that this was Saturday & contemplated writing you a letter tonight as usual.
When George Peterkin came in just now and asked me if there
was any objection to his going to attend service in Orange, I
was highly entertained at his having, as I thought, gained a
day. How I made such a mistake I cannot tell. As the roar of
artillery is again heard this morning, I hasten whilst time is left
me to acknowledge the receipt of yours of last Sunday and to
thank you my dear Bettie, for all that it contains. I cannot tell
you how anxiously I watch the mails when the time arrives

when I think I may reasonably expect a letter. When there is none, I bear my disappointment like a Trojan and patiently await another day. And when the earnestly longed for favor makes its appearance I almost tremble with delight. Oh Bettie, my precious one, your letters are very dear to me. When I read them, I am almost transported with joy to see that you are my own truly my own. My happiness is almost too great when I perceive that you too look forward to our future with anticipations of a happy life together. When we shall be all in all to each other. When I shall study and labor, oh! so earnestly and faithfully to secure your comfort and happiness. Hitherto, dear Bettie, my devotion for you has struggled alone under most adverse circumstances, it could not develop itself because it was unrequited: 'twas not encouraged; but now that it meets with reciprocal sentiment on your part, now that I can properly remove the restraint which I always imposed upon it, it assumes mammoth proportions, it absorbs my whole being. Did I not feel very secure, yes, did I not recognize the kind hand of Providence in bringing us thus together finally after my many hopes, fears and prayers, I should tremble indeed when I realize how entirely dependent I am upon you; when I have to confess that you are all to me, light, life, everything. . . .

But little of importance has occurred in the army since my letter or note of last Saturday. From the papers, you have no doubt learned of our movement to the south side of the Rapidan. Contrary to my expectations the enemy was very tardy in pushing his advantage, after our misfortune at Rappanhannock Station. Soon after my note to you was dispatched, we struck tents, packed the wagons and sent them to the rear—only moving ourselves about twelve o'clock. Before leaving our camp we built the most immense fires in all our new chimneys, to show how nicely they would draw; and wrapped in my overcoat, I stretched out in front of mine upon a pile of straw and soon lost consciousness in a sweet sleep. I was presently awakened by an exclamation from the General addressed to those around to the effect that Major Taylor was a happy fellow, meaning that I could sleep, whether circumstances were propitious or the reverse, at any time. After the chimneys themselves, as well as the wood in the fire places, were consumed, for we were determined the Yankees should not reap the profits of our industry and skill, we commenced our march for the point where it had been arranged HdQtrs should be established for the anticipated engagement. So soon as we arrived there, it being yet some hours before day, the "happy fellow" again composed himself to sleep and awoke about day with a thought of his absent dear one and ready for Meade or "the newest fashions"—(Pray excuse the slang).

But the Yankees were apparently satisfied; at all events evinced no desire to bring on a general engagement and permitted us to remain in line of battle all day Sunday without any serious molestation. Sunday night, in pursuance of the original design of the General, we resumed our march for the Rapidan and encamped on the south side of that river that night. A day or two afterwards we changed camp to our present location— one much nearer Orange CHo. more central to the army and more convenient to all parties. It is a camp of my selection and I am pleased to see it gives general satisfaction. I hope we may have as nice a one for the winter, if we do not remain where we are.

When the thundering of the artillery commenced this morning, a message was received that the enemy was attempting a passage of the river at one of the lower fords; the whole army was at once signaled to be under arms and ready for battle and the General, with all the Staff save me, started for the front. I was left to attend to whatever should arrive in the General's absence, and was to follow when convinced there was really to be a battle and when there was no longer any necessity for my remaining at HeadQtrs. So I have had a nice quiet time to write and what is the best part of it, I have been relieved of all anxiety about the threatened battle, by the receipt of a signal message informing Genl. Lee that the movement was only a cavalry demonstration. So there will be no fight today. When it does come we have no fears as to the result. Don't you mind what you hear in Richmond, wait for my letters, I will always, when it is possible, keep you promptly advised of what is transpiring here. It is needless for me to admonish you as I did Mother yesterday, not to follow and put faith in Dame Rumor, and to deviate from the fashion in the capital, always wear a cheerful, hopeful countenance. Above all, don't wound our pride by feeling any apprehension on our account. Don't imagine that the enemy are to have it all their own way. Our confidence in God and our own strong arms is by no means impaired, and it is not flattering to see our good people doubtful of our ability to manage our old enemy, so often fairly beaten by this army. You ask if there is any prospect of our falling back to Richmond. I see none now. The enemy, I trust, will never force us back so far. I cannot say what we may be compelled to do through a want of forage for our animals; this depends on the departments in Richmond. Personally I would be gratified to be so near you; but with you I think of the country which would be laid open to the enemy and the people who would be exposed to their tyranny and I pray we may never relinquish again so much of the Old Commonwealth. I only wish the General had good Lieutenants. We miss Jackson & Longstreet terribly. Poor Ewell—a cripple—is now laid up and not able to be in the field. . . .

I was very sorry to hear of Mayhew Hobson's death. Poor Mrs. H.—she looked so comfortable and happy when I saw her at home. When I thought how happily fixed the three brothers were, with their beautiful homes, I little dreamed how soon one would be taken away. I received a letter for Mr. John H. a few days ago, enclosed to my care from Pemberton. It was post marked 9th & reached here on the 12th. I presumed it was about his brother and sent it over by a special courier. Mr. Hobson had just been to Stuart's HdQ. to try and get a leave of absence and there learned of his brother's death. I am sorry that he cannot go home now, but Genl. Stuart tells me there is but one Lieut. with his Co. Apart from this, which would preclude any merriment at the Neck so soon as Christmas, I very much fear that my chances for a leave so recently after my last are quite poor. But I can ride to Goochland in a day and when you go there, I shall certainly do likewise if practicable, and if my stay must be limited to one day. Our Staff is very small now and is growing smaller. Two of them, I know, will expect to visit their families next month. This leaves but one other besides me. I expect to lose my tent mate Venable. He is the only congenial spirit I have here, and I shall miss him very much. He is a great friend of Col Preston's and the latter wished him to take a place with increased rank in the

Conscription Bureau. I think he will take it. He has a wife and two children & has seen 3 years field service. He consulted me and I advised him to go. The truth is Genl. Lee doesn't make *our time pleasant here* & when promotion is offered his staff elsewhere, it is not to be wondered at if they accept the offer. Don't say anything of this as Venable has told no one else. As for my promotion, please don't expect it; for I shall feel badly if you think I should advance and I do not. I only care for it on your account but Genl. Lee will not push us up tho every body else goes. I have given over all expectation of being more than a Major—certainly as long as his say governs the matter.

I heard from Frank Huger a few days since. He had just received a letter from Fanny Kerr. Said she was well but not in good spirits. I don't wonder at it, she must have written about the time of Dr. Wright's execution. He tells me Fanny wishes to know if certain rumors regarding you and me are true. He seconded her in her request for information. I think my reply should have satisfied you. Tell Mrs. Jack Preston (that is if you choose) that when her husband applies for leave of absence I will be faithful to my promise & help him. His application the other day was to join Genl. Hampton under orders—that is on duty, & as Genl. H. was then en route to the army, it was not proper that *the Major* should go. My love to all at the Neck; to Pattie & Maria & Mrs Petty. Are my letters too long? Good-bye. God bless you. All is quiet now. Your W. I am glad to say there has been a change of opinion, as regards the person most responsible for the Bristoe Station misfortune. Genl. Heth is not so much blamed. I intended mentioning this before.

Walter

Cornelia Hancock to an
Unknown Correspondent

Cornelia Hancock served as a nurse in army hospitals near Gettysburg until early September. After visiting family in Philadelphia and New Jersey, she went to Washington in late October and began working at the Contraband Hospital in northwest Washington.

———————

Contraband Hospital, Washington.
Nov. 15th, 1863.

I shall depict our wants in true but ardent words, hoping to affect you to some action. Here are gathered the sick from the contraband camps in the northern part of Washington. If I were to describe this hospital it would not be believed. North of Washington, in an open, muddy mire, are gathered all the colored people who have been made free by the progress of our Army. Sickness is inevitable, and to meet it these rude hospitals, only rough wooden barracks, are in use—a place where there is so much to be done you need not remain idle. We average here one birth per day, and have no baby clothes except as we wrap them up in an old piece of muslin, *that* even being scarce. Now the Army is advancing it is not uncommon to see from 40 to 50 arrivals in one day. They go at first to the Camp but many of them being *sick* from exhaustion soon come to us. They have nothing that any one in the North would call clothing. I always see them as soon as they arrive, as they come here to be vaccinated; about 25 a day are vaccinated. This hospital is the reservoir for all cripples, diseased, aged, wounded, infirm, from whatsoever cause; all accidents happening to colored people in all employs around Washington are brought here. It is not uncommon for a colored driver to be pounded nearly to death by some of the white soldiers. We had a dreadful case of Hernia brought in today. A woman was brought here with three children by her side; said she had been

on the road for some time; a more forlorn, wornout looking
creature I never beheld. Her four eldest children are still in
Slavery, her husband is dead. When I first saw her she laid on
the floor, leaning against a bed, her children crying around
her. One child died almost immediately, the other two are still
sick. She seemed to need most, food and rest, and those two
comforts we gave her, but clothes she still wants. I think the
women are more trouble than the men. One of the white
guards called to me today and asked me if I got any pay. I told
him no. He said he was going to be paid soon and he would
give me 5 dollars. I do not know what was running through his
mind as he made no other remark. I ask for clothing for women
and children, both boys and girls. Two little boys, one 3 years
old, had his leg amputated above the knee the cause being his
mother not being allowed to ride inside, became dizzy and
dropped him. The other had his leg broken from the same
cause. This hospital consists of all the lame, halt, and blind escaped from slavery. We have a man & woman here without any
feet theirs being frozen so they had to be amputated. Almost
all have scars of some description and many have very weak
eyes. There were two very fine looking slaves arrived here from
Louisiana, one of them had his master's name branded on his
forehead, and with him he brought all the instruments of tor-
ture that he wore at different times during 39 years of very
hard slavery. I will try to send you a Photograph of him he
wore an iron collar with 3 prongs standing up so he could not
lay down his head; then a contrivance to render one leg entirely stiff and a chain clanking behind him with a bar weighing
50 lbs. This he wore and worked all the time hard. At night
they hung a little bell upon the prongs above his head so that
if he hid in any bushes it would tinkle and tell his whereabouts.
The baton that was used to whip them he also had. It is so
constructed that a little child could whip them till the blood
streamed down their backs. This system of proceeding has
been stopped in New Orleans and may God grant that it may
cease all over this boasted free land, but you may readily imagine what development such a system of treatment would bring
them to. With *this* class of beings, those who wish to do good
to the contrabands must labor. Their standard of morality is
very low.

John Hay: Diary, November 18–19, 1863

In the immediate aftermath of the battle of Gettysburg, Union soldiers and local civilians hastily buried the bodies of about 7,000 men
and burned the carcasses of more than 3,000 horses and mules. David
Wills, a prominent Gettysburg lawyer, was appointed by Governor
Andrew G. Curtin to arrange for the proper reburial of Pennsylvania's
soldiers. In late July Wills proposed to Curtin that the Union dead be
reburied in a new national cemetery at Gettysburg, a plan eventually
supported by the seventeen northern states that had lost men in the
battle. On November 2, Wills officially invited President Lincoln to
the dedication ceremony and asked him to "formally set apart these
grounds to their Sacred use by a few appropriate remarks." Lincoln
was accompanied to Gettysburg by his secretary John Hay.

––––––––––––––––––

18 NOVEMBER 1863, WEDNESDAY

We started from Washington to go to the Consecration of
the Soldiers' Cemetery at Gettysburg. On our train were the
President Seward Usher & Blair: Nicolay & Myself: Mercier &
Admiral Reynaud; Bertinatti & Capt. Isola & Lt. Martinez &
Cora: Mrs Wise: Wayne McVeagh: McDougal of Canada and
one or two others. We had a pleasant sort of a trip. At Baltimore Schenck's staff joined us.

Just before we arrived at Gettysburg the President got into a
little talk with McVeagh about Missouri affairs. McV. talked
radicalism until he learned that he was talking recklessly. The
President disavowed any knowledge of the Edwards case, said
that Bates said to him, as indeed he said to me, that Edwards
was inefficient and must be removed for that reason.

At Gettysburg the President went to Mr. Wills who expected
him and our party broke like a drop of quicksilver spilt.
McVeagh young Stanton & I foraged around for a while—
walked out to the College got a chafing dish of oysters then
some supper and finally loafing around to the Court House
where Lamon was holding a meeting of Marshals, we found

Forney and went around to his place Mr. Fahnestocks and drank a little whiskey with him. He had been drinking a good deal during the day and was getting to feel a little ugly and dangerous. He was particularly bitter on Montgomery Blair. McVeagh was telling him that he pitched into the Tycoon coming up and told him some truths. He said the President got a good deal of that from time to time and needed it.

He says "Hay you are a fortunate man. You have kept yourself aloof from your office. I know an old fellow now seventy who was Private Secretary to Madison. He has lived ever since on its recollection. He thought there was something solemn and memorable in it. Hay has laughed through his term."

He talked very strangely referring to the affectionate and loyal support which he and Curtin had given to the President in Pennsylvania: with references from himself and others to the favors that had been shown the Cameron party whom they regard as their natural enemies. Forney seems identified fully now with the Curtin interest, though when Curtin was nominated he called him a heavy weight to carry and said that Cameron's foolish attack nominated him.

We went out after a while following the music to hear the serenades. The President appeared at the door said half a dozen words meaning nothing & went in. Seward who was staying around the corner at Harper's was called out and spoke so indistinctly that I did not hear a word of what he was saying. Forney and McVeagh were still growling about Blair.

We went back to Forney's room having picked up Nicolay and drank more whiskey. Nicolay sung his little song of the "Three Thieves" and we then sung John Brown. At last we proposed that Forney should make a speech and two or three started out Shannon and Behan and Nicolay to get a band to serenade him. I staid with him. So did Stanton and McVeagh. He still growled quietly and I thought he was going to do something imprudent. He said if I speak, I will speak my mind. The music sounded in the street and the fuglers came rushing up imploring him to come down. He smiled quietly told them to keep cool and asked "are the recorders there." "I suppose so of course" shouted the fugler. "Ascertain" said the imperturbable Forney. "Hay, we'll take a drink." They shouted and begged him to come down The thing would be a failure—it would be his fault &c. "Are the recorders congenial?" he calmly insisted on knowing. Somebody commended prudence He said sternly "I am always prudent." I walked down stairs with him.

The crowd was large and clamorous. The fuglers stood by the door in an agony. The reporters squatted at a little stand in the entry. Forney stood on the Threshold, John Young & I by him. The crowd shouted as the door opened. Forney said "My friends, these are the first hearty cheers I have heard tonight. You gave no such cheers to your President down the street. Do you know what you owe to that Great man? You owe your country—you owe your name as American citizens."

He went on blackguarding the crowd for their apathy & then diverged to his own record saying he had been for Lincoln in his heart in 1860—that open advocacy was not as effectual as the course he took—dividing the most corrupt organization that ever existed—the proslavery Dem. Party. He dwelt at length on this question and then went back to the eulogy of the President that great, wonderful mysterious inexplicable man: who holds in his single hands the reins of the republic: who keeps his own counsels: who does his own purpose in his own way no matter what temporizing minister in his cabinet sets himself up in opposition to the progress of the age.

And very much of this.

After him Wayne McVeagh made a most touching and beautiful speech of five minutes and Judge Shannon of Pittsburg spoke effectively and acceptably to the people.

"That speech must not be written out yet" says Young. He will see further about it, when he gets sober," as we went up stairs. We sang John Brown and went home

In the morning I got a beast and rode out with the President's suite to the Cemetery in the procession. The procession formed itself in an orphanly sort of way & moved out with very little help from anybody & after a little delay Mr. Everett took his place on the stand—And Mr Stockton made a prayer which thought it was an oration—and Mr Everett spoke as he always does perfectly—and the President in a firm free way, with more grace than is his wont said his half dozen lines of consecration and the music wailed and we went home through crowded and cheering streets. And all the particulars are in the daily papers.

I met Genl. Cameron after coming in and he McV. and I went down to dinner on board the railroad U. C. R. R. car. I was more than usually struck by the intimate, jovial relations that exist between men that hate and detest each other as cordially as do those Pennsylvania politicians.

We came home the night of the 19th.

Abraham Lincoln: Address at Gettysburg

November 19, 1863

Lincoln delivered his dedicatory address to an audience of 15,000 to 20,000 people, following a two-hour oration by Edward Everett. The text printed here is his final version, prepared in the spring of 1864 for facsimile reproduction in *Autograph Leaves of Our Country's Authors*, a book published in Baltimore to raise funds for the U.S. Sanitary Commission. A report by the Associated Press, which may be closer to what Lincoln actually said at Gettysburg, is printed in the endnotes to this volume.

———————

FOUR SCORE and seven years ago our fathers brought forth on this continent, a new nation, conceived in Liberty, and dedicated to the proposition that all men are created equal.

Now we are engaged in a great civil war, testing whether that nation, or any nation so conceived and so dedicated, can long endure. We are met on a great battle-field of that war. We have come to dedicate a portion of that field, as a final resting place for those who here gave their lives that that nation might live. It is altogether fitting and proper that we should do this.

But, in a larger sense, we can not dedicate—we can not consecrate—we can not hallow—this ground. The brave men, living and dead, who struggled here, have consecrated it, far above our poor power to add or detract. The world will little note, nor long remember what we say here, but it can never forget what they did here. It is for us the living, rather, to be dedicated here to the unfinished work which they who fought here have thus far so nobly advanced. It is rather for us to be here dedicated to the great task remaining before us—that from these honored dead we take increased devotion to that cause for which they gave the last full measure of devotion—that we here highly resolve that these dead shall not have died in vain—that this nation, under God, shall have a new birth of freedom—and that government of the people, by the people, for the people, shall not perish from the earth.

Petition from the Colored Citizens of Beaufort

Former slaves living within the Union lines were often forced by the military to work for little or no pay. This petition was addressed to Major General Benjamin F. Butler, the commander of the Department of Virginia and North Carolina. It was signed by seventeen individuals whose names were followed by the notation "and fifty outher." There is no record that it ever received a reply.

Beaufort N. Carolina Nov 20th 1863
   the undersigned Colored Citizens of the town of Beaufort in behaf of the Colord population of this Commuinty in view of the manner in which their Brotheren on oppressed by the military authurities in this Vicenity Respeckfuley pitision you are at the Head of this military Department for a redress of grievunces

Your politiness disire to make known to you that they and there brothern to the President of the United States are undiscriminatly inpressed by the authorities to labor upon the Public woorks without compensation   that in Consequence of this System of fource labor they Have no means of paying Rents and otherwise Providing for ther families

Your pitisioners disire futher to Express ther Entire Willingness to Contribute to the Cause of the union in anyway consistant with there cause as Freemen and the Rights of their families

Anything that can Be don By You to relieve us from the Burden which wee are nou Labooring will Be Highly appriciated By Your Pitistiorers

And your pititioners Will Ever pray   Yours Respeckfully & Soforth

William Wrenshall Smith: Journal, November 13–25, 1863

On October 18 Grant met with Secretary of War Stanton in India-napolis and received orders appointing him commander of the new Military Division of the Mississippi, covering almost all of the territory from the Allegheny Mountains to the Mississippi. Grant promptly replaced Rosecrans as commander of the Army of the Cumberland with George H. Thomas, named Sherman as the new commander of the Army of the Tennessee, and then headed for Chattanooga. He arrived there on October 23 after riding over the only route still open into the besieged town, a narrow, muddy wagon road through the mountains north of the Tennessee River. By October 30 Union troops had opened the "Cracker Line," a new supply route that cut across a sharp bend in the river west of Chattanooga. In early November Bragg sent 15,000 men under Longstreet to attack Ambrose Burnside's Army of the Ohio at Knoxville. While Longstreet besieged Knoxville, Grant awaited the arrival at Chattanooga of Sherman and four divisions of the Army of the Tennessee. William Wrenshall Smith, a successful businessman from Washington, Pennsylvania, was a first cousin of Grant's wife, Julia Dent Grant. Wishing to "see a *battle*," Smith traveled by train to Bridgeport, Alabama, then took a steamer up the Tennessee to Kelley's Ferry at the western end of the "Cracker Line."

———————

Friday, Nov. 13 When we awake about 4 oclock this morning (a little before daylight) find we are as far as the Boat goes—Kellie's Ferry—as the enemy have possession of the river above. Get baggage out on bank about daylight and by the kindness of the Mate—(a Pittsburgh Irishman, and a relation of Quails) and the Captain of the Boat—I find a place to wash—and get a tin of Coffee, and some bread and meat—Gen Starkweather says he will take my baggage with his to Chattanooga and, as the Gen's Horses dont come, we all start on foot.

Camps now become plentyer—all I beleave, of Hookers troops. The road was now one continuous stream of wagons. We soon got under the famous Look out moutain and within range of thire cannon and every moment expected a shot from the enemy, but we passed clear to Chattanooga, and over two pon-toon bridges, without any interuption. We all sat down on the bank at this (South) end of the Pontoon Bridge, and waited for some time—From the immense quantity of wagons on the other side, awaiting their turns to pass over, ours would have to be delayed some time—so we seperated—Starkweather and his party going down the river to their camps, and I— north to the town, alone—

When on the principal street I asked an officer for Grant's Head Quarters, and following his direction I soon found it in a neat little white frame house overlooking the river. No one at home but servants, and I wash myself in "the Doctors" room. After waiting some time (½ hour) on the porch Gen Rawlins comes in—recognises me—and gives me a hearty welcome. While talking on the front porch, Lagow dismounts & immediately takes possession of me, and insists on my taking up my quarter in his room—which is opposite the General's.

In a short time the General arrives. He greets me cordially, and takes me into his room. He puts his quarters and horses at my disposal and makes me feel altogether comfortable.

We have a long talk. He tells me all about his children, about his purchases since he has been in the army—his saving all the money he could for the future, not knowing when his fortunes might change, and he be thrown out of his office—Besides buying the ground and beautiful English Villa in which he lived when I was visiting him 5 years ago in Missouri, from Fred Dent,—he has invested five thousand Dollars in U.S. 5/20's; He now wants to buy five thousand Dollars worth of Chicago city Passenger Rail Way Stock, and concludes to send his note for that amount—with the U.S. 5/20's as collateral— for discount, to secure the stock. We have a long pleasant talk till Dinner—which is at 6 oclock. The dinner is very plain— consisting of Roast Beef, Boiled Potatoes, Bread and Butter. The mess consists of the General Dr. Kittoe, Col Lagow, Capt Hudson and (now is added) myself. The General at the head of the table does the carving. None of my baggage has yet arrived. Gen Starkweather promised to send it as soon as his wagons should get to his camp. I am fearful the Gen's bottle of wine will be confiscated.

After Dinner, a little after dark, Col. Lagow, Capt. Hudson and myself start on horse back and see some of Lagow's friends —Dr. & Capt. somebody—who are pretty lively larks. Poker and Cold punch fills in the time. I don't join in the play. Get home about eleven oclock and get to playing Eucre. The General comes in and looks over my hand for half an hour and remarks on my playing.

Saturday Nov. 14. 1863.   There was a little rain this morning which made the road too slippery for horses; so we stay at home all day. I send an orderly with a note to Gen Starkweather for my baggage this afternoon. He sends it all but my shawl and a box of segars, both of which were stolen from the wagons, when they crossed the ferry last night. The Gen is pleased to get his bottle of wine. A good many General officers with the General. The Head Quarters are very quiet, as much so as a private house. Quite a disgraceful party—friends of Col Lagow, stay up nearly all night playing &c. The Gen breaks up the party himself about 4 oclock in the morning.

Sunday Nov. 15.   The horses are to-day sent to Kellie's ferry for General Hunter—who has been ordered here from Washington to inspect the army. An inspection, Grant, says is imposseble as the men are on more important duty—principally making roads. Dead horses and mules are very plenty. Gen Rawlins gives us readings this afternoon—among other things the evening service. He has a fine strong voice.

Lt. Col. Duff, and Lt.s Towner and Dunn are churchmen. Dr. Kittoe also is a Churchman. But all religion is lost in the army. Lagow don't come to table to-day. He is greatly mortified at his conduct last night. Grant is much offended at him and I am fearful it will result in his removal.

Gen Hunter is the guest of the General, and is to stay in his room. Capt. Ross' cot is moved in for him. The cot breaks down and sets him onto the floor—and the Gen. gives up his bed to him & is compelled to "bunk" with Dr Kittoe

Monday Nov. 16.   This morning quite a number of General officers at Head quarters. I was standing in front of quarters as they come out to mount and Grant called to me to get Capt

Hudson's horse and ride with him. Hudson's horse was soon out and I follow just in time to get to the boat (rope ferry) as it was about pushing off. Grant stopped it till I got my horse on. The Boat was crowded and we had some dificulty in making the northern shore. The party was Gen's. Grant, Thomas, Sherman, Smith, Hunter, Reynolds, Branen, Rawlins, Lt. Col. Duff and myself, with three orderlies. After riding up the river less than a mile we turned up the hill to the left into the woods perhaps a mile more where our horses were left behind the hill & we all walked to the edge of the woods overlooking the river and the country beyond all of which was held by the enemy. The field glasses of the Generals closely examined Missionary Ridge & the country this side After about half an hour remounted and went up the river still further to the place selected for the Pontoon bridge to be built. Gens Sherman and Smith went out to examine with their glasses while the balance of the party remained behind the woods. Grant was in a fine humor, and as he leaned against the fence, was telling us about the former great speculations in Real Estate in Chicago and Millwaukee When Gens Smith and Sherman came back, Smith asked Grant if he would walk down and see the spot they had selected for the bridge. We could see them as they picked their way over the rather wide bottom between the wooded hill and the river bank, and thought they were getting too near the rifles of the pickets on the other side.

They come back in about half an hour, when Grant immediately mounts and I with him & we ride rapidly back leaving the others behind. After riding for some time I find that Gen Hunter & Col Duff are the only ones of the party who are in sight. Grant told me about his boys at school—he is very proud of them and fond of talking of them. He also tells me of Col. Hillyer, who after leaving him went to N.Y. and is now doing finely at his profession—the Law The hills we have been traveling over to-day appear to be composed of a porous, (like pomice stone) rock which make the roads over it excellent. I say to Grant I think the hill country is worthless for agricultural purposes, but he says it is the finest country for grapes he has seen.

Gen Hunter and Col Duff overtake us at a farm house on top of the hill, where we commence to descend to the river bottom, and we all stop and get a drink of water without dismounting. As we pass the ferry, find the Boat on the other side and we ride very rapidly to the Pontoon Bridge, but find it broken—by a raft—so we ride back more slowly to the ferry again,—where we find the balance of our party. The enemy are continually sending down large rafts to destroy the Pontoon bridges. But most of them are caught and hauled in by the troops for fire-wood, which is exceedingly scarce. While riding back to the ferry Grant & Hunter were telling stories of old army acquaintenses some of which were very rich and were hugely enjoyed. Grant is in high spirits—and tells a story admirably. In general he is extreemly reserved, but with one or two friends he is very entertaining and agreeable.

As we are coming over on the Boat my horse (Hudsons) insists on drinking a great deal of the clear, cold water of the river. As we get off the boat he rears with me, running me against a pile of amunition boxes and almost against the wheel of a big army waggon. I get off however with only some slight scrapes on my leg.—We have lunch at about 3 oclock, after which go out on Rosses horse with Gen Grant, Hunter, Capt Hudson and others to see the fortifications on this side of the river—From fort Wood we go to an eminence south west of the town, under Lookout Mountain. While there the enemy must have been attracted by so large a party on horseback, for a shell from Lookout no doubt fired at us, exploded midway in the air.

Get back in time for a good dinner. After dark go with Lagow to a meeting of Indiana officers. A large room is crowded by them and as I soon see it is a business meeting I go out on the porch and listen to a fine band playing in the yard. After the meeting every body fell to playing Eucre &c. (I noticed four Generals who had monopolised one table.) We did not stay long, but after a few games with some very clever fellows, went home.

Tuesday Nov. 17, 1863. There is such a dense fog today that we cannot go out. Think of home—and the little Church, which is being consecrated to-day, and console myself by reading the consecration service. Amuse myself by writing and talking to some of the Staff officers. The General has a great many General officers and others to see him on business. At dinner Gen Hunter who is a great Puritan remarked that Card playing was very prevelent in the camps. Grant says he thinks it the best possible amusement the troops can have.

Wednesday Nov. 18, 1863. The 79th Penna Band serenade the General this evening. He comes out on the porch, and when they are through, takes off his hat to them, and without saying a word, walks into his room again.

He is very anxious about Burnsides, and is up every night till 12 and 2 o'clock—writing and sending off dispatches.

Thursday Nov. 19. The General had ordered the horses and we were about mounting when despatches are received from Burnsides—so the General can't go, and we order the horses back—and I spend the morning on the knob or promentory overhaging the river and about the ruined Iron works— reading and throwing stones into the river. The mouth of a great cave is said to be just under me. When I first came here this hill was covered with very large cedar trees—they have now disappeared—stumps and all—for fire wood. There is a good deal of stir about Head Quarter to-day It sounds like business. Gen John E. Smith of Sherman's Army here this afternoon. He looks rough and tired. Capts. Hudson and Ross ride with me about the works and camps. Every thing about them looks very clean and comfortable.

Friday Nov. 20. Cloudy to-day. The General has a good many in this room to-day among whom I notice Gen's Hooker, Howard &c. Business is lively about Head Quarters. The Steamer "Dunbar" which is being fast completed just under the bank below our quarters has her boilers protected by piles of cotton bales. Numbers of pontoon boats are being made every day under cover of the bank and disappear during the night.

Capt. Ross, who to-day, takes charge of the mess—("runing the mess" they call it) expects to have a grand dinner and has invited several guests. As the lunch don't come on at the usual hour we commence complaining, and he informs us he don't intend to have any as Dinner to-day is to be at 4 o'clock. As the hunger of the party increases their complaints grow louder, till Ross, at last, has to order lunch at 3 oclock

At 5 oclock we have Dinner. Besides our own party we have Gen's Meigs, Gen Wilson and Mr. Dana (of the warr office).

Ross don't provide enough plates, and Lagow and Hudson have to retire to curse Ross in private. The General adds further to Ross' discomfort by saying that he had lunch so late and dinner so early that he has no appetite. The guests however enjoy there dinner and we do the talking.

Among other things the General says Bragg sent him word by flag of truce this afternoon, advising him to remove all noncombatants from Chattanooga within forty-eight hours. The Gen. says he did not answer it, but will when Sherman gets up. We have several jokes and laughs over it.

Gen Hooker and Howard here agan to-day

Saturday Nov. 21. As it is a pretty day I ask Gen Hunter to ride with me to Gen A Baird's quarters. He is a Washington man and Gen Hunter is acquainted with him. So after lunch Hunter on the Gen's Celebrated Yellow Stallion, "Jack" (which horse he has monopolized) and myself on Capt Ross' horse, start for a short ride. We find Baird's quarters in a pretty little one-story cottage in the south western part of the town. I introduce myself to the General who immediately recognises me, and asks about our family, and his relations and acquantenses in "little" Washington. He had quite a talk with Gen Hunter explaining with a chart his part in the unfortunate battle of Chikamauga. He is also very attentive to me, and when we are going away repeatedly presses me to come and see him often. I speak to him about getting John Acheson transferred to his staff.

Sunday Nov. 22. Capt. Ross and I ride to Fort Wood and have a look at the enemy. The picket line is about a quarter of a mile in front of us and we can planly see their pickets. This side of Missionary ridge is white with the tents of the Confederates. We hold but a little space on the south side of the river about Chattanooga. In the fort I meet and shake hands with Gen. Baird who again asks me to call on him. Lt's Towner and Duff are doing a great deal of riding on duty—Gen Wilson is also very active, being nearly always on horseback—

Read the Church service in our room. Shermans men are being hurried to their concealed camps on the other side of the river.

Monday Nov. 23. 1863 This morning is cloudy. The heavy guns at Fort Wood keep up quite a regular fire on the

Confederate camps. The battle was to have commenced this morning; but Sherman is not quite ready. Spend the Morning at Fort Wood looking at the fireing. At one o'clock the General tells me to take the elegant brown horse presented to him by Gen. Meigs and ride with him. We go in company with Gen Hunter and others, to fort Wood. Gen Thomas and quite a number of General and Staff officers are there, and it looks very much like business. We sit about on the sand bags, smoking and amuse ourselves looking at the bursting of our shells—when they *do* burst.

About half past two Gen Thomas' troops move out in front of us, as if in review. "By Heaven, tis a splendid sight to see, For one who hath no friend, no brother there." The enemy from Missionary-ridge and the near rifle pits look at the show—supposing no doubt it is a review. At about 2 ½ oclock a long line of battle is formed more than a mile in length and just in front of us. The skirmishers move forward, and then, the whole line advances. As our skirmishers come near the enemys pickets, we see, distinctly, their rifles aimed, and the smoke, followed by the reports. It is like a piece of machenary —Then, in a few minutes, the long line become engaged in the woods and I for the first time hear the heavy roll of musketry. The enemy are driven from their first line of rifle pits and our troops get possession of the rising ground more than a half way to Missionary ridge—No sooner had our men possession of the woods than our wagons and wood-choppers were busy cutting fire-wood and hauling it into camp. Thy wagons & woodchopers were in the woods when the battle commenced

Several squads of prisoners are brought in—in one lot about a hundred. At the very first of the engagement I heard two bullets whistle by my head. About four oclock we go back to our quarters—the General being well pleased at what had been accomplished. He seems perfectly cool, and one could be with him for hours, and not know that any great movements were going on. Its a mere matter of business with him.

While we are at Dinner this evening the cannon fireing increeses, and the explosions shake the windows. Our mess eat their dinner, and talk, as though they were a thousand miles away from what is likely to be one of the greatest battle fields of the war. The firing continues till dark. I spend the evening with Col Lagow, Capt Hudson, Capt Ross, Maj Rowley, Lt Dunn and others. Cadwallader, the correspondent of the Chicago *Times*, amuses us by relating some hair-breadth escapes he made on the field this after-noon. The ten Gal. is nerely out.

Tuesday Nov. 24. 1863. A damp, drizzly, cold day. I wear my "ponchio" most of the morning. After Breakfast—about 7½ oclock—The General sends Cap Ross, Hudson and myself to Fort Wood, with orders to stay there, and report to him any thing of interest. About 2 hours later we see him with Gen Thomas and two or three others riding under the fort to "the front," which is now about a mile from us. We hear that Sherman had succeeded in crossing two thousand troops, by day light, on pontoon bridges made during the night, and we can see his troops taking possession of the north end of Missionary Ridge with but little opposition. During the day one of the most beautiful sights that can be imagined, gives us for a little while some extra excitemt. The beautiful Tenn. river is in view for perhaps 2 miles above us, from Ft. Wood Looking up, a single pontoon boat, filled with men, their bright bayonets bristling in the light, came in sight.—then two or three, then a dosen, then the whole river swarmed with them—all quietly and calmly floating down to-wards us.

About noon as Capts. Parker, Hudson, Ross & myself are standing on the front of the fort talking and wondering why it was so quiet on the left and front—suddenly broke out on the other side of Lookout Mountain, and on either side of the river below us, the fiercest and most tremendeous roars of both cannon and musketry, I ever conceived of. We were fearful that Bragg had precipitated a tremendeous force on Hooker, and was anniheleting him. As the General was to the left and fearing he could not, from his position hear what was going on, we dispatched both Ross and Hudson after him. In about ½ an hour we could see Grant and three or four more riding leisurely to-wards the fort, smoking and appearing more like a farmer out looking at Stock, than a general in a battle. Supposing the General would ride to our right, where this tremendeous attack was being made, I mounted my "Brown" and rode about 5 hundred yards to the bridge over the R.R. to meet him, but looking back at the fort saw him quietly dismounting. So I ride back again and did likewise. The Signal men put their glasses on Lookout, and announced the progress of Hookers forces, as they scaled the mountain, slowly driving the enemy before them. The roar of cannon and the volleys of musketry were made more terrific by the reverberation along the steep, high ridges of the mountains.

As the enemy were driven above the thick mist in which the top of Lookout was enveloped, Grant wrote orders for troops to be sent up the valley to cut off the retreat. As none of the staff, but myself, were about him at the time, I furnshed him the paper and pencel. He wrote on one knee while he knelt, on the ground, with the other. Our successes are reported along the lines of the centre and left, and we hear the loud cheers of the men as they rolled from the right to the left.

At night, from the porch of our quarters, we have a most beautiful view of Lookout. Our camp fires skirt the mountain two thirds of the way up. We stay on the porch most of the evening looking at the beautiful scene—Camp fires and flashes of musketry—till about midnight. The musketry firing, the General says, is extra work—not in the programme. The Gen. says they will evacuate the mountain to night. Many a poor fellow, who this morning, was full of life and health and hope, is, to-night, lying among the crags and bushes of Lookout, cold in death.

> There shall they rot, ambitions honor'd fools
> In these behold the tools—the broken tools
> That Tyrants cast away by myriads

So I went to sleep to dream of the roar of cannon the rattle of musketry and the tramp of charging squadrons

Wednesday, Nov. 25. 63.   A beauteful clear cold day. We find the enemy evacuated Lookout during the night and our flag this morning flouts from its top. After breakfast we all go to Fort Wood. (The General gives me his Bay horse today and he rides the Brown) Generals Grant & Hunter and myself were riding to-gether. As we passed a part of the Anderson troop encamped immediately in the rear of Gen Thomases quarter, I remarked to the Gen. that part of the regiment had been recruted in Western Penna. as a body Guard for Anderson and afterwards Buell. Hunter said that Fremont had run the escort or body Guard so much into the ground that it was now looked on as a want of sense to have one, and remarked that if Fremont had had charge of the war, the rebellion would have been a success in 6 months after it started. To which Grant agreed.

After we had been at the Fort some time and as every thing appears to be quiet Lagow and I ride back to quarters for a drink. We stay'd but a few minutes and rode immediately back to the fort but found the General gone. About 11 oclock Sherman became heavely engaged on the extreeme left—every inch of his attempted progress along the ridge being severly contested. About 11 ½ oclock I ride back again, alone, and ordered "Bill," the General's nigger, to get lunch for me and to put up in a haversack enough for the General and five or six others. While "Bill" is getting the lunch ready I bathe myself and put on a clean shirt.

In less than half an hour I was back to Fort Wood, and found General Hunter mounted, and about starting for Orchard Knob, about a mile to the front, where he had sent us word to meet him. Just as we get under the fort one of the big guns is fired over our heads. The sudden and tremendeous report frightens, for a moment, my horse. He gave a sudden spring to one side but I kept my saddle firmly. We pass quite a body of troops in the valley. Suppose them to be Baird's. We go through the woods a little distance, and soon get to the fort of the stony knob on this side of which are a great many officers' horses, and quite a number of troops, ambulances &c I gave my horse to Bradford, one of the General's orderlies, and climbed to the top of the Knob.

We found Grant, Thomas, and several other General Officers and their staffs. The wind blew quite cold, and our overcoats were very comfortable. We are now in the front of the centre. The top of Missionary Ridge is not more than a mile from us by an air line, and the enemy's rifle pits are immediately below or under us, within musket shot. We can see there troops on the road on top of the ridge. Generals and there staffs ride along the top of the ridge and look down on us, as from the third tier of a Theater, and our batteries a mile back of us are throwing shell over our heads at them. I thought it a dangerous place. It is to me astonishing they did not shell us. General Thomas, remarked to Grant, that if the enemy had known who were there, they would have paid us more attention All this time Sherman is attempting to drive them from his end of the ridge and the enemy's whole attention seems to be drawn to him. His troops have been twice repulsed. We can see them advancing across a large open field on the side of the ridge and twice are they driven back with great loss. The cannonaiding and musketry in that quarter is terriffic and is kept up without intermission. All this time the centre and right is quiet. But they are not idle. Heavy bodies of troops, (Gen. Baird's is part of them) are coming up behind and on either side of us, and taking positions. Sherman gets his signal station in sight and the signaling from our quarter to his, commences.

After two oclock Grant asks me if I have anything to eat— and we go down under the hill sit down on a log near a fire and open the lunch which is divided between the General, Gen. Hunter, Dr Kittoe and myself. They were all hungry and enjoyed the lunch. The General tills us he this morning got a dispatch from the President Thanking him for what had been done the two previous days. After smoking and talking pleasantly for half an hour more we go again to the top of the Knoll.

I think it was about half past three when the General gave the orders to fire the six guns which are planted on the Knoll (They were placed here night before last). It was the signal for the storming of the enemies rifle pits along the whole centre. Such an immence roar I never conceived of. All our guns together with those of the enemy all along Missionary Ridge seemed to open up at once. Our stormers moved forward at the rifle pits of the enemy as if they knew they were going to succeed. The roll of musketry from our lines (about two miles in length) and the reply from the enemies rifle pits near the foot of the ridge, was terrific. As our men charged, the Graybacks broke from behind their protection and up the hill, our men following with chear upon chear and the cannon and musketry on top of the hill pouring shot and shell upon them. Regiment after regiment gained the top and planted their colors —most of them gaining it by the many roads that passed from the valley to the top of the ridge.

As the matter is about decided and expecting to have a long

ride in persuit I mount my horse and fly into town,—fill my flask and get back again to near the Knoll, within about a quarter of an hour,—when I catch up to Maj Rowley who is on his way out. We find the General and his party have just left for the Ridge and, we follow. In the valley just under, where we have been standing, we pass many dead & wounded men. Some of the wounded supported by others that are not so badly wounded. It was a horrible sight, but I, expecting it, was not so much shocked as would be supposed.

We got to the top of the ridge by a very rough road, impasable for any thing but horses and men On the top are several captured cannon, and a great many of our troops, resting, drawn up to repel any attempt to retake the heights. The further we get to the north part of the Ridge, the more loud and sharp is the musketry. It seems one continuous roll. Some poor fellows lying on the road, badly wounded—we stop and give some whiskey. We directly meet the General and party, who are returning, as it is now near dark. I ride home with General Hunter The enemy are routed on all hands, and to-morrow, we expect a big ride after them. The General calls to me and says I was very lucky to be here, as "it wasn't in half a dozen life times one could see so much of a battle with comparatively so little danger." He praised General Baird as a "*fine* officer."

We got back in time to have dinner about an hour and a half after dark. Lt. Towner was wounded when only about a hundred yards from the General, on his way back for amunition for some of the captured cannon. The shot knocked him from his horse—but he is not dangerous. The General orders an ambulance to be got ready in the morning with provetions for the staff for three days, and also a sufficent guard for it. As Capt. Ross and Maj Rowley are ordered to Sherman for his report, I go over with Col Lagow and spend an hour with Capt. Janes—the Staff Comasserry. As we walk home we see Missionary Ridge illuminated by the camp-fires of our men.

Montgomery C. Meigs: Journal, November 23–25, 1863

Brigadier General Montgomery Meigs had served as quartermaster general of the Union army since May 1861. He had arrived in Chattanooga on September 25 while on an inspection tour of supply depots and remained there for much of the siege, advising Rosecrans and then Grant on logistical matters while sending regular reports to Stanton on the overall situation. Meigs would draw on his journal of the battle in preparing a shorter account that he sent to Stanton on November 26. Widely printed in northern newspapers, it would become famous for reporting that the battle for Lookout Mountain "was fought among the clouds."

JOURNAL OF THE BATTLE OF CHATTANOOGA
Nov. 23d. 24th & 25. 1863.

At noon November 23rd 1863 a demonstration ordered to develope the enemy on Mission Ridge.

Rode to Fort Wood with Grants Head Quarters.

At 2 P.M. skirmishers opened on the rebel pickets all along the line, and drove them in with sharp interchange of musketry.

Our troops advanced steadily in line of battle, and drove the rebels from a long line of rifle-pits, and crowned "Orchard Knob" and the low ridge to the right of it, and formed on that front.

Some two hundred prisoners, I judge, were brought in, some men of course were wounded and some, I fear, killed, though no reports have come in.

Two Alabamians were the first brought in, very much excited and very stupid. Did not know the name of their Brigade Commanders, but said Hindman's Division, to which they belonged were all here.

At 3½ P.M. Gen. Grant was back in his quarters, writing his despatches.

The Artillery firing from Fort Wood continues—shelling, I suppose the rebel Camps and works on Mission Ridge, and endeavoring to prevent any massing against our troops in the advance.

General Thomas reports to night 169 prisoners, Alabamians, our loss not yet reported.

Bridges both broken "Dunbar" ferrying at Chattanooga—Mule Boat at Brown's Ferry—Woods Division still waiting to cross at Brown's Ferry.

> Fort Wood Chattanooga
> 24th November 1863. A.M.

Dropping fire among the pickets in front—Troops resting on their arms since daylight—since I have been here.

Visited the lines and watched the battle from various parts of the field. The principal fighting to day was on the nose of Lookout Mountain which General Hooker carried—He rests to the left of the White House holding the cleared ground.

His Camp fires show to night, and picket firing continues. General Sherman crossed above us, and is established on the south side of the River—expects to carry point of Mission Ridge before he rests for the night.

Howard moved up South Bank of the River and effected a junction with Sherman and returned, leaving him a Brigade and posting another half way. The Dunbar towed up two flats and crossed some 6000 troops during the day. She has been of essential service. Granger, Sheridan and Baird rested in the position seized and fortified yesterday.

The enemy has not to us shown himself in force, except on Lookout, where he resisted Hooker and stood at last checking his advance. His wagons were seen coming down the Summertown Road which looks like abandoning the Mountain.

Letters from my wife and children by Mr. Freas the Carpenter, who arrived during the day.

II P.M. Point of Lookout Mt. and the N. E. Hill of Mission Ridge are ablaze with Camp fires of Hooker and Sherman. Rest of both Ridges dark. Bright moonlight—clear North wind—General attack or advance ordered for daybreak. Picket firing seems to have ceased—Rebels have probably evacuated.

And now to bed—I have just returned from Gen. Grant's, Granger will, if the rebels have run, march to-morrow with 20,000 men to relieve Burnside beseiged in Knoxville. Steamer "Paint Rock" will follow him with provisions.

Chattanooga 25th Nov. 1863
Woods Fort 7. A.M.

Sun appeared just above Mission Ridge—Large bodies of troops moving to our left along the summit gaining a position on the high point.

American flag waving from the top of the rock at N. E. end of Lookout Mt. Our troops apparently in possession—no firing.

Clear beautiful morning, smoke and mist hang in the valleys summit clear.

We shall have a battle on Mission Ridge.

Gen. Howard with whom I rode to Woods redoubt parted with me there, and I remained until Mr. C. A. Dana, Asst. Secy. War came up and proposed that we should pay Granger's Head Quarters a visit.

I told him I was waiting for Genl. Grant, near whom I wished to be during the day. But concluding that we could ride to "Orchard Knob" and return by the time any serious movement would be made—I consented to visit Granger.

We found Gen. Wood—Granger was visiting his lines—Gave him the information that the flag waved on Lookout Crest (From wounded prisoner I have since learned that Stevenson evacuated the Mountain about 1 A.M. the night previous.) This was good news to him—Hooker had orders to move to join in a general advance upon the rebel lines.

We rode to the "Orchard Knob" henceforth historical, and there remained 'till Gen. Grant was seen approaching. The first salutation I had on the Knob was from a Rifled piece—a 10 pdr. on the summit of Mission Ridge opposite, which sent a shell whizzing, exploding and sputtering, and dropping its butt into a hole some fifteen feet in front of the group of Gen. W. F. Smith, Major Dana and myself—An officer who saw it fall, I was not looking up being occupied in reading some letters from home, picked it up and handed it to me.

A battery of these 10 pdrs. rifled fired at the "Knob" all day. Head Quarters remained there 'till about 4 P.M., and every few minutes throughout the day, a shell whizzed past the Knob on which stood Generals Grant, Thomas, Granger, Wood, W. F. Smith, Rawlings myself and a crowd of officers of the Staff. No one was hit near us, however, and it was not until Mission Ridge or part of it was carried that any officer of General Grant's Staff was hit. Lt. Towner, when dispatched at my request that some officer should be sent back to bring up artillerists to work against the enemy some of the guns captured on the Heights was shot through the back of the neck and shoulder within a minute after leaving us to execute the order—All others escaped.

The day wore on—cannonade at Sherman's position fortified on the left Knobs of Mission Ridge, and much musketry continued, Orchard Knob replied to the guns on the Ridge, other Batteries to the right joined in the chorus. Woods redoubt with its 30 pdr Parrotts and its 4½" guns sent shell screaming over us towards the guns on Mission Ridge—Occasionally guns to the right and left of our front on Mission Ridge would open but the only rifled guns seemed to be those directly in front of us, and they alone had range to reach us, and they fired at intervals all day, and we were the conspicuous mark. Occasionally they would drop a shell into our picket, or rather skirmish line, which advanced early in the day, and drove in the rebel pickets.

The day wore away, I was impatient at the delay—night was approaching, and so might be Longstreet, recalled from Burnsides front at Knoxville.

A cannonade at Rossville Gap at last opened, It was of short duration. It was Hooker who had descended the Lookout Mountain and crossed the valley and attacked two Regiments and a section of Artillery guarding the pass. A wagon train loading with flour and the troops and Artillery escaped him and the sound died away.

A line was seen deployed in a cleared field on Sherman's right—a blue line which went steadily up the steep ascent.

Soon another followed in support. How gallant an assault, It is impossible for them to succeed were the exclamations. I watched them with my telescope, an excellent one, saw them pass the fence at the upper edge of the field, enter the oak woods, climb to the edge of the crest of the hill, whose profile is thus: and stop A sputtering musketry fire broke out. The men sought shelter from the deadly fire of the log breast-work above them. I saw the reserve brought up to resist the assault, filling the terrepleine of the entrenchment with a mass of gray. I saw officers leaping into the air and waving their swords urging and calling their rebel soldiers to the front. I saw the reserve fall back again out of fire.

I saw a great body of troops move from a Camp between our front and Sherman and pass steadily along the ride to assist in repelling the assault. I saw the men again urged forward slowly, step, first a few, then more, then the whole body over the breast-works, and advance pouring their fire into our men, who stood fast and returned it.

Then the rebels nearer to us advanced and taking our men crowded under shelter of the hills in flank, poured into them a murderous fire, and the right flank of the group dissolved, and the open field below was filled with men running down the hill. The rebels cast stones from their rifle pits into our men thus wounding some, so near were the two hostile bodies during the half hour or hour that they thus stood in deadly array before the rebel charge.

Our men at last gave way, and fled down the hill and through the field in confusion.

Colonel Putnam, Commanding an Illinois Regiment whom I had noticed, riding a brown horse, leading his men up the slope, difficult for a horse to climb, was shot through the head. A Major who gallantly urged a black charger up the hill, escaped the storm unhurt.

General Grant repeated his order for a general advance, now making it an order that all the troops in sight should advance, drive back the rebel pickets and following them closely, run them into and over their breast-works, which solidly constructed of logs and earth, extended in nearly continuous lines for two miles along the base of the Ridge.

The troops were impatient for work. They were formed; a

strong line of skirmishers, a line of battle deployed behind them:—the signal six cannon shots from "Orchard Knob" was given and forward they sprang with a cheer. With a quick step not a run, they crossed the space between us and the breast-works. The rebels fired a volley, our men fired at will, and the rebels swarming out of the rifle-pits covered the lower slopes behind them turned to look at our advance and firing a few shots, again turned and swarmed up the steep roads, which, by oblique ascents led to the summit.

Mission Ridge is 500 feet high its sides nearly denuded of timber cut for Camp fires but still with many oaks upon the slopes.

The order was to form on our side of the breast-works, and then send a regiment or two to wheel to the right and sweep the rebels out of their works and capture as many as possible.

Every gun on Mission Ridge broke out with shell and shrap-nell upon the heads of our gallant troops, who never halted till they reached the breastworks.

Most of them halted there; but the colors of three Regi-ments pushed on and up the slopes of a projecting spur, too steep to be seen from the summit. Mission Ridge is here five hundred feet in height. Slowly the three red silken flags as-cended and the regiments swarmed up after them.

General Grant said it was contrary to orders, it was not his plan—he meant to form the lines and then prepare and launch columns of assault, but, as the men; carried away by their en-thusiasm had gone so far, he would not order them back.

Presently he gave the order for the whole line, now well formed to advance and storm the ridge. It extended some two miles in length, and it pressed forward with cheers. Shot and shell and cannister poured into it right and left, our guns, 10 pdr rifles, on "Orchard Knob" responded firing into the batteries, exploding a caisson, and disturbing the gunners.

The line ceased to be a line. The men gathered towards the points of least difficult ascent, for very steep is this hill-side, a horse cannot ascend or descend except by the obliquely graded roads. The three colors approach the summit, another mass, gathered gradually into a confused column or stream, at an-other point directly, in our front, reaches the summit, the color bearer springs forward and plants his flag upon the crest, a gun gallops wildly to the right, cheer upon cheer rings out from actors and spectators. The men swarm up, color after color reaches the summit, and the rebel line is divided and the confused, astonished and terrified rebels fly this way and that to meet enemies, every way but down the rear slope of the ridge and by this open way they mostly escape.

Bragg whose Head Quarters are in a house in plain sight to the right of our front, astonished at our success leaves the house, passing from the porch through and out the back door, mounts his horse and rides down the hill-side. Our men then crowned the summit, and had they known it, could by a volley, have put an end to this traitors career, as he fled down the road.

Still, between Sherman and Baird, whose division made the left assault, remained a mile of fortified ridge, held by the rebels. Fierce musketry broke out on the summit, for the "unpainted house" guns still blazed each way and Gen. Grant determined to go to the summit, and see that proper order was restored.

I rode with him, soon found three brass pieces, a limber and caisson; but no lanyard and no artillery-men—the cartridges near the piece piled at its wheel were round shot—I directed some of the men lying down behind the rebel breastwork looking to see Bairds line formed across the ridge and hotly engaged give way, while still from the right, at the unpainted house, the cannon blazed,—to bring the limber and caissons behind the breastworks, had the chests examined, found friction tubes and shell, but no lanyard with which to discharge them. An ordnance officer heard me asking for primers and said he had some in his saddle bags. He always carried them and sometimes found them very useful.

The suspension hook from my own and a Captains swordbelt, we wrenched off for hooks, a piece of bed cord, which I found on the ground, completed the Lanyard, and the guns were turned into a battery and ready for use. Gen. Baird spoke to me. I asked Gen. Grant to send back for artillerists and lanyards, and he sent Lt. Towner, who was wounded as he left us.

Gen. Baird requested me to ride with him to the left, now the front, where the musketry roared and raged. We spoke to every officer, many men, wild with excitement—color bearers seeking their Colonels and men their colors—urged the necessity of forming the men at once and that Bragg's army might still by a charge sweep us from the Ridge. Got a line formed across the ridge in the rear of the one so hotly engaged. Set the men to carrying the logs of the rebel-breastworks to the rear edge of the narrow summit, and to forming barricades of timber across the summit. Rode up to the front line and finding that the answer from the part of the hill in rebel possession was dying out, stopped the firing, ordered a breastwork and that the men should lie down behind it, and not fire unless attacked. Ordered a discreet officer and a patrol to be sent out to ascertain what was in front, and finding order being restored and troops regularly organized into bodies which could be handled, marching into position, as it became dark, I, with Gen. Wilson of the Engrs, who had joined me, bade Baird good-night, and rode to my tent.

It was dark as we turned away—the moon just then showed her face above the range, and late I reached my tent—ate a hearty supper and went to Hd Qrs to hear the result.

Hooker came in, reported that we had captured 2000 prisoners on Lookout and 1000 on Mission Ridge, and that Johnson's Division had captured a thousand.

Four thousand to Five thousand prisoners, thirty five guns and many small arms are the trophies. The substantial results are not yet known. Burnside will be relieved at once. Two steam boats arrived at our wharf from Bridgeport during the fight, Hooker having raised the blockade yesterday.

Bragg with a beaten and discontented army in full retreat, burning and destroying behind him. Invasion of Kentucky and Tennessee indefinitely postponed.

The Slave aristocracy broken down. The grandest stroke yet struck for our country.

Our loss is small considering the exploit. The storming of a steep hill five hundred feet high on a front of two miles, every where doubly entrenched by a line of troops which soon lost their formation and streamed upward, aggregating into channels as a sheet of water would have done in descending the same hill. It is unexampled—Another laurel leaf is added to Grant's Crown.

M C MEIGS
Q M Gn
U S A

James A. Connolly to
Mary Dunn Connolly

Major James A. Connolly of the 123rd Illinois Infantry had fought at
Chickamauga, where his brigade, led by Colonel John T. Wilder, had
covered the retreat of the Union right wing. Connolly was then assigned to the staff of Brigadier General Absalom Baird, a division
commander in the Fourteenth Corps of the Army of the Cumberland.
The battle of Chattanooga cost the Union about 5,800 men killed,
wounded, or missing, and the Confederates more than 6,600. While
Bragg retreated to Dalton, Georgia, twenty-five miles southeast of
Chattanooga, Grant sent Sherman to relieve Burnside at Knoxville.
As Sherman approached on December 4, Longstreet abandoned his
siege and retreated to the east. By then Bragg had resigned as commander of the Army of Tennessee.

———————

Chattanooga, Thursday, Nov. 26, 1863.
Dear wife:

I have just come down off Mission Ridge, up which we
fought our way yesterday afternoon. My horse carried me up
there without a girth to my saddle, but I can't tell how. We
captured quite a good sized army in the way of prisoners and
artillery. Right in front of our Division as we climbed the
mountain, were massed 42 pieces of artillery, belching away at
us, but they couldn't even scare us, as they couldn't depress
their guns to reach us, but had to blaze away far over our
heads. We captured all these guns. One of the first officers I
saw at these guns was old Quartermaster General Meigs, wild
with excitement, trying himself, to wheel one of these guns on
the rebels, flying down the opposite side of the mountain and
furious because he couldn't find a lanyard with which to fire
the gun.

Our advance to the base of the Ridge was the grandest sight
I ever saw. Our line stretched along the valley for miles, in the
open field, in plain view of the rebels on the mountain top,

and at a given signal all moved forward as if on parade, through the open valley to the foot of the mountain, then without further orders, slowly, steadily, but broken into irregular groups by the inequalities of the face of the mountain, that long line climbed up the mountain, mostly on hands and knees, amid a terrible storm of shot, shell and bullets; the rebels were driven from their entrenchments on the mountain side, and on our gallant boys went, officers and men mingled together, all rank forgotten, following their old flag away to the mountain top, a struggle for a moment and our flag was planted here and there by scores of color bearers, on the very crest of the Ridge, battery after battery was taken, battle flags and prisoners captured, and the men indeed seemed perfectly frantic—rushing down the opposite side of the mountain after the flying rebels, regardless of officers, orders or anything else.

I slept on the ground on top of the Ridge last night, and when I waked this morning found myself lying within three feet of a dead man who, I thought, was lying there asleep when I laid down there in the dark last night. I have no time to write more; one brigade of our Division started in pursuit this morning, the rest of the Division may be off when I get back to where I left it, so I must hurry.

Thank God I am again unhurt, and in excellent health. Chattanooga is full of prisoners. They are non combatants now, and Grant will remove them to a safe place in accordance with the notice Bragg gave him some days since.

Your husband.

Chattanooga, Dec. 7, 1863.

Dear wife:

I received your letter written Nov. 26, on the 3rd day of this month, and when your letter was brought to my tent I was lying on my cot indulging in some vigorous remarks concerning mules in general, and one mule in particular, which, about two hours before, had given me a hard kick on the leg as I was riding past him, cold and hungry, just returning with my Division from the pursuit of Bragg and his valiant cavaliers whom we so handsomely "cleaned out" as the soldiers say. On

Monday, Nov. 23rd our Division was ordered to move out just in front of the fortifications. We did so, and the rebels, as they looked down on us from Lookout Mountain and Mission Ridge, no doubt thought we had come out for a review. But Sheridan's Division followed us out and formed in line with us. Wonder what the rebels thought then? "Oh, a Yankee review; we'll have some fun shelling them directly." But out came Wood's Division, then Cruft's Division, then Johnson's Division, then Howard's entire Corps of "Potomacs." "What can those Yankee fools mean," Bragg must have thought, as he sat at the door of his tent on Mission Ridge and watched the long lines of blue coats and glistening guns marching around in the valley below him, almost within gun shot of his pickets, and yet not a gun fired. All was peace in Chattanooga valley that day.

The sun shone brightly, the bands played stirring airs; tattered banners that had waved on battle fields from the Potomac to the Mississippi streamed out gaily, as if proud of the battle scars they wore. Generals Grant and Hooker, and Sherman and Thomas and Logan and Reynolds and Sheridan and scores of others, with their staffs, galloped along the lines, and the scene that spread out around me like a vast panorama of war filled my heart with pride that I was a soldier and member of that great army. But what did it all mean? Bragg, from his mountain eyrie, could see what we were doing just as well as Grant who was riding around amongst us. The rebels thought they had us hemmed in so that we dared not move, and so near starved that we could not move. Two o'clock came, and all was yet quiet and peaceful, gay as a holiday review; we could see crowds of rebels watching us from Mission Ridge and Lookout Mountain, but three o'clock came, and a solitary shot away over on our left, among Wood's men, made every fellow think: "Hark"! A few moments and another shot, then a rat-tat-tat-tat made almost every one remark: "Skirmishing going on over there." Wood's line moved forward, a few volleys, still Wood's line moved forward, and Sheridan's started forward, heavy work for a few minutes then all was quiet; two important hills were gained; cheer after cheer rang out in the valley and echoed and reverberated through the gorges of Lookout and Mission Ridge; still it was only 5 o'clock Monday afternoon.

The bands commenced playing and the valley was again peaceful, but we all knew there was "something up," and Bragg
must have thought so too. We lay there all night, sleeping on
our arms.

Tuesday morning, Nov. 24th, broke bright and beautiful;
the sun rose clear; but for whom was it a "sun of Austerlitz"?
Grant or Bragg? We talked of Austerlitz and Waterloo at headquarters that morning. During the night the moon was almost
totally eclipsed. We talked of that also. It was considered a bad
omen among the ancients, on the eve of battle; we concluded
also that it was ominous of defeat, but not for us; we concluded that it meant Bragg because he was perched on the
mountain top, nearest the moon. Daylight revealed the hills
which Wood and Sheridan had won the day before, bristling
with cannon of sufficient calibre to reach Bragg's eyrie on Mission Ridge. About 9 o'clock in the morning some 30 heavy
guns opened on Mission Ridge. It appeared then that we were
to advance right down the valley and attack the rebel centre,
but, hark! Away off on our right—3 miles away, on the opposite side of Lookout—we hear firing. What can that mean?
Suddenly the cannon, with which we have been pounding
away at Mission Ridge, are silent, and all eyes are turned westward toward Lookout Mountain. The sounds of battle increase
there but it is on the other side of the mountain from us and
we can see nothing, but the word passes around: "Hooker is
storming Lookout"! My heart grows faint. Poor Hooker, with
his Potomac boys are to be the forlorn hope! What? Storm
that mountain peak 2400 feet high, so steep that a squirrel
could scarcely climb it, and bristling all over with rebels, bayonets and cannon? Poor boys! far from your quiet New England
homes, you have come a long way only to meet defeat on that
mountain peak, and find your graves on its rugged sides!
Lookout Mountain will only hereafter be known as a monument to a whole Corps of gallant New Englanders who died
there for their country! But hold! Some one exclaims: "The
firing comes nearer, our boys are getting up"! All eyes are
turned toward the Mountain, and the stillness of death reigns
among us in the valley, as we listen to the sounds of battle on
the other side of the Mountain while all was quiet as a Puritan
sabbath on our side of it. How hope and despair alternated in

our breasts! How we prayed for their success and longed to assist them, can only be known by those of us who, in that valley, stood watching that afternoon and listening to the swelling diapason of their battle. But the firing actually did grow nearer, manifestly our men were driving them; Oh! now if they only can continue it, but we fear they cannot! I have a long telescope with which I can distinctly see everything on our side of the mountain. I scan the mountain with it closely and continuously, but not a soul can I see. After hours of anxious suspense I see a single rebel winding his way back from the firing and around to our side of the mountain.

I announce to the crowd of Generals standing around: "There goes a straggler"! and in an instant everybody's glass is to his eye, but no more stragglers are seen, still the battle rages, and the little gleam of hope, that solitary straggler raised in our breasts, dies out. Minutes drag like hours, the suspense is awful, but look! look! Here comes a crowd of stragglers! here they come by hundreds, yes by thousands! The mountain is covered with them! They are broken, running! There comes our flag around the point of the mountain! There comes one of our regiments on the double quick! Oh! such a cheer as then went up in the valley! Manly cheeks were wet with tears of joy, our bands played "Hail to the Chief," and 50 brazen throated cannon, in the very wantonness of joy, thundered out from the fortifications of Chattanooga, a salute to the old flag which was then on the mountain top. The work was done. Lookout was ours, never again to be used as a perch by rebel vultures. Didn't we of the old Army of the Cumberland feel proud though? It was one of the regiments that fought at Chickamauga that carried that first flag to the mountain top. It was a brigade of the old Chickamauga army that led the storming party up the mountain. A straggling skirmish fire was kept up along our (the Eastern) side of the mountain, which we could trace by the flashes of the guns, until 11 o'clock at night, but then all became quiet, and again we passed the night in line of battle, sleeping on our arms. Bragg, no doubt, thought Hooker would continue to press forward across the valley from Lookout and attack his left on Mission Ridge in the morning, so he prepared for that during the night, by moving troops from his right to his left, to meet the anticipated attack of the morning, but Sherman, with his Vicksburg veterans, had all this time been lying concealed behind the hills on the North side of the Tenessee river, just North of the northern end of Mission Ridge, where Bragg's right was, awaiting the proper moment to commence his part of the stupendous plan. The time was now come. Lookout was ours; now for Mission Ridge! Before daylight of Wednesday Nov. 25th, Sherman had his pontoons across the river, about 3 miles north of Chattanooga, and under cover of a dense fog, crossed his whole Corps and took possession of the northern extremity of Mission Ridge, finding nothing there but a few pickets, and there he fell to work fortifying. By this time Bragg saw his mistake. The attack of Wednesday was to be on his right, at the North end of Mission Ridge, instead of his left at the South end of the Ridge, so he hurriedly countermarched his troops back from his left to his right. When the fog rose, about ten o'clock in the morning, Sherman attempted to carry the summit of the Ridge but was repulsed; again he tried it but was again repulsed, still again he tried it and was repulsed. This time the fighting was all to the left of where we were instead of to the right, as it had been the day before. Sherman, after terrible fighting, had been repulsed in three successive efforts to crush the enemy's right on the top of the Ridge, and an order came for our Division to move up the river to his support. We started. The enemy could see us from the top of the Ridge, and quickly understood (or thought they did) our design, so they commenced shelling us, as our long line of 20 regiments filed along, but we moved along until we came to where a thin strip of woodland intervened between us and the Ridge. Sheridan's Division followed us and did the same. The enemy supposed of course that we were moving on up the river to the support of Sherman, but we were not; we halted and formed line of battle in that strip of woodland, facing Mission Ridge. This, I confess, staggered me; I couldn't understand it; it looked as though we were going to assault the Ridge, and try to carry it by storm, lined and ribbed as it was with rifle pits, and its topmost verge crowded with rebel lines, and at least 40 cannon in our immediate front frowning down on us; we never could live a moment in the open spaces of 600 yards between the strip of woods in which we were formed, and the line of rifle pits at the base of the mountain, exposed as we would be to the fire of the 40 cannon massed, and from five to eight hundred feet immediately above us, also to the infantry fire from the rifle pits. I rode down along the line of our Division, and there I found Woods Division formed on our right and facing the Ridge just as we were; I rode on and came to Sheridan's Division formed on Woods right and facing the same. Here was a line of veteran troops nearly two miles long, all facing Mission Ridge, and out of sight of the enemy. The purpose at once became plain to me, and I hurried back to my own Division, and on asking Gen. —— he replied: "When 6 guns are fired in quick succession from Fort Wood, the line advances to storm the heights and carry the Ridge if possible. Take that order to Col. ——" (commanding the third brigade of our Division) "and tell him to move forward rapidly when he hears the signal." I communicated the order at once and that was the last I saw of the brigade commander, for he was killed just as he reached the summit of the Ridge. A few moments elapse, it is about half past three o'clock P. M., when suddenly, 6 guns are rapidly fired from Fort Wood. "Forward"! rings out along that long line of men, and forward they go, through the strip of woods, we reach the open space, say 600 yards, between the edge of the woods and the rifle pits at the foot of the Ridge. "Charge"! is shouted wildly from hundreds of throats, and with a yell such as that valley never heard before, the three Divisions (60 regiments) rushed forward; the rebels are silent a moment, but then the batteries on top of the Ridge, open all at once, and the very heavens above us seemed to be rent asunder; shells go screaming over our heads, bursting above and behind us, but they hurt nobody and the men don't notice them; about midway of the open space a shell bursts directly over my head, and so near as to make my horse frantic and almost unmanageable; he plunges and bursts breast strap and girth and off I tumble with the saddle between my legs. My orderly catches my horse at once, throws the blanket and saddle on him, gives me a "leg lift" and I am mounted again, without girth, but I hold on with my knees and catch up with our madcaps at the first rifle pits, over these we go to the second line of pits, over these we go, some of the rebels lying down to be run over, others scrambling up the hill which is becoming too steep for horses, and the General and staff are forced to abandon the direct ascent at about the second line of rifle pits; the long line of men reach the steepest part of the mountain, and they must crawl up the best way they can 150 feet more before they reach the summit, and when they do reach it, can they hold it? The rebels are there in thousands, behind breastworks, ready to hurl our brave boys back as they reach their works. One flag bearer, on hands and knees, is seen away in advance of the whole line; he crawls and climbs toward a rebel flag he sees waving above him, he gets within a few feet of it and hides behind a fallen log while he waves his flag defiantly until it almost touches the rebel flag; his regiment follows him as fast as it can; in a few moments another flag bearer gets just as near the summit at another point, and his regiment soon gets to him, but these two regiments dare not go the next twenty feet or they would be annihilated, so they crouch there and are safe from the rebels above them, who would have to rise up, to fire down at them, and so expose themselves to the fire of our fellows who are climbing up the mountain. The suspense is greater, if possible, than that with which we viewed the storming of Lookout. If we can gain that Ridge; if we can scale those breastworks, the rebel army is routed, everything is lost for them, but if we cannot scale the works few of us will get down this mountain side and back to the shelter of the woods. But a third flag and regiment reaches the other two; all eyes are turned there; the men away above us look like great ants crawling up, crouching on the outside of the rebel breastworks. One of our flags seems to be moving; look! look! look! Up! Up! Up! it goes and is planted on the rebel works; in a twinkling the crouching soldiers are up and over the works; apparently quicker than I can write it the 3 flags and 3 regiments are up, the close fighting is terrific; other flags go up and over at different points along the mountain top—the batteries have ceased, for friend and foe are mixed in a surging mass; in a few moments the flags of 60 Yankee regiments float along Mission Ridge from one end to the other, the enemy are plunging down the Eastern slope of the Ridge and our men in hot pursuit, but darkness comes too soon and the pursuit must cease; we go back to the summit of the Ridge and there behold our trophies—dead and wounded rebels under our feet by hundreds, cannon by scores scattered up and down the Ridge with yelling soldiers astraddle them, rebel flags lying around in profusion, and soldiers and officers completely and frantically drunk with excitement. Four hours more of daylight, after we gained that Ridge would not have left two whole pieces of Bragg's army together.

Our men, stirred by the same memories, shouted "Chickamauga"! as they scaled the works at the summit, and amid the din of battle the cry "Chickamauga"! "Chickamauga"! could be heard. That is not *fancy* it is *fact*. Indeed the plain unvarnished facts of the storming of Mission Ridge are more like romance to me now than any I have ever read in Dumas, Scott or Cooper. On that night I lay down upon the ground without blankets and slept soundly, without inquiring whether my neighbors were dead or alive, but, on waking found I was sleeping among bunches of dead rebels and Federals, and within a few rods of where Bragg slept the night before, if he slept at all.

You must not think that the General and staff remained at the second line of rifle pits on the side of the mountain, where I left them a few pages back, until the fight was over. The steepness of the mountain compelled us to zigzag back and forth, ascending a little with every zigzag until we reached the summit while the hand to hand melee was going on, before the rebels broke away down the Eastern slope.

Early next morning I rode back to my quarters in the city, where I am now writing, got a new saddle girth and wrote you a brief letter, just to let you know I was safe. That was Nov. 26th, Thanksgiving Day in the United States, I believe, and it was the same with me, though my "Thanksgiving Dinner" was hard tack and raw bacon, but it was toothsome as turkey, for hunger makes fine sauce, you know. You wrote me that same day. After writing my hasty letter to you I hurried back to the Ridge and found my Division gone in pursuit of Bragg, but I soon overtook it, and we bivouacked for the night without having overtaken the enemy. On that night (26th) I rolled up in my saddle blanket and slept on the ground soundly. We started at two o'clock, on the morning of the 27th, and reached Chickamauga Creek, the bridge over which the rebels had burned in their retreat, and by daylight we had a bridge over it and marched to Greyville, where we met Davis' Division, which had moved by a different road and had captured a battery and 300 rebels in a fight there that morning. Davis had moved by a shorter road and arrived there ahead of us. I wasn't *very* sorry for it, for by him getting there before us he saved us a fight, and I like to dodge fights, but appear to have poor success at it, and a fellow stands a chance of getting just as badly hurt in a little fight as in a big one. After halting a few moments at Greyville we started in a Southeasterly direction, toward Ringgold, where we heard the sound of a battle going on, and Gen. ———, our Corps Commander, rightly supposed that Hooker, who had taken that road, had come up with the enemy. After marching ten miles very rapidly we reached Hooker and found him hotly engaged with the enemy; our Division was soon in line and ready for the word to "go in" but the rebels withdrew, and fell back to Dalton. We bivouacked at Ringgold on that night (27th) and the next day one brigade of our Division was sent down the railroad toward Dalton to destroy the railroad bridges. I asked leave to accompany this brigade, as I had been over the road with ———'s brigade of mounted infantry, before the battle of Chickamauga, and knew the country and location of the railroad bridges. The General gave me leave to go and direct the expedition, so I went along. We burned 5 railroad bridges, tore up and burned the ties of a mile of the track, took some prisoners, one of them a lieutenant on the staff of Gen. Joe Johnston, and found the houses along the road filled with dead and wounded rebels, whom we left as we found. We got back to Ringgold, in the rain, before dark, and bivouacked for the night, (28th). Gen. Turchin, who had a couple of tents along in a wagon which he had brought with him, loaned us a tent, and we all, General and staff, rolled up in our saddle blankets and slept together under that tent. I enclose a rough pencil sketch, made by one of our staff officers, depicting a portion of our staff that night just before we got any supper. Gen. ———, you see, is making desperate efforts to fry his own supper, consisting entirely of fresh pork. The African, with frying pan is endeavoring to provide something for the rest of us.

No other incidents of note occurred until we returned to Chattanooga, except, as we were returning, I was riding through the woods in company with Gen. ——, our Corps commander, and his staff, when we came across a caisson, loaded with shells, which the rebels had abandoned.

Gen. —— ordered me to find my Division commander and have him bring the caisson in to Chattanooga. I couldn't find my Division commander nor any team that could haul it in, so I went to work with the assistance of my orderly, and knocked some weatherboards off an old church near by, and built a rousing fire under the caisson, but had to hurry away from it after I got my fire well started, and hadn't gone far until the fire reached the powder, and then I had the fun of hearing 90 rebel shells explode together, and I tell you, it made something of a racket in those old Georgia woods. I am glad now that I didn't ask for leave of absence before the fight, for I should have missed it, and should always have regretted it. I shall now get one as soon as I can. Gen. Reynolds has gone to New Orleans to take command there. I should have been glad to go with him, but if I did I wouldn't have got home until the close of the war, and I couldn't think of that. There are many things I intended to write about when I began this, which I have omitted, but this is long enough, and I'll quit. xxxxxxxxx

Your husband.

Theodore Lyman: Journal,
November 26–December 2, 1863

Aware of Lincoln's mounting frustration over his failure to bring Lee to battle, Meade made plans to turn the Army of Northern Virginia's eastern flank by crossing the Rapidan downriver from the Confederate lines and then marching west through the scrub woods of the Wilderness. One of his aides in the ensuing campaign was Lieutenant Colonel Theodore Lyman, a wealthy Bostonian who had studied natural history at Harvard under Louis Agassiz. While collecting marine specimens in Florida before the war, Lyman had become friends with Meade, who at the time was a first lieutenant in the corps of engineers supervising lighthouse construction projects. After spending the first two years of the war touring Europe, Lyman joined Meade's staff as an (unpaid) volunteer aide in September 1863. In the sketch maps Lyman drew in his notebooks, Union cavalry units are indicated with the letter "C," while corps are indicated by their respective badges: for the First Corps, commanded by Major General John Newton, a disk; for the Second Corps (Major General Gouverneur K. Warren), a three-leaf clover; for the Third Corps (Major General William H. French), a diamond; for the Fifth Corps (Major General George Sykes), a Maltese cross; for the Sixth Corps (Major General John Sedgwick), a Greek cross. The designations "N," "O," "P," and "N'" indicate the order in which the maps appear in Lyman's notebook for the period from August 31, 1863, to March 9, 1864.

November 26, Thursday.

Thanksgiving day, when the fat turkey is served in state. And this was appointed for our flank move on Orange Court House, via our left. At 7¾ A.M. we started. The order of march was 5th followed by 1st Corps to cross by pontoon at Culpeper Mine Ford, advance by a cross road to the Orange C.H. plank road and keep on to "Parker's Store." The 3d followed by the 6th, cross at Jacob's Mills and keep on to form on right of 2d, which crossed at Germanna Mills took a cross

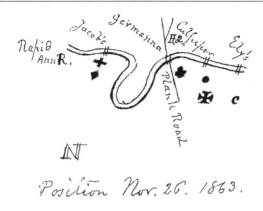

Position Nov. 26. 1863.

road to the Orange Court House turnpike and then keep on to Robertson's Tavern, or, if possible, to Verdiersville.

The 3d Div. of 1st Corps left to guard railroad. Reserve Artillery to follow 1st Corps. Waggon train park at Richardsville, under guard of Merritt's (Buford's) division of cavalry, Custer's division (Kilpatrick's) to hold Raccoon & Morton's Fords. Gregg's Div. to cross at Ely's Ford and cover the advance & left of Sykes. Owing, apparently, to some dullness on part of Gen. Prince, this division did not start till say 7.30, which delayed the rest of the 3d Corps; moreover they had not properly reconnoitred the roads or repaired them, so they took the wrong road, this side of the river, and got their artillery stalled into the bargain! At about 10.30 we got within ½ mile of Germanna Ford & there found the troops massed and the batteries placed, ready to run up and shell the crossing. The Rapidan there runs between high, steep banks whereof the northern dominates the southern, the reverse of what happens at the fords above. Officers were sent to French & Sykes, to find whether they had got up; because it was deemed important to force the river, at the same moment. The communications were difficult, and so the officers did not get back till late, so that our troops (2d Corps) began to cross at about 2 P.M., Sykes having begun at 12, and French not till later. The artillery of the 3d & 6th had finally to come to Germanna and was not over till 5 next morning. We camped at the junction of the

plank and dirt roads on the north side of the river. It was quite
cold and the water froze in the tent.

November 27, Friday.
We were up before daylight, with a magnificent moon glitter-
ing on the hoar frost, but the Staff did not move till 8.45 A.M.
Then we crossed on the pontoons and kept down the plank
road, to a point some 2 or 3 miles from the river where we
struck off, more to the S.W. to make a short cut for the Orange
court house turnpike. Before this turn-off we got to the artillery of the 6th Corps, to whom the General gave a good blowing up, for not knowing their precise road. On this side of the
river, the country is, for some distance, open farming land;
then succeeds dense, scrub-oak wood, penetrated only by farm
roads, narrow and intricate, at best, and in wet weather, impossible for artillery. Near the river had been made long rifle-
pits, with some entrenched epaulements for guns, but they
were quite unoccupied. About midday through the woods we
came on the rear of the 2d Corps, moving briskly, and we filed
past them, with some difficulty. At 9.30 we heard cannon ahead
and, at 10.45 struck the turnpike, along which we advanced to
within say 1¼ miles of Robertson's Tavern, and there halted by
the roadside, at which time (11) there was brisk skirmishing
by Warren, who had gained the ridge of Robertson's Tavern
and pushed back the Rebel advance (part of Ewell's Corps.) And
now we found ourselves with a weak centre, on the pike and
the strong right not heard from, and inexplicably behindhand! Aides were sent to French, under guidance of natives &
niggers. Ludlow, sent to Sykes, reported him well up on the
left. About 12.45 we heard cannon off on our right, which
seemed from the 3d Corps. McBlair came, but he, honest soul,
did display his usual muddleheadedness, as to time & place, and
could only make out, that French was going along somewhere
in the thick woods. At length Cadwalader returned, who had
taken an order to French to attack & smash through to Warren, and reported French's left some 2 miles from Warren's
right. Meanwhile Gregg, in the left advance, had a sharp fight
with the enemy's infantry, in which the cavalry did excellently
and, among them, the 1st Mass. Longfellow and Bowditch were

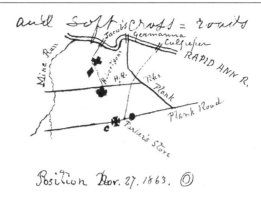

Position Nov. 27. 1863. ⊙

here wounded. An aide from Custer stated he had made a good diversion at Raccoon & Morton's Fords, by charging across both, and forcing the enemy to detach a large force to drive him back again. Meanwhile Warren had received orders to attack without French, or not, at his discretion. He concluded it would not be safe; and so we pitched camp where we stood. After dark came a despatch from French that he had had a sharp action, with very heavy musketry (none of which we had heard) and had driven the enemy from the field, taking 900 prisoners (a number which proved greatly exaggerated) and losing some 900 himself in killed, wounded, &c. His fight, also, was with a portion of Ewell's Corps.

November 28, Saturday.

A pretty place to pass my Wedding-day! Twelve months ago we were in Paris, and enjoying the quiets of the Hotel Wagram. And this morning, behold me, with little Wife hundreds of miles away and a cheery prospect of mud and intermittent rain! At 7.45 we rode to Robertson's Tavern 1¼ m. which stands on a ridge along which the 2d Corps was in line of battle and just advancing. The enemy had disappeared from our front, and many thought them in full retreat. After some talk with Gen. Warren, Gen. Meade went to the tavern, and sat by the fire. However, say at 10.15 there was a report that we had come on the enemy in entrenchments; and we all rode to the front, slop, slop in the mud, and amid infantry, artillery &

ambulances going to the front, also. A little behind the crest of the next ridge, and about 1 m. from the tavern the General halted us, and rode alone to reconnoitre. At 11, a battery opened and fired some time, posted just on the left of the pike. They were in entrenchments, sure enough, and we had only to wait for other troops to come along. The rest of the day was occupied by the corps getting into position, a very laborious thing, midst mud and soft cross-roads. The day previous Meade, anxious for his centre, had brought over both Sykes & Newton, from the plank road; and the 5th Corps was now in reserve at Robertson's Tavern, while the First Corps took position in line.

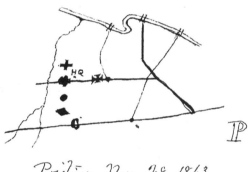

Position Nov. 28. 1863.

November 29, Sunday.

The enemy's position was found to be a very strong one. Along a bold ridge, running nearly north & south across both turnpike and plank road, rising from Mine Run by a steep slope, which in many parts was quite naked, and in others partially wooded, they had thrown up a heavy and continuous breastwork, supported by batteries, for which they had made epaulements. The corresponding high ground east of the Run, and occupied by us, was at least a mile in average distance, so that artillery would be deprived of much of its strong effect, and canister & spherical case pretty much out of the question. Then, at most points the attacking force would be exposed over nearly the whole stretch, to artillery fire, followed by musketry. It was a bad look out! From our ridge we could see the Rebs in hundreds, standing on top their works, or enlarging some portion of them, with logs and earth. The thing was, if possible, to flank. So Warren, with his own corps & a division of the 6th, marched in the morning and passed towards our left, hoping to get beyond the plank road and attack that afternoon; the rest of the line be ready to support. However, the column was delayed by a report of entrenchments that had no existence, and by some skirmishing, so that they did not get on the enemy's flank till too late for an attack. As it was they created great excitement & a brigade was brought on the double-quick to resist an attack. Major Ludlow came back with fine accounts of the prospect in the morning. The General, much encouraged, made immediate disposition for the attack and put French's two flank (left) divisions under Warren (Prince & Carr) greatly to F's indignation. Sykes had already occupied Warren's vacant position. At 8, or earlier, a general cannonade was to open, for an hour, and then the assault to take place. The grand attack on the left, and others, according to opportunity, along the whole line. One division of the 5th Corps occupied the extreme right. Gregg had continued skirmishing, on the left. The day Sykes & Newton moved along the plank road (27th) the enemy's cavalry performed a feat of extraordinary daring. They dashed on the trains, between the tail of the 5th and head of the 1st Corps, cut out a dozen or more waggons and made off with them. They were chiefly ammunition, but one was a Headquarter waggon, so there was Capt. Barnard, quite without blankets or any comfort, poor man; and his general Bartlett, in a similar fix. A brigade from Merritt was sent to reinforce Gregg.

November 30, Monday.

We were up bright & early, for it was necessary to get the trains out of the way about sunrise, as they would be exposed to shell, when the cannonade opened. All was expectation. Yet such is the force of your surroundings that I felt no particular nervousness—to be sure I did not have to lead an assault—which makes a wide difference. The soldiers of the 2d Corps, that morning pinned bits of paper on their clothes, with their names on them! As for Col. Farnum (he of yacht *Wanderer*

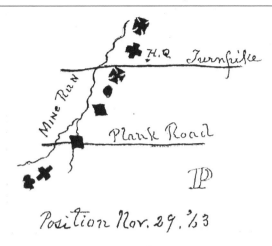

H.Q *Turnpike*

Mine Run

Plank Road

P

Position Nov. 29, '63

fame) he said he considered himself under sentence of death, that morning, for an hour! A little before 8 General Meade mounted & went a little way in search of Gen. Newton; while we rode, at 8.10, a single gun sounded from the right, and then a cannonade, not very heavy, opened along the line, as far as Newton's part. We returned to Headquarters. At 8.30 came Robling with a note from Gen. Warren, saying the enemy had arrived in great force, during the night, had thrown up more rifle pits, and that, on reexamination of the ground he considered an attack there as hopeless!! The General simply turned to Gen. Humphreys, saying "Read that," and exclaimed to Robling "My God! Gen. Warren has half my army." He then issued orders to cease firing; and soon all was still, save an occasional gun. Disappointment was on every face. For about an hour Gen. Meade remained in consultation with Gens. Sedgwick and Humphreys. Then at 9.45, he rode, with Gen. H, Major Biddle, Mitchell & myself, to Gen. Warren's. We passed along the front, in rear of our batteries, proceeded through a wood and emerged on a bare plateau where was Gen. French's command, then through another pine wood and came out on the plank road. We stopped at a run (a branch of Mine Run) and Gen. Warren rode up and dismounted to talk with the two other Generals; and there they sadly stood, over a fire the orderlies had made them, for it was sharp, and thin ice was on the pools. It was then 10.15. After a very long talk, at noon we rode back, stopping at Gen. French's house. He was very mad and talked loudly. He had pushed his skirmishers to within 300 yards of their works, and his troops had counted on success. Warren's troops were in three lines by the Run; French's were on the plateau, behind earthworks. It was of no use! We came back; the moment had passed, the assault was countermanded and the 2d Corps might unpin their bits of paper. That night was cold; 5 of our men on picket, who had been obliged to wade the stream to get to their places, were frozen to death, and the same fate, it is said, befell some rebels.

December 1, Tuesday.

As I looked out of my tent, at daylight, there were the 4½ inch big guns going to the rear, which argued we were soon to follow. It came out shortly that the generals were unanimous in thinking the moment for the assault had passed; and the order was out to fall back. The 1st Corps would start that afternoon, proceeding to Germanna Ford, and halt, to cover the crossing. The 5th Corps would withdraw at dark and be followed by the 6th, marching for Germanna Ford via the Turnpike & the cross wood-road. The 3d would march at dark, on the plank road, and cross at Culpeper Ford; the 2d following. The pickets would be withdrawn at 3 in the morning and, assembling at Robertson's Tavern, march under Col. Hayes (Joe). Some pickets of the 5th Corps had been 3 days on duty without relief! At sunset, went and took a farewell look at Jonny Reb. They were standing in groups on their parapet, while some were walking about in front. At dark we rode as far as Robertson's Tavern, where we built good fires and kept warm, till the 5th Corps should get past. It was a picturesque sight, so many officers, in their long coats, standing, sitting, or lying on the bare floor. Thereto also enter T. F. Meagher "of the Sword" *çi-devant* commander of the Irish Brigade; was in mufti and very drunk! He talked thickly with the English officers (who, by the by, established themselves in a seemingly safe place this morning, but got shelled for their pains, whereat Stephenson returned with a bit of spherical case, as a trophy). We started immediately in rear of the corps, but could go but at a snail's gain; broken bridge ahead and a slough, which kept checking the column. Of the many neglected details in the army none are worse than the repair of essential roads. A slight slough, e.g. makes each rank hesitate as it crosses, and almost stops the column. A working party of 10 men would repair such a place in ½ an hour. A whole corps had preceded, but nothing done! We got mightily cold crawling along this way, but at last got past, and then the General broke into a smart trot and we clattered along the most infernal of pikes, in holes and over rocks till we got to the plank road and turned up, to the left, where we found the holes, if possible worse, among the broken boards. We soon came on a train which had missed the way and we set it right. Then we passed the turn-off to Mine Ford (Culpeper) and, immediately after, came on the head of the 5th Corps, debouching from the woods, on the left and striking the plank road for Germanna Ford, which we reached, crossed by the pontoon bridge, and found our camp pitched at the old spot, at juncture of dirt & plank roads; 2 A.M. of *Dec. 2*, Wednesday. Gregg had followed the army, covering both columns. The enemy made no attempt to follow, not even attacking the rear cavalry. In the afternoon we returned to our old camp in the woods, not getting tents pitched till late at night.

All corps returned to their positions, except the 1st & 5th

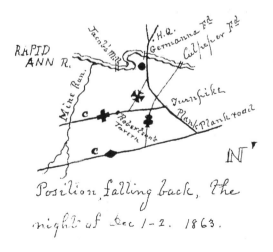

Position, falling back, The night of Dec 1–2. 1863.

which exchanged places. Got a good stock of letters from Deary Mimi and from others. Mrs. Paige is dead. The firm of Paige & Co. is dissolved, which throws out Arthur. It has been very mild north, moving trees as late as the last of November, which is unheard of, almost.

Wilbur Fisk to
The Green Mountain Freeman

Writing to the *Freeman* on November 20, Fisk described a review of
the Sixth Corps and presciently observed that "these reviews almost
always precede an onward movement." The Mine Run campaign cost
the Union about 1,600 men killed, wounded, or missing, and the
Confederates about 600.

———————

Second Vermont Regiment
November 29, 1863

This quiet Sabbath morning while the good people of Vermont are attending their accustomed places of worship, we,
here in the army, are engaged in a manner widely different.
Our regiment is on picket today, close up to the enemy, and
picket firing is going on nearly all the time. I have seated myself
by our little fire on the support, and as it will be several hours
before my turn will come to go on post, perhaps I shall have
no better time to acquaint you with our proceedings for the
last week or so, than the present.

We are in what I am told is called here, the Owl's Wilderness, and certainly it would be hard to conceive of a name
more appropriate. It appears to be one uninterrupted wilderness, extending fifteen or twenty miles either way, without any
other inhabitants than owls, buzzards, and such like animals.
There may be, once in a while, a small clearing with a log
house in the center, and a high fence all around it, and with
some signs of the land having been cultivated in modern times,
but these places have strayed away so far from all civilization
that it will be hardly worth while to take them into account.
The land where we are now, is covered with small second-
growth pine, and looks as if it had been under cultivation
once, but probably worn out and abandoned for more fertile
regions. Part of the woods that we have been through is grown

up to oak and other solid timber of all sizes, and has probably been forest from time immemorial. The land is level, and has the appearance of being good soil, and if I am any judge I should call it just such land as would tempt the eyes of almost any practical farmer, if it was up in our Northern States, instead of being here in decayed Virginia.

As to the latitude and longitude of our present whereabouts, the man in the moon could tell as well as we. We have marched principally in the night, and in all directions, so it has destroyed all our calculations as to distance and directions, and all we can say about the matter is that we have crossed the Rapidan and are still on the rebels' side of the river. It is cheering to be able, under such circumstances, to put confidence in others, for we should be in a woeful plight if we were obliged to act upon our geographical knowledge at the present time. The sun rises in the southwest, and I noticed that the needle of the compass points almost exactly the wrong way. If anybody was going to desert just now, I should be a poor guide to direct their flight.

One week ago today we had divine services in our regiment, held by Mr. Chandler, from Brattleboro. As we have no Chaplain of our own, and consequently very meagre religious privileges of any kind, it was quite a rarity to hear any one preach. He is connected with the Christian Commission, and in anticipation of a battle, had come out here to act the part of the Good Samaritan to the suffering,—as a great many belonging to that Commission have done, to the everlasting gratitude of those who have been wounded in action,—and to preach the gospel and distribute religious reading where such services are needed. He had a large bundle of papers with him that were eagerly received.

On the morning of the 24th, we had orders to be ready to march at an early hour. Accordingly, at precisely three o'clock in the morning, our quiet dreams were broken up by the rattling of drums all through camp, and forthwith we commenced to break up housekeeping—for the most of us had built us tip top houses—and to prepare for another campaign or for whatever was to be accomplished. The weather was grim and forbidding, and the rain drops as they came pattering on our tent that morning, driven by a regular nor'easter, had a very dismal sound in view of the prospect before us. A rainstorm is a very uninviting auxiliary with which to commence a long campaign at any season of the year, but more especially now when cold weather has come and when wet clothes can hardly be made to suggest anything but discomforts of the least desirable kind. Our tents had become wet and heavy, and to carry these in our knapsacks with all the rest of the clothing that we are obliged to carry at this time of the year, was going to make a pretty heavy draft upon the strength of a fellow's back bone. It is the last straw that breaks the camel's back, and the addition of a few extra pounds of water might have the same effect on us, for our packs have hitherto been as heavy as seemed possible for us to carry. You may judge of our satisfaction then, when we heard that the order to march had been postponed for two days. Some think that other reasons besides unpropitious weather, was the cause of the delay; if not it was rather of an anomaly in our war experience but none the less acceptable for all that. We shall certainly think we have one good reason for respecting Gen. Meade.

Although we had been expecting to move somewhere for a long time, we had but little idea where we were going. There have been all sorts of rumors in camp, and there always are at such times, and almost every man had a rumor of his own. No honest man could believe two of them at the same time. Sometimes it was reported that we were going to New York. Gen. Stannard had command there and wanted us to do service under him. I heard that some officers had offered to bet very extravagantly that such would be the case. It is curious how such rumors will thrive and strengthen themselves in a thousand different ways. It was coolly told in the third brigade, and believed there, that orders had been read to us on dress parade to draw clothing suitable for garrison duty, when no such orders had been read to us at all, and more than all that, our regiment had no dress parade while we stayed in our last camp. Another story was that the army was going to move down to the vicinity of Aquia Creek, and go into winter quarters there again. Going across the Rapidan to attack the enemy once more, seemed to be hardly feasible at this late season. Morever attacking Lee in his old chosen position, we have tried so many times and failed, that a great many think it is high time that that method of maneuvering was played out.

The day, before we did move, I was up in one of the New York regiments, and they were trying to enlist the men over again for another three years. They were managing this matter with a great deal of shrewdness. Every man that put his name down was to have a furlough and go home immediately. As it had become pretty certain that we were to have a long, tedious campaign, cold and stormy it might be in pursuit of the enemy, it was quite a tempting bait for a fellow to write down his name and get rid of it all, and go home and have a jolly time instead. In some of the New York regiments, the enlisting officers have been pretty successful; in others, the boys say they want to breathe free air once more before they enlist again.

Thursday morning, the 26th, we were drummed up again, bright and early, to prepare to march. The air was clear, and there were no signs of rain nor any probability that the movement would be postponed again. Our knapsacks were packed, tents struck, huge bonfires were burning all through the camp, consuming material that had cost us a great deal of pains to collect. The sun was just beginning to melt away the frost, when we fell into line and filed off towards Brandy Station. Camps without number were being deserted, some of which had been fixed up as comfortable as would be needed for winter quarters. The whole army was in motion. Infantry, artillery, and baggage wagons *ad infinitum*, had suddenly waked to life and were crowding along, or halting in a field for it to come their turn to start. It was nearly noon before we got hardly so far as Brandy Station. The marching all day was very slow. Sometimes we would hardly get a half mile from one halting place before we would halt again. As it grew towards night, and we believed that we had got to cross the river before we halted for the night, we began to grow impatient of these vexatious delays, and anxious to get to our journey's end. Before we reached the river we had got a couple of miles of woods to go through, and there was only one little road hardly wide enough for a file of four men to walk in abreast, while on each side was a dense thicket of all sorts of timber that nature ever invented. If we could have marched right straight along in this road it would have been all well enough, but, instead of that, we could only march a few steps at a time, then wait for those ahead of us to clear the way. We would march about a rod, then wait five minutes, when we could march a rod more, and then wait another five minutes, and all this while the weight of our knapsacks was increasing, and our patience steadily diminishing, until the boys began to curse patriots and traitors without much discrimination. Finally, we halted and sat down. An hour passed, and still we didn't move. Some of the boys ventured to make coffee, running the risk of being ordered to fall in just as they were divested of their load, and enjoying their warm drink. By and by orders came that we might make us coffee, and eat our supper, and we all pitched into the business with a will. We had ample time allowed us to finish our meal, and when we were at last ordered to fall in, the road was clear and we could march along as fast as we liked.

We crossed the Rapidan between Germanna and Raccoon Ford, at Jacob's Ferry on a pontoon bridge. The opposite bluff was almost perpendicular and as soon as we had climbed to the top we halted and camped for the night, or for what there was left of it, for it was past midnight when we stopped. Before sunrise we were ordered up, and soon on the march again. There was skirmishing ahead of us and our advance was slow. We gained but three or four miles from the river all day. Towards night firing began to be more rapid and we were ordered forward into line. The third corps were ahead of us. Our line extended into the woods to the extreme right. About quarter before four the firing commenced with terrible earnestness. To us it looked as though there would be a chance for us to have a hand in it. We could not see the fight, for the wood was so dense that we could see but a few rods ahead of us, but from the sound of the firing, and from the number of frightened skedaddlers that were making swift tracks to the rear, we had reason to fear that the battle was going against us. The firing continued till long into the night. Evidently the rebels couldn't break our lines or they would have been on to us. It was difficult to get any exact information of the result of the battle, but the "sum and substance" of what we could get was, that we had been flanked and forced to fall back; that the rebels had charged upon our line and been repulsed; that we in turn charged them, drove them back and gained some ground at the close of the struggle. The Tenth Vermont was in the fight, and there was a report that night that they broke and ran;

other reports contradicted it. I have heard that they bore the test and held their ground like men, although a line ahead of them broke and skedaddled back right through their ranks; and for a Vermont regiment, this is decidedly the most rational story to believe.

After a while the firing ceased and everything was quiet as the grave. We commenced to build fires to warm ourselves and to make coffee by, but an order came to allow no fires on the line. Afterward they concluded to let us have a few small fires, and we eat our suppers and laid down. About midnight we were ordered to pack up and fall in. Our line of march was towards the left. By the number of troops that were in motion, I should judge that all hands left that place during the night. It would be impossible to guess how far we marched before daylight, when we maneuvered around and got into a position here. We didn't march very rapidly, nor very straight, but if I was to make a rough guess at the matter, I should say that we came about a half a dozen miles from where the fight was Friday night, and that now we must be pretty well down towards Chancellorsville. Next time I write, I hope I shall be better informed and be able to write a more intelligent letter.

> Second Vermont Regiment
> Near Brandy Station
> Dec. 8, 1863

Being detailed for fatigue, and out a couple of miles from camp, with but little prospect of returning for at least ten days from the commencement of the detail, I have pulled up my knapsack close to the fire, fully determined to write you another letter by firelight, this evening, unless I am driven from my purpose by the smoke, which persists in drifting directly into my face, let me get on to which side of the fire I will. To be bent down over an outdoor's fire on a cold December night, might have a very inspiring effect for a poetical nature, but for me it is a most uncomfortable position, and sometimes places my patience in great jeopardy. But if I wish to narrate the events of the past few days, I shall probably have no better opportunity to do so than now, and to deprive the public of this important delinquency that I never should have the face to ask forgiveness for.

The last time I wrote, I believe we were on picket away out in the wilderness among the rebels, where we expected every hour to be let against the enemy. We were not let against them while we were there, for reasons known only to the higher authorities, though without doubt it was because we found the enemy much stronger in his position than we expected. Gen. Meade did not wish to inaugurate another Lee's Mill's affair. There was a deep creek between us and the enemy, and the rebels had been busy digging rifle-pits and strengthening their position ever since we came up to them. Both banks were abrupt and steep and difficult to get over, while on the rebel side they had added to these disadvantages by placing every conceivable obstacle in the way of our advance. Trees were felled, abattis made, breastworks were thrown up until they occupied a position that if *we* had occupied we should have considered impregnable against all the rebels in the universe.

Army correspondents, I notice, all have it that "the men" were in the best of spirits, and eager for a dash at the enemy. Now all such statements, though meant, I suppose, to be complimentary, need a slight qualification, and admit of some exceptions. We are in "the best of spirits" almost any time when we can get the best of spirits to put into us, and as for being eager for a dash at the enemy, perhaps it is all true; I can speak for but one, but there was certainly a fellow there about my size that felt no such eagerness at all. I couldn't look over to those gray-coated devils and see their position and the means they were providing for our reception, with any desire to be ordered over there amongst them. If the order had been given to charge, of course I should have charged with the rest, and if I could hurt a rebel so that he would have had to go home and stay with his mother until the war was over, I should have done it; but after all, to tell the plain truth about the matter, and there is no use in lying, in the event of a charge, I know I should have had a strong preference for running the other way and placing as much distance as possible between those rebel minnies and my own precious self. Vermonters are the very best fighters in the world, so everybody says that knows anything about it; but you never see a Vermonter manifest any eagerness to get into a fight, nor any desire to back out after he does get in.

It was expected by some, that a charge would be ordered that Sunday afternoon when we were there on picket, but it was postponed until morning. Early in the morning we were relieved from post, and went back to the reserve. At precisely eight o'clock our artillery opened on the enemy. They commenced with energy, and from two points, pouring in a cross fire and throwing in shot and shell among the rebels with terrible rapidity. The rebels hardly knew what to make of it. From the picket outposts they could be seen hurrying in all directions, some scattering in confusion, and some being collected together for resistance. There seemed to be an endless number of them. We had stirred up their hive, and found a pretty lively swarm, and as large a one as we need wish to contend with. The cannonading was to continue for an hour, and then, hurrah boys for a charge. As we are on picket, we should take the lead, and act as skirmishers. In about half an hour the firing ceased. Pretty soon the order came to pack up and fall in. We did so, and were ordered about to the right of the line, a mile or so further. All the way we kept back from the edge of the woods far enough to prevent the rebels from discovering our movement. We picked our way through a dense and almost impenetrable thicket of small trees and underbrush. We passed by where a storming party of the 5th corps had piled up their knapsacks and haversacks, and were stripped for the charge. After a while we got into our position where we should remain until further orders. It was very cold, but no fires were allowed to be built there. The Johnnies were having their nice comfortable fires, and they appeared to be but a short distance from us. They didn't appear to be at all bashful about showing their position by building fires or coming out in sight. But we must keep back in the woods out of sight and keep warm the best way we could. By scuffling, knocking off hats, and running around a ring that we made a path for in the woods, we managed to keep from freezing. We expected to be ordered into action every minute. The companies to be deployed were selected, but the order to advance did not come. The boys were tired of waiting. If they had got to charge on the enemy, they wanted to do it at once, and have it done with, and not stand there and dread it all day in the cold.

But the sun went down and our line had not moved. Soon the order came to "left face place." It was clear and cold. We got into line after about our usual delay in marching and halt-ing, and as soon as we could collect the material, we had a bright, rousing fire to collect around, and to eat supper by. We made our beds around this fire and slept till morning. Some idea of the weather may be understood from the fact that sev-eral of the canteens that I helped fill late in the evening, were frozen solid in the morning, and some had burst open and were spoiled. The next day we had nothing to do but to keep ourselves warm and speculate on the prospects before us. We were on a portion of the plank road that leads from Culpeper to Fredericksburg, and could at any time we chose, move down and take possession of the heights of that place. The enemy were only covering Gordonsville. They were south and west of us, and we were the nearest Fredericksburg. All this looked as if it might be so, but there was an air of mystery and doubt about it that made some of the knowing ones feel in-credulous. Our hesitating to attack the day before looked a little as if everything was not so well for us as some pretended to believe. They had a strong position and doubtless were so disposed that they could move down and occupy their old position by Fredericksburg, or they could fight us there; in either case they held us to a disadvantage. It really looked as if Gen. Meade had failed in some brilliant maneuvre by which he had intended to bring Lee out on an open fight, and in this failure, inasmuch as we had declined to fight and give the reb-els their advantage, it seemed pretty likely that we should fall back across the river once more. This was rendered certain when night came and we were ordered to pack up and fall in. After marching two or three miles, or such a matter, we halted and formed into line. Skirmishers were thrown out, and we were told that we should remain at least two hours.

It was a certain thing then that we were retreating, and that a part of our brigade was acting as rear-guard. We spread down our blankets, determined to steal a little sleep if we could. The next thing we have any recollection of was of being aroused from a good sweet dream, and ordered to form. We had been there three hours instead of two. We were completely chilled through, and it was quite fortunate that we were awakened when we were, for we were shivering with the cold, and trembling like a man of ninety. We fell into line, and before we had marched far we were warm enough.

It was about daylight when we reached and crossed Germanna Ford the next morning. We noticed as we passed down to the river some well constructed rifle-pits and breastworks, from which the enemy had no doubt intended to dispute our passage across the river, and which we were enabled to dodge through the foresight and generalship of Gen. Meade. We marched about a mile this side of the river before we halted for breakfast. The 5th corps had preceded us, and their men were lying in the bushes on each side of the road, as thickly as they could possibly get together. After breakfast we marched on a little further, and finally in a woods for all day, and the next night. Thursday morning we were ordered to pack up and fall in, which we did, and marched towards our old camp. We marched up to Stevensburg and crossed the Mountain Creek at that place, some distance above the place where we crossed the same stream on our way down a week before. As we came along by the camps of the 5th and 3rd corps we noticed that they were occupying the same houses, and, the same places exactly, that they occupied before we moved. At Brandy Station everything was alive with business. One sutler's wagon was actually unloading from a platform car, just as we passed by. This was an important event, for sutler's goods have heretofore been too scarce to be obtained even by officers, and those who feel that they have a special right to these things. We marched straight back into our old camp. Those that had not burned up their houses before they left had only to put their tent overhead for a roof, and they were as comfortably situated as ever; but some had completely destroyed their houses, and material, and consequently if they built again, had to commence anew. We were told that we had better not make any extensive preparations for comfortable quarters, as our regiment intended to move to a more pleasant locality, which has since been done. Friday night the order came into camp to pack up everything, and be ready to move at a moment's notice. The rebel cavalry had crossed to this side of the Rapidan, and possibly we might be attacked. The officers and men had been given a ration of whiskey that night, and all hands were pretty noisy, though nobody supposed that that had anything to do with the rebel scare. Matters quieted down after a while, and so did the boys, and no enemy disturbed us that night. The next morning we were detailed for this "fatigue," and here we have been ever since. We are building a corduroy road along by the side of the railroad from Rappahannock Station to camp. Our supplies they say have got to be carried over this road. The railroad only carries forage to Brandy Station.

But it is getting to be well on towards midnight, and my fire is nearly gone out. No one would disagree with me, if I should say, it is time this tedious letter was brought to a close, for I am beginning to feel almost as dull as what I have written.

George G. Meade to Margaret Meade

Meade wrote to his wife after returning to his headquarters near Brandy Station. In his official report to Halleck on December 7, Meade admitted that the campaign had been "a failure," but insisted the causes of its failure "were beyond my control." He cited French's delays in advancing the Third Corps on November 26–27 as "one of the primary causes of the failure of the whole movement" and criticized Warren's "unfortunate error in judgment" in not attacking on the morning of November 30. The failure at Mine Run caused Lincoln, Stanton, and Halleck to consider replacing Meade with Brigadier General William F. Smith, the chief engineer of the Army of the Cumberland and a former corps commander in the Army of the Potomac, but no decision was made. Meade would remain at his post as his army went into winter quarters.

———————

Head-Quarters, Army of the Potomac,
Decr. 2d.—1863.

Dear Margaret—

I expect your wishes will now soon be gratified;—and that I shall be relieved from the Army of the Potomac. The facts are briefly these.—On the 26th ulto. I crossed the Rapidan intending to turn the right flank of Genl. Lee, and attack him, or compel him to attack me out of his formidable river entrenchments.—I had previously been advised by deserters & others, that he had commenced a line of works running *perpendicular* to the river, but only extending a few miles, by which he designed covering his flank, and permitting him to leave the lower fords unguarded.—I accordingly made my plans to cross in 3 columns, to unite at a common point below his entrenchments, and then to advance rapidly & attack him before he could prepare any defences. The plan was a good one, but owing to the failure of others to whom its execution was necessarily entrusted it failed.—In the first place, one corps was *three* hours behind time in arriving at the river and slow of

movement afterwards, which caused a delay of *one day*—
enabled the enemy to advance & check my columns before
they united, & finally to concentrate his army, in a very formidable position, behind entrenchments almost as strong as
those I was making a long detour to avoid. Again after I had
come up with the enemy one corps commander reported he
had examined a position, where there was not the slightest
doubt he could carry the enemys works & on his positive &
unhesitating judgement, he was given 28,000 men, and directed to attack the next morning at 8 o'clock. At the same
time another attack was to be made by 15,000 men at a point
where the enemy evidently was not fully prepared.—On the
eventful morning, just as the attack was about being made, I
received a despatch from the officer commanding the 28,000
men saying he had changed his opinion, and that the attack on
his front was *so hopeless*, that he had assumed the responsibility
of suspending it, till further orders were received.—This astounding intelligence reached me just 10 minutes before the
hour for attacking, and barely in time to suspend the other attack, which was a secondary one & which even if successful
could not be supported with so large a portion of my force
away for the main attack.—This lost me another day during
which the enemy so strengthened the point threatened by the
secondary attack, as to render it nearly as strong as the rest of
his line, and to have almost destroyed, the before probable
chances of success. Finding no possibility of attacking with
hope of success, and power to follow up success, and that the
only weak point visible, had been strengthened during the
delay caused by the change of opinion of a corps commander—
I determined not to attempt an assault.

I could not move any further round the enemys flank, for
want of roads, and from the danger, at this season of the year
of a storm, which could render locomotion, off the *prepared
roads* a matter of impossibility.—After reviewing all the circumstances, notwithstanding my most earnest desire to give
battle, and in the full consciousness of the fact, that my failure
to do so, was certain personal ruin—I having come to the
conclusion that an attack could not be successful determined
to, & did withdraw the army. I am fully aware it will be said, I
did wrong in deciding this question by reasoning, and that I

ought to have *tried* & then a *failure* would have been evidence
of my good judgement, but I trust I have too much reputation
as a General, to be obliged to encounter certain defeat, in
order to prove that victory was not possible. Political considerations will however enter largely into the decision, and the
failure of the Army of the Potomac to do any thing at this
moment will be considered of vital consequence and if *I* can be
held responsible for this failure, I will be removed to prove
that I am. I therefore consider my fate as settled; but as I have
told you before I would rather be ignominiously dismissed,
and suffer any thing, than knowingly and willfully have thousands of brave men slaughtered for nothing. It was my deliberate judgement that I ought not to attack. I acted on that
judgement, and I am willing to stand or fall by it at all hazards.
I shall write to the President giving him a clear statement of
the case, and endeavoring to free his action as much as possible,
by assuming myself all the responsibility.—I feel of course
greatly disappointed—a little more good fortune, and I should
have met with brilliant success. As it is my conscience is clear—
I did the best I could. If I had thought there was any reasonable degree of probability of success, I would have attacked. I
did not think so—on the contrary believed it would result in a
useless & criminal slaughter of brave men, and might result in
serious disaster to the army—I determined not to attack no
other movements were practicable & I withdrew.

There will be a great howl all over the country. Letter writers & politicians will denounce me. It will be proved as clear as
the light of day, that an attack was perfectly practicable, and
that every one except myself in the army particularly the soldiers, were dying for it and that I had some mysterious object
in view either in connection with politics, or stock-jobbing or
some thing else about as foreign to my thoughts—and finally
the administration will be obliged to yield to popular clamor
and discard me. For all this I am prepared justified as I said
before by a clear conscience, and the conviction that I have
acted from a high sense of duty, to myself as a soldier, to my
men as their General, and to my country and its cause, as the
agent having its vital interests solemnly entrusted to me, which
I have no right to wantonly play with, and to jeopardize either
for my own personal benefit, or to satisfy the demands of

popular clamor, or interested politicians.—I should like this letter shown confidentially to Cortlandt Parker, Mr. Harding, & other friends, whose good opinion I am anxious to preserve. George was sent with one of the messages to suspend the attack—his horse fell with him—he was a little bruised & cut about the eye, but nothing serious.—I have received your letter of the 30th ulto. Good bye.

Ever yours. *G. G. Meade*

————————

Head-Quarters, Army of the Potomac,
Decr. 7th 1863

Dear Margaret,

I received today your letter of the 5th inst.—I am yet on the anxious bench—not one word has been vouchsafed me from Washington. The papers of course you have seen, but there was one article in the Washington Star, said to have been inspired from high official quarters, which was very severe on me. It was headed "Hesitating Generals"—and referred to my failure at Williamsport—to my running away from Lee with *double* the number of men, and to my recent fiasco, as all combining to show I was not competent to command an army. I should hardly suppose any official, claiming respect would choose as a machine for conveying his ideas to the public such a disreputable sheet as the Star whose drunken editor is the horror of all who know him. Still other indications that have reached me would confirm the report that the article was by authority & is a premonition of my approaching fate. I understand from an officer just returned from Washington, that on meeting a prominent member of the Govt, he was asked if the Army of the Potomac has stopped running yet? and whether there were any fighting men in it among the Generals? To day I sent in my official report in which I have told the plain truth—acknowledged the movement was a failure but claimed the causes were not in my plans, but in the want of support & co-operation on the part of subordinates.—I dont know whether my report will be published, but if it is it will make a sensation, and undoubtedly result in some official investigation. I have received a very kind letter from Cortlandt Parker, (written before he had received yours) in which he sympathizes with me in the failure, but says he is satisfied I have done right, and that I have not lost the confidence of intelligent people, and he hopes I will not resign but hold on to the last.—I have also received a very kind & complimentary letter from Gibbon saying he had as much confidence as ever in my ability to command and that military men would sustain me.—I telegraphed Genl. Halleck that I desired to visit Washn. but his reply was couched in such terms, that tho it gave me permission to go, clearly intimated my presence was not desired, so far as he was concerned. I have in consequence not gone, and now shall not go unless they send for me.—I am only concerned for my reputation as a soldier—if I can preserve that they are at liberty to deprive me of command & even of rank.—

I see the Herald inspired by my *friend* Dan Sickles, is constantly harping on the assertion that Gettysburgh was fought by the *corps commanders* (ie D. S.) and the common soldiers & that no Generalship was displayed. I suppose after a while it will be discovered, I was not at Gettysburgh at all. We have had very cold weather, but George & I continue quite well. I hope Sergie will soon be well again. Love & kisses to all the children. Ever yours

G. G. Meade

Frederick Douglass: Our Work Is Not Done

December 4, 1863

Douglass gave this speech at the thirtieth-anniversary meeting of the American Anti-Slavery Society, held in Philadelphia on December 3–4 and devoted to "a general review and survey of the cause." His remarks were in part a response to the views of William Lloyd Garrison, a founder of the society and its president since 1843, who believed that antislavery societies would no longer be needed once emancipation was complete.

―――――――――

LADIES AND GENTLEMEN: I confess at the outset to have felt a very profound desire to utter a word at some period during the present meeting. As it has been repeatedly said here, it has been a meeting of reminiscences. I shall not attempt to treat you to any of my own in what I have now to say, though I have some in connection with the labors of this Society, and in connection with my experience as an American slave, that I might not inappropriately bring before you on this occasion. I desire to be remembered among those having a word to say at this meeting, because I began my existence as a free man in this country with this association, and because I have some hopes or apprehensions, whichever you please to call them, that we shall never, as a Society, hold another decade meeting.

I well remember the first time I ever listened to the voice of the honored President of this association, and I have some recollection of the feelings of hope inspired by his utterances at that time. Under the inspiration of those hopes, I looked forward to the abolition of slavery as a certain event in the course of a very few years. So clear were his utterances, so simple and truthful, and so adapted, I conceived, to the human heart were the principles and doctrines propounded by him, that I thought five years at any rate would be all that would be required for the abolition of slavery. I thought it was only necessary for the slaves, or their friends, to lift up the hatchway of slavery's infernal hold, to uncover the bloody scenes of American thraldom, and give the nation a peep into its horrors, its deeds of deep damnation, to arouse them to almost phrensied opposition to this foul curse. But I was mistaken. I had not been five years pelted by the mob, insulted by the crowds, shunned by the church, denounced by the ministry, ridiculed by the press, spit upon by the loafers, before I became convinced that I might perhaps live, struggle, and die, and go down to my grave, and the slaves of the South yet remain in their chains.

We live to see a better hope to-night. I participate in the profound thanksgiving expressed by all, that we do live to see this better day. I am one of those who believe that it is the mission of this war to free every slave in the United States. I am one of those who believe that we should consent to no peace which shall not be an abolition peace. I am, moreover, one of those who believe that the work of the American Anti-Slavery Society will not have been completed until the black men of the South, and the black men of the North, shall have been admitted fully and completely into the body politic of America. I look upon slavery as going the way of all the earth. It is the mission of the war to put it down. But a mightier work than the abolition of slavery now looms up before the Abolitionist. This Society was organized, if I remember rightly, for two distinct objects; one was the emancipation of the slave, and the other the elevation of the colored people. When you have taken the chains off the slave, as I believe we shall do, we shall find a harder resistance to the second purpose of this great association than we have found even upon slavery itself.

I am hopeful, but while I am hopeful I am thoughtful withal. If I lean to either side of the controversy to which we have listened to-day, I lean to that side which implies caution, which implies apprehension, which implies a consciousness that our work is not done. Protest, affirm, hope, glorify as we may, it cannot be denied that abolitionism is still unpopular in the United States. It cannot be denied that this war is at present denounced by its opponents as an abolition war; and it is equally clear that it would not be denounced as an abolition war, if abolitionism were not odious. It is equally clear that our friends, Republicans, Unionists, Loyalists, would not spin out elaborate explanations, and denials that this is the character of the war, if abolition were popular. Men accept the term Abolitionist with qualifications. They do not come out square and open-handed, and affirm themselves to be Abolitionists. As a general rule, we are attempting to explain away the charge that this is an abolition war. I hold that it is an abolition war, because slavery has proved itself stronger than the Constitution. It has proved itself stronger than the Union, and has forced upon us the necessity of putting down slavery in order to save the Union, and in order to save the Constitution. (Applause.)

I look at this as an abolition war instead of being a Union war, because I see that the lesser is included in the greater, and that you cannot have the lesser until you have the greater. You cannot have the Union, the Constitution, and republican institutions, until you have stricken down that damning curse, and put it beyond the pale of the Republic. For, while it is in this country, it will make your Union impossible; it will make your Constitution impossible. I therefore call this just what the Democrats have charged it with being, an abolition war. Let us emblazon it on our banners, and declare before the world that this is an abolition war, (applause), that it will prosper precisely in proportion as it takes upon itself this character. (Renewed applause.)

My respected friend, Mr. Purvis, called attention to the existence of prejudice against color in this country. This gives me great cause for apprehension, if not for alarm. I am afraid of this powerful element of prejudice against color. While it exists, I want the voice of the American Anti-Slavery Society to be continually protesting, continually exposing it. While it can be said that in this most anti-slavery city in the Northern States of our Union, in the city of Philadelphia, the city of Brotherly Love, in the city of churches, the city of piety, that the most genteel and respectable colored lady or gentleman may be kicked out of your commonest street car, we are in danger of a compromise. While it can be said that black men, fighting bravely for this country, are asked to take $7 per month, while the government lays down as a rule or criterion of pay a complexional one, we are in danger of a compromise. While to be radical is to be unpopular, we are in danger of a compromise.

While we have a large minority, called Democratic, in every State of the North, we have a powerful nucleus for a most infernal re-action in favor of slavery. I know it is said that we have recently achieved vast political victories. I am glad of it. I value those victories, however, more for what they have prevented than for what they have actually accomplished. I should have been doubly sad at seeing any one of these States wheel into line with the Peace Democracy. But, however it may be in the State of Pennsylvania, I know that you may look for abolition in the creed of any party in New York with a microscope, and you will not find a single line of anti-slavery there. The victories were Union victories, victories to save the Union in such ways as the country may devise to save it. But whatever may have been the meaning of these majorities in regard to the Union, we know one thing, that the minorities, at least, mean slavery. They mean submission. They mean the degradation of the colored man. They mean everything but open rebellion against the Federal government in the South. But the mob, the rioters in the city of New York, convert that city into a hell, and its lower orders into demons, and dash out the brains of little children against the curbstones; and they mean anything and everything that the Devil exacts at their hands. While we had in this State a majority of but 15,000 over this pro-slavery Democratic party, they have a mighty minority, a dangerous minority. Keep in mind when these minorities were gotten. Powerful as they are, they were gotten when slavery, with bloody hands, was stabbing at the very heart of the nation itself. With all that disadvantage, they have piled up these powerful minorities.

We have work to do, friends and fellow-citizens, to look after these minorities. The day that shall see Jeff Davis fling down his Montgomery Constitution, and call home his Generals, will be the most trying day to the virtue of this people that this country has ever seen. When the slaveholders shall give up the contest, and ask for re-admission into the Union, then, as Mr. Wilson has told us, we shall see the trying time in this country. Your Democracy will clamor for peace and for restoring the old order of things, because that old order of things was the life of the Democratic party. "You do take away mine house, when you take away the prop that sustains my house," and the support of the Democratic party we all know to be slavery. The Democratic party is for war for slavery; it is for peace for slavery; it is for the *habeas corpus* for slavery; it is against the *habeas corpus* for slavery; it was for the Florida war for slavery; it was for the Mexican war for slavery; it is for jury trial for traitors for slavery; it is against jury trial for men claimed as fugitive slaves for slavery. It has but one principle, one master; and it is guided, governed and directed by it. I say that with this party among us, flaunting its banners in our faces, with the New York *World* scattered broadcast over the North, with the New York *Express*, with the mother and father and devil of them all, the New York *Herald*, (applause), with those papers flooding our land, and coupling the term Abolitionist with all manner of coarse epithets, in all our hotels, at all our crossings, our highways, and byways, and railways, all over the country, there is work to be done—a good deal of work to be done.

I have said that our work will not be done until the colored man is admitted a full member in good and regular standing into the American body politic. Men have very nice ideas about the body politic where I have travelled; and they don't like the idea of having the negro in the body politic. He may remain in this country, for he will be useful as a laborer, valuable perhaps in time of trouble as a helper; but to make him a full and complete citizen, a legal voter, that would be contaminating the body politic. I was a little curious, some years ago, to find out what sort of a thing this body politic was; and I was very anxious to know especially about what amount of baseness, brutality, coarseness, ignorance, and bestiality, could find its way into the body politic; and I was not long in finding it out. I took my stand near the little hole through which the body politic put its votes. (Laughter.) And first among the mob, I saw Ignorance, unable to read its vote, asking *me* to read it, by the way, (great laughter), depositing its vote in the body politic. Next I saw a man stepping up to the body politic, casting in his vote, having a black eye, and another one ready to be blacked, having been engaged in a street fight. I saw, again, Pat, fresh from the Emerald Isle, with the delightful brogue peculiar to him, stepping up—not walking, but leaning upon the arms of two of his friends, unable to stand, passing into the body politic! I came to the conclusion that this body politic was, after all, not quite so pure a body as the representation of its friends would lead us to believe.

I know it will be said that I ask you to make the black man a voter in the South. Yet you are for having brutality and ignorance introduced into the ballot-box. It is said that the colored man is ignorant, and therefore he shall not vote. In saying this, you lay down a rule for the black man that you apply to no other class of your citizens. I will hear nothing of degradation nor of ignorance against the black man. If he knows enough to be hanged, he knows enough to vote. If he knows an honest man from a thief, he knows much more than some of our white voters. If he knows as much when sober as an Irishman knows when drunk, he knows enough to vote. If he knows enough to take up arms in defence of this government, and bare his breast to the storm of rebel artillery, he knows enough to vote. (Great applause.)

Away with this talk of the want of knowledge on the part of the negro! I am about as big a negro as you will find anywhere about town; and any man that does not believe I know enough to vote, let him try it. I think I can convince him that I do. Let him run for office in my district, and solicit my vote, and I will show him.

All I ask, however, in regard to the blacks, is that whatever rule you adopt, whether of intelligence or wealth, as the condition of voting, you should apply it equally to the black man. Do that, and I am satisfied, and eternal justice is satisfied. Liberty, fraternity, equality, are satisfied; and the country will move on harmoniously.

Mr. President, I have a patriotic argument in favor of insisting upon the immediate enfranchisement of the slaves of the South; and it is this. When this rebellion shall have been put down, when the arms shall have fallen from the guilty hand of traitors, you will need the friendship of the slaves of the South, of those millions there. Four or five million men are not of inconsiderable importance at anytime; but they will be doubly important when you come to reorganize and reestablish republican institutions in the South. Will you mock those bondmen by breaking their chains with one hand, and with the other giving their rebel masters the elective franchise and robbing them of theirs? I tell you the negro is your friend. But you will make him not only your friend in sentiment and heart by enfranchising him, you will thus make him your best defender, your best protector against the traitors and the descendants of those traitors who will inherit the hate, the bitter revenge which shall crystalize all over the South, and seek to circumvent the government that they could not throw off. You will need the black man there as a watchman and patrol; and you may need him as a soldier. You may need him to uphold in peace, as he is now upholding in war, the star-spangled banner. (Applause.) I wish our excellent friend, Senator Wilson, would bend his energies to this point as well as the other—to let the negro have a vote. It will be helping him from the jaws of the wolf. We are surrounded by those who, like the wolf, will use their jaws, if you give the elective franchise to the descendants of the traitors, and keep it from the black man. We ought to be voters there! We ought to be members of Congress! (Applause.) You may as well make up your minds that you have got to see something dark down that way! There is no way to get rid of it. I am a candidate already! (Applause.)

For twenty-five years, Mr. President, you know that when I got as far South as Philadelphia, I felt that I was rubbing against my prison wall, and could not go any further. I dared not go over yonder into Delaware. Twenty years ago, when I attended the first Decade meeting of this Society, as I came along the vales and hills of Gettysburg, my good friends, the anti-slavery people along there, warned me to remain in the house during the daytime and travel in the night, lest I should be kidnapped, and carried over into Maryland. My good friend Dr. Fussell was one of the number who did not think it safe for me to attend an anti-slavery meeting along the borders of this State. I can go down there now. I have been to Washington to see the President; and as you were not there, perhaps you may like to know how the President of the United States received a black man at the White House. I will tell you how he received me—just as you have seen one gentleman receive another! (great applause); with a hand and a voice well-balanced between a kind cordiality and a respectful reserve. I tell you I felt big there. (Laughter.) Let me tell you how I got to him; because every body can't get to him. He has to be a little guarded in admitting spectators. The manner in getting to him gave me an idea that the cause was rolling on. The stairway was crowded with applicants. Some of them looked eager; and I have no doubt some of them had a purpose in being there, and wanted to see the President for the good of the country! They were white, and as I was the only dark spot among them, I expected to have a wait at least half a day; I have heard of men waiting a week; but in two minutes after I sent in my card, the messenger came out, and respectfully invited "Mr. Douglass" in. I could hear, in the eager multitude outside, as they saw me pressing and elbowing my way through, the remark, "Yes, damn it, I knew they would let the nigger through," in a kind of despairing voice—a Peace Democrat, I suppose. (Laughter.) When I went in, the President was sitting in his usual position, I was told, with his feet in different parts of the room, taking it easy. (Laughter.) Don't put this down, Mr. Reporter, I pray you; for I am going down there again to-morrow. (Laughter.) As I came in and approached him, the President began to rise, and he continued to rise until he stood over me (laughter); and he reached out his hand and said, "Mr. Douglass, I know you; I have read about you, and Mr. Seward has told me about you;" putting me quite at ease at once.

Now you will want to know how I was impressed by him. I will tell you that, too. He impressed me as being just what every one of you have been in the habit of calling him—an honest man. (Applause.) I never met with a man, who, on the first blush, impressed me more entirely with his sincerity, with his devotion to his country, and with his determination to save it at all hazards. (Applause.) He told me (I think he did me more honor than I deserve), that I had made a little speech somewhere in New York, and it had got into the papers, and among the things I had said was this: That if I were called upon to state what I regarded as the most sad and most disheartening feature in our present political and military situation, it would not be the various disasters experienced by our armies and our navies, on flood and field, but it would be the tardy, hesitating and vacillating policy of the President of the United States; and the President said to me, "Mr. Douglass, I have been charged with being tardy, and the like;" and he went on, and partly admitted that he might seem slow; but he said,

"I am charged with vacillating; but, Mr. Douglass, I do not think that charge can be sustained; I think it cannot be shown that when I have once taken a position, I have ever retreated from it." (Applause.) That I regarded as the most significant point in what he said during our interview. I told him that he had been somewhat slow in proclaiming equal protection to our colored soldiers and prisoners; and he said that the country needed talking up to that point. He hesitated in regard to it when he felt that the country was not ready for it. He knew that the colored man throughout this country was a despised man, a hated man, and he knew that if he at first came out with such a proclamation, all the hatred which is poured on the head of the negro race would be visited on his Administration. He said that there was preparatory work needed, and that that preparatory work had been done. And he added, "Remember this, Mr. Douglass; remember that Milliken's Bend, Port Hudson, and Fort Wagner are recent events; and that these were necessary to prepare the way for this very proclamation of mine." I thought it was reasonable; but I came to the conclusion that while Abraham Lincoln will not go down to posterity as Abraham the Great, or as Abraham the Wise, or as Abraham the Eloquent, although he is all three, wise, great, and eloquent, he will go down to posterity, if the country is saved, as Honest Abraham, (applause); and going down thus, his name may be written anywhere in this wide world of ours side by side with that of Washington, without disparaging the latter. (Cheers.)

But we are not to be saved by the captain this time, but by the crew. We are not to be saved by Abraham Lincoln, but by that power behind the throne, greater than the throne itself. You and I and all of us have this matter in hand. Men talk about saving the Union, and restoring the Union as it was. They delude themselves with the miserable idea that that old Union can be brought to life again. That old Union, whose canonized bones we so quietly inurned under the shattered walls of Sumter, can never come to life again. It is dead, and you cannot put life into it. The first shot fired at the walls of Sumter caused it to fall as dead as the body of Julius Caesar when stabbed by Brutus. We do not want it. We have outlived the old Union. We had outlived it long before the rebellion came to tell us—

I mean the Union under the old pro-slavery interpretation of it—and had become ashamed of it. The South hated it with our anti-slavery interpretation, and the North hated it with the Southern interpretation of its requirements. We had already come to think with horror of the idea of being called upon here in our churches and literary societies, to take up arms and go down South, and pour the leaden death into the breasts of the slaves, in case they should rise for liberty; and the better part of the people did not mean to do it. They shuddered at the idea of so sacrilegious a crime. They had already become utterly disgusted with the idea of playing the part of blood-hounds for the slave-masters, and watch-dogs for the plantations. They had come to detest the principle upon which the slaveholding States had a larger representation in Congress than the free States. They had come to think that the little finger of dear old John Brown was worth more to the world than all the slaveholders in Virginia put together. (Applause.) What business, then, have we to fight for the old Union? We are not fighting for it. We are fighting for something incomparably better than the old Union. We are fighting for unity; unity of object, unity of institutions, in which there shall be no North, no South, no East, no West, no black, no white, but a solidarity of the nation, making every slave free, and every free man a voter. (Great applause.)

Abraham Lincoln:
Annual Message to Congress

In his annual message and the proclamation accompanying it, President Lincoln outlined a program for the reconstruction of the rebelling states. While some abolitionists criticized his plan for being too lenient to secessionists and for failing to extend the franchise to freed slaves, it was initially well received by a wide range of Republicans. Many Radicals praised it for making emancipation a precondition for the restoration of the Union, while conservatives applauded Lincoln's refusal to endorse the theory, advanced by some Radicals, that the Confederate states had lost their sovereignty and reverted to the status of federal territories.

December 8, 1863

Fellow citizens of the Senate and House of Representatives:

Another year of health, and of sufficiently abundant harvests has passed. For these, and especially for the improved condition of our national affairs, our renewed, and profoundest gratitude to God is due.

We remain in peace and friendship with foreign powers.

The efforts of disloyal citizens of the United States to involve us in foreign wars, to aid an inexcusable insurrection, have been unavailing. Her Britannic Majesty's government, as was justly expected, have exercised their authority to prevent the departure of new hostile expeditions from British ports. The Emperor of France has, by a like proceeding, promptly vindicated the neutrality which he proclaimed at the beginning of the contest. Questions of great intricacy and importance have arisen out of the blockade, and other belligerent operations, between the government and several of the maritime powers, but they have been discussed, and, as far as was possible, accommodated in a spirit of frankness, justice, and mutual good will. It is especially gratifying that our prize courts, by the impartiality of their adjudications, have commanded the respect and confidence of maritime powers.

The supplemental treaty between the United States and Great Britain for the suppression of the African slave trade, made on the 17th. day of February last, has been duly ratified, and carried into execution. It is believed that, so far as American ports and American citizens are concerned, that inhuman and odious traffic has been brought to an end.

I shall submit, for the consideration of the Senate, a convention for the adjustment of possessory claims in Washington Territory, arising out of the treaty of the 15th. June, 1846, between the United States and Great Britain, and which have been the source of some disquiet among the citizens of that now rapidly improving part of the country.

A novel and important question, involving the extent of the maritime jurisdiction of Spain in the waters which surround the island of Cuba, has been debated without reaching an agreement, and it is proposed in an amicable spirit to refer it to the arbitrament of a friendly power. A convention for that purpose will be submitted to the Senate.

I have thought it proper, subject to the approval of the Senate, to concur with the interested commercial powers in an arrangement for the liquidation of the Scheldt dues upon the principles which have been heretofore adopted in regard to the imposts upon navigation in the waters of Denmark.

The long pending controversy between this government and that of Chili touching the seizure at Sitana, in Peru, by Chilian officers, of a large amount in treasure belonging to citizens of the United States, has been brought to a close by the award of His Majesty, the King of the Belgians, to whose arbitration the question was referred by the parties. The subject was thoroughly and patiently examined by that justly respected magistrate, and although the sum awarded to the claimants may not have been as large as they expected, there is no reason to distrust the wisdom of his Majesty's decision. That decision was promptly complied with by Chili, when intelligence in regard to it reached that country.

The joint commission, under the act of the last session, for carrying into effect the convention with Peru on the subject of claims, has been organized at Lima, and is engaged in the business intrusted to it.

Difficulties concerning inter-oceanic transit through Nicaragua are in course of amicable adjustment.

In conformity with principles set forth in my last annual message, I have received a representative from the United States of Colombia, and have accredited a minister to that republic.

Incidents occurring in the progress of our civil war have forced upon my attention the uncertain state of international questions, touching the rights of foreigners in this country and of United States citizens abroad. In regard to some governments these rights are at least partially defined by treaties. In no instance, however, is it expressly stipulated that, in the event of civil war, a foreigner residing in this country, within the lines of the insurgents, is to be exempted from the rule which classes him as a belligerent, in whose behalf the government of his country cannot expect any privileges or immunities distinct from that character. I regret to say, however, that such claims have been put forward, and, in some instances, in behalf of foreigners who have lived in the United States the greater part of their lives.

There is reason to believe that many persons born in foreign countries, who have declared their intention to become citizens, or who have been fully naturalized, have evaded the military duty required of them by denying the fact, and thereby throwing upon the government the burden of proof. It has been found difficult or impracticable to obtain this proof from the want of guides to the proper sources of information. These might be supplied by requiring clerks of courts, where declarations of intention may be made or naturalizations effected, to send, periodically, lists of the names of the persons naturalized, or declaring their intention to become citizens, to the Secretary of the Interior, in whose department those names might be arranged and printed for general information.

There is also reason to believe that foreigners frequently become citizens of the United States for the sole purpose of evading duties imposed by the laws of their native countries, to which, on becoming naturalized here, they at once repair, and though never returning to the United States, they still claim the interposition of this government as citizens. Many altercations and great prejudices have heretofore arisen out of this abuse. It is therefore, submitted to your serious consideration. It might be advisable to fix a limit, beyond which no Citizen of the United States residing abroad may claim the interposition of his government.

The right of suffrage has often been assumed and exercised by aliens, under pretences of naturalization, which they have disavowed when drafted into the military service. I submit the expediency of such an amendment of the law as will make the fact of voting an estoppel against any plea of exemption from military service, or other civil obligation, on the ground of alienage.

In common with other western powers, our relations with Japan have been brought into serious jeopardy, through the perverse opposition of the hereditary aristocracy of the empire, to the enlightened and liberal policy of the Tycoon designed to bring the country into the society of nations. It is hoped, although not with entire confidence, that these difficulties may be peacefully overcome. I ask your attention to the claim of the Minister residing there for the damages he sustained in the destruction by fire of the residence of the legation at Yedo.

Satisfactory arrangements have been made with the Emperor of Russia, which, it is believed, will result in effecting a continuous line of telegraph through that empire from our Pacific coast.

I recommend to your favorable consideration the subject of an international telegraph across the Atlantic ocean; and also of a telegraph between this capital and the national forts along the Atlantic seaboard and the Gulf of Mexico. Such communications, established with any reasonable outlay, would be economical as well as effective aids to the diplomatic, military, and naval service.

The consular system of the United States, under the enactments of the last Congress, begins to be self-sustaining; and there is reason to hope that it may become entirely so, with the increase of trade which will ensue whenever peace is restored. Our ministers abroad have been faithful in defending American rights. In protecting commercial interests, our Consuls have necessarily had to encounter increased labors and responsibilities, growing out of the war. These they have, for the most part, met and discharged with zeal and efficiency. This acknowledgment justly includes those Consuls who, residing in Morocco, Egypt, Turkey, Japan, China, and other oriental countries, are charged with complex functions and extraordinary powers.

The condition of the several organized Territories is generally satisfactory, although Indian disturbances in New Mexico have not been entirely suppressed. The mineral resources of Colorado, Nevada, Idaho, New Mexico, and Arizona are proving far richer than has been heretofore understood. I lay before you a communication on this subject from the governor of New Mexico. I again submit to your consideration the expediency of establishing a system for the encouragement of immigration. Although this source of national wealth and strength is again flowing with greater freedom than for several years before the insurrection occurred, there is still a great deficiency of laborers in every field of industry, especially in agriculture and in our mines, as well of iron and coal as of the precious metals. While the demand for labor is thus increased here, tens of thousands of persons, destitute of remunerative occupation, are thronging our foreign consulates, and offering to emigrate to the United States if essential, but very cheap, assistance can be afforded them. It is easy to see that, under the sharp discipline of civil war, the nation is beginning a new life. This noble effort demands the aid, and ought to receive the attention and support of the government.

Injuries, unforseen by the government and unintended, may, in some cases, have been inflicted on the subjects or citizens of foreign countries, both at sea and on land, by persons in the service of the United States. As this government expects redress from other powers when similar injuries are inflicted by persons in their service upon citizens of the United States, we must be prepared to do justice to foreigners. If the existing judicial tribunals are inadequate to this purpose, a special court may be authorized, with power to hear and decide such claims of the character referred to as may have arisen under treaties and the public law. Conventions for adjusting the claims by joint commission have been proposed to some governments, but no definitive answer to the proposition has yet been received from any.

In the course of the session I shall probably have occasion to request you to provide indemnification to claimants where decrees of restitution have been rendered, and damages awarded by admiralty courts; and in other cases where this government may be acknowledged to be liable in principle, and where the amount of that liability has been ascertained by an informal arbitration.

The proper officers of the treasury have deemed themselves required, by the law of the United States upon the subject, to demand a tax upon the incomes of foreign consuls in this country. While such a demand may not, in strictness, be in derogation of public law, or perhaps of any existing treaty between the United States and a foreign country, the expediency of so far modifying the act as to exempt from tax the income of such consuls as are not citizens of the United States, derived from the emoluments of their office, or from property not situated in the United States, is submitted to your serious consideration. I make this suggestion upon the ground that a comity which ought to be reciprocated exempts our Consuls, in all other countries, from taxation to the extent thus indicated. The United States, I think, ought not to be exceptionally illiberal to international trade and commerce.

The operations of the treasury during the last year have been successfully conducted. The enactment by Congress of a national banking law has proved a valuable support of the public credit; and the general legislation in relation to loans has fully answered the expectations of its favorers. Some amendments may be required to perfect existing laws; but no change in their principles or general scope is believed to be needed.

Since these measures have been in operation, all demands on the treasury, including the pay of the army and navy, have been promptly met and fully satisfied. No considerable body of troops, it is believed, were ever more amply provided, and more liberally and punctually paid; and it may be added that by no people were the burdens incident to a great war ever more cheerfully borne.

The receipts during the year from all sources, including loans and the balance in the treasury at its commencement, were $901,125,674.86, and the aggregate disbursements $895,796,630.65, leaving a balance on the 1st. July, 1863, of $5,329,044.21. Of the receipts there were derived from customs, $69,059,642.40; from internal revenue, $37,640,787.95; from direct tax, $1,485,103.61; from lands, $167,617.17; from miscellaneous sources, $3,046,615.35; and from loans, $776,682,361.57; making the aggregate, $901,125,674.86. Of the disbursements there were for the civil service, $23,253,922.08; for pensions and Indians, $4,216,520.79; for interest on public debt, $24,729,846.51; for the War Department, $599,298,600.83; for the Navy Department, $63,211,105.27; for payment of funded and temporary debt, $181,086,635.07; making the aggregate, $895,796,630.65, and leaving the balance of $5,329,044.21. But the payment of funded and temporary debt, having been made from moneys borrowed during the year, must be regarded as merely nominal payments, and the moneys borrowed to make them as merely nominal receipts; and their amount, $181,086,635 07, should therefore be deducted both from receipts and disbursements. This being done, there remains as actual receipts $720,039,039.79; and the actual disbursements, $714,709,995.58, leaving the balance as already stated.

The actual receipts and disbursements for the first quarter, and the estimated receipts and disbursements for the remaining three quarters, of the current fiscal year, 1864, will be shown in detail by the report of the Secretary of the Treasury, to which I invite your attention. It is sufficient to say here that it is not believed that actual results will exhibit a state of the finances less favorable to the country than the estimates of that officer heretofore submitted; while it is confidently expected that at the close of the year both disbursements and debt will be found very considerably less than has been anticipated.

The report of the Secretary of War is a document of great interest. It consists of—

1. The military operations of the year, detailed in the report of the general-in-chief.

2. The organization of colored persons into the war service.

3. The exchange of prisoners, fully set forth in the letter of General Hitchcock.

4. The operations under the act for enrolling and calling out the national forces, detailed in the report of the provost marshal general.

5. The organization of the invalid corps; and

6. The operation of the several departments of the quartermaster general, commissary general, paymaster general, chief of engineers, chief of ordnance, and surgeon general.

It has appeared impossible to make a valuable summary of this report except such as would be too extended for this place, and hence I content myself by asking your careful attention to the report itself.

The duties devolving on the naval branch of the service during the year, and throughout the whole of this unhappy contest, have been discharged with fidelity and eminent success. The extensive blockade has been constantly increasing in efficiency, as the navy has expanded; yet on so long a line it has so far been impossible to entirely suppress illicit trade. From returns received at the Navy Department, it appears that more than one thousand vessels have been captured since the blockade was instituted, and that the value of prizes already sent in for adjudication amounts to over thirteen millions of dollars.

The naval force of the United States consists at this time of five hundred and eighty-eight vessels, completed and in the course of completion, and of these seventy-five are iron-clad or armored steamers. The events of the war give an increased interest and importance to the navy which will probably extend beyond the war itself.

The armored vessels in our navy completed and in service, or which are under contract and approaching completion, are believed to exceed in number those of any other power. But while these may be relied upon for harbor defence and coast service, others of greater strength and capacity will be necessary for cruising purposes, and to maintain our rightful position on the ocean.

The change that has taken place in naval vessels and naval warfare, since the introduction of steam as a motive-power for ships-of-war, demands either a corresponding change in some of our existing navy yards, or the establishment of new ones, for the construction and necessary repair of modern naval vessels. No inconsiderable embarrassment, delay, and public injury have been experienced from the want of such governmental establishments. The necessity of such a navy yard, so furnished, at some suitable place upon the Atlantic seaboard, has on repeated occasions been brought to the attention of Congress by the Navy Department, and is again presented in the report of the Secretary which accompanies this communication. I think it my duty to invite your special attention to this subject, and also to that of establishing a yard and depot for naval purposes upon one of the western rivers. A naval force has been created on those interior waters, and under many disadvantages, within little more than two years, exceeding in numbers the whole naval force of the country at the commencement of the present administration. Satisfactory and important as have been the performances of the heroic men of the navy at this interesting period, they are scarcely more wonderful than the success of our mechanics and artisans in the production of war vessels which has created a new form of naval power.

Our country has advantages superior to any other nation in our resources of iron and timber, with inexhaustible quantities of fuel in the immediate vicinity of both, and all available and in close proximity to navigable waters. Without the advantage of public works the resources of the nation have been developed and its power displayed in the construction of a navy of such magnitude which has, at the very period of its creation, rendered signal service to the Union.

The increase of the number of seamen in the public service, from seven thousand five hundred men, in the spring of 1861, to about thirty four thousand at the present time has been accomplished without special legislation, or extraordinary bounties to promote that increase. It has been found, however, that the operation of the draft, with the high bounties paid for army recruits, is beginning to affect injuriously the naval service, and will, if not corrected, be likely to impair its efficiency, by detaching seamen from their proper vocation and inducing them to enter the Army. I therefore respectfully suggest that Congress might aid both the army and naval services by a definite provision on this subject, which would at the same time be equitable to the communities more especially interested.

I commend to your consideration the suggestions of the

Secretary of the Navy in regard to the policy of fostering and training seamen, and also the education of officers and engineers for the naval service. The Naval Academy is rendering signal service in preparing midshipmen for the highly responsible duties which in after life they will be required to perform. In order that the country should not be deprived of the proper quota of educated officers, for which legal provision has been made at the naval school, the vacancies caused by the neglect or omission to make nominations from the States in insurrection have been filled by the Secretary of the Navy.

The school is now more full and complete than at any former period, and in every respect entitled to the favorable consideration of Congress.

During the past fiscal year the financial condition of the Post office Department has been one of increasing prosperity, and I am gratified in being able to state that the actual postal revenue has nearly equalled the entire expenditures; the latter amounting to $11,314,206.84, and the former to $11,163,789 59, leaving a deficiency of but $150,417 25. In 1860, the year immediately preceding the rebellion the deficiency amounted to $5,656,705 49, the postal receipts of that year being $2,645,722 19 less than those of 1863. The decrease since 1860 in the annual amount of transportation has been only about 25 per cent, but the annual expenditure on account of the same has been reduced 35 per cent. It is manifest, therefore, that the Post Office Department may become self-sustaining in a few years, even with the restoration of the whole service.

The international conference of postal delegates from the principal countries of Europe and America, which was called at the suggestion of the Postmaster General, met at Paris on the 11th of May last, and concluded its deliberations on the 8th of June. The principles established by the conference as best adapted to facilitate postal intercourse between nations, and as the basis of future postal conventions, inaugurate a general system of uniform international charges, at reduced rates of postage, and cannot fail to produce beneficial results.

I refer you to the report of the Secretary of the Interior, which is herewith laid before you, for useful and varied information in relation to the public lands, Indian affairs, patents, pensions, and other matters of public concern pertaining to his department.

The quantity of land disposed of during the last and the first quarter of the present fiscal years was three million eight hundred and forty one thousand five hundred and forty nine acres, of which one hundred and sixty one thousand nine hundred and eleven acres were sold for cash, one million four hundred and fifty six thousand five hundred and fourteen acres were taken up under the homestead law, and the residue disposed of under laws granting lands for military bounties, for railroad and other purposes. It also appears that the sale of the public lands is largely on the increase.

It has long been a cherished opinion of some of our wisest statesmen that the people of the United States had a higher and more enduring interest in the early settlement and substantial cultivation of the public lands than in the amount of direct revenue to be derived from the sale of them. This opinion has had a controlling influence in shaping legislation upon the subject of our national domain. I may cite, as evidence of this, the liberal measures adopted in reference to actual settlers; the grant to the States of the overflowed lands within their limits in order to their being reclaimed and rendered fit for cultivation; the grants to railway companies of alternate sections of land upon the contemplated lines of their roads which, when completed, will so largely multiply the facilities for reaching our distant possessions. This policy has received its most signal and beneficent illustration in the recent enactment granting homesteads to actual settlers.

Since the first day of January last the before-mentioned quantity of one million four hundred and fifty-six thousand five hundred and fourteen acres of land have been taken up under its provisions. This fact and the amount of sales furnish gratifying evidence of increasing settlement upon the public lands, notwithstanding the great struggle in which the energies of the nation have been engaged, and which has required so large a withdrawal of our citizens from their accustomed pursuits. I cordially concur in the recommendation of the Secretary of the Interior suggesting a modification of the act in favor of those engaged in the military and naval service of the United States. I doubt not that Congress will cheerfully adopt such measures as will, without essentially changing the general features of the system, secure to the greatest practicable extent, its benefits to those who have left their homes in the defence of the country in this arduous crisis.

I invite your attention to the views of the Secretary as to the propriety of raising by appropriate legislation a revenue from the mineral lands of the United States.

The measures provided at your last session for the removal of certain Indian tribes have been carried into effect. Sundry treaties have been negotiated which will, in due time, be submitted for the constitutional action of the Senate. They contain stipulations for extinguishing the possessory rights of the Indians to large and valuable tracts of land. It is hoped that the effect of these treaties will result in the establishment of permanent friendly relations with such of these tribes as have been brought into frequent and bloody collision with our outlying settlements and emigrants.

Sound policy and our imperative duty to these wards of the government demand our anxious and constant attention to their material well-being, to their progress in the arts of civilization, and, above all, to that moral training which, under the blessing of Divine Providence, will confer upon them the elevated and sanctifying influences, the hopes and consolation of the Christian faith.

I suggested in my last annual message the propriety of re-modelling our Indian system. Subsequent events have satisfied me of its necessity. The details set forth in the report of the Secretary evince the urgent need for immediate legislative action.

I commend the benevolent institutions, established or patronized by the government in this District, to your generous and fostering care.

The attention of Congress, during the last session, was engaged to some extent with a proposition for enlarging the water communication between the Mississippi river and the north-eastern seaboard, which proposition, however, failed for the time. Since then, upon a call of the greatest respectability a convention has been held at Chicago upon the same subject, a summary of whose views is contained in a memorial addressed to the President and Congress, and which I now have the honor to lay before you. That this interest is one which, ere long, will force its own way, I do not entertain a doubt, while it is submitted entirely to your wisdom as to what can be done now. Augmented interest is given to this subject by the actual commencement of work upon the Pacific railroad, under auspices so favorable to rapid progress and completion. The enlarged navigation becomes a palpable need to the great road.

I transmit the second annual report of the Commissioner of the Department of Agriculture, asking your attention to the developments in that vital interest of the nation.

When Congress assembled a year ago the war had already lasted nearly twenty months, and there had been many conflicts on both land and sea, with varying results.

The rebellion had been pressed back into reduced limits; yet the tone of public feeling and opinion, at home and abroad, was not satisfactory. With other signs, the popular elections, then just past, indicated uneasiness among ourselves, while amid much that was cold and menacing the kindest words coming from Europe were uttered in accents of pity, that we were too blind to surrender a hopeless cause. Our commerce was suffering greatly by a few armed vessels built upon and furnished from foreign shores, and we were threatened with such additions from the same quarter as would sweep our trade from the sea and raise our blockade. We had failed to elicit from European governments anything hopeful upon this subject. The preliminary emancipation proclamation, issued in September, was running its assigned period to the beginning of the new year. A month later the final proclamation came, including the announcement that colored men of suitable condition would be received into the war service. The policy of emancipation, and of employing black soldiers, gave to the future a new aspect, about which hope, and fear, and doubt contended in uncertain conflict. According to our political system, as a matter of civil administration, the general government had no lawful power to effect emancipation in any State, and for a long time it had been hoped that the rebellion could be suppressed without resorting to it as a military measure. It was all the while deemed possible that the necessity for it might come, and that if it should, the crisis of the contest would then be presented. It came, and as was anticipated, it was followed by dark and doubtful days. Eleven months having now passed, we are permitted to take another review. The rebel borders are pressed still further back, and by the complete opening of the Mississippi the country dominated by the rebellion is divided into distinct parts, with no practical communication between them. Tennessee and Arkansas have been substantially cleared of insurgent control, and influential citizens in each, owners of slaves and advocates of slavery at the beginning of the rebellion, now declare openly for emancipation in their respective States. Of those States not included in the emancipation proclamation, Maryland, and Missouri, neither of which three years ago would tolerate any restraint upon the extension of slavery into new territories, only dispute now as to the best mode of removing it within their own limits.

Of those who were slaves at the beginning of the rebellion, full one hundred thousand are now in the United States military service, about one-half of which number actually bear arms in the ranks; thus giving the double advantage of taking so much labor from the insurgent cause, and supplying the places which otherwise must be filled with so many white men. So far as tested, it is difficult to say they are not as good soldiers as any. No servile insurrection, or tendency to violence or cruelty, has marked the measures of emancipation and arming the blacks. These measures have been much discussed in foreign countries, and contemporary with such discussion the tone of public sentiment there is much improved. At home the same measures have been fully discussed, supported, criticised, and denounced, and the annual elections following are highly encouraging to those whose official duty it is to bear the country through this great trial. Thus we have the new reckoning. The crisis which threatened to divide the friends of the Union is past.

Looking now to the present and future, and with reference to a resumption of the national authority within the States wherein that authority has been suspended, I have thought fit to issue a proclamation, a copy of which is herewith transmitted. On examination of this proclamation it will appear, as is believed, that nothing is attempted beyond what is amply justified by the Constitution. True, the form of an oath is given, but no man is coerced to take it. The man is only promised a pardon in case he voluntarily takes the oath. The Constitution authorizes the Executive to grant or withhold the pardon at his own absolute discretion; and this includes the power to grant on terms, as is fully established by judicial and other authorities.

It is also proffered that if, in any of the States named, a State government shall be, in the mode prescribed, set up, such government shall be recognized and guarantied by the United States, and that under it the State shall, on the constitutional conditions, be protected against invasion and domestic violence. The constitutional obligation of the United States to guaranty to every State in the Union a republican form of government, and to protect the State, in the cases stated, is explicit and full. But why tender the benefits of this provision only to a State government set up in this particular way? This section of the Constitution contemplates a case wherein the element within a State, favorable to republican government, in the Union, may be too feeble for an opposite and hostile element external to, or even within the State; and such are precisely the cases with which we are now dealing.

An attempt to guaranty and protect a revived State government, constructed in whole, or in preponderating part, from the very element against whose hostility and violence it is to be protected, is simply absurd. There must be a test by which to separate the opposing elements, so as to build only from the sound; and that test is a sufficiently liberal one, which accepts as sound whoever will make a sworn recantation of his former unsoundness.

But if it be proper to require, as a test of admission to the political body, an oath of allegiance to the Constitution of the United States, and to the Union under it, why also to the laws and proclamations in regard to slavery? Those laws and proclamations were enacted and put forth for the purpose of aiding in the suppression of the rebellion. To give them their fullest effect, there had to be a pledge for their maintenance. In my judgment they have aided, and will further aid, the cause for which they were intended. To now abandon them would be not only to relinquish a lever of power, but would also be a cruel and an astounding breach of faith. I may add at this point, that while I remain in my present position I shall not attempt to retract or modify the emancipation proclamation; nor shall I return to slavery any person who is free by the terms of that proclamation, or by any of the acts of Congress. For these and other reasons it is thought best that support of these measures shall be included in the oath; and it is believed the Executive may lawfully claim it in return for pardon and restoration of forfeited rights, which he has clear constitutional power to withhold altogether, or grant upon the terms which he shall deem wisest for the public interest. It should be observed, also, that this part of the oath is subject to the modifying and abrogating power of legislation and supreme judicial decision.

The proposed acquiescence of the national Executive in any reasonable temporary State arrangement for the freed people is made with the view of possibly modifying the confusion and destitution which must, at best, attend all classes by a total revolution of labor throughout whole States. It is hoped that the already deeply afflicted people in those States may be somewhat more ready to give up the cause of their affliction, if, to this extent, this vital matter be left to themselves; while no power of the national Executive to prevent an abuse is abridged by the proposition.

The suggestion in the proclamation as to maintaining the political framework of the States on what is called reconstruction, is made in the hope that it may do good without danger of harm. It will save labor and avoid great confusion.

But why any proclamation now upon this subject? This question is beset with the conflicting views that the step might be delayed too long or be taken too soon. In some States the elements for resumption seem ready for action, but remain inactive, apparently for want of a rallying point—a plan of action. Why shall A adopt the plan of B, rather than B that of A? And if A and B should agree, how can they know but that the general government here will reject their plan? By the proclamation a plan is presented which may be accepted by them as a rallying point, and which they are assured in advance will not be rejected here. This may bring them to act sooner than they otherwise would.

The objections to a premature presentation of a plan by the national Executive consists in the danger of committals on points which could be more safely left to further developments. Care has been taken to so shape the document as to avoid embarrassments from this source. Saying that, on certain terms, certain classes will be pardoned, with rights restored, it is not said that other classes, or other terms, will never be included. Saying that reconstruction will be accepted if presented in a specified way, it is not said it will never be accepted in any other way.

The movements, by State action, for emancipation in several of the States, not included in the emancipation proclamation, are matters of profound gratulation. And while I do not repeat in detail what I have heretofore so earnestly urged upon this subject, my general views and feelings remain unchanged; and I trust that Congress will omit no fair opportunity of aiding these important steps to a great consummation.

In the midst of other cares, however important, we must not lose sight of the fact that the war power is still our main reliance. To that power alone can we look, yet for a time, to give confidence to the people in the contested regions, that the insurgent power will not again overrun them. Until that confidence shall be established, little can be done anywhere for what is called reconstruction. Hence our chiefest care must still be directed to the army and navy, who have thus far borne their harder part so nobly and well. And it may be esteemed fortunate that in giving the greatest efficiency to these indispensable arms, we do also honorably recognize the gallant men, from commander to sentinel, who compose them, and to whom, more than to others, the world must stand indebted for the home of freedom disenthralled, regenerated, enlarged, and perpetuated. ABRAHAM LINCOLN

Washington, December 8, 1863.

Abraham Lincoln:
Proclamation of Amnesty and Reconstruction

The proclamation excluded Virginia from the list of states without a loyal government because the Lincoln administration had already recognized the unionist "restored government" of Virginia established in Wheeling in June 1861. When West Virginia was admitted as a state on June 20, 1863, Governor Francis H. Pierpont had relocated the restored government to Alexandria, where it exercised authority over areas occupied by Union forces.

December 8, 1863
By the President of the United States of America:
A Proclamation.

Whereas, in and by the Constitution of the United States, it is provided that the President "shall have power to grant reprieves and pardons for offences against the United States, except in cases of impeachment;" and

Whereas a rebellion now exists whereby the loyal State governments of several States have for a long time been subverted, and many persons have committed and are now guilty of treason against the United States; and

Whereas, with reference to said rebellion and treason, laws have been enacted by Congress declaring forfeitures and confiscation of property and liberation of slaves, all upon terms and conditions therein stated, and also declaring that the President was thereby authorized at any time thereafter, by proclamation, to extend to persons who may have participated in the existing rebellion, in any State or part thereof, pardon and amnesty, with such exceptions and at such times and on such conditions as he may deem expedient for the public welfare; and

Whereas the congressional declaration for limited and conditional pardon accords with well-established judicial exposition of the pardoning power; and

Whereas, with reference to said rebellion, the President of the United States has issued several proclamations, with provisions in regard to the liberation of slaves; and

Whereas it is now desired by some persons heretofore engaged in said rebellion to resume their allegiance to the United States, and to reinaugurate loyal State governments within and for their respective States; therefore,

I, Abraham Lincoln, President of the United States, do proclaim, declare, and make known to all persons who have, directly or by implication, participated in the existing rebellion, except as hereinafter excepted, that a full pardon is hereby granted to them and each of them, with restoration of all rights of property, except as to slaves, and in property cases where rights of third parties shall have intervened, and upon the condition that every such person shall take and subscribe an oath, and thenceforward keep and maintain said oath inviolate; and which oath shall be registered for permanent preservation, and shall be of the tenor and effect following, to wit:

"I, ——, do solemnly swear, in presence of Almighty God, that I will henceforth faithfully support, protect and defend the Constitution of the United States, and the union of the States thereunder; and that I will, in like manner, abide by and faithfully support all acts of Congress passed during the existing rebellion with reference to slaves, so long and so far as not repealed, modified or held void by Congress, or by decision of the Supreme Court; and that I will, in like manner, abide by and faithfully support all proclamations of the President made during the existing rebellion having reference to slaves, so long and so far as not modified or declared void by decision of the Supreme Court. So help me God."

The persons excepted from the benefits of the foregoing provisions are all who are, or shall have been, civil or diplomatic officers or agents of the so-called confederate government; all who have left judicial stations under the United States to aid the rebellion; all who are, or shall have been, military or naval officers of said so-called confederate government above the rank of colonel in the army, or of lieutenant in the navy; all who left seats in the United States Congress to aid the rebellion; all who resigned commissions in the army or navy of the United States, and afterwards aided the rebellion; and all who have engaged in any way in treating colored persons or white persons, in charge of such, otherwise than lawfully as prisoners of war, and which persons may have been found in the United States service, as soldiers, seamen, or in any other capacity.

And I do further proclaim, declare, and make known, that whenever, in any of the States of Arkansas, Texas, Louisiana, Mississippi, Tennessee, Alabama, Georgia, Florida, South Carolina, and North Carolina, a number of persons, not less than one-tenth in number of the votes cast in such State at the Presidential election of the year of our Lord one thousand eight hundred and sixty, each having taken the oath aforesaid and not having since violated it, and being a qualified voter by the election law of the State existing immediately before the so-called act of secession, and excluding all others, shall re-establish a State government which shall be republican, and in no wise contravening said oath, such shall be recognized as the true government of the State, and the State shall receive thereunder the benefits of the constitutional provision which declares that "The United States shall guaranty to every State in this union a republican form of government, and shall protect each of them against invasion; and, on application of the legislature, or the executive, (when the legislature cannot be convened,) against domestic violence."

And I do further proclaim, declare, and make known that any provision which may be adopted by such State government in relation to the freed people of such State, which shall recognize and declare their permanent freedom, provide for their education, and which may yet be consistent, as a temporary arrangement, with their present condition as a laboring, landless, and homeless class, will not be objected to by the national Executive. And it is suggested as not improper, that, in constructing a loyal State government in any State, the name of the State, the boundary, the subdivisions, the constitution, and the general code of laws, as before the rebellion, be maintained, subject only to the modifications made necessary by the conditions hereinbefore stated, and such others, if any, not contravening said conditions, and which may be deemed expedient by those framing the new State government.

To avoid misunderstanding, it may be proper to say that this proclamation, so far as it relates to State governments, has no reference to States wherein loyal State governments have all the while been maintained. And for the same reason, it may be proper to further say that whether members sent to Congress from any State shall be admitted to seats, constitutionally rests exclusively with the respective Houses, and not to any extent with the Executive. And still further, that this proclamation is intended to present the people of the States wherein the national authority has been suspended, and loyal State governments have been subverted, a mode in and by which the national authority and loyal State governments may be re-established within said States, or in any of them; and, while the mode presented is the best the Executive can suggest, with his present impressions, it must not be understood that no other possible mode would be acceptable.

Given under my hand at the city, of Washington, the 8th. day of December, A.D. one thousand eight hundred and sixty-three, and of the independence of the United States of America the eighty-eighth.

ABRAHAM LINCOLN

By the President:
WILLIAM H. SEWARD, Secretary of State.

George Templeton Strong:
Diary, December 11–13, 1863

Strong recorded his response to Lincoln's message and proclamation
and to a message sent by Jefferson Davis to the Confederate Congress
on December 7. The report that Strong noted regarding Alexander
H. Stephens, "Vice-President of Rebeldom," turned out to be false.

———————

December 11.   Visited by unknown author of *The New Gospel of Peace*, which has been attributed to a score of people,
myself among them. The Cincinnati Sanitary Commission Fair
people had written to his publisher, Tousey, to ask for the
original manuscript that they might make merchandise thereof,
whereupon, Mr. X. Y., the evangelist, came to me to say that
our Metropolitan Fair could have it for the asking. I closed
with the offer, for the manuscript will bring money. Though
the squib does not seem to me very particularly clever, it has
hit the average popular taste very hard. Seventy thousand copies of the first part and forty thousand of the second have been
sold. The author is ——. Who'd have thought it!

President's message and proclamation of conditional amnesty to the rebels, certain classes excepted, finds very general
favor. Uncle Abe is the most popular man in America today.
The firmness, honesty, and sagacity of the "gorilla despot"
may be recognized by the rebels themselves sooner than we
expect, and the weight of his personal character may do a great
deal toward restoration of our national unity.

Rebeldom has just played us a pretty prank; its audacity is
wonderful. Sixteen "passengers" on the peaceful propeller
Chesapeake, which left New York for Portland last Saturday,
took possession of her during her voyage, killed some of her
officers and crew, put the rest ashore near St. Johns, and then
steamed off with their prize in triumph under Confederate

colors. A whole armada has been sent in pursuit, but they won't catch her.

There is almost universal feeling that rebellion has received its death-blow and will not survive through the winter. It is premature, but being coupled with no suggestion that our efforts may safely be slackened, it will do no harm. The *soi-disant* Chivalry shews no sign of disposition to back down and is as rampant, blatant, and blustering as ever. The most truculent and foul-mouthed bravoes and swashbucklers of the South feel a certain amount of discouragement, no doubt, but they generally keep it to themselves. There will be no enduring peace while the class that has hitherto governed the South continues to exist. They are almost universally given over to a reprobate mind and past possibility of repentance. Southern aristocracy must be dealt with as the Clans were after 1745. Parton's life of Butler (a readable book) tells how that general treated their case in New Orleans. Even his remedies were too mild, but they come nearer to what is required than any others yet administered. That book will do much to raise Butler in popular favor. It paints him as of that Jacksonesque type of beauty which we especially appreciate and admire. Parton colors very high and tries to make a demigod of his hero, but I have always thought Butler among the strongest men brought forward by the war.

December 13, SUNDAY.   Dr. Peters brings news of a bulletin at Union League Club announcing that A. H. Stephens, Vice-President of Rebeldom, has just presented himself once more at Fortress Monroe with a couple of colleagues as Peace Commissioners, that Butler refused to receive them in any official character, but offered to hear what they had to say as prominent citizens of Secessia, and that they thereupon went back again in a huff, sending a vindictive Parthian shaft behind them in the shape of a notification that they would no longer allow supplies to be sent our starving prisoners at Richmond. If they have done this, it won't much help their cause abroad; but that's a small matter. Government should notify them that inasmuch as they have declared their inability to give their prisoners rations sufficient to sustain life, their refusal to allow us to make up the deficiency will be followed by the execution of the rebel officers in our hands *per diem*, till such refusal is revoked.

Message of Jefferson Davis, "anti-President," to the squad of malefactors now gathered at Richmond and styling themselves members of Congress from Kentucky, Tennessee, Missouri, and other states, is long and doleful and dull—a mélange of lies, sophistry, swagger, lamentation, treason, perjury, and piety. He admits that rebellion has been drifting to leeward during the past year, but refers his gang for consolation to the boundless capacities of the future. He is moral, also, and objects to any action inconsistent with the letter or the spirit of "the constitution we have sworn to obey." This is cool. He and probably the majority of his pals and councillors in Congress assembled had held not less than twenty offices apiece before they concluded to rebel. How many hundred broken oaths to uphold another constitution were represented on the floor while this pious message was being read? Could all these several perjuries have been combined in one colossal act of blasphemy, I think the earth would necessarily have opened and swallowed the perpetrator. Jefferson's act of hypocrisy is (time, place, and presence considered) of like enormity, though less criminal and black. I wonder the assembled peers of Secessia were not startled by a vast resounding guffaw from the Powers of Nature, reverberating from the Chesapeake to the Alleghenies. Jefferson Davis has outbrazened Louis Napoleon himself.

Catherine Edmondston:
Diary, December 11, 1863

Catherine Edmondston reflected on the causes of the recent Confederate defeats in Tennessee and the strengths and weaknesses of Jefferson Davis as a leader.

———————

DECEMBER 11, 1863

A fortunate thing it is for us in this Confederacy that it is not 'de rigueur' to testify greif on the receipt of bad news by rending one's clothes! Did that ancient custom prevail the frequency with which one misfortune follows another would tell sadly upon our slender wardrobes! Perhaps, however, the ancients mingled economy in their sorrow and rent their clothes at the seams only. Even that, with thread at 1.75 cts per spool, which I this day paid for one in Clarksville, would be rather hard on us. But to go back to the bad news which has metaphorically rent all the clothes in the country within the past few days. Official dispatches have been received from Gen Longstreet from a point thirty miles from Knoxville in full retreat from that place to Virginia. What he has accomplished the Examiner says may be summed up in a few words —*nothing*. Gild the pill as ye may, Mr Davis, it is a bitter one to swallow. I say Mr Davis for he is, we are told, who detached Longstreet from Bragg's command before the late battle. By his orders, too, was the army of Northern Geo reorganized in the face of the foe & to this cause is the late disaster at Lookout ascribed. Brigades were recast, divisions remoddled, & when the shock of battle came men were led into action by generals who had never led them before. Regiments had lost their old & tried supporters, their fellow regiments in their Brigades, & had to rely on men whom they had never seen before & upon whose support they could not with confidence, *which experience* gives, rely. *Hence* our defeat & hence the small loss we endured, for some Regiments gave way without waiting to see how their new comrades fought. A want of sense it appears to us to reorganize thus in the face of the foe. Mr Davis Message came last night, an able document especially in reference to our *foreign relations*. Lord John Russel, her Majesty's Secretary for foreign affairs, is shown in his true light, petty & deceitful, under the mask of neutrality, claiming credit with the U S. for favouring it. Faugh! If he be a diplomat—I'll none of them! His lies have not the merit of plausibility!

The President's summary of Home affairs is rather gloomy. The currency & the soldiers whose term of enlistment is to expire in the spring are knotty points, but God has led us heretofore & He will lead us still. It is sad to myself to realize how my admiration has lessened for Mr Davis, lessened since the loss of Vicksburg, a calamity brought on us by his obstinacy in retaining Pemberton in command, & now still further diminished by his indomitable pride of opinion in upholding Bragg.

The Examiner says, "It is some comfort we grant to have a President who does not disgrace us by Hoosier English but it is a comfort which is dearly bought at the price of a Memminger & a Bragg." His favourites have cost us much: Mallory, a Navy; Memminger has flooded the land with useless Treasury notes, sapped the fountain head of our prosperity; Huger cost us Roanoke Island & in consequence Norfolk. (He also let McClellan escape at [   ]; Lovel, New Orleans; Pemberton, Vicksburg and the two together the greater part of the Mississippi Valley. Bragg lost us first Kentucky and then Tennessee. His obstinacy in refusing to give Price the command lost Missouri & now the incapable Holmes, also his favourite, is clinching the loss and letting Arkansas slip away likewise. Truly I fear that to him is not given the first element of a ruler—"the discerning of Spirits." He upheld Sidney Johnston when unjustly assailed, however. "No general have I, if indeed great Johnston be not one." Here let us do him justice, but to give such a man as [   ] a Lieut Gen'ship for "auld acquaintance sake" only seems trifling with the interests of the country. But let me "not speak" too much "evil of dignities." Mr Davis whilst he has made many mistakes has presided over our fortunes with dignity & Christian forbearance. Toward a man so harrassed with care as he is, & with such heavy responsibilities resting upon him as he has, requires that we should judge him kindly. Who would have done better if placed in his seat?

Sue, Rachel, & Col Clark dined with us today. Col C gives a melancholly picture of the country late in his command—below Hamilton. The Yankees have destroyed everything & burnt upon a large scale, many plantations being left without a house upon them. They misinterpret our forbearance in Penn last summer, think we abstained from devastating the country through fear, & this is the return they make us. Have been riding on horse back every afternoon latterly & enjoy my rides with Mr E greatly.

Mary Chesnut: Diary, January 1, 1864

Mary Chesnut spent the New Year in Richmond, where her husband Colonel James Chesnut, a former U.S. senator from South Carolina, served as an aide to Jefferson Davis. During the 1860s Mary Chesnut kept a diary that she would later revise and expand between 1881 and 1884. Her diary for the winter of 1863–64 is not known to have survived, and the text printed here is taken from the revised version.

———————

January 1st, 1864.   God help my country.

Table talk.

"After the battles around Richmond, hope was strong in me. All that has insensibly drifted away."

"I am like David after the child was dead. Get up, wash my face, have my hair cut, &c&c."

"That's too bad. I think we are more like the sailors who break into the spirits closet when they find out the ship must sink. There seems to be for the first time a resolute feeling to enjoy the brief hour and never look beyond the day."

"I now long, pine, pray, and grieve—and—well, I have no hope. Have you any of old Mr. Chesnut's brandy here still?"

"It is a good thing never to look beyond the hour. Laurence, take this key—look in such a place for a decanter marked &c&c&c."

General Hood's an awful flatterer—I mean an awkward flatterer. I told him to praise my husband to someone else—not to me. He ought to praise me to somebody who would tell J. C., and then praise J. C. to another person who would tell me. Man and wife are too much one person to receive a compliment straight in the face that way—that is, gracefully.

"That"—as an American demonstrative adjective pronoun, or adjective pure and simple—we give it illimitable meaning. Mrs. King, now, we were "weeping and commenting over a stricken deer," one who would say yes but was not asked. "Do you mean to say she is looking to marry him?" Mrs. King, with eyes uplifted and hands clasped: "*That* willing!" Again, of a wounded soldier: "Do you mean to say he is willing to leave the army for so slight an excuse?" Again: "Willing indeed! *That* willing!"

A peculiar intonation, however, must be given to *that* to make it bear its mountain of meaning.

Again, Grundy père was said to be a man of "des absences délicieuses."

"That's Madame Deffand's wit. I made a note of it—fits so many households."

"List of the halfhearted ones—at least we all know they never believed in this thing. Stephens—vice president—No. 1. Ashmore, Keitt, Boyce—of the South Carolina delegation. Orr—he was lugged in, awfully against the grain.

"There now, look at our wisdom. Mr. Mason! We grant you all you are going to say. Who denies it? He is a grand old Virginia gentleman. Straightforward, honest-hearted, blunt, high-headed, and unchangeable in his ways as—as the Rock of Gibraltar. Mr. Hunter, you need not shake your wise head. You know it set all the world a-laughing when we sent Mr. Mason abroad as a *diplomat!*"

"About tobacco, now—the English can't stand chewing—&c&c. They say at the lordliest table Mr. Mason will turn round halfway in his chair and spit in the fire!"

Jack Preston says the parting of high Virginia with its sons at the station is a thing to see—tears streaming from each eye, a crystal drop, from the corner of each mouth a yellow stream of tobacco juice.

"You know yourself, General Lee and General Huger's hearts were nearly rent asunder when they had to leave the old army."

"Oh! Did not Mrs. Johnston tell you of how General Scott thought to save the melancholy, reluctant, slow Joe for the Yankees? But he is a genuine F.F., and he came."

"One more year of Stonewall would have saved us."

"Chickamauga is the only battle we have gained since Stonewall went up!"

"And no results—as usual."

"Stonewall was not so much as killed by a Yankee. He was shot by Mahone's brigade. Now, that is hard."

"General Lee can do no more than keep back Meade."

"One of Meade's armies, you mean. They have only to double on him when he whips one of theirs."

"General Edward Johnson says he got Grant a place. Esprit de corps, you know, would not bear to see an old army man driving a wagon. That was when he found him out west. Put out of the army for habitual drunkenness."

"He is their man, a bullheaded Suwarrow. He don't care a snap if they fall like the leaves fall. He fights to win, that chap. He is not distracted by a thousand side issues. He does not see them. He is narrow and sure, sees only in a straight line."

"Like Louis Napoleon—from a bath in the gutters, he goes straight up."

"Yes, like Lincoln, they have ceased to carp at him because he is a rough clown, no gentleman, &c&c. You never hear now of his nasty fun—only of his wisdom. It don't take much soap and water to wash the hands that the rod of empire sways. They talked of Lincoln's drunkenness, too. Now, since Vicksburg they have not a word to say against Grant's habits."

"He has the disagreeable habit of not retreating before irresistible veterans—or it is reculer pour mieux sauter—&c&c. You need not be afraid of a little dirt on the hands which wield a field marshal's baton, either."

"General Lee and Albert Sidney Johnston, they show blood and breeding. They are of the Bayard, the Philip Sidney order of soldiers."

"Listen, if General Lee had Grant's resources, he would have bagged the last Yankee or had them all safe back, packed up in Massachusetts."

"You mean, if he had not the weight of the negro question on him?"

"No, I mean, if he had Grant's unlimited allowance of the powers of war—men, money, ammunition, arms—[   ].

"His servant had a stray pair of French boots down here,

and he was admiring his small feet and moving one so as to bring his high instep in better line of vision. For an excuse to give him a furlough, they sent some Yankee prisoners down here by him. I said, 'What sort of creatures are they?'"

"Damn splay-footed Yankees, every man jack of them."

"As they steadily tramp this way, I must say, I have ceased to admire their feet myself. How beautiful are the feet &c&c, says the Scriptures."

"Eat, drink, and be merry—tomorrow ye die—they say that, too."

"Why do you call General Preston 'Conscript Father'? On account of those girls?"

"No, indeed. He is at the head of the Conscription Bureau."

"General Young says, 'Give me those daredevil dandies I find in Mrs. C's drawing room. I like fellows who fight and don't care what all the row's about.'"

"Yes, and he sees the same daredevils often enough, stiff and stark, stripped, stone-dead on the battlefield."

"Oh, how can you bring all that to our eyes here!"

"What? Not compliment your drawing-room friends, the fellows who dance and fight with light hearts—who battle fire and famine, nakedness, mud, snow, frost, gunpowder, and—well, no words about it. Take it all as it comes."

"Talking feet—the bluest-blooded American you know, you call him 'the giant foot.'"

"They found that name for him in Bulwer's last. In the last page. A giant foot comes out of the darkness and kicks over the sort of Medea's cauldron of a big pot they were brewing."

Mr. Ould says Mrs. Lincoln found the gardener of the White House so nice she would make him a major general.

Lincoln said to the secretary, "Well! the little woman must have her way—sometimes."

She has the Augean perquisite of cleaning the military stables. She says it pays so well. She need never touch the president's saddle.

"The Roman emperor found all money of good odor."

"We do pitch into our enemies."

"As the English did into the French. And, later, into the Russians."

"They got up in a theater and huzzahed—when they heard the emperor of Russia was dead."

Marriage in high life. Senator Johnson of Arkansas—somewhere out West, I may not "locate" him properly—his friends fondly say "Bob Johnson."

He explained his marriage to Mrs. Davis. He is a devoted friend of the president.

With his foot on the carriage steps, so to speak, he married his deceased wife's sister. He wished to leave her power over his children, to protect them and take care of them while he was away.

Mrs. Davis asked, "Pray, why did you not tell us before?"

"I did not think it a matter worth mentioning. I only proposed it to her the morning I left home, and it was done at once. And now my mind is easy. I can stay here and attend to my business, as a man should. She is quite capable of looking after things at home."

We did not know Mrs. Lawton, and I inquired of Mary P, who did, if she was not unusually clever.

"*That* clever!" said Mary P, imitating the gesture attributed to Mrs. King. "How did you guess it?"

"General Lawton will hear every word I say. No matter how 'superior' the men are who surround us, I knew he was accustomed to hear things worth listening to at home."

Know now why the English, who find out the comfort of life in everything, send off a happy couple to spend the honeymoon out of everybody's way or shut them up at home and leave them. Today the beautiful bride and the happy bridegroom came to see me. They had not one thought to give, except to themselves and their wedding. Or their preliminary love affairs. How it all was, when it was, &c&c&c. She did tell a capital story—if I could write it!

Mrs. Wright of Tennessee came for me to go with her on a calling expedition. Found one cabinet minister's establishment in a state of republican simplicity. Servant who asked us in—out at elbows and knees.

The next a widower, whose house is presided over by a relative.

"Bob Johnson?" whispered Mrs. Wright.

"Not quite," answered another visitor. "Splendid plan, though. Like the waiter in Dickens's book—'Here on suiting—and she suits.'"

"Wigfall's speech—'Our husbandless daughters.'" Said Isabella: "No wonder. Here we are, and our possible husbands and lovers killed before we so much as knew them. Oh! the widows and old maids of this cruel war."

Read *Germaine*—About's. It is only in books that people fall in love with their wives. The arsenic story more probable—science, then, and not theory. After all, is it not as with any other copartnership, say, traveling companions? Their future opinion of each other, "the happiness of the association," depends entirely on what they really are, not what they felt or thought about each other before they had any possible way of acquiring accurate information as to character, habits, &c. Love makes it worse. The pendulum swings back further, the harder it was pulled the other way.

Mrs. Malaprop to the rescue—"Better begin with a little aversion." Not of any weight either way, what we think of people before *we know them*. Did two people ever live together so stupid as to be deceived? What they pretend does not count.

The *Examiner* gives this amount of pleasant information to the enemy.

He tells them we are not ready, and we cannot be before spring. And that now is their time.

Our safeguard, our hope, our trust is in beneficent mud, impassable mud. And so feeling, I hail with delight these long, long rainy days and longer nights. Things are deluging, sloppy, and up to the ankles in water and dirt, enough to satisfy the muddiest-minded croaker of us all.

We have taken prisoner some of Averell's raiders.

Somebody in secret session kicked and cuffed Foote, Foote of Mississippi, in the Senate.

So ends the old year.

The last night of the old year. Gloria Mundi sent me a cup of strong, *good* coffee. I drank two cups, and so I did not sleep a wink.

Like a fool I passed my whole life in review—and bitter memories maddened me quite. Then came a happy thought. I mapped out a story of the war. The plot came to hand, for it was true. Johnny is the hero—light dragoon and heavy swell. I will call it F.F.'s, for it is F.F.'s both of South Carolina and Virginia. It is to be a war story, and the filling out of the skeleton is the pleasantest way to put myself to sleep.

Old Hickory fought for Aunt Rachel of questionable fame. That is, she was married before her other husband died, or before her divorce was settled, or something wrong, but she did not know she was doing wrong. She is said to have been a good woman, but it is all a little confused to my straitlaced ideas. They say when someone asked if old Hickory was a Christian, the answer: "I don't know, but if he wants to go to heaven, the devil can't keep him out of it." And then he stood by Mrs. Eaton in good report and in evil. And now Richmond plays old Hickory with its beautiful Mrs. M.

I can forgive Andrew Jackson the headlong wedding business, but that duel! when he deliberately waited—and after the other man had missed, or failed in some way to shoot at him—slowly and coolly killed him. But the pious North swallowed Andrew Jackson because he put his sword in the balance where we nullifiers were concerned.

England declined Nelson's legacy of Lady Hamilton, but she accepts his glory and his fame as a typical naval hero. English to the core.

There are breaking hearts this beautiful New Year's Day.

Young Frasier, on his way back to Maryland to be married, was shot dead by a Yankee picket.

Read *Volpone* until J. C. emerged for his breakfast. He asked me to make out his list for his New Year's calls.

Mrs. Davis, Mrs. Preston, Mrs. Randolph, Mrs. Elzey, Mrs. Stanard, Mrs. MacFarland, Mrs. Wigfall, Mrs. Miles, Mrs. John Redman Coxe Lewis.

At the president's, J. C. saw L. Q. C. Lamar who, unconfirmed by the Senate, has had to come home from Russia. They must have refused to confirm his nomination simply to annoy and anger Jeff Davis. Everybody knows there is not a cleverer man on either side of the water than Mr. Lamar, or a truer patriot. J. C. said Lamar put his arms round him (he has a warm heart) and said, "*You* are glad to see me, eh?" Lamar is changed so much that at first J. C. did not recognize him. Colonels Browne and Ives there, in full fig, swords and sashes, gentlemen ushers. J. C. was in citizen's dress and stood behind Mrs. Davis all the time, out of the fray. So he enjoyed the fun immensely. No responsibility.

The *Examiner* indulges in a horse laugh. "Is that your idea? England come to the help of a slave power?" Turkey! Why not, O Daniel come to judgment? and India?

But slavery was the sore spot on this continent, and England touched up the Yankees *that they so hated* on the raw when they were shouting hurrah for liberty, hurrah for General Jackson, whom the British turned their backs on, but who did not turn his back on the exconquerors of Waterloo! English writers knew where to flick. They set the Yankees on us by incessant nagging, jeering at the inconsistency. Now the Yankees have the bit in their teeth. After a while they will ascend higher and higher in virtue, until maybe they will even attack Mormonism in its den.

"Little Vick is going to do the best she can for her country. The land of our forefathers is not squeamish but looks out for No. 1," said the irreverent Wigfall. And then he laid sacrilegious hands on the father of his country! He always speaks of him as an old granny, or the mother of his country, because he looked after the butter and cheese on Madam Martha's *Mount Vernon* farm.

"There is one thing that always makes my blood rise hot within me—this good slave-owner who *left* his negroes free when he no longer needed them. He rides his fine horse along the rows where the poor African hoes corn. He takes out his beautiful English hunting watch and times Cuffy. Cuffy, under his great master's eyes, works with a will. With his watch still in hand, Farmer George sees what a man can do in a given time. And by that measure he tasks the others—strong, weak, slow, swift, able-bodied, and unable. There is magnanimity for you! George the 1st of America—the founder of the great U.S. America."

"But Wigfall! You exaggerate. He was not a severe disciplinarian. He was the very kindest of men. Everyone knows that. But you only rave in this manner and say such stuff to be different from other people."

"I get every word of it from his own letters."

"He was no harder on Cuffy than English, French, German landlords are to their white tenants."

"Do you mean to say a poor man must not work for his living, but his rich neighbor must support him in idleness?" &c&c&c.

After he had gone: "You see, we did not expect Wigfall, who shoots white men with so little ceremony, to be so thoughtful, so tender of the poor and helpless—but it is so, it seems. He was in bitter earnest. Did you notice his eyes?" At this moment Dangerfield Lewis and Maria came—and in another second L. Q. Washington was at their heels. J. C. said,

"If walls could speak, what a tale these would have to tell you!"

"How? what?"

"Oh, Louis Wigfall's perversity. He says Lamar is as model a diplomat as Mr. Mason!" I hastily put in, "I really thought the *Washington Lewis* family ought not to hear—well! how aggravating Louis Wigfall can be—so I stopped you. For one thing, he is the very best husband I know and the kindest father."

Judith W. McGuire: Diary, January 1, 1864

Judith W. McGuire and her husband, John P. McGuire, the principal
of the Episcopal High School of Virginia, had fled their home in Alexandria in May 1861 when the town was occupied by Union troops.
In February 1862 the McGuires settled in Richmond, where she later
found work as a clerk in the Confederate commissary department. On
New Year's Day she wrote in her diary about Lieutenant Colonel
Raleigh T. Colston, the son of her sister, Sarah Jane Brockenbrough
Colston. The commander of the 2nd Virginia Infantry, Colston had
his left leg amputated below the knee after being shot at Payne's Farm
on November 27, 1863, during the Mine Run campaign.

January 1, 1864.—A melancholy pause in my diary. After
returning from church on the night of the 18th, a telegram was
handed me from Professor Minor, of the University of Virginia, saying, "Come at once, Colonel Colston is extremely
ill." After the first shock was over, I wrote an explanatory note
to Major Brewer, why I could not be at the office next day,
packed my trunk, and was in the cars by seven in the morning.
That evening I reached the University, and found dear R. desperately ill with pneumonia, which so often follows, as in the
case of General Jackson, the amputation of limbs. Surgeons
Davis and Cabell were in attendance, and R's uncle, Dr. Brockenbrough, arrived the next day. After ten days of watching and
nursing, amid alternate hopes and fears, we saw our friend Dr.
Maupin close our darling's eyes, on the morning of the 23d;
and on Christmas-day, a military escort laid him among many
brother soldiers in the Cemetery of the University of Virginia.
He died in the faith of Christ, and with the glorious hope of
immortality. His poor mother is heart-stricken, but she, together with his sisters, and one dearer still, had the blessed,
and what is now the rare privilege, of soothing and nursing
him in his last hours. To them, and to us all, his life seemed as
a part of our own. His superior judgment and affectionate

temper made him the guide of his whole family. To them his loss can never be supplied. His country has lost one of its earliest and best soldiers. Having been educated at the Virginia Military Institute, he raised and drilled a company in his native County of Berkeley, at the time of the John Brown raid. In 1861 he again led that company to Harper's Ferry. From that time he was never absent more than a week or ten days from his command, and even when wounded at Gaines's Mills, he absented himself but three days, and was again at his post during the several last days of those desperate fights. His fatal wound was received in his nineteeth general engagement, in none of which had he his superior in bravery and devotion to the cause. He was proud of belonging to the glorious Stonewall Brigade, and I have been told by those who knew the circumstances, that he was confided in and trusted by General Jackson to a remarkable degree.

Thus we bury, one by one, the dearest, the brightest, the best of our domestic circles. Now, in our excitement, while we are scattered, and many of us homeless, these separations are poignant, nay, overwhelming; but how can we estimate the sadness of heart which will pervade the South when the war is over, and we are again gathered together around our family hearths and altars, and find the circles broken? One and another gone. Sometimes the father and husband, the beloved head of the household, in whom was centred all that made life dear. Again the eldest son and brother of the widowed home, to whom all looked for guidance and direction; or, perhaps, that bright youth, on whom we had not ceased to look as still a child, whose fair, beardless cheek we had but now been in the habit of smoothing with our hands in fondness—one to whom mother and sisters would always give the good-night kiss, as his peculiar due, and repress the sigh that would arise at the thought that college or business days had almost come to take him from us. And then we will remember the mixed feeling of hope and pride when we first saw this household pet don his jacket of gray and shoulder his musket for the field; how we would be bright and cheerful before him, and turn to our chambers to weep oceans of tears when he is fairly gone. And does he, too, sleep his last sleep? Does our precious one fill a hero's grave? O God! help us, for the wail is in the whole land!

"Rachel weeping for her children, and will not be comforted, because they are not." In all the broad South there will be scarcely a fold without its missing lamb, a fireside without its vacant chair. And yet we must go on. It is our duty to rid our land of invaders; we must destroy the snake which is endeavouring to entwine us in its coils, though it drain our heart's blood. We know that we are right in the sight of God, and that we must

> "With patient mind our course of duty run.
> God nothing does, or suffers to be done,
> But we would do ourselves, if we could see
> The end of all events as well as He."

The Lord reigneth, be the earth never so unquiet.

Patrick R. Cleburne: Memorandum on Emancipation and Enlisting Black Soldiers

January 2, 1864

Born in Cork County, Ireland, Patrick R. Cleburne served as a private in the British army before immigrating to the United States in 1849. He settled in Helena, Arkansas, where he worked as a druggist before passing the bar. Elected colonel of the 1st Arkansas Infantry in 1861, Cleburne later led a brigade at Shiloh and Perryville and a division at Stones River, Chickamauga, and Chattanooga. He read this memorandum at a meeting of the corps and division commanders of the Army of Tennessee held on January 2, 1864, at the Dalton, Georgia, headquarters of Joseph E. Johnston, Bragg's replacement. It was co-signed by thirteen officers, all past or present brigade and regimental commanders in Cleburne's division. Although corps commanders William J. Hardee and Thomas Hindman, a prewar friend of Cleburne's, were sympathetic to his proposal, other generals condemned it in private letters to fellow officers. Alexander P. Stewart wrote that the memorandum was "at war with my social, moral, and political principles," while Patton Anderson described it as a "monstrous proposition" and "revolting to Southern sentiment, Southern pride, and Southern honor." A copy was sent to Jefferson Davis, who told Johnston that the "dissemination or even promulgation of such opinions" could only cause "discouragement, distraction, and dissension." Davis ordered the suppression of the memorandum and of all discussion about it. Cleburne would continue to lead his division until his death in battle at Franklin, Tennessee, on November 30, 1864. His memorandum was first published by the War Department as part of the *Official Records* series in 1898.

————————

COMMANDING GENERAL, THE CORPS, DIVISION, BRIGADE, AND REGIMENTAL COMMANDERS OF THE ARMY OF TENNESSEE:

GENERAL: Moved by the exigency in which our country is now placed, we take the liberty of laying before you, unofficially, our views on the present state of affairs. The subject is so

677

grave, and our views so new, we feel it a duty both to you and the cause that before going further we should submit them for your judgment and receive your suggestions in regard to them. We therefore respectfully ask you to give us an expression of your views in the premises. We have now been fighting for nearly three years, have spilled much of our best blood, and lost, consumed, or thrown to the flames an amount of property equal in value to the specie currency of the world. Through some lack in our system the fruits of our struggles and sacrifices have invariably slipped away from us and left us nothing but long lists of dead and mangled. Instead of standing defiantly on the borders of our territory or harassing those of the enemy, we are hemmed in to-day into less than two-thirds of it, and still the enemy menacingly confronts us at every point with superior forces. Our soldiers can see no end to this state of affairs except in our own exhaustion; hence, instead of rising to the occasion, they are sinking into a fatal apathy, growing weary of hardships and slaughters which promise no results. In this state of things it is easy to understand why there is a growing belief that some black catastrophe is not far ahead of us, and that unless some extraordinary change is soon made in our condition we must overtake it. The consequences of this condition are showing themselves more plainly every day; restlessness of morals spreading everywhere, manifesting itself in the army in a growing disregard for private rights; desertion spreading to a class of soldiers it never dared to tamper with before; military commissions sinking in the estimation of the soldier; our supplies failing; our firesides in ruins. If this state continues much longer we must be subjugated. Every man should endeavor to understand the meaning of subjugation before it is too late. We can give but a faint idea when we say it means the loss of all we now hold most sacred—slaves and all other personal property, lands, homesteads, liberty, justice, safety, pride, manhood. It means that the history of this heroic struggle will be written by the enemy; that our youth will be trained by Northern school teachers; will learn from Northern school books their version of the war; will be impressed by all the influences of history and education to regard our gallant dead as traitors, our maimed veterans as fit objects for derision. It means the crushing of Southern manhood, the hatred of our former slaves, who will, on a spy system, be our secret police. The conqueror's policy is to divide the conquered into factions and stir up animosity among them, and in training an army of negroes the North no doubt holds this thought in perspective. We can see three great causes operating to destroy us: First, the inferiority of our armies to those of the enemy in point of numbers; second, the poverty of our single source of supply in comparison with his several sources; third, the fact that slavery, from being one of our chief sources of strength at the commencement of the war, has now become, in a military point of view, one of our chief sources of weakness.

The enemy already opposes us at every point with superior numbers, and is endeavoring to make the preponderance irresistible. President Davis, in his recent message, says the enemy "has recently ordered a large conscription and made a subsequent call for volunteers, to be followed, if ineffectual, by a still further draft." In addition, the President of the United States announces that "he has already in training an army of 100,000 negroes as good as any troops," and every fresh raid he makes and new slice of territory he wrests from us will add to this force. Every soldier in our army already knows and feels our numerical inferiority to the enemy. Want of men in the field has prevented him from reaping the fruits of his victories, and has prevented him from having the furlough he expected after the last reorganization, and when he turns from the wasting armies in the field to look at the source of supply, he finds nothing in the prospect to encourage him. Our single source of supply is that portion of our white men fit for duty and not now in the ranks. The enemy has three sources of supply: First, his own motley population; secondly, our slaves; and thirdly, Europeans whose hearts are fired into a crusade against us by fictitious pictures of the atrocities of slavery, and who meet no hindrance from their Governments in such enterprise, because these Governments are equally antagonistic to the institution. In touching the third cause, the fact that slavery has become a military weakness, we may rouse prejudice and passion, but the time has come when it would be madness not to look at our danger from every point of view, and to probe it to the bottom. Apart from the assistance that home and foreign prejudice against slavery has given to the North, slavery is a source of great strength to the enemy in a purely military point of view, by supplying him with an army from our granaries; but it is our most vulnerable point, a continued embarrassment, and in some respects an insidious weakness. Wherever slavery is once seriously disturbed, whether by the actual presence or the approach of the enemy, or even by a cavalry raid, the whites can no longer with safety to their property openly sympathize with our cause. The fear of their slaves is continually haunting them, and from silence and apprehension many of these soon learn to wish the war stopped on any terms. The next stage is to take the oath to save property, and they become dead to us, if not open enemies. To prevent raids we are forced to scatter our forces, and are not free to move and strike like the enemy; his vulnerable points are carefully selected and fortified depots. Ours are found in every point where there is a slave to set free. All along the lines slavery is comparatively valueless to us for labor, but of great and increasing worth to the enemy for information. It is an omnipresent spy system, pointing out our valuable men to the enemy, revealing our positions, purposes, and resources, and yet acting so safely and secretly that there is no means to guard against it. Even in the heart of our country, where our hold upon this secret espionage is firmest, it waits but the opening fire of the enemy's battle line to wake it, like a torpid serpent, into venomous activity.

In view of the state of affairs what does our country propose to do? In the words of President Davis "no effort must be spared to add largely to our effective force as promptly as possible. The sources of supply are to be found in restoring to the army all who are improperly absent, putting an end to substitution, modifying the exemption law, restricting details, and placing in the ranks such of the able-bodied men now employed as wagoners, nurses, cooks, and other employés, as are doing service for which the negroes may be found competent." Most of the men improperly absent, together with many of the exempts and men having substitutes, are now without the Confederate lines and cannot be calculated on. If all the exempts capable of bearing arms were enrolled, it will give us the boys below eighteen, the men above forty-five, and those persons who are left at home to meet the wants of the country and the army, but this modification of the exemption law will remove from the fields and manufactories most of the skill that directed agricultural and mechanical labor, and, as stated by the President, "details will have to be made to meet the wants of the country," thus sending many of the men to be derived from this source back to their homes again. Independently of this, experience proves that striplings and men above conscript age break down and swell the sick lists more than they do the ranks. The portion now in our lines of the class who have substitutes is not on the whole a hopeful element, for the motives that created it must have been stronger than patriotism, and these motives added to what many of them will call breach of faith, will cause some to be not forthcoming, and others to be unwilling and discontented soldiers. The remaining sources mentioned by the President have been so closely pruned in the Army of Tennessee that they will be found not to yield largely. The supply from all these sources, together with what we now have in the field, will exhaust the white race, and though it should greatly exceed expectations and put us on an equality with the enemy, or even give us temporary advantages, still we have no reserve to meet unexpected disaster or to supply a protracted struggle. Like past years, 1864 will diminish our ranks by the casualties of war, and what source of repair is there left us? We therefore see in the recommendations of the President only a temporary expedient, which at the best will leave us twelve months hence in the same predicament we are in now. The President attempts to meet only one of the depressing causes mentioned; for the other two he has proposed no remedy. They remain to generate lack of confidence in our final success, and to keep us moving down hill as heretofore. Adequately to meet the causes which are now threatening ruin to our country, we propose, in addition to a modification of the President's plans, that we retain in service for the war all troops now in service, and that we immediately commence training a large reserve of the most courageous of our slaves, and further that we guarantee freedom within a reasonable time to every slave in the South who shall remain true to the Confederacy in this war. As between the loss of independence and the loss of slavery, we assume that every patriot will freely give up the latter—give up the negro slave rather than be a slave himself. If we are correct in this assumption it only remains to show how this great national sacrifice is, in all human probabilities, to change the current of success and sweep the invader from our country.

Our country has already some friends in England and France, and there are strong motives to induce these nations to recognize and assist us, but they cannot assist us without helping slavery, and to do this would be in conflict with their policy for the last quarter of a century. England has paid hundreds of millions to emancipate her West India slaves and break up the slave-trade. Could she now consistently spend her treasure to reinstate slavery in this country? But this barrier once removed, the sympathy and the interests of these and other nations will accord with our own, and we may expect from them both moral support and material aid. One thing is certain, as soon as the great sacrifice to independence is made and known in foreign countries there will be a complete change of front in our favor of the sympathies of the world. This measure will deprive the North of the moral and material aid which it now derives from the bitter prejudices with which foreigners view the institution, and its war, if continued, will henceforth be so despicable in their eyes that the source of recruiting will be dried up. It will leave the enemy's negro army no motive to fight for, and will exhaust the source from which it has been recruited. The idea that it is their special mission to war against slavery has held growing sway over the Northern people for many years, and has at length ripened into an armed and bloody crusade against it. This baleful superstition has so far supplied them with a courage and constancy not their own. It is the most powerful and honestly entertained plank in their war platform. Knock this away and what is left? A bloody ambition for more territory, a pretended veneration for the Union, which one of their own most distinguished orators (Doctor Beecher in his Liverpool speech) openly avowed was only used as a stimulus to stir up the anti-slavery crusade, and lastly the poisonous and selfish interests which are the fungus growth of the war itself. Mankind may fancy it a great duty to destroy slavery, but what interest can mankind have in upholding this remainder of the Northern war platform? Their interests and feelings will be diametrically opposed to it. The measure we propose will strike dead all John Brown fanaticism, and will compel the enemy to draw off altogether or in the eyes of the world to swallow the Declaration of Independence without the sauce and disguise of philanthropy. This delusion of fanaticism at an end, thousands of Northern people will have leisure to look at home and to see the gulf of despotism into which they themselves are rushing.

The measure will at one blow strip the enemy of foreign sympathy and assistance, and transfer them to the South; it will dry up two of his three sources of recruiting; it will take from his negro army the only motive it could have to fight against the South, and will probably cause much of it to desert over to us; it will deprive his cause of the powerful stimulus of fanaticism, and will enable him to see the rock on which his so-called friends are now piloting him. The immediate effect of the emancipation and enrollment of negroes on the military strength of the South would be: To enable us to have armies numerically superior to those of the North, and a reserve of any size we might think necessary; to enable us to take the offensive, move forward, and forage on the enemy. It would open to us in prospective another and almost untouched source of supply, and furnish us with the means of preventing temporary disaster, and carrying on a protracted struggle. It would instantly remove all the vulnerability, embarrassment, and inherent weakness which result from slavery. The approach of the enemy would no longer find every household surrounded by spies; the fear that sealed the master's lips and the avarice that has, in so many cases, tempted him practically to desert us would alike be removed. There would be no recruits awaiting the enemy with open arms, no complete history of every neighborhood with ready guides, no fear of insurrection in the rear, or anxieties for the fate of loved ones when our armies moved forward. The chronic irritation of hope deferred would be joyfully ended with the negro, and the sympathies of his whole race would be due to his native South. It would restore confidence in an early termination of the war with all its inspiring consequences, and even if contrary to all expectations the enemy should succeed in overrunning the South, instead of finding a cheap, ready-made means of holding it down, he would find a common hatred and thirst for vengeance, which would break into acts at every favorable opportunity, would prevent him from settling on our lands, and render the South a very unprofitable conquest. It would remove forever all selfish taint from our cause and place independence above every question of property. The very magnitude of the sacrifice itself, such as no nation has ever voluntarily made before, would appal our enemies, destroy his spirit and his finances, and fill our hearts with a pride and singleness of purpose which would clothe us with new strength in battle. Apart from all other aspects of the question, the necessity for more fighting men is upon us. We can only get a sufficiency by making the negro share the danger and hardships of the war. If we arm and train him and make him fight for the country in her hour of dire distress, every consideration of principle and policy demand that we should set him and his whole race who side with us free. It is a first principle with mankind that he who offers his life in defense of the State should receive from her in return his freedom and his happiness, and we believe in acknowledgment of this principle. The Constitution of the Southern States has reserved to their respective governments the power to free slaves for meritorious services to the State. It is politic besides. For many years, ever since the agitation of the subject of slavery commenced, the negro has been dreaming of freedom, and his vivid imagination has surrounded that condition with so many gratifications that it has become the paradise of his hopes. To attain it he will tempt dangers and difficulties not exceeded by the bravest soldier in the field. The hope of freedom is perhaps the only moral incentive that can be applied to him in his present condition. It would be preposterous then to expect him to fight against it with any degree of enthusiasm, therefore we must bind him to our cause by no doubtful bonds; we must leave no possible loop-hole for treachery to creep in. The slaves are dangerous now, but armed, trained, and collected in an army they would be a thousand fold more dangerous; therefore when we make soldiers of them we must make free men of them beyond all question, and thus enlist their sympathies also. We can do this more effectually than the North can now do, for we can give the negro not only his own freedom, but that of his wife and child, and can secure it to him in his old home. To do this, we must immediately make his marriage and parental relations sacred in the eyes of the law and forbid their sale. The past legislation of the South concedes that a large free middle class of negro blood, between the master and slave, must sooner or later destroy the institution. If, then, we touch the institution at all, we would do best to make the most of it, and by emancipating the whole race upon reasonable terms, and within such reasonable time as will prepare both races for the change, secure to ourselves all the advantages, and to our enemies all the disadvantages that can arise, both at home and abroad, from such a sacrifice. Satisfy the negro that if he faithfully adheres to our standard during the war he shall receive his freedom and that of his race. Give him as an earnest of our intentions such immediate immunities as will impress him with our sincerity and be in keeping with his new condition, enroll a portion of his class as soldiers of the Confederacy, and we change the race from a dreaded weakness to a position of strength.

Will the slaves fight? The helots of Sparta stood their masters good stead in battle. In the great sea fight of Lepanto where the Christians checked forever the spread of Mohammedanism over Europe, the galley slaves of portions of the fleet were promised freedom, and called on to fight at a critical moment of the battle. They fought well, and civilization owes much to those brave galley slaves. The negro slaves of Saint Domingo, fighting for freedom, defeated their white masters and the French troops sent against them. The negro slaves of Jamaica revolted, and under the name of Maroons held the mountains against their masters for 150 years; and the experience of this war has been so far that half-trained negroes have fought as bravely as many other half-trained Yankees. If, contrary to the training of a lifetime, they can be made to face and fight bravely against their former masters, how much more probable is it that with the allurement of a higher reward, and led by those masters, they would submit to discipline and face dangers.

We will briefly notice a few arguments against this course. It is said Republicanism cannot exist without the institution. Even were this true, we prefer any form of government of which the Southern people may have the molding, to one forced upon us by a conqueror. It is said the white man cannot perform agricultural labor in the South. The experience of this army during the heat of summer from Bowling Green, Ky., to Tupelo, Miss., is that the white man is healthier when doing reasonable work in the open field than at any other time. It is said an army of negroes cannot be spared from the fields. A sufficient number of slaves is now administering to luxury alone to supply the place of all we need, and we believe it would be better to take half the able-bodied men off a plantation than to take the one master mind that economically regulated its operations. Leave some of the skill at home and take some of the muscle to fight with. It is said slaves will not work after they are freed. We think necessity and a wise legislation will compel them to labor for a living. It is said it will cause terrible excitement and some disaffection from our cause. Excitement is far preferable to the apathy which now exists, and disaffection will not be among the fighting men. It is said slavery is all we are fighting for, and if we give it up we give up all. Even if this were true, which we deny, slavery is not all our enemies are fighting for. It is merely the pretense to establish sectional superiority and a more centralized form of government, and to deprive us of our rights and liberties. We have now briefly proposed a plan which we believe will save our country. It may be imperfect, but in all human probability it would give us our independence. No objection ought to outweigh it which is not weightier than independence. If it is worthy of being put in practice it ought to be mooted quickly before the people, and urged earnestly by every man who believes in its efficacy. Negroes will require much training; training will require time, and there is danger that this concession to common sense may come too late.

P. R. Cleburne, major-general, commanding division; D. C. Govan, brigadier-general; John E. Murray, colonel Fifth Arkansas; G. F. Baucum, colonel Eighth Arkansas; Peter Snyder, lieutenant-colonel, commanding Sixth and Seventh Arkansas; E. Warfield, lieutenant-colonel, Second Arkansas; M. P. Lowrey, brigadier-general; A. B. Hardcastle, colonel Thirty-second and Forty-fifth Mississippi; F. A. Ashford, major Sixteenth Alabama; John W. Colquitt, colonel First Arkansas; Rich. J. Person, major Third and Fifth Confederate; G. S. Deakins, major Thirty-fifth and Eighth Tennessee; J. H. Collett, captain, commanding Seventh Texas; J. H. Kelly, brigadier-general, commanding Cavalry Division.

William T. Sherman to Roswell M. Sawyer

In late December Sherman sent the four divisions he had brought to Chattanooga into winter quarters in southern Tennessee and northern Alabama. He then returned to Vicksburg and began planning a campaign to destroy the railroads in eastern Mississippi around Meridian. Sherman wrote to one of his staff officers in northern Alabama shortly before the start of the Meridian campaign.

Head Qrs. Dept. of the Tenn.
Vicksburg, Jan. 31-1864.

Major R. M. Sawyer
A. A. G. Army of the Tenn., Huntsville, Alabama
Dear Sawyer,

In my former letters I have answered all your questions save one, and that relates to the treatment of inhabitants known or suspected to be hostile or "Secesh." This is in truth the most difficult business of our Army as it advances & occupies the Southern Country. It is almost impossible to lay down Rules and I invariably leave this whole subject to the local commander, but am willing to give them the benefit of my acquired Knowledge and experience.

In Europe whence we derive our principles of war Wars are between Kings or Rulers through hired Armies and not between Peoples. These remain as it were neutral and sell their produce to whatever Army is in possession. Napoleon when at War with Prussia, Austria and Russia bought forage & provisions of the Inhabitants and consequently had an interest to protect the farms and factories which ministered to his wants. In like manner the Allied Armies in France could buy of the French Habitants, whatever they needed, the produce of the soil or manufactures of the Country. Therefore the General Rule was & is that War is confined to the Armies engaged, and should not visit the houses of families or private Interests. But in other examples a different Rule obtained the Sanction of

Historical Authority. I will only instance one when in the reign of William and Mary the English Army occupied Ireland then in a state of revolt. The inhabitants were actualy driven into foreign lands and were dispossessed of their property and a new population introduced. To this day a large part of the North of Ireland is held by the descendants of the Scotch emigrants sent there by Williams order & an Act of Parliament. The War which now prevails in our land is essentially a war of Races. The Southern People entered into a clear Compact of Government with us of the North, but still maintained through State organizations a species of seperate existence with seperate interests, history and prejudices. These latter became stronger and stronger till at last they have led to war, and have developed the fruits of the bitterest Kind. We of the North are beyond all question Right in our Cause but we are not bound to ignore the fact that the people of the South have prejudices which form a part of their nature, and which they cannot throw off without an effort of reason, or by the slower process of natural change. The question then arises Should we treat as absolute enemies all in the South who differ from us in opinion or prejudice, Kill or banish them, or should we give them time to think and gradually change their conduct, so as to conform to the new order of things which is slowly & gradually creeping into their country?

When men take up Arms to resist a Rightful Authority we are compelled to use like force, because all reason and argument cease when arms are resorted to. When the provisions, forage, horses, mules, wagons, &c. are used by our enemy it is clearly our duty & Right to take them also; because otherwise they might be used against us. In like manner all houses left vacant by an inimical people are clearly our Right, and such as are needed as Storehouses, Hospitals & Quarters. But the question arises as to dwellings used by women, children & non-combatants. So long as non-combatants remain in their houses & Keep to their accustomed peaceful business, their opinions and prejudices can in no wise influence the War & therefore should not be noticed; but if any one comes out into the public streets & creates disorder he or she should be punished, restrained or banished, Either to the rear or front as the officer in Command adjudges. If the People or any of them

Keep up a correspondence with parties in hostility they are spies & can be punished according to Law with death or minor punishment. These are well established principles of War & the People of the South having appealed to *War* are barred from appealing for protection to our Constitution which they have practically and publicly defied. They have appealed to War and must abide *its* Rules & Laws. The United States as a belligerent party, claiming Rights in the soil as the ultimate Sovereign, has a right to change the population—and it may be & is both politic and just we should do so in certain districts; When the Inhabitants persist too long in hostility, it may be both politic and right we should banish them and appropriate their lands to a more loyal and useful population. No man could deny but that the United States would be benefited by dispossessing a single prejudiced, hard headed and disloyal planter and substituting in his place a dozen or more patient industrious good families, even if they were of foreign birth. I think it does good to present this view of the case to many Southern Gentlemen, who grew Rich and wealthy, not by virtue *alone* of their personal industry and skill, but in great part by reason of the protection and impetus to prosperity given by our hitherto moderate & magnanimous Government. It is all idle nonsense for these Southern planters to say that they made the South, that they own it, and that they can do as they please, even to break up our Government & shut up the natural avenues of trade, intercourse and Commerce. We Know and they Know if they are inteligent beings, that as compared with the whole World, they are but as 5 millions to one thousand millions— that they did not create the land, that the only title to its use & usufruct is the deed of the U.S. and that if they appeal to War they hold their all by a very insecure tenure. For my part I believe that this War is the result of false Political Doctrine for which we are all as a people more or less responsible, and I would give all a chance to reflect & when in error to recant. I know that Slave owners, finding themselves in possession of a species of property in opposition to the growing sentiment of the whole Civilized World, conceived their property to be in danger and foolishly appealed to War, and that by skilled political handling they involved with themselves the whole South on this Result of error & prejudice. I believe that some of the

Rich & slave holding are prejudiced to an extent that nothing but death & ruin will ever extinguish, but I hope that as the poorer & industrial classes of the South realize their relative weakness, and their dependence upon the fruits of the earth & good will of their fellow men, they will not only discover the error of their ways & repent of their hasty action, but bless those who persistently have maintained a Constitutional Government strong enough to sustain itself, protect its citizens, and promise peaceful homes to millions yet unborn.

In this belief, whilst I assert for our Govt. the highest Military prerogatives, I am willing to bear in patience the political nonsense of Slave Rights, State Rights uncontrolled freedom of conscience, License of the press and such other trash which have deluded the Southern People and carried them into War, Anarchy, & blood shed, and the perpetration of some of the foulest Crimes that have disgraced any time or any people.

I would advise the Commanding officer at Huntsville and such other towns as are occupied by our troops to assemble the Inhabitants & explain to them these plain, selfevident propositions & tell them that it is for them *now* to say whether they and their children shall inherit the beautiful lands which by the accidents of nature have fallen to their share.

The Government of the United States has in North Alabama any and all the rights of Sovereignty which they choose to enforce in War, to take their lives, their homes, their lands, their every thing, because they cannot deny that War does exist by their acts, and War is simply Power unrestrained by Constitution or Compact. If they want Eternal War, well & good. We must accept the issue & will be forced to dispossess them and put our own people who at a simple notice, would come to North Alabama & accept the elegant houses & Plantations now there.

If the People of Huntsville think differently, let them persist in this War three years longer and then they will not be consulted.

Three years ago by a little reflection and patience they could have had a hundred years of Peace & Prosperity, but they *preferred* War. Last year they could have saved their Slaves but now it is too late, all the Powers of Earth cannot restore to them their slaves any more than their dead Grandfathers. Next year in all probability their lands will be taken, for in War we can take them & rightfully too, and in another year they may beg in vain for their lives, for sooner or later there must be an end to strife.

A People who will persevere in a War beyond a certain limit ought to Know the consequences. Many, Many People with less pertinacity than the South has already shown have been wiped out of national Existence.

My own belief, is that even now the non-slaveholding classes of the South are alienating from their associates in War. Already I hear Crimination & recrimination. Those who have property left should take warning in time.

Since I have come down here I have seen many Southern Planters, who now hire their own negroes & acknowledge that they were mistaken and knew not the earthquake they were to make by appealing to secession. They thought that the Politicians had prepared the way, and that they could part the states of this Union in Peace. They now see that we are bound together as one nation by indissoluble ties, and that any interest or any fraction of the people that set themselves up in antagonism to the Nation must perish.

Whilst I would not remit one jot or tittle of our Nations Rights in Peace or War, I do make allowances for past political errors and prejudices.

Our National Congress and the Supreme Court are the proper arenas on which to discuss conflicting opinions & not the Battle field.

You may not hear from me again for some time and if you think it will do any good, Call some of the better people of Huntsville together & explain to them my view. You may even read to them this letter & let them use it, so as to prepare them for my coming.

To those who submit to the Rightful Laws & authority of their State & National Government promise all gentleness and forbearance, but to the petulant and persistant secessionist, why death or banishment is a mercy, and the quicker he or she is disposed of the better. Satan & the rebellious saints of Heaven, were allowed a continuance of existence in Hell, merely to swell their just punishment.

To such as would rebel against a Government so mild and

just as ours was in Peace, a punishment equal would not be unjust.

We are progressing well in this quarter, but I have not changed my opinion that although we may soon make certain the existence of the Power of our National Government yet years must pass before ruffianism, murder & Robbery will cease to afflict this region of our country. Your friend,

W. T. Sherman
Maj. Genl. Comdg.

Lois Bryan Adams to the
Detroit Advertiser and Tribune

A journalist, schoolteacher, and poet who had edited the literary and household departments of the *Michigan Farmer* for several years, Lois Bryan Adams moved to Washington in the summer of 1863 and began working as a clerk for the recently established Department of Agriculture. Adams contributed regular letters to the *Detroit Advertiser and Tribune* while also serving as a volunteer for the Michigan Soldiers' Relief Association. She wrote about a White House reception and a fund-raising fair held at the Patent Office (where the Department of Agriculture was housed) in letters that appeared in the *Advertiser and Tribune* on February 16 and February 29, 1864.

———————

Life in Washington
A LADY'S FIRST DAY AT THE PRESIDENTS
Correspondence of the *Advertiser and Tribune*
Washington, February 8, 1864

Saturdays are public reception days at the White House. From 11 till 3 o'clock all who choose can go and pay their respects to the President and his lady, pass through the room and conservatories and go on their way.

One mile west of the Capitol, directly through the heart of the city, stands the Presidential mansion. It is Saturday, the 6th of February, a chilly, cloudy day, with a lowering sky threatening rain; but let us go. Standing at the Seventh street crossing we turn our face to the east, up Pennsylvania Avenue. Look a moment; does it seem possible that we can ever work our way through that thronging, crowding mass, pouring down the broad pavement in one incessant stream? You say no, and look toward the street cars passing each way every two or three minutes, but they are full, too—crowded to suffocation; the sidewalk will be better; there, at least, one may breathe more of Heaven's breath than of their neighbors.

We are on the fashionable, north side of the avenue; but glance across—the other side is nearly as crowded as this and all the broad space between is thronged with double lines of heavy army wagons drawn by four or six mules each, and seemingly endless in each direction; squads and companies of cavalry are passing, some one way and some another; state and private carriages, rattling hacks, omnibuses, street cars and every sort of vehicle imaginable seem mixed up in inextricable confusion; the noise is deafening and the ground trembles; but everybody is hurrying on; let us pass too, if pass we may.

Soldiers are here too, in companies and singly, in every style of uniform, and most uniformly gathered in knots and platoons about the hotel and restaurant doors. There, tearing along through the crowd, come 30 or 40 little negro boot-blacks, following the rattling music of a fifer and drummer who are beating up recruits for some low theater tonight; and here are elegantly dressed ladies and gentlemen, and young misses and children, with their jaunty hats and showy scarlet plumes—crowds of everybody, going and coming, and standing at corners gathered about the handsome show windows of the stores and shops. We press on, following close upon the train of those rustling silks that sweep across and dip into the filthy gutters at every crossing, and draw little waving lines of wet dust from every brimming runnel of slop-water running down from back yards and alleys. These silks are going to the President's.

Ah, now, the way is uphill, and growing tiresome. We are passing Willards, and rounding the corner of the Treasury, that immense marble caudle-cup, whose recesses we hope to explore some day, and explain to the public how that wonderful "pap" is made, on which so many Government pets get full. Now the silks have taken themselves into the cars. We go north past the Treasury, and its grounds, and then turn again to the west. All around this square on either side of the avenue the pavement is plastered with sticky mud some inches deep; but passing this we come in front of the President's grounds and find ourselves on broad, dry, granite flagstones clean and white. The avenue here runs east and west again, and the White

House is on the south side some little distance from it. Between the house and the street is a semi-circular park planted with evergreens and other trees, and having a bronze statue of Gen. Lafayette in the center. Around this little park sweeps the broad graveled carriage drive, bordered on the outer side by the wide granite footwalk and passing directly under the deep colored porch of the mansion. The park and drive are surrounded and protected by high iron palings. Iron gates lead into the drive and walk which are nearly always open.

Today guards armed with swords, mounted on handsome black horses, sit facing each other just within the gates at each end of the drive, and two more are stationed directly in front of the house. Between these guards the carriages freighted with their brocades and velvets and plumes make their entrance and exit. Foot guards are at all times pacing up and down the pavement before the house. Let us go up the steps and enter the open doors. Here is a mother plainly dressed, leading her little boy of ten to whom she is telling the story of Abraham Lincoln's youth. In the vestibule a waiter stands, motioning with his hand the way for visitors to go. The mother and child pass on; we follow. There is no crowd, nobody going in just now but us. Just inside the door of the blue room stands the President between two young men, and a plump, round-faced, smiling man stands opposite him. Between these two the mother leads her boy. The President takes her hand in one of his, places the other on the boy's brown curls, says some kindly words to both, and they pass on.

The same hand takes mine, the eyes look down as kindly; he bows low and says, "How do you do?" in a tone that seems to demand a friendly reply. But no reply comes. My heart is on my lips, but there is no shape or sound of words. In one glance at that worn yet kindly face I read a history that crushes all power of speech, and before I am fairly conscious that I have touched the hand and looked into the eyes of our honored Father Abraham, I find myself on the opposite side of the room. Doubtless if he had a thought about me it was, "What a stupid creature! who does not know enough to give a name or answer a civil question!"

Six months had I been in Washington without seeing the President. Six months of anxious waiting for friends whose long-promised "some day" never seemed to draw any nearer, till at last, tired of patience and friends together, I went alone. And that was the way I met him. I, who had honored him from the first moment he put his hand so firmly to the helm of our mighty ship of state, to steer her through the perilous sea of blood and strife; I, who could have knelt to touch the hand that first swept the curse from the nation's capitol, and then proclaimed freedom to all, in the name of God and humanity; I, the child of a State so loyal and true to her very heart's core that her veteran troops, almost to a man, have re-pledged themselves to stand by him till the fiery ordeal is past; I, who had sung for him, knowing he had not time to sing for himself, and had longed for the day to come when I might speak to him as well as for him—that was the way I did it!

It is late, for it has taken at least two hours' walking on the streets, to say nothing of numerous advances and retreats up and down the sweep of the semi-circle, to get resolution up to the point of accomplishing even this. There is but time to glance about us and then retire with the already departing crowd.

The blue room is a circular apartment, papered, draped, and furnished with the color from which it takes its name. In the center, under the massive chandelier, is a white marble table, supporting a vase of rare flowers, and beside it stands Mrs. Lincoln, now in animated conversation with the ladies and gentlemen gathered about her. We need not speak to her—she will never know we have been in the room—many others come in the same way, only to look and go. Another time we shall have confidence to pay her the respect due to her station.

It is a general remark that Mrs. Lincoln, at her receptions and parties, is always dressed with the most perfect taste—always richly and elegantly, and never over-dressed. Today she was robed in purple velvet; she wears a postilion basque, waist or body of the same, made high at the throat, and relieved by an elegant point lace collar, fastened by a knot of some dainty white material, in the center of which glistens a single diamond. The seams of the basque and skirt are corded in white, and the skirt, basque, and full open sleeves all richly trimmed with a heavy fringe of white chenille. The delicate head-dress is of purple and white to match the dress. It is all very becoming, and she is looking exceedingly well, receiving and dismissing her guests with much apparent ease and grace. Mrs. Lincoln is short in stature, plump, and round favored, with a very pleasant countenance.

But the President with his attendants has already left the room; the guests are fast departing; the conservatory doors are closed; we pass out with the rest, and pass a resolution to make better use of the next reception day at the White House.

L.

From Washington
Opening of the Great Fair at the Patent Office
From Our Own Correspondent
Washington, February 23, 1864

Washington celebrated the birthday of its great namesake in a very appropriate manner. The 22nd was the day set apart for the inauguration of the grand Fair got up by the ladies for the benefit of the Christian Commission and the families of the District volunteers. Although quite a little army of soldiers, clerks, and others, officered by the lady managers had been at work on the decorations of the hall, all was not yet quite complete when the hour for admitting the public arrived, but amid the blaze of splendor that everywhere met the eye, these little deficiencies were quite unnoticed.

The hall itself is the grandest place that could have been selected for such an exhibition. It is in the third story of the Patent Office building, on the partially finished and unoccupied north side, and is 300 feet in length by 75 feet wide, and high in proportion. The floor is of marble, and the walls, though yet unplastered, have been so wreathed and draped with evergreens and the national colors, that scarcely a blemish is visible. Down the center and along each side, stands, booths, bowers, and fairy-like arbors are ranged, all brilliant with the "red, white, and blue," draped, festooned, and bound and blended with the twining wreaths of evergreen. These booths and bowers all bear appropriate mottoes, and are all filled with the beautiful and tempting things that Fairs are made of, with pleasant-faced ladies adding still stronger temptations for visitors to invest in the great charity scheme. The hall is warmed by registers, and well lighted with gas, and presents by night a scene of bewildering beauty and dazzling splendor.

At the extreme west of the hall a handsome stage is built up, at the back of which is a large brazen shield, from which spears and lances radiate like sunbeams, bearing on their points small crimson pennons, while behind them flash the everywhere present stars and stripes. The front of this stage is handsomely draped and festooned, like everything else, with red, white and blue, and evergreens fashioned in various symbolic forms. On each side of the front is a splendid stand of arms, surmounted by armor and an ancient plumed helmet, and intertwined with evergreens.

It was expected that Edward Everett would have been here to deliver the opening address, but he did not come, and his place was very happily supplied by the Hon. L. E. Chittenden. The vast hall was crowded almost to suffocation long before the speaker was announced, and the passing time was somewhat enlivened by the martial music of the band present.

A little before eight, a general buzz and clapping of hands went through the crowd, and it was whispered that the President was coming up the hall. Very soon, accompanied by his son Robert, the Rev. Mr. Sunderland, Hon. B. B. French, and other gentlemen, he passed through to the rear of the stage, came upon it and quietly took his seat on a sofa in one corner, with his son beside him. Prayer was offered by Mr. Sunderland in a most fervent and patriotic spirit, after which Mr. Chittenden was introduced. His address was of considerable length, but so earnest, patriotic, and eloquent, that it was listened to throughout with rapt attention, the audience frequently showing their hearty approval by sincere and merited applause. After the address, the Hon. B. B. French, Commissioner of Public Buildings, read an original poem on the occasion of the present gathering and exhibition. It was also radically patriotic and anti-slavery in its tone, and was loudly applauded by the audience.

When Mr. French retired there was a universal clapping of hands for the President to come forward. It continued so long and so earnest that several gentlemen on the stage went to him to persuade him to gratify the general desire; but it was some moments before he would allow himself to be moved at all, and when he did rise and come forward, it was evidently with very great reluctance. He was looking extremely pale and worn, but smiled good-naturedly as he remarked that he thought the Committee who had invited him to be present had practiced a little fraud upon him, as no intimation had been given that he would be expected to say a word. He was unprepared for a speech, and felt that after the eloquent address and poem to which the audience had listened, any attempt of his would be a failure; besides, from the position he occupied everything that he said necessarily went into print, therefore, it was advisable that he should say nothing foolish. (Laughter and applause, and a voice, "Nothing foolish ever comes from our President.") It was very difficult to say sensible things. In speaking without preparation he might make some bad mistake, which, if published, would do both the nation and himself harm. Therefore, he would only say that he thanked the managers of the fair for the persevering manner in which they had prosecuted the enterprise for so good an object, and with this expression of his gratitude, he hoped they would accept his apology and excuse him from speaking.

He then retired to his seat amidst the hearty applause of the multitude. Soon after this the benediction was pronounced, and the President and his party withdrew. There was music by the band, and some singing on the stage afterward, and the hall was filled till midnight and after by the crowds who on this first day of opening came more to see than to buy.

One of the most attractive features among the decorations at this fair, is a miniature representation of Gen. U. S. Grant's headquarters at Chattanooga. Near the center of the hall a space some 14 feet square is inclosed, and within are built up two little mountains of rock work, mosses, and branches of evergreen. On the top of one mountain is a fort, with soldiers, cannon, and everything complete; on the other a lookout; a rustic bridge spans the gorge between them, and at the bottom of the gorge is a small body of water with a boat and ducks on its surface; and along its banks and scattered among the rocks are turtles, cattle, goats, and birds, as like as life. A winding gravel road runs from the fort to the lookout, and heavily laden wagons are ascending the heights of each mountain. On the low ground beneath the foot and protected by it, is a rustic building, with the name "U. S. Grant" over the door. Around the whole enclosure slender columns with evergreens springing up, from the tops of which light arches meet over the center, forming a sort of airy dome. Altogether it is very beautiful and draws crowds of admirers.

As a sort of side scene some enterprising ladies have got up a representation of a New England kitchen a hundred years ago. Here several hoopless dames may be seen in petticoat and short gown, with high-crowned cambric caps and other evidences of antiquity; one is spinning at the big wheel, another at the little one; one winding yarn from old-time swifts, one carding; young girls churning, knitting and paring apples; visitors coming in with their antique calash sunbonnets; the fortune-teller in her red cloak and hood, the circulating snuff-box, strings of dried apples along the wall, the wooden mortar and pestle and iron candlesticks on the chimney-piece, old-fashioned pitchers and pewter dishes on the dresser—all are there, and the identical old fire-place, that some of us may remember, with the pot hanging from the crane, and the fore-stick burned in two. It all seems very well done except the talking. When people here attempt Yankee talk, they slide down at once into the negro slang, which is quite another thing. However, the New England kitchen at the Washington fair promises to be a very attractive and remunerative feature.

L.

Francis J. Higginson to John A. Dahlgren

The U.S.S. *Housatonic*, a wooden steam sloop armed with eleven guns, had joined the South Atlantic Blockading Squadron off Charleston in September 1862. Over the next seventeen months she helped capture several blockade runners, fought a gun duel with two Confederate ironclad rams, and supported Union troops during the battle for Charleston Harbor. On February 17, 1864, the *Housatonic* was sunk by an underwater explosive charge. Her executive officer, Lieutenant Francis J. Higginson, reported the loss of his vessel, unaware that the *Housatonic* was the first ship ever to be sunk in combat by a submarine.

U. S. S. Canandaigua.
Off Charleston, S. C., February 18, 1864.

Sir: I have the honor to make the following report of the sinking of the U. S. S. *Housatonic*, by a rebel torpedo off Charleston, S. C., on the evening of the 17th instant:

About 8:45 P. M. the officer of the deck, Acting Master J. K. Crosby, discovered something in the water about 100 yards from and moving toward the ship. It had the appearance of a plank moving in the water. It came directly toward the ship, the time from when it was first seen till it was close alongside being about two minutes.

During this time the chain was slipped, engine backed, and all hands called to quarters.

The torpedo struck the ship forward of the mizzenmast, on the starboard side, in a line with the magazine. Having the after pivot gun pivoted to port we were unable to bring a gun to bear upon her.

About one minute after she was close alongside the explosion took place, the ship sinking stern first and heeling to port as she sank.

Most of the crew saved themselves by going into the rigging, while a boat was dispatched to the *Canandaigua*. This vessel came gallantly to our assistance and succeeded in rescuing all but the following-named officers and men, viz, Ensign E. C. Hazeltine, Captain's Clerk C. O. Muzzey, Quartermaster John Williams, Landsman Theodore Parker, Second-Class Fireman John Walsh.

The above officers and men are missing and are supposed to have been drowned.

Captain Pickering was seriously bruised by the explosion and is at present unable to make a report of the disaster.

Very respectfully, your obedient servant,

F. J. HIGGINSON,
Lieutenant.

Rear-Admiral JOHN A. DAHLGREN,
Commanding South Atlantic Blockading Squadron.

James H. Tomb:
Notes on the H. L. Hunley

In 1863 a group of engineers in Mobile designed and built a forty-foot-long submarine that was named for Horace L. Hunley, a Louisiana lawyer and merchant who helped finance the project. Driven by a hand-cranked propeller, the *H. L. Hunley* was equipped with diving planes, hand-pumped ballast tanks, and a primitive snorkel device, and could remain underwater for two hours. Sent to Charleston by rail, the submarine sank during a test on August 29, drowning five of its crew. After being raised from the harbor, she sank again on October 15, killing Hunley and seven other men. The second sinking was witnessed by James H. Tomb, an engineer who served on the *David*, a small steam-driven boat with a low silhouette designed for making night attacks on Union warships. Like the *David*, the *Hunley* was armed with a spar torpedo intended to be rammed into an enemy hull and then detonated from a distance. On February 17, 1864, the *Hunley* disappeared shortly after she sank the *Housatonic*. In 1995 the submarine was located four miles off the coast and one hundred yards from the wreck of her target. The *Hunley* was raised in 2000, and in 2004 the remains of Lieutenant George E. Dixon and his seven crew members were buried in Charleston.

CHARLESTON, S. C., *January, 1865*

There was a submarine torpedo boat, not under the orders of the Navy, and I was ordered to tow her down the harbor three or four times by Flag-Officer Tucker, who also gave me orders to report as to her efficiency as well as safety. In my report to him I stated, "The only way to use a torpedo was on the same plan as the 'David'—that is, a spar torpedo—and to strike with his boat on the surface, the torpedo being lowered to 8 feet. Should she attempt to use a torpedo as Lieutenant Dixon intended, by submerging the boat and striking from below, the level of the torpedo would be above his own boat, and as she had little buoyancy and no power, the chances were the suction caused by the water passing into the sinking ship would prevent her rising to the surface, besides the possibility of his own boat being disabled." Lieutenant Dixon was a very brave and cool-headed man, and had every confidence in his boat, but had great trouble when under the water from lack of air and light. At the time she made the attempt to dive under the receiving ship in Charleston Harbor, Lieutenant Dixon, James A. Eason, and myself stood on the wharf as she passed out and saw her dive, but she did not rise again, and after a week's effort she was brought to the surface and the crew of 7 men were found in a bunch near the manhole. Lieutenant Dixon said they had failed to close the after valve.

The last night the "David" towed him down the harbor his torpedo got foul of us and came near blowing up both boats before we got it clear of the bottom, where it had drifted. I let him go after passing Fort Sumter, and on my making report of this, Flag-Officer Tucker refused to have the "David" tow him again. The power for driving this boat came from 7 or 8 men turning cranks attached to the propeller shaft, and when working at their best would make about 3 knots. She was very slow in turning, but would sink at a moment's notice and at times without it. The understanding was that from the time of her construction at Mobile up to the time when she struck *Housa-tonic* not less than 33 men had lost their lives in her. She was a veritable coffin to this brave officer and his men.

J. H. TOMB.

Judith W. McGuire:
Diary, February 28, 1864

McGuire had noted in her diary on December 12, 1863, that the price of bacon was $2.50 a pound, and then wrote: "How are the poor to live? Though it is said that the *poor genteel* are the real sufferers. Money is laid aside for paupers by every one who can possibly do it, but persons who do not let their wants be known are the really poor." On February 15, 1864, she recorded that bacon was now selling for $8 a pound.

———————

28*th.*—Our hearts ache for the poor. A few days ago, as E. was walking out, she met a wretchedly dressed woman, of miserable appearance, who said she was seeking the Young Men's Christian Association, where she hoped to get assistance and work to do. E. carried her to the door, but it was closed, and the poor woman's wants were pressing. She then brought her home, supplied her with food, and told her to return to see me the following afternoon. She came, and with an honest countenance and manner told me her history. Her name is Brown; her husband had been a workman in Fredericksburg; he joined the army, and was killed at the second battle of Manassas. Many of her acquaintances in Fredericksburg fled last winter during the bombardment; she became alarmed, and with her three little children fled too. She had tried to get work in Richmond; sometimes she succeeded, but could not supply her wants. A kind woman had lent her a room and a part of a garden, but it was outside of the corporation; and although it saved house-rent, it debarred her from the relief of the associations formed for supplying the city poor with meal, wood, etc. She had evidently been in a situation little short of starvation. I asked her if she could get bread enough for her children by her work? She said she could sometimes, and when she could not, she "got turnip-tops from her piece of a garden, which were now putting up smartly, and she boiled them, with a little salt, and fed them on that." "But do they satisfy your hunger," said I? "Well, it is something to go upon for awhile, but it does not stick by us like as bread does, and then we gets hungry again, and I am afraid to let the children eat them too often, lest they should get sick; so I tries to get them to go to sleep; and sometimes the woman in the next room will bring the children her leavings, but she is monstrous poor." When I gave her meat for her children, taken from the bounty of our Essex friends, tears of gratitude ran down her cheeks; she said they "had not seen meat for so long." Poor thing, I promised her that her case should be known, and that she should not suffer so again. A soldier's widow shall not suffer from hunger in Richmond. It must not be, and will not be when her case is known. Others are now interested for her. This evening Mrs. R. and myself went in pursuit of her; but though we went through all the streets and lanes of "Butcher Flat" and other vicinities, we could get no clue to her. We went into many small and squalid-looking houses, yet we saw no such abject poverty as Mrs. Brown's. All who needed it were supplied with meal by the corporation, and many were supporting themselves with Government work. One woman stood at a table cutting out work; we asked her the stereotyped question—"Is there a very poor widow named Brown in this direction?" "No, ladies; I knows two Mrs. Browns, but they ain't so poor, and ain't no widows nuther." As neither of them was our Mrs. B., we turned away; but she suddenly exclaimed, "Ladies, will one of you read my husband's last letter to me? for you see I can't read writing." As Mrs. R. took it, she remarked that it was four weeks old, and asked if no one had read it to her? "Oh yes, a gentleman has read it to me four or five times; but you see I loves to hear it, for may-be I shan't hear from him no more." The tears now poured down her cheeks. "He always writes to me every chance, and it has been so long since he wrote that, and they tell me that they have been fighting, and may-be something has happened to him." We assured her that there had been no fighting—not even a skirmish. This quieted her, and Mrs. R. read the badly written but affectionate letter, in which he expresses his anxiety to see her and his children, and his inability to get a furlough. She then turned to the mantel-piece, and with evident pride took from a nail an old felt hat, through the crown of which were two bullet-holes. It was her husband's hat, through which a bullet had passed in the battle of Chancellorsville, and, as she remarked, must have come "very nigh grazing his head." We remarked upon its being a proof of his bravery, which gratified her very much; she then hung it up carefully, saying that it was just opposite her bed, and she never let it be out of her sight. She said she wanted her husband to fight for his country, and not "to stand back, like some women's husbands, to be drafted; she would have been ashamed of that, but she felt uneasy, because something told her that he would never get back." Poor woman! we felt very much interested in her, and tried to comfort her.

John Paris: Sermon Preached at Kinston

February 28, 1864

On February 1, 1864, Confederate forces began an unsuccessful attempt to retake New Bern, North Carolina, held by the Union since March 1862. Before withdrawing on February 3, Brigadier General Robert F. Hoke's North Carolina brigade overran several Union outposts and captured more than 300 prisoners. Among them were fifty-three soldiers from the 2nd North Carolina Union Volunteers, one of two white Union regiments recruited in the coastal areas of the state. When Major General George E. Pickett, the commander of the Department of North Carolina, learned that some of the prisoners had deserted from the Confederate army before enlisting in the Union forces, he ordered their court-martial. Between February 5 and February 22, twenty-two men from the 2nd North Carolina Union Volunteers were convicted of desertion and treason and hanged in Kinston, thirty miles northwest of New Bern. The executions were witnessed by Hoke's brigade and, in many cases, by the families of the men who were hanged (most of the condemned were from nearby counties). At least twenty-one of the remaining unionist prisoners would later die from disease in Confederate prison camps. John Paris, a Methodist clergyman who had served as chaplain of the 54th North Carolina Infantry since July 1862, preached a sermon on the executions before Hoke's brigade on February 28 and later published it as a pamphlet.

NOTE

On the morning of the first of February, Brig. Gen. R. F. Hoke forced the passage of Batchelor's Creek, nine miles west from Newbern; the enemy abandoned his works and retreated upon the town. A hot and vigorous pursuit was made, which resulted in the capture of a large number of prisoners, and the surrender to our forces of many others, who were cut off from escape by the celerity of the pursuit, and our troops seizing and holding every avenue leading into the town, near the enemy's batteries.

Among the prisoners taken, were about fifty native North Carolinians, dressed out in Yankee uniform, with muskets upon their shoulders. Twenty-two of these men were recognized as men who had deserted from our ranks, and gone over to the enemy. Fifteen of them belonged to Nethercutt's Battalion. They were arraigned before a court martial, proved guilty of the charges, and condemned to suffer death by hanging.

It became my duty to visit these men in prison before their execution, in a religious capacity. From them I learned that bad and mischievous influences had been used with every one to induce him to desert his flag, and such influences had led to their ruin. From citizens who had known them for many years, I learned that some of them had heretofore borne good names, as honest, harmless, unoffending citizens. After their execution I thought it proper, for the benefit of the living, that I should deliver a discourse before our brigade, upon the death of these men, that the eyes of the living might be opened, to view the horrid and ruinous crime and sin of desertion, which had become so prevalent. A gentleman from Forsyth county, who was present at the delivery of the discourse, solicited a copy for publication, which has been granted.

For the style and arrangement, as it was preached as well as written in the camp, no apology is offered. Having no pecuniary interest in its publication, it is respectfully submitted to all who go for the unqualified independence of the Southern Confederacy.

J. PARIS,

Hoke's Brigade, April 1st, 1864.

SERMON

MATTHEW XXVII CHAPTER 3, 4, AND 5TH VERSES.

3. Then Judas which had betrayed him, when he saw that he was condemned, repented himself, and brought again the thirty pieces of silver to the chief priests and elders,

4. Saying, I have sinned in that I have betrayed the innocent blood. And they said, what is that to us? See thou to that.

5. And he cast down the pieces of silver in the temple, and departed, and went and hanged himself.

You are aware, my friends, that I have given public notice that upon this occasion I would preach a funeral discourse upon the death of the twenty-two unfortunate, yet wicked and deluded men, whom you have witnessed hanged upon the gallows within a few days. I do so, not to eulogize or benefit the dead. But I do so, solely, for the benefit of the living: and in doing so, I shall preach in my own way, and according to my own manner, or rule. What I shall say will either be true or false. I therefore request that you will watch me closely; weigh my arguments in the balance of truth; measure them by the light of candid reason, and compare them by the Standard of Eternal Truth, the Book of God; what is wrong, reject, and what is true, accept, for the sake of the truth, as responsible beings.

Of all deserters and traitors, Judas Iscariot, who figures in our text, is undoubtedly the most infamous, whose names have found a place in history, either sacred or profane. No name has ever been more execrated by mankind: and all this has been justly done. But there was a time and a period when this man wore a different character, and had a better name. A time when he went forth with the eleven Apostles at the command of the Master to preach the gospel, heal the sick and cast out devils. And he, too, returned with this same chosen band, when the grand, and general report was made of what they had done and what they had taught.

But a change came over this man. He was the treasurer of the Apostolic board; an office that warranted the confidence and trust of his compeers. "He bare the bag and kept what was put therein." Possibly this was the grand and successful temptation presented him by the evil One. He contracted an undue love for money, and Holy Writ informs us "the love of money is the root of all evil;" so must it ever be when valued above a good name, truth or honor. Now comes his base and unprincipled desertion of his blessed Master. He goes to the chief priests. His object is selfish, base and sordid,—to get money.

He enters into a contract with them, to lead their armed guards to the place to which the Saviour had retired, that they might arrest him. Thirty pieces of silver is the price agreed upon,— about twenty-two dollars and fifty cents of our money. A poor price, indeed, for any man to accept for his reputation, his life, his soul, his all. When Judas saw that the Saviour was condemned, it is stated in the text that "he repented himself, and brought again the thirty pieces of silver to the chief priests and elders, saying, I have sinned in that I have betrayed the innocent blood." "And he cast down the thirty pieces of silver in the temple, and departed and went and hanged himself." The way of transgressors is truly hard. As sure as there is a God in heaven, justice and judgment will overtake the wicked; though he may flourish as a green bay tree for awhile, yet the eye of God is upon him and retribution must and will overtake him.

Let us now consider what this man gained by his wicked transaction. First, twenty-two dollars and fifty cents. Secondly, a remorse of conscience too intolerable to be borne. An immortality of infamy without a parallel in the family of man. What did he lose? His reputation. His money. His apostleship. His peace of conscience, his life, his soul, his all.

Well may it be said that this man is the most execrable of all whose names stand on the black list of deserters and traitors that the world has furnished from the beginning until now.— Turning to the history of our own country, I find written high on the scroll of infamy the name of Benedict Arnold, who at one time stood high in the confidence of the great and good Washington. What was his crime? Desertion and treason. He too hoped to better his condition by selling his principles for money, to the enemies of his country, betraying his Washington into the hands of his foes, and committing the heaven-insulting crime of perjury before God and man. Verily, he obtained his reward; an immortality of infamy; the scorn and contempt of the good and the loyal of all ages and all countries.

Thus, gentlemen, I have brought before you two grand prototypes of desertion, whose names tower high over all on the scroll of infamy. And I now lay down the Proposition, that every man who has taken up arms in defence of his country, and basely deserts or abandons that service, belongs in principle and practice to the family of Judas and Arnold. But what was the status of those twenty-two deserters whose sad end and just fate you witnessed across the river in the old field? Like you they came as volunteers to fight for the independence of their own country. Like you they received the bounty money offered by their country. Like you they took upon themselves the most solemn obligations of this oath: "I, A. B. do solemnly swear that I will bear true allegiance to the Confederate States of America, and that I will serve them honestly and faithfully against all their enemies or opposers whatsoever, and observe and obey the orders of the Confederate States, and the orders of the officers appointed over me, according to the rules and articles for the government of the Confederate States, so help me God."

With all the responsibilities of this solemn oath upon their souls, and all the ties that bind men to the land that gave them birth, ignoring every principle that pertains to the patriot, disowning that natural as well as lawful allegiance that every man owes to the government of the State which throws around him the ægis of its protection, they went, boldly, Judas and Arnold-like, made an agreement with the enemies of their country, took an oath of fidelity and allegiance to them, and agreed with them for money to take up arms and assist in the unholy and hellish work of the subjugation of the country which was their own, their native land! These men have only met the punishment meted out by all civilized nations for such crimes. To this, all good men, all true men, and all loyal men who love their country, will say, Amen!

But who were those twenty-two men whom you hanged upon the gallows? They were your fellow-beings. They were citizens of our own Carolina. They once marched under the same beautiful flag that waves over our heads; but in an evil hour, they yielded to mischievous influence, and from motives or feelings base and sordid, unmanly and vile, resolved to abandon every principle of patriotism, and sacrifice every impulse of honor; this sealed their ruin and enstamped their lasting disgrace. The question now arises, what are the influences and the circumstances that lead men into the high and damning crimes, of perjury and treason? It will be hard to frame an answer that will fit every case. But as I speak for the benefit of those whom I stand before to-day, I will say I have made the answer to this question a matter of serious inquiry for more than eighteen months. The duties of my office as Chaplain have brought me much in contact with this class of men. I have visited twenty-four of them under sentence of death in their cells of confinement, and with death staring them in the face, and only a few short hours between them and the bar of God. I have warned them to tell the whole truth, confess everything wrong before God and man, and yet I have not been able to obtain the full, fair and frank confession of everything relating to their guilt from even one of them, that I thought circumstances demanded, although I had baptized ten of them in the Name of the Holy Trinity. In confessing their crimes, they would begin at Newbern, where they joined the enemy, saying nothing about perjury and desertion. Every man of the twenty-two, whose execution you witnessed, confessed that bad or mischievous influences had been used with him to influence him to desert. All but two, willingly gave me the names of their seducers. But none of these deluded and ruined men seemed to think he ought to suffer the penalty of death, because he had been persuaded to commit those high crimes by other men.

But gentlemen, I now come to give you my answer to the question just asked. From all that I have learned in the prison, in the guard house, in the camp, and in the country, *I am fully satisfied, that the great amount of desertions from our army are produced by, and are the fruit of a bad, mischievous, restless, and dissatisfied, not to say disloyal influence that is at work in the country at home.* If in this bloody war our country should be overrun, this same mischievous home influence will no doubt be the prime agent in producing such a calamity. Discontentment has, and does exist in various parts of the State. We hear of these malcontents holding public meetings, not for the purpose of supporting the Government in the prosecution of the war, and maintenance of our independence, but for the purpose of finding fault with the Government. Some of these meetings have been dignified with the name of "peace meetings;" some have been ostensibly called for other purposes, but they have invariably been composed of men who talk more about their "rights," than about their duty and loyalty to their country. These malcontents profess to be greatly afflicted in mind about the state of public affairs. In their doleful croakings they are apt to give vent to their melancholy lamentations in such words as these: "The country is ruined!" "We are whipt!" "We might as well give up." "It is useless to attempt to fight any longer!" "This is the rich man's war and the poor man's fight;" &c. Some newspapers have caught the mania and lent their influence to this work of mischief; whilst the pulpit, to the scandal of its character for faith and holiness, has belched forth in some places doctrines and counsels through the ministrations of unworthy occupants, sufficient to cause Christianity to blush under all the circumstances. I would here remark, standing in the relation which I do before you, that the pulpit and the press, when true and loyal to the Government which affords them protection, are mighty engines for good but when they see that Government engaged in a bloody struggle for existence, and show themselves opposed to its efforts to maintain its authority by all constitutional and legal means, such a press, and such pulpits should receive no support for an hour from a people that would be free. The seal of condemnation should consign them to oblivion.

Such sentiments as we have just alluded to, are sent in letters to our young men in the army, by writers professing to be friends; often with an urgent and pressing invitation to come home; and some have even added that execrable and detestable falsehood, the quintescence of treason, "the State is going to secede." Letters coming into our camps on the Rappahannock and Rapidan sustain this position. What are the effects produced upon our young men in the ranks? With the illiterate, they are baleful indeed. The incautious youth takes it for granted that the country is ruined and that the Government is his enemy. The poisonous contagion of treason from home gets hold in his mind and steals into his feelings. This appeal from home has overcome him. The young man of promise and of hope once, now becomes a deserter. Is guilty by one false step of the awful crimes of perjury and desertion. The solemn obligations of his oath are disregarded; he takes to the woods, traverses weary roads by night for days, until he reaches the community in which he claims his home; but for what? To engage in any of the honorable vocations of life? No, gentlemen. But to lie hidden from the face of all good, true and loyal men. But for what purpose? To keep from serving his country as a man and a citizen. To consume the provisions kept in the country for the support of the women and children, families of soldiers who are serving their country, indeed; and lastly, to get his living in part, at least, by stealing and robbing. And here allow me to say, I am not sufficiently skilled in language to command words to express the deep and unutterable detestation I have of the character of a deserter. If my brother were to be guilty of such a high crime, I should certainly make an effort to have his name changed to something else, that I, and my children after me, might not feel the deep and lasting disgrace which his conduct had enstamped upon it.

I hold, gentlemen, that there are few crimes in the sight of either God or man, that are more wicked and detestable than desertion. The first step in it is perjury. Who would ever believe such an one in a court of justice again? The second, is treason. He has abandoned the flag of his country; thus much he has aided the common enemy. Those are startling crimes, indeed, but the third is equally so. He enstamps disgrace upon the name of his family and children.

From amidst the smoke and flames of Sinai God has declared that He "is a jealous God, visiting the iniquities of the fathers upon the children unto the third and fourth generations of them that hate me." The infamy that the act of disloyalty on the part of a father places his children in after him, is a disability they cannot escape: it was his act, not theirs; and to them it has become God's visitation according to the text quoted above. The character of infamy acquired by the tories of the revolution of 1776, is to this day imputed to their descendants, in a genealogical sense. Disloyalty is a crime that mankind never forget and but seldom forgive; the grave cannot cover it.

Many cry out in this the day of our discontent, and say, "we want peace." This is true, we all want peace, the land mourns on account of the absence of peace, and we all pray for peace. You have often heard me pray for peace, but I think you will bear me witness to-day that you have never heard me pray for peace without independence. God forbid that we should have a peace that brought no independence.

But how are we to obtain peace? There are but two modes

known by which to obtain this most desirable boon. First: to lay down our arms, cease to fight, and submit to the terms of our enemy, the tyrant at Washington. Fortunately for us, we already know what those terms are. They stand recorded in his law books, and in his published orders and edicts,—and constitute with our enemies, *the law of the land*, so far as we are concerned.

1. The lands of our citizens are to be sold for the purpose of paying the enormous public debt of the Yankees. This part of the programme has already been put into operation at points held by the enemy, as in Fairfax county, Va., and Beaufort, S. C. In the latter place, the lands have been laid off into thirty acre lots, and bought mostly by negroes.

2. The negroes, everywhere, to be declared free, and placed upon a state of equality with the whites.

3. Every man who has taken any part in the war, denied the right of voting at the polls.

4. Our Governors and Judges appointed by the Federal Government at Washington, and sent to rule over us at his pleasure.

5. Even the men selected to administer to us in holy things at the altars of our God, must be men approved and appointed by his military authorities; as it is now done in Norfolk and Portsmouth, where I am acquainted.

In addition to this, Gentlemen, we of course will have to endure the deep and untold mortification of having bands of negro soldiers stationed in almost every neighborhood, to enforce these laws and regulations.

These things would be some of the "*blessings*," we would obtain by such a peace. Tell me to-day, sons of Carolina, would not such a peace bring ten-fold more horrors and distress to our country than this war has yet produced? Can any people on the face of this earth, fit to be freemen, ever accept a peace that will place them in such a condition? Never! never! never!

The great and good Stonewall Jackson, a few weeks before his death was talking with a friend about the probable issue of the war; the conversation turned upon the possibility of the Confederate States being brought again under the rule and authority of the United States; when our illustrious chief remarked, that if he could have his choice in view of such a contingency, he would prefer the grave as his refuge. What patriot would not? What soldier would not? What freeman would not? This was the noble sentiment of a man whom we all believed to be fit to live, or fit to die.

The other mode by which to obtain peace, is to fight it out to the bitter end, as our forefathers did in the revolution of 1776, and reduce our enemies, by our manly defence, to the necessity of acknowledging our independence, and "letting us alone." We are involved in this bloody war, and the question before us is, not how did we get into it, but how shall we get out of it?

Many tell us the war cloud looks dark and impenetrable to mortal vision. This is all true. But are we not men? Have we not buckled on the armor, putting our trust in the Lord of hosts, as the arbiter of our destiny as a nation? Shall we then lay down our arms before we are overthrown? God forbid! Sons of Carolina, let your battle-cry be, Onward! Onward! until victory shall crown the beautiful banner that floats over us to-day with such a peace as freemen only love, and brave men only can accept. We are engaged in a mighty work, the establishment of an empire, which we trust by the blessing of God will become the freest, the best and the greatest on the face of the earth. Every man must act his part in this great work. Let us then look to the manner in which we perform the part which duty assigns, that there may be no regrets or heart-burnings hereafter. For just as sure as this cruel war began, it will have an end, and that end is nearer now than when it began. And when the sweet and lovely days of delightful peace return to cheer us, and friend meets with friend, and talk over the trials, the perils and sufferings we have endured in freedom's cause; with what emotions of pleasure shall we speak of the soldier ever true and faithful who stood by us, faithful alike both in the sunshine and storm of war. But what will then be said of the miserable skulker? May God give him a better heart that he may become a better man and a better soldier.

From the position which I occupy, I have been enabled to notice deserters and skulkers closely, and I have made it my business to inquire into their history, and I am happy to say for the credit of Christianity, that among the multitude I have known guilty of desertion, only three of that number professed to be members of any Church, and they had been no credit to the religion they professed, as it lived only upon their lips and was a stranger in their hearts.

The true christian is always a true patriot. Patriotism and Christianity walk hand in hand. When perils and dangers gather around the country that protects him, he then belongs to no party but his country's party; his loyalty must stand unquestioned and unquestionable. As one that fears God, he knows that, *if a man is not for his country, he is against it.* Hence, there is no neutral ground or position for him to occupy; but to stand by his country as its fast, unwavering friend, that its triumph may be his triumph, and its destiny his destiny. There is no toryism in a Christian's heart. The two principles cannot dwell together.

War is the scourge of nations. God is no doubt chastising us for our good. When the ends of His providence are accomplished, He will no doubt remove the rod. But the ways of His providence are generally dark to mortal vision. Yet he is able to bring light out of darkness. We are only drinking now from a cup, from which every nation upon the face of the earth have drank before us. We have walked the bloody road of revolution for three years; and still we face the foe. Our fathers trod it for seven, and in the end were successful.

The pious Dr. Watts tells us in one of his beautiful hymns, that,

> "God moves in a mysterious way,
> His wonders to perform;
> He plants his footsteps in the sea,
> And rides upon the storm."

His ways with the nations of the earth are deeply mysterious to mortal vision and whilst they are the exhibitions of His majesty and power, we should regard them likewise as the evidence of his goodness and mercy towards fallen man. As He deals with individuals, so does He deal with nations. He lifteth up one and putteth down another; but all this is done for the good of the whole. Righteousness exalteth a nation, but sin is a reproach to any people, is the doctrine laid down in Holy Writ. Proud Egypt, the cradle of the arts and sciences, has sadly fallen from her ancient glory and splendor. Ezekiel, speaking as the oracle of God, and accusing her of her sins, declared "she shall become the basest of the kingdoms," and the words of the Seer have become verified to the letter. For transgression, the chosen people of God, the Israelites, were compelled to wander forty years in the Arabian desert, thus suffering the chastisement of the disfavor of offended Deity. And when they were permitted to cross over Jordan into the land of promise, they were required to do a strange and wondrous work; namely, to destroy the nations of this goodly land and possess it for their own inheritance. The sins of these nations had cried unto heaven, and Israel became the instrument in the hand of God by which the judgments of offended Justice was meted out to the guilty nations. Jerusalem, the lovely, queenly Jerusalem, whose beautiful temple was the glory of the whole earth, in which the presence of the Eternal Shekinah was visible annually to mortal eye, and where Solomon in all his glory once reigned—sinned with an high hand against God; she knew not the day of her visitation, the cup of her iniquity was full; the judgment of offended heaven overtook her; her glory departed; the besom of destruction swept over her, and she is now trodden down by the gentiles—a crumbling monument of her departed greatness.

Babylon, once the proud mistress of the East, whose spacious walls, hanging gardens, and lofty temples stood as the wonders of the world, and Daniel, the prophet, robed in the vestments of royal honors, once spake, and wrote by heaven's prompting of things to come has fallen; her greatness is lost; her walls have perished; her palaces have crumbled; her temples are entombed, and the wandering Arab now nightly pitches his tent over the spot where Belshazzar held his impious feast. Where is the Nineveh? The mighty Nineveh? And Tadmor, and Persepolis, and hundred-gated Thebes? They belong only to the past, the silence of death has spread its sepulchral pall over them, and the relics of fallen greatness alone remain to mark the spot where they lie entombed. Sparta has departed from the map of nations, and Athens is but the tomb of the Athens that was. These have all sinned, and "there is a God that judgeth in the earth."

Four years ago, these Confederate States formed an integral part of the U. States. Perhaps no nation of people ever sinned against more light, and abused more privileges than the United States. The Northern pulpits hatched and fostered the spirit that produced this cruel and bloody war: but cruel and bloody as it is, I believe in God, to-day, that great good to us of the South as a people, if we will only depart from our sins and lean upon the Almighty Arm. If He be for us, who can stand successfully against us? He gave to our fathers a Washington, a man who feared God, to guide them through the revolution of 1776. He has given to us a Lee, a man of like faith and of like hopes, to be our leader in these dark days of trial, and we all love to follow where he leads.

He lent to us a Jackson, that bright and shining light of Christianity, whose ardent piety and strong faith always presented the same beauties, in the halls of science, at the altars of God, around the camp-fires, or on the battle-field. Oh, what a model of a Christian soldier! Well do I remember how his presence cheered us as he rode along our line on the morning of the first battle of Fredericksburg, after the artillery began to roar heavily. His very appearance seemed to be the presage of victory. He seemed like one sent by God. But God has seen proper in His providence to take him away, and whatsoever He doeth is right. Let us then bow, to the hand that afflicts in such dispensations as this, take courage and press onward.

Let us then humble ourselves before God as a people, confess our sins, and implore His protecting power to guide us through this mighty struggle to a successful issue. He has certainly done great things for us as a people, whereof we should be glad.

I think you will bear me witness that I have never been hopeful of an early peace in my intercourse among you. But to-day I fancy that I can discover a little cloud, in the political heavens as large as a man's hand at least, that seems to portend peace. Take courage, then, companions in arms. All things around us to-day bid us be of good courage. History fails to tell us of ten millions of freemen being enslaved, who had determined to be free. A braver or more patriotic army than we have, never followed their chief to victory. Their endurance challenges the admiration of the world. When I have seen our brave men in winter's cold and summer's heat, marching from battle-field to battle-field, bare-footed as they were born, and without a murmur, I could not doubt our final success. *Such men as these, were never born to be slaves.* Again when I have turned my eye homeward from the camp, and witnessed the labors of our fair country women, in preparing clothing to meet the wants of the suffering in the field, and witnessed their untiring devotion to the relief of the sick and wounded in the hospitals, I knew that the history of no country, and of no age afforded anything like a parallel, and my faith assured me we never were born to be slaves of the Yankees. Then let your trust to-day be strong in the God of nations.

Surely, then, no man can be found in all our land who owes allegiance to his country, that is so lost to himself, and to all that is noble and patriotic, as to say, "I am for the Union as it was." Such an one could only merit the good man's scorn, and desire the tory's infamy for himself, and disgrace for his children.

Gentlemen, I have followed your fortunes for twenty months, leaving wife and children far behind me. I have rejoiced in your prosperity, and mourned over your adversity. Marches, battles, sufferings are before us still. By the help of God I am with you, and hope still to be with you to share in your triumphs, your sufferings and your joys. If these be the days to try men's souls, for my country's sake I am willing to be tried, by bearing my humble part in this mighty struggle.

For, standing before you to-day, you must permit me to say in the language of a noble patriot, "I am for my country right, yea, for my country wrong." My loyalty to her is unqualified, and without any conditions. Her cause is always my cause. If her cause be right, she shall have my free support; if it be wrong she shall have my unqualified support. Therefore, when I shall sleep in the dust, you must not say to my children, "your father was a conservative, (or any other name,) when his country was engaged in a bloody struggle for existence." Then you would do me wrong, and do them wrong also. I belong only to my country's party. But it may be said, that I can afford to use strong language when I am not required to take position in the front ranks on the battle-field. The duties of my office require me, as you are aware, to take position in the rear, to assist with the wounded, but yet at Fredericksburg, Williamsport, Mine Run, and Batchelor's Creek, I was under the fire of both artillery and musketry, and I will here add that if ever my country calls upon me to fall into ranks in her defence with a musket on my shoulder, my answer shall be, "here am I."

Then, to-day, in the light of this beautiful Sabbath sun, let us take courage, and with renewed trust in God, resolve to do our whole duty as patriots and soldiers, and leave the event to the Arbiter of nations. *Amen!*

Oliver W. Norton to Elizabeth Norton Poss

Oliver W. Norton had been commissioned as a first lieutenant in the 8th U.S. Colored Infantry in November 1863 and joined the regiment the following month at its training camp near Philadelphia. Recruited mainly in eastern Pennsylvania and Delaware, the regiment sailed to South Carolina in January and was then sent to Florida. On February 7, Union troops occupied Jacksonville, beginning a campaign intended to gain control of northern Florida and, if possible, establish a loyal government in the state. Norton and the 8th U.S. Colored Infantry were among the 5,000 Union troops under Brigadier General Truman B. Seymour who encountered 5,000 Confederate defenders in the pine woods near Olustee Station, about fifty miles west of Jacksonville, on February 20. In the battle that followed, the Confederates lost 964 men killed, wounded, or missing, while Union losses totaled 1,861, including an unknown number of black soldiers who were killed after being captured. The 54th Massachusetts Infantry helped cover the Union retreat, which continued until Seymour's command reached Jacksonville on February 22. "If there is a second lieutenant in our regiment who couldn't plan and execute a better battle, I would vote to dismiss him for incompetency," Norton wrote to his father the day after he had described the fighting in a letter to his sister.

———————

Jacksonville, Fla.,
Monday, Feb. 29, 1864.

Dear Sister L.:—

You will probably see accounts of the battle of Olustee, or Ocean Pond, in the papers. I have ordered a copy of the Brookville Republican, containing a letter from Dr. Heichold, descriptive of the battle, sent to you, but I will give you some of my own ideas about it, too; you always express a preference for them, you know.

Well, the morning of Saturday, the 20th, found us at Barber's Ford on the St. Mary's river ready to march and loaded down with ten days' rations. Our force consisted of the One hundred-fifteenth, Forty-seventh and Forty-eighth New York Regiments, Seventh New Hampshire and Seventh Connecticut (repeating rifles), Fifty-fourth Massachusetts (colored) of Fort Wagner memory, the First North Carolina Colored and the Eighth, twenty pieces of artillery, one battalion cavalry and the Fortieth Massachusetts (mounted infantry).

We started marching in three columns, artillery in the road, flanked by the infantry on either side. After marching twelve miles we halted near a few desolate houses called Sanders and while resting heard a few musket shots in advance. We supposed our cavalry had met a few of the enemy's pickets. Their force was supposed to be at Lake City, twelve miles distant, so we moved on up the railroad. The skirmishing increased as we marched, but we paid little attention to it. Pretty soon the boom of a gun startled us a little, but not much, as we knew our flying artillery was ahead, but they boomed again and again and it began to look like a brush. An aide came dashing through the woods to us and the order was—"double quick, march!" We turned into the woods and ran in the direction of the firing for half a mile, when the head of the column reached our batteries. The presiding genius, General Seymour, said: "Put your regiment in, Colonel Fribley," and left.

Military men say it takes veteran troops to maneuver under fire, but our regiment with knapsacks on and unloaded pieces, after a run of half a mile, formed a line under the most destructive fire I ever knew. We were not more than two hundred yards from the enemy, concealed in pits and behind trees, and what did the regiment do? At first they were stunned, bewildered, and knew not what to do. They curled to the ground, and as men fell around them they seemed terribly scared, but gradually they recovered their senses and commenced firing. And here was the great trouble—they could not use their arms to advantage. We have had very little practice in firing, and, though they could stand and be killed, they could not kill a concealed enemy fast enough to satisfy my feelings.

After seeing his men murdered as long as flesh and blood could endure it, Colonel Fribley ordered the regiment to fall back slowly, firing as they went. As the men fell back they gathered in groups like frightened sheep, and it was almost impossible to keep them from doing so. Into these groups the rebels poured the deadliest fire, almost every bullet hitting some one. Color bearer after color bearer was shot down and the colors seized by another. Behind us was a battery that was wretchedly managed. They had but little ammunition, but after firing that, they made no effort to get away with their pieces, but busied themselves in trying to keep us in front of them. Lieutenant Lewis seized the colors and planted them by a gun and tried to rally his men round them, but forgetting them for the moment, they were left there, and the battery was captured and our colors with it.

Colonel Fribley was killed soon after his order to fall back, and Major Burritt had both legs broken. We were without a commander, and every officer was doing his best to do something, he knew not what exactly. There was no leader. Seymour might better have been in his grave than there. Many will blame Lieutenant Lewis that the colors were lost. I do not think he can be blamed. Brave to rashness, he cannot be accused of cowardice, but man cannot think of too many things.

Some things in this story look strange. Officers should know exactly what to do, you may say. Certainly, but it is a damper on that duty when there is a certainty on the mind that the commander does not know. When, with eight or ten regiments ready, you see only two or three fighting, and feel you are getting whipped from your general's incompetency, it is hard to be soldierly.

I saw from the commencement of our retreat that the day was lost, but I confess to you that I was in doubt whether I ought to stay and see my men shot down or take them to the rear. Soldierly feelings triumphed, but at what a cost!

Captain Dickey was shot early in the fight and the command of the company devolved on me. He was not seriously wounded, a ball through the face.

Captain Wagner was standing by me when he fell, pierced by three balls. I seized him and dragged him back a few rods and two of his men then took him to the rear. I carried his sword through the fight. Several times I was on the point of throwing it away, thinking he must be dead, but I saved it and had the pleasure of giving it to him and hearing that he is likely to recover.

Of twenty-two officers that went into the fight, but two escaped without marks. Such accurate firing I never saw before. I was under the impression all the time that an inferior force was whipping us, but the deadly aim of their rifles told the story.

Well, you are wanting to know how I came off, no doubt. With my usual narrow escapes, but escapes. My hat has five bullet holes in it. Don't start very much at that—they were all made by one bullet. You know the dent in the top of it. Well, the ball went through the rim first and then through the top in this way. My hat was cocked up on one side so that it went through in that way and just drew the blood on my scalp. Of course a quarter of an inch lower would have broken my skull, but it was too high. Another ball cut away a corner of my haversack and one struck my scabbard. The only wonder is I was not killed, and the wonder grows with each succeeding fight, and this is the fifteenth or sixteenth, Yorktown, Hanover, Gaines' Mill, Charles City, Malvern, Bull Run, Antietam, Shepherdstown Ford, Fredericksburg, Richards Ford, Chancellorsville, Loudon Valley, Gettysburg, Manassas Gap, Rappahannock Station and Olustee, to say nothing of the shelling at Harrison's Landing or the skirmish at Ely's Ford. Had any one told me when I enlisted that I should have to pass through so many I am afraid it would have daunted me. How many more?

Company K went into the fight with fifty-five enlisted men and two officers. It came out with twenty-three men and one officer. Of these but two men were not marked. That speaks volumes for the bravery of negroes. Several of these twenty-three were quite badly cut, but they are present with the company. Ten were killed and four reported missing, though there is little doubt they are killed, too.*

* *Note.*—The regiment went into the battle with five hundred and fifty-four officers and enlisted men. Of these, three hundred and nineteen were killed or disabled by serious wounds. Many others were slightly wounded, but remained on duty.

A flag of truce from the enemy brought the news that prisoners, black and white, were treated alike. I hope it is so, for I
have sworn never to take a prisoner if my men left there were
murdered.

This is the first letter I have written since the fight, and it is
to you, my best beloved sister. It is written in haste, in a press
of business, but you will excuse mistakes and my inattention to
the matter of your own letter. You may pray for me—I need
that, and do write to me as often as you find time.

John B. Jones: Diary,
March 1–2 and 5, 1864

The prisoner exchange cartel signed by the opposing sides in July 1862 began to collapse in the summer of 1863 because of the Confederate refusal to treat black soldiers and their officers as prisoners of war. Union officials insisted that black and white prisoners be treated equally under the cartel, and later protested when men paroled at Vicksburg returned to the Confederate ranks without being properly exchanged. By February 1864 some 5,000 Union prisoners were being held in Richmond, where they suffered from hunger, disease, and exposure. Brigadier General Judson Kilpatrick, a division commander in the Army of the Potomac's cavalry corps, gained approval from Lincoln and Stanton for a raid on the Confederate capital aimed at freeing the prisoners. On February 28 Kilpatrick and 3,500 men crossed the Rapidan sixty miles north of Richmond, then split up the next day. The main force under Kilpatrick encountered unexpectedly strong resistance when it reached the northern outskirts of the city on March 1, while a smaller body of 460 men led by Colonel Ulric Dahlgren was unable to cross the James River and attack Richmond from the south. While Kilpatrick and most of his command reached the Union lines on the Peninsula, Dahlgren was killed in an ambush on March 2. In papers found on his body Dahlgren wrote that once the prisoners were released and the city captured, "it must be destroyed and Jeff Davis and Cabinet killed." The papers were given to Davis on March 4 and published in the Richmond press the next day. Kilpatrick would later deny having given or received orders to burn the city or to kill Confederate leaders.

MARCH 1ST.—Dark and raining.

As the morning progressed, the city was a little startled by the sound of artillery in a northern direction, and not very distant. Couriers and horsemen from the country announced the approach of the enemy *within* the outer fortifications; a column of 5000 cavalry. Then Hon. James Lyons came in, reporting that the enemy were shelling his house, one and a half miles from the city. And Gen. Elzey (in command) said, at the department, that a fight was in progress; and that Brig.-Gen. Custis Lee was directing it in person. But an hour or so after the report of artillery ceased, and the excitement died away. Yet the local troops and militia are marching out as I write; and a caisson that came in an hour ago has just passed our door, returning to the field. Of course the city is full of rumors, and no one yet knows what has occurred. I presume it was only distant shelling, as no wounded men have been brought in.

It is reported that the enemy captured Mr. Seddon's family twenty-five miles distant,—also Gen. Wise's. To-morrow we shall know more; but no *uneasiness* is felt as to the result. In a few hours we can muster men enough to defend the city against 25,000.

A letter from Gen. Whiting suggests that martial law be proclaimed in North Carolina, as a Judge Pearson—a traitor, he thinks—is discharging men who have in conscripts as substitutes, on the ground that the act of Congress is unconstitutional. The President suggests a General Order, etc., complying with Gen. W.'s request.

Col. A. C. Myers, late Quartermaster-General, writes again, indignantly resenting the President's indorsement, etc. as unfounded and injurious, etc.

The President indorses this letter as follows: "Unless this letter is designed to ask whether Col. M. is still in the army, or discharged by the appointment of a successor, I find nothing which changes the case since my indorsement referred to, as causing resentment and calling for vindication. Your orders were certainly official communications. Not having seen them, I can express no opinion upon their terms.—JEFFERSON DAVIS."

MARCH 2D.—A slight snow on the ground this morning—but bright and cool. Last night, after I had retired to bed, we heard a brisk cannonading, and volleys of musketry, a few miles distant.

This morning an excitement, but no alarm, pervaded the city. It was certainly a formidable attempt to take the city by surprise. From the number of disgraceful failures heretofore, the last very recently, the enemy must have come to the desperate resolution to storm the city this time at all hazards. And indeed the coming upon it was sudden, and if there had been a column of 15,000 bold men in the assault, they might have penetrated it. But now, twenty-four hours subsequently, 30,000 would fail in the attempt.

The Department Clerks were in action in the evening in five minutes after they were formed in line. Capt. Ellery, Chief Clerk of 2d Auditor, was killed, and several were wounded. It rained fast all the time, and it was very dark. The enemy's cavalry charged upon them, firing as they came; they were ordered to lie flat on the ground. This they did, until the enemy came within fifteen yards of them, when they rose and fired, sending the assailants to the right and left, helter-skelter. How many fell is not yet known.

To-day Gen. Hampton sent in 77 prisoners, taken six miles above town—one lieutenant-colonel among them; and Yankee horses, etc. are coming in every hour.

Gov. Vance writes that inasmuch as Judge Pearson still grants the writ of *habeas corpus*, and discharges all who have put substitutes in the army, on the ground of the unconstitutionality of the act of Congress, he is bound by his oath to sustain the judge, even to the summoning the military force of the State to resist the Confederate States authorities. But to avoid such a fatal collision, he is willing to abide the decision of the Supreme Court, to assemble in June; the substitute men, meantime, to be left unmolested. We shall soon see the President's decision, which will probably be martial law.

Last night, when it was supposed probable that the prisoners of war at the Libby might attempt to break out, Gen. Winder ordered that a large amount of powder be placed under the building, with instructions to blow them up, if the attempt were made. He was persuaded, however, to consult the Secretary of War first, and get his approbation. The Secretary would give no such order, but said the prisoners must not be permitted to escape under any circumstances, which was considered sanction enough. Capt. —— obtained an order for, and procured several hundred pounds of gunpowder, which were placed in readiness. Whether the prisoners were advised of this I know not; but I told Capt. —— it could not be justifiable to spring such a mine in the absence of their knowledge of the fate awaiting them, in the event of their attempt to break out,—because such prisoners are not to be condemned for striving to regain their liberty. Indeed, it is the *duty* of a prisoner of war to escape if he can.

Gen. Winder addressed me in a friendly manner to-day, the first time in two years.

The President was in a bad humor yesterday, when the enemy's guns were heard even in his office.

The last dispatch from Gen. Lee informs us that Meade, who had advanced, had fallen back again. But communications are cut between us and Lee; and we have no intelligence since Monday.

Gen. Wilcox is organizing an impromptu brigade here, formed of the furloughed officers and men found everywhere in the streets and at the hotels. This looks as if the danger were not yet regarded as over.

The Secretary of War was locked up with the Quartermaster and Commissary-Generals and other bureau officers, supposed to be discussing the damage done by the enemy to the railroads, etc. etc. I hope it was not a consultation upon any presumed necessity of the abandonment of the city!

We were paid to-day in $5 bills. I gave $20 for half a cord of wood, and $60 for a bushel of common white cornfield beans. Bacon is yet $8 per pound; but more is coming to the city than usual, and a decline may be looked for, I hope. The farmers above the city, who have been hoarding grain, meat, etc., will lose much by the raiders.

MARCH 5TH.—Clear and pleasant, after a slight shower in the morning.

The raid is considered at an end, and it has ended disastrously for the invaders.

Some extraordinary memoranda were captured from the raiders, showing a diabolical purpose, and creating a profound sensation here. The cabinet have been in consultation many hours in regard to it, and I have reason to believe it is the present purpose to deal summarily with the captives taken with Dahlgren, but the "sober second thought" will prevail, and they will not be executed, notwithstanding the thunders of the press. Retaliation for such outrages committed on others having been declined, the President and cabinet can hardly be expected to begin with such sanguinary punishments when *their own* lives are threatened. It would be an act liable to grave criticism. Nevertheless, Mr. Secretary Seddon has written a letter to-day to Gen. Lee, asking his views on a matter of such importance as the execution of some *ninety* men of Dahlgren's immediate followers, not, as he says, to divide the responsibility, nor to effect a purpose, which has the sanction of the President, the cabinet, and *Gen. Bragg*, but to have his *views*, and information as to what would probably be its effect on the army under his command. We shall soon know, I hope, what Gen. Lee will have to say on the subject, and I am mistaken if he does not oppose it. If these men had been put to death in the heat of passion, on the field, it would have been justified, but it is too late now. Besides, *Gen. Lee's son* is a captive in the hands of the enemy, designated for retaliation whenever we shall execute any of their prisoners in our hands. It is cruelty to Gen. Lee!

It is already rumored that Gen. Butler has been removed, and a flag of truce boat is certainly at City Point, laden with prisoners sent up for exchange.

The Commissary-General has sent in a paper saying that unless the passenger cars on the Southern Road be discontinued, he cannot supply half enough meal for Lee's army. He has abundance in Georgia and South Carolina, but cannot get transportation. He says the last barrel of flour from Lynchburg has gone to the army.

We have news from the West that Morgan and his men will be in the saddle in a few days.

After all, Mr. Lyon's house was not touched by any of the enemy's shells. But one shell struck within 300 yards of one house in Clay Street, and not even the women and children were alarmed.

The price of a turkey to-day is $60.

Ulysses S. Grant to William T. Sherman

On December 14, 1863, Elihu B. Washburne introduced a bill in the House of Representatives reviving the grade of lieutenant general, a rank previously held only by George Washington and, by brevet (honorary) appointment, Winfield Scott. President Lincoln signed the bill on February 29 and nominated Grant for the position. The nomination was confirmed by the Senate on March 2. As he prepared to leave for Washington, Grant acknowledged his debt to Sherman and to Major General James B. McPherson, who had served as Grant's chief engineer at Fort Donelson and Shiloh and commanded a corps in the Army of the Tennessee during the Vicksburg campaign.

———————————

Nashville Tennessee,
March 4th 1864.

DEAR SHERMAN,

The bill reviving the grade of Lieut. Gen. in the Army has become a law and my name has been sent to the Senate for the place. I now receive orders to report to Washington, *in person*, immediately, which indicates either a confirmation or a likelyhood of confirmation. I start in the morning to comply with the order but I shall say very distinctly on my arrival there that I accept no appointment which will require me to make that city my Hd Qrs. This however is not what I started out to write about.

Whilst I have been eminently successful in this War, in at least gaining the confidence of the public, no one feels more than me how much of this success is due to the energy, skill, and harmonious puting forth of that energy and skill, of those who it has been my good fortune to have occupying a subordinate position under me. There are many officers to whom these remarks are applicable to a greater or less degree, proportionate to their ability as soldiers, but what I want is to express my thanks to you and McPherson as *the men* to whom, above all others, I feel indebted for whatever I have had of success. How far your advice and suggestions have been of assistance you know. How far your execution of whatever has been given you to do entitles you to the reward I am receiving you cannot know as well as me. I feel all the gratitude this letter would express, giving it the most flattering construction.

The word *you* I use in the plural intending it for Mc. also. I should write to him, and will some day, but starting in the morning I do not know that I will find time just now.

Your friend
U. S. GRANT
Maj. Gen.

William T. Sherman to Ulysses S. Grant

Grant arrived in Washington on March 8 and met Lincoln for the first time that night. He received his commission as lieutenant general the next day and was assigned command of the Union armies on March 10, the same day he went to Virginia to meet with Meade. By the time Grant received Sherman's letter, he had decided on a course different from the one Sherman had recommended. Grant would make his headquarters in the field with the Army of the Potomac while keeping Meade as its commander. Sherman would succeed Grant as commander of the Military Division of the Mississippi, and McPherson would replace Sherman as commander of the Army of the Tennessee.

[private and confidential]

Near Memphis, March 10, 1864

General Grant

Dear General:

I have your more than kind and characteristic letter of the 4th, and will send a copy of it to General McPherson at once.

You do yourself injustice and us too much honor in assigning to us so large a share of the merits which have led to your high advancement. I know you approve the friendship I have ever professed to you, and will permit me to continue as heretofore to manifest it on all proper occasions.

You are now Washington's legitimate successor, and occupy a position of almost dangerous elevation; but if you can continue as heretofore to be yourself, simple, honest, and unpretending, you will enjoy through life the respect and love of friends, and the homage of millions of human beings who will award to you a large share for securing to them and their descendants a government of law and stability.

I repeat, you do General McPherson and myself too much honor. At Belmont you manifested your traits, neither of us being near; at Donelson also you illustrated your whole character. I was not near, and General McPherson in too subordinate a capacity to influence you.

Until you had won Donelson, I confess I was almost cowed by the terrible array of anarchical elements that present themselves at every point; but that victory admitted the ray of light which I have followed ever since.

I believe you are as brave, patriotic, and just, as the great prototype Washington; as unselfish, kind-hearted, and honest, as a man should be; but the chief characteristic in your nature is the simple faith in success you have always manifested, which I can liken to nothing else than the faith a Christian has in his Saviour.

This faith gave you victory at Shiloh and Vicksburg. Also, when you have completed your best preparations, you go into battle without hesitation, as at Chattanooga—no doubts, no reserve; and I tell you that it was this that made us act with confidence. I knew wherever I was that you thought of me, and if I got in a tight place you would come—if alive.

My only points of doubt were as to your knowledge of grand strategy, and of books of science and history; but I confess your common-sense seems to have supplied all this.

Now as to the future. Do not stay in Washington. Halleck is better qualified than you are to stand the buffets of intrigue and policy. Come out West; take to yourself the whole Mississippi Valley; let us make it dead-sure, and I tell you the Atlantic slope and pacific shores will follow its destiny as sure as the limbs of a tree live or die with the main trunk! We have done much; still much remains to be done. Time and time's influences are all with us; we could almost afford to sit still and let these influences work. Even in the seceded States your word *now* would go further than a President's proclamation, or an act of Congress.

For God's sake and for your country's sake, come out of Washington! I foretold to General Halleck, before he left Corinth, the inevitable result to him, and I now exhort you to come out West. Here lies the seat of the coming empire; and from the West, when our task is done, we will make short work of Charleston and Richmond, and the impoverished coast of the Atlantic. Your sincere friend,

W. T. Sherman

Chronology
January 1863–March 1864

1863   President Abraham Lincoln issues Emancipation Proclamation, freeing all slaves in enumerated Confederate-held areas on January 1. General William T. Sherman withdraws his troops from the Yazoo River north of Vicksburg, Mississippi, on January 2. (Sherman had unsuccessfully attacked the Confederate positions at Chickasaw Bluffs on December 29, 1862, as part of a failed Union attempt to capture Vicksburg.) After a lull on New Year's Day, General Braxton Bragg resumes attacks on Union forces along Stones River near Murfreesboro, Tennessee, January 2 (battle had begun on December 31). On January 3 Bragg withdraws his Army of Tennessee to Tullahoma, thirty-five miles to the south. Confederates lose approximately 12,000 men killed, wounded, or missing at Stones River, while General William S. Rosecrans's Army of the Cumberland loses about 13,000. General John A. McClernand, a politically influential War Democrat and former Illinois congressman who had been authorized by Lincoln to raise and lead troops against Vicksburg, assumes command of Sherman's forces at Milliken's Bend, Louisiana, January 4. The same day, Lincoln responds to protests by revoking General Ulysses S. Grant's order of December 17, 1862, expelling all Jews from the Department of the Tennessee. Lincoln nominates John P. Usher on January 5 to replace Caleb P. Smith as secretary of the interior. On January 11, Union forces under McClernand capture Fort Hindman and almost 4,800 Confederate prisoners at Arkansas Post, fifty miles up the Arkansas River, at the cost of 1,061 men killed, wounded, or missing. The same day, the Confederate raider *Alabama* sinks the Union gunboat *Hatteras* off Galveston, Texas. Jefferson Davis sends message to new session of the Confederate Congress on January 12 in which he praises recent military successes at Fredericksburg and Vicksburg, criticizes Britain and France for failing to recognize southern independence, and calls the Emancipation Proclamation "the most execrable measure recorded in the history of guilty man," one which makes restoration of the Union "forever impossible." In Virginia General Ambrose Burnside, commander of the Army of the Potomac, begins offensive on January 20 designed to cross the Rappahannock River above Fredericksburg and outflank General Robert E. Lee's Army of Northern Virginia. When heavy rain makes the roads impassable, Burnside abandons the movement, which becomes known as the "Mud March," on January 22. Burnside asks Lincoln on January 24 to either remove several of his generals, including Joseph Hooker, or accept his resignation. The next day, Lincoln replaces Burnside with Hooker as commander of the Army of the Potomac. Union navy bombards Fort McAllister outside of Savannah, Georgia, on January 27 (attack is designed to test effectiveness of modern naval guns against earth fortifications). Grant assumes direct command of operations against Vicksburg on January 30 and assigns McClernand to command of one of four infantry corps in the Army of the Tennessee. On Grant's orders Union troops continue work on canal cutting across peninsula opposite Vicksburg, and begin attempt to open a water route through several Louisiana lakes, rivers, and bayous to the Mississippi below the city. Confederate ironclad rams *Chicora* and *Palmetto State* damage two Union gunboats off Charleston, South Carolina, on January 31, but are unable to break the blockade of the port.

Fort McAllister is bombarded again on February 1. Union ram *Queen of the West* runs past Confederate batteries at Vicksburg, Mississippi, on February 2, and begins capturing ships bringing supplies down the Red River to the Confederate garrison at Port Hudson, Louisiana, the other remaining Confederate stronghold on the Mississippi. On February 3 Union forces cut through Mississippi River levee at Yazoo Pass, beginning attempt to open route through the waterways of the Mississippi Delta to the Yazoo River northeast of Vicksburg. The same day, Secretary of State William H. Seward rejects proposal by French foreign minister Édouard Drouyhn de Lhuys for peace negotiations between the Union and the Confederacy. Queen Victoria declares in address to Parliament on February 5 that her government believes a British attempt to mediate the conflict would be unsuccessful. Union ironclad gunboat *Indianola* runs Vicksburg batteries on

February 13. *Queen of the West* runs aground on the Red River below Alexandria, Louisiana, on February 14 and is abandoned by crew. Cherokee National Council meets at Cowskin Prairie in northeastern Indian Territory, February 17, and votes to revoke its October 1861 treaty of alliance with the Confederacy and to abolish slavery in the Cherokee Nation. (Cherokees remain divided between pro-Union faction led by John Ross and Thomas Pegg and pro-Confederate faction headed by Stand Watie.) Four Confederate vessels, including the captured *Queen of the West*, sink the *Indianola* in shallow water south of Vicksburg on February 24. Lincoln signs legislation creating Arizona Territory, February 24, and establishing national banking system authorized to issue banknotes, February 25. U.S.S. *Vanderbilt* seizes the British merchant vessel *Peterhoff* in the Danish West Indies, February 25, on suspicion that the ship, bound for Matamoros, Mexico, was carrying contraband cargo intended for importation into the Confederacy. British protest removal of official mailbag from the *Peterhoff*, raising Anglo-American tensions. (Incident is resolved in April 1863 when U.S. officials return the mail unopened.) Confederates abandon attempt to salvage the *Indianola* and destroy the ship on February 26 after Union forces float a coal barge disguised as a gunboat downriver.

On March 3 Lincoln signs conscription act making most males between twenty and forty-five eligible for service if voluntary enlistments fail to meet the recruitment quotas for their district. The law allows individuals who are drafted to avoid service by hiring a substitute or paying a $300 commutation fee. Lincoln also signs into law on March 3 a bill adding a tenth justice to the Supreme Court, as well as an act authorizing the president to suspend the writ of habeas corpus during the "present rebellion" while limiting his power to detain persons indefinitely without charge. Union naval force bombards Fort McAllister on March 3 and then withdraws to prepare for attack on Charleston, South Carolina. Jacksonville, Florida, is occupied by Union troops, March 10–29, who gather provisions and recruit freed slaves for service in the 1st and 2nd South Carolina Volunteer regiments. In the *Prize Cases*, decided March 10, the U.S. Supreme Court upholds 5–4 the legality of the blockade proclamations issued by

Lincoln in April 1861. Lincoln issues proclamation on March 10 granting amnesty to soldiers absent without leave who return to duty by April 1. Confederates at Fort Pemberton on the Tallahatchie River repel Union gunboats attempting to reach the Yazoo River by way of Yazoo Pass, March 11. Two ships from Union squadron led by Rear Admiral David G. Farragut run past the Confederate defenses at Port Hudson on night of March 14. Union gunboats make unsuccessful attacks on Fort Pemberton, March 13 and March 16, then withdraw. Grant and Acting Rear Admiral David D. Porter send expedition up Steele's Bayou on March 16 in attempt to open route through the southern Mississippi Delta to the Yazoo northeast of Vicksburg. In Virginia, Union cavalry cross the Rappahannock River at Kelly's Ford on March 17 and skirmish with Confederate cavalry before withdrawing. French banking house Erlanger & Cie floats £3 million loan to the Confederacy financed by sale of cotton bonds, March 19. (Proceeds from loan eventually total about $8.5 million, which Confederate agents use to buy arms and war supplies in Europe.) Porter abandons Steele's Bayou expedition on March 22 when Confederates block passage of Union gunboats up Deer Creek in the southern delta. West Virginia voters overwhelmingly approve amendment to state constitution abolishing slavery through gradual emancipation, March 26. The same day, the Confederate Congress passes law authorizing government agents to impress property, including slaves, in support of military operations. On March 29 Grant orders McClernand's corps to begin marching to New Carthage, Louisiana, in preparation for a possible crossing of the Mississippi south of Vicksburg.

Farragut begins blockading the mouth of the Red River on April 1. Several hundred women riot in Richmond, Virginia, on April 2 to protest food shortages. Nine Union ironclads bombard Fort Sumter and other fortifications guarding Charleston Harbor on April 7, but are repulsed by artillery fire that sinks one ship and seriously damages five others. In southeastern Virginia two divisions detached from the Army of Northern Virginia under General James Longstreet begin siege of Suffolk, April 11, while gathering forage and supplies for Lee's army. Union forces under General Nathaniel P. Banks attack Fort Bisland on

Bayou Teche in southern Louisiana, April 12–13. The Confederates evacuate the fort on April 14, the same day Union gunboats sink the *Queen of the West* on nearby Grand Lake. Ship carrying 453 former slaves sails from Fort Monroe, Virginia, on April 14, beginning colonization project on Île à Vache off Haiti authorized by Lincoln in 1862. Union gunboats and transports run past the batteries at Vicksburg on the night of April 16, providing Grant with the means to cross the Mississippi south of the city. Union cavalry brigade led by Colonel Grierson conducts raid from La Grange, Tennessee, through central Mississippi to Baton Rouge, Louisiana, April 17–May 2, destroying railroads and further confusing Confederate commanders as to Union intentions. Second Union fleet of transport steamers runs past the Vicksburg batteries on April 22 as most of Grant's army moves down the west bank of the Mississippi below the city. Confederate Congress passes its first comprehensive tax law, April 24, laying taxes on income, licenses, and products, and imposing a 10 percent "tax in kind" on agricultural produce for the year. (Law is resented by many small farmers for not taxing the land and slaves of plantation owners.) Union army issues General Orders No. 100, a comprehensive code of the laws of war drafted by jurist Francis Lieber, April 24. In Virginia, Hooker begins offensive on April 27, sending one wing of his army up the Rappahannock to turn Lee's left flank while the other wing prepares to cross the river at Fredericksburg. Union troops cross the Rappahannock and Rapidan rivers west of Fredericksburg, April 29, as cavalry forces begin raid on railroad lines supplying Lee's army. On April 30 Hooker halts Union advance at Chancellorsville, ten miles west of Fredericksburg. Grant has Sherman feint an attack along the Yazoo on April 29, then crosses the Mississippi with more than 20,000 men at Bruinsburg, thirty miles southwest of Vicksburg, on April 30.

On May 1 Grant defeats Confederate forces at Port Gibson, Mississippi. Lee leaves 10,000 men to defend Fredericksburg and sends the rest of his army to face Hooker. Fighting begins on May 1 as Hooker resumes advance toward Fredericksburg, then withdraws to defensive positions around Chancellorsville. On May 2 Lee sends General Thomas J. (Stonewall) Jackson with about

30,000 men on a twelve-mile march to strike Hooker's
exposed right flank west of Chancellorsville. Jackson attacks in the late afternoon and routs the Union Eleventh
Corps, but is then accidentally shot by his own men while
attempting to continue his offensive in darkness. On the
morning of May 3 Lee's army drives Union forces from
Chancellorsville north toward the Rappahannock after
Hooker is concussed by debris from the impact of a Confederate cannonball. The same day, the other wing of
Hooker's army captures Marye's Heights at Fredericksburg and advances toward Chancellorsville, but is stopped
by Confederate defenders at Salem Church. In Mississippi,
Grant captures Grand Gulf on May 3 and learns that General Nathaniel P. Banks's expedition against Port Hudson
has been delayed. Grant abandons plan to cooperate with
Banks and decides instead to advance into central Mississippi and have his men live off the countryside as they
march. Longstreet abandons siege of Suffolk on May 4
and moves north to reinforce Lee. The same day, Lee attacks at Salem Church, and the Union forces there withdraw across the Rappahannock on the night of May 4. Lee
plans attack on Hooker's defensive line near the Rappahannock, but the Union troops withdraw north of the
river on the night of May 5. Chancellorsville costs the
Union about 17,000 men killed, wounded, or missing,
and the Confederates about 13,000. In Ohio, former
Democratic congressman Clement L. Vallandigham is arrested in Dayton by Union soldiers on May 5 on orders
from General Ambrose Burnside, commander of the Department of the Ohio. Vallandigham is convicted by a
military commission on May 7 of having expressed "disloyal
sentiments and opinions" in a recent speech and is sentenced to imprisonment for the duration of the war. Banks
occupies Alexandria, Louisiana, on May 7. The same day,
Sherman's corps crosses the Mississippi and joins Grant's
army as it advances into central Mississippi. Jackson dies
from his wounds at Guiney Station, Virginia, on May 10.
Grant's army defeats Confederates at Raymond, Mississippi,
May 12, and captures Jackson, May 14, frustrating attempt
by General Joseph E. Johnston to assemble reinforcements
there. While Sherman's men destroy factories and railroads
in Jackson, Grant turns most of his army west toward Vicksburg. Grant's forces defeat General John C. Pemberton's

army at Champion Hill, May 16, and capture crossings on the Big Black River, May 17, forcing the Confederates to retreat inside the Vicksburg fortifications. Banks evacuates Alexandria on May 17 and begins advance on Port Hudson. Grant orders assault on Vicksburg that fails, May 19. The same day, Lincoln commutes Vallandigham's sentence to banishment in Confederate-held territory. Banks begins siege of Port Hudson, May 21. Grant orders second assault on Vicksburg, May 22, which also fails, then begins siege operations. Vallandigham is expelled across the lines in Tennessee, May 25. Union troops, including two black Louisiana regiments, make unsuccessful assault on fortifications at Port Hudson on May 27. Lee reorganizes the infantry of the Army of Northern Virginia, previously divided into two corps led by Longstreet and Jackson, into three corps commanded by Longstreet, Richard S. Ewell, and A. P. Hill, May 30.

On June 1 Burnside orders the suppression of the *Chicago Times*, an anti-administration Democratic newspaper, for "repeated expression of disloyal and incendiary sentiments" (Lincoln revokes suppression order on June 4). Army of Northern Virginia begins moving toward Shenandoah Valley of Virginia on June 3 as Lee plans an invasion of the North. French troops occupy Mexico City, June 7, as part of attempt by Napoleon III to install the Hapsburg archduke Maximilian as emperor of Mexico. On June 7, Confederate forces attack Union supply depot at Milliken's Bend, Louisiana, defended by brigade of black troops; after several hours of intense fighting, the Confederates retreat under fire from Union gunboats. In Virginia the largest cavalry battle of the war is fought on June 9 when Union forces cross the Rappahannock and engage Confederate cavalry near Brandy Station before withdrawing. (Although inconclusive, the engagement increases confidence of the Army of the Potomac's cavalry corps.) Ohio Democratic convention nominates Vallandigham for governor, June 11. Grant receives significant reinforcements at Vicksburg, some of which he uses to guard against a possible offensive from central Mississippi by Joseph E. Johnston. Second Union assault at Port Hudson is repulsed on June 14. Ewell defeats Union forces at Winchester, Virginia, June 15, opening the Shenandoah Valley to the remainder of Lee's army. The same day, Confederate

troops cross the Potomac into western Maryland as
Hooker moves north, keeping his army between Lee and
Washington, D.C. Vallandigham sails for Bermuda from
Wilmington, North Carolina, on June 17. (After arriving
in Halifax, Nova Scotia, on July 5, he will campaign for
governor of Ohio from exile in Canada.) As the siege of
Vicksburg continues, Grant relieves McClernand for insubordination on June 18 and replaces him with General
Edward O. C. Ord. West Virginia becomes the thirty-fifth
state on June 20. Advance Confederate forces cross into
Pennsylvania on June 22. William S. Rosecrans's Army of
the Cumberland begins offensive on June 23, advancing
from Murfreesboro toward Tullahoma with objective of
driving the Confederates out of central Tennessee. On
June 25 General J.E.B. Stuart, Lee's cavalry commander,
begins weeklong raid through Virginia, Maryland, and
Pennsylvania. (Stuart's absence will deprive Lee of his
main source of intelligence regarding Union troop movements.) The same day, Hooker's army starts to cross the
Potomac into Maryland. After series of disputes with
General-in-chief Henry W. Halleck, Hooker offers his resignation as commander of the Army of the Potomac on
June 27, and Lincoln replaces him with General George G.
Meade. On June 28 Meade assumes command at Frederick, Maryland, and orders advance north toward Pennsylvania. The same day, Lee learns that the Army of the
Potomac is in Maryland and issues orders reuniting his
three infantry corps in preparation for battle. Union cavalry enters Gettysburg, Pennsylvania, on June 30 and de-
ploys north and west of the small crossroads town.
     Fighting begins outside Gettysburg on the morning of
July 1 as Confederate infantry advancing from the west
encounters dismounted Union cavalry. As both sides bring
up reinforcements, the Confederates capture Gettysburg
but are unable to prevent Union troops from establishing
defensive line on the high ground south of the town.
Confederate attacks on both Union flanks on July 2 result
in heavy casualties on both sides but fail to drive the Army
of the Potomac from the high ground. Lee orders assault
against the Union center on July 3 that is repulsed with
heavy Confederate losses. The battle costs the Confederates about 28,000 men killed, wounded, or missing, and
the Union about 23,000. In Mississippi Pemberton opens

negotiations, July 3, and surrenders Vicksburg and its garrison of 30,000 on July 4 after Grant agrees to parole the Confederate prisoners. Confederate attack against Union garrison at Helena, Arkansas, is repulsed the same day. Lee begins retreat from Gettysburg on evening of July 4. Lincoln refuses on July 6 to receive Confederate vice president Alexander H. Stephens, who had requested safe passage to Washington in attempt to open peace negotiations. Bragg retreats with his army to Chattanooga, Tennessee, July 7, after being outmaneuvered by Rosecrans during Union advance from Murfreesboro. Union authorities begin implementing conscription, July 7. General John Hunt Morgan and 2,000 Confederate cavalry cross Ohio River at Brandenburg, Kentucky, July 8, and begin raid through southern Indiana and Ohio. Confederate garrison of 6,000 surrenders at Port Hudson, Louisiana, on July 9, giving the Union control of the entire length of the Mississippi. Union troops land on Morris Island at the southern entrance to Charleston Harbor, July 10, but fail to capture Fort Wagner at the northern end of the island, July 11. Meade plans attack on Lee's army at Williamsport, Maryland, July 12, but then postpones it. Mob in New York City burns draft office on July 13, beginning riots in which blacks and prominent Republicans become targets. Lee's army crosses Potomac River from Williamsport into West Virginia, July 13–14, shortly before planned Union advance on the Confederate lines. Union troops led by Sherman force Joseph E. Johnston to abandon Jackson, Mississippi, on July 16. New York draft riots are suppressed by Union troops on July 17 after at least 105 people are killed. In South Carolina, Union forces led by the 54th Massachusetts Infantry, a black regiment, are repulsed with heavy losses in unsuccessful assault on Fort Wagner, July 18. Union troops and gunboats defeat Morgan at Buffington Island on the Ohio River, July 19, and capture most of his command. Attempt by Meade to cut off Lee's withdrawal through the Shenandoah Valley fails when Union forces are blocked at Manassas Gap, Virginia, on July 23. Morgan is captured in Salineville, Ohio, July 29. Lincoln issues order on July 30 pledging retaliation for the execution or enslavement of black Union prisoners of war on July 30.

On August 1 Jefferson Davis offers amnesty to soldiers absent without leave if they report for duty within twenty days. Horatio Seymour, the Democratic governor of New York, asks Lincoln to suspend conscription in his state on August 3; on August 7 Lincoln refuses. In Virginia, Lee withdraws south of the Rapidan River on August 4. Union forces at Helena, Arkansas, begin advance on Little Rock, August 10. Rosecrans resumes offensive in Tennessee on August 16 with Chattanooga as his objective, while Burnside's Army of the Ohio begins advance from Kentucky toward Knoxville in eastern Tennessee. Union siege artillery on Morris Island engages in intensive bombardment of Fort Sumter, August 17–23, causing heavy damage. Confederate guerrillas from Missouri led by William C. Quantrill raid Lawrence, Kansas, on August 21, killing 180 men. Union artillery shells city of Charleston, August 22–24. In Missouri, Union general Thomas Ewing issues General Orders No. 11 on August 25, expelling almost the entire civilian population of four counties along the Kansas border in an effort to suppress Confederate guerrillas. (Order will result in the expulsion of between 10,000 and 20,000 persons.) Alabama legislature adopts resolution on August 29 asking the Confederate Congress to consider using slaves as soldiers. Rosecrans's Army of the Cumberland crosses the Tennessee River below Chattanooga, August 29–September 4. Union artillery resumes intense bombardment of Fort Sumter, August 30–September 1.

Burnside's army occupies Knoxville on September 2. In response to protests from U.S. minister Charles Francis Adams, on September 3 British foreign secretary Lord Russell orders that two ironclad rams built for the Confederacy by the Laird shipyards in Liverpool be detained in port. On September 5 Adams sends another note to Russell, warning that the United States will go to war with Great Britain if the rams are allowed to sail. Confederates evacuate Fort Wagner on night of September 6 after weeks of bombardment, giving Union forces control of all of Morris Island. Confederate artillery repulses attempt by Union gunboats and troop transports to sail up Sabine Pass on the Texas-Louisiana border, September 8. Attempt by landing party of Union sailors and marines to capture Fort Sumter on night of September 8 is defeated. Rosecrans's army occupies Chattanooga, September 9, as Bragg retreats into northwest Georgia. The same day, Burnside's army captures Confederate garrison at the Cumberland

Gap, a mountain pass at the juncture of Kentucky, Tennessee, and Virginia. Davis sends Longstreet and two divisions from the Army of Northern Virginia by rail to reinforce Bragg, September 9 (Bragg also receives reinforcements from Mississippi and eastern Tennessee). Union forces occupy Little Rock, Arkansas, September 10. Lincoln issues proclamation on September 15 suspending the writ of habeas corpus, including in cases where judges issue writs releasing draftees from the military. In northwest Georgia the opposing armies skirmish on September 18 as Rosecrans concentrates his forces along the western side of Chickamauga Creek. Battle begins on September 19 as Bragg attacks Union positions with limited success. On September 20 Confederate assault splits the Union center. Rosecrans and the Union right wing retreat toward Chattanooga, while General George H. Thomas and the Union left hold defensive position on Snodgrass Hill for several hours before withdrawing at nightfall. Battle costs Confederates about 18,000 men killed, wounded, or missing, and the Union about 16,000. Rosecrans establishes defensive line around Chattanooga on September 22, the same day Grant begins sending reinforcements from Mississippi to Tennessee. Bragg seizes heights overlooking Chattanooga from the south and east on September 23 and begins laying siege to the city. On night of September 23 Lincoln approves proposal by Secretary of War Edwin M. Stanton to send two corps from the Army of the Potomac west under the command of Joseph Hooker. First Union troops leave Virginia on September 25 and arrive in Bridgeport, Alabama, about thirty miles west of Chattanooga, on September 30 after traveling 1,200 miles by train (rail movement of more than 20,000 men is completed on October 8).

Confederate cavalry led by General Joseph Wheeler raids eastern Tennessee, October 1–9, attacking wagon trains and depots used to supply Rosecrans's army at Chattanooga. Confederate attorney general Thomas H. Watts resigns on October 1 after winning election as governor of Alabama. On night of October 5, Confederate steamboat *David* uses a torpedo (underwater explosive charge) mounted on a spar to damage the Union ironclad *New Ironsides* off Charleston. Jefferson Davis leaves Richmond on October 6 to visit Bragg's army. Lord Russell orders

seizure of Laird rams on October 8. Lee begins offensive
in northern Virginia on October 9 that turns the right
flank of the Army of the Potomac and forces Meade to
retreat across the Rappahannock and fall back toward
Centreville. Davis arrives at headquarters of the Army of
Tennessee near Chattanooga on October 9 and tries to
resolve conflict between Bragg and his generals, many of
whom seek his replacement. On October 13, Republicans
win victories in several state elections, including Ohio,
where John A. Brough, a War Democrat running for governor on the Union ticket, defeats Vallandigham by more
than 100,000 votes, and Pennsylvania, where Republican
governor Andrew G. Curtin defeats George W. Woodward, a Peace Democrat. Confederate attack on Union
rearguard at Bristoe Station, Virginia, October 14, fails to
disrupt Meade's withdrawal to Centreville. The same day,
Davis leaves Bragg's headquarters and begins tour through
Georgia, Alabama, Mississippi, and the Carolinas in effort
to rally public support for the war. Lincoln issues proclamation on October 17 calling for 300,000 new volunteers
and ordering draft for January 1864 (draft is postponed).
Lee abandons offensive in northern Virginia and begins
withdrawal to the Rappahannock, October 18. Secretary of
War Edwin M. Stanton meets with Grant at Indianapolis
on October 18 and gives Grant order appointing him commander of the newly created Military Division of the Mississippi (division covers the territory between the
Alleghenies and the Mississippi, except for Louisiana).
Grant replaces Rosecrans with George H. Thomas and
makes Sherman the new commander of the Army of the
Tennessee. After arriving in Chattanooga on October 23,
Grant orders implementation of plan devised by General
William F. Smith to open new supply line to the Army of
the Cumberland. Union artillery resumes heavy bombard-
ment of Fort Sumter, October 26–December 5. New sup-
ply route into Chattanooga is opened, October 27.
Attempt by Longstreet to break the new line is repulsed at
Wauhatchie, Tennessee, on night of October 28.

Union forces land on Brazos Island at the mouth of the
Rio Grande, November 2. During his return to Richmond,
Jefferson Davis visits Charleston and inspects its harbor
defenses, November 2–4, as bombardment of Fort Sumter
continues. On November 4 Bragg sends Longstreet and

his two divisions to retake Knoxville. Elections held in the eleven seceding states for the Second Confederate Congress, May 28–November 4, result in increased number of representatives opposed to Davis, although supporters of the administration still hold a majority in the new Congress, which will meet in May 1864. (Confederate soldiers and refugees from Kentucky and Missouri elect representatives, February 10–May 2, 1864.) In Texas, Union forces occupy Brownsville on November 6. Union troops capture Confederate bridgehead at Rappahannock Station, Virginia, on November 7. Lee withdraws across the Rapidan, November 10. Sherman and the first of four divisions from the Army of the Tennessee reach Bridgeport, Alabama, on November 13 as Grant plans offensive against Bragg. In fighting at Campbell's Station, Tennessee, on November 16 Longstreet fails to prevent Burnside from retreating inside the fortifications around Knoxville. Union forces occupy Corpus Christi, Texas, November 16. The same day, Union artillery resumes bombardment of Charleston, South Carolina. Lincoln delivers address at dedication of national cemetery at Gettysburg on November 19. Union offensive at Chattanooga begins on November 23 as Thomas captures advance Confederate position at Orchard Knob. On November 24, Hooker's troops seize Lookout Mountain while Sherman occupies hill near the north end of Missionary Ridge. Sherman's attack on November 25 fails to push back the Confederate right and Hooker's advance against the Confederate left is delayed, but Thomas's men break the Confederate center on Missionary Ridge and force Bragg to retreat into northern Georgia. Meade crosses the Rapidan River on November 26 in attempt to turn Lee's right flank. Attempt by Longstreet to capture Fort Sanders outside of Knoxville is repulsed on November 29. Meade cancels attack against Lee's positions along Mine Run south of the Rapidan on November 30. Davis accepts Bragg's resignation as commander of the Army of Tennessee, November 30.

Meade withdraws the Army of the Potomac across the Rapidan on December 1 and goes into winter quarters. As relief force led by Sherman approaches Knoxville, Longstreet abandons siege on December 4 and withdraws into northeast Tennessee. Davis sends message to the Confederate Congress on December 7, acknowledging defeat at

Chattanooga and grave "reverses" at Vicksburg and Port Hudson while calling for continued resistance. In his annual message to Congress on December 8, Lincoln outlines his plan for restoring loyal governments in the insurrectionary states. The same day, he issues a proclamation of amnesty and reconstruction. Republican congressmen James M. Ashley of Ohio and James F. Wilson of Iowa introduce proposals in the House of Representatives on December 14 to abolish slavery by constitutional amendment. Davis names Joseph E. Johnston as commander of the Army of Tennessee on December 16. Confederate Congress abolishes the hiring of substitutes for military service on December 28. Davis appoints George Davis (no relation) as Confederate attorney general, December 31.

1864   On January 2 General Patrick R. Cleburne proposes to meeting of senior commanders in the Army of Tennessee in Dalton, Georgia, that the Confederacy emancipate slaves and enlist them as soldiers. John B. Henderson, a Unionist from Missouri, introduces proposal in the Senate on January 11 for a constitutional amendment abolishing slavery. Confederate raider *Alabama* burns merchant vessel *Emma Jane* off southern India on January 14, the thirty-seventh American ship it has captured since sinking the *Hatteras* in January 1863. Convention of Arkansas Unionists meeting in Little Rock adopts new state constitution abolishing slavery, January 19. Lincoln writes letter on January 23 approving efforts by plantation owners in Mississippi and Arkansas to hire former slaves as free laborers and resume growing cotton.

On February 1 Lincoln orders draft on March 10 of up to 500,000 men, depending on number of voluntary enlistments (draft is postponed to April 15). The same day, Lincoln orders ship sent to the Île à Vache off Haiti to evacuate those colonists wishing to leave. (Ship returns to the United States on March 20 with all 368 surviving colonists.) In North Carolina, Confederate forces under General George E. Pickett make an unsuccessful attempt to capture Union-held New Bern, February 1–3. Sherman leaves Vicksburg on February 3 with 25,000 men and begins marching across central Mississippi toward Meridian, destroying railroads and war materials and stripping the countryside of food and forage. The same day, Davis sends message to the Confederate Congress warning of increasing "discontent, disaffection, and disloyalty" within the Confederacy and asking that the privilege of the writ of habeas corpus be suspended (previous suspension had expired in February 1863). Union forces occupy Jacksonville, Florida, on February 7. Illinois Republican Lyman Trumbull, chairman of the Senate Judiciary Committee, reports text of proposed constitutional amendment abolishing slavery to the Senate on February 10. General William Sooy Smith and 7,000 Union cavalry leave Collierville, Tennessee, on February 11 with orders to destroy railroads in northern Mississippi before joining Sherman at Meridian. Sherman's troops occupy Meridian, February 14–20, destroying railroads, storehouses, and an arsenal. On February 15 the Confederate Congress suspends writ of habeas corpus through August 1, 1864, including in cases of desertion and draft evasion, and on February 17 it requires all Confederate soldiers to serve for the duration of the war and makes all white males from seventeen to fifty eligible for conscription. Experimental Confederate submarine *H. L. Hunley* uses spar torpedo to sink the Union sloop *Housatonic* off Charleston on the night of February 17; the *Hunley* also sinks, with the loss of all seven crew members. The "Pomeroy Circular," confidential letter sent to influential Republicans by Senator Samuel C. Pomeroy criticizing Lincoln and supporting the nomination of Secretary of the Treasury Salmon P. Chase, is published in the Washington press on February 20. Union advance toward Lake City, Florida, is defeated at Olustee, February 20. Confederate cavalry led by General Nathan Bedford Forrest defeats William Sooy Smith's raiding force at Okolona, Mississippi, February 22. Davis appoints Braxton Bragg as his chief military advisor on February 24. General Judson Kilpatrick crosses Rapidan on February 28 with 3,500 men on cavalry raid aimed at freeing Union prisoners of war held in Richmond. Lincoln signs legislation reestablishing the rank of lieutenant general and nominates Grant for the position, February 29.

On March 1 Kilpatrick abandons attempt to enter Richmond and begins retreat toward Union lines. Senate confirms Grant's nomination on March 2. Embarrassed by the publication of the "Pomeroy Circular," Chase declares on

March 5 that he is not a candidate for president. The same day, the Richmond newspapers publish documents found during the Kilpatrick raid on the body of Union colonel Ulric Dahlgren outlining a plot to kill Jefferson Davis and burn Richmond. Grant arrives in Washington on March 8, and meets Lincoln for the first time that evening at a White House reception. He receives his commission the following day, and on March 10 is named general-in-chief of the armies of the United States.

Biographical Notes

Henry Livermore Abbott (January 21, 1842–May 6, 1864) Born in Lowell, Massachusetts, the son of a lawyer active in Democratic politics. Graduated from Harvard College in 1860 and began studying law in his father's office. Commissioned second lieutenant, 20th Massachusetts Volunteer Infantry Regiment, July 10, 1861. Formed close friendship with his fellow officer Oliver Wendell Holmes Jr. Fought at Ball's Bluff. Promoted to first lieutenant, November 1861. Fought at Fair Oaks and in the Seven Days' Battles, where he was wounded in the arm at Glendale. Older brother Edward killed at Cedar Mountain. Fought at Fredericksburg (December 1862 and May 1863) and Gettysburg; promoted to captain, December 1862, and major, October 1863. Became acting commander of the 20th Massachusetts after all of the regimental officers senior to him were killed or wounded at Gettysburg. Led the regiment at Briscoe Station and fought at Mine Run and at the battle of the Wilderness, where he was fatally wounded on May 6, 1864.

Charles Francis Adams (August 18, 1807–November 21, 1886) Born in Boston, Massachusetts, the son of John Quincy Adams and Louisa Johnson Adams and grandson of John and Abigail Adams. Graduated from Harvard in 1825. Admitted to the bar in 1829. Married Abigail Brown Brooks the same year. Served as a Whig in the Massachusetts house of representatives, 1841–43, and in the state senate, 1844–45. Vice-presidential candidate of the Free Soil Party in 1848. Edited *The Works of John Adams* (1850–56). Served in Congress as a Republican, 1859–61. As U.S. minister to Great Britain, 1861–68, helped maintain British neutrality in the Civil War. Served as the U.S. representative on the international arbitration tribunal that settled American claims against Great Britain for losses caused by Confederate commerce raiders built in British shipyards, 1871–72. Edited the *Memoirs of John Quincy Adams* (1874–77). Died in Boston.

Henry Adams (February 16, 1838–March 27, 1918) Born in Boston, Massachusetts. Brother of Charles Francis Adams Jr., son of lawyer Charles Francis Adams and Abigail Brooks Adams, grandson of John Quincy Adams, great-grandson of John Adams. Graduated Harvard 1858; studied law in Berlin and Dresden until 1860. Served as secretary to father while Charles Francis Adams served in Congress, 1860–61, and as U.S. minister to Great Britain, 1861–68. Reported British reaction to the American Civil War as anonymous London correspondent of *The New York Times*, 1861–62. Returned to Washington, D.C., in 1868 to work as journalist. Appointed assistant professor of history at Harvard (1870–77); assumed editorship of *North American Review* (1870–76). Married Marion Hooper in 1872. Published *The Life of Albert Gallatin* (1879), biography; *Democracy* (1880), a novel that appeared anonymously; *John Randolph* (1882), a biography; *Esther* (1884), a novel that appeared pseudonymously; *History of the United States during the Administrations of Thomas Jefferson and James Madison* (1889–91); *Mont-Saint-Michel and Chartres: A Study of Thirteenth-Century Unity* (1904); *The Education of Henry Adams* (1907). Died in Washington.

Lois Bryan Adams (October 14, 1817–June 28, 1870) Born in Whitestown, New York, the daughter of a carpenter. Family moved in 1823 to Michigan Territory and settled near Ypsilanti, then moved to the Constantine area in 1835. Attended White Pigeon Academy, branch of the University of Michigan, in 1839. Married James R. Adams, a newspaper editor, in 1841. Moved to Kentucky after her husband died of consumption in 1848, and taught school for three years before returning to Michigan in 1851. Began writing for the monthly (later weekly) *Michigan Farmer* and for the *Detroit Advertiser and Tribune*. Moved to Detroit in 1853 to work on the *Michigan Farmer*, and became its copublisher in 1854 and household editor in 1856. Sold her interest in the publication in 1861. Published *Sybelle and Other Poems* (1862). Moved to Washington, D.C., in 1863 to take post as clerk in the recently formed Department of Agriculture and became assistant to the director of the agricultural museum. Volunteered during the war for the Michigan Soldiers' Relief Association while contributing columns to the *Detroit Advertiser and Tribune*. Continued work at the Department of Agriculture after the war. Died in Washington, D.C.

John A. Andrew (May 31, 1818–October 30, 1867) Born in Windham, Maine, the son of a storekeeper and a former schoolteacher. Graduated from Bowdoin College in 1837. Studied law in Boston and began practice there after being admitted to the bar in 1840. An antislavery Whig, Andrew helped organize the Free Soil Party in Massachusetts in 1848. Married Eliza Jane Hersey in 1848. Elected as a Republican in 1857 to one-year term in the state house of representatives. Raised money for John Brown's legal defense after the Harpers Ferry raid in 1859. Elected governor of Massachusetts in 1860 and was reelected four times, serving from January 1861 to January 1866. Began strengthening state militia immediately after taking office in 1861, and became a strong supporter of the Union war effort and of emancipation. Urged enlistment of black soldiers, and organized the 54th and

55th Massachusetts Infantry in 1863, the first black infantry regiments raised by a northern state. Resumed law practice after retiring from office in 1866. Died in Boston.

George Richard Browder (January 11, 1827–September 3, 1886) Born in Logan County, Kentucky, the son of a slave-owning farmer. Attended Male Academy in Clarksville, Tennessee. Licensed as a Methodist preacher in 1846, ordained as a deacon in 1848 and as an elder in 1850. Married Ann Elizabeth Warfield in 1850. Received farm in Logan County as gift from his father in 1853. Preached on Logan circuit, 1861–63, and at Hadensville, 1863–65. Continued preaching after the war despite recurring illness. Appointed presiding elder of the Louisville Conference in 1876 and served until his death in Logan County.

Joshua Lawrence Chamberlain (September 8, 1828–February 24, 1914) Born in Brewer, Maine, the son of a farmer. Graduated from Bowdoin College in 1852 and from Bangor Theological Seminary, a Congregational institution, in 1855. Accepted professorship at Bowdoin, where he taught natural theology, logic, rhetoric, and modern languages. Married Frances (Fanny) Caroline Adams in 1855. Used two-year leave of absence, originally granted by the college to study languages in Europe, to obtain commission as lieutenant colonel in the newly formed 20th Maine Infantry in August 1862. Served in reserve at Antietam and saw action at Shepherdstown and Fredericksburg. Became colonel of the 20th Maine in late May 1863 and led the regiment at Gettysburg, where it helped defend Little Round Top on July 2. Promoted to command the Third Brigade, First Division, Fifth Corps in August 1863, but fell ill with malaria in November. Served on court-martial duty in early 1864 before rejoining the 20th Maine at Spotsylvania in May 1864. Led regiment at the North Anna River and Cold Harbor before becoming commander of the First Brigade, First Division, Fifth Corps. Seriously wounded by gunshot to the pelvis while leading brigade in assault at Petersburg on June 18, 1864. Promoted to brigadier general. Returned to brigade command in November 1864. Wounded in arm and chest at Quaker Road, March 29, 1865. Led brigade at White Oak Road, Five Forks, and in the Appomattox campaign. Received formal surrender of the Army of Northern Virginia on April 12, where he ordered his men to salute the defeated Confederates. Mustered out on January 15, 1866, and returned to professorship at Bowdoin. Served four one-year terms as governor of Maine, 1867–71. President of Bowdoin, 1871–83. Taught moral philosophy, 1874–79, and published *Maine, Her Place in History* (1877). Resigned as college president in 1883 from ill health due to war wounds. Wrote memoir of the final campaign in Virginia,

The Passing of the Armies (published posthumously in 1915). Died in Portland, Maine.

John Hampden Chamberlayne (June 2, 1838–February 18, 1882) Born in Richmond, Virginia, the son of a physician. Attended the University of Virginia, 1855–58, read law in Richmond, and was admitted to Virginia bar in 1860. Enlisted in the 21st Virginia Regiment and served in western Virginia, 1861–62. Became artillery sergeant in the Army of Northern Virginia, February 1862, and was promoted to lieutenant, June 1862. Served at Mechanicsville, Gaines's Mill, Glendale, Cedar Mountain, Second Manassas, Antietam, Fredericksburg, and Chancellorsville. Captured at Millerstown, Pennsylvania, on June 28, 1863. Exchanged in March 1864. Served in Overland campaign and the siege of Petersburg. Promoted to captain, August 1864. Evaded surrender at Appomattox Court House and joined Confederate forces in North Carolina before giving his parole at Atlanta, Georgia, on May 12, 1865. Became journalist at the *Petersburg Index* in 1869. Married Mary Walker Gibson in 1873. Edited the *Norfolk Virginian*, 1873–76. Founded *The State* newspaper in Richmond in 1876 and edited it until his death. Died in Richmond.

Mary Chesnut (March 31, 1823–November 22, 1886) Born Mary Boykin Miller in Statesburg, Sumter County, South Carolina, the daughter of Stephen Miller, a former congressman who later served as governor of South Carolina and in the U.S. Senate, and Mary Boykin Miller. Educated at a French boarding school in Charleston. Married James Chesnut Jr. in 1840 and lived on Mulberry, the Chesnut family plantation near Camden, South Carolina. Lived in Washington, D.C., while husband served in the Senate, 1859–60. Spent much of the Civil War in Richmond, Virginia, where her husband served as an advisor to Jefferson Davis, and formed close friendship with Varina Davis. Wrote three unfinished novels after the war, and extensively revised and expanded her wartime journal from 1881 to 1884. Died in Camden.

William Henry Harrison Clayton (June 1840–December 18, 1917) Born in Pittsburgh, Pennsylvania. Moved with family to Cincinnati, Ohio, in 1842 and to western Van Buren County, Iowa, where his father bought a farm in 1855. Enlisted in Company H, 19th Iowa Infantry, in August 1862, and was made the company clerk. Served in southern Missouri and northern Arkansas, September 1862–May 1863, and fought in the battle of Prairie Grove. Promoted to sergeant in April 1863. Sent with regiment to Vicksburg in mid-June and served in siege until Confederate surrender on July 4, 1863. Remained in Mississippi until late July, when the 19th Iowa was posted to

Louisiana. Captured along with two hundred men from his regiment at Sterling's Plantation near Morganza, Louisiana, on September 29, 1863. Held as prisoner of war at Shreveport, Louisiana, and Marshall and Tyler, Texas, before being exchanged in July 1864. Rejoined regiment and served at Fort Barrancas near Pensacola, Florida, August–December 1864, and at the entrance to Mobile Bay and in southeastern Mississippi, December 1864–March 1865. Saw action in the siege of Spanish Fort near Mobile, March 27–April 8, 1865. Remained at Mobile after Confederate surrender until July 1865, when his regiment was mustered out. Returned to Iowa, then moved in fall 1865 to Pittsburgh, where he worked as a bookkeeper. Married cousin Elizabeth Cooper in 1869; she died in 1876. Moved in 1879 to farm in Orange, California. Married cousin Ora Clayton in 1879. Gave up farming in 1887 to become public notary and sell insurance and real estate. Served as Orange city treasurer, 1888–92 and 1898–1904, and as city councilman, 1894–98. Died in Orange.

Patrick R. Cleburne (March 16, 1828–November 30, 1864) Born in Ovens, County Cork, Ireland, the son of a physician. Apprenticed in 1844 to a physician in Mallow. Applied to study medicine at Apothecaries' Hall in Dublin, but was rejected for failing to meet the Greek and Latin requirements. Enlisted as private in the 41st Regiment of Foot in 1846 and served on garrison duty in Ireland during the Great Famine. Promoted to corporal in 1849. Purchased discharge and emigrated to United States with his sister and two brothers; arrived in New Orleans on December 25, 1849. Settled in 1850 in Helena, Arkansas, where he managed and later co-owned a drugstore. Sold his share in the store in 1854 and read law. Admitted to bar in January 1856 and began successful legal practice. Became close friend of Democratic politician Thomas C. Hindman (later a Confederate general). Feud between Hindman and Know-Nothing leader Dorsey Rice resulted in gunfight in May 1856 in which Cleburne killed Rice's brother-in-law and was himself seriously wounded. Elected captain of Yell Rifles, a local militia company, in summer 1860 and colonel of the 1st Arkansas Infantry in May 1861. Appointed brigade commander in Army of Central Kentucky in October 1861. Promoted to brigadier general in March 1862. Led brigade at Shiloh, Richmond (Kentucky), and Perryville, and was shot in mouth at Richmond. Promoted to major general in December 1862. Commanded division at Stones River, Chickamauga, and Chattanooga. Proposed emancipating and arming slaves in address to generals of the Army of Tennessee, January 2, 1864. Led division in Atlanta campaign and in General John B. Hood's invasion of Tennessee. Killed in battle of Franklin.

Richard Cobden (June 3, 1804–April 2, 1865) Born in Heyshott, near Midhurst, West Sussex, England, the son of a farmer. Attended Bowes Hall School in Yorkshire before entering his uncle's calico trading firm in London in 1819. Formed his own trading partnership in 1828 and opened calico printing works in Sabden, Lancashire, in 1831. Moved to Manchester in 1832. Traveled to the United States, Europe, and the Middle East. Published pamphlets *England, Ireland, and America* (1835) and *Russia* (1836), criticizing military expenditures and advocating free trade. Helped form Anti-Corn-Law League to campaign for repeal of duties on imported grain. Began friendship and political collaboration with orator John Bright. Married Catherine Anne Williams in 1840. Elected to Parliament in 1841. Following the repeal of the Corn Laws in 1846, traveled to France, Spain, Italy, and Russia. Campaigned for free trade, international arbitration, and the reduction of armaments. Opposed the Crimean War and criticized British policy in China. Lost parliamentary seat in 1857 but was elected by another constituency in 1859. Helped negotiate commercial treaty with France in 1860, and organized international peace conferences. Publicly supported the Union and opposed British intervention in the Civil War. Died in London.

James A. Connolly (March 8, 1838–December 15, 1914) Born in Newark, New Jersey, the son of a tanner. Moved with family around 1850 to Chesterville, Ohio. Graduated from Selby Academy in Chesterville and studied law. Admitted to the bar in 1859 and served as assistant clerk of the Ohio state senate, 1859–60. Moved to Charleston, Illinois, in 1860. Mustered into service as major of the newly-formed 123rd Illinois Infantry in September 1862. Fought at Perryville. Married Mary Dunn, sister of the judge with whom he had read law, in February 1863. Fought at Milton (Vaught's Hill) and Chickamauga. Joined staff of the Third Division, Fourteenth Corps, commanded by Brigadier General Absalom Baird. Served at Chattanooga, in the Atlanta campaign, and in Sherman's marches through Georgia and the Carolinas. Helped escort Abraham Lincoln's body to Springfield. Returned to law practice in Charleston before moving to Springfield in 1886. Served in Illinois state house of representatives, 1872–76, as U.S. attorney for the Southern District of Illinois, 1876–85 and 1889–94, and as a Republican congressman, 1895–99. Died in Springfield.

Richard Cordley (September 6, 1829–July 11, 1904) Born in Nottingham, England. Family moved to farm in Livingston County, Michigan Territory, in 1833. Attended Ann Arbor Classical School. Graduated from the University of Michigan in 1854 and Andover Theological Seminary in 1857. Recruited by American Home Missionary Society to settle in Kansas. Became minister of Plymouth Congregational Church in Lawrence in December 1857. Founded quarterly (later monthly) publication *Congregational Record* and married Mary Ann Minta Cox in 1859. Established Sunday and night schools to educate runaway slaves, helped other fugitives flee to Canada, and founded the Second Congregational Church ("Freedman's Church") for freed slaves in 1862. Escaped injury during William Quantrill's raid on Lawrence on August 21, 1863, although his house and office were destroyed. Helped found the University of Kansas in 1866. Resigned position at Plymouth Congregational in 1875. Served as pastor in Flint, Michigan, 1875–78, and Emporia, Kansas, 1878–84. Returned to Lawrence and served as pastor of Plymouth Congregational from 1884 until his death. Published *A History of Lawrence, Kansas* (1895) and *Pioneer Days in Kansas* (1903). Died in Lawrence.

Kate Cumming (December 1826–June 5, 1909). Born Catherine Cumming in Edinburgh, Scotland. Moved with family to Montreal and then to Mobile, Alabama, arriving there by 1845. Volunteered after the battle of Shiloh in April 1862 to help nurse Confederate soldiers in northern Mississippi. Returned to Mobile after two months, then began serving in September 1862 as hospital matron in Chattanooga, where she was officially enrolled as a member of the Confederate army medical department. Following the evacuation of Chattanooga in the summer of 1863, served at several field hospitals in Georgia and Alabama. Returned to Mobile after the war. Published *A Journal of Hospital Life in the Confederate Army of Tennessee* (1866). Moved with father in 1874 to Birmingham, Alabama, where she taught school and gave music lessons. Published *Gleanings from Southland* (1895). Died in Birmingham.

William Parker Cutler (July 12, 1812–April 11, 1889) Born in Warren Township, Washington County, Ohio, the son of a farmer active in local and state politics. Attended Ohio University at Athens, then returned to work on family farm. Elected to Ohio house of representatives as a Whig, 1844–47, and served as speaker, 1846–47. Married Elizabeth P. Voris in 1849. Trustee of Marietta College, 1849–89, and was a delegate to the state constitutional convention in 1850. President of Marietta & Cincinnati Railroad, 1850–54 and 1858–60. Served in U.S. Congress as a Republican, 1861–63; defeated for reelection. President of Marietta & Pittsburgh Railroad, 1868–72, and served as contractor on railroad construction projects in Indiana and Illinois, 1869–73. Died in Marietta, Ohio.

Maria Lydig Daly (September 12, 1824–August 21, 1894) Born Maria Lydig in New York City, the daughter of a wealthy grain merchant and landowner. Married Judge Charles P. Daly of the New York Court of Common Pleas, the son of poor Irish immigrants, in 1856 despite opposition from many members of her family who objected to his Catholicism and family background. Supported the Woman's Central Association of Relief during the Civil War and visited sick and wounded soldiers. Died at her country home in North Haven, New York.

Jefferson Davis (June 3, 1808–December 6, 1889) Born in Christian (now Todd) County, Kentucky, the son of a farmer. Moved with his family to Mississippi. Graduated from West Point in 1828 and served in the Black Hawk War. Resigned his commission in 1835 and married Sarah Knox Taylor, who died later in the year. Became a cotton planter in Warren County, Mississippi. Married Varina Howell in 1845. Elected to Congress as a Democrat and served 1845–46, then resigned to command a Mississippi volunteer regiment in Mexico, 1846–47, where he fought at Monterrey and was wounded at Buena Vista. Elected to the Senate and served from 1847 to 1851, when he resigned to run unsuccessfully for governor. Secretary of war in the cabinet of Franklin Pierce, 1853–57. Elected to the Senate and served from 1857 to January 21, 1861, when he withdrew following the secession of Mississippi. Inaugurated as provisional president of the Confederate States of America on February 18, 1861. Elected without opposition to six-year term in November 1861 and inaugurated on February 22, 1862. Captured by Union cavalry near Irwinville, Georgia, on May 10, 1865. Imprisoned at Fort Monroe, Virginia, and indicted for treason. Released on bail on May 13, 1867; the indictment was dropped in 1869 without trial. Published *The Rise and Fall of the Confederate Government* in 1881. Died in New Orleans.

Theodore A. Dodge (May 28, 1842–October 25, 1909) Born in Pittsfield, Massachusetts, the son of a manufacturer. Educated at Berlin, Heidelberg, and University College, London. Commissioned first lieutenant in Company G, 101st New York Infantry, in February 1862. Led company in the Seven Days' Battles at Oak Grove, Glendale, and Malvern Hill. Became regimental adjutant during the summer of 1862. Fought at Second Bull Run and was wounded in leg at Chantilly. Resigned from 101st New York and became adjutant of the 119th New York Infantry in November 1862. Fought at Chancellorsville. Wounded in ankle at Gettysburg on July 1 and had right leg amputated below the knee five days later. Commissioned as captain in the Veteran Reserve Corps in November 1863. Served in the enrollment and desertion branches of the Provost Marshal General's office in Washington, D.C. Married Jane Marshall Neil in 1865. Attended Columbia Law School and was admitted to the District of Columbia bar in 1866. Commissioned as captain in the regular army and served as superintendent of military buildings in Washington, 1866–70.

Moved to Cambridge, Massachusetts, and became successful manufacturer of tires and other rubber products. Published *The Campaign of Chancellorsville* (1881), *A Bird's-eye View of Our Civil War* (1883), *Patroclus and Penelope* (1886), *Great Captains* (1889), *Alexander* (1890), *Hannibal* (1891), *Caesar* (1892), *Riders of Many Lands* (1894), *Gustavus Adolphus* (1895), *Army and Other Tales* (1899), and *Napoleon* (1904–7). Following the death of his wife, married Clara Isabel Bowden in 1892. Moved to Paris in 1900. Died in Nanteuil-le-Hadouin, Oise, France.

Francis Adams Donaldson (June 7, 1840–May 3, 1928). Born in Philadelphia, where he was raised by his aunt after the death of his parents. Worked as clerk in a shipping company. Enlisted in June 1861 in the 1st California Regiment (later the 71st Pennsylvania Infantry) and became a sergeant in Company H. Captured at Ball's Bluff and was a prisoner in Richmond until his exchange in February 1862. Returned to his regiment and was promoted to second lieutenant. Served in Peninsula campaign and was wounded in the arm at Fair Oaks on May 31, 1862. Commissioned as captain of Company M, 118th Pennsylvania Infantry, in August 1862. Served at Antietam, Shepherdstown, Fredericksburg, Chancellorsville, Gettysburg, and in the Bristoe and Mine Run campaigns. Feuded with his commanding officer, Lieutenant Colonel James Gwyn, who refused to give Donaldson permission to resign from the regiment. In December 1863 Donaldson publicly insulted and threatened Gwyn, resulting in Donaldson's court-martial and dismissal from the army. (Sentence was changed in March 1864 to dismissal without "disability" after Donaldson made a personal appeal to President Lincoln.) Returned to Philadelphia and entered the insurance business. Founded his own company in 1866 and remained at its head until 1917. Married Mary Heyburger Landell in 1872. Died in Philadelphia.

Frederick Douglass (February 1818–February 20, 1895) Born Frederick Bailey in Talbot County, Maryland, the son of a slave mother and an unknown white man. Worked on farms and in Baltimore shipyards. Escaped to Philadelphia in 1838. Married Anna Murray, a free woman from Maryland, and settled in New Bedford, Massachusetts, where he took the name Douglass. Became a lecturer for the American Anti-Slavery Society, led by William Lloyd Garrison, in 1841. Published *Narrative of the Life of Frederick Douglass, An American Slave* (1845). Began publishing *North Star*, first in a series of antislavery newspapers, in Rochester, New York, in 1847. Broke with Garrison and became an ally of Gerrit Smith, who advocated an antislavery interpretation of the Constitution and participation in electoral politics. Published *My Bondage and My Freedom* (1855).

Advocated emancipation and the enlistment of black soldiers at the outbreak of the Civil War. Met with Abraham Lincoln in Washington in August 1863 and August 1864, and wrote public letter supporting his reelection in September 1864. Continued his advocacy of racial equality and women's rights after the Civil War. Served as U.S. marshal for the District of Columbia, 1877–81, and as its recorder of deeds, 1881–86. Published *Life and Times of Frederick Douglass* (1881). After the death of his wife Anna, married Helen Pitts in 1884. Served as minister to Haiti, 1889–91. Died in Washington, D.C.

Lewis Douglass (October 9, 1840–September 19, 1908) Born in New Bedford, Massachusetts, oldest son of abolitionist Frederick Douglass and Anna Murray Douglass. Moved with family in 1848 to Rochester, New York, where he attended public schools and later worked as a printer for *Frederick Douglass' Paper* and *Douglass' Monthly*. Along with his brother Charles, enlisted in the 54th Massachusetts Infantry in March 1863. Promoted to sergeant major in April. Fought at Fort Wagner. Given medical discharge on May 10, 1864, after months of illness. Moved to Denver, Colorado, with brother Frederick in 1866 and worked as secretary for a mining company. Returned east in 1869 to work in the Government Printing Office in Washington, D.C. Married Amelia Loguen in 1869. Assisted father in editing and publishing weekly Washington newspaper *The New National Era*, 1870–74. Served on legislative council for the District of Columbia, 1872–73, and as assistant U.S. marshal for the District, 1877–81. Began successful real estate business. Died in Washington.

Catherine Edmondston (October 10, 1823–January 3, 1875) Born Catherine Ann Devereux in Halifax County, North Carolina, the daughter of a plantation owner. Married Patrick Edmondston in 1846. Lived on Looking Glass, plantation in Halifax County. Published pamphlet *The Morte d'Arthur: Its Influence on the Spirit and Manners of the Nineteenth Century* (1872), in which she accused the Union army of barbarism. Died in Raleigh.

Wilbur Fisk (June 7, 1839–March 12, 1914). Born in Sharon, Vermont, the son of a farmer. Family moved to Lowell, Massachusetts, in 1852 to work in woolen mills, then returned to Vermont in 1854 and settled on farm in Tunbridge. Worked as hired farm laborer and taught in local schools. Enlisted in September 1861 in Company E, 2nd Vermont Infantry. Contributed regular letters under the name "Anti-Rebel" to *The Green Mountain Freeman* of Montpelier from December 11, 1861, to July 26, 1865. Saw action in the siege of Yorktown and in the Seven Days' Battles. Hospitalized with severe diarrhea in Washington, D.C., in early September 1862. Recovered in convalescent camp in Fairfax, Virginia, then went absent without leave and married Angelina Drew of Lawrence, Massachusetts, in February 1863. Returned to regiment in March 1863 and served at Chancellorsville, Gettysburg, Rappahannock Station, Mine Run, the Wilderness, Spotsylvania, North Anna, Cold Harbor, and Petersburg. Sent with regiment in July 1864 to help defend the capital against Jubal Early's Washington raid. Served in the Shenandoah Valley at Winchester, Fisher's Hill, and Cedar Creek before returning to Petersburg siege lines in December 1864. Detached for guard duty at Sixth Corps hospital at City Point, Virginia, in January 1865, and served there for remainder of the war. Rejoined family, who had moved to Geneva, Kansas, and worked on farm. Licensed as Congregational preacher in 1874, and the following year became pastor of a church in Freeborn, Minnesota, where he served until his retirement in 1909. Following the death of his first wife in 1898, married Amanda Dickerson Dickey in 1909. Died in Geneva, Kansas.

Samuel W. Fiske (July 23, 1828–May 22, 1864) Born in Shelburne, Massachusetts. Graduated from Amherst College in 1848. Taught school, studied for three years at the Andover Theological Seminary, then returned to Amherst in 1853 as a tutor. Traveled in Europe and the Middle East. Published *Dunn Browne's Experiences in Foreign Parts* (1857), travel letters written to the *Springfield Republican* under a nom de plume. Became pastor of the Congregational church in Madison, Connecticut, in 1857. Married Elizabeth Foster in 1858. Became second lieutenant in the 14th Connecticut Infantry in August 1862. Signing himself Dunn Browne, wrote weekly letters to the *Springfield Republican* describing campaigns and camp life (collected in 1866 under the title *Mr. Dunn Browne's Experiences in the Army*). Served at Antietam and Fredericksburg. Promoted to captain in early 1863. Captured at Chancellorsville on May 3, 1863, he was paroled in late May and exchanged in June. Served at Gettysburg. Wounded in the battle of the Wilderness on May 6, 1864, and died in Fredericksburg, Virginia.

Charlotte Forten (August 17, 1837–July 22, 1914) Born in Philadelphia, the daughter of Robert Bridges Forten, a sail maker, and Mary Virginia Woods Forten; both parents were members of prominent black Philadelphia families and active abolitionists. Mother died in 1840. Moved to Salem, Massachusetts, in 1853 and lived with family of black abolitionist Charles Lenox Remond while attending Higginson Grammar School and Salem Normal School. Graduated in 1856. Taught school in Salem and Philadelphia and tutored her cousins in Byberry, Pennsylvania, 1856–62, while suffering several bouts of illness. Published poems and essays in *The Liberator*, *Christian Recorder*, and *National Anti-Slavery Standard*. Moved to St. Helena Island, South Carolina, in October 1862 to teach freed slaves, becoming one of the first black schoolteachers in the Sea Islands. Helped nurse wounded soldiers of the 54th Massachusetts after the battle of Fort Wagner in July 1863. Returned to Philadelphia in May 1864. Published essay "Life on the Sea Islands" in the *Atlantic Monthly*, May–June 1864. Moved to Boston in 1865 to work as secretary at the New England Freedmen's Union Commission, an organization that supplied financial and material support to teachers of freed slaves. Published translation of French novel *Madame Thérèse; or, The Volunteers of '92* by Emile Erckman and Alexandre Chatrain in 1869. Taught school in Charleston, South Carolina, 1871–72, and Washington, D.C., 1872–73. Worked as clerk in U.S. Treasury Department, 1873–78. Married the Reverend Francis Grimké, nephew of abolitionists Sarah and Angelina Grimké, in 1878. Lived in Jacksonville, Florida, 1885–89, where her husband pastored the Laura Street Presbyterian Church. Returned to Washington, D.C., in 1889 when Francis Grimké became the pastor of the Fifteenth Street Presbyterian Church. Continued to publish essays and poems. Became a founding member of the National Association of Colored Women in 1896. Died in Washington.

Arthur James Lyon Fremantle (November 11, 1835–September 25, 1901). The son of a major general in the British army, Fremantle graduated from the Royal Military College at Sandhurst and entered the army in 1852. Commissioned in Coldstream Guards in 1853. Promoted to captain in the Coldstream and lieutenant colonel in the army in 1860. Posted the same year to Gibraltar, where he met Confederate naval commander Raphael Semmes in 1862. Became increasingly sympathetic to the Confederate cause and obtained six months' leave to go to North America. Entered Texas from Mexico in April 1863 and traveled through the Confederacy, meeting Sam Houston, Joseph E. Johnston, Braxton Bragg, Pierre G. T. Beauregard, Jefferson Davis, Robert E. Lee, and James Longstreet. Witnessed the battle of Gettysburg, then crossed the lines in western Maryland and sailed from New York in July 1863. Published *Three Months in the Southern States, April–June 1863* in late 1863. Married Mary Hall in 1864. Commanded a battalion in the Coldstream Guards, 1877–80, and served as aide-de-camp to the Duke of Cambridge, commander-in-chief of the army, 1881–82. Promoted to major general in 1882. Served in Sir Garnet Wolseley's expeditionary force in the Sudan as governor of Suakin, 1884–85, commander of the Brigade of Guards, and chief of staff before returning to England in 1886. Served as governor of Malta, 1894–99. Died at Cowes on the Isle of Wight.

Benjamin B. French (September 4, 1800–August 12, 1870) Born in Chester, New Hampshire, the son of a lawyer who later served as the state attorney general. Admitted to the bar in 1825, the same year he married Elizabeth S. Richardson. Served in New Hampshire house of representatives, 1831–33. Assistant clerk of the U.S. House of Representatives, 1833–45; clerk of the House, 1845–47. President of the Magnetic Telegraphic Company, 1847–50. Commissioner of public buildings in Washington, 1853–55. Left Democratic Party and became a Republican. Appointed commissioner of public buildings in 1861. After the death of his wife in 1861, married Mary Ellen Brady, 1862. Oversaw completion of the U.S. Capitol and helped organize Lincoln's funeral. Worked as clerk in the Treasury Department after position of commissioner of public buildings was abolished in 1867 by Radical Republicans angered by his support of President Andrew Johnson. Died in Washington, D.C.

Isaac Funk (November 17, 1797–January 29, 1865) Born in Clark County, Kentucky, the son of a farmer. Family moved to farm in Fayette County, Ohio, in 1807. Attended school for parts of three winters before age thirteen. Spent year working in the Kanawha salt works in western Virginia before returning to Ohio in 1821. Began trading in cattle and hogs with his father and brother Absalom. Moved with Absalom in 1824 to McLean County, Illinois, and settled on farm in area later known as Funk's Grove. Married Cassandra Sharp in 1826. Expanded livestock business, eventually owning 25,000 acres of land on which he raised cattle and hogs for sale in Chicago and other markets. Served as a Whig in the Illinois house of representatives, 1840–42. Helped found Illinois Wesleyan University in 1850. A friend and supporter of Abraham Lincoln, Funk was a delegate to the 1860 Republican convention in Chicago and campaigned for Lincoln in the fall. Served as a Republican in the Illinois state senate from 1862 until his death in Bloomington, Illinois.

James Henry Gooding (August 28, 1838–July 19, 1864). Born into slavery in North Carolina, Gooding had his freedom purchased by James M. Gooding, possibly his father, and was brought to New York City. Enrolled in September 1846 in the New York Colored Orphan Asylum, where he was educated. Indentured in 1850, possibly to a dentist, but left position in 1852. Signed on to whaling ship *Sunbeam* in New Bedford, Massachusetts, claiming to be a freeborn man from Troy, New York, and sailed in July 1856. Worked in galley as ship hunted sperm whales in the Indian and Pacific oceans before returning to New Bedford in April 1860. Made second whaling voyage as steward on *Black Eagle*, May 1860–November 1861, hunting right whales off western Greenland. Sailed for Montevideo as cook and steward on merchant ship *Richard Mitchell* in January 1862. Returned to New Bedford in late summer and married Ellen Louisa Allen in September 1862. Wrote six poems during his voyages that were printed in broadside form. Enlisted in the 54th Massachusetts Infantry on February 14, 1863, and became a private in Company C. Wrote forty-eight letters from the 54th Massachusetts that were printed in the New Bedford *Mercury*, March 1863–February 1864, signed "J.H.G." and "Monitor." Fought at Fort Wagner. Wrote letter to President Lincoln in September 1863 protesting unequal pay for black soldiers. Promoted to corporal in December 1863. Wounded in leg and taken prisoner at battle of Olustee, February 20, 1864. Died in prison camp at Andersonville, Georgia.

Ulysses S. Grant (April 22, 1822–July 23, 1885) Born in Point Pleasant, Ohio, the son of a tanner. Graduated from West Point in 1843. Served in the U.S.-Mexican War, 1846–48, and promoted to first lieutenant in 1847. Married Julia Dent in 1848. Promoted to captain, 1854, and resigned commission. Worked as a farmer, real estate agent, and general store clerk, 1854–61. Commissioned colonel, 21st Illinois Volunteers, June 1861, and brigadier general of volunteers, August 1861. Promoted to major general of volunteers, February 1862, after victories at Forts Henry and Donelson. Defeated Confederates at Shiloh, April 1862, and captured Vicksburg, Mississippi, July 1863. Promoted to major general in the regular army, July 1863, and assigned to command of Military Division of the Mississippi, covering territory between the Alleghenies and the Mississippi, October 1863. Won battle of Chattanooga, November 1863. Promoted to lieutenant general, March 1864, and named general-in-chief of the Union armies. Accepted surrender of Robert E. Lee at Appomattox Court House, April 9, 1865. Promoted to general, July 1866. Served as secretary of war ad interim, August 1867–January 1868. Nominated for president by the Republican Party in 1868. Defeated Democrat Horatio Seymour, and won reelection in 1872 by defeating Liberal Republican Horace Greeley. President of the United States, 1869–77. Made world tour, 1877–79. Failed to win Republican presidential nomination, 1880. Worked on Wall Street, 1881–84, and was financially ruined when private banking firm of Grant & Ward collapsed. Wrote *Personal Memoirs of U.S. Grant*, 1884–85, while suffering from throat cancer, and completed them days before his death at Mount McGregor, New York.

Edward O. Guerrant (February 28, 1838–April 26, 1916). Born in Sharpsburg, Kentucky, the son of a physician. Graduated from Centre College in Danville, Kentucky, in 1860. Briefly attended Danville Seminary and taught school in Flat Creek. Enlisted as private in the Confederate 1st Battalion Kentucky Mounted Rifles at Gladesville,

Virginia, in February 1862. Became clerk on staff of Brigadier General Humphrey Marshall, the Confederate commander in southwestern Virginia, and was commissioned as his assistant adjutant general in December 1862. Continued his staff duties under Marshall's successors William Preston, John S. Williams, and John Hunt Morgan, serving in southwestern Virginia, eastern Kentucky, and northeastern Tennessee and seeing action in several engagements. Surrendered in eastern Kentucky in late April 1865. Studied medicine at Jefferson Medical College, Philadelphia, and Bellevue Hospital, New York. Established medical practice in Mount Sterling, Kentucky, in 1867. Married Mary Jane DeVault in 1868. Entered Union Theological Seminary at Hampden-Sydney College in Virginia in 1873 and was licensed as a Presbyterian preacher in 1875. Served as minister of the First Presbyterian Church in Louisville, 1879–82. Appointed by the Kentucky Synod in 1882 as evangelist to eastern Kentucky. Became minister of churches in Troy and Wilmore in 1885. Contributed two articles to the *Century Magazine* "Battles and Leaders of the Civil War" series. Helped establish several schools in eastern Kentucky. Published *Bloody Breathitt* (1890), *The Soul Winner* (1896), *Forty Years Among the Highlanders* (1905), *The Galax Gatherers: The Gospel among the Highlanders* (1910), and *The Gospel of the Lilies* (1912). Founded the Inland Mission, also known as the Society of Soul Winners, in 1897 to continue evangelical work in Appalachia. Died in Douglas, Georgia.

Henry W. Halleck (January 16, 1814–January 9, 1872) Born in Westernville, New York, the son of a farmer. Educated at Union College. Graduated from West Point in 1839. Published *Elements of Military Art and Science* (1846). Served in California during the U.S.-Mexican War. Resigned from the army in 1854 as captain. Married Elizabeth Hamilton, granddaughter of Alexander Hamilton, in 1855. Practiced law in California. Published *International Law, or, Rules Regulating the Intercourse of States in Peace and War* (1861). Commissioned as a major general in the regular army in August 1861. Commanded the Department of the Missouri, November 1861–March 1862, and the Department of the Mississippi, March–July 1862. General-in-chief of the Union army from July 11, 1862, to March 12, 1864, when he was succeeded by Ulysses S. Grant. Served as chief of staff for the remainder of the war. Commanded Military Division of the Pacific, 1866–69, and the division of the South, 1869–72. Died in Louisville, Kentucky.

Cornelia Hancock (February 8, 1840–December 31, 1927) Born in Hancock's Bridge, near Salem, New Jersey, the daughter of a Quaker fisherman. Educated in Salem schools. Brother and several cousins enlisted in Union army in 1862. Traveled to Gettysburg with her brother-in-law Dr. Henry T. Child in July 1863 and served as volunteer nurse in Second Corps and general army hospitals until September. Volunteered as nurse at the Contraband Hospital for escaped slaves in Washington, D.C., October 1863–February 1864, and at army hospitals in Virginia at Brandy Station, February–April 1864; Fredericksburg and White House, May–June 1864; and City Point, June 1864–May 1865. Founded the Laing School for freed slaves in Pleasantville, South Carolina, in 1866 with funds from the Freedmen's Bureau and donations from the Philadelphia Yearly Meeting of the Society of Friends. Resigned as principal in 1875 and returned to Philadelphia. Visited England and studied efforts to help the poor in London. Helped found the Philadelphia Society for Organizing Charitable Relief in 1878 and the Children's Aid Society of Philadelphia in 1882. Engaged in philanthropic work in the Sixth Ward and in "Wrightsville," a slum neighborhood in South Philadelphia. Retired in 1914 to Atlantic City, New Jersey, where she died.

John Hay (October 8, 1838–July 1, 1905) Born in Salem, Indiana, the son of a doctor. Family moved to Warsaw, Illinois. Graduated from Brown University in 1858. Studied law in office of his uncle in Springfield, Illinois. Traveled to Washington in 1861 as assistant private secretary to Abraham Lincoln, serving until early in 1865. First secretary to American legation in Paris, 1865–67; chargé d'affaires in Vienna, 1867–68; and legation secretary in Madrid, 1868–70. Published *Castilian Days* (1871) and *Pike County Ballads and Other Pieces* (1871). Married Clara Louise Stone in 1874. Served as assistant secretary of state, 1879–81. Political novel *The Bread-Winners*, an attack on labor unions, published anonymously in 1884. In collaboration with John G. Nicolay, wrote *Abraham Lincoln: A History* (10 volumes, 1890) and edited *Complete Works of Abraham Lincoln* (2 volumes, 1894). Ambassador to Great Britain, 1897–98. Served as secretary of state in the administrations of William McKinley and Theodore Roosevelt, 1898–1905. Among first seven members elected to American Academy of Arts and Letters in 1904. Died in Newbury, New Hampshire.

Charles B. Haydon (1834–March 14, 1864) Born in Vermont. Raised in Decatur, Michigan. Graduated from the University of Michigan in 1857, then read law in Kalamazoo. Joined the Kalamazoo Home Guard on April 22, 1861, then enlisted on May 25 for three years' service in the 2nd Michigan Infantry. Fought at Blackburn's Ford during the First Bull Run campaign. Commissioned second lieutenant in September 1861 and promoted to first lieutenant in February 1862. Fought at Williamsburg, Fair Oaks, the Seven Days' Battles, Second Bull Run, and Fredericksburg; promoted to captain in September 1862. Regiment was sent to Kentucky in April 1863 and to Vicksburg in June as part of the Ninth Corps. Wounded in the shoulder while leading his company at Jackson, Mississippi, on July 11, 1863. Returned to active duty in December 1863 and was made lieutenant colonel of the 2nd Michigan. Died of pneumonia in Cincinnati while returning to Michigan on a thirty-day furlough after reenlisting.

William W. Heartsill (October 17, 1839–July 27, 1916) Born in Louisville, Tennessee. Educated at local schools. Began working in a wholesale merchandise firm in Nashville in 1856. Moved to Marshall, Texas, in 1859, where he became a clerk in a dry goods store. Enlisted in W. P. Lane Rangers, a cavalry company, in April 1861. Helped guard Texas frontier against Indian raids until November 1862, when his company was sent to Arkansas. Taken prisoner in the surrender of Fort Hindman at Arkansas Post, January 1863. Exchanged at City Point, Virginia, in April 1863 and sent to central Tennessee, where the enlisted men from the Lane Rangers became part of a consolidated Texas infantry regiment. Fought at Chickamauga and served in siege of Chattanooga. Deserted in early November 1863 along with several other Lane Rangers and returned to Texas, where he resumed service under his former commander in the Rangers. Served as guard at prisoner-of-war camp at Tyler, Texas, in spring 1864. Posted to Louisiana and Arkansas in summer 1864 before returning to Texas, where he served until the Confederate surrender there in May 1865. Returned to Marshall and acquired a grocery and saddle store. Married Judith Elizabeth Stevens. Printed memoir *Fourteen Hundred and 91 Days in the Confederate Army* one page at a time on his personally owned press, 1874–76. Elected mayor, 1876, and member of the board of aldermen, 1881. Died in Waco, Texas.

Francis J. Higginson (July 19, 1843–September 13, 1931) Born in Boston and raised in Deerfield, Massachusetts. Graduated from U.S. Naval Academy in 1861. Assigned to frigate *Colorado* and was wounded during raid in September 1861 that burned schooner *Judah* in Pensacola harbor. Served on gunboat *Cayuga* in passage of Forts Jackson and St. Philip and the capture of New Orleans. Promoted to lieutenant in August 1862. Assigned to South Atlantic Blockading Squadron and served on gunboat *Vixen*, frigate *Powhatan*, and the sloop *Housatonic*. Participated in bombardment of Charleston Harbor and served in the landing party that unsuccessfully attempted to capture Fort Sumter in September 1863. Executive officer of the *Housatonic* when it was sunk by Confederate submarine *H. L. Hunley*, February 17, 1864. Promoted to lieutenant commander, 1866, and commander, 1876. Married Grace Glenwood Haldane in 1878. Promoted to captain in 1891. Commanded battleship *Massachusetts* in Spanish-American War, 1898, taking part in naval blockade of Cuba and invasion of Puerto Rico. Promoted to commodore, 1898, and rear admiral, 1899. Commanded North Atlantic Fleet, 1901–3. Published *Naval Battles of the Century* (1903). Retired from navy in 1905. Died in Kingston, New York.

Thomas Wentworth Higginson (December 22, 1823–May 9, 1911) Born in Cambridge, Massachusetts, the son of the bursar of Harvard College. Graduated from Harvard in 1841. Taught school and tutored in Boston suburbs before entering Harvard Divinity School. Graduated in 1847 and was ordained by the Unitarian First Religious Society in Newburyport, Massachusetts. Married Mary Elizabeth Channing in 1847. Became active in abolitionism, temperance, women's rights, and other reform movements. Resigned pulpit in 1849. Lectured and wrote for newspapers before becoming minister of nondenominational Free Church in Worcester, Massachusetts, in 1852. Helped lead unsuccessful attempt to free fugitive slave Anthony Burns from the Boston courthouse in 1854 in which a guard was killed. Traveled to Kansas in 1856 with group of antislavery settlers he had helped recruit and outfit. Began contributing essays and stories to the *Atlantic Monthly*. Became member of the "Secret Six," group of radical abolitionists who financed and supported John Brown's raid on Harpers Ferry, 1858–59. Began correspondence with Emily Dickinson in 1862. Joined 51st Massachusetts Infantry as captain in September 1862. Accepted colonelcy of 1st South Carolina Volunteers, regiment of freed slaves raised in the Sea Islands, in November 1862. Led series of expeditions that gathered supplies and freed slaves in coastal Georgia, Florida, and South Carolina from January until July 1863, when he was wounded. Fell ill with malaria in October 1863. Wrote letters to newspapers calling for equal pay for black soldiers. Left South Carolina in May 1864 and moved to Newport, Rhode Island. Resigned commission in October 1864. Continued writing for magazines and became advocate for woman suffrage. Published novel *Malbone: An Oldport Romance* (1869), memoir *Army Life in a Black Regiment* (1870), and *Young Folks' History of the United States* (1875). Wife died in 1877. Moved to Cambridge, Massachusetts, in 1878. Married Mary (Minnie) Potter Thatcher, 1879. Served as Republican in the Massachusetts house of representatives, 1879–83. Edited *Poems* (1890) of Emily Dickinson with Mabel Loomis Todd. Published memoirs *Cheerful Yesterdays* (1898) and *Parts of a Man's Life* (1905). Died in Cambridge.

Emma Holmes (December 17, 1838–January 1910) Born in Charleston, South Carolina, the daughter of a physician and plantation owner. Family moved to Camden, South Carolina, in June 1862, where she began teaching. Returned after the war to Charleston, where she continued to teach and tutor. Died in Charleston.

Jedediah Hotchkiss (November 30, 1828–January 17, 1899). Born near Windsor, New York, the son of a farmer. Graduated from Windsor Academy in 1846. Taught school for a year in Lykens Valley, Pennsylvania, then became tutor to family living on Mossy Creek in the Shenandoah Valley of Virginia. Taught himself mapmaking. Became principal of the newly established Mossy Creek Academy in 1852. Married Sara Ann Comfort in 1853. Moved in 1859 to Churchville, Virginia, where he opened the Loch Willow Academy. Closed the academy in June 1861 and offered services to Confederate army. Served as mapmaker for Confederate forces in western Virginia until August 1861, when he contracted typhoid fever. Resumed military service in March 1862 and became topographical engineer on the staff of Thomas J. (Stonewall) Jackson. Performed reconnaissances and made detailed maps during Jackson's Shenandoah Valley campaign in the spring of 1862. Remained in the valley until July 1862, then rejoined Jackson's staff and served in the Second Manassas and Maryland campaigns and at Fredericksburg and Chancellorsville. Following Jackson's death, continued mapmaking and reconnaissance duties under Richard S. Ewell during Gettysburg campaign. Served under Jubal Early in his raid on Washington and in the subsequent campaign in the Shenandoah Valley. Performed reconnaissance duties in western Virginia in the spring of 1865. Kept a school in Staunton, Virginia, 1865–67. Published *The Battlefields of Virginia; Chancellorsville* with William Allan (1867). Continued to work as topographer, and became promoter and investor in mining and land development projects in western Virginia and West Virginia. Published *Virginia: A Geographical and Political Summary* (1876) and, with Joseph A. Waddell, *Historical Atlas of Augusta County* (1885). Contributed maps to the *Atlas of the War of the Rebellion* (1880–1901). Wrote *Virginia*, third volume in twelve-volume series *Confederate Military History* (1899). Died in Staunton, Virginia.

David Hunter (July 21, 1802–February 2, 1886) Born in Princeton, New Jersey, the son of a Presbyterian minister. Graduated from West Point in 1822. Married Maria Indiana Kinzie, 1829. Resigned commission in July 1836, but reentered the army in November 1841 as paymaster. Commissioned as brigadier general of volunteers, May 1861, and promoted to major general, August 1861. Led brigade at First Bull Run, where he was wounded. Commanded Department of Kansas, November 1861–March 1862, and Department of the South, March–September 1862 and January–June 1863. Declared military emancipation of slaves in Department of the South, May 9, 1862; his order was revoked by President Lincoln on May 19. Attempted to recruit black regiments in the spring of 1862 but failed to receive War

Department authorization. Served as president of the court-martial that convicted General Fitz John Porter in January 1863. Commanded the Army of West Virginia in the Shenandoah Valley, May–June 1864. Retreated from the valley following his defeat at Lynchburg, and resigned command in August 1864. President of the military commission that tried the conspirators in the Lincoln assassination, May–June 1865. Resigned commission on July 31, 1866. Died in Washington, D.C.

John S. Jackman (December 1841–December 21, 1912). Born in Carroll County, Kentucky. Worked as carpenter and schoolteacher. Moved to Bardstown. Enlisted in September 1861 at Bowling Green in the Confederate 5th (later the 9th) Kentucky Infantry. Saw action at Shiloh, Stones River, Chickamauga, Chattanooga, and in the Atlanta campaign. Wounded in the head by shell fragment at Pine Mountain, Georgia, on June 14, 1864. Rejoined regiment in December 1864 in Georgia, where he spent the remainder of the war. Studied law in Russellville, Kentucky, after the war and began successful chancery practice in Louisville in 1871. Helped publish the Confederate veterans' journal *Southern Bivouac*, 1882–87. Died in Louisville.

Harriet Ann Jacobs (1813–March 7, 1897) Born in Edenton, North Carolina, the daughter of slaves. After the death of her mother in 1819, she was raised by her grandmother and her white mistress, Margaret Horniblow, who taught her to read, write, and sew. In 1825 Horniblow died, and Jacobs was sent to the household of Dr. James Norcom. At sixteen, to escape Norcom's repeated sexual advances, Jacobs began a relationship with a white lawyer, Samuel Tredwell Sawyer (later a member of the U.S. House of Representatives), with whom she had two children, Joseph (b. 1829) and Louisa Matilda (b. 1833). In 1835, Jacobs ran away and spent the next seven years hiding in a crawl space above her freed grandmother's storeroom. In 1842, escaped to New York City, where she was reunited with her children. Worked as a nurse for the family of Nathaniel Parker Willis; moved to Boston in 1843 to avoid recapture by Norcom. Moved to Rochester in 1849, where she became part of a circle of abolitionists surrounding Frederick Douglass. In 1852, Cornelia Grinnell Willis, second wife of Nathaniel Parker Willis, purchased Jacobs's manumission. Published *Incidents in the Life of a Slave Girl, Written by Herself* pseudonymously in 1861. From 1862 to 1868 Jacobs engaged in Quaker-sponsored relief work among former slaves in Washington, D.C.; Alexandria, Virginia; and Savannah, Georgia. She then lived with her daughter in Cambridge, Massachusetts, and in Washington, D.C., where she died.

Hannah Johnson (c. 1820–?) The daughter of a slave who escaped from Louisiana to the North before her birth, Johnson was self-taught and was living in Buffalo, New York, in 1863 when she wrote to President Lincoln about her son, who was serving in the 54th Massachusetts Volunteer Infantry.

Charles C. Jones Jr. (October 28, 1831–July 19, 1893) Born in Savannah, Georgia, the son of minister Charles C. Jones and Mary Jones. Educated at South Carolina College and the College of New Jersey (Princeton). Graduated from Dane Law School at Harvard, 1855. Practiced law in Savannah, where he served as alderman, 1859–60, and mayor, 1860–61. Married Ruth Berrien Whitehead, 1858, and after her death, Eva Berrien Eve, 1863. Commissioned lieutenant in Chatham Artillery, August 1861. Promoted to lieutenant colonel and made chief of artillery for Georgia, October 1862. Practiced law in New York City, 1866–77, then returned to Georgia. Published several historical and archaeological studies, including *Indian Remains in Southern Georgia* (1859), *The Monumental Remains of Georgia* (1861), *Antiquities of the Southern Indians* (1873), and *The History of Georgia* (1883). Died in Augusta, Georgia.

Charles C. Jones Sr. (December 20, 1804–March 16, 1863) Born in Liberty County, Georgia, the son of a plantation owner. Educated at Phillips Andover Academy, Andover Theological Seminary, and Princeton Theological Seminary. Married first cousin Mary Jones in 1830. Pastor of the First Presbyterian Church, Savannah, 1831–32. Returned to Liberty County, where he owned three plantations. Taught at Columbia Theological Seminary, South Carolina, 1837–38 and 1848–50. Published *Catechism of Scripture Doctrine and Practice* (1837) and *The Religious Instruction of the Negroes of the United States* (1842). Lived in Philadelphia, 1850–53, while serving as the corresponding secretary of the board of domestic missions of the Presbyterian Church. Died in Liberty County.

John B. Jones (March 6, 1810–February 4, 1866) Born in Baltimore, Maryland. Lived in Kentucky and Missouri as a boy. Married Frances Custis in 1840. Became editor of the *Saturday Visitor* in Baltimore, 1841. Published several novels, including *Wild Western Scenes* (1841), *The War Path* (1858), and *Wild Southern Scenes* (1859). Established weekly newspaper *Southern Monitor* in Philadelphia, 1857. Fearing arrest as a Confederate sympathizer, Jones moved in 1861 to Richmond, Virginia, where he worked as a clerk in the Confederate War Department. Died in Burlington, New Jersey, shortly before the publication of *A Rebel War Clerk's Diary*.

Elizabeth Blair Lee (June 20, 1818–September 13, 1906) Born in Frankfort, Kentucky, daughter of journalist Francis Preston Blair and

Elizabeth Gist Blair, sister of Montgomery Blair (postmaster general, 1861–64) and Frank Blair (a Union major general, 1862–65). Moved with family in 1830 to Washington, D.C., where her father edited the *Globe* and advised Andrew Jackson. Educated at boarding school in Philadelphia. Married naval officer Samuel Phillips Lee, a cousin of Robert E. Lee, in 1843. Became board member and active patron of the Washington City Orphan Asylum in 1849. Lived in Washington and at the Blair estate in Silver Spring, Maryland. Died in Washington.

Robert E. Lee (January 19, 1807–October 12, 1870) Born in West-moreland County, Virginia, the son of Revolutionary War hero Henry "Light-Horse Harry" Lee and Ann Carter Lee. Graduated from West Point in 1829. Married Mary Custis, great-granddaughter of Martha Washington, in 1831. Served in the U.S.-Mexican War, and as superinten-dent of West Point, 1852–55. Promoted to colonel in March 1861. Re-signed commission on April 20, 1861, after declining offer of field command of the Federal army. Served as commander of Virginia military forces, April–July 1861; commander in western Virginia, August–October 1861; commander of the southern Atlantic coast, November 1861–March 1862; and military advisor to Jefferson Davis, March–May 1862. Assumed command of the Army of Northern Virginia on June 1, 1862, and led it until April 9, 1865, when he surrendered to Ulysses S. Grant at Appo-mattox. Named general-in-chief of all Confederate forces, January 1865. Became president of Washington College (now Washington and Lee), September 1865. Died in Lexington, Virginia.

Francis Lieber (March 18, 1798–October 2, 1872) Born Franz Lieber in Berlin, Prussia. Fought in the Prussian army in the Waterloo cam-paign and was seriously wounded at Namur. Imprisoned for four months for anti-government activities in 1819. Received degree in mathematics from Jena in 1820. Studied at Dresden, then served briefly as volunteer in the Greek War of Independence in 1822. Left Greece and traveled to Rome, where the Prussian ambassador, the historian Barthold Niebuhr, encouraged him to publish a book on his experiences in Greece (it appeared in 1823). Returned to Berlin in 1823 and continued his study of mathematics. Arrested in 1824 and imprisoned for six months for alleged subversion. Fled to England in 1826. Immigrated to Boston in 1827, where he served as director of a newly established gymnasium and swimming school. After the gym-nasium venture failed, edited the *Encyclopaedia Americana*, published successfully in thirteen volumes, 1829–33. Married Mathilda Oppen-heimer in 1829. Moved to Philadelphia in 1834 and published a con-stitution and plan of education for Girard College. Accepted a chair in history and political economy at South Carolina College (later University of South Carolina) in Columbia in 1835. Published numerous books and essays on law, government, and politics, including *Legal and Political Hermeneutics* (1837), *Manual of Political Ethics* (1838–39), and *On Civil Liberty and Self-Government* (1853). Resigned position in South Carolina in 1855. Appointed professor of history and political science at Columbia College in New York in 1857. During the Civil War one of his sons was killed fighting for the Confederacy in 1862, while his other two sons fought for the Union, one of them losing an arm at Fort Donelson. Became adviser to Henry W. Halleck on the laws of war. Wrote *A Code for the Government of Armies*, issued in revised form by the Union War Department as General Orders No. 100 in April 1863. Became professor at Columbia Law School in 1865. Helped gather and preserve the records of the Confederate government. Appointed in 1870 to commission settling claims arising from the U.S.-Mexican War. Died in New York City.

Abraham Lincoln (February 12, 1809–April 15, 1865) Born near Hodgenville, Kentucky, the son of a farmer and carpenter. Family moved to Indiana in 1816 and to Illinois in 1830. Settled in New Salem, Illinois, and worked as a storekeeper, surveyor, and postmaster. Served as a Whig in the state legislature, 1834–41. Began law practice in 1836 and moved to Springfield in 1837. Married Mary Todd in 1842. Elected to Congress as a Whig and served from 1847 to 1849. Became a public opponent of the extension of slavery after the passage of the Kansas-Nebraska Act in 1854. Helped found the Republican Party of Illinois in 1856. Campaigned in 1858 for Senate seat held by Stephen A. Douglas and debated him seven times on the slavery issue; although the Illinois legislature reelected Douglas, the campaign brought Lincoln national prominence. Received Republican presidential nomination in 1860 and won election in a four-way contest; his victory led to the secession of seven southern states. Responded to the Confederate bombardment of Fort Sumter by calling up militia, proclaiming the blockade of southern ports, and suspending habeas corpus. Issued preliminary and final emancipation proclamations on September 22, 1862, and January 1, 1863. Appointed Ulysses S. Grant commander of all Union forces in March 1864. Won reelection in 1864 by defeating Democrat George B. McClellan. Died in Washington, D.C., after being shot by John Wilkes Booth.

Theodore Lyman (August 23, 1833–September 9, 1897) Born in Waltham, Massachusetts, the son of a wealthy merchant and textile manufacturer. Graduated from Harvard in 1855. Studied natural history with Louis Agassiz after graduation. Traveled to Florida in 1856 to collect marine specimens for the Harvard Museum of Comparative Zoology. Graduated from Lawrence Scientific School at Harvard in 1858. Married Elizabeth Russell, a cousin of Robert Gould Shaw in

1858. Traveled in Europe, 1861–63. Joined staff of George G. Meade in September 1863 with rank of lieutenant colonel and served until Lee's surrender. Returned to home in Brookline and resumed work at Museum of Comparative Zoology. Served in Congress as an independent, 1883–85. Retired from scientific work in 1887 due to failing health. Died in Brookline.

Judith W. McGuire (March 19, 1813–March 21, 1897) Born Judith White Brockenbrough near Richmond, Virginia, the daughter of a judge. Married John P. McGuire, an Episcopalian rector, in 1846. Moved to Alexandria in 1852 when husband became principal of the Episcopal High School of Virginia. Fled Alexandria in May 1861 and settled in Richmond in February 1862. Worked as a clerk in the Confederate commissary department, November 1863–April 1864. Published *Diary of a Southern Refugee, During the War* (1867). Kept a school with her husband in Essex County in the 1870s. Published *General Robert E. Lee: The Christian Soldier* (1873). Died in Richmond.

Lafayette McLaws (January 15, 1821–July 24, 1897) Born in Augusta, Georgia, the son of a cotton broker. Attended the University of Virginia, 1837–38. Graduated from West Point in 1842 and was commissioned in the infantry. Saw action in the war with Mexico at Fort Brown, Monterrey, and the siege of Veracruz. Married Emily Taylor, niece of Zachary Taylor, in 1849. Served in New Mexico, Indian Territory, and Utah. Resigned commission as captain in March 1861 and joined the Confederacy. Commissioned colonel of the 10th Georgia Infantry in June 1861. Promoted to brigadier general, September 1861, and major general, May 1862. Led division at Williamsburg, Savage's Station, Malvern Hill, Harpers Ferry, Antietam, Fredericksburg, Chancellorsville, Gettysburg, the siege of Chattanooga, and Knoxville, Relieved of his command in December 1863 by his corps commander James Longstreet for failing to capture Fort Sanders during the Knoxville campaign. Assigned to defend Savannah, Georgia, in May 1864. Commanded division in the Carolinas campaign and at Bentonville. Served as court clerk in Richmond County, Georgia, 1866–68. Bought farm in Effingham County, Georgia, in 1870. Appointed postmaster for Savannah by Ulysses S. Grant in 1876 and served until 1885. President of company that sought to build canal from the Atlantic to the Gulf of Mexico, 1876–84. Died in Savannah.

George G. Meade (December 31, 1815–November 6, 1872) Born in Cádiz, Spain, the son of an American merchant. Family returned to Philadelphia in 1816. Graduated from West Point in 1835. Resigned in 1836 to work as engineer and surveyor. Married Margaretta Sergeant in 1840. Reentered army in 1842 as topographical engineer. Served under Zachary Taylor in the U.S.-Mexican War at Palo Alto, Resaca de la Palma, and Monterrey, and under Winfield Scott in the siege of Veracruz. Engaged in engineering and surveying duties in Delaware Bay, Florida, and the northern lakes, 1847–61. Commissioned as brigadier general of volunteers, August 1861. Became brigade commander in the Army of the Potomac, October 1861. Fought at Mechanicsville, Gaines's Mill, and Glendale, where he was wounded. Returned to duty in August 1862. Commanded brigade at Second Bull Run and a division at South Mountain and Antietam, where he temporarily led the First Corps after Joseph Hooker was wounded. Promoted to major general of volunteers, November 1862. Commanded division at Fredericksburg. Appointed commander of the Fifth Corps in December 1862 and led it at Chancellorsville. Replaced Hooker as commander of the Army of the Potomac on June 28, 1863, and led it until the end of the war. Received the thanks of Congress for his victory at Gettysburg. Promoted to major general in the regular army, September 23, 1864. Held postwar commands in the South and in the mid-Atlantic states. Died in Philadelphia.

Montgomery C. Meigs (May 3, 1816–January 2, 1892) Born in Augusta, Georgia, the son of a physician. Moved with family to Philadelphia. Graduated from West Point in 1836 and began service in engineering corps. Married Louisa Rodgers in 1841. Supervised construction of the Washington Aqueduct, 1852–60, and of the wings and dome of the Capitol, 1853–59. Promoted to brigadier general, May 1861, and made army quartermaster general, a post he held throughout the war. Designed the Pension Building in Washington, D.C., after retiring from the army in 1882. Died in Washington.

Herman Melville (August 1, 1819–September 28, 1891) Born in New York City, the son of a merchant. Educated at schools in New York City and in upstate New York. Worked as bank clerk, bookkeeper, and schoolteacher. Sailed for Pacific on whaling ship in 1841 and returned in 1844 on frigate *United States*. Published *Typee* (1846) and *Omoo* (1847), fictionalized accounts of his experiences in the South Seas. Married Elizabeth Shaw in 1847. Published *Mardi* (1849), *Redburn* (1849), *White-Jacket* (1850), *Moby-Dick* (1851), *Pierre; or, The Ambiguities* (1852), *Israel Potter* (1855), *The Piazza Tales* (1856), and *The Confidence-Man* (1857). Visited Union lines in Virginia in spring 1864. Published poetry collection *Battle-Pieces and Aspects of the War* (1866). Worked as customs inspector in New York City, 1866–85. Published long poem *Clarel* (1876) and two small books of poetry, *John Marr and Other Sailors* (1888) and *Timoleon* (1891). Died in New York City, leaving *Billy Budd, Sailor*, in manuscript.

Matthew M. Miller (November 28, 1840–1918) Born in Galena, Illinois. Attended Yale College but left school to enlist as a private in the 45th Illinois Volunteers. Fought at Shiloh. Promoted to first lieutenant, June 1862, and became captain of Company I, 9th Louisiana (African Descent) Infantry, November 1862. Fought at Milliken's Bend. Mustered out in May 1865. Returned to Illinois and practiced law. Married Anna Florence Woodbury in Boston in 1873. Moved to Kansas, where he died.

Sarah Morgan (February 28, 1842–May 5, 1909) Born in New Orleans, the daughter of a lawyer. Family moved in 1850 to Baton Rouge, where father served as a judge. Spent war with widowed mother and sisters in Baton Rouge, in the countryside near Port Hudson, and in Union-occupied New Orleans. Two of her brothers died of illness in January 1864 while serving in the Confederate army. Moved with mother to brother's plantation near Columbia, South Carolina, in 1872. Began writing editorials for the Charleston *News and Courier* in 1873 as "Mr. Fowler." Married Francis Warrington Dawson, editor of the *News and Courier*, in 1874. Husband killed in 1889 by doctor who had been paying unwanted attentions to family's governess. Moved in 1899 to Paris, where her son lived. Published *Les Aventures de Jeannot Lap*, version of Brer Rabbit stories, in 1903. Died in Paris.

Charles F. Morse (September 22, 1839–December 11, 1926) Born in Boston, Massachusetts. Graduated from Harvard in 1858. Commissioned as first lieutenant in Company B of the 2nd Massachusetts Infantry in May 1861. Became friends with fellow officer Robert Gould Shaw. Fought at Front Royal. Promoted to captain in July 1862 and fought at Cedar Mountain and Antietam. Served as provost marshal of the Twelfth Corps during the Chancellorsville campaign. Promoted to major and fought with 2nd Massachusetts at Gettysburg. Sent with regiment to Tennessee in early autumn 1863. Promoted to lieutenant colonel. Served in Atlanta campaign and in Sherman's march across Georgia. Led regiment in the Carolinas campaign until March 16, 1865, when he was wounded at Averasborough, North Carolina. Mustered out in July 1865. After failed attempt at cotton farming in Georgia, became general superintendent of the Atchison, Topeka, and Santa Fe Railroad in 1870. Married Ellen Mary Holdrege in 1874. Appointed general manager of the Kansas City Stockyards Company in 1879 by Charles Francis Adams, Jr., the company president. Successfully increased stockyard business and later served as company president. Published *Letters Written During the Civil War, 1861–1865* (1898). Retired to Falmouth, Massachusetts, in 1913. Wrote memoir *A Sketch of My Life Written for My Children: And a Buffalo*

Hunt in Nebraska in 1871, posthumously published in 1927. Died in Falmouth.

William H. Neblett (March 2, 1826–May 4, 1871) Born in Winchester, Mississippi, the son of a physician. Family moved to Texas in 1839. Attended school in Anderson and studied law. Married Elizabeth Rowan Scott in 1852. Moved in 1855 to Corsicana, where he practiced law and raised cotton and corn on plantation. Edited weekly secessionist newspaper *Navarro Express* in 1860. Moved to Lake Creek in Grimes County in 1861. Enlisted as private in the 20th Texas Infantry in March 1863. Served at Galveston as guard for gunboat *Bayou City* before obtaining position as clerk in brigade headquarters. Transferred to quartermaster department in Houston in July 1864 on grounds of ill health, suffering from rheumatism and neuralgia. Returned to plantation after war. Died in Anderson, Texas.

Oliver W. Norton (December 17, 1839–October 1, 1920) Born in Angelica, New York, the son of a Presbyterian minister. Educated at academy in Montrose, Pennsylvania. Taught school in 1858 in Waites Corner, New York. Family moved to Springfield, Pennsylvania, in 1860, where he taught school and worked on a farm. Enlisted in Company K, 83rd Pennsylvania Infantry, in 1861. Served as brigade bugler under Daniel Butterfield and became first bugler to play "Taps." Saw action in the Seven Days' Battles, Second Bull Run, Fredericksburg, Chancellorsville, and Gettysburg, where he served as Strong Vincent's brigade bugler during the fighting for Little Round Top. Commissioned first lieutenant with the 8th U.S. Colored Troops in November 1863. Fought at Olustee, Petersburg, and Darbytown Road. Mustered out in November 1865. Worked as bank clerk in New York City. Married Lucy Coit Fanning in 1870. Moved to Chicago and established business manufacturing cans and sheet-metal goods with his brother Edwin. Published *Army Letters 1861–1865* (1903), *Strong Vincent and his brigade at Gettysburg, July 2, 1863* (1909), and *The Attack and Defense of Little Round Top* (1913). Died in Chicago.

Frederick Law Olmsted (April 26, 1822–August 23, 1903) Born in Hartford, Connecticut, the son of a merchant. Attended schools in Hartford and boarded with several tutors in Connecticut and Massachusetts. Worked in dry goods importing firm in New York City, 1840–42. Traveled to Canton (Guangzhou), China, 1842–43. Studied farming and moved in 1848 to a farm his father purchased for him on Staten Island, New York, where he experimented with new agricultural and landscaping methods. Visited Europe in 1850. Published *Walks and Talks of an American Farmer in England* (1852). Traveled through the South, 1852–54. Published *A Journey in the Seaboard*

Slave States (1856), later much expanded as *The Cotton Kingdom: A Traveler's Observations on Cotton and Slavery in the American Slave States* (1861). Won contest along with Calvert Vaux to design new Central Park in Manhattan and was named architect-in-chief of the project in 1858. Married Mary Cleveland Olmsted, his brother's widow, in 1859. Became general secretary of the U.S. Sanitary Commission in 1861. Directed operations of hospital ships during the Peninsula campaign, May–July 1862. Made inspection tour of the Midwest and Mississippi valley, February–April 1863. Resigned from Sanitary Commission in September 1863 and became manager of the Mariposa Estate in northern California. Returned to New York in 1865 and established landscape architecture firm with Vaux, working on park and college campus projects across the United States. Moved to Brookline, Massachusetts, in 1881. Retired in 1895. Suffering from senility, became a patient in 1898 at McLean Asylum in Belmont, Massachusetts, where he died.

John Paris (September 1, 1809–October 6, 1883). Born in Orange County, North Carolina. Licensed to preach in the Methodist Protestant Church in 1839. Ordained as a deacon in 1842 and chosen as a church elder in 1844. Married Sally Ann Bellamy in 1845. Following her death, married Maria Yancey in 1849. Published *History of the Methodist Protestant Church* (1849) and *Baptism, Its Mode, Its Design, and Its Subjects* (1852). Moved to Virginia in 1852. Became chaplain of the 54th North Carolina Infantry in July 1862 and served with regiment at Fredericksburg, Chancellorsville, Plymouth, Drewry's Bluff, and in the Shenandoah Valley and Appomattox campaigns. Served as pastor on the Albemarle Circuit in North Carolina after the war. Published "Soldier's History of the War" in periodical *Our Living and Our Dead* (1874–76), "Causes Which Produced the War" in *Southern Historical Monthly* (1876), and *The Methodist Protestant Manual* (1878). Died in Buffalo Springs, Virginia.

Edmund DeWitt Patterson (March 20, 1842–May 22, 1914). Born Lorain County, Ohio, the son of a farmer and a schoolteacher. Raised by his grandfather and uncle after his mother's death in 1852. Attended local schools to age seventeen. Sold books and magazines in Tennessee and Alabama. Taught school and worked as a store clerk in Waterloo, Alabama. Enlisted in May 1861 in Company D, 9th Alabama Infantry. Saw action at Williamsburg and Fair Oaks and was seriously wounded at Glendale. Rejoined regiment in November 1862. Fought at Chancellorsville and Gettysburg, where he was captured on July 2, 1863. Held in prison camp at Johnson's Island, Ohio, until prisoner exchange in March 1865. Studied law after the war. Married Eleanor Mildred McDougal in 1869 and entered law partnership with her father, serving as clerk and master of chancery court for Hardin County, Tennessee, 1870–82. Elected to Tennessee state senate for one term in 1882. Served as circuit court judge, 1886–97. Died in Redlands, California.

Catharine Peirce (March 16, 1828–April 2, 1867) Born Catharine Milner in Pennsylvania, the daughter of a schoolteacher. Married Taylor Peirce in York County, Pennsylvania, in 1846. Joined husband, who had been working as a farm laborer, in Union, Iowa, in 1851. Spent war with children, brother, and sister-in-law in Des Moines, Iowa, helping brother to run boardinghouse for transient soldiers while her husband served in the Union army. Died in Des Moines while giving birth to her daughter Catharine, who survived.

Taylor Peirce (July 20, 1822–November 21, 1901) Born in Chester County, Pennsylvania. Married Catharine Milner in York County, Pennsylvania, in 1846. Traveled to Iowa to trade with Fox and Sac Indians. Became farm laborer in Iowa in 1850. Enlisted in 22nd Iowa Infantry at Newton in August 1862 and became sergeant in Company C. Served in southern Missouri, in the Vicksburg campaign, and in southern Louisiana and coastal Texas. Sent with regiment to the Shenandoah Valley in August 1864 and fought at Winchester and Cedar Creek. Served with regiment on garrison duty at Savannah, Georgia, and Morehead City, North Carolina, in winter and spring of 1865. Returned after the war to Des Moines, Iowa, where his wife died in 1867. Served as city clerk of Des Moines, 1871–79, and city auditor, 1874–77. Married Eliza Ann Van Horn in 1873. After 1879 worked in grain business and in a plow factory. Died in Des Moines.

George Hamilton Perkins (October 20, 1836–October 24, 1899) Born in Hopkinton, New Hampshire, the son of a lawyer. Graduated from the U.S. Naval Academy in 1856. Returned to the United States from West Africa in summer 1861 and was assigned to the gunboat *Cayuga* as first lieutenant in December 1861. Served in passage of Forts Jackson and St. Philip and the capture of New Orleans, April 1862. Patrolled the lower Mississippi River and served on blockade duty off Mobile, Alabama and the Texas coast, 1862–64. Promoted to lieutenant commander, December 1862. Assumed command of the ironclad monitor *Chickasaw* in July 1864. Fought in battle of Mobile Bay, August 5, 1864. Commanded *Chickasaw* on Gulf blockade duty for remainder of the war. Married Anna Minot Weld in 1870. Retired as captain in 1891. Died in Boston.

Samuel Pickens (June 9, 1841–September 9, 1890) Born in Greensboro, Alabama, the son of a wealthy plantation owner. Attended University of Virginia. Helped manage family plantation before the war. Enlisted in Company D, 5th Alabama Infantry, in September 1862. Fought at Chancellorsville and Gettysburg. Wounded at Winchester on September 19, 1864. Captured at Petersburg on April 2, 1865. Returned to family plantation after war.

Whitelaw Reid (October 27, 1837–December 15, 1912). Born near Cedarville, Ohio, the son of a farmer. Graduated from Miami University in 1856. Edited and published the *Xenia News*, 1857–60. Supported Abraham Lincoln in the 1860 presidential election. In 1861 began contributing to the *Cincinnati Times*, *Cleveland Herald*, and *Cincinnati Gazette*. Reported on the 1861 Union offensive in western Virginia and the battle of Shiloh for the *Gazette*. Became the Washington correspondent for the *Gazette* in June 1862, signing his dispatches "Agate," while also contributing reports to the *Chicago Tribune* and newspapers in St. Louis, Cleveland, Detroit, and Pittsburgh. Reported from the field at Gettysburg. Published *After the War* (1866), describing his travels through the South following the Confederate surrender. Unsuccessfully tried to raise cotton in Louisiana and Alabama, 1866–67. Published *Ohio in the War: Her Statesmen, Her Generals, and Soldiers* (1868). Reported on the impeachment trial of President Andrew Johnson and the 1868 political conventions for the *Gazette*. Joined the *New York Tribune* in 1868 and served as its managing editor, 1869–72. Following the death of Horace Greeley, he became the *Tribune*'s editor, 1872–1905, and publisher, 1872–1912. Served as U.S. minister to France, 1889–92. Nominated by the 1892 Republican convention as vice presidential running mate for President Benjamin Harrison (election was won by former president Grover Cleveland). Served as member of the commission that negotiated peace treaty with Spain in 1898 and as U.S. ambassador to Great Britain, 1905–12. Died in London.

John M. Schofield (September 29, 1831–March 4, 1906) Born in Gerry, New York, the son of a Baptist minister. Family moved to Bristol, Illinois, in 1843. Worked as surveyor and teacher before being nominated for West Point. Graduated in 1853 and commissioned in artillery. Taught natural philosophy at West Point, 1855–60. Married Harriet Whitehorn Bartlett in 1857. Obtained leave of absence in 1860 to teach physics at Washington University in St. Louis. Commissioned as major in 1st Missouri Infantry in April 1861. Served as chief of staff to Nathaniel Lyon and saw action at Wilson's Creek, where Lyon was killed. Promoted to brigadier general in November 1861 and held series of positions in Missouri. Commanded Department of the Missouri, May 1863–January 1864. Commanded the Army of the Ohio in the Atlanta campaign. Promoted to major general in May 1864. Commanded Twenty-third Corps at Franklin and Nashville and in

North Carolina, where he joined Sherman's army in March 1865. Served as agent of the State Department in France, 1865–66, negotiating withdrawal of French troops from Mexico. Commanded the Department of the Potomac, August 1866–June 1868, implementing Reconstruction in Virginia. Secretary of War under President Andrew Johnson, June 1868–March 1869. Commanded Department of the Missouri, 1869–70, and the Department of the Pacific, 1870–76. Traveled to Hawaii in 1872 and recommended acquisition of naval base at Pearl Harbor. Superintendent of West Point, 1876–81. Commanding general of United States Army, 1888–95. After death of first wife, married Georgia Kilburne in 1891. Published *Forty-six Years in the Army* (1897). Died in St. Augustine, Florida.

Raphael Semmes (September 27, 1809–August 30, 1877) Born in Charles County, Maryland. Raised by his uncle in Washington, D.C., after being orphaned in early childhood. Appointed midshipman in U.S. Navy in 1826. Served in Mediterranean, West Indies, and in Florida during the Second Seminole War. Promoted to lieutenant in 1837. Married Anne Elizabeth Spencer in 1837, the same year he was promoted to lieutenant. Assigned to blockade duty at the outbreak of the U.S.-Mexican War and took command of the brig *Somers* in October 1846. Exonerated by court of inquiry after *Somers* sank in a sudden squall on December 8, 1846, with the loss of more than half its crew. Served in landing at Veracruz and subsequent march to Mexico City. Practiced law in Mobile, Alabama, after the war while awaiting orders. Published *Service Afloat and Ashore during the Mexican War* (1851). Promoted to commander in 1855. Resigned from U.S. Navy in February 1861. Commissioned as commander in the Confederate navy in March 1861 and given command of commerce raider *Sumter*. Escaped blockade in the Gulf of Mexico in June 1861 and captured or burned eighteen American merchant vessels in the Caribbean and Atlantic before being blockaded in Gibraltar in January 1862. Promoted to captain and assumed command of raider *Alabama* in August 1862. Captured or destroyed sixty-four American ships in the Caribbean, Atlantic Ocean, and Indian Ocean before the *Alabama* was sunk off Cherbourg, France, by the Union sloop *Kearsarge* on June 19, 1864. Escaped to England on a British yacht and returned to Virginia in January 1865. Commanded James River Squadron until the end of the war. Arrested for treason in December 1865 but was released in April 1866. Taught literature and philosophy at Louisiana State Seminary (later Louisiana State University) and edited *Memphis Daily Bulletin* before returning to law practice in Mobile. Published *Memoirs of Service Afloat during the War Between the States* (1869). Died at Point Clear, Alabama.

Robert Gould Shaw (October 10, 1837–July 18, 1863) Born in Boston, the son of a wealthy merchant and lawyer; both parents were active abolitionists. Family moved to West Roxbury, Massachusetts, in 1841 and to Staten Island, New York, in 1847. Traveled with family in Europe, 1851–56, and was educated at boarding school in Switzerland and by private tutors in Hanover, Germany. Attended Harvard, 1856–59. Worked for uncle's mercantile company in New York City, 1859–61. Commissioned as second lieutenant in 2nd Massachusetts Infantry in May 1861 and was later promoted to captain. Fought at Front Royal, Cedar Mountain, and Antietam. Accepted colonelcy of 54th Massachusetts Infantry, the first black regiment to be raised by a northern state, in January 1863. Married Annie Kneeland Haggerty on May 2, 1863, shortly before regiment left for South Carolina. Led regiment in raid on Darien, Georgia, June 11, 1863. Killed while leading assault on Fort Wagner in Charleston Harbor and was buried in mass grave with his soldiers.

William T. Sherman (February 8, 1820–February 14, 1891) Born in Lancaster, Ohio, the son of an attorney. Graduated from West Point in 1840. Served in Florida and California, but did not see action in the U.S.-Mexican War. Married Ellen Ewing in 1850. Promoted to captain; resigned his commission in 1853. Managed bank branch in San Francisco, 1853–57. Moved in 1858 to Leavenworth, Kansas, where he worked in real estate and was admitted to the bar. Named first superintendent of the Louisiana State Seminary of Learning and Military Academy at Alexandria (now Louisiana State University) in 1859. Resigned position when Louisiana seceded in January 1861. Commissioned colonel, 13th U.S. Infantry, May 1861. Commanded brigade at First Bull Run, July 1861. Appointed brigadier general of volunteers, August 1861, and ordered to Kentucky. Assumed command of the Department of the Cumberland, October 1861, but was relieved in November at his own request. Returned to field in March 1862 and commanded division under Ulysses S. Grant at Shiloh. Promoted major general of volunteers, May 1862. Commanded corps under Grant during Vicksburg campaign, and succeeded him as commander of the Army of the Tennessee, October 1863, and as commander of the Military Division of the Mississippi, March 1864. Captured Atlanta, September 1864, and led march through Georgia, November–December 1864. Marched army through the Carolinas and accepted the surrender of Confederate general Joseph E. Johnston at Durham Station, North Carolina, April 26, 1865. Promoted to lieutenant general, 1866, and general, 1869, when he became commander of the army. Published controversial *Memoirs of General W. T. Sherman* (1875, revised 1886). Retired from army in 1884 and moved to New

York City. Rejected possible Republican presidential nomination, 1884. Died in New York City.

William Wrenshall Smith (August 15, 1830–c. 1904) Born in Washington, Pennsylvania, where he graduated from Washington College in 1852. Worked in the family dry goods business and banking office. His mother was the sister of Ellen Wrenshall Dent, Ulysses S. Grant's mother-in-law, and during the Civil War he visited Grant's headquarters several times. Married Emma Willard McKennan in 1867. Founded Trinity Hall, a boys' school, in Washington, Pennsylvania, in 1879.

George E. Stephens (1832–April 24, 1888) Born in Philadelphia, the son of free blacks who had fled from Virginia after the Nat Turner rebellion. Worked as upholsterer and cabinetmaker. An active abolitionist, he helped found the Banneker Institute, a literary society and library for blacks, in Philadelphia in 1853. Served on coastal survey ship *Walker* in 1857–58 and visited Charleston, South Carolina. Became cook and personal servant to Lieutenant Colonel Benjamin Tilghman of the 26th Pennsylvania Infantry in 1861 while serving as war correspondent for the New York *Weekly Anglo-African*, an influential black newspaper. Helped recruit in early 1863 for the 54th Massachusetts Infantry, the first black regiment raised by a northern state, then enlisted in the regiment as a sergeant. Served in siege of Charleston, South Carolina, and fought in the assault on Fort Wagner on July 18, 1863. Continued to write for the *Anglo-African* and protested the failure of black soldiers to receive equal pay. Commissioned as first lieutenant before being mustered out in July 1865. Worked for the Freedman's Bureau in Virginia educating freed slaves, 1866–70. Returned to Philadelphia before moving in 1873 to Brooklyn, where he worked as an upholsterer until his death.

Kate Stone (May 8, 1841–December 28, 1907) Born Sarah Katherine Stone in Hinds County, Mississippi, the daughter of a plantation owner. Family moved to plantation in Madison Parish, Louisiana, thirty miles northwest of Vicksburg. Educated at boarding school in Nashville. Two of her five brothers died while serving in the Confederate army in 1863. Family fled plantation in April 1863 during the Vicksburg campaign and went to eastern Texas. Returned to plantation in November 1865. Married Henry Bry Holmes in 1869. Founded local chapter of the United Daughters of the Confederacy. Died in Tallulah, Louisiana.

George Templeton Strong (January 26, 1820–July 21, 1875) Born in New York City, the son of an attorney. Graduated from Columbia College in 1838. Read law in his father's office and was admitted to the bar in 1841. Joined father's firm. Married Ellen Ruggles in 1848. Served on Columbia board of trustees and as vestryman of Trinity Episcopal Church. Helped found the U.S. Sanitary Commission, June 1861, and served as its treasurer through the end of the war; also helped found the Union League Club of New York in 1863. Died in New York City.

Walter H. Taylor (June 13, 1838–March 1, 1916) Born in Norfolk, Virginia, the son of a commission merchant. Graduated from Norfolk Military Academy. Attended Virginia Military Institute, 1854–55. Worked in Norfolk branch of Bank of Virginia, 1855–61. Joined 6th Virginia Infantry in April 1861. Became assistant adjutant general on staff of Robert E. Lee in May 1861 and served with him in Richmond, western Virginia, and South Carolina. Continued in position when Lee took command of the Army of Northern Virginia in June 1862 and served until Lee's surrender at Appomattox. Promoted to lieutenant colonel in January 1864. Married Elizabeth Selden Saunders in Richmond, Virginia, on night of April 2, 1865. Returned to Norfolk after the war and worked in hardware business before becoming president of the Marine Bank in 1876. Served as director of several insurance and railroad companies. Published *Four Years with General Lee* (1878) and *General Lee: His Campaigns in Virginia, 1861–1865* (1906). Died in Norfolk.

James H. Tomb (March 16, 1839–May 25, 1929) Born in Savannah, Georgia, the son of a painter. Family moved in 1852 to New Berlin, Florida, where father operated a sawmill. Commissioned in Confederate navy in June 1861. Served on the Mississippi as engineer on gunboats *Jackson* and *McRae*. Captured at Forts Jackson and St. Phillip in April 1862. Exchanged in October 1862. Assigned to ironclad ram *Chicora* and served in successful attack on Union fleet blockading Charleston, South Carolina, on January 31, 1863. Worked on design of torpedoes (underwater explosive devices). Became engineer of ironclad ram *David*, which damaged U.S.S. *New Ironsides* in a night attack off Charleston on October 5, 1863. Made unsuccessful attack on the U.S.S. *Memphis* in March 1864. Served at Charleston until its evacuation in February 1865. Surrendered and paroled in Florida in May 1865. Served with Brazilian navy during the Paraguayan War, 1866–67. Opened hotel in St. Louis in 1872. Married Sarah Green in 1880. Retired in 1905 to Jacksonville, Florida, where he died.

Clement L. Vallandigham (July 29, 1820–June 17, 1871) Born in New Lisbon, Ohio, the son of a Presbyterian minister. Attended New Lisbon Academy and Jefferson College in Washington, Pennsylvania. Served as principal of Union Academy in Snow Hill, Maryland,

1838–40. Returned to Ohio in 1840 to study law. Admitted to bar in 1842. Served as a Democrat in the Ohio house of representatives, 1845–46. Married Louisa Anna McMahon in 1846. Moved in 1847 to Dayton, where he practiced law and edited the *Dayton Western Empire*, 1847–49. Served in Congress, 1858–63, and became a leading "Peace Democrat" opposed to emancipation and the continued prosecution of the war. Arrested in Dayton on May 5, 1863, and tried before military commission for expressing "disloyal sentiments and opinions." Expelled across lines into Confederate-held territory in Tennessee. Made his way to Canada in June 1863 after receiving Democratic nomination for governor of Ohio and campaigned from exile, but was defeated in October 1863. Returned to United States in June 1864 and helped draft peace platform adopted by Democratic national convention in August. Resumed law practice. Accidentally shot himself on June 16, 1871, while demonstrating to other attorneys how his client's alleged victim could have accidentally shot himself during an altercation (his client was later acquitted). Died the following day in Lebanon, Ohio.

Charles S. Wainwright (December 31, 1826–September 13, 1907) Born in New York City, the son of a farmer from Dutchess County in the Hudson Valley. Helped manage family estate near Rhinebeck. Served in New York state militia. Commissioned as major in the 1st New York Artillery on October 17, 1861. Served as chief of artillery in Hooker's division, Army of the Potomac, from January 1862. Promoted to lieutenant colonel, April 1862, and colonel, May 1862. Fought at Williamsburg and Fair Oaks before falling ill in early June 1862. Returned from sick leave in August 1862 and became chief of artillery in the First Corps in September 1862; joined his command after the battle of Antietam. Served at Fredericksburg, Chancellorsville, and Gettysburg. Commanded artillery brigade in Fifth Corps, 1864–65, and served in the Overland campaign, the siege of Petersburg, and the Appomattox campaign. Returned to farming in Dutchess County before moving to Washington, D.C., around 1884. Died in Washington.

Henry C. Whelan (January 8, 1835–March 2, 1864) Born in Philadelphia, the son of a merchant. Attended University of Pennsylvania for two years. Worked in shoe store. Commissioned as captain in 6th Pennsylvania Cavalry in September 1861. Promoted to major in March 1863. Fought at Brandy Station and in Mine Run campaign. Returned in December 1863 to Philadelphia, where he died of pulmonary disease.

Walt Whitman (May 31, 1819–March 26, 1892) Born in Huntington

Township, New York, the son of a farmer and carpenter. Moved with
family to Brooklyn in 1823. Learned printing trade at Brooklyn newspapers. Taught school on Long Island, 1836–38. Became freelance
journalist and printer in New York and Brooklyn. Published first edition of *Leaves of Grass* in 1855 (revised editions appeared in 1856, 1860,
1867, 1870, 1881, and 1891). Traveled to northern Virginia in December 1862 after learning that his brother George had been wounded at
Fredericksburg. Became volunteer nurse in Washington, D.C., army
hospitals. Published *Drum-Taps* and *Sequel to Drum-Taps* in 1865.
Worked as clerk at the Interior Department, 1865, and the office of
the attorney general, 1865–73. Published prose recollections of his war
experiences in *Memoranda During the War* (1875) and *Specimen Days
and Collect* (1882). Died in Camden, New Jersey.

Charles B. Wilder (August 28, 1802–May 7, 1882) Born in Needham,
Massachusetts. Married Mary Ann Guild in 1827. Became successful
paper merchant. Appointed superintendent of contrabands at Fort
Monroe, Virginia, in February 1863 and commissioned as captain.
Charged with embezzlement in 1865 after he purchased confiscated
land in Virginia with the intent of distributing it to freed slaves, but
was acquitted at court-martial. Mustered out in March 1866. Moved
to Jacksonville, Florida, where he died.

Alpheus S. Williams (September 20, 1810–December 21, 1878) Born
in Deep River, Connecticut, the son of a manufacturer. Graduated
from Yale College in 1831. Admitted to the bar in 1834. Moved to
Detroit in 1836, where he practiced law and joined the local militia
company. Married Jane Hereford Pierson in 1839; she died in 1848.
Served as probate judge of Wayne County, 1840–44, and published
the *Detroit Daily Advertiser*, 1843–48. Commissioned as brigadier
general of volunteers in August 1861. Commanded brigade in the
Army of the Potomac, October 1861–March 1862. Led a division in
the Shenandoah Valley campaign and at Cedar Mountain and Second
Bull Run. Assumed temporary command of Twelfth Corps at Antietam following the death of General Mansfield. Commanded division
at Chancellorsville and was temporary commander of the Twelfth
Corps at Gettysburg. Sent with his division in September 1863 to Tennessee, where they guarded railroads. Served in the Atlanta campaign
and commanded the Twentieth Corps in the march through Georgia
and the Carolinas. Mustered out on January 15, 1866. Served as U.S.
minister to San Salvador, 1866–69. Returned to Detroit. Married
Martha Ann Tillman in 1873. Elected to Congress as a Democrat and
served from 1875 until his death in Washington, D.C.

William Winters (1830–April 8, 1864?) Born in Connecticut.

Married Harriet J. Smith in Cincinnati, Ohio, in 1853. Moved to Hawes Creek Township in Bartholomew County, Indiana, where he worked as a saddle and harness maker. Enlisted in Company I, 67th Indiana Infantry, in August 1862. Taken prisoner along with his regiment when the Union garrison at Munfordville, Kentucky, surrendered on September 17, 1862. Returned to Indiana after being paroled the day after his capture. Exchanged in late November 1862. Regiment joined Sherman's expedition against Vicksburg. Saw action at Chickasaw Bayou. Served as hospital attendant during expedition to capture Arkansas Post and in army camps near Vicksburg. Saw action at Port Gibson, Champion Hill, Big Black River, and in the siege of Vicksburg. Sent with regiment to southern Louisiana in August 1863 and to Matagorda Bay, Texas, in December. Returned to southern Louisiana in February 1864 and served in Red River campaign. Missing in action and presumed killed in the battle of Sabine Crossroads.

Jonathan Worth (November 18, 1802–September 5, 1869) Born in Guilford County, North Carolina, the son of a physician. Attended Caldwell Institute in Greensboro. Married Martitia Daniel in 1824, the same year he began practicing law in Asheboro. Served in North Carolina house of commons, 1830–32, where he opposed nullification. Served in state senate, 1840–41 and 1858–61. Opposed secession in 1861. Elected state treasurer in 1862 and served until 1865, when he was elected governor. Reelected in 1866. Opposed ratification of the Fourteenth Amendment and the Reconstruction Act of 1867, which made southern state governments subject to military authority. Declined to run for reelection in 1868 and refused to recognize the election of William W. Holden as his successor. Removed from office by military authority in July 1868. Died in Raleigh.

Note on the Texts

This volume collects nineteenth-century writing about the Civil War, bringing together public and private letters, newspaper and magazine articles, memoranda, speeches, journal and diary entries, proclamations, messages, commission testimony, poems, and sermons written by participants and observers and dealing with events in the period from January 1863 to March 1864. Most of these documents were not written for publication, and most of them existed only in manuscript form during the lifetimes of the persons who wrote them. With ten exceptions, the texts presented in this volume are taken from printed sources. In cases where there is only one printed source for a document, the text offered here comes from that source. Where there is more than one printed source for a document, the text printed in this volume is taken from the source that appears to contain the fewest editorial alterations in the spelling, capitalization, paragraphing, and punctuation of the original. In ten instances where no printed sources (or no complete printed sources) were available, the texts in this volume are printed from manuscripts.

This volume prints texts as they appear in the sources listed below, but with a few alterations in editorial procedure. The bracketed conjectural readings of editors, in cases where original manuscripts or printed texts were damaged or difficult to read, are accepted without brackets in this volume when those readings seem to be the only possible ones; but when they do not, or when the editor made no conjecture, the missing word or words are indicated by a bracketed two-em space, i.e., [   ]. In cases where a typographical error or obvious misspelling in manuscript was marked by earlier editors with "[*sic*]," the present volume omits the "[*sic*]" and corrects the typographical error or slip of the pen. In some cases, obvious errors were not marked by earlier editors with "[*sic*]" but were printed and then followed by a bracketed correction; in these instances, this volume removes the brackets and accepts the editorial emendation. Bracketed editorial insertions used in the source texts to identify persons or places, to expand contractions and abbreviations, or to clarify meaning have been deleted in this volume. In instances where canceled, but still legible, words were printed in the source texts with lines through the deleted material, or where canceled words were printed and indicated with an asterisk, this volume omits the canceled words.

In *The Papers of Jefferson Davis*, material that was written in interlined form in manuscript is printed within diagonal marks; this volume prints the interlined words and omits the diagonals.

The texts of the letters from Matthew M. Miller to his aunt and from George Hamilton Perkins to Susan G. Perkins were presented as quoted material in the sources used in this volume, with quotation marks placed at the beginning of each paragraph and at the end of the text; this volume omits the quotation marks.

Sherman's Civil War: Selected Correspondence of William T. Sherman, 1860–1865 (1999), edited by Brooks D. Simpson and Jean V. Berlin, presents Sherman's letter to Ellen Ewing Sherman of June 27, 1863, in a text in which erased material is indicated by "<erased>," "<sentence erased>," "<remainder of sentence erased>," and "<phrase erased>." In this volume, the erased material is indicated by a bracketed two-em space, i.e., [   ].

Inside Lincoln's White House: The Complete Civil War Diary of John Hay (1997), edited by Michael Burlingame and John R. Turner Ettlinger, prints a paragraph in the July 15, 1863, entry describing Hay's visits to concert saloons with Robert Todd Lincoln (page 376.28–31 in this volume) as canceled material because it was crossed out in the manuscript. This volume prints the paragraph without cancelation marks because it is likely that it was crossed out by someone other than Hay, possibly after his death. Similarly, in the instances in his diary where Hay originally referred to Lincoln as "the Tycoon," the word "Tycoon" was later crossed out in the manuscript and "President" added. These instances are printed in *Inside Lincoln's White House* with "Tycoon" canceled and then followed by "President," but in this volume at pages 376.32 and 563.5 "Tycoon" is printed without cancelation and "President" is omitted.

The text of the journal of Jedediah Hotchkiss presented in *Make Me a Map Of the Valley: The Civil War Journal of Stonewall Jackson's Topographer* (1973), edited by Archie P. McDonald, is based on a typescript prepared under Hotchkiss's personal supervision. In the typescript of the entry for May 2, 1863, there are two blank spaces where the names of a house on the Chancellorsville battlefield and of a Confederate officer were omitted. The text presented in *Make Me a Map Of the Valley* supplies the missing names in brackets. In this volume, these bracketed insertions are deleted, a two-em space is left blank at pages 178.24 and 179.11, and the names are printed in the notes. Similarly, there are three blank spaces in the entry for May 15, 1863, in the diary of Edward O. Guerrant where two dates and the name of a battle were omitted. In the text presented in *Bluegrass Confederate: The Headquarters Diary of Edward O. Guerrant* (1999), edited by William C. Davis and Meredith L. Swentor, the omitted dates and names are supplied in brackets. This volume deletes the bracketed insertions, leaves a two-em space blank at pages 220.37, 221.5, and 221.14, and prints the dates and the name of the battle in the notes.

Two setting errors that appeared in the printed source texts are corrected in this volume: at 465.34, "while it could prevent depredations" becomes "while it could not prevent depredations," and at 593.5, "Tuesday morning, Dec. 24th" becomes "Tuesday morning, Nov. 24th." Eight slips of the pen in documents printed from manuscript sources are also corrected: at 17.13–14, "seemed in in excellent spirits, said they" becomes "seemed in excellent spirits, said they"; at 334.9, "when the skirmisher on both flanks" becomes "when the skirmishers on both flanks"; at 334.11, "only two offices besides myself" becomes "only two officers besides myself"; at 335.23, "before & the the rest as quick" becomes "before & the rest as quick"; at 393.25–26, "have troops enough to built them" becomes "have troops enough to build them"; at 457.24, "privalege" becomes "privilege"; at 458.1, "theory in practice of Government" becomes "theory in practice of the Government"; at 458.14–15, "regret this his bill" becomes "regret that his bill."

The following is a list of the documents included in this volume, in the order of their appearance, giving the source of each text. The most common sources are indicated by these abbreviations:

CWAL   *The Collected Works of Abraham Lincoln*, ed. Roy P. Basler (8 vols., New Brunswick, N.J.: Rutgers University Press, 1953). Copyright © 1953 by the Abraham Lincoln Association. Used by permission.

DCDT   *Dear Catharine, Dear Taylor: The Civil War Letters of a Union Soldier and His Wife*, ed. Richard L. Kiper, letters transcribed by Donna B. Vaughn (Lawrence: University Press of Kansas, 2002). Copyright © 2002 by University Press of Kansas.

Norton   Oliver Willcox Norton, *Army Letters, 1861–1865* (Chicago: O. L. Deming 1903).

OR   *The War of the Rebellion: A Compilation of the Official Records of the Union and Confederate Armies* (128 vols., Washington, D.C.: Government Printing Office, 1880–1901).

ORN   *Official Records of the Union and Confederate Navies in the War of the Rebellion* (30 vols., Washington, D.C.: Government Printing Office, 1894–1922).

PJD   *The Papers of Jefferson Davis* (13 vols. to date, Baton Rouge: Louisiana State University Press, 1971–2012). Volume 9 (1997), ed. Lynda Lasswell Crist and Mary Seaton Dix, Volume 10 (1999), ed. Lynda Lasswell Crist. Copyright © 1997, 1999 by Louisiana State University Press. Used by permission of the publisher.

PUSG   *The Papers of Ulysses S. Grant*, ed. John Y. Simon (31 vols.
         to date, Carbondale: Southern Illinois University Press,
         1967–2009). Volume 8 (1979), Volume 9 (1982), Volume
         10 (1982). Copyright © 1979, 1982 by The Ulysses S. Grant
         Association. Published with the permission of The Ulysses
         S. Grant Association.

SCW   *Sherman's Civil War: Selected Correspondence of William
         T. Sherman, 1860–1865*, ed. Brooks D. Simpson and Jean V.
         Berlin (Chapel Hill: The University of North Carolina
         Press, 1999). Copyright © 1999 by The University of
         North Carolina Press, www.uncpress.unc.edu. Used by
         permission of the publisher.

Edmund DeWitt Patterson: Journal, January 20, 1863. *Yankee Rebel: The
    Civil War Journal of Edmund DeWitt Patterson*, ed. John G. Barrett
    (Chapel Hill: The University of North Carolina Press, 1966), 93–94.
    Copyright © 1966 by The University of North Carolina Press, www
    .uncpress.unc.edu. Used by permission of the publisher.

Theodore A. Dodge: Journal, January 21–24, 1863. *On Campaign
    with the Army of the Potomac: The Civil War Journal of Theodore
    Ayrault Dodge*, ed. Stephen W. Sears (New York: Cooper Square
    Press, 2001), 150–56. Copyright © 2001 by Stephen W. Sears.

Henry Adams to Charles F. Adams Jr., January 23, 1863. *The Letters of
    Henry Adams*, vol. I, ed. J. C. Levenson, Ernest Samuels, Charles
    Vandersee, Viola Hopkins Winner (Cambridge: The Belknap Press
    of Harvard University Press), 326–27. Copyright © 1982 by the
    Massachusetts Historical Society. Used by permission of the Adams
    Family Papers, Massachusetts Historical Society.

George G. Meade to Margaret Meade, January 23, 26, and 28, 1863.
    Manuscript, George Gordon Meade Papers, Historical Society of
    Pennsylvania, Philadelphia.

Abraham Lincoln to Joseph Hooker, January 26, 1863. *CWAL*, vol.
    VI, 78–79.

John A. Andrew to Francis Shaw, January 30, 1863. Manuscript, John
    A. Andrew Papers, Massachusetts Historical Society, Boston. Used
    by permission.

William Parker Cutler: Diary, February 2 and 9, 1863. Allan G. Bogue,
    "William Parker Cutler's Congressional Diary of 1862–63," *Civil
    War History*, vol. 33, no. 4 (December 1987), 329–330. Copyright ©
    1987 by Kent State University Press.

George Templeton Strong: Diary, February 3–5, 1863. George Tem-
    pleton Strong, *Diary of the Civil War, 1860–1865*, ed. Allan Nevins
    (New York: The Macmillan Publishing Company, 1962), 293–95.
    Reprinted with permission of Scribner, a Division of Simon &

Schuster, Inc., from *The Diary of George Templeton Strong* by Allan Nevins and Milton Halsey Thomas. Copyright © 1952 by The Macmillan Publishing Company; copyright renewed © 1980 by Milton Halsey Thomas. All rights reserved.

Oliver W. Norton to Edwin Norton, February 6, 1863. *Norton*, 134–37.

Robert E. Lee to Mary Lee, February 8, 1863. *The Wartime Papers of Robert E. Lee*, ed. Clifford Dowdey and Louis H. Manarin (Boston: Little, Brown, 1961), 401–2. Copyright © 1961 by Commonwealth of Virginia.

Robert Gould Shaw to Annie Haggerty, February 8, 1863. *Blue-Eyed Child of Fortune: The Civil War Letters of Colonel Robert Gould Shaw*, ed. Russell Duncan (Athens: The University of Georgia Press, 1992), 285–86. Copyright © 1992 by The University of Georgia Press. Used by permission of The University of Georgia Press.

Richard Cobden to Charles Sumner, February 13, 1863. *American Historical Review*, vol. 2, no. 2 (January 1897), 308–9.

Isaac Funk: Speech in the Illinois State Senate, February 14, 1863. *Copperheads Under the Heel of an Illinois Farmer* (New York: 1863), 1–3.

Taylor Peirce to Catharine Peirce, February 16, 1863. *DCDT*, 79–81.

William T. Sherman to Thomas Ewing Sr., February 17, 1863, and to John Sherman, February 18, 1863. *SCW*, 398–405.

Clement L. Vallandigham: Speech in Congress, Washington, D.C., February 23, 1863. *Congressional Globe Appendix*, 37th Congress, 3rd Session, 172–77.

Samuel W. Fiske to the *Springfield Republican*, February 25, 1863. *Mr. Dunn Browne's Experiences in the Army: The Civil War Letters of Samuel W. Fiske*, ed. Stephen W. Sears (New York: Fordham University Press, 1998), 58–60. Copyright © 1998 by Stephen W. Sears.

Charles C. Jones Jr. to Charles C. Jones Sr. and Mary Jones, March 3, 1863. *The Children of Pride: A True Story of Georgia and the Civil War*, Abridged Edition, ed. Robert Manson Myers (New Haven: Yale University Press, 1984), 351–52. Copyright © 1972, 1984 by Robert Manson Myers.

Charles C. Jones Sr. to Charles C. Jones Jr., March 4, 1863. *The Children of Pride: A True Story of Georgia and the Civil War*, Abridged Edition, ed. Robert Manson Myers (New Haven: Yale University Press, 1984), 352–53. Copyright © 1972, 1984 by Robert Manson Myers. Used by permission of the publisher.

Harriet Jacobs to Lydia Maria Child, March 18, 1863. *The Harriet Jacobs Family Papers*, vol. II, ed. Jean Fagan Yellin (Chapel Hill: The University of North Carolina Press), 468–70. Copyright © 2008 Jean Fagan Yellin. Used by permission of the publisher.

William Henry Harrison Clayton to Nide and Rachel Pugh, March 26, 1863. *A Damned Iowa Greyhound: The Civil War Letters of*

William Henry Harrison Clayton, ed. Donald C. Elder III (Iowa City: University of Iowa Press, 1998), 52–55. Copyright © 1998 by University of Iowa Press. Used by permission of the publisher.

Henry W. Halleck to Ulysses S. Grant, March 31, 1863. *OR*, series 1, vol. XXIV, part 3, 156–57.

Frederick Law Olmsted to John Olmsted, April 1, 1863. *The Papers of Frederick Law Olmsted, Volume IV: Defending the Union, 1861–1863*, ed. Jane Turner Censer (Baltimore: The Johns Hopkins University Press, 1986), 570–76. Copyright © 1986 by The Johns Hopkins University Press.

Frederick Douglass: Why Should a Colored Man Enlist?, *Douglass' Monthly*, April 1863. *The Life and Writings of Frederick Douglass*, vol. III, ed. Philip S. Foner (New York: International Publishers, 1952), 340–44. Copyright © 1952 by International Publishers Co. Inc.

Jefferson Davis to William M. Brooks, April 2, 1863. *PJD*, vol. 9, 122–24. Used by permission of the publisher.

John B. Jones: Diary, April 2–4, 1863. J. B. Jones, *A Rebel War Clerk's Diary at the Confederate States Capital*, vol. I (Philadelphia: J. B. Lippincott & Co., 1866), 284–87.

Whitelaw Reid to the *Cincinnati Gazette*, April 4, 1863. *A Radical View: The "Agate" Dispatches of Whitelaw Reid 1861–1865*, vol. 1, ed. James G. Smart (Memphis, Tenn.: Memphis State University Press), 257–58.

Charles S. Wainwright Diary, April 5–12, 1863. *A Diary of Battle: The Personal Journals of Colonel Charles S. Wainwright*, ed. Allan Nevins (New York: Harcourt, Brace & World, Inc., 1962), 176–79. Copyright © 1962 by Allan Nevins.

Francis Lieber: No Party Now, But All for Our Country, April 11, 1863. Francis Lieber, *No Party Now, But All for Our Country* (New York: C.S. Westcott & Co., 1863), 1–8.

Catharine Peirce to Taylor Peirce, April 12, 1863. *DCDT*, 97–98.

James A. Connolly to Mary Dunn Connolly, April 20, 1863. "Major James Austin Connolly," *Transactions of the Illinois State Historical Society for the Year 1928* (Springfield: Illinois State Historical Library, 1928), 241–43. Used by permission of the Abraham Lincoln Presidential Library.

Ulysses S. Grant to Jesse Root Grant, April 21, 1863. *PUSG*, vol. 8, 109–10.

David Hunter to Jefferson Davis, April 23, 1863. *PJD*, vol. 9, 152.

Kate Stone: Journal, April 25, 1863. *Brokenburn: The Journal of Kate Stone, 1861–1868*, ed. John Q. Anderson (Baton Rouge: Louisiana State University Press, 1955), 194–99. Copyright © 1989 by Louisiana State University Press. Used by permission of the publisher.

Wilbur Fisk to *The Green Mountain Freeman*, April 26, 1863. *Hard Marching Every Day: The Civil War Letters of Private Wilbur Fisk,*

1861–1865, ed. Emil and Ruth Rosenblatt (Lawrence: University Press of Kansas, 1992), 70–74. Copyright © 1983, 1992 by Emil Rosenblatt.

John Hampden Chamberlayne to Martha Burwell Chamberlayne, April 30, 1863. *Ham Chamberlayne—Virginian: Letters and Papers of an Artillery Officer in the War for Southern Independence 1861–1865*, ed. C. G. Chamberlayne (Richmond, Va.: Dietz Printing Co., 1932), 171–72. Copyright © 1932 by C. G. Chamberlayne.

Sarah Morgan: Diary, April 30, 1863. *The Civil War Diary of Sarah Morgan*, ed. Charles East (Athens: The University of Georgia Press, 1991), 489–92. Copyright © 1991 by The University of Georgia Press. Used by permission of The University of Georgia Press.

Samuel Pickens: Diary, May 1–3, 1863. *Voices from Company D: Diaries by the Greensboro Guards, Fifth Alabama Infantry Regiment, Army of Northern Virginia*, ed. G. Ward Hubbs (Athens: The University of Georgia Press, 2003), 159–63. Copyright © 2003 by The University of Georgia Press. Used by permission of the Pickens Family Papers, The Doy Leale McCall Sr. Collection, The Doy Leale McCall Rare Book and Manuscript Library, University of South Alabama, Mobile, AL.

Jedediah Hotchkiss: Journal, May 2–6, 1863. Jedediah Hotchkiss, *Make Me a Map Of the Valley: The Civil War Journal of Stonewall Jackson's Topographer*, ed. Archie P. McDonald (Dallas: Southern Methodist University Press, 1973), 137–42. Copyright © 1973 by Southern Methodist University Press. Used by permission of the publisher.

Taylor Peirce to Catharine Peirce, May 4, 1863. *DCDT*, 105–9.

Catherine Edmondston: Diary, May 5–7, 9, and 11–12, 1863. *"Journal of a Secesh Lady": The Diary of Catherine Ann Devereux Edmondston, 1860–1866*, ed. Beth G. Crabtree and James W. Patton (Raleigh: North Carolina Division of Archives and History, 1979), 387–90, 390–91, 391–92. Copyright © 1979 by the North Carolina Division of Archives and History. Used by permission.

Charles Morse to His Family, May 7, 1863. Charles Fessenden Morse, *Letters Written During the Civil War, 1861–1865* (Boston: T. R. Marvin & Son, 1898), 127–39.

Samuel W. Fiske to the *Springfield Republican*, May 9 and 11, 1863. *Mr. Dunn Browne's Experiences in the Army: The Civil War Letters of Samuel W. Fiske*, ed. Stephen W. Sears (New York: Fordham University Press, 1998), 76–84. Copyright © 1998 by Stephen W. Sears.

Charles B. Wilder: Testimony before the American Freedmen's Inquiry Commission, May 9, 1863. *Freedom: A Documentary History of Emancipation, 1861–1867. Series I, Volume I: The Destruction of Slavery*, ed. Ira Berlin, Barbara J. Fields, Thavolia Glymph, Joseph P. Reidy, Leslie S. Rowland (New York: Cambridge University Press, 1985), 88–90. Copyright © 2010 by Cambridge University Press. Reprinted with permission of Cambridge University Press.

Thomas Wentworth Higginson: Journal, May 10, 1863. *The Complete Civil War Journal and Selected Letters of Thomas Wentworth Higginson*, ed. Christopher Looby (Chicago: The University of Chicago Press, 2000), 143–45. Copyright © 2000 by The University of Chicago. Reprinted with permission of The University of Chicago Press.

Edward O. Guerrant: Diary, May 15, 1863. *Bluegrass Confederate: The Headquarters Diary of Edward O. Guerrant*, ed. William C. Davis and Meredith L. Swentor (Baton Rouge: Louisiana State University Press, 1999), 275–77. Copyright © 1999 by Louisiana State University Press. Used by permission of the publisher.

George Richard Browder: Diary, May 17–26, 1863. *The Heavens Are Weeping: The Diaries of George Richard Browder, 1852–1886*, ed. Richard L. Troutman (Grand Rapids, Mich.: Zondervan Publishing House, 1987). Copyright © 1987 by Richard L. Troutman.

Harper's Weekly: The Arrest of Vallandigham, May 30, 1863. *Harper's Weekly*, May 30, 1863.

Oliver W. Norton to Elizabeth Norton Poss, June 8, 1863. *Norton*, 158–61.

Robert Gould Shaw to Annie Haggerty Shaw, June 9–13, 1863. *Blue-Eyed Child of Fortune: The Civil War Letters of Colonel Robert Gould Shaw*, ed. Russell Duncan (Athens: The University of Georgia Press, 1992), 341–45. Copyright © 1992 by The University of Georgia Press. Used by permission of The University of Georgia Press.

William Winters to Harriet Winters, June 9, 1863. *The Musick of the Mocking Birds, the Roar of the Cannon: The Civil War Diary and Letters of William Winters*, ed. Steven E. Bloodworth (Lincoln: University of Nebraska Press, 1998), 55–57. Copyright © 1998 by University of Nebraska Press.

Matthew M. Miller to His Aunt, June 10, 1863. *OR*, series 3, vol. III, 452–53.

Robert E. Lee to Jefferson Davis, June 10, 1863. *The Wartime Papers of Robert E. Lee*, ed. Clifford Dowdey and Louis H. Manarin (Boston: Little, Brown, 1961), 507–9. Copyright © 1961 by Commonwealth of Virginia.

William T. Sherman to John T. Swayne, June 11, 1863. *SCW*, 479–81.

Henry C. Whelan to Mary Whelan, June 11, 1863. Typescript, Cadwalader Family Collection, Historical Society of Pennsylvania, Philadelphia.

Abraham Lincoln to Erastus Corning and Others, June 12, 1863. *New-York Daily Tribune*, June 15, 1863.

William Henry Harrison Clayton to Amos and Grace Clayton and to George Washington Clayton and John Quincy Adams Clayton,

June 18 and 28, 1863. *A Damned Iowa Greyhound: The Civil War Letters of William Henry Harrison Clayton*, ed. Donald C. Elder III (Iowa City: University of Iowa Press, 1998), 73–77. Copyright © 1998 by University of Iowa Press. Used by permission of the publisher.

Charles B. Haydon: Journal, June 20, 1863. *For Country, Cause & Leader: The Civil War Journal of Charles B. Haydon*, ed. Stephen W. Sears (New York: Ticknor & Fields, 1993), 331–33. Copyright © 1993 by Stephen W. Sears.

William T. Sherman to Ellen Ewing Sherman, June 27, 1863. *SCW*, 489–93.

Edmund DeWitt Patterson: Journal, June 24–30, 1863. *Yankee Rebel: The Civil War Journal of Edmund DeWitt Patterson*, ed. John G. Barrett (Chapel Hill: The University of North Carolina Press, 1966), 109–12. Copyright © 1966 by The University of North Carolina Press, www.uncpress.unc.edu. Used by permission of the publisher.

Lafayette McLaws to Emily McLaws, June 28, 1863. *A Soldier's General: The Civil War Letters of Major General Lafayette McLaws*, ed. John C. Oeffinger (Chapel Hill: The University of North Carolina Press, 2002), 192–94. Copyright © 2002 by The University of North Carolina Press, www.uncpress.unc.edu. Used by permission of the publisher.

Alpheus S. Williams to Irene and Mary Williams, June 29, 1863. *From the Cannon's Mouth: The Civil War Letters of Alpheus S. Williams*, ed. Milo M. Quaife (Detroit: Wayne State University Press, 1959), 220–22.

Samuel W. Fiske to the *Springfield Republican*, June 30, 1863. *Mr. Dunn Browne's Experiences in the Army: The Civil War Letters of Samuel W. Fiske*, ed. Stephen W. Sears (New York: Fordham University Press, 1998), 99–102. Copyright © 1998 by Stephen W. Sears. Reprinted with permission by Stephen W. Sears.

Arthur James Lyon Fremantle: Diary, July 1–4, 1863. Arthur James Lyon Fremantle, *Three Months in the Southern States, April–June 1863* (New York: John Bradburn, 1864), 251–76.

Samuel Pickens: Diary, July 1–3, 1863. *Voices from Company D: Diaries by the Greensboro Guards, Fifth Alabama Infantry Regiment, Army of Northern Virginia*, ed. G. Ward Hubbs (Athens: The University of Georgia Press, 2003), 182–84. Copyright © 2003 by The University of Georgia Press. Used by permission of the Pickens Family Papers, The Doy Leale McCall Sr. Collection, The Doy Leale McCall Rare Book and Manuscript Library, University of South Alabama, Mobile, AL.

Francis Adams Donaldson, Narrative of Gettysburg, July 2–3, 1863. *Inside the Army of the Potomac: The Civil War Experience of Captain Francis Adams Donaldson*, ed. J. Gregory Acken (Mechanicsburg,

Pa.: Stackpole Books, 1998), 298–310. Copyright © 1998 by Stackpole Books. Used by permission of the publisher.

Elizabeth Blair Lee to Samuel Phillips Lee, July 3 and 4–5, 1863. *Wartime Washington: The Civil War Letters of Elizabeth Blair Lee*, ed. Virginia Laas (Urbana: University of Illinois Press, 1990), 281–83. Copyright © 1991 by the Board of Trustees of the University of Illinois. Reprinted from the Blair and Lee Family Papers, Manuscripts Division, Department of Rare Books and Special Collections, Princeton University Library.

Joshua Lawrence Chamberlain to George B. Herendeen, July 6, 1863. Manuscript, Maine State Archives, Augusta.

Henry Livermore Abbott to Josiah Gardner Abbott, July 6, 1863. Manuscripts, Abbott Family Civil War Letters (MS Am 800.26). Houghton Library, Harvard University, series III, folder 19. Used by permission of the Houghton Library, Harvard University, MS Am 800.26.

Lafayette McLaws to Emily McLaws, July 7, 1863. *A Soldier's General: The Civil War Letters of Major General Lafayette McLaws*, ed. John C. Oeffinger (Chapel Hill: The University of North Carolina Press, 2002), 195–97. Copyright © 2002 by The University of North Carolina Press, www.uncpress.unc.edu. Used by permission of the publisher.

Cornelia Hancock to Her Cousin, July 7, 1863, and to Ellen Hancock Child, July 8, 1863. *Letters of a Civil War Nurse: Cornelia Hancock, 1863–1865*, ed. Henrietta Stratton Jaquette (Lincoln: University of Nebraska Press, 1998), 7–12.

Catharine Peirce to Taylor Peirce, July 5, 1863. *DCDT*, 126–27.

William Henry Harrison Clayton to Amos and Grace Clayton, July 5, 1863. Donald C. Elder, ed., *A Damned Iowa Greyhound: The Civil War Letters of William Henry Harrison Clayton* (Iowa City: University of Iowa Press, 1998), 78–81. Copyright © 1998 by University of Iowa Press. Used by permission of the publisher.

William T. Sherman to Ellen Ewing Sherman, July 5, 1863. *SCW*, 499–502.

William Winters to Harriet Winters, July 6, 1863. Stephen E. Woodworth, ed., *The Musick of the Mocking Birds, the Roar of the Cannon* (Lincoln: University of Nebraska Press, 1998), 63–65. Used by permission of the publisher.

Benjamin B. French: Journal, July 8, 1863. Benjamin Brown French, *Witness to the Young Republic: A Yankee's Journal, 1828–1870*, ed. Donald B. Cole and John J. McDonough (Hanover, N.H.: University Press of New England, 1989), 426. Copyright © 1989 by University Press of New England, Lebanon, N.H. Used by permission of the publisher.

Catherine Edmondston: Diary, July 8–11, 1863. *"Journal of a Secesh Lady": The Diary of Catherine Ann Devereux Edmondston, 1860–1866*, ed. Beth G. Crabtree and James W. Patton (Raleigh: North Carolina Division of Archives and History, 1979), 424–29. Copyright © 1979 by the North Carolina Division of Archives and History. Used by permission.

George Hamilton Perkins to Susan G. Perkins, July 29, 1863. *Letters of Capt. Geo. Hamilton Perkins* (Concord, N.H.: Ira C. Evans, 1886), 116–19.

Charles B. Haydon: Journal, July 11, 1863. *For Country, Cause & Leader: The Civil War Journal of Charles B. Haydon*, ed. Stephen W. Sears (New York: Ticknor & Fields, 1993), 337–39. Copyright © 1993 by Stephen W. Sears.

John Hay: Diary, July 11–15, 1863. *Inside Lincoln's White House: The Complete Civil War Diary of John Hay*, ed. Michael Burlingame and John R. Turner Ettlinger (Carbondale and Edwardsville: Southern Illinois University Press, 1997), 61–63. Copyright © 1997 by the Board of Trustees, Southern Illinois University. Used by permission.

Abraham Lincoln to Ulysses S. Grant, July 13, 1863. *CWAL*, vol. VI, 326.

Abraham Lincoln to George Meade, July 14, 1863. *CWAL*, vol. VI, 327–28.

Samuel Pickens: Diary, July 14, 1863. *Voices from Company D: Diaries by the Greensboro Guards, Fifth Alabama Infantry Regiment, Army of Northern Virginia*, ed. G. Ward Hubbs (Athens: The University of Georgia Press, 2003), 186–87. Copyright © 2003 by The University of Georgia Press. Used by permission of the Pickens Family Papers, The Doy Leale McCall Sr. Collection, The Doy Leale McCall Rare Book and Manuscript Library, University of South Alabama, Mobile, AL.

George Templeton Strong: Diary, July 13–17, 1863. George Templeton Strong, *Diary of the Civil War, 1860–1865*, ed. Allan Nevins (New York: The Macmillan Company, 1962), 335–41. Reprinted with permission of Scribner, a Division of Simon & Schuster, Inc., from *The Diary of George Templeton Strong* by Allan Nevins and Milton Halsey Thomas. Copyright © 1952 by Macmillan Publishing Company; copyright renewed © 1980 by Milton Halsey Thomas. All rights reserved.

Emma Holmes: Diary, July 16–19, 1863. Manuscript, South Caroliniana Library, University of South Carolina, Columbia.

Walter H. Taylor to Richard Taylor, July 17, 1863. R. Lockwood Tower, ed., *Lee's Adjutant: The Wartime Letters of Colonel Walter Herron Taylor, 1862–1865* (Columbia: University of South Carolina Press, 1995), 59–63. Copyright © 1995 by University of South Carolina. Used by permission of the publisher.

James Henry Gooding to the *New Bedford Mercury*, July 20, 1863. James Henry Gooding, *On the Altar of Freedom: A Black Soldier's Civil War Letters From the Front*, ed. Virginia M. Adams (Amherst:

The University of Massachusetts Press, 1991), 36–39. Copyright ©
1991 by The University of Massachusetts Press. Used by permission
of the publisher.

Lewis Douglass to Amelia Loguen, July 20, 1863. *The Mind of the Negro
as Reflected in Letters Written During the Crisis, 1800–1860*, ed. Carter
G. Woodson (Washington, D.C.: The Association for the Study of
Negro Life and History, Inc., 1926), 544. Copyright © 1926 by The
Association for the Study of Negro Life and History, Inc.

Charlotte Forten: Journal, July 20–24, 1863. *The Journals of Charlotte
Forten Grimké*, ed. Brenda Stevenson (New York: Oxford University
Press), 494–98. Copyright © 1988 by Oxford University Press, Inc.
Used by permission of Brenda Stevenson.

Maria Lydig Daly: Diary, July 23, 1863. Maria Lydig Daly, *Diary of
a Union Lady, 1861–1865*, ed. Harold Earl Hammond (New York:
Funk & Wagnalls, 1962), 249–52. Copyright © 1962 by Funk and
Wagnalls Company, Inc.

Herman Melville: The House-top. Herman Melville, *Battle-Pieces and
Aspects of the War* (New York: Harper & Brothers, 1866), 86–87.

Henry Adams to Charles Francis Adams Jr., July 23, 1863. *The Letters
of Henry Adams*, vol. I, ed. J. C. Levenson, Ernest Samuels, Charles
Vandersee, Viola Hopkins Winner (Cambridge: The Belknap Press
of Harvard University Press), 373–76. Copyright © 1982 by the Massachusetts Historical Society. Reprinted courtesy of the Adams Family Papers, Massachusetts Historical Society. Used by permission.

George G. Meade to Henry W. Halleck, July 31, 1863. *OR*, series I,
vol. XXVII, part I, 108–10.

Robert E. Lee to Jefferson Davis, July 31, 1863. *The Wartime Papers of
Robert E. Lee*, ed. Clifford Dowdey and Louis H. Manarin (Boston:
Little, Brown, 1961), 564–65. Copyright © 1961 by Commonwealth
of Virginia.

Hannah Johnson to Abraham Lincoln, July 31, 1863. *Freedom: A Documentary History of Emancipation, 1861–1867. Series II: The Black Military
Experience*, ed. Ira Berlin (Cambridge and New York: Cambridge University Press, 1982), 582–83. Copyright © 2010 by Cambridge University Press. Reprinted with permission of Cambridge University Press.

Frederick Douglass to George L. Stearns, August 1, 1863. *The Life and
Writings of Frederick Douglass*, vol. III, ed. Philip S. Foner (New York:
International Publishers, 1952), 367–69. Copyright © 1952 by Interna-
tional Publishers Co. Inc. Used by permission of the publisher.

Frederick Douglass: The Commander-in-Chief and His Black Soldiers.
The Life and Writings of Frederick Douglass, vol. III, ed. Philip S.
Foner (New York: International Publishers, 1952), 369–72. Copyright
© 1952 by International Publishers Co. Inc. Used by permission of the
publisher.

Walt Whitman to Lewis Kirk Brown, August 1, 11, and 15, 1863. *Walt Whitman and the Civil War: A Collection of Original Articles and Manuscripts*, ed. Charles I. Glicksberg (Philadelphia: University of Pennsylvania Press, 1933), 94–98. Copyright © 1933 by University of Pennsylvania Press.

George E. Stephens to the *Weekly Anglo-African*, August 7, 1863. *A Voice of Thunder: The Civil War Letters of George E. Stephens*, ed. Donald Yacovone (Urbana: University of Illinois Press, 1997), 250–55. Copyright © 1997 by the Board of Trustees of the University of Illinois.

Robert E. Lee to Jefferson Davis, August 8, 1863. *PJD*, vol. 9, 326–27.

Jefferson Davis to Robert E. Lee, August 11, 1863. *PJD*, vol. 9, 337–38.

Wilbur Fisk to *The Green Mountain Freeman*, August 10, 1863. *Hard Marching Every Day: The Civil War Letters of Private Wilbur Fisk, 1861–1865*, ed. Emil and Ruth Rosenblatt (Lawrence: University Press of Kansas, 1992), 129–32. Copyright © 1983, 1992 by Emil Rosenblatt.

Frederick Douglass to George L. Stearns, August 12, 1863. Manuscript, Historical Society of Pennsylvania, Philadelphia.

William H. Neblett to Elizabeth Scott Neblett, August 18, 1863. Erika L. Murr, ed., *A Rebel Wife in Texas: The Diary and Letters of Elizabeth Scott Neblett, 1852–1864* (Baton Rouge: Louisiana State University Press, 2001), 137–40. Copyright © 2001 by Louisiana State University Press. Used by permission of the publisher.

Richard Cordley: Narrative of the Lawrence Massacre. *The Congregational Record*, September and October 1863, vol. V, nos. 9 and 10, 98–115.

Ulysses S. Grant to Abraham Lincoln, August 23, 1863. *PUSG*, vol. 9, 195–97.

Jonathan Worth to Jesse G. Henshaw, August 24, 1863. *The Correspondence of James Worth*, vol. I, ed. J. G. de Roulhac Hamilton (Raleigh: North Carolina Historical Commission, 1909), 257–58.

John M. Schofield to Thomas Ewing Jr., August 25, 1863. *OR*, series I, vol. XXII, part 2, 471–72.

Abraham Lincoln to James C. Conkling, August 26, 1863. *CWAL*, vol. VI, 406–10.

Ulysses S. Grant to Elihu B. Washburne, August 30, 1863. *PUSG*, vol. 9, 217–18.

Charles Francis Adams to Lord Russell, September 5, 1863. *Papers Relating to Foreign Affairs, Accompanying the Annual Message of the President to the first session of the Thirty-Eighth Congress, 1863*, part I (Washington, D.C.: Government Printing Office, 1864), 367–68.

Charles C. Jones Jr. to Mary Jones, September 6 and 9, 1863. *The Children of Pride: A True Story of Georgia and the Civil War*, Abridged Edition, ed. Robert Manson Myers (New Haven: Yale

University Press, 1984), 397–98. Copyright © 1972, 1984 by Robert Manson Myers. Used by permission of the publisher.

Raphael Semmes: Journal, September 16–24, 1863. *ORN*, series I, vol. II, 765–67.

William T. Sherman to Henry W. Halleck, September 17, 1863. *SCW*, 543–50.

William W. Heartsill: Journal, September 17–28, 1863. W. W. Heartsill, *Fourteen Hundred and 91 Days in the Confederate Army* (Wilmington, N.C.: Broadfoot Publishing Company, 1992), 271–77. Copyright © 1992 by Broadfoot Publishing Company.

John S. Jackman: Diary, September 18–21, 1863. *Diary of a Confederate Soldier: John S. Jackman of the Orphan Brigade*, edited by William C. Davis (Columbia: University of South Carolina Press, 1990), 86–89. Copyright © 1990 by University of South Carolina. Used by permission of the publisher.

Kate Cumming: Journal, September 28–October 1, 1863. Kate Cumming, *A Journal of Hospital Life in the Confederate Army of Tennessee, from the battle of Shiloh to the end of the war* (Louisville, Ky.: 1866), 94–99.

Jefferson Davis: Speech at Missionary Ridge, Tennessee, October 10, 1863. *PJD*, vol. 10, 21–22.

Oliver W. Norton to Elizabeth Norton Poss, October 15, 1863. *Norton*, 183–85.

Jefferson Davis: Speech at Wilmington, North Carolina, November 5, 1863. *PJD*, vol. 10, 49–51.

Walter H. Taylor to Bettie Saunders, November 15, 1863. R. Lockwood Tower, ed., *Lee's Adjutant: The Wartime Letters of Colonel Walter Herron Taylor, 1862–1865* (Columbia: University of South Carolina Press, 1995), 86–89. Copyright © 1995 by University of South Carolina. Used by permission of the publisher.

Cornelia Hancock to an Unknown Correspondent, November 15, 1863. *Letters of a Civil War Nurse: Cornelia Hancock, 1863–1865*, ed. Henrietta Stratton Jaquette (Lincoln: University of Nebraska Press, 1998), 31–32.

John Hay: Diary, November 18–19, 1863. *Inside Lincoln's White House: The Complete Civil War Diary of John Hay*, ed. Michael Burlingame and John R. Turner Ettlinger (Carbondale and Edwardsville: Southern Illinois University Press, 1997), 111–14. Copyright © 1997 by the Board of Trustees, Southern Illinois University. Used with permission.

Abraham Lincoln: Address at Gettysburg, November 19, 1863. *CWAL*, vol. VII, 22–23.

Petition from the Colored Citizens of Beaufort, November 20, 1863. *Freedom: A Documentary History of Emancipation, 1861–1867. Series I, Volume II: The Wartime Genesis of Free Labor: The Upper South*, ed. Ira Berlin, Steven F. Miller, Leslie S. Rowland (New

York: Cambridge University Press, 1993), 166. Copyright © 1993 by Cambridge University Press. Reprinted with the permission of Cambridge University Press.

William W. Smith: Journal, November 13–25, 1863. Smith, William Wrenshall, "Holocaust Holiday: The Journal of a Strange Vacation to the War-torn South and a Visit with U.S. Grant," *Civil War Times Illustrated*, XVIII, 6 (Oct. 1979), 28–40. Copyright © 1979 by Historical Times Inc.

Montgomery C. Meigs: Journal, November 23–25, 1863. "First Impressions of Three Days' Fighting: Quartermaster General Meigs's 'Journal of the Battle of Chattanooga,'" ed. John M. Hoffman, in *Ulysses S. Grant: Essays and Documents*, ed. David L. Wilson and John Y. Simon (Carbondale and Edwardsville: Southern Illinois University Press, 1981), 70–76. Copyright © 1981 by The Ulysses S. Grant Association. Used by permission of The Ulysses S. Grant Association.

James A. Connolly to Mary Dunn Connolly, November 26 and December 7, 1863. "Major James Austin Connolly," *Transactions of the Illinois State Historical Society for the Year 1928* (Springfield: Illinois State Historical Library, 1928), 297–304. Used by permission of the Abraham Lincoln Presidential Library.

Theodore Lyman: Journal, November 26–December 2, 1863. David W. Lowe, ed., *Meade's Army: The Private Notebooks of Lt. Col. Theodore Lyman* (Kent, Ohio: Kent State University Press, 2007), 70–76. Copyright © 2007 by Kent State University Press. Used by permission of the publisher.

Wilbur Fisk to *The Green Mountain Freeman*, November 29 and December 8, 1863. *Hard Marching Every Day: The Civil War Letters of Private Wilbur Fisk, 1861–1865*, ed. Emil and Ruth Rosenblatt (Lawrence: University Press of Kansas, 1992), 166–74. Copyright © 1983, 1992 by Emil Rosenblatt.

George G. Meade to Margaret Meade, December 2 and 7, 1863. Manuscript, George Gordon Meade Papers, Historical Society of Pennsylvania, Philadelphia.

Frederick Douglass: Our Work Is Not Done, December 4, 1863. *The Frederick Douglass Papers, Series One: Speeches, Debates, and Interviews*, vol. 3, ed. John W. Blassingame (New Haven: Yale University Press, 1985), 598–609. Copyright © 1985 by Yale University. Reprinted by permission. Used by permission of the publisher.

Abraham Lincoln: Annual Message to Congress, December 8, 1863. *CWAL*, vol. VII, 36–53.

Abraham Lincoln: Proclamation of Amnesty and Reconstruction, December 8, 1863. *CWAL*, vol. VII, 53–56.

George Templeton Strong: Diary, December 11–13, 1863. George Templeton Strong, *Diary of the Civil War, 1860–1865*, ed. Allan

Nevins (New York: The Macmillan Publishing Company, 1962), 379–80. Reprinted with permission of Scribner, a Division of Simon & Schuster, Inc., from *The Diary of George Templeton Strong* by Allan Nevins and Milton Halsey Thomas. Copyright © 1952 by The Macmillan Publishing Company; copyright renewed © 1980 by Milton Halsey Thomas. All rights reserved.

Catherine Edmondston: Diary, December 11, 1863. *"Journal of a Secesh Lady": The Diary of Catherine Ann Devereux Edmondston, 1860–1866,* ed. Beth G. Crabtree and James W. Patton (Raleigh: North Carolina Division of Archives and History, 1979), 505–6. Copyright © 1979 by the North Carolina Division of Archives and History. Used by permission.

Mary Chesnut: Diary, January 1, 1864. *Mary Chesnut's Civil War*, ed. C. Vann Woodward (New Haven: Yale University Press, 1981), 519–26. Copyright © 1981 by C. Vann Woodward, Sally Bland Meets, Barbara C. Carpenter, Sally Bland Johnson, and Katherine W. Herbert. Used by permission of the publisher.

Judith W. McGuire: Diary, January 1, 1864. Judith W. McGuire, *Diary of a Southern Refugee, during the war*, 3rd edition (Richmond, Va.: J.W. Randolph & English, Publishers, 1889), 248–50.

Patrick R. Cleburne: Memorandum on Emancipation and Enlisting Black Soldiers, January 2, 1864. *OR*, series 1, vol. LII, part 2, 586–92.

William T. Sherman to Roswell M. Sawyer, January 31, 1864. *SCW*, 598–602.

Lois Bryan Adams to the *Detroit Advertiser and Tribune*, February 8, 23, 1864. Lois Bryan Adams, *Letter from Washington, 1863–1865*, ed. Evelyn Leasher (Detroit: Wayne State University Press, 1999), 77–80, 83–85. Copyright © 1999 by Wayne State University Press.

Francis J. Higginson to John A. Dahlgren, February 18, 1864. *ORN*, series I, vol. XV, 328.

James H. Tomb: Notes on the *H. L. Hunley*, January 1865. *ORN*, series I, vol. XV, 334–35.

Judith W. McGuire: Diary, February 28, 1864. Judith W. McGuire, *Diary of a Southern Refugee, during the war*, 3rd edition (Richmond, Va.: J.W. Randolph & English, Publishers, 1889), 252–55.

John Paris: Sermon Preached at Kinston, N.C., February 28, 1864. *A Sermon: preached before Brig.-Gen. Hoke's Brigade, at Kinston, N.C., on the 28th of February, 1864, by Rev. John Paris, Chaplain Fifty-Fourth Regiment N.C. Troops, upon the death of twenty-two men, who had been executed in the presence of the brigade for the crime of desertion* (Greensborough, N.C.: A. W. Ingold & Co., 1864).

Oliver W. Norton to Elizabeth Norton Poss, February 29, 1864. *Norton*, 197–201.

John B. Jones: Diary, March 1–2 and 5, 1864. J. B. Jones, *A Rebel War Clerk's Diary at the Confederate States Capital*, vol. II (Philadelphia: J. B. Lippincott & Co., 1866), 162–65, 166–67.

Ulysses S. Grant to William T. Sherman, March 4, 1864. *PUSG*, vol. 10, 186–87.

William T. Sherman to Ulysses S. Grant, March 10, 1864. *SCW*, 602–04.

This volume presents the texts of the printings and manuscripts chosen as sources here but does not attempt to reproduce features of their typographic design or physical layout. In the texts that have been printed from manuscript, dashes at the end of sentences have been changed to periods, the beginnings of sentences have been capitalized, and punctuation at the end of sentences and closing quotation marks have been supplied. The texts are printed without alteration except for the changes previously discussed and the correction of typographical errors. Spelling, punctuation, and capitalization are often expressive features, and they are not altered, even when inconsistent or irregular. The following is a list of typographical errors corrected, cited by page and line number: 1.22, fours.; 26.40, *montem*; 74.8, accused-; 74.9, point.; 74.10, amend,/ments.; 111.18–19, arrangments; 123.37, truy; 126.15, to-dry; 128.9, not be; 136.11, no pursue; 144.10, thal may; 151.32, than any; 170.1, haven; 184.13, lnftry; 213.22, Carolina There; 213.26, A.; 214.15, them One; 219.17, unkindest" stroke of all"; 221.25, 4000000; 221.29, 40000,000; 266.4, sevral; 296.10, right, Our; 365.28, this It; 368.26, 20th; 405.16, 3 killed; 432.12, be; 475.25, burning But; 479.19, head; 482.33, manths; 486.1, consnmed.; 544.6, answred,; 547.16, fulfilled He; 552.1, of government; 554.2–3, degredation; 554.10, shackless; 572.40, decend; 573.37, consecreated; 576.35, movemnts; 579.39, of of; 581.21, doszen; 594.32, mounain; 653.12, hertofore; 674.14, diary After; 696.22, it's name.; 709.32, Chapter,; 729.19, suggest.

Notes

In the notes below, the reference numbers denote page and line of this volume (the line count includes headings, but not rule lines). No note is made for material included in the eleventh edition of *Merriam-Webster's Collegiate Dictionary*. Biblical references are keyed to the King James Version. Quotations from Shakespeare are keyed to *The Riverside Shakespeare*, ed. G. Blakemore Evans (Boston: Houghton Mifflin, 1974). Footnotes and bracketed editorial notes within the text were in the originals. For further historical and biographical background, references to other studies, and more detailed maps, see James McPherson, *Battle Cry of Freedom: The Civil War Era* (New York: Oxford University Press, 1988); *Encyclopedia of the American Civil War: A Political, Social, and Military History*, edited by David S. Heidler and Jeanne T. Heidler (New York: W. W. Norton, 2002); *The Library of Congress Civil War Desk Reference*, edited by Margaret E. Wagner, Gary W. Gallagher, and Paul Finkelman (New York: Simon & Schuster, 2002); and Aaron Sheehan-Dean, *Concise Historical Atlas of the U.S. Civil War* (New York: Oxford University Press, 2008).

4.8   Stahel's Division] The First Division of the Eleventh Corps had been commanded by Brigadier General Julius Stahel (1825–1912) until January 10, 1863, when Stahel was succeeded by Brigadier General Nathaniel C. McLean (1815–1905).

4.23–24   Colonel and Lieutenant Col.] Colonel Elias Peissner (1825–1863), a Bavarian-born professor of German and political economy at Union College in Schenectady, recruited the 119th New York Infantry in the summer of 1862 and commanded the regiment until May 2, 1863, when he was killed at Chancellorsville. Lieutenant Colonel John T. Lockman (1834–1912), a native of New York City, succeeded Peissner and led the regiment for the remainder of the war.

5.12   three letters from you] Theodore A. Dodge mailed portions of his wartime journal to his family in New York.

5.25   Von Steinwehr] Brigadier General Adolph von Steinwehr (1822–1877) commanded the Second Division of the Eleventh Corps.

6.32–33   Grand Divisions . . . Franklin] In November 1862 Burnside had organized the Army of the Potomac into three Grand Divisions: the Right, commanded by Major General Edwin V. Sumner (1797–1863); the Center, commanded by Major General Joseph Hooker (1814–1879); and the Left, commanded by Major General William B. Franklin (1823–1903). Each Grand Division was composed of two infantry corps and was assigned its own cavalry and artillery.

9.18   John] John Quincy Adams II (1833–1894), older brother of Henry Adams and Charles Francis Adams Jr. A lawyer, he served during the war on the staff of Massachusetts governor John A. Andrew.

10.8   Mary] Mary Adams (1845–1928), younger sister of Henry Adams and Charles Francis Adams Jr.

10.17   Lebe wohl.] Farewell.

12.36   Markoe] Captain Francis Markoe Bache (1833–1867), the son of Meade's sister, Maria Del Carmen Meade Bache (1810–1877), and Lieutenant Colonel Hartman Bache (1798–1872), an officer in the Army Corps of Engineers. Francis Markoe Bache joined Meade's staff in the summer of 1863 after the battle of Gettysburg.

12.37   Halleck] Major General Henry W. Halleck (1815–1872), general-in-chief of the Union armies from July 1862 to March 1864.

13.12   George] Lieutenant George Meade (1843–1897), General Meade's son, was serving with the 6th Pennsylvania Cavalry.

13.15   *Doubleday . . . Reserves*] Major General Abner Doubleday (1819–1893) had been assigned to command the Third Division of the First Corps, which Meade had led at South Mountain, Antietam, and Fredericksburg. The division included thirteen infantry regiments that were formerly part of the Pennsylvania Reserve Volunteer Corps, organized by the state authorities in May 1861 when Pennsylvania raised more troops than the federal government had initially called for.

13.18   Mr. Meredith] William M. Meredith (1799–1873) was secretary of the treasury, 1849–50, and attorney general of Pennsylvania, 1861–67.

13.21   my nomination] Meade had been appointed major general of volunteers on November 29, 1862.

14.8   Grand Division organization broken up] Hooker abolished the Grand Divisions on February 5, 1863, and Meade resumed command of the Fifth Corps.

14.27–28   *Dan Butterfield* & *Dan Sickles*] Major General Daniel Butterfield (1831–1901), a former superintendent of the American Express Company, had commanded a brigade in the Peninsula campaign and at Second Bull Run and a corps at Fredericksburg. Hooker appointed Butterfield chief of staff of the Army of the Potomac on January 29, 1863, and he served until July 9, 1863, when Meade replaced him with Major General Andrew A. Humphreys. Brigadier General Daniel E. Sickles (1819–1914) had served as a Democratic congressman from New York, 1857–61. Sickles had commanded a brigade during the Peninsula campaign and a division at Fredericksburg. Appointed commander of the Third Corps by Hooker on February 3, 1863, he served until July 2, 1863, when he was seriously wounded at Gettysburg.

15.18   Gibbons]   Brigadier General John Gibbon (1827–1896) commanded a brigade at Second Bull Run, South Mountain, and Antietam, and a division at Fredericksburg.

15.39–40   we go to the James River]   A week after the Union defeat at Fredericksburg, Major Generals William B. Franklin and William F. Smith had proposed to President Lincoln that the Army of the Potomac abandon its position on the Rappahannock River and instead advance on Richmond along the north and south banks of the James River.

16.12–13   General . . . Fremont, Hunter]   Major Generals John C. Frémont (1813–1890), the Republican presidential nominee in 1856, and David Hunter (1802–1886) were both abolitionists.

16.20–21   Couch . . . Sedgewick]   Darius Couch (1822–1897), commander of the Second Corps; Franz Sigel (1824–1902), commander of the recently formed Reserve Grand Division; Henry W. Slocum (1827–1894), commander of the Twelfth Corps; William F. Smith (1824–1903), commander of the Sixth Corps; John Sedgwick (1813–1864), who succeeded William F. Smith as commander of the Sixth Corps in February 1863.

16.23   Reynolds]   John Reynolds (1820–1863), commander of the First Corps.

16.26   *Stoneman*]   George Stoneman (1822–1894), commander of the Third Corps, who became commander of the Army of the Potomac's newly established Cavalry Corps in February 1863.

16.37   the Regulars.—Humphreys]   Two brigades of regular U.S. infantry served in the Second Division of the Fifth Corps. Brigadier General Andrew A. Humphreys (1810–1883) commanded the Third Division in the Fifth Corps.

17.2   Secy.]   Edwin M. Stanton (1814–1869), secretary of war, 1862–68.

17.5   *Berry*]   Major General Hiram G. Berry (1824–1863) had led a brigade in the Peninsula campaign and at Fredericksburg. He commanded the First Division of the Third Corps from February 1863 to May 3, when he was killed at Chancellorsville. Like Butterfield and Sickles, Berry had not attended West Point.

17.14   en Prince]   In a princely manner; lavishly.

17.21   South Mountain]   The battle of South Mountain was fought in western Maryland on September 14, 1862.

18.30–32   I have heard, . . . a Dictator.]   Henry J. Raymond (1820–1869), the editor of *The New York Times*, was told by his correspondent William Swinton on January 22, 1863, that Hooker had recently denounced Burnside as incompetent, described "the President and Government at Washington as imbecilic and 'played out,'" and called for a dictator. Raymond had repeated these remarks to Lincoln at a White House reception on January 24.

21.9–10   Capt. Hallowell of the 20th Mass. Infantry]   Captain Norwood Penrose (Pen) Hallowell (1839–1914), an 1861 graduate of Harvard College, had fought at Ball's Bluff and Fair Oaks and had been wounded at Glendale and Antietam.

22.6   Oliver T. Beard]   Lieutenant Colonel Oliver T. Beard of the 48th New York Infantry had led a company of the 1st South Carolina Volunteers, a recently organized black regiment, in successful raids along the Georgia and Florida coasts in November 1862. Beard resigned his commission on December 24, 1862.

23.18   Mr Stevens]   Thaddeus Stevens (1792–1868) served in Congress as an antislavery Whig from Pennsylvania, 1849–53, and as a Republican from 1859 until his death.

24.2–3   *"Our God is marching on."*]   Julia Ward Howe (1819–1910), "The Battle Hymn of the Republic" (1862).

24.6   Capt Carpenter . . . Jessie Scouts]   Captain Charles C. Carpenter commanded the Jessie Scouts, an irregular intelligence-gathering detachment formed in Missouri in 1861 by John C. Frémont and named in honor of his wife, Jessie Benton Frémont. After Frémont was relieved of his command in November 1861, Carpenter collected intelligence in Missouri, Kentucky, and Tennessee until the spring of 1862, when Major General Ulysses S. Grant ordered him expelled from his military district for horse stealing. Carpenter then rejoined Frémont in western Virginia, where he gave a dramatic account of his alleged exploits behind Confederate lines to the *Philadelphia Inquirer* in June 1862.

24.22   Washburne of Ill.]   Elihu B. Washburne (1816–1887) was a Whig, and then Republican, congressman from Illinois, 1853–69. Washburne met Ulysses S. Grant shortly after the outbreak of the war and became his political patron.

24.24–27   the canal . . . the Yazoo]   See Chronology, January–March 1863.

24.29–30   the gun boat . . . Vicksburg blockade]   The *Queen of the West*. See Chronology, February 1863.

25.11   Joe Kernochan and Aspinwall]   Joseph Kernochan (1789–1864) was a retired dry goods merchant. William H. Aspinwall (1807–1875) was a founder and former president of the Pacific Mail Steamship Company who had financed the construction of a railroad across the Isthmus of Panama in the 1850s.

25.13   at 823]   823 Broadway, between 12th and 13th Streets, the headquarters of the U.S. Sanitary Commission.

25.14 Murray Hoffman] Hoffman (1791–1878) was assistant vice-chancellor of New York, 1839–43, a judge of the New York Superior Court, 1853–61, and the author of several legal treatises.

25.15 Dr. Bellow's] Henry Bellows (1814–1882), a Unitarian pastor from New York City, helped found the U.S. Sanitary Commission in 1861 and served as its president throughout the war.

25.16 Gibbs and Agnew] Oliver Wolcott Gibbs (1822–1908) was professor of chemistry at the Free Academy (later City College of New York), 1849–63, and at Harvard, 1863–87. Cornelius Rea Agnew (1830–1888), an ophthalmologist, was surgeon general of New York state, 1859–62. Both men served on the executive committee of the Sanitary Commission.

25.33 Rosecrans] Major General William S. Rosecrans (1819–1898) commanded the Union Army of the Cumberland, which was deployed around Murfreesboro, Tennessee.

26.20 vibices] Patches of effused blood beneath the skin.

26.39–40 *fortem . . . mentem*] Latin: to keep a resolute attitude in difficult circumstances.

27.6 *adynamia*] Lack of strength.

27.7 Bidwell] Marshall S. Bidwell (1799–1872), Strong's law partner.

28.14 Wicks] Sergeant Oscar Wicks had served with Norton in Company K of the 83rd Pennsylvania Infantry. Wicks was medically discharged on January 21, 1863.

28.21 Malvern Hill] Union troops and artillery repulsed Confederate attacks at Malvern Hill near the James River on July 1, 1862, in the last of the Seven Days' Battles.

28.28 L.] Norton's sister Elizabeth Norton Poss, known as Libby.

29.9 hog-car] A railroad freight car used for transporting hogs.

29.19 Hanover Court House . . . Gaines' Mill] The battle of Hanover Court House, fought north of Richmond on May 27, 1862, was a Union victory. Gaines' Mill, the third of the Seven Days' Battles, was fought on June 27, 1862, and ended with the Confederates driving Union forces south across the Chickahominy River.

33.20 Agnes] Eleanor Agnes Lee (1841–1873), Lee's daughter.

33.25–27 Mrs. Jones . . . her husband] Sarah Taylor Jones (1831–1917), a niece of Zachary Taylor, was the widow of Major General David R. Jones, a division commander in Lee's army who died of heart disease in Richmond on January 15, 1863.

33.27–28 Fitzhugh . . . Charlotte] Brigadier General William Henry

Fitzhugh Lee (1837–1891), Lee's son, who commanded a cavalry brigade in the Army of Northern Virginia; Charlotte Wickham Lee (d. 1863), the wife of W.H.F. Lee.

33.32–33   George . . . Perry]   The brothers George and Perry Parks were slaves owned by Lee's father-in-law, George Washington Parke Custis (1781–1857). Under the terms of Custis's will, they were freed on December 29, 1862.

34.3   *Annie Haggerty*]   The daughter of a wealthy New York auctioneer, Annie Kneeland Haggerty (1835–1907) met Shaw in 1861 and became engaged to him at the end of 1862.

34.30   Susie's]   Sarah Susannah Shaw Minturn (1839–1926), Shaw's sister.

37.3   vast gathering at Exeter Hall]   A public meeting held by the London Emancipation Society on January 29, 1863, at Exeter Hall on the Strand, which could hold three thousand people in its main hall and another thousand in a smaller room. Henry Adams attended the event, and wrote to his brother Charles the following day: "Every allusion to the South was followed by groaning, hisses and howls, and the enthusiasm for Lincoln and for everything connected with the North, was immense."

38.4–5   "they who take . . . the sword."]   Cf. Matthew 26:52.

38.9–10   when your Senatorial . . . the 4th,]   The third session of the 37th Congress ended on March 3, 1863, after which the Senate held a special session, March 4–14.

40.3   Mr. Speaker]   Francis Hoffmann (1822–1903), Republican lieutenant governor of Illinois, 1861–65. (Under the 1848 Illinois constitution, the lieutenant governor served as speaker of the senate.)

41.6   Colonel Mack]   Alonzo W. Mack (1822–1871), an attorney, served in the Illinois house of representatives, 1858–60, and the state senate, 1860–68. Mack organized the 76th Illinois Infantry in August 1862 and served as its colonel until January 1863, when he resigned his commission in order to return to the state senate.

44.18   Col Stone]   William M. Stone (1827–1893) commanded the 22nd Iowa Infantry from August 1862 to August 1863, when he resigned to run for governor on the Republican ticket. He served as governor of Iowa, 1864–68.

44.29   Gen Bentons]   Brigadier General William P. Benton (1828–1867) commanded the First Division of the Union Army of Southeast Missouri.

45.33   Lieutenant Murray]   Neill Murray (1827–1899) was the first lieutenant of Company C, 22nd Iowa Infantry. Murray was wounded in the assault on Vicksburg on May 22, 1863, and resigned his commission on May 27.

45.36   Cyrus & Mary . . . the babys]   Cyrus Milner (1822–1881), brother of Catharine Peirce and husband of Mary Milner (1824–1900), Taylor Peirce's sister. Catharine and Taylor Peirce had three children: Sarah, born 1853; Frank, born 1858; and Ellis, born 1862.

45.34   Capt Ault] Adam T. Ault (1822–1883) commanded Company C until August 1863, when he resigned due to chronic dysentery.

47.3–4   *Thomas Ewing Sr. . . . John Sherman*] Thomas Ewing (1789–1871) served as a senator from Ohio, 1831–37 and 1850–51; as secretary of the treasury, 1841; and as secretary of the interior, 1849–50. William T. Sherman had married Ellen Ewing, his eldest daughter, in 1850. John Sherman (1823–1900) served as a Republican congressman from Ohio, 1855–61; as a senator, 1861–77 and 1881–97; as secretary of the treasury, 1877–81; and as secretary of state, 1897–98.

47.29–30   slips . . . Cincinnati Commercial] Ellen Ewing Sherman (1824–1888) had sent clippings of favorable pieces about Sherman's leadership that appeared on January 24 and February 2, 1863.

48.10   Andre] Major John André (1750–1780), an aide to Sir Henry Clinton, was captured in civilian disguise by New York militiamen on September 23, 1780, after he secretly met with Benedict Arnold to arrange for the surrender of West Point. André was tried as a spy and hanged on October 2, 1780.

48.32–33   the Manassas movement . . . McDowell] Brigadier General Irvin McDowell (1818–1885) advanced with 30,000 men into northeastern Virginia on July 16, 1861, with the objective of defeating the 20,000 Confederate troops at Manassas Junction under General Pierre G. T. Beauregard (1818–1893). General Joseph E. Johnston (1807–1891) shifted his command of 11,000 men by rail out of the Shenandoah Valley and reinforced Beauregard at Manassas, leading to the Union defeat at the first battle of Bull Run on July 21.

48.36–37   Beauregard at Corinth] Beauregard moved his headquarters to Corinth, Mississippi, in late March 1862 and retreated there after the battle of Shiloh, April 6–7. His army remained at Corinth until May 29, when Beauregard ordered its evacuation.

48.40   Halleck . . . Forts Henry & Donaldson] As commander of the Department of the Missouri, Halleck was Grant's immediate superior in February 1862 when Grant's forces captured the two forts.

49.4   post of Arkansas] See Chronology, January 1863.

50.13–15   Dr. Hewit . . . Dr. McMillan] Henry S. Hewit (1825–1873) became the medical director of Grant's army in February 1862. Correspondent Whitelaw Reid, writing as "Agate," published a report in the *Cincinnati Gazette* on April 4 accusing Hewit of incompetence, drunkenness, and disloyalty. Hewit was removed from his post in late April, but was reinstated later in the year. Charles McMillan (c. 1825–1890) was the medical director of Sherman's corps.

50.35   do.] Ditto.

52.20 Peter Hagner] Hagner (1772–1850) was an accounting clerk in the War Department, 1793–1817, and auditor of the U.S. Treasury, 1817–49.

53.26–27 The Captain . . . badly, cowardly] Frank W. Flanner was dismissed from the service on March 2, 1863.

53.30–31 Island No. 10] An island in the Mississippi near New Madrid, Missouri.

57.22 Mr. SPEAKER] Schuyler Colfax (1823–1885) was presiding as speaker pro tempore. A Republican congressman from Indiana, 1855–69, he was speaker of the house, 1863–69, and vice president of the United States, 1869–73.

57.31 Mr. OLIN] Abram B. Olin (1808–1879) was a Republican congressman from New York, 1857–63.

58.4 Mr. CAMPBELL] James H. Campbell (1820–1895) was a Republican congressman from Pennsylvania, 1859–63.

58.13 His threat] In his speech earlier in the day, Campbell had defended the Lincoln administration for arresting "spies and traitors" in the North and said: "Let me tell gentlemen on the other side that so far from condemning these arrests, it would be better for them if they could read the writing on the wall, and make their peace with liberty and their country while there is yet time. If they cannot see the evidence of a healthy reaction among the masses they are blind to the signs of the times. The error of the Government has been *leniency.* If it had given to traitors a drum-head court-martial and hempen cord, it would have better pleased the loyal men of the United States. [Applause in the galleries.] If I mistake not, the day is not far distant when the people will be so aroused against rebellion that traitors, their aiders and abettors, will call upon the rocks and mountains to cover them."

58.40 Mr. ROBINSON] James Robinson (1823–1886) was a Democratic congressman from Illinois, 1859–65 and 1871–75.

59.4 Mr. COX] Samuel Cox (1824–1889) was a Democratic congressman from Ohio, 1857–65, and from New York, 1869–73, 1873–85, and 1886–89.

59.17 Mr. ROSCOE CONKLING] Conkling (1829–1888) was a Republican congressman from New York, 1859–63 and 1865–67, and a senator, 1867–81.

59.22 Mr. JOHNSON] Philip Johnson (1818–1867) was a Democratic congressman from Pennsylvania, 1861–67.

59.33 Mr. VERREE] John Paul Verree (1817–1889) was a Republican congressman from Pennsylvania, 1859–63.

60.17–21 a gentleman . . . State and city] John Van Buren (1810–1866), son of Martin Van Buren, was a prominent New York Democrat who had supported John C. Breckinridge in the 1860 presidential election. Speaking to a

Democratic meeting on February 10, 1863, Van Buren had said that "until the South can put down the men who led her into rebellion, the war must go on." In a speech to a Democratic campaign rally on October 13, 1862, Van Buren proposed that McClellan "be authorized" to take Richmond, after which a convention would be held at which "our Southern brethren" would be free to either rejoin the Union "under the Constitution as it is" or to separate.

60.22–23　"wayward sisters depart in peace."]　In his October 13, 1862, speech, John Van Buren had read a letter sent by General Winfield Scott to William H. Seward on March 3, 1861, outlining four alternative policies the new administration could adopt toward the seceding states: offer new constitutional concessions, impose a blockade, launch an invasion with an army of 300,000 men, or "Say to the seceded States—wayward sisters, depart in peace."

60.34　the recent election]　In the fall 1862 elections, the Democrats won the governorships of New Jersey and New York, legislative majorities in Illinois, Indiana, and New Jersey, and gained thirty-four seats in the House of Representatives, although the Republicans retained control of Congress.

61.29–30　"healthy reaction" . . . Mr. CAMPBELL]　See note 58.13.

63.22　Baba]　Turkish for "father," sometimes used as an honorific in the Ottoman Empire.

63.25　Turkish bow-string and the sack]　Enemies of the Ottoman sultan were sometimes strangled with a bow-string or thrown in sacks into the Bosphorus.

65.3　Mr. WHITE]　Chilton White (1826–1900) was a Democratic congressman from Ohio, 1861–65.

65.29　insurrection in Poland]　An insurrection against Russian rule began in Poland on January 22, 1863. It was suppressed in 1864.

67.22–23　a single day . . . the king]　The prohibition of a political banquet by the government of King Louis-Philippe led to demonstrations in Paris on February 22, 1848, that quickly turned into a popular revolution. Louis-Philippe abdicated on February 24, and the Second Republic was proclaimed that evening.

68.34–37　"inquire into . . . treasonable practices"]　This provision was omitted from the seventh section of the final bill, which gave provost marshals the power to arrest deserters and spies.

69.8　act . . . twenty-fifth Edward III]　The Treason Act of 1351, passed in the twenty-fifth year of the reign of Edward III.

69.15　act of Henry IV]　The Treason Act of 1399, which repealed several laws expanding the crime of high treason enacted during the reign of Richard II (1377–99).

69.19   Lord Hale observes] Sir Matthew Hale (1609–1676), in his post-humously published *Historia Placitorum Coronæ: The History of the Pleas of the Crown* (2 vols., 1736).

69.37   Blackstone remarks,] William Blackstone (1723–1780), *Commentaries on the Laws of England* (4 vols., 1765–69), bk. IV, ch. 6.

70.23–24   Erskine . . . Hardy] Thomas Erskine (1750–1823) success-fully defended Thomas Hardy (1752–1832), secretary of the radical London Corresponding Society, against charges of high treason in 1794. The speech quoted by Vallandigham was given by Erskine on February 5, 1781, at the trial of the anti-Catholic agitator Lord George Gordon (1751–1793), who had been charged with high treason for inciting the London "No Popery" riots of 1780. Gordon was acquitted.

70.39–40   declaration of Montesquieu] Charles de Secondat, Baron de Montesquieu (1689–1755), *The Spirit of the Laws* (1748), bk. XII, ch. 7.

71.2   Madison, in the Federalist] *The Federalist* No. 43, January 23, 1788.

71.11–12   Story, . . . declared] Joseph Story (1779–1845), *Commentaries on the Constitution of the United States* (3 vols., 1833), bk. III, ch. 39, sec. 1793. Story was an associate justice of the U.S. Supreme Court, 1811–45.

72.30   Barré] Isaac Barré (1726–1802) was a member of Parliament, 1761–90.

72.35–36   Ohio Senator . . . who said] Thomas Corwin (1794–1865), in a speech in the Senate on February 11, 1847, said: "If I were a Mexican, I would tell you, 'Have you not room in your own country to bury your dead men? If you come into mine, we will greet you with bloody hands, and wel-come you to hospitable graves.'" Corwin was a Whig congressman, 1831–40; governor of Ohio, 1840–42; a U.S. senator, 1845–50; and secretary of the treasury, 1850–53. He served in Congress as a Republican, 1859–61, and as U.S. minister to Mexico, 1861–64.

72.40–73.2   Abraham Lincoln . . . this House?] In a speech delivered on January 12, 1848.

74.1   Forts Warren and La Fayette?] Fort Warren, on Georges Island in Boston Harbor, and Fort Lafayette, on the Brooklyn side of the entrance to New York harbor, were used to hold political prisoners during the Civil War.

75.32–33   Hamilton . . . Federalist] Cf. *The Federalist* No. 84, May 28, 1788.

77.7–11   twenty-fifth section . . . confinement indefinitely] Under the twenty-fifth section of the final bill, persons convicted of resisting the draft were subject to a $500 fine and two years' imprisonment.

77.12–13   the draft . . . complete] The Militia Act of July 17, 1862, made all able-bodied male citizens from eighteen to forty-five members of their respective state militias and authorized the president to call state militia into federal service for up to nine months. On August 4 the Lincoln administration summoned 300,000 militia into service, subject to the number of voluntary enlistments in each state. Although many states filled their recruiting quotas with volunteers, several states conducted militia drafts.

77.30–32 Keyes . . . Mr. MAY] John W. Kees, the editor of the *Circleville Watchman*, a Democratic weekly in Ohio, was arrested on June 29, 1862, and held in the Old Capitol prison in Washington, D.C., for seventeen days before being released. Edson B. Olds (1802–1869), a former Democratic congressman from Ohio, was arrested on August 12, 1862, and held in Fort Lafayette until his release on December 12, 1862. During his imprisonment Olds was elected to the Ohio house of representatives. Dennis A. Mahony (1821–1879), editor of the *Dubuque Herald*, was arrested on August 14, 1862, and David Sheward (1825–after 1895), editor of the Fairfield *Constitution and Union*, was detained three days later. The two Iowa Democrats were held in the Old Capitol prison until November 11, 1862, when they were discharged after swearing allegiance to the United States. Mahony wrote about his arrest and detention in his book *The Prisoner of State* (1863). Kees, Olds, Mahony, and Sheward were all arrested on orders from Secretary of War Stanton for disloyalty and discouraging enlistments, although none of the men were ever charged. William J. Allen (1829–1901) was a Democratic congressman from Illinois, 1862–65, who advocated letting southern Illinois decide whether it should join the Confederacy. Allen was arrested on August 14, 1862, two months after winning a special election to Congress, and taken to Washington, where he was paroled to a hotel because of illness. President Lincoln ordered his discharge on September 16, 1862. Henry May (1816–1866) was a Unionist congressman from Maryland, 1861–63. He was arrested on suspicion of disloyalty on September 13, 1861, and imprisoned at Fort Lafayette. May was paroled on October 14 and discharged on December 12, 1861.

78.26 Festus] See Acts 25:16.

79.2 prisoner of Chillon] Poem (1816) by Lord Byron.

79.10 Weed] Thurlow Weed (1797–1882), editor of the *Albany Evening Journal*, 1830–62, and a close political associate of William H. Seward.

79.15–16 minion of Mr. Seward] Seth C. Hawley (1810–1884), a New York attorney Seward had engaged to examine the cases of political prisoners being held in New York and Boston.

80.37–81.2 lad of fifteen . . . "disloyal practices"] A similar story, regarding an unnamed thirteen-year-old boy, appeared in the Columbus *Crisis* on December 24, 1862, and was later circulated in Democratic campaign literature in 1864.

81.10–13 hump-back carrier . . . Fort La Fayette] George A. Hubbell, a news agent on the Naugatuck Railroad who suffered from a spinal deformity, was arrested on September 20, 1861, and imprisoned in Fort Lafayette on the orders of Secretary of War Simon Cameron for selling the *New York Daily News* after its circulation in Connecticut had been banned by U.S. marshal David H. Carr. Nathan Hubbell, a Methodist preacher and Republican, wrote to President Lincoln on September 21 vouching for his brother's loyalty, and Hubbell was released on Seward's orders on September 26, 1861. Benjamin Wood (1820–1900), a Democratic congressman from New York, 1861–65 and 1881–83, was editor and publisher of the *New York Daily News*, 1860–1900. His brother, Fernando Wood (1812–1881), was the Democratic mayor of New York, 1855–57 and 1860–61, and served in Congress, 1841–43, 1863–65, and 1867–81.

81.17   Hamilton declares]   In *The Federalist* No. 84, May 28, 1788.

81.19   Blackstone declares]   In *Commentaries on the Laws of England* (4 vols., 1765–69), bk. I, ch. I.

81.26   "the pestilence . . . darkness."]   Psalm 91:6.

83.4   Patrick Henry, in the Virginia Convention]   Cf. Patrick Henry's speech in the Virginia Ratifying Convention, June 5, 1788.

83.17   Hamilton, in the Federalist]   *The Federalist* No. 29, January 9, 1788.

84.7   answer of Hamilton]   In *The Federalist* No. 29.

85.6   indemnity and suspension bill]   The bill, which became law on March 3, 1863, authorized the president to suspend the privilege of the writ of habeas corpus "during the present rebellion" and indemnified government officials against legal proceedings brought against them for arrests made under presidential authority.

85.9   an Attorney General]   Edward Bates (1793–1869) served as attorney general, 1861–64. He submitted an opinion to Congress on July 13, 1861, defending the constitutionality of Lincoln's suspension of the writ of habeas corpus.

85.19–21   Chief Justice . . . supreme court of Wisconsin]   While sitting as a U.S. circuit court judge in Baltimore, Chief Justice Roger B. Taney ruled in *Ex parte Merryman* on May 28, 1861, that President Lincoln lacked the constitutional authority to suspend the writ of habeas corpus. The Supreme Court of Wisconsin issued a writ of habeas corpus on December 4, 1862, for Nicholas Kemp, who had been arrested by the military for participating in a riot against the militia draft in Port Washington on November 10. When the army refused to respond, the court ruled 3–0 on January 13, 1863, that Lincoln's suspension of the writ was legally void, but did not attempt to enforce its decision.

85.40   opinion of Story]   In *Commentaries on the Constitution of the United States* (3 vols., 1833), bk. III, ch. 32, sec. 1336.

86.24   Mr. SHEFFIELD]   William P. Sheffield (1820–1907) was a Union congressman from Rhode Island, 1861–63.

86.29–30   the bill . . . Senate in 1807] On January 22, 1807, President Thomas Jefferson sent a special message to Congress in which he accused former vice president Aaron Burr of conspiring to foment war with Spain and detach the western states from the Union. William Branch Giles, a Democratic-Republican senator from Virginia, immediately introduced a bill in Congress suspending the writ of habeas corpus in cases of treason for three months. It passed the Senate on January 23 with only one dissenting vote, but was rejected by the House of Representatives, 113–19, on January 26.

87.33–34   the words . . . Job] Job 2:4.

87.38   Mr. BIDDLE] Charles J. Biddle (1819–1873) was a Democratic congressman from Pennsylvania, 1861–63.

90.25   Hartford Times] A Democratic newspaper that supported Thomas H. Seymour's candidacy for governor.

91.3   western Egypt] "Egypt" was a popular name for southern Illinois.

91.33–34   "winter of our discontent"] *Richard III* I.i.1.

93.22–23   columbiad] A large cannon used for coastal defense.

94.21   Genesis Point] The peninsula on which Fort McAllister was built.

94.38–40   General Walker . . . Taliaferro] Brigadier General William H. T. Walker (1816–1864), Brigadier General Thomas L. Clingman (1812–1897), Brigadier General William B. Taliaferro (1822–1898).

97.25   Your dear baby] Mary Ruth Jones (1861–1934) was born on June 25, 1861, seven days before the death of her sister Julia Berrien Jones (1859–1861) from scarlet fever, and twelve days before the death of her mother Ruth Berrien Jones (1837–1861) from puerperal fever.

97.26–27   Daughter, Robert, . . . Stiles] Mary Sharpe Jones Mallard (1835–1889), daughter of Charles C. Jones Sr. and Mary Jones; her husband, Robert Q. Mallard (1830–1904), a Presbyterian clergyman; Katherine Clay Stiles (1832–1916), a family friend.

98.17   L. M. CHILD] Lydia Maria Child (1802–1880), a novelist and author of popular advice books, had edited the *National Anti-Slavery Standard* from 1841 to 1843; her antislavery works included *An Appeal in Favor of that Class of Americans Called Africans* (1833) and *Correspondence between Lydia Maria Child and Gov. Wise and Mrs. Mason of Virginia* (1860).

99.27   New York *Evangelist*] The *Home Evangelist*, a monthly magazine published in New York by the American Baptist Home Mission Society, printed an article, "A Visit to the Freedmen," in its March 1863 number that said: "The three vices that prevail are lying, thieving and licentiousness. Drunkenness is increasing."

99.30   Gen. Saxton] Brigadier General Rufus Saxton (1824–1908), the Union military governor of coastal South Carolina and Georgia, 1862–65.

102.1 butternuts] A term, derived from the use of butternut dyes in homespun clothing and military uniforms, for upland southerners; for upland southerners who had settled in the southern counties of Illinois, Indiana, and Ohio; and for Confederate soldiers.

102.5 Yellville] Town in northern Arkansas, about forty miles southeast of Forsyth, Missouri.

102.25 Hindman at Prairie Grove] Major General Thomas C. Hindman (1828–1868) unsuccessfully attacked Union forces at Prairie Grove in north-west Arkansas on December 7, 1862, before retreating the next day. The battle engaged about 11,000 Confederate and 9,000 Union soldiers, and cost the Confederates about 1,300 men killed, wounded, or missing, and the Union about 1,250.

102.30 Blunt] Brigadier General James G. Blunt commanded a Union division at Prairie Grove.

104.16 "Nincy" and Ab. Buckles] Absalom Nincehelser (1833–1907) and Abner J. Buckles (1833–1909) served with Clayton in Company H of the 19th Iowa Infantry.

104.21–22 Lt. Ferguson . . . Lt. Sommerville] Walter Ferguson commanded Company H in January 1863 before being sent home due to illness. He was discharged on February 26, 1863. George W. Sommerville (1819–1896) later commanded Company H and published a history of the unit in 1890.

105.29–30 General Banks] Major General Nathaniel P. Banks (1816–1894) commanded the Army of the Gulf, December 1862–May 1864.

106.35–36 "hewers of . . . of water."] Joshua 9:23.

108.27 Gen'l Hurlbert] Major General Stephen A. Hurlbut (1815–1882) commanded the Sixteenth Corps in the Army of the Tennessee.

108.28 Columbus] Columbus, Kentucky.

108.29 Jackson] Jackson, Tennessee.

108.31 Gen'l McPherson] Major General James B. McPherson (1828–1864) commanded the Seventeenth Corps in the Army of the Tennessee.

109.5–6 Col. Bissell's . . . Regiment] Josiah Wolcott Bissell (1818–1891) commanded the "Engineer Regiment of the West," organized in the fall of 1861 with men from Michigan, Illinois, Iowa, and Missouri.

109.14–15 Admiral Porter] Acting Rear Admiral David D. Porter (1813–1891), commander of the Mississippi Squadron.

109.18 Sunflower and Blackwater expeditions] Unsuccessful Union attempts to reach the Yazoo River to the northeast of Vicksburg via Steele's Bayou and the Sunflower River, and by way of Yazoo Pass and the Coldwater River. See Chronology, February–March 1863.

109.28 Parrotts] Muzzle-loading rifled cannon, named after the New York ordnance manufacturer Robert R. Parrott (1804–1877).

109.32 Hewit] See note 50.13–15.

110.37 Captain Janney] William L. Jenney (1832–1907) was a civilian engineer who had joined the Union army in 1861.

111.1 Cranch] Christopher Pearse Cranch (1813–1892), a Unitarian minister, poet, and painter who lived in Paris, 1853–63.

111.2 Politechnique and Centrale] The École Polytechnique, scientific school founded in Paris in 1794 to train managers for the French civil service, and the École Centrale des Arts et Manufactures, engineering school founded in Paris in 1829. Janney had studied at the École Centrale.

111.10–11 Farragut's . . . Hartford] Rear Admiral David G. Farragut (1801–1870), commander of the West Gulf Blockading Squadron, had run past the batteries at Port Hudson, Louisiana, on the night of March 14 in his flagship, the steam sloop *Hartford*.

111.12 Dick Taylor's] Major General Richard Taylor (1826–1879), the son of Zachary Taylor, commanded the Confederate District of West Louisiana. Olmsted had visited his sugar plantation near New Orleans in 1853.

111.13–17 McMillan . . . Herald's correspondent.] Charles McMillan had been accused of "criminal oversight" by Thomas W. Knox (1835–1896), correspondent for the *New York Herald*, in a January 18, 1863, dispatch story that led to Knox's court-martial; see headnote on p. 47 in this volume.

111.26 Gen'l Steele] Major General Frederick Steele (1819–1868) commanded the First Division in Sherman's Fifteenth Corps.

111.30 Gen'l Blair's] Brigadier General Frank Blair (1821–1875) commanded a brigade in Sherman's corps. Blair served as a Republican congressman from Missouri, 1857–59, 1861–62, and 1863–64. He was the brother of Montgomery Blair, postmaster general, 1861–64, and the son of Francis Preston Blair, an adviser to President Lincoln.

114.24 Governors of Iowa and Wisconsin] Samuel J. Kirkwood (1813–1894) was the Republican governor of Iowa, 1860–64 and 1876–77; a senator, 1866–67 and 1877–81; and secretary of the interior, 1881–82. Edward Salomon (1828–1909) was the Republican governor of Wisconsin, 1862–64.

114.27 Governor of Illinois] Richard Yates (1815–1873) was the Republican governor of Illinois, 1861–65. Yates served in Congress as a Whig, 1851–55, and in the Senate as a Republican, 1865–71.

115.4–5 Governor of Indiana] Oliver Perry Morton (1823–1877) was the Republican governor of Indiana, 1861–67, and a senator, 1867–77.

115.20–21 his adjutant General] Lieutenant Colonel John A. Rawlins (1831–1869).

115.32   Breese his flag-captain]   Lieutenant Commander Kidder Randolph
Breese (1831–1881) was the captain of Porter's flagship *Black Hawk*, a converted river steamboat.

118.10   "*A man's . . . a' that.*"]   Song (1795) by Robert Burns.

118.11–12   American citizen, . . . highest legal adviser]   Attorney General Edward Bates issued an opinion on November 29, 1862, declaring that
free black persons born in the United States were American citizens.

120.14   another Detroit]   William Faulkner, a Detroit tavern keeper, was
arrested on February 26, 1863, for allegedly raping a nine-year-old white girl.
Although Faulkner claimed to be of Spanish and American Indian ancestry,
he was identified in the newspapers as a "negro." The case was extensively
covered in the *Detroit Free Press*, a Democratic newspaper that for months had
been warning its readers that the Emancipation Proclamation would result
in racial "amalgamation" and the loss of jobs for white labor. Faulkner was
convicted of rape on March 6 and sentenced to life imprisonment. After an
attempt to lynch him outside the courthouse failed, white mobs began attacking black residents and setting fire to their homes and businesses. Two men,
one white and one black, were killed and approximately thirty-five buildings
destroyed before troops ended the rioting before midnight. Faulkner was pardoned in 1870 after his accuser recanted her story.

123.2–3   Tallahatchie and at Deer Creek,]   See Chronology, March 1863.

123.27   Governor Letcher]   John Letcher (1813–1884) was governor of Virginia, 1860–64. He had previously served in Congress as a Democrat, 1851–59.

123.34   Col. I. W. Garrett]   Isham W. Garrott (1816–1863) and William
M. Brooks had practiced law together in Marion, Alabama, before the war.
Garrott became the colonel of the 20th Alabama Infantry in 1861 and led the
regiment until June 17, 1863, when he was killed at Vicksburg.

125.10   Judge Campbell]   John A. Campbell (1811–1889) was an associate
justice of the U.S. Supreme Court, 1853–61, and an assistant secretary in the
Confederate War Department, 1862–65.

125.11   Judge Meredith]   John A. Meredith (1814–1882) was judge of the
Richmond circuit court, 1852–69. Meredith had ruled on February 24, 1863,
in a habeas corpus case that every citizen of Maryland, and every foreigner,
who had previously enlisted in the Confederate service for any length of time
was subject to conscription.

125.14–15   the mayor]   Joseph C. Mayo (1795–1872) was mayor of Richmond, 1853–65 and 1866–68.

125.38–39   Gen. Elzey . . . Secretary of War]   Major General Arnold
Elzey (1816–1871), commander of the Richmond defenses; Brigadier General
John H. Winder (1800–1865), the Confederate provost marshal; James A. Sed-
don (1815–1880), Confederate secretary of war, 1862–65.

126.11   Gen. D. H. Hill] Major General Daniel Harvey Hill (1821–1889), commander of the Confederate Department of North Carolina and Southern Virginia.

126.23–24   the tax bill] See Chronology, April 24, 1863.

126.25–26   Gen. Blanchard . . . Massachusetts] Brigadier General Albert G. Blanchard (1810–1891) had been relieved of his command in northern Louisiana for failing to stop raids by the Union forces camped along the Mississippi near Vicksburg. A West Point graduate, Blanchard had settled in Louisiana after resigning from the army in 1840.

126.31–32   the capture . . . five guns] The Union gunboat *Diana* ran aground in Berwick Bay, Louisiana, on March 28, 1863, after being damaged by Confederate artillery fire and was captured by troops from the 13th Battalion Texas Cavalry and the 28th Louisiana Infantry. On April 14, 1863, the Confederates burned the *Diana* to prevent her from being retaken by Union forces after their victory at Bayou Teche.

126.34–35   Charleston . . . the forts] See Chronology, April 7, 1863.

129.22   Liverpool Point] On the Maryland shore of the lower Potomac, about thirty-five miles south of Washington.

130.5–6   General Hunt] Brigadier General Henry J. Hunt (1819–1889) was chief of artillery of the Army of the Potomac, 1862–65.

130.7–8   Fifth . . . Franklin] Major General Fitz John Porter (1822–1901) commanded the Fifth Corps, May–November 1862. He was cashiered from the army on January 21, 1863, after being convicted at court-martial of disobedience and misconduct at Second Bull Run. Major General William B. Franklin commanded the Sixth Corps from May to November 1862, when he became commander of the Left Grand Division of the Army of the Potomac (see note 6.32–33).

130.12–13   Major DePeyster . . . Howe's division] John Watts De Peyster Jr. (1841–1873) was commissioned in 1862 as a major in the 1st New York Light Artillery, Wainwright's regiment, and later assigned to command the artillery in the Second Division of the Sixth Corps, led by Brigadier General Albion P. Howe (1818–1897).

130.26   Colonel Von Vegesack] Ernst von Vegesack (1820–1903), a Swedish military officer, came to the United States in 1861 to join the Union army. He commanded the 20th New York Infantry at South Mountain, Antietam, Fredericksburg, and Chancellorsville, then returned to Sweden after the regiment mustered out at the end of its two-year enlistment term in June 1863.

131.9   one of his sons] Thomas (Tad) Lincoln (1853–1871).

132.25–26   Sanderson] Lieutenant Colonel James M. Sanderson (1815?–1871), a former New York hotel manager and author of *Camp Fires and Camp*

Cooking; or, Culinary Hints for the Soldier (1862), was the commissary of subsistence of the First Corps.

132.29–30   Dupont's fleet . . . *Keokuk* sunk] Rear Admiral Samuel Francis Du Pont (1803–1865), commander of the South Atlantic Blockading Squadron, 1861–63, led the unsuccessful naval assault on Charleston Harbor. The *Keokuk* was badly damaged by Confederate shore batteries on April 7 and sank the next day.

132.36–37   first report . . . Conduct of the War] The seven-member Joint Committee on the Conduct of the War, made up of three senators and four representatives and dominated by Radical Republicans, was established by Congress on December 10, 1861, in response to the Union defeats at Bull Run and Ball's Bluff. It issued its first report, which focused primarily on the operations of the Army of the Potomac, on April 6, 1863.

133.5–7   War Department order . . . treasonable sentiments] General Orders No. 89, issued by the adjutant general's office in the War Department on April 6, 1863, announced that Lieutenant John M. Garland of the 42nd New York Infantry had been dishonorably discharged for writing that the Emancipation Proclamation was "as unconstitutional as it is unjust" and that the "principles" and "hearts" of the administration were "blacker than the 'nigger' they are fighting for." (Garland's letter, addressed to the Reverend Elliott H. Thompson in Shanghai, was opened by the post office because it carried insufficient postage.)

138.5–6   fair Italy has risen] Victor Emmanuel II of Sardinia-Piedmont was proclaimed king of a united Italy in 1861.

138.27–28   "corner-stone] In a widely reported speech given in Savannah, Georgia, on March 21, 1861, Confederate vice president Alexander H. Stephens (1812–1883) said that the "corner-stone" of the Confederacy "rests upon the great truth, that the negro is not equal to the white man; that slavery—subordination to the superior race—is his natural and normal condition."

139.25   our Crawfords?] Thomas Crawford (1814–1857), American sculptor born and raised in New York City who spent much of his career in Italy. His work included the design for the Statue of Freedom on top of the U.S. Capitol dome.

142.18–19   James Louis Petigru] Petigru (1789–1863) was attorney general of South Carolina, 1822–30, and led the opposition to nullification in the state house of representatives, 1830–32. He later served as the U.S. attorney for South Carolina, 1850–53, and opposed secession in 1860.

142.19–20   Baphomet] A pagan idol allegedly worshipped by the medieval Knights Templar.

145.6–11   foreign minister . . . breach] Henri Mercier (1816–1886), the French minister to the United States from July 1860 to December 1863, was considered by many northerners to be sympathetic to the Confederacy. In January 1863 Mercier had become involved with the Colorado mining promoter William Cornell Jewett (1823–1893), Horace Greeley of the *New York Tribune*, and Congressman Clement L. Vallandigham in an unsuccessful attempt to gain support for European mediation of the war.

148.19   the 19th regulars] The 19th U.S. Infantry.

148.25   my long illness] Connolly had fallen ill with typhoid fever in November 1862.

149.26   Morgan . . . Forrest] Brigadier General John Hunt Morgan (1825–1864), Major General Joseph Wheeler (1836–1906), Brigadier General John Wharton (1828–1865), and Brigadier General Nathan Bedford Forrest (1821–1877). Wheeler was a cavalry corps commander, and Morgan, Wharton, and Forrest were cavalry division commanders, in the Army of Tennessee.

149.34   Burnsides' armies] Major General Ambrose Burnside (1824–1881) had taken command of the Department of the Ohio on March 17, 1863.

152.16   Hains Bluff] Hayne's Bluff, overlooking the Yazoo River about eleven miles northeast of Vicksburg.

153.21   this Department] The Department of the South, which included South Carolina, Georgia, and most of Florida.

154.6   Mr. Jefferson has beautifully said] Cf. Query XVIII, *Notes on the State of Virginia* (1785).

155.17   Van Dorn] Major General Earl Van Dorn (1820–1863) commanded a cavalry corps in the Army of Tennessee. On April 10, 1863, Van Dorn conducted a reconnaissance of the Union positions at Franklin, Tennessee, before withdrawing to Spring Hill.

155.18–19   Brother Coley and Dr. Buckner] Coleman Stone (c. 1844–1863) served with the 28th Mississippi Cavalry. He died on September 22, 1863, from injuries he received by being thrown from his horse. Dr. C. B. Buckner, a druggist and planter who served as a captain with the 28th Mississippi Cavalry, was married to Kate Stone's aunt, Laura Ragan Buckner.

157.3   Little Sister] Amanda Stone (c. 1850–1934).

157.24   Mrs. Alexander] The mother of Mary Hardison.

158.5   Jimmy] Kate Stone's brother, James A. Stone (c. 1847–1905).

158.15   Mamma] Kate Stone's widowed mother, Amanda Ragan Stone (c. 1824–1892).

158.25   Webster] A slave who worked as a dining room servant and coachman on the Stone plantation.

158.29   Beverly] Laura Ragan Buckner's daughter, who was about three years old.

159.29   Johnny's lap]   Kate Stone's brother, John B. Stone (c. 1848–1930).

160.9   Charles]   A slave who worked with Webster in the dining room of the Stone plantation.

160.17–18   Finish this another day.]   In her journal for April 27, 1863, Stone described how her family traveled in two dugouts through bayous and swamps to the plantation of Dr. James G. Carson, where they stayed for nearly three weeks before resuming their westward flight.

163.29   this brigade]   The Second Brigade of the Second Division in the Sixth Corps was made up of the 2nd, 3rd, 4th, 5th, and 6th Vermont Infantry and the 26th New Jersey Infantry.

165.20   a disgraceful affair]   On the night of April 19, 1863, as many as a dozen soldiers from the 5th Vermont Infantry attacked a black family living in a cabin near their picket line, beating John Frazier and raping his wife and her twelve-year-old niece. When the picket guard was alerted and approached the cabin, they were fired upon and returned fire, wounding one of the assailants. Although the victims were unable to identify most of their attackers, Sergeant Lawson M. Perkins was court-martialed and sentenced to five years in prison on May 22, 1863. Perkins was released on December 16, 1864, and returned to duty with the 5th Vermont before mustering out in June 1865. Private Moses D. Emerson was also convicted and imprisoned, but was released on August 8, 1864, and returned to the 5th Vermont, where he served for the remainder of the war.

167.34   Rhodes']   Brigadier General Robert E. Rodes (1829–1864) commanded a division in the Second Corps of the Army of Northern Virginia, led by Lieutenant General Thomas J. (Stonewall) Jackson.

167.37   A. P. Hill]   Major General Ambrose Powell Hill (1825–1865) led a division in Jackson's corps. (A. P. Hill was not related to Major General Daniel Harvey Hill.)

167.38   Trimble & Early]   The division in Jackson's corps assigned to Major General Isaac R. Trimble (1802–1888) was led in the Chancellorsville campaign by Brigadier General Raleigh E. Colston (1825–1896) because Trimble was still recovering from being wounded at Second Manassas. Major General Jubal A. Early (1816–1894) led a division in Jackson's corps.

170.5–6   Revocation . . . Nantes]   In 1685 Louis XIV revoked the Edict of Nantes, issued by Henry IV in 1598, which had granted religious and political rights to French Protestants.

170.20   Brother's]   Philip Hicky Morgan (1825–1900), Sarah Morgan's half brother, was a successful attorney in New Orleans who had remained loyal to the Union.

170.24   Gen. Bowen]   Brigadier General James Bowen (1808–1886) was the provost marshal of the Union Department of the Gulf.

171.6   Miriam]   Sarah Morgan's older sister, Miriam Morgan (1840–1898), later Miriam Morgan Dupré.

171.17–18   George and Gibbes]   Sarah Morgan's brothers George M. Morgan (1838–1864) and Thomas Gibbes Morgan (1835–1864) were serving with the Confederate army in Virginia. George M. Morgan would die of illness at Orange Court House on January 12, 1864; Thomas Gibbes Morgan was captured at Rappahannock Station on November 7, 1863, and died of illness in the prison camp at Johnson's Island, Ohio, on January 21, 1864.

171.19   Banks . . . Attakapas]   A region of southern Louisiana that includes Bayou Teche. See Chronology, April 1863.

172.31–32   the river]   The Rappahannock.

172.33   Hamilton's Crossing]   A railroad depot five miles southeast of Fredericksburg.

173.8   Col. Sam. B. Pickens]   Colonel Samuel B. Pickens (1839–1891) commanded the 12th Alabama Infantry, 1862–65.

175.11   Capt. Williams]   Captain Jonathan W. Williams (1840–1908) commanded Company D of the 5th Alabama Infantry, in which Pickens served.

175.21–22   Col. Hobson]   Lieutenant Colonel Edwin Lafayette Hobson (1835–1901), second in command of the 5th Alabama Infantry.

176.40   Col. Oneil]   Colonel Edward A. O'Neal (1818–1890), Pickens's brigade commander.

178.11   The Generals]   Jackson and Lee.

178.15   General Stuart]   Major General J.E.B. Stuart (1833–1864) commanded the cavalry corps of the Army of Northern Virginia.

178.23   the   house]   The Luckett house.

179.11   Smith and   .]   Smith and Wilbourn. Lieutenant James Power Smith (1837–1923) was one of Jackson's aides; Captain Richard E. Wilbourn (1838–1875) was the chief signal officer in Jackson's corps.

179.14   Dr. McGuire]   Hunter H. McGuire (1835–1900) was the medical director of Jackson's corps.

179.15   Lacey]   The Reverend Beverly Tucker Lacy (1819–1900), a Presbyterian minister who served as the chaplain of Jackson's corps.

179.30   Colonel Long]   Armistead L. Long (1825–1891), one of Lee's staff officers.

179.34–36   Anderson . . . McLaws]   Major General Richard Anderson (1821–1879) and Major General Lafayette McLaws (1821–1897) commanded divisions in the First Corps of the Army of Northern Virginia, led by Lieutenant General James Longstreet. During the Chancellorsville campaign

Anderson and McLaws reported directly to Lee while Longstreet was on detached duty in southeast Virginia.

180.8   the Irish Battalion] The 1st Virginia Infantry Battalion.

180.11   Major A. S. Pendleton] Alexander S. Pendleton (1840–1864), Jackson's assistant adjutant general (chief of staff).

180.32   Boswell] Captain James K. Boswell (1838–1863), a topographical engineer serving on Jackson's staff.

181.3   Major J. Horace Lacey] Lacey (1823–1906) was the brother of Beverly Tucker Lacy (see note 179.15).

181.7   Brown] Sergeant Samuel Howell Brown (1831–1905), who had served as surveyor of Jefferson County, Virginia, before the war.

181.22–23   Morrison . . . Mrs. Jackson] Lieutenant Joseph G. Morrison (1842–1906), one of Jackson's aides, was the brother of Mary Anna Morrison Jackson (1831–1915).

181.25–26   Colonel Crutchfield] Colonel Stapleton Crutchfield (1835–1865), the chief of artillery in Jackson's corps, had his leg amputated after being wounded on May 2.

181.40   Col. French] Colonel Samuel Bassett French (1820–1898) served as a military aide to Virginia governor John Letcher.

182.4   Stoneman] Major General George Stoneman led a cavalry raid against the railroads between Richmond and Fredericksburg, April 29–May 8, that failed to seriously disrupt Lee's supply line.

182.17   United States Ford] A ford across the Rappahannock.

184.30–32   Genl Carr . . . Genl McClernand] Brigadier General Eugene A. Carr (1830–1910), Brigadier General Alvin P. Hovey (1821–1891), and Brigadier General Peter J. Osterhaus (1823–1917) commanded divisions in the Thirteenth Corps of the Army of the Tennessee. Major General John A. McClernand (1812–1900), the corps commander, had been a Democratic congressman from Illinois, 1843–51 and 1859–61.

185.37–38   Genl Green . . . Baldwin] Brigadier General Martin E. Green (1815–1863), Brigadier General Edward D. Tracy (1833–1863), and Brigadier General William E. Baldwin (1827–1864) commanded brigades in the division led by Brigadier General John S. Bowen (1830–1863). Tracy was killed at Port Gibson, Green was killed during the siege of Vicksburg, and Bowen died of dysentery shortly after Vicksburg surrendered.

186.12   about 3,500 of their men] Confederate losses at Port Gibson were reported as sixty killed, 340 wounded, and 387 missing.

186.35–36   the 23 Iowa . . . the loss] The regiment's casualties at Port Gibson were reported as nine killed and twenty-six wounded.

187.12   Lt Col Glasgow] Lieutenant Colonel Samuel L. Glasgow (1838–1916) led the 23rd Iowa Infantry at Port Gibson.

187.32   Genl Quinbys brigade] Brigadier General Isaac F. Quinby (1821–1891) commanded a division in the Seventeenth Corps.

187.33   Smiths Divisions] Brigadier General Andrew J. Smith (1815–1897) led a division in the Thirteenth Corps.

190.23   Libby Prison] Prison for Union soldiers in Richmond that was established in a warehouse formerly used by Libby & Sons, a ship provisioning company.

190.26–27   "One blast . . . men."] Cf. Sir Walter Scott, *The Lady of the Lake* (1810), Canto VI, stanza 18.

191.20–21   "With His . . . the victory."] Cf. Psalm 98:1.

191.34–35   His brother in Law] Edmondston confused D. H. Hill, whose wife Isabella was a sister of Mary Anna Morrison Jackson, with A. P. Hill.

192.16–17   Col Duke of Wise's Legion] Colonel Richard T. W. Duke (1822–1898) was the commander of the 46th Virginia Infantry. Organized in 1861 as part of Wise's Legion, a force in northwestern Virginia commanded by Brigadier General Henry A. Wise, the regiment was later posted to Chaffin's Bluff along the James River south of Richmond. Wise (1806–1876) had served as a congressman from Virginia, 1833–44, and as governor, 1856–60.

192.19   Tunstall's] Tunstall Station, about fifteen miles east of Richmond.

193.19–20   Gen Paxton . . . Stonewall Brigade] Brigadier General Elisha F. Paxton (1828–1863) was killed at Chancellorsville on May 3. The Stonewall brigade was recruited from the Shenandoah Valley of Virginia in April 1861 and was commanded by Thomas J. Jackson at the first battle of Manassas, July 21, 1861, where both the brigade and its commander earned the nickname "Stonewall" for their defensive stand on Henry Hill.

193.23–24   Van Dorn is dead] Major General Earl Van Dorn was shot to death in Spring Hill, Tennessee, on May 7, 1863, by Dr. George B. Peters, who claimed Van Dorn was having an affair with his wife.

193.33   Hascosea] Plantation in Halifax County, North Carolina, used as a summer home by the Edmondstons.

194.14–15   "Little children . . . idols."] 1 John 5:21.

194.23–24   Thomas Jones . . . wife] Thomas Devereux Jones (1838–1863) and Martha (Pattie) Ann Skinner (1842–1889) were married on January 1, 1863. A captain in the 27th North Carolina Infantry, Jones was wounded at Bristoe Station, Virginia, on October 14, 1863, and died in Richmond on November 6.

194.27   Hill's repulse at Washington] Major General D. H. Hill unsuccessfully besieged the Union garrison at Washington, North Carolina, March 30–April 15, 1863.

196.18   Colonel McVicars]   Lieutenant Colonel Duncan McVicar (1827–1863) of the 6th New York Cavalry.

197.4   General Geary]   Brigadier General John W. Geary (1819–1873) commanded the Second Division of the Twelfth Corps.

197.20   General Howard]   Major General Oliver Otis Howard (1830–1909), commander of the Eleventh Corps since April 1863.

197.28   General Williams' Division]   Brigadier General Alpheus S. Williams (1810–1878) commanded the First Division of the Twelfth Corps.

198.22   Dutchmen]   Many of the soldiers in the Eleventh Corps were German-American.

199.5   General Birney's Division]   Brigadier General David B. Birney (1825–1864) commanded the First Division of the Third Corps.

201.32   General Patrick]   Brigadier General Marsena R. Patrick (1811–1888), provost marshal of the Army of the Potomac.

203.18   The old Second]   The 2nd Massachusetts Infantry.

205.26   general of brigade]   Colonel Samuel S. Carroll (1832–1893) commanded the First Brigade in the Third Division of the Second Corps.

205.33   French's division]   Brigadier General William H. French (1815–1881) commanded the Third Division of the Second Corps.

208.25   "the best army . . . planet,"]   At a dinner held on April 8, 1863, during President Lincoln's visit to army headquarters, Hooker had called the Army of the Potomac "the finest army on the planet."

208.34–209.1   Longstreet didn't come up at all]   See Chronology, May 4–5, 1863.

214.17   the Merrimack]   In 1861, Union forces scuttled and burned the steam frigate U.S.S. *Merrimack* when they evacuated the Norfolk navy yard. The Confederates raised and rebuilt the ship as the ironclad ram C.S.S. *Virginia* and used it to attack the Union fleet in Hampton Roads on March 8, 1862. After fighting its historic duel with the ironclad U.S.S. *Monitor* on March 9, the *Virginia* remained at Norfolk until May 11, 1862, when it was blown up to prevent its capture following the Confederate evacuation of the city.

216.21   Dr Rogers]   Dr. Seth Rogers (1823–1893), a friend of Higginson's and the owner of the Worcester Hydropathic Institution, served as surgeon of the 1st South Carolina Volunteers.

217.14–18   Maj Strong . . . Lt. Col. Billings]   Lieutenant Colonel Liberty Billings (1823–1877) was dismissed from the army for incompetence by an examining board on July 28, 1863, at which time Major John D. Strong was promoted to lieutenant colonel and became the regiment's second in command. Strong resigned his commission on August 15, 1864.

218.29   The Tribune correspondent]   Clarence A. Page (1838–1873) was a war correspondent for the *New-York Daily Tribune*, 1862–65.

219.11   Col. Hawkins']   Colonel Hiram Hawkins (1826–1914) commanded the Confederate 5th Kentucky Infantry.

219.17   "That is . . . of all"!]   Maria Edgeworth (1767–1849), *The Modern Griselda* (1804).

220.26–27   "*He gave . . . away*".]   Cf. Job 1:21.

220.37   on   at]   On May 10 at.

221.3   Major Hawkes]   Major Wells J. Hawks (1814–1873), the chief commissary officer in Jackson's corps.

221.5   on   where]   On May 11 where.

221.13   Gen Ewell]   Richard S. Ewell (1817–1872) commanded a division under Jackson, March 1862–August 1862, and the Second Corps of the Army of Northern Virginia, May 1863–May 1864.

221.14   the battle of   ]   The battle of Groveton (or Brawner Farm), August 28, 1862, was part of the Second Manassas campaign.

221.18   "fame is . . . brass"]   See Horace, *Odes*, bk. III. xxx.

221.31–32   *Balaams numerical horse*]   See Numbers 22:21–35.

222.19–20   Brig Genl Shackelford]   A native of Lincoln County, Kentucky, James M. Shackelford (1827–1909) commanded a Union brigade with its headquarters in Russellville.

223.3   "submit to . . . that be"]   See Romans 13:1.

223.22–23   Buckner . . . Boone & Burnett]   Camp Boone and Camp Burnett were set up near Clarksville in northwestern Tennessee in the summer of 1861 to recruit and train Kentucky Confederate troops. Brigadier General Simon Bolivar Buckner (1823–1914) took command of the camps in September 1861 and led several regiments into Kentucky in order to occupy Bowling Green.

224.20   Lizzie]   Browder's wife, Ann Elizabeth Warfield Browder (d. 1897).

224.26   Bro Alexander]   William Alexander (1818–1883), a Methodist preacher who shared the Logan County circuit with Browder.

227.17–18   General Burnside . . . Cincinnati Court]   Vallandigham applied for a writ of habeas corpus in the U.S. Circuit Court for the Southern

District of Ohio on May 9, 1863, two days after his conviction by a military commission. On May 11 Burnside submitted a written statement to the court in which he declared that "my duty requires me to stop license and intemperate discussion, which tends to weaken the authority of the Government and army." After hearing arguments from attorneys representing Vallandigham and Burnside, Judge Humphrey H. Leavitt refused to issue a writ and stated that Burnside, as an agent of the president, had the power during time of war to "arrest persons who, by their mischievous acts of disloyalty, impede or endanger the military operations of the government."

228.3   Fernando Wood's party]   Fernando Wood (see note 81.10–13) was a leading New York Peace Democrat.

232.23   Colonel Montgomery]   James Montgomery (1814–1871) later commanded a brigade of black troops in South Carolina and Florida before resigning his commission in 1864.

233.1   Mr. Butler King's]   Thomas Butler King (1800–1864), a lawyer and planter who served in Congress as a Whig, 1839–43 and 1845–50.

234.31   Effie]   Shaw's sister, Josephine Shaw (1843–1905), who married Colonel Charles Russell Lowell Jr. (1835–1864) in October 1863. Lowell was fatally wounded at Cedar Creek, Virginia, on October 19, 1864, while leading the 2nd Massachusetts Cavalry.

235.13   "Semmes"]   Raphael Semmes (1809–1877), captain of the Confederate commerce raider *Alabama*, 1862–64.

235.33–37   Pierce Butler . . . three hundred slaves]   In 1836 Pierce Butler (1810–1867) inherited a half-share in the coastal Georgia rice and cotton plantations of his grandfather Pierce Butler (1744–1822), a South Carolina delegate to the Constitutional Convention who later served in the Senate. Heavily in debt from gambling and financial losses in the panic of 1857, Butler sold 429 men, women, and children at a Savannah race course in March 1859 for $303,850.

236.2   Miss Fanny]   English actress and writer Frances Anne (Fanny) Kemble (1809–1893) married Pierce Butler in 1834. They separated in 1845 and were divorced in 1849, in part because of her opposition to slavery. Kemble published an account of her stay on the Butler plantations, *Journal of a Residence on a Georgian Plantation in 1838–1839*, in 1863.

236.25   the young ladies]   Sarah Butler Wister (1835–1908) and Frances Butler Leigh (1838–1910), the daughters of Fanny Kemble and Pierce Butler.

237.24   Mr. Ritchie]   Lieutenant John Ritchie (1836–1919) served as the quartermaster of the 54th Massachusetts, 1863–65.

241.20   Colonel Page]   Lieutenant Colonel Page of the 9th Louisiana Infantry (African Descent), who took command of the regiment after Colonel Hermann Lieb (1826–1908) was wounded.

241.32   enemy cried, "No quarters"]   In a report dated June 8, 1863, Colonel Lieb wrote that in the fighting along the levee the Confederates charged "madly on with cries of 'No quarters for white officers, kill the damned Abolitionists, but spare the niggers' &c." Captain Corydon Heath of the 9th Louisiana (African Descent) and Second Lieutenant George Conn of the 11th Louisiana (African Descent) were recorded in Union army records as having been killed after being taken prisoner at Milliken's Bend.

241.34–35   Colonel Allen . . . Brigadier-General Walker]   Colonel Robert T. P. Allen (1813–1888), the commander of the 17th Texas Infantry, survived the battle. Major General John G. Walker (1821–1893) commanded the division that attacked the Union lines at Milliken's Bend, but was not present on the battlefield.

246.21–23   General Hurlbut . . . Lawyer]   Major General Stephen A. Hurlbut (1815–1882) was born in South Carolina and was admitted to the bar there in 1837. Hurlbut moved to Illinois in 1845 and served as a Republican in the Illinois house of representatives, 1859–61.

249.21   Haseltine]   Major James Henry Hazeltine.

249.26–29   Captain Treichel . . . Captain Leiper]   William P. C. Treichel was discharged from the army as a major in July 1864; William White (b. 1843) was mustered out as a captain in November 1864; Charles B. Davis was killed at Brandy Station, June 9, 1863; Samuel R. Colladay (1842–1884) was captured at Brandy Station, exchanged in March 1864, and resigned from the army; Charles Lewis Leiper (1842–1899) was promoted to major in September 1864 and served as the last commander of the 6th Pennsylvania Cavalry.

249.31   Major Morris]   Robert Morris (1837–1863), the great-grandson of the Revolutionary financier Robert Morris, commanded the 6th Pennsylvania Cavalry at Brandy Station. He was taken prisoner during the battle and died of scurvy in Libby prison at Richmond on August 13, 1863.

251.13   Captain Rodenbaugh]   Theophilus F. Rodenbough (1838–1912) of the 2nd U.S. Cavalry.

251.33   Frazier's]   Captain William West Frazier (1839–1921), commander of Company B in the 6th Pennsylvania Cavalry.

252.13   5th Cavalry]   The 5th U.S. Cavalry.

252.25   Lieut. Lennig]   Thompson Lennig (1841–1911) was taken prisoner at Brandy Station and exchanged in March 1864.

252.30   Bulwer's "What will he do with it"]   Novel (1858) by Edward Bulwer-Lytton, originally published under the pseudonym Pisistratus Caxton.

252.39   General Buford]   Brigadier General John Buford (1826–1863) commanded the First Division of the Cavalry Corps of the Army of the Potomac.

253.17   Rudolph Ellis] Captain Rudolph Ellis (1837–1915) commanded Company B of the 6th Pennsylvania Cavalry.

258.29–30   General John C. Breckinridge] Breckinridge (1821–1875), vice president of the United States, 1857–61, and the southern Democratic candidate for president in 1860, commanded a division in the Army of Tennessee.

258.31   Gen. John B. Magruder, Gen. William B. Preston] Magruder (1807–1871) commanded the Confederate forces in Texas; Preston (1816–1887), the U.S. minister to Spain, 1858–61, commanded a brigade in the Army of Tennessee.

258.32   Commodore Franklin Buchanan] Buchanan (1800–1874) commanded the Confederate squadron at Mobile, Alabama.

261.27–31   the judge . . . President Jackson] Humphrey H. Leavitt (1796–1873) was appointed as federal district judge for Ohio by Andrew Jackson in 1834 and served until 1871.

261.37–38   battle of New-Orleans . . . treaty of peace] The battle of New Orleans was fought on January 8, 1815. News of the Treaty of Ghent, signed on December 24, 1814, reached New Orleans on February 25, but official confirmation did not arrive in the city until March 13.

262.3   Mr. Louiallier] Louis Louaillier, a member of the state senate, published an article in the *Louisiana Courier* on March 3, 1815, criticizing Jackson's continued imposition of martial law. Jackson had Louaillier arrested on March 5 and court-martialed two days later on charges of spying, mutiny, libel, disobedience, and misconduct. Although the court-martial cleared Louaillier of all charges, Jackson refused to release him.

262.5   Judge Hall] Dominic A. Hall (1765–1820), U.S. district judge for New Orleans, 1804–12, and for Louisiana, 1812–20.

262.7   arrested both the lawyer and the judge] Jackson did not order the arrest of Pierre L. Morel, the attorney who obtained the writ of habeas corpus from Judge Hall.

262.21–22   Congress refunded . . . Douglas,] Congress passed a bill indemnifying Jackson for the fine in 1843. Stephen A. Douglas (1813–1861) served as Democratic congressman from Illinois, 1843–47, and as a senator, 1847–61.

266.27   Johnston . . . reinforcements] See Chronology, May–June 1863.

269.6   at Salem.] The 19th Iowa Infantry was camped near Salem in southern Missouri from May 2 to June 3, 1863.

269.9   Chequest boys] Men from the Chequest Valley in southeastern Iowa, where the Clayton family farm was located.

269.17–18   Col. Kent . . . Mrs. Wittemeyer] Lieutenant Colonel Daniel

Kent (1819–1898), commander of the 19th Iowa Infantry at Vicksburg; Annie Turner Wittenmyer (1827–1900), an agent for the Iowa State Army Sanitary Commission (an auxiliary of the U.S. Sanitary Commission) and the Keokuk Ladies' Soldiers' Aid Society.

269.19   Gen. Herron] The 19th Iowa Infantry was assigned in Missouri and at Vicksburg to the division commanded by Major General Francis J. Herron (1837–1902).

271.5   Lt. Col. May] Dwight May (1822–1880) had commanded Company I of the 2nd Michigan Infantry, in which Haydon served, until his resignation in December 1861. He was commissioned as lieutenant colonel of the 25th Michigan Infantry in October 1862.

271.20   "Eat drink . . . you die."] See Ecclesiastes 8:15, Isaiah 22:13, and Luke 12:19.

271.27–28   "Let joy be unconfined."] Lord Byron, *Childe Harold's Pilgrimage*, Canto III (1816), stanza 23.

274.12–13   Charley . . . Hugh] Ellen Ewing Sherman's brothers Charles Ewing (1835–1883), a lieutenant colonel who was serving as inspector general of the Fifteenth Corps, and Hugh Boyle Ewing (1826–1905), a brigadier general who commanded a brigade in the Fifteenth Corps.

274.37   Tom Bartley] Thomas W. Bartley (1812–1885) married Susan Denman Sherman (1825–1876), Sherman's sister, in 1848. A former state legislator, Bartley served on the Ohio supreme court, 1852–59, and was its chief justice, 1853–54 and 1856–59.

275.38–39   the invariable Hill] John Hill, a black servant hired by Sherman.

276.5   McCoy] Lieutenant James C. McCoy (d. 1875), who served as one of Sherman's aides, 1862–65.

276.10–11   Genl. Sherman of New Orleans] Union brigadier general Thomas W. Sherman (1813–1879), a division commander in the Army of the Gulf who lost a leg in the assault on Port Hudson, May 27, 1863.

276.18   Mrs. Wilkinson] Mary Stark Wilkinson (1809–1901).

276.19–20   her husband . . . Manassas] Robert A. Wilkinson (1809–1862) was killed in the second battle of Manassas, August 30, 1862, while serving as lieutenant colonel of the 15th Louisiana Infantry.

276.24   General Wilkinson of the old wars] James Wilkinson (1757–1825), grandfather of Robert A. Wilkinson, served in the Revolution, on the frontier, and in the War of 1812. He was accused of complicity in Aaron Burr's conspiracy to detach the western states from the Union, but was acquitted by a court of inquiry.

276.25–26   the famous Land case of Penrose St. Louis]   Thomas Ewing
Sr. successfully argued *Bissell v. Penrose*, a case involving conflicting claims to a
valuable land tract in St. Louis, before the U.S. Supreme Court in 1850.

276.26   at Alexandria]   Sherman was the founding superintendent of the
Louisiana State Seminary of Learning and Military Academy at Alexandria,
1859–61.

276.30–31   Vicksburg . . . his fate.]   On July 3, 1863, Sherman wrote to
Grant, asking him to help Mary Wilkinson see her son once the Vicksburg
garrison had surrendered.

277.30–31   Minnie & Willy . . . Tom & Lizzy]   Sherman's children Maria Boyle Ewing Sherman (1851–1913), William Tecumseh Sherman Jr. (1854–
1863), Thomas Ewing Sherman (1856–1915), and Mary Elizabeth Sherman
(1852–1925).

278.17–19   General Wright . . . General's son]   Brigadier General Ambrose R. Wright (1826–1872) commanded a brigade in A. P. Hill's Third
Corps. Lieutenant William A. Wright (1844–1929), the brigade ordnance officer, was exchanged in May 1864.

278.20   Manassas]   Lieutenant Wright was wounded at the second battle
of Manassas on August 30, 1862.

279.31   sing "Rally round the flag,"]   "The Battle Cry of Freedom"
(1862), song with words and music by George F. Root (1820–1895).

279.34   Florence or Athens, Alabama]   A Union cavalry brigade commanded by Colonel Florence M. Cornyn (1829–1863) raided Florence, Alabama, on May 28, 1863, and burned seven cotton mills and several other
buildings. Union troops from a brigade commanded by Colonel John B.
Turchin (1822–1901) pillaged Athens, Alabama, on May 2, 1862.

279.38   "Gaine's Mills,"]   See note 29.19.

280.1   "squirrel tail rifles."]   The 13th Regiment of the Pennsylvania Reserves (see note 13.15), also known as the 1st Pennsylvania Rifles and the Buck-
tail Rifles.

280.19   Heath's and Pender's divisions]   Major General Henry Heth
(1825–1899) and Major General William Dorsey Pender (1834–1863) commanded divisions in A. P. Hill's corps. Pender was wounded at Gettysburg
on the afternoon of July 2 and died on July 18 after having his leg amputated.

280.26–27   "The Bonnie Blue Flag,"]   A popular Confederate marching
song, written in 1861 by the variety performer Harry Macarthy (1834–1888)
and sung to the tune of "The Irish Jaunting Car."

280.28   Hood . . . McLaws]   Major General John B. Hood (1831–1879)
and Major General Lafayette McLaws (1821–1897) commanded divisions in
Lieutenant General James Longstreet's First Corps.

281.35–282.1   Charles J. Faulkner] Faulkner (1806–1884) had served in Congress as a Whig and as a Democrat, 1851–59, and as U.S. minister to France, 1860–61. He resigned his military commission in June 1863.

283.4   Mr Roman] James D. Roman (1809–1867), a lawyer and banker, served in Congress as a Whig, 1847–49.

284.1–2   Thadeus Stevens] See note 23.18.

284.11–13   WmR . . . Laura & Bet.] McLaws's brother, William Raymond McLaws (1818–1880); his sister, Anna Laura McLaws (1816–1894); and his niece, Lillie Huguenin McLaws (b. 1860).

285.3–4   *Irene and Mary Williams*] Irene Williams (1843–1907) and Mary Williams (1846–1935) lived with their father's relatives in Connecticut. Their mother had died in 1849.

285.20   Dr. Steiner] Lewis H. Steiner (1827–1892), a physician and medical writer, was the chief inspector for the U.S. Sanitary Commission with the Army of the Potomac.

287.29–30   "Divinity which shapes . . . as we will."] *Hamlet*, V.ii.10–11.

289.17–19   "chief burgess" . . . surrender the city] David Small (1809–1885), publisher of the *York Gazette* and chief burgess (mayor) of York, went outside of the city on June 28, 1863, to arrange its surrender with Brigadier General John B. Gordon (1832–1904). The Confederates occupied the town until June 30.

291.10–11   "a little more sleep . . . slumber"] See Proverbs 6:10.

292.27   Colonel Walton] James B. Walton (1813–1885), the senior artillery officer in Longstreet's corps, commanded the Washington Artillery, a battalion from New Orleans, 1861–64.

293.2   Johnson's] Major General Edward Johnson (1816–1873).

294.32–33   General Reynolds] Major General John Reynolds (1820–1863), commander of the First Corps, was killed late in the morning of July 1 west of the town of Gettysburg.

295.28   Lawley] Francis Lawley (1825–1901) reported from the Confederacy for *The Times* of London, October 1862–April 1865.

295.30   Major Clark] Major John J. Clarke (1832?–1880), an engineer who served on Longstreet's staff.

295.31–32   the stout Austrian . . . Major Walton] Captain Fitzgerald Ross (b. 1825), an Englishman who joined the Austrian cavalry in 1850, traveled through the Confederacy from May 1863 to April 1864 while on a leave of absence and later wrote *A Visit to the Cities and Camps of the Confederate States* (1865). Major William M. Walton (1832–1915) was one of Longstreet's staff officers.

295.33   *ciréd*]   Waxed.

295.35   Colonel Sorrell]   Lieutenant Colonel Gilbert Moxley Sorrell (1838–1901), Longstreet's chief of staff, 1862–64.

296.2   Captain Schreibert]   Justus Scheibert (1831–1903), a Prussian engineer sent to observe the American Civil War for professional purposes, later wrote *Seven Months in the Rebel States during the North American War, 1863* (1868).

296.32   Pickett]   Major General George E. Pickett (1825–1875).

296.34–35   Colonel Manning]   Peyton T. Manning (1837–1868), Longstreet's ordnance officer.

298.12   Hill's Florida brigade]   The brigade, commanded at Gettysburg by Colonel Daniel Lang (1838–1917), was assigned to the division led by Major General Richard H. Anderson (1821–1879) in A. P. Hill's Third Corps. Previous to Lee's reorganization of the Army of Northern Virginia in late May 1863, Anderson's division had been part of Longstreet's First Corps.

298.20   General Barksdale . . . Semmes]   Brigadier General William Barksdale (1821–1863), who had served as a Democratic congressman from Mississippi, 1853–61, died on July 3. Brigadier General Paul J. Semmes (1815–1863), a cousin of Confederate naval officer Raphael Semmes, died on July 10. Both men led brigades assigned to McLaws's division in Longstreet's corps.

298.27   Major Fairfax]   Major John W. Fairfax (1828–1908), one of Longstreet's aides.

299.35   Heth and Pettigrew]   Brigadier General James J. Pettigrew (1828–1863) led one of the brigades in Heth's division, and had assumed command of the division after Heth was wounded on July 1. Another division from Hill's corps, commanded by Major General Isaac Trimble (1802–1888), also participated in the July 3 assault on the Union center.

299.36–37   absence of two brigades]   The brigades had been detached for service in North Carolina.

300.36   Oxford-street]   A main shopping street in the West End of London.

301.36–38   Major Latrobe . . . Captain Goree]   Osmun Latrobe (1835–1915) and Thomas J. Goree (1835–1905), officers on Longstreet's staff.

302.38   This officer . . . the Potomac.]   Pettigrew was mortally wounded in a rearguard action near Williamsport, Maryland, on July 14 and died three days later.

303.9–11   General Willcox . . . state of his brigade.]   Brigadier General Cadmus M. Wilcox (1824–1890) commanded a brigade in Anderson's division that had been ordered to advance on Pickett's right flank. In his official report of July 17, 1863, Wilcox wrote that his brigade had lost 577 men killed, wounded, or missing, on July 2 and another suffered another 204 casualties on July 3.

303.30–31 Generals Garnett . . . Kemper] Garnett, Armistead, and Kemper commanded the three brigades in Pickett's division. Brigadier General Richard B. Garnett (1817–1863) was killed during the assault; Brigadier General Lewis A. Armistead (1817–1863) died of his wounds in a Union hospital on July 5; and Brigadier General James L. Kemper (1823–1895), who was left behind when the Confederates retreated on July 4, survived his wound and was exchanged in September 1863.

304.19–21 Johnson's division . . . advantages there.] The Confederates made a series of unsuccessful attacks on Culp's Hill on the morning of July 3.

304.25–27 Yankee cavalry . . . have escaped.] On the afternoon of July 3 a Union cavalry brigade led by Brigadier General Elon J. Farnsworth (1837–1863) unsuccessfully attacked Hood's division on the Confederate right flank. Farnsworth was killed, and his brigade lost another 106 men killed, wounded, or missing.

304.29 Moses's] Major Raphael Moses (1812–1893), Longstreet's chief commissary officer.

305.7 Dr. Barksdale] Randolph Barksdale (1831–1907), the medical inspector of Longstreet's corps, was not related to Brigadier General William Barksdale.

305.25 General Pendleton (the parson)] Brigadier General William N. Pendleton (1809–1883), chief of artillery of the Army of Northern Virginia, 1862–65. A West Point graduate, Pendleton had resigned from the army in 1833 and become an Episcopal clergyman.

307.15 General Milroy] Brigadier General Robert H. Milroy (1816–1890), a division commander in the Eighth Corps, was driven out of Winchester, Virginia, by Ewell, June 14–15, 1863.

308.34 Doles'] Brigadier General George P. Doles (1830–1864) commanded a brigade in the division led by Major General Robert E. Rodes.

309.17 26th Regt.] The 26th Alabama Infantry.

309.18 Mr. Mushat] Dr. John Patrick Mushat (1830–1890), assistant surgeon of the 5th Alabama Infantry.

310.20 Col. Hall] Colonel Josephus M. Hall (1828–1915), commander of the 5th Alabama Infantry.

311.9 Ramseur . . . Iversons] Brigadier General Stephen D. Ramseur (1837–1864) and Brigadier General Alfred Iverson commanded brigades in Rodes's division.

311.11–15   Tom Biscoe . . . 5th La. Regt.]   Captain Thomas H. Biscoe (c. 1839–1864) was originally from Greene County, Alabama, but had been living in New Orleans when he joined the 5th Louisiana Infantry. Biscoe assumed command of the regiment after Major Alexander Hart was wounded on July 2 during an attack on Cemetery Hill. The 5th Louisiana was part of a brigade led by Brigadier General Harry T. Hays (1820–1876) in the division commanded by Jubal A. Early.

312.30   our division]   The First Division of the Fifth Corps, commanded by Brigadier General James Barnes (1801–1869). Donaldson's regiment, the 118th Pennsylvania Infantry, was part of the division's First Brigade.

313.7   our Colonel]   Lieutenant Colonel James Gwyn (1828–1906).

314.35   Capt. John Fassitte . . . General Birney]   Captain John B. Fassett (1836–1905), an aide to Brigadier General David B. Birney (1825–1864). Birney commanded the First Division of the Third Corps, which held the north side of the salient formed by Sickles's advance toward the Emmitsburg Road.

314.39   Captain Crocker]   Lemuel B. Crocker (1829–1885), commander of Company K of the 118th Pennsylvania Infantry.

315.11   P.V.]   Pennsylvania Volunteers.

317.37   Capt. Richd. W. Davids]   Davids (1825–1863) was the commander of Company G of the 118th Pennsylvania Infantry.

318.12   Maj. Herring]   Major Charles S. Herring (1829–1889), second in command of the 118th Pennsylvania Infantry at Gettysburg.

318.25   Maj. Biddle]   James Cornell Biddle (1835–1898).

319.12–14   Pennsylvania Reserves . . . Genl. Crawford]   Nine regiments of the Pennsylvania Reserves that had previously been assigned to the Third Division of the First Corps (see note 13.15) fought at Gettysburg as part of the Third Division of the Fifth Corps, commanded by Brigadier General Samuel W. Crawford (1829–1892).

319.23–24   the 2nd and 3rd brigade]   The Second Brigade, First Division, Fifth Corps fought alongside the First Brigade in the woods of the Rose Farm, while the Third Brigade fought on Little Round Top.

319.26–28   The 16th Mich. . . . colonel being bayonetted]   Lieutenant Colonel Norval E. Welch (1835–1864) commanded the 16th Michigan Infantry, which fought on July 2 on Little Round Top as part of the Third Brigade. Colonel Harrison H. Jeffords (1834–1863), the commander of the 4th Michigan Infantry in the Second Brigade, was bayoneted on July 2 in the wheat field of the Rose Farm and died the following day.

320.8   news of the 22nd Virginia Regt.]   Donaldson's brother, John P. Donaldson (1838–1901), moved from Philadelphia to Charleston, Virginia (later West Virginia), in 1858. He joined the Confederate army in 1861 and was serving as a captain with the 22nd Virginia Infantry in southern West Virginia during the battle of Gettysburg. John P. Donaldson was captured at Cold Harbor on June 3, 1864, and remained a Union prisoner for the rest of the war.

320.9–10   Bradley Johnson]   Colonel Bradley T. Johnson (1829–1903), a prominent Maryland Confederate.

322.27   Capt. O'Neill]   Captain Henry O'Neill, the commander of Company A of the 118th Pennsylvania Infantry.

325.25   tete monte]   *Tête montée*: swelled head.

325.31–32   Genl McClellands dismissal by Grant]   Grant, who had long been unhappy with John A. McClernand's performance, removed him from command of the Thirteenth Corps on June 18 after Sherman and McPherson strongly protested McClernand's publication of a self-congratulatory order in the newspapers without authorization.

326.13   Blair]   Francis Preston Blair Lee (1857–1944), the only child of Elizabeth Blair Lee and Samuel Phillips Lee.

326.26   Betty]   Elizabeth Blair (1841–1872), daughter of Montgomery Blair.

326.36   Robt]   Robert Leamy Meade (1817–1841), brother of George G. Meade.

327.1   Apo]   Apolline Alexander Blair (1828–1908), the wife of Frank Blair.

327.11–12   Dahlgren son a Capt. . . . Robt. Lee]   Captain Ulric Dahlgren (1842–1864), a Union cavalry officer, was the son of Rear Admiral John A. Dahlgren (1809–1870), commander of the South Atlantic Blockading Squadron. On July 2 Dahlgren captured a courier in Greencastle, Pennsylvania, and seized an unenciphered letter in which Davis told Lee not to expect to receive reinforcements from North Carolina or the Richmond area. Dahlgren lost his right leg in a skirmish in Hagerstown, Maryland, on July 6. Promoted to colonel, he was killed on March 2, 1864, during a failed cavalry raid on Richmond (see pp. 728–32 in this volume).

327.17   Cooper]   Brigadier General Samuel Cooper (1798–1876), adjutant general of the Confederate War Department.

327.18   Beauregard]   Lee had proposed that General Pierre G. T. Beauregard, the Confederate commander at Charleston, South Carolina, be sent to northern Virginia with the purpose of threatening an attack on Washington while Lee's army was in Pennsylvania.

327.21–22   the White House]   White House Landing on the Pamunkey River, twenty-three miles east of Richmond.

328.36–329.1   Col. Vincent commanding the Brigade,]   Colonel Strong

Vincent (1837–1863) commanded the Third Brigade of the First Division in the Fifth Corps.

330.40–331.1   Col. Rice . . . mortally wounded]   Colonel James C. Rice (1828–1864), the commander of the 44th New York Infantry, took over the brigade after Vincent was wounded.

331.6   "Wolf Hill"]   A hill three miles northeast of Big Round Top.

331.28   Genl. Laws]   Brigadier General Evander M. Law (1836–1920) led one of the brigades in Hood's division and took over command of the division when Hood was wounded on the afternoon of July 2.

332.18–21   Lt. W. L. Kendall . . . Lieut. A. N. Linscott]   Lieutenant Warren L. Kendall of Company G died on July 5, Captain Charles W. Billings of Company C died on July 15, and Lieutenant Arad N. Linscott of Company I died on July 27.

332.29–31   Capt Woodward . . . Adjt. Gifford]   Captain Orpheus S. Woodward (1835–1919) and Lieutenant Martin Van Buren Gifford (1837–1922).

333.18–19   Henry Ropes]   First Lieutenant Henry Ropes (1839–1863), the commander of Company K of the 20th Massachusetts Infantry, had joined the regiment in November 1861 and fought at Fair Oaks, the Seven Days' Battles, Antietam, Fredericksburg, and Chancellorsville. He was killed at Gettysburg by the premature explosion of a Union shell on the morning of July 3 while reading a novel by Charles Dickens.

333.24   Col. Hall]   Colonel Norman J. Hall (1837–1867) commanded the Third Brigade, Second Division, Second Corps, at Fredericksburg, Chancellorsville, and Gettysburg.

333.31–33   pique against Revere . . . he is regretted]   Colonel Paul Joseph Revere (1832–1863), a grandson of the Revolutionary War hero, was appointed major of the 20th Massachusetts in July 1861, but left the regiment in August 1862 to serve on the staff of Major General Edwin V. Sumner. Abbott and several other officers had opposed his appointment as regimental commander in May 1863, believing the colonelcy should have been given to Lieutenant Colonel George N. Macy, who had led the regiment at Fredericksburg and Chancellorsville. Revere was wounded by a shell burst at Gettysburg on the evening of July 2 and died two days later.

334.1–2   Macy . . . Herbert Mason]   Lieutenant Colonel George N. Macy (1837–1875) was wounded on July 3 and lost his left hand. He resumed command of the 20th Massachusetts in late October 1863. Captain Herbert Mason, the commander of Company H, was wounded on July 3 and medically discharged in March 1864.

334.7   Patten]   Captain Henry Lyman Patten (1836–1864), the commander of Company D, was wounded on July 2. He returned to the regiment later in the year and was mortally wounded at Deep Bottom, Virginia, on August 17, 1864, while serving as acting commander of the 20th Massachusetts.

334.18   Paine]   Second Lieutenant Sumner Paine (1845–1863) was killed on July 3.

335.16–17   Baxter's Pennsylvania men]   Colonel DeWitt C. Baxter commanded the 72nd Pennsylvania Infantry. The gap in the line to the right of the 20th Massachusetts was caused by the retreat of several companies from the 71st Pennsylvania.

335.32   Gen Webb]   Brigadier General Alexander Webb (1835–1911) commanded the Second Brigade, Second Division, Second Corps, which was posted to the right of Hall's brigade on July 3. It was made up of the 71st, 72nd, 69th, and 106th Pennsylvania regiments.

335.35   miserable rowdy named Hays]   Brigadier General Alexander Hays (1819–1864) commanded the Third Division in the Second Corps.

335.38–40   Hays . . . Gibbon]   Brigadier General William Hays (1819–1875) took command of the Second Corps on July 3 after Major General Winfield Scott Hancock was wounded during the Confederate assault on Cemetery Ridge. Hancock (1824–1886) had replaced Major General Darius N. Couch as commander of the Second Corps on May 22, 1863. Brigadier General John Gibbon (1827–1896), commander of the Second Division of the Second Corps, was wounded on July 3.

336.25–26   first day's . . . second day's]   July 2 and July 3, 1863.

337.11   Wm Kelly]   Corporal William P. Kelley (c. 1843–1865) was captured at Spotsylvania on May 12, 1864, and died in a Confederate prison camp at Wilmington, North Carolina, on March 5, 1865.

337.17   Fletcher]   Fletcher Abbott (1843–1925), Henry Livermore Abbott's younger brother, was serving as a Union staff officer in Louisiana. He was medically discharged from the army in December 1863.

337.18–19   George & Mary Welch . . . John]   George B. Perry was commissioned as a first lieutenant in the 20th Massachusetts in July 1861 and served until September 1862, when he was discharged because of illness. Perry became formally engaged to Caroline Abbott (1839–1872), Henry Livermore Abbott's sister, early in 1864. His cousin, John Gardner Perry (1840–1926), who joined the 20th Massachusetts as an assistant surgeon in April 1863, had his leg broken by a horse on June 15, 1863. He returned to the regiment in September 1863 and served until his discharge in August 1864. Mary Ann Welch was a young woman from Lowell, Massachusetts, whom Abbott corresponded with during the war.

339.10–12   Kershaw . . . Wofford]   Brigadier General Joseph B. Kershaw (1822–1894) and Brigadier General William T. Wofford (1824–1884).

339.21–23   Colonel Carter . . . Lt. Col. Fiser]   James W. Carter (c. 1830–1863), Thomas M. Griffin (1816–1878), William D. Holder (1824–1900), William De Saussure (1819–1863), and John C. Fiser (1838–1876).

341.19   Will]   William N. Hancock (1832–1911), Cornelia Hancock's brother.

341.28–29   Mrs. Harris]   Ellen Orbison Harris (1816–1902), field secretary for the Ladies' Aid Society of Philadelphia.

342.20–22   Major General Schenk . . . Miss Dix]   Major General Robert C. Schenck (1809–1890), commander of the Middle Department, which included Baltimore. Dorothea Dix (1802–1887) served as superintendent of female nurses for the Union army, 1861–65. In an account of her Gettysburg experiences written after the war, Hancock recalled that at the Baltimore Depot Dix had "immediately objected to my going farther on the score of my youth and rosy cheeks. I was then just twenty-three years of age." (It was Dix's policy not to use women under the age of thirty as nurses.) Despite Dix's objections, Hancock boarded the train for Gettysburg.

342.24   Doctor Horner's house]   Dr. Robert Horner (1825–1899), who lived on Chambersburg Street.

343.25   E. W. Farnham]   A writer, lecturer, and social reformer who had served as matron of the female prison at Sing Sing, Eliza W. Farnham (1815–1864) helped organize nursing care for the wounded at Gettysburg.

345.3–4   First Minnesota Regiment . . . the late battle.]   During the fighting on Cemetery Ridge on July 2, General Hancock personally ordered the 1st Minnesota Infantry to counterattack an advancing Confederate brigade so as to gain time for other Union reinforcements to arrive. The survivors of the charge then helped defend Cemetery Ridge against the Confederate assault on July 3. The regiment had reported 399 men present for duty on June 30, and lost 233 men killed, wounded, or missing at Gettysburg.

345.9   The Colonel]   Colonel William J. Colvill (1830–1905).

345.29–30   Senator Wilson, Mr. Washburn]   Henry Wilson (1812–1875) was a Republican senator from Massachusetts, 1855–73; for Elihu B. Washburne, see note 24.22.

345.34   Dr. Child]   Henry T. Child (c. 1816–1890), a Quaker physician and philanthropist from Philadelphia and the husband of Hancock's sister Ellen.

346.18   Mr Palmer]   Frank W. Palmer (1827–1907) was the publisher of the *Iowa State Register*, 1861–66, and its editor, 1861–68.

346.25–26   Rachel . . . Aunt Hannah]   Taylor Peirce's sister, Rachel Peirce Gibson (b. 1827), and his aunt, Hannah Kirk Peirce.

349.19 the National salute] A Fourth of July salute in which one gun was fired for each state in the Union, i.e., in 1863 a thirty-five-gun salute.

349.20 Ormes] Brigadier General William W. Orme (1832–1866) commanded the Second Brigade in the division led by Major General Francis J. Herron.

350.31 Lizzie Cooper] A cousin of Clayton's who lived in Pittsburgh. She married Clayton in 1869 and died in 1876.

352.23 Ords corps . . . Parkes] On June 18 Grant had named Major General Edward O. C. Ord (1818–1883) to replace McClernand as commander of the Thirteenth Corps. Major General John G. Parke (1827–1900) commanded the Ninth Corps, which had reinforced Grant at Vicksburg in June.

354.34–35 reach the same points by Grenada] That is, by advancing on Vicksburg from the north along the Mississippi Central Railroad.

355.15 Dayton] Captain Lewis M. Dayton (1835–1891), one of Sherman's aides.

355.27 Carter] A former slave Sherman had hired to care for his horses.

355.28 Hammond] Captain John H. Hammond (1833–1890), an officer on Sherman's staff.

361.11–12 Sound the loud . . . people are FREE!] Opening lines of "Miriam's Song" (1816), also known as "Sound the Loud Timbrel," by Thomas Moore (1779–1852). The poem was inspired by Exodus 15:20.

362.16 Scales] Alfred M. Scales (1827–1892) commanded a brigade in Pender's division in A. P. Hill's corps. Wounded on July 1, Scales returned to duty in August 1863.

362.19–20 Sickles, . . . assassinate no more men] Major General Daniel E. Sickles (see note 14.27–28), the commander of the Third Corps, was wounded on the afternoon of July 2 and had his right leg amputated. In 1859 he had shot and killed Philip Barton Key (1818–1859), U.S. attorney for Washington and the son of Francis Scott Key, because Key was having an affair with his wife, Teresa Bagioli Sickles (1836–1867). Sickles became the first defendant to be acquitted on grounds of temporary insanity in an American murder case.

362.25–29 Gen Lee has issued . . . Pope's and Steinwehr's!] Lee issued General Orders No. 72 on June 21, 1863, forbidding the pillaging of private property but allowing designated officers to requisition supplies and pay for them with Confederate currency and vouchers. Major General John Pope (1822–1892), commander of the Army of Virginia, issued a series of orders from July 18 to July 23, 1862, regarding the treatment of southern civilians. General Orders No. 5 authorized his troops to seize the property of disloyal citizens without compensation; General Orders No. 7 made captured guerrillas

subject to execution without civil trial; and General Orders No. 11 allowed Union
commanders to expel across the lines male citizens who refused to take the oath of
allegiance, to execute persons who violated the oath, and to treat expelled persons
who returned, and persons who communicated across the lines, as spies. Brigadier
General Adolph von Steinwehr (1822–1877), one of Pope's division commanders,
seized five prominent citizens in Luray, Virginia, on July 13, 1862, and declared
that one of them would be executed for every Union soldier killed by "bushwhackers." There is no record of civilians being executed or expelled under Pope's
orders, and von Steinwehr later released his hostages unharmed.

362.29   A no 20.]   Edmondston placed newspaper clippings regarding
Lee's orders in another part of her journal.

363.4–5   Brashear city]   Renamed Morgan City in 1876.

363.14   the R R at Magnolia]   The Wilmington and Weldon Railroad,
which ran through Magnolia, North Carolina.

363.16   Gen Martins]   Brigadier General James G. Martin (1819–1878)
commanded a Confederate brigade in North Carolina.

363.17   Murad the Unlucky]   Story by Maria Edgeworth (1768–1849),
published in her *Popular Tales* (1804).

363.20   her brother, Col Evans,]   Colonel Peter G. Evans (1822–1863),
the commander of the 5th North Carolina Cavalry, was wounded and captured at Upperville, Virginia, on June 21, 1863, and died in Washington, D.C.,
on July 24.

363.24   German Gen Weitzel]   Brigadier General Henry W. Wessells
(1809–1889), who was born in Connecticut, commanded the Union expedition against Williamstown. Brigadier General Godfey Weitzel (1835–1884),
who was born in Ohio, commanded a division in Louisiana in the Port Hudson campaign.

363.26   Rainbow Banks]   A bluff on the Roanoke River two miles below
Hamilton, North Carolina.

363.28   the Gunboat]   The ironclad ram C.S.S. *Albemarle*, which was
commissioned on April 17, 1864, and sunk on the night of October 27.

364.5–6   like "Widrington" in "*doleful dumps*,"]   A reference to a
seventeenth-century version of the medieval "Ballad of Chevy-Chase": "For
Withrington needs must I wail / As one in doleful dumps; / For when his legs
were smitten off, / He fought upon the stumps."

364.8   Com Barron]   Commodore Samuel Barron (1809–1888), a Confederate naval officer.

365.1   Loring]   Major General William W. Loring (1818–1886) commanded a division under Johnston in Mississippi.

365.36   Hannah More's ill "*bile*"]   In a letter to Sir William Weller Pepys of July 1, 1823, the English evangelical writer and philanthropist Hannah More (1745–1833) wrote that there were "but two great evils in the world, sin and bile."

365.38 Petigru again wounded!] James J. Pettigrew (see notes 299.35 and 302.40) was wounded at Fair Oaks (Seven Pines) on May 31, 1862, and at Gettysburg on July 3, 1863, before being mortally wounded near Williamsport, Maryland, on July 14.

366.19 Northern Generals . . . Lovel & New Orleans] Major General Mansfield Lovell (1822–1884), the Confederate commander in Louisiana when New Orleans surrendered to Union naval forces on April 25, 1862, was born in Washington, D.C., to northern parents. An 1842 graduate of West Point who served in the war with Mexico, Lovell resigned from the army in 1854 and worked at an ironworks in Trenton and as deputy street commissioner in New York City before joining the Confederate army in the fall of 1861.

366.26–27 Londonderry . . . Antwerp] Protestants loyal to William of Orange held out in Londonderry (Derry) under siege from Irish and French Jacobite forces, April 18–July 31, 1689. The Dutch held Antwerp against the Spanish from July 1584 to August 1585, when they were forced to surrender.

366.32 court of Inquiry . . . Lovels conduct] At Lovel's request, a court of inquiry examined his conduct at New Orleans. Its findings, published in November 1863, largely exonerated him.

366.40 French] Major General William H. French (1815–1881) commanded the Union garrison at Harpers Ferry during the Gettysburg campaign until July 7, when he became commander of the Third Corps.

367.2–3 "fight him . . . Shrewsbury clock"] Cf. *1 Henry IV*, V.iv.146–148.

367.8 Keyes] Major General Erasmus D. Keyes (1810–1895) commanded a Union division on the Virginia Peninsula.

367.22 "The King does not dine today."] See Henry Wadsworth Longfellow, *Hyperion: A Romance* (1839): "But perhaps you have never heard that, at the court of Naples, when the dead body of a monarch lies in state, his dinner is carried up to him as usual, and the court physician tastes it, to see that it be not poisoned, and then the servants bear it out again, saying, 'The king does not dine today.'"

367.29 Suffolk] Union forces evacuated Suffolk, Virginia, on July 3, 1863.

367.32 Dix] Major General John A. Dix (1798–1879), commander of the Department of Virginia.

371.8 Abner Read] Commander Abner Read (1821–1863) was wounded on July 7 and died July 12.

371.14 Captain Cooke] Lieutenant Commander Augustus P. Cooke (1836–1896), captain of the gunboat *Estrella*.

372.26   Chas. Smith . . . severe shot] Smith later returned to duty with
the 2nd Michigan. He was taken prisoner at Peebles' Farm, Virginia, on September 30, 1864, during the siege of Petersburg, and was mustered out in
1865.

373.1   Kearney's] The 2nd Michigan fought in the Peninsula and Second
Bull Run campaigns in the division commanded by Brigadier General Philip
Kearny (1815–1862), who was killed at Chantilly, Virginia, on September 1, 1862.

373.30   Sergt. Keyser] Sylvester Keyser (1843–1916) was later promoted
to captain and commanded Company E of the 2nd Michigan at the end of
the war.

374.10   Lt. Montague . . . severe flesh wound] Calvin S. Montague (b.
1838) was commissioned as a captain in the 102nd U.S. Colored Infantry in
March 1864 and mustered out as a major in 1865.

375.31   Eckert says Kelly] Major Thomas T. Eckert (1825–1910), superintendent of the War Department telegraph office, and Brigadier General Benjamin Franklin Kelley (1807–1891), commander of the Department of West
Virginia.

376.28–31   Went with R.T.L. . . . trinkt and raucht] This paragraph was
crossed out in the manuscript of Hay's diary. "R.T.L." refers to Robert Todd
Lincoln (1843–1926), Abraham Lincoln's eldest son, then a student at Harvard
College. "Where mann sauft and trinkt and raucht": where people drink and
drink and smoke.

378.22   Gen. Couch . . . Gen. Smith] Major General Darius N. Couch
(1822–1897), commander of the Department of the Susquehanna, and his subordinate Brigadier General William F. Smith (1824–1903) commanded Pennsylvania militia levies during the Gettysburg campaign.

382.15–17   Charley . . . Wall Street] Charles E. Strong (1824–1897),
George Templeton Strong's cousin, and Marshall S. Bidwell (1799–1872) were
law partners with Strong; their firm had its office at 68 Wall Street.

383.37–38   No. 823 . . . Fifth Avenue] 823 Broadway, between 12th and
13th Streets, the headquarters of the U.S. Sanitary Commission; the Colored
Half-Orphan Asylum was located on Fifth Avenue between 43rd and 44th
Streets.

383.39   reservoir] The Croton Distributing Reservoir, on the west side of
Fifth Avenue between 40th and 42nd Streets.

384.5   Wolcott Gibbs] See note 25.16.

384.6   Maison Dorée] A restaurant on 14th Street between Broadway
and Fourth Avenue.

384.18   St. Nicholas Hotel] The hotel was on Broadway between Broome
and Spring Streets.

384.19–21   John Jay . . . John Austin Stevens, Jr.] John Jay (1817–1894), a grandson of the Chief Justice, was a lawyer who had helped organize the New York Republican Party. George W. Blunt (1802–1878) was a publisher of nautical books and maps and a member of the U.S. Coastal Survey and the New York board of harbor pilot commissioners. Frank E. Howe (1829–1883), a merchant originally from Boston, served as Massachusetts state agent in New York, arranging housing and provisions for Massachusetts soldiers in transit through the state and assistance for its sick and wounded men in New York hospitals. John Austin Stevens Jr. (1827–1910) was a New York financier and merchant. All four men were members of the Union League Club, which Strong and other leaders of the Sanitary Commission had helped found in February 1863.

384.25–26   Opdyke . . . Wool] George Opdyke (1805–1880) was the Republican mayor of New York, 1862–63. Major General John E. Wool (1784–1869), a veteran of the War of 1812, commanded the Department of the East.

384.30–31   Colonel Cram] Thomas J. Cram (1804–1883) served as Wool's aide-de-camp, 1861–65.

384.35   Union League Club] The clubhouse was located at 26 East 17th Street.

384.38   We telegraphed] The telegram to President Lincoln was signed by John Jay, George Templeton Strong, Wolcott Gibbs, and James Wadsworth (1819–1891), a lawyer, businessman, and former Democratic mayor of Buffalo who served as chairman of the Loyal League of Union Citizens.

385.13–14   Ellie . . . Johnny] Ellen Caroline Ruggles Strong (1825–1891), George Templeton Strong's wife, and his son, John Ruggles Strong (1851–1941).

385.26   black man hanged] At least eleven African American men were lynched in New York during the draft riots.

385.27   Opdyke's house] At 79 Fifth Avenue, between 15th and 16th Streets.

385.31   *Herald, World,* and *News*] Democratic New York newspapers.

385.36   Tiffany's shop, Ball & Blacks] Tiffany & Co. was located at 550 Broadway, between Spring and Prince Streets. Ball, Black & Co., another jewelry store, was located at 565 Broadway at the corner of Prince Street.

386.7   Bellows . . . home] Henry Bellows (see note 25.15). Strong lived at 74 East 21st Street (renumbered 113 East 21st in 1867).

386.10–12   Dudley Field, Jr. . . . his father's] David Dudley Field (1805–1894) was a prominent lawyer who had helped organize the New York Republican Party. His son Dudley Field (1830–1880) was also an attorney.

387.1   "Swinging slow with sullen roar."] John Milton, "Il Penseroso," line 76.

387.15–16   Cisco . . . his establishment] John Jay Cisco (1806–1884), assistant treasurer of the United States, was in charge of the Sub-Treasury building at the corner of Wall and Nassau Streets.

387.18–19   "so cool, so calm, so bright"] See George Herbert, "Virtue," line 1: "Sweet day, so cool, so calm, so bright!"

387.20   Assay Office] Located at 30 Wall Street, next to the Sub-Treasury.

387.21–22   called on Collector Barney] Hiram Barney (1811–1895), collector of customs at New York, 1861–64. The Custom House was located at 55 Wall Street.

387.27   Hoppin] William Jones Hoppin (1813–1895), an attorney and the treasurer of the Union League Club.

387.34   Lieutenant Colonel Jardine] Edward Jardine (1828–1893) had served with the 9th New York Infantry, a two-year regiment, until it was mustered out in May 1863. Jardine was leading a volunteer group of veterans from the 9th New York when his leg was broken by the impact of a homemade bullet. He was sheltered from the mob in a nearby house.

387.39   General Frémont's . . . Craven's] Major General John C. Frémont moved to New York City in 1863. Alfred W. Craven (1810–1879) was chief engineer of the Croton Aqueduct system, 1849–68.

388.27–28   Governor Seymour] Horatio Seymour (1810–1886), the Democratic governor of New York, 1863–64, had repeatedly criticized the draft as unconstitutional. In a speech given at the Academy of Music in New York City on July 4, 1863, Seymour had attacked the Lincoln administration for curtailing civil liberties and warned that "the bloody and treasonable and revolutionary doctrine of public necessity can be proclaimed by a mob as well as by a government."

389.1–2   McCunn . . . the Brookses] John H. McCunn (1825–1872) was a city judge in New York and a prominent Peace Democrat. James Brooks (1810–1873) was a Democratic congressman from New York, 1863–66 and 1867–73, and the editor and part-owner of the *New York Express*. His brother Erastus Brooks (1815–1886) was a co-owner of the *Express*.

390.14–15   James I. . . . negro troops] See headnote, page 402 in this volume.

390.19   some captured to be hung] Several dozen black soldiers captured during the fighting in Charleston Harbor were transferred from a military prison to the city jail in August 1863 to face charges of engaging in slave insurrection. Four men were tried by a South Carolina state tribunal, September 8–10, that ruled it lacked jurisdiction over enemy soldiers in wartime. No further trials were held at Charleston, and in December 1864 the prisoners were returned to military custody.

391.11   Henry Young] Louis Gourdin Young (1833–1922), a Charleston resident, served as Pettigrew's aide; his brother, Henry Edward Young (1831–1918), held several staff positions with the Army of Northern Virginia.

391.32–33   Superintendent Kennedy several wounded]   John A. Kennedy (1803–1873), the superintendent of the New York City Police, 1860–70, was badly beaten by rioters on the morning of July 13.

392.13   the Ironsides]   The U.S.S. *New Ironsides*, an ironclad commissioned in 1862 that carried eighteen guns, had joined the blockading squadron off Charleston in January 1863.

394.21–23   Capt. Ryan . . . Maj. David Ramsey]   Captain William H. Ryan commanded Company C, known as the Irish Volunteers, in the 1st South Carolina Infantry Battalion, known as the Charleston Battalion. Major David Ramsay (1830–1863), the second in command of the Charleston Battalion, died of his wounds on August 4, 1863.

394.31–32   Lieut. Col. Simpkins, commanding the fort]   Lieutenant Colonel John C. Simpkins (1827–1863) of the 1st South Carolina Infantry. The Confederate garrison at Fort Wagner was commanded by Brigadier General William B. Taliaferro.

394.34   Clingman's North Carolinians]   Brigadier General Thomas L. Clingman (1812–1897), a former congressman and U.S. senator from North Carolina, commanded a brigade that included two regiments in the Fort Wagner garrison, the 31st and 51st North Carolina Infantry.

395.1   Lieut. James Powe]   Powe (1835–1898), an officer in the 1st South Carolina Infantry.

395.9–10   Col. Putnam . . . Gen. Israel Putnam]   Colonel Haldimand S. Putnam (1835–1863), commander of the 7th New Hampshire Infantry, led a specially organized brigade in the assault on Fort Wagner. He was the grandson of Israel Putnam (1718–1790), a Connecticut officer in the French and Indian War and the Revolutionary War.

396.7–8   Morgan . . . Indiana]   See Chronology, July 8, July 19–29, 1863.

397.3   *Richard Taylor*]   Taylor (1835–1917) was a Confederate artillery officer who was wounded and captured at Fort Harrison near Richmond in September 1864.

397.11   Mary Lou]   Mary Louisa Taylor (1832–1902), Taylor's sister.

397.15   Rob]   Taylor's brother, Captain Robertson Taylor (1840–1924), assistant adjutant general of the brigade led by Brigadier General William Mahone in A.P. Hill's corps of the Army of Northern Virginia.

397.19   John]   Taylor's brother, Captain John Cowdrey Taylor (b. 1842), an aide to Pemberton who was paroled at the surrender of Vicksburg. He was later captured at Fort Morgan near Mobile on August 23, 1864, and spent the remainder of the war as a prisoner.

401.8   Sally] Sally Louisa Tompkins (1833–1916), a friend of the Taylor family who ran the Robertson Hospital in Richmond, 1861–65.

402.34   Gen. Stevenson] Brigadier General Thomas G. Stevenson (1836–1864) commanded the First Brigade in the First Division of the Department of the South during the siege of Charleston. He was killed at Spotsylvania on May 10, 1864.

403.18   Gen. Terry's brigade] Brigadier General Alfred H. Terry (1827–1890) commanded a division during the Charleston campaign.

404.1–2   Saturday] July 18, 1863.

404.4   Gen. Strong] Brigadier General George C. Strong (1832–1863) commanded the brigade the 54th Massachusetts was assigned to for the assault on Fort Wagner. Strong was wounded during the attack and died on July 30.

404.9   Sebastopol] During the Crimean War the British and French besieged Sevastopol, the main Russian naval base in the Black Sea, from October 1854 until its evacuation by the Russians in September 1855.

404.32   Lieut. Grace] James W. Grace (b. 1833), a merchant from New Bedford, was later promoted to captain and mustered out in August 1865.

405.26–28   DeForrest . . . Chas Creamer] All of the men mentioned by Douglass were from Syracuse, where Helen Amelia Loguen (1843–1936) lived with her father, the Reverend Jermain Loguen, a prominent black abolitionist. Andrew DeForest, Jacob Carter, Charles Whiten, and Charles Creamer were discharged from the 54th Massachusetts in August 1865. George Washington died in a Union military hospital at Beaufort, South Carolina, on August 3, 1863, and Charles Reason died at Beaufort on July 27, 1863.

407.26–27   Mrs. L's . . . Dr. R.] Jean Davenport Lander (1829–1903), an English actress and the widow of Union brigadier general Frederick W. Lander (1821–1862), was the supervisor of nursing at Beaufort, South Carolina; Colonel Thomas Wentworth Higginson (1823–1911), commander of the 1st South Carolina Volunteers; for Dr. Seth Rogers, see note 216.21.

408.6   Mrs. S.] Maltilda Thompson Saxton (1840–1915), a schoolteacher from Philadelphia who had married General Rufus Saxton (see note 99.30) on March 11, 1863.

408.12–13   "Many and low . . . of a friend."] Elizabeth Barrett Browning, "A Court Lady," line 16.

410.6   Mr. P.] Edward L. Pierce (1829–1897), a Boston lawyer and friend of Charles Sumner who had served as a treasury department agent at Port Royal in 1862.

410.10   Major Hallowell] Edward N. Hallowell (1837–1871), a former officer of the 20th Massachusetts, became second in command of the 54th Massachusetts after his brother, Norwood Penrose Hallowell (see note 21.9–10), was commissioned colonel of the black 55th Massachusetts Infantry in June 1863. Edward Hallowell returned to duty in October 1863 and was colonel of the 54th Massachusetts for the remainder of the war.

411.19   Colonel O'Brian] Henry O'Brien (c. 1823–1863), the colonel of the recently formed 11th New York Infantry, was repeatedly beaten and dragged through the streets on the afternoon of July 14 after he failed to disperse a mob at Second Avenue and 34th Street.

411.23–24   Father . . . his house] Philip M. Lydig (1799–1872), a wealthy landowner and retired merchant, owned a house at 84 Laight Street.

411.28   our own block] The Dalys lived at 84 Clinton Place (now West 8th Street).

412.2–3   to see Judge Hilton] Henry Hilton (1824–1899), a Democratic judge on the court of common pleas, lived at 222 Madison Avenue.

412.10   he had $300.] The amount of the commutation fee needed under the 1863 conscription act to avoid being drafted; see the headnote on page 57 in this volume.

412.28   Leonard, the Superintendent of Police] Inspector James Leonard (c. 1820–1869), who helped restore order in several downtown neighborhoods during the riots.

412.38   Mrs. Jarvis and James T. Brady] Maria Louisa Brady Jarvis, the wife of Nathaniel Jarvis, clerk of the court of common pleas; her brother, James T. Brady (1815–1869), a prominent New York lawyer who had successfully defended Daniel E. Sickles (see note 362.18–19) and Lewis Baker, who was charged with murder in the 1855 shooting death of Nativist gang leader William (Bill the Butcher) Poole.

412.39   Susanna Brady] A sister of James T. Brady.

413.19–20   Judge Pierrepont] Edwards Pierrepont (1817–1892), a Democratic former judge of the New York superior court who would support Lincoln's reelection in 1864.

413.23   General Dix] Major General John A. Dix (1798–1879) replaced John E. Wool as commander of the Department of the East on July 18, 1863. Dix had served as a Democratic senator from New York, 1845–49.

415.11   Roman, never to be scourged.] Under Roman law the scourging of citizens was prohibited, and the punishment was reserved for slaves and foreigners.

417.11   Monckton Milnes] Richard Monckton Milnes (1809–1885), a poet, writer, literary patron, biographer of John Keats, and member of Parliament from 1837 to August 1863, when he was made Baron Houghton.

417.15   W. H. Russell]   William Howard Russell (1820–1907), British war correspondent who had reported for *The Times* from America on the secession crisis and the war from March 1861 to April 1862.

417.18   Cosmopolitan Club]   A club on Berkeley Square in London, founded in 1852, whose members included artists, writers, senior civil servants, and political figures.

417.30   case of the iron-clads]   The Laird shipyards in Liverpool were building two ironclad rams for the Confederate navy; see pp. 502–4 in this volume.

418.3–4   Dana, John]   Richard Henry Dana, author of *Two Years Before the Mast* (1840), who served as U.S. district attorney for Massachusetts, 1861–66; John Quincy Adams II (see note 9.18).

418.10–11   Judge Goodrich]   Aaron Goodrich (1807–1887), secretary to the U.S. legation in Brussels, 1861–69, had previously served as chief justice of the Minnesota territorial supreme court, 1849–51.

418.18   the Trent affair]   On November 8, 1861, Captain Charles Wilkes of the U.S.S. *San Jacinto* boarded the British mail packet *Trent* off Cuba and seized the Confederate envoys James M. Mason and John Slidell. The incident caused a major diplomatic crisis that continued until the Lincoln administration decided on December 26 to release the envoys in order to avoid a possible war with Great Britain.

418.30   Pendennis]   *The History of Pendennis*, novel (1848–50) by William Makepeace Thackeray.

418.36   Brooks]   Brooks Adams (1848–1927), younger brother of Henry Adams and Charles Francis Adams Jr.

418.37–38   Isle of Skye . . . Dr. Johnson]   Samuel Johnson and James Boswell traveled through western Scotland together in 1773. Their travels were described by Johnson in *Journey to the Western Islands of Scotland* (1775) and by Boswell in *The Journal of a Tour to the Hebrides, with Samuel Johnson, LL.D.* (1785).

419.20   the Index]   A pro-Confederate weekly newspaper published in London, May 1862–August 1865, by Henry Hotze (1833–1887), a Swiss-born journalist from Mobile who was sent to England as a propaganda agent by the Confederate State Department.

421.19   Generals Sedgwick, Wright, Slocum, Hays, Sykes]   Major General John Sedgwick commanded the Sixth Corps; Brigadier General Horatio G. Wright (1820–1899) led the First Division of the Sixth Corps; Major General Henry W. Slocum commanded the Twelfth Corps; Brigadier General William Hays was the acting commander of the Second Corps; Major General George Sykes (1822–1880) led the Fifth Corps.

429.20–21   free men . . . slavery in Texas.]   Charles Fairfax Revaleon (1845–1910) and his cousin Charles Gerrish Amos were personal servants to the colonel and staff of the 42nd Massachusetts Infantry. They were captured at Galveston on January 1, 1863, and sold into slavery in Texas. Revaleon and Amos returned to Massachusetts in the summer of 1865.

429.27   slaughtered teamsters at Murfreesboro.]   Reports in the northern press claimed that Confederate cavalrymen had killed twenty black teamsters during a raid on the Union supply line during the battle of Stones River (Murfreesboro), December 31, 1862–January 2, 1863. Other reports alleged that the Confederates captured and then killed twenty black teamsters along the Murfreesboro Pike in late January 1863.

430.4   "Hold, enough!"]   *Macbeth*, V.8.34.

432.37–40   two white men . . . will retaliate]   On July 6, 1863, Confederate authorities selected by lot Henry Sawyer and John Flinn, two Union captains held in Libby Prison in Richmond, and announced that they would be executed in retaliation for the deaths of Captain William Francis Corbin and Lieutenant Thomas Jefferson McGraw, who had been shot as spies on May 15 after being captured within the Union lines in northern Kentucky while secretly recruiting for the Confederate army. President Lincoln responded on July 15 by declaring that if Sawyer and Flinn were executed, the Union would retaliate by hanging Brigadier General William Henry Fitzhugh Lee (see note 33.27–28), who had been captured by Union cavalry in Virginia on June 26. The threatened executions were not carried out, and on March 14, 1864, Sawyer, Flinn, and Brigadier General Neal Dow were exchanged for Lee and another Confederate officer who had been held as a hostage, Captain Robert H. Tyler.

433.26   "shame extremest hell."]   John Greenleaf Whittier, "Stanzas for the Times" (1835), line 26.

435.31   Johnny Mahay]   Mahay, a soldier in the 101st New York Infantry who was wounded at Second Bull Run by a bullet that perforated his bladder, died in 1864. Whitman later wrote about him in "A Case from Second Bull Run" in *Specimen Days* (1882).

437.29   Dr. Bliss]   D. Willard Bliss (1825–1889) was the superintendent of Armory Square Hospital.

442.27   "eternal vigilance . . . liberty."]   Cf. the Irish attorney and orator John Philpot Curran, in his speech on the right of election of Lord Mayor of Dublin (1790): "The condition upon which God hath given liberty to man is eternal vigilance; which condition, if he break, servitude is at once the consequence of his crime and the punishment of his guilt."

443.6   Mr. Blair]   In a speech to a Union mass meeting in Cleveland on May 20, 1863, Postmaster General Montgomery Blair (1813–1883) had described proposals to colonize freed slaves outside the United States as "a deliverance" from "a war of races which could only end in the extermination of the negro race or amalgamation with it."

443.38   Col. Littlefield] Colonel Milton S. Littlefield (1830–1899) of the 4th South Carolina Volunteers.

444.18–20   Our First Sergeants, . . . $10 a month] The monthly pay for white noncommissioned officers was $17 for a sergeant, $20 for a first sergeant, and $21 for a sergeant major.

445.18–19   anniversary of British West India Emancipation] The Abolition Act of August 28, 1833, went into effect on August 1, 1834.

445.40   decision of Attorney-General Bates] See note 118.11–12.

446.10   day of Jubilee] See Leviticus 25:8–13.

446.25   "Who would be free, . . . the blow."] See Lord Byron, *Childe Harold's Pilgrimage*, Canto II (1812), stanza 76: "Hereditary bondsmen! Know ye not, / Who would be free, themselves must strike the blow?"

447.21   your proclamation] See Chronology, August 1, 1863.

448.17   attack I experienced last spring.] Lee had suffered from chest pains in the spring of 1863.

450.18–20   Sydney Johnston] After he was criticized for a series of Confederate reverses in Kentucky and Tennessee, Confederate general Albert Sidney Johnston (1803–1862) wrote to Davis on March 18, 1862, that "the test of merit in my profession with the people is success."

452.16–17   last Wednesday] August 5, 1863.

457.11   Head Quars 1210 Chesnut St] The headquarters of the Supervisory Committee for Recruiting Colored Regiments.

458.12   the bill drawn up by himself] Stanton presumably refers to the bill regarding black troops introduced in the House of Representatives by Thaddeus Stevens; see pp. 23–24 in this volume.

458.28   Gen Thomas] Brigadier General Lorenzo Thomas (1804–1875), the adjutant general of the U.S. Army, was assigned in March 1863 to recruit black troops.

461.29   Col Lucketts Reg] Colonel Philip N. Luckett (c. 1823–1869) commanded the 3rd Texas Infantry.

461.31   Debray] Colonel Xavier B. DeBray (1818–1895) commanded a brigade at Galveston.

462.4   Cooks Reg] Colonel Joseph J. Cook (1826–1869) commanded the 1st Texas Heavy Artillery.

462.9 Browns Battallion] Lieutenant Colonel Reuben R. Brown (1808–1894) led the 12th Texas Cavalry Battalion.

462.13 Gen Magruder] See note 258.31.

462.36 the capture of Morgan] See Chronology, July 8, July 19–29, 1863.

463.24 Bettie] Elizabeth Neblett (1863–1928), the fifth child of William and Elizabeth Neblett, was born on May 26.

463.27 Mary] Mary Caroline Neblett (1853–1936), their first child.

463.33 Walters] Walter Scott Neblett (1860–1957), their fourth child.

465.30–31 Springfield . . . Lexington] Confederate forces defeated Union troops at Wilson's Creek near Springfield, Missouri, on August 10, 1861, and captured Lexington, Missouri, on September 20, 1861.

466.7–8 Gen. Ewing's staff] Brigadier General Thomas Ewing Jr. (1829–1896) commanded the District of the Border, which covered part of western Missouri and most of Kansas.

466.20–21 "welcomed with bloody hands to hospitable graves."] See note 72.35–36.

467.18 Jim. Lane] James H. Lane (1814–1866) was a Republican senator from Kansas, 1861–66. Lane had commanded an irregular Kansas brigade that looted and burned the town of Osceola, Missouri, on September 23, 1861.

469.15 Kansas Fourteenth] The 14th Kansas Cavalry.

474.12–13 Gov. Robinson] Charles L. Robinson (1818–1894) had served as the Republican governor of Kansas, February 1861–January 1863.

475.16 Gen. Collamore] George W. Collamore (1818–1863), the quartermaster general of the Kansas militia, was elected mayor of Lawrence in the spring of 1863.

477.5–11 His wife . . . wife's sister] Mary Barber Carpenter (1837–1917) and Abigail Barber Morse (1833–1925).

480.14–22 Mr. Rothrock . . . may recover.] Abraham Rothrock (1796–1870) survived, but lost the use of his left arm.

480.22–24 Rev. H. D. Fisher . . . Rev. Mr. Paddock] Hugh Dunn Fisher (1824–1905) and George Washington Paddock (1823–1908) were both Methodist ministers. Fisher had served as the chaplain of the 5th Kansas Cavalry and accompanied it on raids into Missouri during which a number of slaves were freed.

481.27–30 "Uncle Henry" . . . Mr. Ellis] Charles Henry, Benjamin Stonestreet, and Frank Ellis.

482.25 My wife] Elizabeth Acheson Fisher (1826–1901).

485.12   A son of John Speer]   John Speer Sr. (1817–1906) was the editor of the *Kansas Weekly Tribune* and the former editor of the *Lawrence Republican*. His nineteen-year-old son John Speer Jr. was killed during the raid, while his fifteen-year-old son William survived. Another son, seventeen-year-old Robert, disappeared during the raid, and may have been burned beyond identification in the fire that destroyed the *Tribune* building.

491.35   the Conservative party]   A coalition of former Whigs and conditional unionists that had supported Zebulon B. Vance in the 1862 election for governor.

493.2–4   policy of removing . . . bushwhackers.]   Ewing had issued orders on August 18, 1863, authorizing the removal of slaves from rebels and the banishing of the families of "known guerrillas" from Missouri.

500.22   Dana]   Charles A. Dana (1819–1897), managing editor of the *New-York Tribune*, 1849–62, served as Secretary of War Stanton's special emissary at Grant's headquarters.

501.4   Col. Chetlain]   Augustus L. Chetlain (1824–1914), a merchant from Galena, was the colonel of the 12th Illinois Infantry. Chetlain was promoted to brigadier general in December 1863 and assigned to recruit and organize black troops in Tennessee and western Kentucky.

501.9–10   Vice President Stevens . . . corner stone]   See note 138.27–28.

501.22   Rawlins & Maltby]   John A. Rawlins (1831–1869) served as Grant's adjutant general, 1861–65. Jasper A. Maltby (1826–1867), the colonel of the 45th Illinois Infantry, commanded a brigade for the remainder of the war.

503.3   the Warrior]   H.M.S. *Warrior*, an ironclad steamship commissioned in 1861 that carried forty guns and was considered the most powerful warship of its time.

505.25–26   Battery Haskell]   The battery was located on James Island.

506.9   large Blakely gun]   A muzzle-loading rifled cannon with a 12.75-inch-diameter bore that could fire a 470-pound shell or a 650-pound solid shot more than five miles. It was named after its designer, the British artillery officer Captain Alexander Blakely.

506.34–35   surrendered by Anderson]   Major Robert Anderson (1805–1871) surrendered Fort Sumter to Confederate forces on April 13, 1861.

508.29   *Vanderbilt*]   The U.S.S. *Vanderbilt* was a converted sidewheel mail steamer armed with fifteen guns.

509.3–4   the admiral . . . *Narcissus*]   Rear Admiral Sir Baldwin Walker (1802–1876) was the commander of the Royal Navy squadron, based at the Cape of Good Hope, that patrolled off West Africa in order to suppress the slave trade. The *Narcissus*, a steam frigate, was the flagship of the West Africa squadron.

509.30   Captain J. H. Coxon]   An officer of the Royal Navy.

510.39   Cape Agulhas and Point Danger]   Cape Agulhas and Point Danger are, respectively, about one hundred miles and sixty miles southeast of Simon's Town.

514.21   Tiers-etat]   Third Estate.

515.16   Jackson]   Brigadier General William H. Jackson (1835–1903) commanded a cavalry division in Mississippi.

515.21–22   Cosby . . . Stephen D. Lee]   Brigadier General George B. Cosby (1830–1909), an 1852 West Point graduate who had resigned from the U.S. Army in May 1861; Brigadier General John W. Whitfield (1818–1879); Major General Stephen D. Lee (1833–1908). Stephen D. Lee was not related to Robert E. Lee.

515.26   Mr. Chase's]   Salmon P. Chase (1808–1873) was secretary of the treasury in the Lincoln administration, 1861–64.

519.24–25   Napoleons design in Mexico]   See Chronology, June 7, 1863.

521.31   Whartons Cavalry]   See note 149.26.

522.12–13   Adams Brigade]   Confederate brigadier general Daniel W. Adams (1821–1872) led a brigade in the division commanded by Major General John C. Breckinridge.

523.32   Gen Hills HcQts]   Daniel H. Hill commanded the corps that Heartsill served in at Chickamauga.

524.17   Col Wilkes]   Colonel Franklin C. Wilkes (c. 1822–1881) commanded a regiment in Deshler's Brigade that had been formed by the consolidation of the dismounted 17th, 18th, 24th, and 25th Texas Cavalry.

524.21   7th Texas]   The 7th Texas Infantry.

524.34–35   Cheathams men]   Major General Benjamin F. Cheatham (1820–1886) commanded a division in the Army of Tennessee.

525.5   Col Mills]   Colonel Roger Q. Mills (1832–1911) commanded Heartsill's regiment, a consolidation of the 6th and 10th Texas Infantry and the dismounted 15th Texas Cavalry.

525.15   W P L Rs]   W. P. Lane Rangers.

525.29   suffered . . . Woods Brigade]   Brigadier General Sterling A. M. Wood (1823–1891) reported that his brigade lost 776 men killed or wounded at Chickamauga.

531.29   Capt. N . . . Dr. S.]   Captain Price C. Newman and First Sergeant James W. Ford of Company C, 9th Kentucky Infantry, and Dr. Preston B. Scott, a surgeon with the 1st Kentucky Brigade. Jackman was a member of Company B of the 9th Kentucky, but served as a regimental clerk during the Chickamauga campaign.

532.4 Cobbs' . . . Slocums'] Captain Robert Cobb (1836–1914) and Captain Culbert H. Slocomb commanded artillery batteries assigned to Breckinridge's division.

532.26 the Col.] Colonel John W. Caldwell (1837–1903), commander of the 9th Kentucky Infantry.

532.36 Napoleon gun] A smoothbore muzzle-loading field artillery gun that fired a twelve-pound projectile with a maximum range of 1,600 yards. It was developed in France under the auspices of Napoleon III.

533.5 Maj. Wilson . . . Gen'l Helm] Major James Wilson, Breckinridge's adjutant; Brigadier General Ben Hardin Helm (1831–1863), who had commanded the 1st Kentucky Brigade since late January 1863.

533.27 J. H.] James Hunter.

533.30 Lt. Col. W.] Lieutenant Colonel John C. Wickliffe.

533.35–36 Col. H. . . . Maj. Hope] Colonel Thomas H. Hunt (1815–1884) commanded the 9th Kentucky Infantry from the fall of 1861 to the spring of 1863. Major John S. Hope was an officer with the 2nd Kentucky Infantry.

535.31 Dr. Heustis] James F. Heustis (1828–1891), a surgeon from Mobile.

536.14 Colonel Colyer] Arthur St. Clair Colyar (1818–1907), a member of the Second Confederate Congress, 1864–65.

537.15 Dr. Ushery] Benjamin W. Ussery (1829–1894), a surgeon with the 42nd Tennessee Infantry.

538.8 Professor Pickett] Joseph Desha Pickett (1822–1900), a minister in the Christian Church (Disciples of Christ), was the chaplain of the 1st Kentucky Brigade and a former professor of rhetoric at Bethany College in Virginia (now West Virginia).

538.27 Colonels Walter] Colonel Harvey W. Walter (1819–1878) served as a judge advocate on Bragg's staff.

539.5 Dr. Stout] Samuel H. Stout (1822–1903) was superintendent of hospitals for the Army of Tennessee.

539.19 Neal Brown] Neill Smith Brown (1810–1886) was the Whig governor of Tennessee, 1847–49, and served as U.S. minister to Russia, 1850–53.

540.36 Hindman's] Major General Thomas C. Hindman (1828–1868) commanded a division in the Army of Tennessee.

541.11 Claiborne's Division] Cleburne's Division.

541.23–24 Managault's Brigade] Brigadier General Arthur M. Manigault (1824–1886) commanded a brigade in Hindman's division.

542.32   Captain O'Brien] Captain William J. O'Brien of the Alabama 24th Infantry, who had practiced law in Mobile before the war.

543.9   Cowper . . . tea] See William Cowper (1731–1800), *The Task* (1785), Book IV, "A Winter Evening."

544.1–2   Dr. Foard] Andrew J. Foard (c. 1829–1868), the field medical director for the Department of the West.

544.5   Flewellyn] Edward A. Flewellen (1819–1910), the field medical director for the Army of Tennessee.

544.22   Deus's Brigade] Brigadier General Zachariah C. Deas (1819–1882) commanded a brigade in Hindman's division.

545.5–6   like Rachel . . . her children] See Jeremiah 31:15.

545.8–9   "O, what a field . . . Faulkland] See James Montgomery (1771–1854), "Lord Falkland's Dream" (1831): "'Can this,' he sigh'd, 'be virtuous fame and clear? / Ah! what a field of fratricide is here!'" Lucius Cary, second Viscount Falkland (c. 1610–1643), was a royalist member of Parliament who unsuccessfully sought a negotiated end to the English Civil War before being killed at the first battle of Newbury.

548.25–26   Galusha A. Grow] A congressman from Pennsylvania, Grow (1823–1907) served as a Democrat, 1851–57, and as a Republican, 1857–63 and 1894–1903. He was Speaker of the House, 1861–63.

548.34–35   Major General Casey] Silas Casey (1807–1882) headed the board that examined prospective officers for the U.S. Colored Troops.

549.11   Casey's Tactics] Silas Casey, *Infantry Tactics, for the Instruction, Exercise, and Manoeuvres of the Soldier, a Company, Line of Skirmishers, Battalion, Brigade, or Corps D'Armee* (1862).

549.28   rumors of another great battle] See Chronology, October 9–18, 1863.

549.39–40   Curtin . . . Brough] See Chronology, October 13, 1863.

551.10   Mr. Wright] William A. Wright (1807–1878) was a Wilmington banker, lawyer, and railroad investor.

551.21   best soldiers in the Confederate army] Major General William H. C. Whiting (1824–1865) led a division in the Army of Northern Virginia in the Peninsula campaign before being appointed commander of the Wilmington district in November 1862. Whiting was fatally wounded during the Union capture of Fort Fisher, North Carolina, on January 15, 1865.

552.20   President . . . through Wilmington] Davis had spoken in Wilmington on May 28, 1861, while on his way to Richmond.

553.14   great Bethel] Confederate troops repulsed a Union advance at Big Bethel, Virginia, on June 10, 1861.

555.29 George Peterkin] Lieutenant George Peterkin (1841–1916), an aide to Brigadier General William N. Pendleton, chief of artillery of the Army of Northern Virginia.

558.16 Poor Ewell—a cripple—is now laid up] Lieutenant General Richard S. Ewell had lost his left leg at the battle of Groveton in 1862 and was suffering from an abscess caused by an ill-fitting wooden prosthesis. Ewell was temporarily relieved of command of the Second Corps on November 15 and returned to duty on December 5, 1863, after being fitted with a new leg.

558.23 John H. . . . Pemberton] John Hobson, Mahew Hobson's brother. Pemberton was a post office village in Goochland County, Virginia.

558.37–39 Venable . . . Col Preston] Major Charles Venable (1827–1900), a mathematician and astronomer in civilian life, served on Lee's personal staff, 1862–65. Colonel John S. Preston (1809–1881) was chief of the Confederate bureau of conscription, 1863–65.

559.15 Dr. Wright's execution.] On July 11, 1863, Dr. David M. Wright (1809–1863) shot and killed Lieutenant Anson L. Sanborn (1834–1863), a white officer marching through Norfolk, Virginia, at the head of his company of the 1st U.S. Colored Infantry. Wright was convicted by a military commission and hanged on October 23, 1863.

559.18–21 Mrs. Jack Preston . . . Genl. Hampton] Celestine Pinckney Huger Preston (1843–1878) was married to Major John S. Preston Jr. (1836–1880), the son of Colonel John S. Preston. Major Preston was an aide to Major General Wade Hampton (1818–1902), who commanded a cavalry division in the Army of Northern Virginia.

562.19–21 Usher & Blair . . . McDougal of Canada] John P. Usher (1816–1889), secretary of the interior, 1863–65; Montgomery Blair (1813–1883), postmaster general, 1861–64; John G. Nicolay (1832–1901), secretary to Abraham Lincoln, 1860–65; Henri Mercier (1816–1886), the French minister to the United States, 1860–63; Aimé Félix Sainte-Elme Reynaud (1808–1876), the French naval commander in the Gulf of Mexico; Joseph (Giuseppe) Bertinatti (1808–1881), the Italian minister to the United States, 1861–66; Ulissa Isola and Martinez were Italian naval officers whose ships were visiting New York harbor; Cora was the secretary of the Italian legation; Charlotte Brooks Everett Wise (1825–1879), the daughter of Edward Everett; Isaac Wayne MacVeagh (1833–1917), district attorney of Chester County, Pennsylvania, and chairman of the Republican state central committee; William McDougall (1822–1905), commissioner of crown lands in the provincial government of Canada.

562.27 the Edwards case] Attorney General Edward Bates had removed William W. Edwards as U.S. attorney for the Eastern District of Missouri on November 2, 1863, for "active participation in political enterprises hostile to the known views and wishes of the Executive Government." Edwards had joined other Radicals in an unsuccessful attempt to have John

Schofield replaced as the Union military commander in Missouri with Benjamin F. Butler.

562.32   young Stanton]   Edwin L. Stanton (1842–1877), son of Secretary of War Edwin M. Stanton.

562.35   Lamon]   Ward Hill Lamon (1828–1893), an Illinois lawyer and friend of Lincoln's who served as U.S. marshal for the District of Columbia, 1861–65. He was the marshal for the dedication ceremony at Gettysburg.

563.1   Forney . . . Mr. Fahnestocks]   John W. Forney (1817–1881) was the editor of the *Philadelphia Press* and the *Washington Chronicle*. Harris C. Fahnestock (1835–1914), a banker from Harrisburg, Pennsylvania, was a partner in the Washington branch of Jay Cooke & Company.

563.14   Curtin]   Andrew G. Curtin (1815–1894), Republican governor of Pennsylvania, 1861–66.

563.16   the Cameron party]   Supporters of Simon Cameron (1799–1889), who served as a Democratic senator from Pennsylvania, 1845–49; Republican senator, 1857–61; secretary of war, 1861–62; and U.S. minister to Russia, 1862–63.

563.24   Harper's]   The home of Robert G. Harper (1799–1870), publisher and editor of the *Adams Sentinel*.

563.35   fuglers]   A political handler; also, a person who leads crowds in cheering.

564.6   John Young]   John Russell Young (1840–1899), managing editor of the *Philadelphia Press* and the *Washington Chronicle*.

564.14–15   in 1860 . . . course he took]   Forney had supported Stephen A. Douglas, the northern Democratic candidate, in the 1860 election.

564.26   Judge Shannon]   Peter C. Shannon (1821–1899), a Republican member of the Pennsylvania house of representatives, 1862–63, had served as a judge on the Allegheny County district court, 1852–53.

564.34–35   Mr. Everett . . . Mr Stockton]   Edward Everett (1794–1865), a Unitarian clergyman, was professor of Greek at Harvard, 1819–25; a Whig congressman from Massachusetts, 1825–35; governor of Massachusetts, 1836–40; U.S. minister to Great Britain, 1841–45; president of Harvard, 1846–49; secretary of state, 1852–53; a senator from Massachusetts, 1853–54; and the vice presidential candidate of the Constitutional Union Party, 1860. Thomas H. Stockton (1808–1868), a Methodist clergyman, was chaplain of the U.S. House of Representatives, 1861–63.

565.3   Genl. Cameron]   Simon Cameron, who had served as adjutant general of the Pennsylvania militia, 1829–31.

566.2   *Address at Gettysburg*]   The Associated Press report, prepared by

Joseph L. Gilbert, appeared in three major New York newspapers on November 20 as follows:

> Four score and seven years ago our fathers brought forth upon this continent a new Nation, conceived in Liberty, and dedicated to the proposition that all men are created equal. [Applause.] Now we are engaged in a great civil war, testing whether that Nation or any Nation so conceived and so dedicated can long endure. We are met on a great battle-field of that war. We are met to dedicate a portion of it as the final resting-place of those who gave their lives that that nation might live. It is altogether fitting and proper that we should do this. But in a larger sense we cannot dedicate, we cannot consecrate, we cannot hallow this ground. The brave men living and dead who struggled here have consecrated it far above our power to add or detract. [Applause.] The world will little note or long remember what we say here, but it can never forget what they did here. [Applause.] It is for us, the living, rather to be dedicated here to the refinished work that they have thus far so nobly carried on. [Applause.] It is rather for us to be here dedicated to the great task remaining before us, that from these honored dead we take increased devotion to the cause for which they here gave the last full measure of devotion; that we here highly resolve that the dead shall not have died in vain [applause]; that the nation shall, under God, have a new birth of freedom; and that Governments of the people, by the people, and for the people, shall not perish from the earth. [Long-continued applause.]

Subsequent printings of the Associated Press text in other newspapers corrected three likely errors in the New York version: "our power" became "our poor power," "refinished work" became "unfinished work," and "the dead" became "these dead."

569.32–33   Gen Starkweather]   Brigadier General John C. Starkweather (1830–1890) commanded a brigade in the First Division, Fourteenth Corps, in the Army of the Cumberland.

570.1–2   Hookers troops]   See Chronology, September 23, 1863.

570.19   Lagow]   Colonel Clark B. Lagow (1828–1867) had served as an aide to Grant since August 1861.

570.31   Fred Dent]   Frederick Dent (1786–1873), Grant's father-in-law.

570.32   5/20's]   Treasury bonds redeemable after five years and maturing in twenty years that carried 6 percent interest.

570.38–39   Dr. Kittoe . . . Capt Hudson]   Edward D. Kittoe (1814–1887), a surgeon from Galena, Illinois, who served on Grant's staff; Captain Peter D. Hudson (d. 1892), one of Grant's aides.

571.23   General Hunter]   Major General David Hunter (1802–1886); see Biographical Notes.

571.29   Lt. Col. Duff, and Lts. Towner and Dunn]   Lieutenant Colonel William L. Duff (1822–1894), Grant's chief of artillery; Lieutenant Horatio N. Towner (1836–1873), assistant chief of artillery; Lieutenant William M. Dunn Jr. (1843–1891), one of Grant's aides.

571.31–33   Lagow . . . his removal.]   Lagow submitted his resignation on November 18 and left Grant's headquarters in December 1863.

571.35   Capt. Ross]   Captain Orlando H. Ross (1835–1892), a cousin of Grant and one of his aides.

572.5–6   Thomas . . . Branen]   Major General George H. Thomas (1816–1870), commander of the Army of the Cumberland; Brigadier General William F. Smith (1824–1903), who was serving as Grant's chief engineer; Major General Joseph J. Reynolds (1822–1899), chief of staff of the Army of the Cumberland; Brigadier General John M. Brannan (1819–1892), chief of artillery of the Army of the Cumberland.

572.32   Col. Hillyer]   Colonel William S. Hillyer (1830–1874) served as an aide to Grant, 1861–62, and as provost marshal of the Department of the Tennessee, 1862–63.

573.22   fort Wood]   The fort was part of the Union defensive line around Chattanooga.

574.8   very anxious about Burnsides]   See Chronology, November 4 and November 16, 1863.

574.20   Gen John E. Smith]   Brigadier General John E. Smith (1816–1897) commanded a division in the Seventeenth Corps, Army of the Tennessee.

574.26   Howard]   Major General Oliver Otis Howard (1830–1909), commander of the Eleventh Corps, which had been sent west under Hooker's command along with the Twelfth Corps.

574.40   Gen's Meigs, Gen Wilson]   Brigadier General Montgomery C. Meigs (1816–1892), quartermaster general of the Union army; Brigadier General James H. Wilson (1837–1925), an engineering officer serving on Grant's staff.

575.13–14   Gen A Baird's . . . Washington man]   Brigadier General Absalom Baird (1824–1905), commander of the Third Division, Fourteenth Corps, Army of the Cumberland. Baird and William Wrenshall Smith were both from Washington, Pennsylvania.

575.25   John Acheson]   John W. Acheson (1837–1872), a cousin of Baird from Washington, Pennsylvania, was a first lieutenant in the 85th Pennsylvania Infantry who was serving in the Charleston Harbor campaign. He was assigned to Baird's staff in 1864.

577.2   Maj Rowley]   Major William R. Rowley (1824–1886) served as an aide to Grant, 1862–64.

577.3–4   Cadwallader . . . Chicago *Times*] Sylvanus Cadwallader (1825–1908).

577.25   Capts. Parker] Captain Ely S. Parker (1828–1895), a Seneca Indian, was an assistant adjutant general on Grant's staff and later served as his military secretary.

578.26–28   There shall . . . by myriads] Lord Byron, *Childe Harold's Pilgrimage*, Canto I (1812), stanza 42.

578.36   the Anderson troop] The 15th Pennsylvania Cavalry, recruited in 1862 by Colonel William J. Palmer (1836–1909). Palmer had earlier raised a troop of cavalry in the autumn of 1861 to serve as a headquarters guard for Brigadier General Robert Anderson, the commander of the Department of the Cumberland and former defender of Fort Sumter.

579.1   Buell] Major General Don Carlos Buell (1818–1898) commanded the Army of the Ohio, November 1861–October 1862.

583.10   Woods Division] Brigadier General Thomas J. Wood (1823–1906) commanded the Third Division, Fourth Corps, Army of the Cumberland.

583.28   Granger, Sheridan] Major General Gordon Granger (1822–1876) commanded the Fourth Corps in the Army of the Cumberland; Major General Philip H. Sheridan (1831–1888) commanded the Second Division in the Fourth Corps.

584.28   Stevenson] Major General Carter L. Stevenson (1817–1888) was a division commander in the Confederate Army of Tennessee.

584.38   Major Dana] Charles A. Dana.

586.29   Colonel Putnam] Colonel Holden Putnam (1820–1863), commander of the 93rd Illinois Infantry, died from his wound.

589.20   Johnson's Division] Brigadier General Richard W. Johnson (1827–1897) commanded the First Division, Fourteenth Corps, Army of the Cumberland.

591.26   notice Bragg gave him] See p. 575.6–8 in this volume.

592.8   Cruft] Brigadier General Charles Cruft (1826–1883) commanded the First Division of the Fourth Corps in the Army of the Cumberland.

592.20   Logan] Major General John A. Logan (1826–1886), a division commander in the Army of the Tennessee, had been named to succeed Sherman as the commander of the Fifteenth Corps, but did not reach Tennessee until December because of his duties in Mississippi. During the battle of Chattanooga the Fifteenth Corps was led by Major General Frank Blair.

593.6   "sun of Austerlitz"] The sun breaking through morning mist on the battlefield became the symbol of Napoleon's victory over the Austrian-Russian army at Austerlitz on December 2, 1805.

596.11   Gen. ——]   General Baird.

596.14   Col. ——"]   Colonel Edward H. Phelps (c. 1829–1863), formerly commander of the 38th Ohio Infantry.

599.1   Davis' Division,]   Brigadier General Jefferson C. Davis (1828–1879) commanded the Second Division of the Fourteenth Corps in the Army of the Cumberland. (General Davis was not related to the president of the Confederate states.)

599.11   Gen. ——]   Major General John M. Palmer (1817–1900) led the Fourteenth Corps.

599.20–21   with —— 's brigade]   Colonel John T. Wilder (1830–1917).

599.29–30   Gen. Turchin]   Brigadier General John B. Turchin (1822–1901) commanded the First Brigade in Baird's division.

599.33   a rough pencil sketch]   The sketch is not reproduced in this volume.

599.35   Gen. ——]   General Baird.

600.1–4   Gen. ——, . . . Gen. ——]   General Palmer.

602.5–6   Merritt's . . . (Kilpatrick's)]   Brigadier General Wesley Merritt (1836–1910) led the First Division of the Cavalry Corps of the Army of the Potomac during the Mine Run campaign after its commander, Brigadier General John Buford (1826–1863), fell ill with typhoid fever (Buford died on December 16). Brigadier General George Armstrong Custer (1839–1876) led the Third Division of the Cavalry Corps during the campaign after Brigadier General Judson Kilpatrick (1836–1881) went on leave following the death of his wife.

602.7   Gregg's Div.]   Brigadier General David M. Gregg (1833–1916) commanded the Second Division of the Cavalry Corps.

602.9   Gen. Prince]   Brigadier General Henry Prince (1811–1892) commanded the Second Division of the Third Corps.

603.28–30   Ludlow . . . McBlair]   Major Benjamin C. Ludlow (1831–1898), an inspector of artillery on Meade's staff; Captain John G. McBlair, one of Meade's aides.

603.33   Cadwalader]   Charles Evert Cadwalader (1839–1907), one of Meade's aides.

603.38   Longfellow and Bowditch were here wounded]   Second Lieutenant Charles Appleton Longfellow (1844–1893), son of the poet Henry Wadsworth Longfellow, and Captain Henry Pickering Bowditch (1840–1911), grandson of the mathematician and astronomer Nathaniel Bowditch, were both medically discharged from the 1st Massachusetts Cavalry on February 15, 1864. Bowditch was later commissioned as major of the 5th Massachusetts Cavalry, a black regiment.

606.16   Carr]   Brigadier General Joseph B. Carr (1828–1895) commanded the Third Division in the Third Corps.

606.27–29   Capt. Barnard . . . Bartlett]   Captain George M. Barnard (1835–1898) served on the staff of the First Division, Fifth Corps, which was commanded by Brigadier General Joseph J. Bartlett (1834–1893).

606.39–607.1   Col. Farnum (he of yacht *Wanderer* fame)]   Colonel John Egbert Farnum (1824–1870) led the 70th New York Infantry in the Second Division, Third Corps. A veteran of the war with Mexico and of filibustering expeditions in Cuba and Nicaragua, Farnum had served as supercargo on the *Wanderer*, a schooner that illegally landed four hundred African slaves on the Georgia coast in November 1858. His trial on federal piracy charges in Savannah, Georgia, in May 1860 ended in a hung jury.

607.7   Robling]   Lieutenant Washington A. Roebling (1837–1926), an aide to Major General Gouverneur K. Warren. He later served as chief engineer in the construction of the Brooklyn Bridge, 1869–83.

607.11   Gen. Humphreys]   Major General Andrew A. Humphreys (1810–1883), chief of staff of the Army of the Potomac.

608.24–25   Col. Hayes (Joe)]   Colonel Joseph Hayes (1835–1912) commanded the Third Brigade, First Division, Fifth Corps.

608.32–33   T. F. Meagher "of the Sword"]   Thomas F. Meagher (1823–1867), a member of the Young Ireland movement, became known as "Meagher of the Sword" after he declared in a speech in Dublin on July 28, 1846: "Be it in the defense, or be it in the assertion of a people's liberty, I hail the sword as a sacred weapon." Meagher was convicted of high treason in 1848 and exiled the following year to Van Diemen's Land (Tasmania). He escaped to the United States in 1852 and commanded the Irish Brigade in the Second Corps of the Army of the Potomac from November 1861 until May 1863, when he resigned his commission as a brigadier general shortly after the battle of Chancellorsville.

608.34–35   the English officers]   Lieutenant Colonel William Earle (1833–1885) and Lieutenant William Cuffed (1845–1898) of the Grenadier Guards and Captain John Floyd Peel (1827–1910) and Captain Sussex Vane Stephenson (1833–1878) of the Scots Fusilier Guards visited Meade's headquarters, November 14–December 3, 1863.

610.2   Mimi]   Lyman's wife, Elizabeth Russell Lyman (1836–1911).

610.3   Arthur]   Lyman's cousin, Arthur Theodore Lyman (1832–1915).

612.23   the Christian Commission]   Established in 1861 by the Young Men's Christian Association, the United States Christian Commission supplied Union soldiers with food, medical supplies, volunteer nursing care, and religious literature.

613.25   Gen. Standard]   Brigadier General George J. Standard (1820–1886) had served as lieutenant colonel of the 2nd Vermont Infantry, June 1861–May 1862. Standard commanded the harbor defenses at New York in late 1863 while recovering from a leg wound he suffered at Gettysburg.

613.29   the third brigade] The Third Brigade, Second Division, Sixth Corps. Fisk served in the Second Brigade of the Second Division.

615.39   The Tenth Vermont] The 10th Vermont Infantry was assigned to the First Brigade, Third Division, Third Corps.

617.9–10   Lee's Mill's affair] On April 16, 1862, the Vermont Brigade (the 2nd, 3rd, 4th, 5th, and 6th Vermont Infantry) made an unsuccessful attack across the Warwick River near Lee's Mill on the Virginia Peninsula. The action cost the brigade 165 men killed, wounded, or missing.

625.2   Cortland Parker, Mr. Harding] Cortland Parker (1818–1907), a prominent New Jersey lawyer who served as public prosecutor of Essex County, 1857–67; George Harding (1827–1902), a leading Philadelphia patent attorney.

625.4   George] Captain George Meade (1843–1897), General Meade's son, was now serving as one of his aides.

625.23   the Star . . . editor] William D. Wallach (1812–1871) was owner and editor of the *Washington Evening Star*, 1855–67.

626.5   Gibbon] Brigadier General John Gibbon (1827–1896), the commander of the Second Division in the Second Corps of the Army of the Potomac, was recovering from a wound suffered at Gettysburg.

626.15   the Herald] The *New York Herald*.

629.25   Mr. Purvis] Robert Purvis (1810–1898), an antislavery activist of mixed racial background, was a founding member of the American Anti-Slavery Society who served as president of the Pennsylvania Anti-Slavery Society, 1845–50. Purvis headed two vigilance committees, 1839–44 and 1852–57, that assisted fugitive slaves in Philadelphia, while also campaigning for the rights of free blacks in Pennsylvania.

630.36   Mr. Wilson] See note 345.29–30.

630.39–631.1   "You do take away . . . my house,"] Cf. *The Merchant of Venice*, IV.i.375–76.

633.30   Dr. Fussell] Dr. Bartholomew Fusel (1794–1871), a Quaker physician and advocate of medical education for women, was a founding member of the American Anti-Slavery Society.

638.24–25   long pending controversy . . . seizure at Sitana] During the Chilean war of independence Chilean forces seized $70,400 in silver in 1821 from an American merchant ship captain in southern Peru, claiming that it was Spanish property. King Leopold I settled the dispute on May 15, 1863, by awarding the American claimants $42,400.

640.16   the Tycoon] Tokugawa Iemochi (1846–1866), shogun of Japan, 1858–66.

640.20–21   the Minister . . . legation at Yedo] Robert H. Pruyn (1815–1882) was U.S. minister to Japan, 1862–65. Most of the American legation at Edo (Tokyo) was destroyed on May 24, 1863, in a fire set by anti-Western samurai.

641.7   Indian disturbances in New Mexico] In the summer of 1863 Colonel Kit Carson (1809–1868) and the 1st New Mexico Cavalry began a campaign designed to end Navaho raiding against settlements in New Mexico and Arizona. The campaign continued until March 1864, when thousands of Navahos were forced by the destruction of their dwellings, crops, and livestock to move onto the reservation at Bosque Redondo in New Mexico.

643.39   General Hitchcock] Major General Ethan Allen Hitchcock (1798–1870) served as the Union commissioner for prisoner exchanges from November 1862 until the end of the war.

649.11–653.8   When Congress assembled . . . any other way.] These eleven paragraphs are in Lincoln's hand in the incomplete preliminary draft, indicating that he himself composed the message from this point on. The preceding parts were probably written by the various members of the cabinet, with the likely exception of the opening paragraph.

658.9–10   The New Gospel of Peace] The New Gospel of Peace According to St. Benjamin, a pamphlet satirizing Fernando Wood and other prominent Peace Democrats, including his brother Benjamin (see note 81.10–13). The first part ("Book First") was published on July 27, 1863, and the second part on October 24, 1863; subsequent parts appeared on July 22, 1864, and May 19, 1866.

658.12   publisher, Tousey] Sinclair Tousey (1815–1887), a successful New York bookseller and news agent.

658.20   The author is ——.] Richard Grant White (1822–1885), a New York lawyer, literary and music critic, and the editor of a twelve-volume edition of Shakespeare (1857–65).

658.30–31   Chesapeake . . . killed] The second engineer of the Chesapeake was killed and two other crew members wounded when the ship was seized off Cape Cod on the night of December 7, 1863, by sixteen Confederate sympathizers from the Canadian maritime provinces who planned to refuel in a Canadian port and then sail to Wilmington, North Carolina. A boarding party from the U.S.S. Ella and Annie recaptured the Chesapeake in Sambro Harbor, Nova Scotia, on December 17 after most of the raiders had fled, and subsequent attempts to prosecute them for piracy in the Canadian courts were unsuccessful.

659.15   the Clans were after 1745] Many Scottish Highland clan leaders were executed or forced into exile after the failed Jacobite uprising of 1745–46. Their estates were confiscated, and parliamentary legislation ended the hereditary power of clan leaders to administer justice in their domains.

659.15–16   Parton's life of Butler]   *General Butler in New Orleans* (1863) by James Parton (1822–1891), a New York journalist who had published popular biographies of Horace Greeley, Aaron Burr, and Andrew Jackson.

659.25   Dr. Peters]   John Charles Peters (1819–1893), a New York physician and medical writer.

659.26–28   A. H. Stephens, . . . once more at Fortress Monroe]   Stephens had approached Fort Monroe on a Confederate flag of truce boat on July 4, 1863, and requested safe passage to Washington in an attempt to open peace negotiations. Lincoln and his cabinet refused to receive him, and Stephens returned to Richmond.

662.19   The Examiner]   The *Richmond Examiner*, in an editorial published on December 3, 1863.

662.21–22   Memminger . . . Mallory]   Christopher G. Memminger (1803–1888), Confederate secretary of the treasury, February 1861–July 1864; Stephen R. Mallory (c. 1813–1873), Confederate secretary of the navy, February 1861–May 1865.

662.24–26   Huger . . . let McClellan escape]   Major General Benjamin Huger (1805–1877), the commander of the Department of Norfolk, May 1861–April 1862, was criticized for not sending sufficient supplies and reinforcements to Roanoke Island in Pamlico Sound before its capture by Union forces on February 8, 1862. Huger later commanded a division in the Army of Northern Virginia during the Seven Days' Battles and was blamed for the Confederate failure to destroy the retreating Union army at Glendale (Frayser's Farm), June 30, and at Malvern Hill, July 1, 1862.

662.26   Lovel, New Orleans]   See notes 366.19 and 366.32.

662.29–30   Price . . . Holmes]   Sterling Price (1809–1867), the leader of the pro-secession Missouri State Guard, shared command in the state in 1861 with Confederate brigadier general Benjamin McCulloch (1811–1862). In January 1862 both men were placed under Earl Van Dorn, whose defeat at Pea Ridge (Elkhorn Tavern) in northwestern Arkansas, March 7–8, 1862, ended Confederate hopes of gaining control of Missouri. Lieutenant General Theophilus H. Holmes (1804–1880) commanded Confederate forces in Arkansas, September 1863–March 1864.

662.32–33   "the discerning of Spirits."]   See 2 Corinthians 12:4–10.

662.38   "not speak" . . . "evil of dignities."]   See 2 Peter 2:10.

663.4   Col Clark]   Edmondston's brother-in-law, Colonel William J. Clarke (1827–1886), commander of the 24th North Carolina Infantry.

664.14–15   like David . . . my hair cut]   See 2 Samuel 12:19–20.

664.25   General Hood's]   Major General John B. Hood (1831–1875) was recovering from the loss of his right leg at Chickamauga on September 20, 1863.

664.33   Mrs. King,]   Susan Petrigu King (1824–1875), daughter of James L. Petrigru (see note 142.18–19), was a novelist and story writer whose works included *Busy Moments of an Idle Woman* (1854), *Lily* (1855), and *Sylvia's World; and, Crimes Which the Law Does Not Reach* (1859).

665.8   Grundy père]   Thomas Billop Grundy (1827–1879), Chestnut's downstairs neighbor in Richmond.

665.10   Madame Deffand]   Marie Anne de Vichy-Chamrond, Marquise du Deffand (1697–1780), hostess of a Parisian literary salon who corresponded with Voltaire, Montesquieu, Horace Walpole, and Madame de Staël.

665.14–15   Ashmore, . . . Orr]   John D. Ashmore (1819–1871) was a Democratic congressman from South Carolina, 1859–60. Laurence M. Keitt (1824–1864) was a Democratic congressman from South Carolina, 1853–60; a delegate to the Provisional Confederate Congress, 1861–62; and colonel of the 20th South Carolina Infantry, 1862–64. Keitt was mortally wounded at Cold Harbor, Virginia, on June 1, 1864, and died the following day. William W. Boyce (1818–1890) was a Democratic congressman from South Carolina, 1853–60; a delegate to the Provisional Confederate Congress, 1861–62; and a member of the Confederate house of representatives, 1862–65. James L. Orr (1822–1873) was a Democratic congressman from South Carolina, 1849–59, and a Confederate senator, 1862–65.

665.16   Mr. Mason]   James M. Mason (1798–1871) was a Democratic congressman from Virginia, 1837–39, and a senator, 1847–61, who served as Confederate envoy to Great Britain and France, 1861–65.

665.20   Mr. Hunter]   Robert M. T. Hunter (1809–1887) was a congressman from Virginia, 1837–43 and 1845–47, and a senator, 1847–61. A delegate to the Confederate Provisional Congress in 1861 and a Confederate senator, 1862–65, Hunter served as the secretary of state of the Confederacy, July 1861–February 1862.

665.26   Jack Preston]   See note 559.18–21.

665.33   General Scott]   Major General Winfield Scott (1786–1866), a native of Virginia, was general-in-chief of the U.S. Army, 1841–61.

665.35   F.F.]   First Family.

666.4–5   Stonewall . . . Mahone's brigade.]   Brigadier General William Mahone (1826–1895) commanded an infantry brigade composed of five Virginia regiments at Chancellorsville. Jackson was accidentally shot by men of the 18th North Carolina Infantry, one of five North Carolina regiments that made up the brigade commanded by Brigadier General James H. Lane (1833–1907).

666.9   General Edward Johnson]   Major General Edward Johnson (1816–1873) commanded a division in the Army of Northern Virginia.

666.13   Suwarrow]   Aleksandr Vasilyevich Suvorov (1729–1800), Russian general who successfully commanded troops in the Seven Years' War, 1756–63; in wars with the Turkish Empire, 1768–74 and 1787–91; in suppressing the Polish insurrection of 1794; and in a campaign against the French in Italy and Switzerland in 1799.

666.26   reculer pour mieux sauter]   French: step back to make a better jump.

666.30   Bayard . . . Philip Sidney]   Pierre Terrail, seigneur de Bayard (1473–1524), French soldier killed at the Sesia River in Italy who became known as "le chevalier sans peur et sans reproche" (the knight without fear and beyond reproach); Sir Philip Sidney (1554–1586), English poet, soldier, and courtier, fatally wounded at the battle of Zutphen in the Netherlands.

667.7   How beautiful are the feet]   See Song of Solomon 7:1.

667.11   General Preston]   See note 558.37–39.

667.14   General Young]   Brigadier General Pierce M. B. Young (1836–1896) led a cavalry brigade in the Army of Northern Virginia.

667.25–26   'the giant foot' . . . Bulwer's last.]   A "giant Foot" appears in chapter 87 of Edward Bulwer-Lytton's novel of the occult, *A Strange Story* (1862).

667.29   Mr. Ould]   Robert Ould (1820–1882), an attorney from Washington, D.C., was the Confederate commissioner for prisoner exchanges, 1862–65.

667.36   "The Roman emperor . . . good odor."]   The Latin saying "pecunia non olet" (money does not smell) is attributed to the emperor Vespasian (9–79 CE).

668.4–5   theater and huzzahed . . . dead."]   Theater audiences in London and Manchester cheered the news of the death of Nicholas I in 1855 during the Crimean War.

668.6   Senator Johnson of Arkansas]   Robert Ward Johnson (1814–1879) was a Democratic senator from Arkansas, 1853–61, and a Confederate senator, 1862–65.

668.21   Mrs. Lawton, . . . Mary P]   Sarah Alexander Lawton (1826–1897); Mary Cantey Preston (1840–1891), daughter of Colonel John S. Preston.

668.25   General Lawton]   Brigadier General Alexander R. Lawton (1818–

1896), a former brigade commander in the Army of Northern Virginia who served as Confederate quartermaster general, 1863–65.

668.31–32   beautiful bride . . . happy bridegroom] Probably James Chesnut's cousin John Redman Coxe Lewis (1834–1898) and Maria Freeland Lewis (1838–1920), who were married in December 1863.

669.8   Wigfall] Louis T. Wigfall (1816–1874) was a South Carolina native who moved to Texas in 1846. He served in the Texas house of representatives, 1850–57; in the Texas senate, 1857–59; in the U.S. Senate, 1859–61; and in the Confederate senate, 1862–65.

669.12   *Germaine*] Novel (1857) by Edmond About (1828–1885).

669.22–23   Mrs. Malaprop . . . begin with a little aversion."] See Richard Brinsley Sheridan, *The Rivals* (1775), Act 2, scene 1: "'Tis safest in matrimony to begin with a little aversion."

670.1   Averell's raiders] Brigadier General William W. Averell (1832–1900) led a cavalry brigade that attacked the Virginia & Tennessee Railroad at Salem, Virginia, on December 16, 1863, and then withdrew into West Virginia. Averell reported that 122 of his men were captured during the raid.

670.2–3   Foote of Mississippi] Henry S. Foote (1804–1880) was a Democratic senator from Mississippi, 1847–52, and its governor, 1852–54. He served as representative from Tennessee in the Confederate Congress, 1862–65. During a committee hearing Thomas B. Hanly (1812–1880) of Arkansas brawled with Foote after Foote laughed at him.

670.15   Old Hickory . . . Aunt Rachel] Andrew Jackson and Rachel Donelson Robards (1767–1828) were married in 1791 before her divorce from Lewis Robards was finalized. They were remarried in 1794.

670.23   Mrs. Eaton] Margaret (Peggy) O'Neale Timberlake (1799–1879) married Senator John H. Eaton (1790–1856) of Tennessee, an old friend of Andrew Jackson, on January 1, 1829, less than a year after the death of her first husband. Jackson then named Eaton as secretary of war in his first cabinet despite widespread gossip about Peggy Eaton's character, and defended her reputation after she was snubbed by the wives of the other cabinet members.

670.24   Mrs. M.] Marion Twiggs Myers (c. 1838–1893), wife of Colonel Abraham C. Myers (1811–1889), who served as Confederate quartermaster general, 1861–63. Jefferson Davis's decision to replace Myers with Alexander R. Lawton (see note 668.25) led to a dispute in the Confederate Congress between supporters and opponents of the Davis administration. The conflict was exacerbated by reports that Marion Twiggs Myers had called Varina Howell Davis an "old squaw."

670.25–28   Andrew Jackson . . . coolly killed him.] Jackson shot and killed Charles Dickinson, a young Tennessee lawyer, in a duel in 1806 after being wounded by Dickinson's first shot. Although the duel overtly resulted from a quarrel arising from a horse race bet, it was rumored that Dickinson had insulted Rachel Jackson.

670.31   England declined . . . Lady Hamilton] In a codicil to his will written in 1805 shortly before his death at Trafalgar, Lord Nelson left his mistress, Lady Emma Hamilton (1765–1815), and their daughter Horatia (1801–1881) to the care of the nation. Despite his wishes, the government failed to provide for Lady Hamilton, who died in poverty.

671.1   *Volpone*] Comedy (1606) by Ben Jonson.

671.6   L. Q. C. Lamar] Lucius Quintus Cincinnatus Lamar (1825–1893) was a Democratic congressman from Mississippi, 1857–60, and a member of the Mississippi secession convention. He was appointed as special envoy to Russia by Davis in November 1862 but was recalled in June 1863 after the Confederate senate failed to confirm his nomination. During his time in Europe Lamar visited Paris and London, but did not attempt to go to St. Petersburg because he doubted that the Russian government would receive him.

671.14   Colonels Browne and Ives] William M. Browne and Joseph M. Ives, military aides to Jefferson Davis.

671.20   Daniel comes to judgment] See *The Merchant of Venice*, IV.i.223: "A Daniel come to judgment! yea, a Daniel!"

672.1   "Little Vick] Queen Victoria.

672.29–30   Wigfall, who shoots white men] In 1840 Wigfall became involved in a political feud in South Carolina with Whitfield Brooks, Brooks's son Preston, and their ally, James Carroll. After posting Whitfield Brooks as a scoundrel and coward, Wigfall fatally shot Thomas Bird, Whitfield's nephew, in a gunfight outside the Edgefield District courthouse. He then fought a bloodless duel with Carroll, and a duel with Preston Brooks in which both men were seriously wounded. (While serving in Congress, Preston Brooks would assault Charles Sumner on the Senate floor in 1856.)

672.33–34   Dangerfield Lewis . . . L.Q. Washington] Henry Llewellyn Dangerfield Lewis (1841–1893), a cavalry officer who served as a courier with Stuart's headquarters; his sister-in-law, Maria Freeland Lewis (see note 668.31); Littleton Quinton Washington (1825–1902), chief clerk of the Confederate state department and grandson of Lund Washington, a distant cousin of George Washington.

673.3   *Washington Lewis*] Henry Llewellyn Dangerfield Lewis and his brother, John Redman Coxe Lewis (see note 668.31), were the grandsons of George Washington's nephew, Lawrence Lewis (1767–1839), and of Martha Custis Washington's granddaughter, Eleanor (Nelly) Parke Custis Lewis (1779–1852).

674.16   Professor Minor] John B. Minor (1813–1895) was a professor of law at the University of Virginia, 1845–95.

674.23–25   Surgeons Davis and Cabell . . . Dr. Brockenbrough]   Dr. John S. Davis (1824–1885), professor of anatomy at the University of Virginia, 1856–85; Dr. John L. Cabell (1813–1889), professor of anatomy and surgery at the University of Virginia, 1837–89, and superintendent of the Confederate military hospital at Charlottesville; Dr. William Spencer Roane Brockenbrough (1819–1880), Judith W. McGuire's brother, was a physician in Hanover County, Virginia.

674.27   Dr. Maupin]   Dr. Socrates Maupin (1808–1871), a physician, was professor of chemistry at the University of Virginia, 1853–71, and dean of the faculty, 1854–70.

675.8   Gaines's Mill]   See note 29.19.

676.1–2   "Rachel weeping . . . they are not."]   See Jeremiah 31:15.

676.9–12   "With patient mind . . . as well as He."]   Cf. John Byrom (1692–1763), *Miscellaneous Poems*, "Miscellaneous Pieces" (1773); "With peaceful Mind thy Race of Duty run; / God Nothing does, or suffers to be done, / But what thou wouldst Thyself, if thou couldst see / Through all Events of Things, as well as He."

676.13   The Lord . . . so unquiet.]   Cf. Psalm 99:1, in the 1662 *Book of Common Prayer*.

680.27   words of President Davis]   In his message to the Confederate Congress, December 7, 1863.

682.34   Beecher in his Liverpool speech]   During a speaking tour of Great Britain, Henry Ward Beecher, the pastor of Plymouth Congregational Church in Brooklyn, New York, addressed a public meeting in Liverpool on October 16, 1863. "It is said that the North is fighting for Union, and not for emancipation. The North is fighting for Union, for that ensures emancipation," Beecher said. "But the motive determines the value; and why are we fighting for the Union? Because we shall never forget the testimony of our enemies. They have gone off declaring that the Union in the hands of the North was fatal to slavery."

685.18   Lepanto]   Naval battle fought off western Greece on October 7, 1571, in which Spanish and Venetian naval forces defeated the main Turkish fleet.

685.23–25   slaves of Saint Domingo, . . . French troops]   In the Haitian Revolution, 1791–1804.

685.25–26   negro slaves of Jamaica . . . Maroons]   The first Maroons were slaves who left Spanish plantations during the English invasion of Jamaica in 1655. Maroon resistance to colonial rule continued until the Second Maroon War in 1795–96.

686.28–38   D. C. Govan, . . . J. H. Kelly]   Daniel C. Govan (1829–1911) and Mark P. Lowrey (1828–1885) led brigades in Cleburne's division;

John E. Murray (1843–1864), George F. Baucum (1837–1905), Peter Snyder (1829–1865), Elisha Warfield (1838–1894), Aaron B. Hardcastle (1836–1914), Frederick A. Ashford (1830–1864), John W. Colquitt (1840–1903), Richard J. Person (1843–1909), George S. Deakins (1832–1902), and James H. Collett (1825–1916) commanded regiments in Cleburne's division; John H. Kelly (1840–1864) had commanded the 8th Arkansas Infantry in Cleburne's division at Stones River. Murray was killed at Atlanta on July 22, 1864; Snyder died of typhoid fever at Raleigh, North Carolina, on April 19, 1865; Ashford was killed at Franklin, Tennessee, on November 30, 1864; and Kelly was fatally wounded at Franklin on September 2, 1864.

687.13   A. A. G.] Assistant adjutant general.

694.30   Willards] A popular hotel established in 1847 at the corner of 14th Street and Pennsylvania Avenue.

697.26   Patent Office . . . partially finished] Construction of the building, located at 8th and F Streets N.W., began in 1836 and was not completed until 1868. The building now houses the National Portrait Gallery and the Smithsonian American Art Museum.

698.17   Hon. L. E. Chittenden] A lawyer from Vermont, Lucius E. Chittenden (1824–1900) served as register of the treasury, April 1861–August 1864.

698.24   Rev. Mr. Sunderland, Hon. B. B. French] Byron Sunderland (1819–1901), Presbyterian minister who served as chaplain of the U.S. Senate, 1861–64 and 1873–79. For Benjamin B. French, see Biographical Notes.

703.27   Flag-Officer Tucker] Captain John R. Tucker (1812–1883) commanded the Confederate naval forces at Charleston, 1863–65.

703.32–33   Lieutenant Dixon] George E. Dixon (1837?–1864), a steamboat engineer, had been wounded at Shiloh while serving as a lieutenant with the 21st Alabama Infantry. He became involved with Horace L. Hunley's submarine project after being posted to the Mobile garrison.

704.6–7   attempt to dive . . . receiving ship] On October 15, 1863, the *Hunley* attempted to dive beneath the *Indian Chief,* a schooner used by the Confederate navy as a receiving ship—i.e., a vessel where new recruits were sent to await their permanent assignments.

704.8   James A. Eason] Probably James M. Eason (1819–1887), a Charleston machinist and foundry operator.

704.24   not less than 33 men] A total of twenty-one men died in the *Hunley;* see headnote, p. 703.

709.7   Nethercutt's Battalion] The 8th North Carolina Partisan Rangers, commanded by Major John H. Nethercutt (1824–1867), was a local home guard unit organized in 1862. In August 1863 the battalion became part of the 66th North Carolina Infantry.

710.33–34   "He bare the bag . . . put therein."]   Cf. John 12:6.

710.36–37   "the love . . . all evil;"]   1 Timothy 6:10.

711.7–11   "he repented . . . hanged himself."]   Matthew 27:3–5.

711.14   flourish as a green bay tree]   See Psalm 37:35: "I have seen the wicked in great power, and spreading himself like a green bay tree."

711.26   Benedict Arnold]   Major General Benedict Arnold (1741–1801) conspired in 1780 to betray West Point in return for £20,000. He fled to the British lines after his plot was discovered and commanded British and Loyalist troops in Virginia and Connecticut, 1780–81.

713.37–38   "peace meetings"]   See pp. 490–91 in this volume.

714.26–27   "the State is going to secede."]   Some opponents of the war in North Carolina advocated that the state should secede from the Confederacy and negotiate a separate peace with the Union.

715.23–25   "is a jealous God . . . hate me."]   See Deuteronomy 5:9.

717.8–9   "letting us alone."]   In his message to the Provisional Confederate Congress of April 29, 1861, Jefferson Davis wrote: "We feel that our cause is just and holy; we protest solemnly in the face of mankind that we desire peace at any sacrifice save that of honor and independence; we seek no conquest, no aggrandizement, no concession of any kind from the States with which we were lately confederated; all we ask is to be let alone; that those who never held power over us shall not now attempt our subjugation by arms."

718.26–29   "God moves . . . rides upon the storm."]   From "Light Shining Out of Darkness" (1773) by William Cowper (1731–1800).

719.2   "she shall become . . . kingdoms,"]   See Ezekiel 29:15.

719.30   Belshazzar held his impious feast.]   See Daniel 5.

719.31   Tadmor]   Semitic name for Palmyra.

719.37–38   "there is a God . . . the earth."]   See Psalm 58:11.

720.18   first battle of Fredericksburg]   The battle of December 13, 1862. The Union capture of Marye's Heights on May 3, 1863, during the Chancellorsville campaign is sometimes called the second battle of Fredericksburg.

723.30   Brookville Republican . . . Dr. Heichold]   The *Brookville Republican* was a weekly newspaper published in Jefferson County, Pennsylvania. Alexander P. Heichold, surgeon of the 8th U.S. Colored Infantry, was a resident of Jefferson County.

724.22   Colonel Fribley]   Colonel Charles W. Fribley (1835–1864) served as a captain in the 84th Pennsylvania Infantry before being appointed colonel of the 8th U.S. Colored Infantry in November 1863.

725.12 Major Burritt] Loren Burritt (1837–1889), a former lieutenant in the 56th Pennsylvania Infantry, was promoted to lieutenant colonel and took command of the 8th U.S. Colored Infantry in September 1864, but was unable to continue in the position because of his Olustee wounds. He served on recruiting and court-martial duty for the remainder of the war.

725.16 Lieutenant Lewis] Lieutenant Elijah Lewis (1833–1913) of Company F was mustered out as a captain in 1865.

725.30 Captain Dickey] Captain Alexander G. Dickey (1836–1864), the commander of Company K, was fatally wounded near Richmond in the battle of Darbytown Road on October 13, 1864.

725.33 Captain Wagner] Captain George E. Wagner (1842–1904) was medically discharged in December 1864 because of the wounds he received at Olustee.

726.21 Charles City] Battle fought on June 30, 1862, also known as Glendale, White Oak Swamp, and Frayser's Farm.

726.22 Richards Ford] A ford across the Rappahannock River.

726.25 Harrison's Landing . . . Ely's Ford] A landing on the north bank of the James River, where the Army of the Potomac retreated after the Seven Days' Battles; a ford across the Rapidan River.

728.35 Hon. James Lyons] Lyons (1801–1882) was a Richmond lawyer who served in the Confederate Congress, February 1862–February 1864.

729.1 Gen. Elzey] See note 125.38–39.

729.2–3 Brig.-Gen. Custis Lee] Brigadier General George Washington Custis Lee (1832–1913), son of Robert E. Lee, commanded a brigade in the Richmond defenses.

729.10–11 captured Mr. Seddon's . . . Gen. Wise's] Union cavalry led by Colonel Ulric Dahlgren reached Sabot Hill, the plantation of Confederate secretary of war James A. Seddon (see note 125.38–39), and Eastwood, the nearby home of the daughter and son-in-law of Brigadier General Henry A. Wise (see note 192.16–17), on March 1. Neither family was harmed during the raid.

729.15 Gen. Whiting] See note 551.21.

729.16–19 Judge Pearson . . . unconstitutional.] Richmond M. Pearson (1805–1878) was an associate justice of the North Carolina supreme court, 1848–59, and its chief justice, 1859–78. The conscription act passed by the Confederate Congress on April 16, 1862, had permitted men eligible to be drafted to hire substitutes, but the hiring of substitutes was subsequently abolished on December 28, 1863, and an act passed on January 5, 1864, made persons who had previously provided substitutes eligible for conscription. On February 19 Pearson ruled in *Ex parte Walton* that the act of January 5 violated the contracts clause of the Confederate constitution. Pearson had earlier angered the Davis administration by ruling in April 1863 that the North Carolina militia could not legally be used to apprehend Confederate deserters, and by consistently interpreting the conscription laws in favor of applicants seeking to be discharged from the army.

729.21   Col. A. C. Myers]   See note 670.24.

730.16   Gov. Vance]   An opponent of the Davis administration, Zebulon B. Vance (1830–1894) was governor of North Carolina, 1862–65. He later served as governor, 1877–79, and in the U.S. Senate, 1879–94.

730.23   Supreme Court, to assemble in June]   Pearson had ordered the Walton case to be reargued before the full North Carolina supreme court in June 1864. The court overturned his earlier decision, 2–1, and upheld the act of January 5, 1864. (Although the Confederate constitution provided for a Confederate supreme court, the Confederate Congress never established one, leaving constitutional questions to be decided in various state courts.)

730.27–28   Gen. Winder]   Brigadier General John Henry Winder (1800–1865), the Confederate provost marshal, was in charge of the prisoner-of-war camps in the Richmond area.

731.12   Gen. Wilcox]   Major General Cadmus M. Wilcox (1824–1890), a division commander in the Army of Northern Virginia who was in Richmond on furlough at the time of the raid.

732.6–7   Mr. Secretary Seddon . . . Gen. Lee]   Lee replied to Seddon on March 6 and recommended that none of the Union prisoners captured during the raid be executed.

732.11   *Gen. Bragg*]   General Braxton Bragg, who was in Richmond serving as a military advisor to Jefferson Davis.

732.17–18   *Gen. Lee's son* . . . designated for retaliation]   See note 432.37–40.

732.21   Gen. Butler has been removed]   Major General Benjamin F. Butler had been appointed as the Union agent for prisoner exchanges in December 1863.

732.30   Morgan]   Brigadier General John Hunt Morgan escaped from the Ohio state penitentiary in Columbus on November 27, 1863, and reached Confederate-held territory in Tennessee on December 18.

735.33   Belmont]   Grant led 3,000 men in a raid against the Confederate camp at Belmont, Missouri, on November 7, 1861.

Index

*This book is set in 10 point ITC Galliard Pro, a
face designed for digital composition by Matthew Carter
and based on the sixteenth-century face Granjon. The paper
is acid-free lightweight opaque and meets the requirements
for permanence of the American National Standards Institute.
The binding material is Brillianta, a woven rayon cloth made
by Van Heek–Scholco Textielfabrieken, Holland.
Composition by Dedicated Book Services. Printing and
binding by Edwards Brothers Malloy, Ann Arbor.
Designed by Bruce Campbell.*

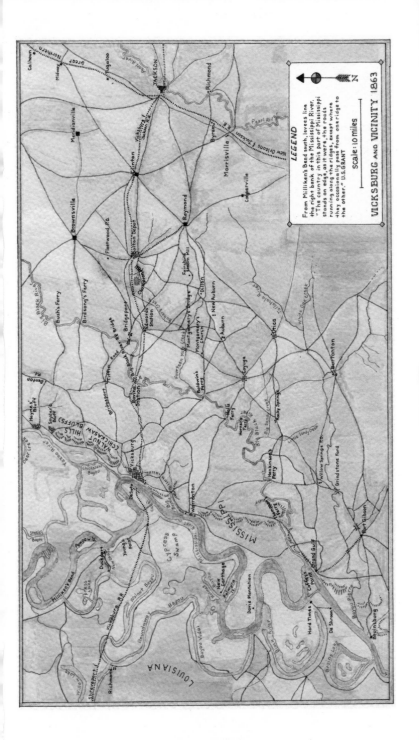